# Doing Well and Doing Good

# Doing Well
# *and* Doing Good

## ROSS & GLENDINING
## Scottish Enterprise in New Zealand

S.R.H. Jones

OTAGO

Published by Otago University Press,
Level 1 / 398 Cumberland Street
PO Box 56, Dunedin, New Zealand
Email: university.press@otago.ac.nz
Fax: 64 3 479 8385

First published 2010
ISBN 978 1 877372 74 2

Published with the assistance of the
Ministry for Culture and Heritage

Publisher: Wendy Harrex
Designer: Fiona Moffat
Maps: Allan Kynaston
Index: Andrew Parsloe

Printed in Hong Kong through Condor Production Ltd.

# CONTENTS

CHARTS AND MAPS

# ACKNOWLEDGEMENTS

When I became director of the Centre for Business History at the University of Auckland in 1991, it was suggested to me that what was urgently required was a comprehensive history of the development of business in New Zealand. I began my research by visiting the Hocken Library at Otago University as I had heard that the Hocken Librarian, Stuart Strachan, had a considerable collection of business archives in his care. While discussing my project with Stuart, he pointed out that the history of Ross & Glendining Ltd, at one stage New Zealand's largest manufacturing enterprise, had yet to be written. Clearly, a properly informed business history of the country as a whole could not be written before a study of Ross & Glendining was complete. Fortunately, the Hocken Library holds a splendid collection of archives relating to this company. For the past sixteen years I have been slowly working my way through them.

Many friends and colleagues have helped me while preparing this book, although I am especially grateful to Stuart Strachan and his staff at the Hocken Library. They have always been welcoming and extremely helpful. Their knowledge of sources and the general development of Otago has proved invaluable. Thanks are also due to the staff of National Archives, both in Dunedin and Wellington, who have happily fielded my requests for information, to Steve Innes of the New Zealand & Pacific Collection at Auckland University Library, to the reference librarians at Dunedin City Library and Auckland City Library, and to the New Zealand Collection librarians at the University of Edinburgh.

I am indebted to the University of Auckland and the University of Dundee for granting me periods of sabbatical leave to work at the Hocken Library, and to the Pasold Research Fund for travel assistance. In 2000, I spent time as Bamforth Research Fellow in the Department of History at the University of Otago and benefited greatly from the many conversations I had whilst there. The Economics Department at Otago has constituted an alternative home for me on the numerous occasions that I have visited Dunedin, providing me with office facilities, arranging accommodation and generally supporting me in my research. I also owe thanks to the Auckland University of Technology, where I spent two semesters as Visiting Fellow.

A number of fellow researchers have generously shared the fruits of their scholarship with me, including Richard and Marianne Davis, who allowed me to read their manuscript on Messrs Thompson & Shannon, and Ali Clarke who sent me chapters of her forthcoming history of Knox College. Gael Ferguson sourced materials from National Archives for me and provided personal information relating to manpower planning; Janet Thomson supplied family details relating to her ancestor, James Elliott; Richard Higham helped with the history of the United Empire Box Co., and Jim McAloon managed to cast light on the background and career of James Lillico. Some understanding of the dynamics of the Ross family has been gleaned from conversations with Tom Ross and Jennie Coleman, while the more technical aspects of sheep breeding have been explained to me by Christine Martyn. Gordon Parsonson kindly showed me around Central Otago.

I wish to thank a number of people for the helpful comments they have made on various versions of my manuscript, particularly Tom Brooking, Graham Brownlow, Gael Ferguson, Harry Hutchinson, Ken Jackson, Michael Keenan, Gray Maingay, Patricia Prime and Simon Ville. I have also benefited from comments made at seminars at both Auckland and Otago Universities, Victoria University Wellington, and at sessions of the Business History Conference, Glasgow 1999, and the Australian and New Zealand Economic History Conference held in Brisbane, 2006.

I am especially grateful to Alan King, who has rectified some of the many deficiencies I have as a researcher. When I have failed to extract the necessary information from records, Alan has obliged, spending hours in the Hocken and Otago University Libraries and trawling through the Otago Run Registers at National Archives in Dunedin on my behalf. He has commented in detail on my manuscript, helping to make sure that it is both more economically literate and historically accurate than it otherwise would be. Needless to say, neither he nor any of the other commentators are responsible for any errors or omissions that remain.

Finally, I must acknowledge the help and encouragement of my wife, Lynn. Quite apart from acting as unpaid research assistant, she has tolerated my long absences from home – and inattention to domestic duties when I was at home – with cheerful forbearance. This book would not have been written without her support.

STEPHEN JONES,
*Dundee, June 2009*

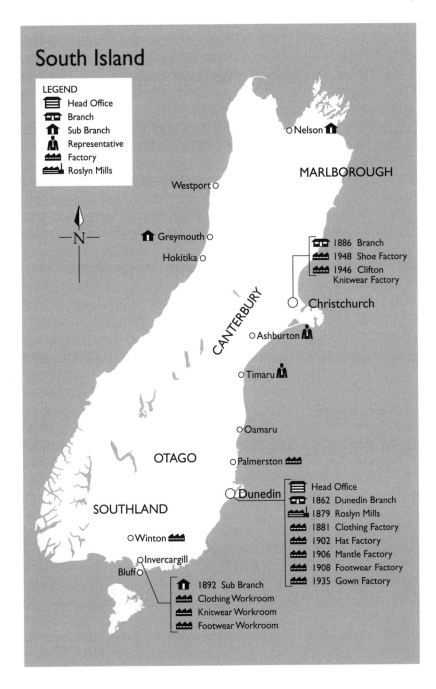

Location of Ross & Glendinning Ltd manufacturing and distributing units, 1953. *Annual Report*, 1953.

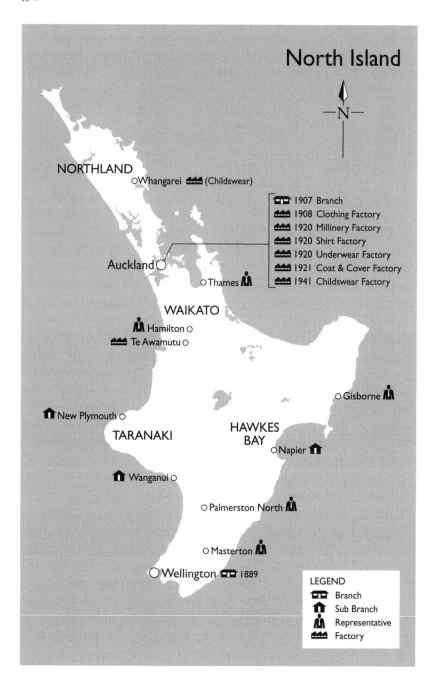

# North Island

—N—

**NORTHLAND**
O Whangarei 🏭 (Childswear)

| 🚃 | 1907 | Branch |
| 🏭 | 1908 | Clothing Factory |
| 🏭 | 1920 | Millinery Factory |
| 🏭 | 1920 | Shirt Factory |
| 🏭 | 1920 | Underwear Factory |
| 🏭 | 1921 | Coat & Cover Factory |
| 🏭 | 1941 | Childswear Factory |

Auckland O

O Thames 👥

**WAIKATO**

👥 Hamilton O
🏭 Te Awamutu O

O Gisborne 👥

🏠 New Plymouth O

**TARANAKI**

**HAWKES BAY**

O Napier 🏠

🏠 Wanganui O

O Palmerston North 👥

O Masterton 👥

O Wellington 🚃 1889

**LEGEND**
🚃 Branch
🏠 Sub Branch
👥 Representative
🏭 Factory

# INTRODUCTION

The view of the Scots as a hardy, enterprising race, willing to travel the world in search of their fortunes seems well founded. From the late seventeenth century onwards, Scottish merchants were to the forefront in developing the American tobacco and West Indian sugar trades, with Glasgow developing as a major commercial centre in the process. Thereafter the sons of merchants and minor landowners flocked to that other outpost of Empire, India. Service in the East India Company offered rich pickings, at least to those who survived, and some returned to Scotland wealthy beyond the dreams of avarice.

Yet it was not only the relatively well off who sought to better themselves abroad. Scottish professional classes were well represented, especially in North America, where their advanced ideas on education ensured that university students were tutored in a broad range of secular subjects. Poorer members of society, on the other hand, often found the costs of emigration beyond their means. For some, the British army offered a lifeline, the need for soldiers to police the Empire allowing many young men to fight, settle and die abroad.[1]

The Scottish Diaspora continued throughout the nineteenth century, although the character of migration changed somewhat. Until around 1800, Scottish landowners regarded labour as a valuable resource, to be kept at home if at all possible. The rage for improvement that followed reversed the situation as crofters were forcibly cleared from the land to make way for sheep. Some of those evicted from their homes moved to newly established coastal settlements where they were expected to find employment in the herring fisheries. Others emigrated, passage money being paid wholly or in part by landlords, emigration societies, family and friends. At the same time, a stream of migrants from the slightly better off in Scottish society continued to make their way abroad, often to the new Imperial frontiers in Africa, Australia and New Zealand. Here they immersed themselves in industry, commerce, the professions and government.

To contemporaries, Scots emigrants appeared to be unusually successful, whatever their origins or calling. Charles Dilke, touring the Empire in 1867, commented that 'for every Englishman you meet who has worked himself up from small beginnings, without external aid, you find ten Scotchmen'.[2] Certainly the disproportionate number of Scots abroad helped them to build strong networks which, in many cases, had originally been forged through business and family connections back home. Inevitably this gave rise to accusations of clannishness. Their competitive edge, however, came not only from cooperation but also from a superior education. In 1696 the Scottish Parliament had passed an act to establish a school in every parish, with the result that standards of literacy were far higher than those in England. One of the motives for the legislation was that Presbyterians believed that both boys and girls should be able to read the Bible for themselves. Indeed, religion provided the driving force for most Scots in the eighteenth and nineteenth centuries, a Calvinist belief that worldly success was a reflection of virtue being an integral part of Scottish culture. The individual single-mindedly pursuing his or her own self-interest was thus seen to serve a moral as well as an economic purpose. Doing good and doing well were inextricably linked.[3]

From the very first, New Zealand attracted Scots determined to do well. The establishment of the capital in Auckland in 1841 saw Dr John Logan Campbell and his compatriot, William Brown, quickly cast aside their professions to commence trading 'in anything and everything in both a large and small way'.[4] They were as good as their word, combining the activities of auctioneers, commission agents, and general merchants as they supplied goods to the struggling settlement. The following year the number of Scots in Auckland was swollen when two vessels arrived from Greenock with some 500 souls on board. Mainly poor migrants who had benefited from assisted passages, their lack of capital concerned Campbell, who saw few immediate openings for the new arrivals. In 1845 the local economy began to move forwards as George Grey, the new Governor, embarked on a period of sustained military expenditure. Soon Brown & Campbell were making very considerable profits, the importation of blankets being particularly lucrative.[5]

There was also a sizeable Scottish contingent in other parts of New Zealand. In 1839, the New Zealand Company dispatched the *Bengal Merchant* from Glasgow, with 161 settlers on board, to what was to become Wellington. The decision to locate the capital in Auckland, however, together with a severe earthquake and disputes with local Maori meant that Wellington languished by comparison, with some early settlers quickly moving north.[6] By the early 1850s the European population of Wellington, at just over 6,000, was still only two thirds that of Auckland.

It was the settlement in Otago, established in 1848 by the Lay Association of the Free Church of Scotland in conjunction with the New

Zealand Company, which was to prove particularly attractive to Scots migrants. Around 145,000 acres had been purchased by the Company to be subdivided into 2,400 properties. The main township, originally to be called New Edinburgh, was named Dunedin, the Gaelic form for Edinburgh, with a street plan that supposedly followed that of its northern namesake. Topography, unfortunately, resulted in a number of quirks, with Princes St ultimately running into George St instead of being parallel to it. Lower High St was partially under water.

Once the land had been subdivided and funds raised by the sale of sections, formal settlement could commence. The first two migrant ships arrived in the autumn of 1848 and a year later the European population within the town belt amounted to 444 persons.[7] A growing flood of migrants arrived during the following decade, the majority Scots Presbyterian, and by 1860 the population of the province numbered over 12,000. The principal export was wool.

The discovery of gold in Central Otago in 1861 completely changed the pattern of economic development within the province. Thousands of miners, many from the Victorian and Californian goldfields, poured into Dunedin en route for the diggings. The settlement, little more than a sprawling harbour-side village, was rapidly transformed into a major port and it soon became the leading commercial centre in New Zealand. Mining settlements inland underwent a similar metamorphosis to become small country towns. The influx of miners and others meant that, by 1870, Otago was the most heavily populated province in New Zealand, with more than 67,000 European inhabitants.

The expansion of the market not only fostered the growth of industry and commerce but also encouraged firms to specialise. This was most evident within the mercantile community, where general merchants soon gave up trading in 'anything and everything'. Thus stock and station agents emerged to handle rapidly expanding exports of wool while drapery, the principal import into the colony, was marketed and distributed by a relatively small group of soft goods warehousemen. The growth in the domestic market saw the warehousemen progressively extend the scope of their enterprises, introducing the latest techniques to manufacture clothing, footwear and textiles themselves. The lead was taken by Dunedin-based merchants who were to dominate the New Zealand soft goods trade for almost a hundred years.

John Ross, a sober and staunch supporter of the Free Church, arrived in Dunedin just as the gold rush was getting under way. A Highlander from Caithness, he had served his apprenticeship as a draper and gained commercial experience in both Glasgow and Edinburgh before returning to manage a drapery in Sutherland. When he was offered a partnership in a Dunedin business that had been established by his employer's brother, he jumped at the chance.

Robert Glendining was from Dumfries, close to the Scottish borders. Younger and rather more colourful than Ross, Glendining too had served an apprenticeship as a draper before arriving in Dunedin. Both men came from relatively humble origins, although between them they had access to sufficient capital to set up in business as importers and distributors of draperies – or soft goods as they were known in the trade. In August 1862, they entered into partnership and promptly opened for business, trading as Ross & Glendining & Co.

The story of Ross & Glendining exemplifies many aspects of the transition from merchant to manufacturer in New Zealand's economic history. The firm accumulated capital during the gold rush years; integrated backwards into woollen mills and sheep stations on the proceeds of the Vogel boom of the 1870s; diversified into worsted manufacturing to cope with the depression of the 1880s; developed branches nationwide in the 1890s; and, at the turn of the century, began making shirts, hats and footwear to meet the needs of increasingly affluent New Zealanders. In 1900, the partners adopted joint stock limited liability both to reduce death duties and to ensure the smooth continuation of the enterprise when they died.

A new management team, led by Ross's son, eventually took over in the 1920s. It was not an easy time. As the price of wool and meat dipped and consumer demand slackened, the firm was obliged to restrict both their manufacturing and merchandising activities. The depression of the 1930s and the collapse in agricultural prices led to further retrenchment, the massive Napier earthquake of 1931 – which flattened their branch warehouse and killed a number of customers – adding to the firm's problems. The election of a Labour Government in 1935, which used unorthodox policies to stimulate the economy, saw consumer demand expand once more. By the outbreak of war, Ross & Glendining Ltd was working at full capacity.

Like many other manufacturers and merchants, the firm struggled to meet government demands in both world wars but they still made excellent profits. The trading environment after World War II proved to be rather more problematic, the maintenance of price and import controls, shortages of labour and changes in government policy all squeezing profitability. Matters were made worse by a decade of poor management, characterised by underinvestment in new machinery and a failure to produce a modern range of products. Belatedly, the firm attempted to adjust both strategy and internal management structure but with limited success. In 1966, with its share price falling, Ross & Glendining Ltd was taken over by the United Empire Box

Company. Following acquisition, the firm was broken up and its assets were sold off, thus bringing to an end more than a century of enterprise.

Much has been written in recent years about the growth of big business, both in terms of internal organisation and the use of external networks. Even by international standards, Ross & Glendining Ltd was not exactly a minnow. Around 1,000 hands were employed in its textile mills, clothing factories and warehouses at the turn of the century, a figure that rose to well over 2,000 by the early 1940s. The systems the firm used to collect and process information, the way it managed that information, and the incentive structures and decision-making processes it employed set it apart from many of its rivals. Paradoxically, it was a failure of these control systems to cope with the increasing scale of the enterprise that ultimately contributed to its downfall.

The founders undoubtedly benefited from the fact that they were part of a network of Scottish businessmen, able to draw on the knowledge, expertise – and sometimes the capital – of fellow Scots, both in New Zealand and back home. Caithnessmen on the staff of the Bank of New South Wales in London were happy to advance Ross credit. Ross, in turn, was well able to judge the creditworthiness of the mainly Scots drapers that he served in Otago. Indeed, they would have differed little to those customers he had visited in the Highlands, especially as the majority spoke with a Scottish brogue. Ross certainly preferred to employ 'Scotchmen' and relied heavily on Scots contacts for advice. This policy proved to be particularly valuable when the Roslyn Woollen Mills were being established in 1879, with a Glasgow consulting engineer employed to design the works. For the next fifty years labour was recruited with the help of friends and acquaintances in the Borders woollen industry. Roslyn Mills, it seems, worked to a Hawick rather than Galashiels 'cut'.

How John Ross and Robert Glendining first met is unclear, although as Scottish drapers and staunch adherents to the Free Church they clearly had much in common. Their relationship became even closer when they married two Scottish migrant sisters, Mary and Margaret Cassels. Yet in some ways they were contrasting characters, with Ross the more careful of the two, initially taking charge of finances and travelling while Glendining busied himself with operational matters relating to stock. When Ross returned to the United Kingdom in 1870 to run the firm's London buying office, he left financial matters in the hands of accountant George Hercus, a strict Baptist and fellow Caithnessman. Glendining now had the freedom to run the firm as he wished although the conservative Hercus, a master of financial detail, kept Ross fully informed of all developments. Nevertheless, Glendining's greater local knowledge often enabled him to persuade a reluctant Ross to

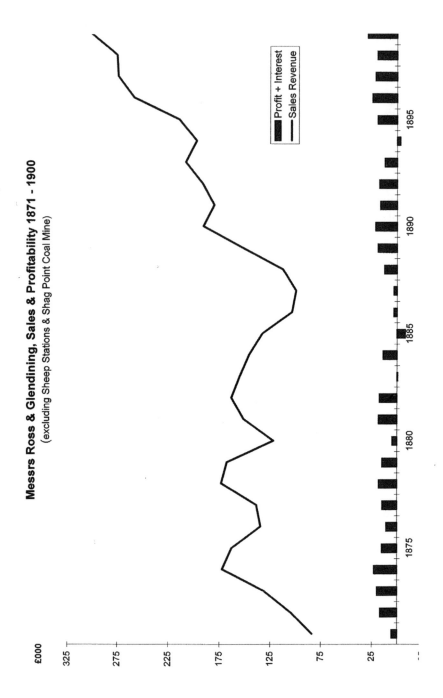

**Messrs Ross & Glendining, Sales & Profitability 1871 - 1900**
(excluding Sheep Stations & Shag Point Coal Mine)

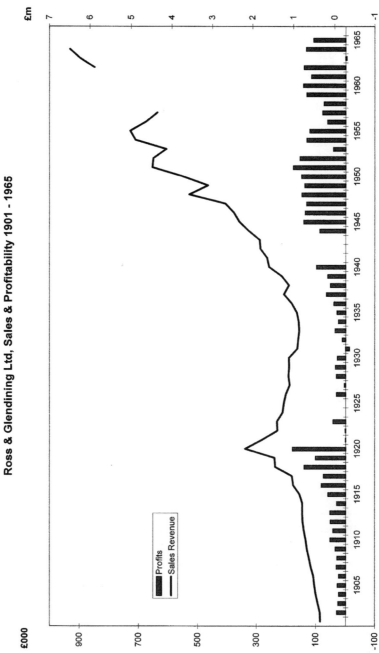

Ross & Glendining Ltd, Sales & Profitability 1901 - 1965

embark on schemes that others might have considered too risky. Thus it was he who was the driving force behind the construction of Roslyn Mills on the outskirts of Dunedin; the leasing of Lauder sheep station in Central Otago; and the acquisition of the ill-fated Shag Point coal mine.

The partnership worked well for a number of years, with Ross an ideal foil for the increasingly reckless Glendining. When John Ross returned to New Zealand in 1899, however, he was shocked by the intemperate habits of Glendining and his son, Bob, and the chaos that characterised parts of the business. The conversion of the firm to a limited liability company in 1900 provided Ross with an opportunity to assume control, though he met with strong resistance from his former partner. With Glendining cutting his consumption of alcohol to one glass of champagne a day – and his son doing his best to dry out – Ross reluctantly agreed that they might continue to run Roslyn Mills. Ross managed the rest of the business until after World War I.

Limited liability did little to separate ownership from control, the tightly held shares meaning that Ross & Glendining Ltd remained essentially a family firm. As in many family firms, the succeeding generations were not as enterprising as the founders. Under the long chairmanship of Ross's eldest son, John Sutherland Ross, the firm became a follower rather than a leader. In a sector in which fashion was of paramount importance, the failure to embrace new styles and new fabrics had dire consequences.

The evidence suggests that Ross & Glendining were model employers. They came out of the sweating enquiry of 1890 with a relatively clean bill of health, with the leading protagonist against sweating, the Reverend Rutherford Waddell, ultimately placing funds with the firm to earn interest. During World War I they continued to pay reduced wages to those who had entered the services, at the same time supporting their workers at home by opening a staff canteen that served subsidised meals. Subsequently profit-sharing schemes were introduced, while the Ross Foundation was established to assist members of the workforce who had fallen on hard times.

The general approach of John Ross and Robert Glendining to business and to those who worked for them undoubtedly reflected their Christian values as committed Presbyterians. For them doing good was undoubtedly as important as doing well. Both gave their time and money to worthy causes. Robert Glendining was heavily involved with the Knox Presbyterian Church in the centre of Dunedin, built an orphanage in Anderson's Bay and helped finance the construction of a winter garden in Dunedin's Botanic Garden. He died in 1917 after being unwell for some years.

Little is known of Ross's London life but he continued a life-long involvement in church affairs when he returned to New Zealand. His main contribution was in helping to fund the construction of Knox College, a Presbyterian theological college that also acted as a hall of residence for students at the University of Otago. He also contributed to the local YMCA and a home for the elderly. Scotland was not neglected either. In 1909 he took steps to secure the site of his childhood school in Caithness, upon which he erected a social and educational institute. This, he hoped, would help the young resist the temptations of drink. Ross was knighted in 1922, retired as chairman of Ross & Glendining in 1925, and died two years later at the age of 92.

John Ross and Robert Glendining were extremely wealthy by the standards of the day, each being worth well in excess of £175,000 by the turn of the century. But they were, in Jim McAloon's words, 'no idle rich'.[8] Hardworking and resourceful, they made a significant contribution to the wealth and prosperity of those in Dunedin and beyond. The demise of their enterprise just over a century after they first started out in business was unfortunate, especially as it resulted in unemployment for many. At the same time, it reflected the fact that the business environment in New Zealand was changing and that the days of the traditional soft goods merchant were rapidly coming to an end.

# From Scotland to New Zealand

# SCOTTISH FOUNDATIONS

John Ross, some seven years older than his partner Robert Glendining, was born in November 1834 in the hamlet of Gerston, northern Caithness. His family had moved there from the parish of Kildonan, Sutherland, in 1814. The move was not voluntary but the result of the clearances implemented by the Duke and Duchess of Sutherland towards the end of the Napoleonic Wars. Dwellings and grazing in the parish were set on fire by the Duke's factors and agents as they drove the tenants from the land to make way for sheep. Some crofters were persuaded to emigrate to the Red River Valley settlement in Manitoba where they were offered land by the Earl of Selkirk. Many were to remain in Scotland. Even so, by 1831 the population of Kildonan had fallen to 257, one fifth of what it had been in 1811.[1]

The Ross family may have been a little better off than the typical crofter, having been tenant flour millers on the River Helmsdale for many years. Grandfather John Ross died around 1812, his son Murdoch apparently taking over the mill and helping to provide for his mother and six younger siblings. This was the family unit that was ejected during the Sutherland clearances of 1814. Not all went north to Gerston. Uncle Roderick emigrated to Nova Scotia, while Uncle Alexander went to Edinburgh, where he was to start a grocery business in Cowgate.[2]

The decision to move to Gerston may have been due to the fact that it was very close to Halkirk, a planned settlement just south of Thurso that had been laid out in 1803 to absorb the surplus agricultural population. More probably, the availability of employment was the deciding factor, Murdoch taking up the tenancy of a mill owned by a Mr Swanson, the local landowner and proprietor of the celebrated Gerston distillery. Much later Murdoch moved to another mill at Auldichlevan, near Lybster, but not before he had trained his younger brother, also named John, in the arts of flour milling.

John Ross senior took over the tenancy of the mill in Gerston and in 1832 married Janet Sutherland, the daughter of Donald Sutherland, a farmer from nearby Rangag. It was to this couple that John Ross the draper, merchant, manufacturer and knight was born on 24 November 1834. He was their second child, an elder sister having died soon after birth. Another five children followed in rapid succession.[3]

## 1. A Free Church upbringing

John Ross frequently claimed that he came from a humble background and this was undoubtedly true. In return for operating the Gerston mill, his father was provided with a free house, potato ground, keep for a cow, pigs, and hens, and as much peat as the family wished to cut. Wages were £7 per annum and 36 bushels of meal. Whether Ross senior was allowed to use the mill to grind flour for others is not clear but, with six children to provide for, it is evident that the family was not well off.[4]

Yet the extended Ross family was in many ways far from poor. Murdoch Ross, the head of the family, was a leading churchman to whose home many northern preachers found their way. The bookshelves of Uncle Murdoch's home were well stocked, with 'Bunyan, Boston and William Guthrie rubbing shoulders with one another'. His sons, William and John, were close friends with the young John Ross, the former gaining the necessary qualifications to teach Gaelic before he went on to study at Edinburgh University. William Ross subsequently became Secretary to the Highland Committee of the Free Church of Scotland, was heavily involved in the temperance movement – ultimately becoming Right Worthy Chief Templar of the World – and spent many years in evangelical work in Glasgow.[5]

The excitement surrounding the split in the Church of Scotland in 1843, when nearly 450 ministers left to form the 'Free Protesting Church of Scotland', was well remembered in later life by John Ross. As a member of a family closely associated with the more evangelical Free Church, he was able to recall attending outdoor meetings in the glens before the local dissenters built their own kirk. Like his cousin William, he became imbued with the social concerns of the Free Church. He also spoke Gaelic, a useful accomplishment for a travelling Scots draper, and his Gaelic Bible remained with him to the end of his days.[6]

During his early years, John Ross appears to have spent much time with his grandparents at their farm in Rangag. The tiny settlement was located on the edge of the bleak Flow Country, a large area of bog some twelve miles south of Halkirk which had little in the way of houses. Even here, though, the Scottish preoccupation with education was evident, for there was a small school to which farming children of all ages went in the winter months. The school was a one-roomed building although, unlike the aptly named 'black houses' found in the Highlands and Islands, smoke from an open peat fire went out through a hole in the roof rather than drifting through the thatch. In the Scottish tradition, pupils brought a peat to school each day to keep the school fire burning. Ross was around seven when he first attended the school. He spent the summer months herding his grandfather's cattle while the teacher, a future minister, furthered his education in Edinburgh.[7]

More serious learning commenced a year or so later when he returned home to live with his family at Gerston. For a while he walked to school at Calder, some two miles to the west of the mill, and it was here that he learnt arithmetic, for which he apparently had an aptitude. The establishment of a Free Church school around 1846 in the much closer Halkirk saw John Ross walking in the opposite direction. For the next couple of years he was taught by the Reverend Mr Gunn who, for six days every week, instructed his single room of pupils in the three 'r's and subjects as diverse as Latin, Greek and agricultural chemistry. On Saturdays, the Shorter Catechism was repeated from beginning to end.[8]

## 2. AN APPRENTICE DRAPER

Although obviously bright, the limited resources of the family meant that John Ross was obliged to leave school after his fourteenth birthday. Initially he spent time working for his father's landlord, Swanson, driving carts and engaging in general farm work. This, it seems, was merely a stopgap. By the autumn of 1849 the school had secured him a position as apprentice to Robert Wallace, who lived in the planned fishing settlement of Lybster, some twenty miles to the east. A former peddler turned shopkeeper, Wallace did a general business in drapery, groceries and ironmongery. Here the young Ross learnt about the practicalities of wrapping snuff, weighing nails and handling treacle but, apparently, little else. After three years Wallace, who could barely read or write, failed.

The failure of Wallace proved to be a blessing in disguise for John Ross, who now entered the employment of Lybster draper, Tom Forbes. The shop was not particularly busy, Forbes having bought the business after inheriting money rather than establishing it himself, but it did allow Ross to become better acquainted with the drapery trade. Seriously underemployed in the shop, he found himself tending his employer's garden and making and repairing nets for the rapidly expanding local fishing fleet.[9] With plenty of spare time, he also proceeded to read each and every book he could lay his hands on. He was encouraged in his literary interests by his cousins William and John Ross, visiting them regularly at their home nearby. The young man also began to develop his social interests, including attending temperance meetings. It was at this juncture that he decided to sign the pledge.[10]

## 3. A RESTLESS SPIRIT

It was while he was in the employment of Tom Forbes that John Ross began to think about emigration. The potato famine of 1846, which affected not only Ireland but Scotland to a lesser degree, gave rise to the establishment of a Highland Emigration Fund. A Scottish Patriotic Society, formed in 1846, also saw emigration as one way of improving the lot of the crofting community. For many Highland Scots, therefore, emigration once again became a familiar and accepted way of getting ahead in life. With Forbes' business in the doldrums and the hard times of the potato famine fresh in Ross's memory, the opportunities offered by emigration must have appealed to the eighteen-year-old apprentice draper.

The Ross family was not unaccustomed to emigration. In addition to Uncle Roderick in Canada, a relative of Janet Ross had sailed for New Zealand in 1839, possibly on the *Bengal Merchant* bound for Wellington. As committed members of the Free Church, the family would also have been aware of the establishment of the Free Church settlement in Otago in 1848. Even so, it was the offer of work in Canada, not New Zealand, that first caught the attention of the young man. The nature of the work is not recorded but the offer was insufficiently attractive and Ross turned it down.[11]

At around this time his father decided to move, taking a mill and farm at Westerdale just to the south of Halkirk. Ross, also unsettled, now took a position as assistant with draper James Gerry who had a shop in the market town and port of Thurso. With a population of around 3,000, Thurso was a major outlet for the produce of northern Caithness and was the principal social centre of the area.[12] The drapery, as a consequence, was far busier than that of Forbes, with Ross, his employer and another assistant, Willie Lunn, spending long hours in the shop. The close relationship persisted after the shop closed, with Ross and Lunn being obliged to sleep in the same bed.[13]

After a year of hard toil, Ross received an invitation to work for the brothers W. & R.L. Begg, who owned a general store at Golspie in east Sutherland. Although Golspie was smaller than Thurso, the Begg brothers drove an extensive business throughout Sutherland, serving the scattered community with groceries, drapery, stationery and medicine. William Begg was the druggist while Robert was the draper, John Ross being employed to assist with the drapery while the latter was away travelling.

Ross had been working in Golspie for a little while when, in June 1854, Robert Begg set off on his regular trip to Glasgow and London to buy stock for the summer season. When he returned, Begg unexpectedly announced that he had decided to migrate to New Zealand. What prompted this decision is not known, although he may have been attracted by a drive for Scottish migrants then being undertaken by the Otago Provincial Council.[14] In any event, after purchasing a selection of spades, ploughs and other trade goods, Robert Begg and his younger brother, Sandy, set sail for Dunedin where they were to set up as general merchants. At nineteen years of age, John Ross was left in Golspie in sole charge of the drapery side of the business.

## 4. GAINING EXPERIENCE

The young Ross remained in Golspie for another two years before he, too, decided he would like to see more of the world. For a few months he worked for Arnold Cannock & Co. of Glasgow, a firm that specialised in handling bankrupt stock. It was here that Ross would have enhanced his skills regarding stock valuation and the trading margins necessary to survive in business. There was a lot to be learned in Glasgow, not only the leading commercial centre in Scotland but the main industrial centre too, but apparently Ross soon tired of the city with its 'congestion, squalor and vice'.[15] At the age of twenty-two he moved to Edinburgh to work for Messrs Lewis & Beater of 77–80, Leith St.

Lewis & Beater variously described themselves as general drapers, warehousemen, lace-men and mercers.[16] Their shop, just off the end of Princes St under the shadow of Calton Hill, was ideally placed to capture the burgeoning trade of the middle-class New Town. Here Ross was engaged as a window dresser, a very different job to that in Glasgow, requiring the ability to discern trends in fashion and the creative capacity to display those trends in a visually attractive manner. Whether the Highland boy brought up in homespun trews had a strong sense of fashion when he arrived in Edinburgh is difficult to say. What is quite clear, however, is that his sense of fashion was very finely developed by the time he began to buy for Ross & Glendining in the mid-1860s. When yellow and green were 'all the rage' and spots were not, Ross knew.[17]

While in Edinburgh, Ross lodged in the Old Town close to the university, doubtless seeing something of his cousin, William, a student there at the time. The hours at Lewis & Beater were nevertheless rather long. Consequently, when the young man received a letter from W. Begg inviting him to go back to Golspie to assist in the management of the business, he was happy to return.

Ross had far greater responsibilities in his new post, being required to travel throughout Sutherland, both by mail gig and on foot, taking orders and settling accounts. He sold a wide range of goods, 'tea, tar and testaments' being amongst the many items stocked at Golspie. With Begg being a druggist, Ross was required to read and dispense prescriptions – with a little help from the dispensers' guide, *Materia Medica*. He also learned how to keep the books.[18]

The years spent as a traveller undoubtedly stood Ross in good stead for his future life in New Zealand, for it required him to be able to assess the creditworthiness of a potential customer and develop the necessary firmness when demanding payment. Travelling in rural Sutherland was probably little different to travelling in rural Otago, both in terms of clientele, business practice and the physical demands placed on the individual by the often inhospitable conditions. On one of his journeys he almost perished in a snowstorm, only to be rescued by a shepherd who apparently revived him with a glass of whisky. Thus ended a strict adherence to abstinence. Ross nevertheless remained temperate for the rest of his life, disapproving greatly of alcoholic excess.[19]

The second spell with the Beggs also enabled Ross to develop another skill which was to be of vital importance to him in the future, namely, that of buying. Many leading wholesale houses at this time were located in either Glasgow or London. Like Robert Begg before him, John Ross was obliged to travel to these cities several times a year to purchase goods for the forthcoming season. The journey to London was far from straightforward, with Ross being obliged to travel down the coast to the Moray Firth, take a ferry to Burghead, on to Aberdeen, and thence by steamer to London.[20] Once in London, he had to visit the various wholesalers and merchant outfitters, select the assortment and quantity of goods that he judged was required for the forthcoming season, and then negotiate the most advantageous price and credit terms possible. Where draperies were concerned, he also had to choose the styles and colours that were currently in demand. For the business to succeed, Ross had to buy well.

### 5. OPPORTUNITIES AND EMIGRATION

John Ross spent another four agreeable years at Golspie. While there he continued to improve himself by attending lectures on a variety of subjects, although he still retained a desire to pursue his fortunes elsewhere. During this period he was offered a position at a post office in the west of Scotland but it was not particularly well paid and he rejected it. However, when a visiting minister attempted to persuade people to emigrate to the Presbyterian settlement in Carlton County, New Brunswick, by offering them cheap land, Ross was sorely tempted. Talking things over with his parents, he convinced them that the entire family should emigrate. A deposit of £1 was duly paid to secure 100 acres. For some reason they decided not to go, leaving the Presbyterian minister £1 the richer.[21]

Ultimately it was his employer, W. Begg, who provided John Ross with the opportunity he sought. Begg had remained in partnership with his two brothers after they departed for New Zealand, receiving a share of the profits they made from their general business in Dunedin. The quality of their management began to concern Begg, however, and so he turned to his restless assistant, offering him a partnership in the New Zealand venture if he would go there and straighten out affairs. This was agreeable to Ross and articles of partnership were signed.[22]

The partnership of Begg & Ross came into effect in 1861, John Ross sailing on the barque *Velore*, which cleared outwards from Gravesend on 13 March. After paying £42 for a cabin passage and giving £20 to his parents, he had little more than £50 left in his pocket. On the *Velore* were thirty passengers, as well as a £3,000 consignment of general merchandise belonging to the Beggs. As well as drapery, the consignment included musical instruments, opera glasses, pouches for shot, electroplated kitchen-ware, other hardware and an old Begg staple, tea. These items were to be sold by Ross, who was to receive a share of the profits realised.[23]

The voyage of the *Velore* proved to be exceptionally slow, the vessel being set back in the Channel for several weeks by adverse winds, becalmed at the Equator and running into heavy seas in the Southern ocean. Troubles amongst the crew also slowed progress, the *Velore* being obliged to put back in to Portsmouth on 28 March to replace a drunken cook. Friction between the master and mate led to the latter being put in irons. The lack of sobriety on the part of the master as the ship entered New Zealand waters lengthened the voyage still further, for the vessel completely missed the Otago heads and sailed up the coast as far as the Waitaki River. It finally arrived back in Port Chalmers, short of food, water and crockery, on 8 August 1861, having been given up as lost.[24]

Upon disembarkation at Port Chalmers, Ross took a steam ferry, *The Pride of the Yarra*, up the harbour to the jetty at Dunedin. It was, he thought, the most beautiful sight he had ever seen.[25] Had he known that, while at sea, a gold rush had occurred in Central Otago and the demand for all types of goods had soared, he would doubtless have regarded his new home with even greater enthusiasm.[26]

# EARLY DAYS IN DUNEDIN

Prior to the gold rush, Dunedin was little more than a scattered village at the top of the Otago harbour inlet. The roads were as yet largely unmade, the streets unlit, and drainage was described by Dr Hocken as 'natural'.[1] Yet even at this stage the settlement was not without prospects. Initially profits were to be made by exporting grain from Otago to Australia, where food prices had soared as a result of the Victorian gold rush. Grain prices were highly volatile, however, and many settlers, especially those with access to capital, found it more profitable to develop sheep runs. Exports of grain were soon overhauled by the value of wool sent to the United Kingdom and by 1859 some 290,000 sheep grazed on 112 runs.[2] Supported by assisted immigration and easy access to land, the population of Otago doubled between 1858 and 1860. Still, with barely 12,000 inhabitants, the province lagged behind Auckland, Wellington and Canterbury.[3]

The discovery of gold transformed the fortunes of Otago, the population increasing fourfold by 1865. Limited quantities of gold had been found in North Otago during the 1850s, a find in the Lindis Pass early in 1861 resulting in a small influx of miners into the area. Then in May, 1861, Gabriel Read, an 'old Californian and Australian digger', discovered gold in the Tuapeka field in Central Otago, just north of present-day Lawrence. The richness of the field was very quickly proved, a second strike occurring at Waitahuna, just south of Lawrence, two months later.[4]

Word of the discoveries spread rapidly and, by the spring, shiploads of miners had started to arrive from the Victorian goldfields, Great Britain and beyond. Inevitably the character of Otago and its settlements changed, even though there seems to have been a disproportionate number of miners of Scots origin.[5] By the end of 1861, some 20,000 people had disembarked at Dunedin. Further discoveries followed as the miners worked their way inland and up the Clutha, Arrow, Shotover and Manuherikia rivers. The value of gold exports from Otago, negligible before 1860, rose from £727,000 in 1861 to a peak of over £2 million in 1863. Thereafter production of the Otago fields fell but fresh strikes on the West Coast of the South Island provided new employment for the diggers.[6] By the end of the decade, miners were turning their attention to discoveries at Thames, east of Auckland, and on the Palmer River in Queensland.

## 1. A TIMELY ARRIVAL

The gold rush was just getting under way when John Ross stepped ashore in Dunedin in early August 1861. A short walk from the jetty took Ross to a draper's shop on the corner of Manse and Princes St where he found Robert Begg. When they met, he was surprised to find that Robert and Sandy Begg had quarrelled and that Robert Begg had formed a new partnership with a man called Christie. They had leased the shop, used as a drapery by a Mrs Bain since 1849, and were themselves carrying on the business of general drapers.[7] Not knowing anyone else in the settlement and unfamiliar with the local business environment, Ross agreed to join Begg, Christie & Co. as a partner.

The consignment of general merchandise brought out on the *Velore* still had to be disposed of, however. Rather than transfer the goods to the new partnership, Ross thought it best to sell them independently. The gold rush meant that the drapery and hardware found ready buyers amongst boarding-house keepers, shopkeepers and the like, the proceeds being remitted to Golspie.[8] Ross retained £600 as his half share of the profits, which provided him with the capital he needed to become a partner in Begg, Christie & Co. William Begg, back in Scotland, was not at all happy with what had transpired but after arbitration found for Ross, he was obliged to settle.[9]

Robert Begg and his new partner, Christie, would have been well satisfied with this turn of events. With support no longer forthcoming from Golspie and trade expanding rapidly, any additional capital was welcome. More importantly, the young Ross was known to be honest, a hard worker, well versed in selling drapery and an accomplished bookkeeper. There is little doubt that in the ensuing months both Ross and his capital were fully employed as miners and others passed through Dunedin. Moleskin trousers, shirts, blankets and other drapers' goods were very much in demand on the goldfields. The exhausted Ross found himself serving behind the counter during the day, doing accounts in the evening, and spending the nights sleeping in the shop. The New Year, which is a happy occasion in Scotland, brought little relief. 'I cannot say that I enjoyed New Year's Day very much. Although the middle of summer, the rain poured down in torrents, and the mud in the streets was about half a foot deep'.[10]

## 2. GOLD AND GROWTH

New strikes of gold during 1862 ensured that people continued to pour into the town on their way to the goldfields. Whether anyone from Begg, Christie & Co. travelled inland and sold to the growing number of mining settlements is not clear. There was plenty of business to be done in Dunedin, however, which expanded in all directions as the population grew. The cutting through Bell Hill, which linked Princes St to the northern part of the town, was widened and much of the hill removed and used for harbour reclamation. Additional jetties were erected at the foot of Stuart and Rattray Streets, the latter jetty being 1200 feet long and faced with stone. The number of retail establishments also increased rapidly. The imposing Royal Arcade, consisting of a double row of fifty-four shops, was built between High St and Maclaggan St. The shop leases were quickly sold at auction, annual rentals reaching up to £150 each, with an additional £20 per annum being paid to the city as ground rent. Retailers also began to spread along George St away from the centre towards North East Valley. In 1863 the much-improved streets were lit with gas.[11] By this stage the city boasted forty-two hotels and restaurants, seven insurance offices, three banks, three daily newspapers, concert halls, public gardens and numerous clubs and societies.[12] Further down the harbour, the growth in shipping meant that Port Chalmers, which had facilities for ocean-going vessels, also expanded. When a census was taken at the end of 1864, it was found that 15,264 people resided in Dunedin City with another 939 located at the port.[13]

The growth in population, improved coastal steamer services, and regular stagecoach and cartage links to the goldfields led to the progressive expansion of the market. As Adam Smith, yet another Scotsman, might have predicted, the division of labour increased as the extent of the market grew. This resulted in larger drapers abandoning a general trade in order to specialise as importers and wholesalers of soft goods. Australian merchants were equally alive to the opportunities in the rapidly developing colony. In 1862, Sargood, King & Co., the largest importers in Melbourne, offered their Castlemaine traveller, John Ewen, a partnership and sent him to Dunedin to open a warehouse.[14] At the same time, some of the more ambitious drapers decided to expand their retail operations. Several, including I. Hallenstein & Co., William McBeath, and the optimistically named Isaacs (Wonder of the World) operated stores in more than one gold-mining settlement.[15]

The changing nature of business did not escape the attention of John Ross. Certainly he was not happy with the way the existing partnership was being run, the incessant toil beginning to affect his health. In the winter of 1862, after working in Princes St for almost a year, he offered either to withdraw from Begg, Christie & Co. or to buy his partners out. They opted for the latter.[16]

## 3. Ross and Glendining become partners

The large profits to be made by selling draperies during the gold rush meant that the original £600 invested by Ross had now become £1,906. This sum, it seems, was insufficient to establish the type of business that he had in mind. Rather than borrow additional funds, he decided to take on a partner, a stratagem that both spread risks and provided him with assistance in running the business. His choice of partner was Robert Glendining, a 22-year-old draper from Dumfries who had arrived in Dunedin a year before Ross on the 811 ton liner, *Evening Star*. Most of the 130 passengers on this vessel were assisted migrants, but Glendining already possessed sufficient means to pay for himself, albeit in a second class cabin.[17]

Robert Glendining was born in Dumfries in 1840, the first of five children. He was of humble origins, his father, John, being employed as an agricultural labourer and then a stone cutter. Like Ross, Glendining benefited from a sound, if basic, Scottish education before leaving school to take up an apprenticeship as a draper. His brother John, some two years his junior, followed him into the drapery trade and then to New Zealand where he became one of Ross & Glendining's earliest employees. Their youngest brother, Thomas, was to join the firm later on.[18]

How well Ross knew Glendining before they set up in business together is not known but, given the size of Dunedin and their common calling, they probably enjoyed more than a passing acquaintance. Being staunch members of the Free Church, they may even have worshipped together. In any event, Glendining certainly appears to have been widely regarded as a sound and trustworthy character, for he was able to borrow the £1,500 necessary to join John Ross in business. On 6 August 1862, the two young Scotsmen commenced trading as Ross & Glendining & Co.[19]

The partners concentrated on soft goods, the generic term given to cotton, linen and woollen fabrics, household furnishings, all types of clothing, millinery, trimmings and haberdashery. They also continued to rent the wooden shop on the corner of Princes St, which had been considerably extended during the previous tenancy. At £850 a year it was not cheap, but it was in a prime location and convenient to the main jetty. Half a dozen men and one woman were initially employed to unpack stock, serve customers, and dispatch orders. Shortly afterwards three women, probably with some pretence to being seamstresses, were engaged in a workroom to make up dresses and millinery. Patterns were sent out to customers – post free.[20]

Ross & Glendining advertised the commencement of their business with a notice that somewhat inflated both their experience and the resources behind them. It read, 'With all the advantages of a home connection and direct importations, combined with long experience and attention to the wants of customers, we hope to merit a share of their public patronage.'[21] Such puffery was commonplace in early Dunedin, the suggestion that goods were bought 'at home' and imported direct conveying the impression that prices were keen owing to the absence of middlemen. Goods from home, moreover, may have possessed connotations of quality, as well as providing an added pull to a migrant community missing the familiar things in life.

Whether Ross & Glendining had a home connection that specifically bought for them so early in their partnership seems doubtful. Instead, they appear to have relied on merchant outfitters in the United Kingdom, such as the London firm of S.W. Silver & Co. and Anderson & Co. of Glasgow, both of which supplied goods on credit to small colonial enterprises. That a newly established firm in a distant land was able to obtain credit suggests that Ross may have had previous dealings with these suppliers. The partners also bought some of their requirements from soft goods warehouses in Melbourne, many of which did have a buyer in the United Kingdom.[22] Buying through intermediaries, at home or in Melbourne, was not the cheapest way to source goods. Even so, the ability to buy specific lines in bulk undoubtedly provided the firm with a cost advantage over those rivals forced to buy odd lots at the quayside auctions that were commonplace in New Zealand.

### 4. Supplying a wider market

The relatively large numbers of staff employed indicates that, from the very beginning, Ross & Glendining were intent on serving not only retail customers but the growing wholesale trade of the province as well. There was competition both from across the Tasman and from local merchants. One of the largest wholesale suppliers was Wolf Harris who, after importing goods from Melbourne for a short while, opened a general store in Maclaggan St in 1858 in partnership with Adolphe Bing. Bing, Harris & Co. soon outgrew its original premises, moving to accommodation at the back of Turnbull & Co.'s property in High St. In 1862, they opened their own purpose-built two-storey warehouse in Lower High St, where 'an extensive assortment of drapery and the newest fashions of clothing' was to be found.[23]

The rapid increase in business meant that by May 1863, Ross & Glendining also found themselves pressed for space, being obliged to rent additional storage facilities. A year later they secured a small warehouse at an annual rental of £350.[24] Growth was partly attributable to the expansion of the retail trade in Dunedin, which benefited both the wholesale and retail side of their enterprise. The main increase in demand, however, came from the rapid spread of the wholesale trade in Otago and adjacent Southland – declared a province in 1861 – where new settlements constantly sprang up.

Some settlements came into being to service the local agricultural community, the emergence of Milton, forty miles southwest of Dunedin, being fairly typical. Established around a flour mill in the late 1850s, by 1860 two general stores had opened for business, a draper's shop appearing in 1862 and another in 1864. Several tailors also set up around this time, a third draper's shop being added by 1870.[25]

Although Milton may have come into existence to meet the needs of the growing number of farmers on the Tokomairiro plains, the discovery of gold at the Waitahuna and Tuapeka fields just over twenty miles away provided the settlement with an added impetus. As a gateway to the early goldfields, it both supplied and serviced the mining community. An agency of the Bank of New Zealand was opened in the township in 1862 to conduct general business, staff also making visits to the diggings to buy gold.[26] Over the next few years a number of other firms set up in Milton, including a brickworks, pottery works and cement works, thereby adding to the general demand for goods and services.

The bulk of the miners' needs, however, were met on the goldfields themselves. Some of the first storekeepers, like the gold buyers from the banks, operated out of tents. The tented settlements were often transient affairs, with miners frequently abandoning the diggings when news reached them of a new and supposedly better strike elsewhere. Thus in November 1862, the settlement of Weatherstones contained banks, stores, and fourteen hotels as well as dance halls and saloons, all built of wood and canvas. A year later the place was deserted.[27] When gold was discovered on the West Coast of the South Island in 1864, large numbers left Otago altogether. From a peak of around 23,000 in February, by November 1865 the total population of the Otago goldfields had fallen to just under 11,000 persons, of whom only 6,000 or so were miners.[28] By way of comparison, the European population of Otago at the end of 1865 was estimated to be just under 47,000.[29]

While many miners departed for the West Coast, Auckland and Australia, some remained, often combining mining with agriculture. Pastoral agriculture increasingly became the mainstay of Central Otago and, as it did so, the number of permanent settlements grew. Some, such as Lawrence in the south, Naseby in the north, and Clyde and Queenstown over to the west, rapidly developed into important service centres. Within a few years of foundation, these townships possessed their own commercial areas, with banks, a variety of hotels and boarding houses, a number of general stores, specialist retailers such as butchers and bakers, boot makers and, invariably, a draper or two.[30] Lesser settlements were also surprisingly well served, with storekeepers and hoteliers seemingly arriving soon after gold had been discovered. Most appeared to prosper, notwithstanding the decline in gold mining, and by the end of the 1860s commercial activity in Central Otago appeared to be greater than ever (see Table 2.1).

The commencement of Cobb & Co. stagecoach services to the goldfields and elsewhere meant that it became relatively easy for provincial shopkeepers and others to visit Dunedin to buy goods. In an effort to attract customers, Ross & Glendining frequently placed large advertisements in the *Otago*

## TABLE 2.1
## COMMERCIAL ACTIVITY ON THE GOLDFIELDS, 1865–1869

|  | 1865 | | | 1869 | | |
|---|---|---|---|---|---|---|
|  | Drapers | Store-keepers | All trades & profs. | Drapers | Store-keepers | All trades & profs. |
| Lawrence District | 2 | 29 | 104 | 4 | 17 | 126 |
| Waipori Junction | 2 | 6 | 32 | 1 | 9 | 29 |
| Roxburgh/Teviot | – | 1 | 17 | 2 | 12 | 42 |
| Switzers | – | – | – | – | 10 | 47 |
| Alexandra | 1 | 3 | 9 | 3 | 5 | 40 |
| Clyde | 3 | 6 | 29 | 3 | 3 | 46 |
| Cromwell | 1 | 1 | 6 | 2 | 4 | 28 |
| Queenstown Dist. | 2 | 6 | 32 | 4 | 8 | 91 |
| Cardrona/Bendigo | – | – | – | 1 | 9 | 28 |
| St Bathans Dist. | 2 | 6 | 28 | 1 | 21 | 85 |
| Naseby/Hamilton | – | 13 | 31 | 4 | 10 | 73 |
| Hyde/Macraes Flat | – | 2 | 9 | 1 | 7 | 28 |

Source: Mackays Otago Provincial and Goldfields Almanac (Dunedin, 1866 & 1870).

*Witness* and the *Otago Daily Times*. Thus double-column spreads appeared in the papers announcing 'Summer Fashions' in 'All the new shades and styles', or their 'Annual Cheap Sale of Summer Goods'.[31] Flyers were sent out to customers, two thousand copies of the firm's stock list being circulated when the partners commenced in business.[32]

Ross & Glendining also placed copy in the pages of the 1865 *Goldfields Almanac*, advertising themselves as 'Wholesale and Retail Drapers, Importers, Silk Mercers, and General Outfitters'. They solicited orders from 'parties furnishing hotels'; aimed directly at the rural and mining community with their 'choice selection' of trousers, riding pants, lambs wool underclothing, and waterproof garments; and were equally happy to supply wedding outfits or 'family mournings'. Country orders, they promised, would be executed with 'punctuality and dispatch'.[33]

## 5. Travelling 'on the outside of a horse'

While advertisements and flyers may have alerted country folk as to what was available in town, the principal means used by Ross & Glendining to push rural business was the commercial traveller. For wholesale warehousemen such as themselves, a competent traveller was absolutely essential, not only through the sales they created but also because of the information that they were able to gather concerning the creditworthiness of customers, the profitability of a particular locality, and the prospects for new business. Regular visits by travellers also had the added advantage of enabling customers to keep their stocks up to date, at the same time helping to ensure that accounts did not get out of hand. Over a period of years, close relationships between traveller and customer might engender goodwill, allowing the firm to retain trade even when undersold by rivals.

Much of Ross & Glendining's early travelling appears to have been undertaken by John Ross. He already had considerable experience as a traveller and, as a partner rather than an employee, had every incentive to ensure that the accounts opened were safe. In January 1863 he took a journey through Otago and on into Southland, travelling four days 'on the outside of a horse', visiting Milton and other settlements en route. He sold purely on a wholesale basis, leaving private individuals to buy their goods either from local shopkeepers or peddlers.[34]

In June 1863 Ross repeated the trip, this time going as far as the township of Invercargill, which had been settled some seven years earlier. Rather than suffer the discomfort of returning overland, he embarked on a coastal steamer, the *William Miskin,* arriving back in Otago Harbour on the night of 3 July. Early next morning Ross, together with other passengers, boarded the harbour ferry, *The Pride of the Yarra,* which was to take them up the harbour to the jetty at Dunedin. Half-way up the harbour and in poor light, the ferry was in collision with the paddle steamer *Favourite.* Ross was on deck as the collision occurred and, with the *Yarra* sinking fast, he grabbed on to the bow of the *Favourite.* Forming a bridge between the vessels, 'he was, so to speak, walked over by a number of others and his clothes, even his trousers, were torn to strips'. Such selflessness, which was widely reported, doubtless constituted excellent public relations for Ross & Glendining. Sadly, of the thirty-nine people on board the *Yarra,* fourteen drowned, including the newly appointed principal to the High School, his wife and their five children.[35]

The following year the firm opened up new ground when Ross travelled northwards into Canterbury. Whether a detour was made to incorporate the gold mining settlements of Naseby and St Bathans is not clear but Waikouaiti and Palmerston, both gateways to the northern fields, were on the way. Yet in spite of conducting a more extensive trade, the profits of the business steadily fell, from £7,000 in the thirteen months ending September 1863 to around £3,500 in the year to September 1864, and continued to fall thereafter. These profits were still considerable, bearing in mind that the firm's eleven employees earned only £35 per week between them, but the downward trend inevitably gave cause for concern.[36]

The decline in profitability is not surprising, for the splendid returns earned by Ross & Glendining and the other early merchants inevitably attracted competition. The short-lived nature of the gold rush also contributed to the decline, the departure of many miners to the West Coast in 1864 and 1865 resulting in the loss of business to Melbourne-based merchants who dominated the trade there.[37] The late arrival of shipments in 1864 further depressed profits, several consignments having to be sold at reduced prices to maintain cash flow.[38]

## 6. THE NEW ZEALAND EXHIBITION

The decline in trade and pressure on margins might help to explain why Ross & Glendining were happy to support the New Zealand Exhibition, held in Dunedin in 1865. The idea for a small industrial exhibition was originally conceived in the minds of local Anglican churchmen as a means of supplementing the St Paul's Church building funds. When they saw how enthusiastically their proposal was received, they realised that the colony as a whole might benefit by holding an industrial exhibition on an altogether grander scale. The principal objective was to demonstrate to the world the suitability of New Zealand 'for almost every species of production'.

Modelled along the lines of the Great Exhibition of 1851, it was hoped that an exhibition, in which products were displayed in a pavilion, would both stimulate old industries and give rise to new ones. Worthy items were to be sent to London for permanent display where, it was hoped, they might induce both capital and labour to flow to New Zealand. It was also intended that Maori should benefit, both as exhibitors and visitors. Although the exhibition site was in Dunedin, exhibits were to be drawn from the entire country with local committees set up to coordinate affairs.[39]

The benefits of an exhibition to industry and commerce were not lost on the Dunedin business community and, in December 1863, a local committee was formed. The Provincial Government almost immediately declared its support, voting £4,000 to support the exhibition and, on 18 February 1864, the cornerstone of the exhibition building was laid. At a final cost of over £18,000, it turned out to be a stunning piece of architecture. Three storeys high and with a floor area at ground level of around 10,000 square feet, the building was decorated with balconies and Italianate towers that soared above the muddy streets and wooden premises round about. Located on

Great King St, a short walk from the centre of town, it was finally handed over to the organisers on 11 November 1864, a declaration of faith in the future of Otago.

The exhibits on display were divided into thirty-six classes, from Class 1 which consisted of 'Mining, Quarrying, Metallurgy and Mineral Products' to Class 36B 'Maori and other Aboriginal Manufactures and Implements'. There were a number of sub-classes such as 10B, 'Sanitary Improvements and Accoutrements' and 31A, 'Iron Manufactures'. There were also classes for clothing, carpets, cotton manufactures, woollen and worsted mixed fabrics, silk and velvet, tapestry, lace and embroidery, just the sorts of things that would appeal to the customers of the soft goods warehousemen. The ground floor of the main building was divided into bays devoted to displays of the various provinces, with English exhibitors relegated to a back corner. In a galleried area on the first floor were to be found exhibits from Australia, India and France, together with a display of furniture made in Otago. An outside annex provided space for the display of machinery and iron fencing. Here, too, patrons could obtain refreshments, while those of the appropriate gender might visit the 'Ladies Private Rest Rooms'.[40]

The Exhibition was as much a showcase as to what might be imported into New Zealand as to the state of domestic production. Under the class for 'Clothing, Accoutrements, Woven Fabrics, Boots & Shoes', the London merchants S.W. Silver & Co. exhibited tweed jumpers, Bedford cord trousers, ladies waterproof jackets and other items. British manufacturers were also represented with, amongst others, E. Firth of Heckmondwike displaying blankets and Clark & Co. of Paisley their world famous cotton threads. Ross & Glendining, classified as 'Importers', had two exhibits in Class 20; No. 636 which was a display of British textiles manufactured in silk, velvet, woollen and worsteds and No. 637 which included cashmere squares, French embroidered handkerchiefs and 'A Baby Basket – Complete'.

## 7. BACK HOME TO IMPROVE THE SUPPLY CHAIN

The Exhibition, which remained open from 13 January to 5 May 1865, attracted more than 30,000 visitors and undoubtedly provided a boost to flagging trade. By this time, however, Ross & Glendining had decided to put their business on a more competitive footing by making arrangements to buy and ship goods from the United Kingdom themselves. Early that year, with the Exhibition in full flow, John Ross departed for London, taking the quickest route possible. This involved taking a mail ship to Suez via Sydney and coaling stations in the Indian Ocean, overland to Alexandria, and thence by steamer to Marseilles. He arrived in London, 'along with the Marseilles portion of the mail', on 15 March 1865.[41]

His first thought was for his parents and so that evening he took an overnight train to Glasgow. Combining business with pleasure, Ross bought some fancy goods in the city before making his way to Caithness. He arrived at his parents' home at 7.00 a.m. Saturday morning, quite unexpected, to find all in bed except his mother. The following Tuesday he left, finally arriving back in London on Thursday morning. Once in the city, he began his round of the merchants, paying accounts and settling a dispute with S.W. Silver & Co. over goods they had shipped. His next task was 'to get someone to look after us in the world of London, which would not be so difficult a manner under ordinary circumstances as at the present time owing to the news of failures coming to hand by this mail, one in Sydney and the other in Melbourne'.[42] Not for the last time were events in the other Australasian colonies to impinge on business in New Zealand.

On the voyage from Sydney, Ross had been fortunate enough to share a cabin with an Englishman, Thomas Geard. An experienced soft goods buyer, Geard had just visited Australia to wind up a business on behalf of merchants Dalgety, Rattray & Co. Although considerably older than Ross, the two men rapidly became firm friends and it was to his new-found friend that Ross now turned. In many respects, Geard was the ideal contact. Brought up in the retail drapery trade, he had been working on his own account for more than twenty years buying soft goods on commission for colonial merchants. He was, Ross thought, a first-rate character, 'well to do in the world and is on intimate terms with all the first houses in the trade'. After satisfying himself that his impressions were correct, Ross decided to see if he could secure Geard's services. Geard was equally cautious but once he had established Ross & Glendining's credentials, he agreed to act as their London buyer. He was to receive $2^{1}/_{2}$ per cent commission on all goods bought.[43]

The first thing Geard did was to introduce Ross to the leading drapery merchants in London. At one establishment, Ross informed Glendining, 'I underwent a severe catechising, viz Brown, Davis & Hulse. Mr. Davis is the counting house man and has the reputation of being not only the sharpest but the most sagacious man in our trade in London. At the end of our interview he paid me the compliment of telling me that my head was screwed on all right'. More importantly for Ross & Glendining, Davis said that they might call upon his firm for references should they wish to open accounts elsewhere.[44]

Ross was equally fortunate when he called upon the Bank of New South Wales in London for a bill of exchange. To his surprise, the manager, the secretary and all the clerks were Caithnessmen, the result being that a business account, with permission to obtain credit by drawing bills of exchange on the Bank, was opened without delay.[45] Being a Scotsman clearly had its advantages, at least at this particular institution.

Having arranged trade references and banking facilities, Ross spent the next three weeks in and around London visiting warehouses and manufacturers and placing orders for stock. The vagaries of fashion meant that deciding what was best for New Zealand was not always straightforward. He informed Glendining, '... yellow and light green appears to be all the rage. ... I may mention that there has been a good deal of light ground and laines and mohairs with printed spots shown this season but I cannot say that I have seen much of it moving around, in fact, Londoners are still dressing in winter materials'. In spite of his experience as an Edinburgh window dresser, Ross was 'frightened off such extreme colours' and bought sparingly.[46]

Geard was of great assistance when it came to selecting suppliers. Following his advice, orders for hats and caps were placed with a Messrs Brannans of London, stays were manufactured in Surrey, most hosiery requirements were obtained from a manufacturer in Nottingham, manchester (cotton goods) was to be supplied by Hocken, Bird, Cole & Co., and the orders for slops (clothing) were divided between two London manufacturers with more to be obtained from Glasgow. There was also a case of goods bought from Messrs Brown, Davis and Co. containing glove boxes, jet ornaments and other fancy stuff which, unlike clothing and textiles, was admitted into New Zealand duty free.

The first batch of orders cost over £6,000, most of which had to be paid for in nine months or less. Wherever possible, the goods had been purchased either direct from the manufacturers or their principal agents. Ross was confident that they were 'as well bought' as any goods in the market and should yield 'a larger profit than we have hitherto been getting'. Even so, he was anxious not to order too liberally, for Otago was no longer as prosperous as hitherto. With 'the prospect of hard times and dull trade' he had no wish to overextend the business.[47]

The downturn in trade in Otago had other consequences as well. Since Ross had left there had been two severe fires in Dunedin, the first late in January breaking out in Princes St and destroying the Bank of New Zealand, several restaurants, the First Church and a number of other buildings. A second fire, barely two weeks later, started in the Octagon and again spread to Princes St, a hotel, three shops, and another ten buildings being burnt out.[48] The news soon spread to London, with insurers being advised not to take fire risks in Dunedin because, as trade was very bad, 'there would be lots of fires in consequence'. Whether the fires were acts of God or the result of arson is not clear, but Ross found it very difficult to arrange insurance. As a practical measure, however, he purchased and shipped a large iron safe.[49]

London was not the best place to buy all the firm's requirements and on 28 April Ross made his way back to Glasgow, via Sheffield, Manchester, Liverpool and Dumfries, placing orders as he went.[50] While in Glasgow he visited J. & P. Coats in Paisley, purchasing reels of cotton for cash, before travelling on to Belfast to obtain linens.[51] Finally, he made his way to Dublin to attend an exhibition. At thirty years old and unmarried, Ross also had other matters on his mind, commenting that 'the Dublin girls are the prettiest I have ever seen'.[52]

The three months that John Ross spent in London contributed enormously to the success of Ross & Glendining. It also allowed him to gain an insight into the ways his competitors in New Zealand operated, several of whom were also in the United Kingdom buying goods: 'You would be astonished if you knew the inner workings of the business of our more bouncing friends', he wrote to Glendining. 'I met Butterworth on Saturday, he was going to Lancashire …. Harris has been down to Glasgow and back but I do not think he is getting on so well.'[53] The 'bouncing friends' clearly did not welcome the additional competition for, by the time Ross arrived in Dublin, he suspected they were trying to ruin his reputation. They evidently failed. On 20 June he left for New Zealand, having successfully completed his business.[54]

## 8. A PASSIONLESS PASSAGE

Ross paid a brief visit to Paris and then travelled on to Marseilles, where he took a steamer for Alexandria. Once on board, he settled down to shipboard life, writing a number of letters to family and friends. A particularly long and familiar letter was addressed to a Miss Geard, although the relationship was evidently a platonic one. His preoccupation with his single status yet again came to the fore,

> We have only five ladies on board in all, and all of them married; no widows of any sort! But I am living in hope that there will be a larger sprinkling of the fairer sex when we meet the Southampton passengers.
>
> The presence of cholera in Alexandria and Egypt is a source of great concern and we are hoping to get right through from Alexandria to Suez.[55]

Fortunately, cholera did not prevent the vessel on which Ross was travelling from entering Alexandria and a week later he was sailing down the Red Sea on the SS *Candia*.

The passage to Aden, he informed his parents, was both airless and hot, with a lot of passengers sleeping on deck. Early each morning they were obliged to take refuge as the crew hosed down the decks. Ross had the benefit of a cabin to himself. After taking on bunkers at Aden for half a day, the *Candia* then set off for Point De Galle in Ceylon where passengers for Australia were to disembark. A day out from Aden and the monsoon began to blow, 'laying the greater part of the passengers on their beam ends, and the ladies, with one exception, were all sick'. Deprived of female company yet again, Ross arrived in Ceylon only to find that he was to transfer to an Australian mail ship, reputedly one of the most uncomfortable of the P & O fleet.[56] In Australia he changed ships once more, arriving in Dunedin on 26 August, some two months after he had left London.

Once back at work, Ross began to busy himself with stocktaking and drawing up the annual balance sheet. The departure of miners from Otago to the West Coast inevitably affected turnover, although the loss of trade was felt more by up-country drapers than retailers in town. Under the circumstances profits held up well, £2,500 having been earned in the year to September after exceptional items had been deducted. These included £600 for extensions to premises and £500 in expenses for the trip home. Bad debts were quite modest at £700, from which it was expected to receive something. Thomas Geard, who now had an interest in such matters, received a comforting note from Dunedin in which he was assured that Ross & Glendining would be able to meet all their liabilities as they fell due. The firm still required a renewal of credit from certain suppliers but, as this had already been arranged, it did not constitute a problem.[57]

The unsettled conditions in Otago were not sufficient to deter either John Ross or Robert Glendining from encouraging their relatives to emigrate. In December 1865, Ross was to be found negotiating for purchase of an iron-mongery on behalf of his brother, Murdoch, and a partner, Sandy Gunn. The two men were expected to bring out Glendining's younger brother, Thomas, with them.[58] Murdoch, it seems, did not come out straight away although he and his partner ultimately did arrive to set up business in New Zealand.

## 9. SPECIALISING IN WHOLESALE

The summer season of 1865 which, in the drapery trade, lasted from September to February, was one of substantial progress, with the partnership turning over about £35,000 in six months. Encouraged by this performance, Ross and Glendining decided to give up the retail trade to devote themselves 'entirely to wholesale in future'. The restructured enterprise was to come into being on 1 September 1866.[59] Their retail business, by now a valuable asset, was purchased by three of the firm's salesmen, Thomas Brown, Ralph Ewing, and Glendining's younger brother, John. The buyers, trading as Brown, Ewing & Co., were to retain the shop premises on the corner of Princes and Manse St, while the now-expanding wholesale business was to relocate in more suitable accommodation.[60]

As vacant sites in appropriate locations were difficult to come by, Ross & Glendining first tried to secure one of the existing city warehouses. For a short while negotiations took place with Bing, Harris & Co., who were apparently willing to vacate their warehouse on Lower High St – providing the price was right.[61] Agreement proved to be difficult to reach with the ever-opportunistic Harris, and ultimately the partners decided to build.

The best site they were able to obtain was part of a leasehold section at 28 Stafford St, albeit one street further away from the centre than High St. It was not ideal, for although it was 165 feet deep the site had only a relatively narrow frontage of 29 feet in width. Fortunately, there appears to have been the prospect of acquiring more of the section later and, possibly with this in mind, the partners started to build.[62] By September 1866 their new warehouse was ready and its doors opened for business.

The decision to give up retail was a bold step, for retailing was a largely cash business in which margins were usually generous. The wholesale trade, on the other hand, while yielding slimmer margins and requiring more in the way of advances to customers, offered greater scope for expansion. The risks attached to the latter were obviously greater, but so were the rewards. This fundamental change in the nature of their business – from general drapers and outfitters to importers and warehousemen – proved instrumental in laying the basis for future success.[63]

3

# DEVELOPING THE WAREHOUSE BUSINESS

The importation of draperies, woollens and cottons and other apparel increased enormously during the 1860s, although growth was far from even. By the end of the decade such goods accounted for almost a quarter of all imports, the total bill for which amounted to £4.6 million. The population of Canterbury and Otago also continued to grow. Of the quarter of a million Europeans living in New Zealand in 1870, more than half resided in the lower South Island. The market facing Ross & Glendining thus underwent considerable expansion in this period, although keeping it well supplied proved to be far from straightforward. A downturn in the late 1860s, difficulties in shipping, and constant competition both from local competitors and Melbourne-based firms forced the partners to change the way in which they did business. Having adapted to changing circumstances, they were in a good position to take full advantage of the booming economy of the 1870s.

## 1. THE NEW VENTURE

Their new Dunedin warehouse on Stafford St, completed in September 1866, was an imposing affair that was built to the latest designs. Constructed of brick and stone and costing over £3,000, it not only provided Ross & Glendining with ample storage space and well-lit showrooms, but it also served to advertise the firm to the world at large.[1] During the first month it was open, sales amounted to around £7,500. More might have been done had consignments arrived on time.

Ross found the slow passage of the *Olive Mount* and its consignment of millinery particularly annoying, the season being over by the time she arrived. Losses were also made on other goods on this vessel as the market had been falling since they were shipped. This, together with the late arrival of other ships, meant that the firm started to run short of cash. As a result, Ross was forced to ask suppliers for further extensions of credit.[2] Matters were made worse when he also agreed to buy the closing stock of the Dunedin drapers, J. & J.H. Barr, in an attempt to alleviate the shortfall of seasonal goods. The purchase proved to be a costly error. Not only was the price paid too generous, but it left the firm even more short of cash than before. It was a mistake that Ross vowed he would never make again.[3]

Other Dunedin warehousemen also failed to receive goods on time, with Melbourne firms quick to take advantage of the situation. Encouraged by large orders from shopkeepers early in the summer season, Australian salesmen arrived in the South Island 'in shoals'. 'A few days ago', Geard was told, 'there were no fewer than 13 softgoods travellers in one town in New Zealand at one time'. Ross & Glendining also employed a traveller to help them meet the opposition, but Ross was not overly optimistic. 'We do not expect that he will do a paying trade at first,' he wrote to Geard, 'nor do we expect to be any richer at the end of the year than we were at the commencement.'[4] Even so, the firm turned over more than £43,000 in the six months from October 1866, up 25 per cent on the corresponding period in the previous year.[5]

The year was not all gloom. While Ross had been away, Robert Glendining had sailed to Australia to marry a tailor's daughter, Mary Cassels, whose family had lived in New Zealand for a short while.[6] In November she had presented him with his first son, John Ross Glendining. Thomas Geard, too, had married earlier in 1866. The still single Ross was clearly not at ease with his continuing bachelorhood, writing to Geard, 'You are indeed a lucky man in gaining such an estimable lady for a wife, and she no doubt is lucky getting a husband who can so well appreciate her many virtues. I wish you would select for me another'.[7]

Whether Ross was quite ready for marriage seems doubtful. His correspondence with Miss Reid, the proprietress of a school for young ladies in Thurso, suggests a certain lack of tact and understanding. Upon learning that his sisters had been excluded from her school because they had once been in domestic service he wrote, 'I cannot for one moment suppose that you would be guilty of anything so unjust to my sisters or unbusinesslike to yourself, or that the ladies of Thurso could so forget their duty to their sex as to be instrumental in excluding anyone from the benefits of education on account of their humble birth or dependent circumstances.'[8] How Miss Reid received these strictures from a thirty-two year old bachelor on how her business should be run, the right of the poor to self-improvement, or the duties of the fairer sex in Thurso, can only be imagined. One suspects, though, that the Ross sisters were not allowed to pursue their schooling at her establishment.

## 2. STRUGGLE FOR SURVIVAL

The difficulties experienced by Ross & Glendining towards the end of 1866 continued into the New Year as the economy deteriorated still further. Trading conditions in the North Island, where the wars between Maori and settlers saw over seventy engagements fought between 1864 and 1868, had been difficult for some time.[9] The lack of economic integration at the time, however, meant that business in the South Island had not been much affected by the fighting. Gold, grain and pastoralism combined to sustain trade in Canterbury and Otago although, as the gold discoveries were worked out, activity there began to slow down also.

The slow-down in trade, already evident in Dunedin by 1865, became more general thereafter as a reduction in Government loan expenditure began to affect incomes. There were also worries about the state of public finances, the level of both government and provincial indebtedness affecting New Zealand's ability to raise loans in the City of London.[10] The excessive borrowing upset businessmen in the South Island, annoyed that their taxes were being spent to support the land wars in the north. Ross, along with many others, called for the political separation of the two islands.[11] The uncertainty that this caused inevitably affected business confidence and, from this point onwards, it took little to push the economy over the edge. When, early in 1867, wheat and wool prices began to fall, incomes declined sharply. By the middle of the year, it was reported that widespread depression existed throughout the colony.[12]

The depression inevitably led to acute competition as warehousemen tried to push goods on an overstocked market. Once again, it was the Melbourne firms that Ross complained about most. Having over-imported in the previous season, the Australians were now dumping goods in New Zealand that, in many cases, 'they sold at a loss giving five to six months credit'.[13] To make matters worse, the Dunedin branch of Sargood, Son & Ewen had poached Ross & Glendining's new traveller, 'for no better reason than doing us an injury'. This was inconvenient but, as the traveller had proved unsatisfactory, the partners 'did not mind very much'. For the benefit of the trade in London – which soon learned of Sargoods' coup – Ross was quick to point out to Geard that Sargoods had also found the traveller unsatisfactory and had fired him.[14]

The attempt by Ross to put this episode in perspective is a reflection of the fact that he was worried about his firm's credit standing amongst suppliers. He assured Geard that Ross & Glendining were not losing money and had actually turned over £46,000 in the half-year to July 1867, although slow trade and heavy stocks had again left the firm short of cash. The promised remittance of £7,000 for July was thus £2,000 short – and it looked as though the August remittance would be short as well. If this proved to be the case, Ross promised to come home 'either by next Panama or overland mail' to help Geard arrange fresh credit facilities.[15]

### 3. AN ADDITIONAL PARTNER

When Ross wrote to Geard a month later he was altogether more cheerful. In spite of bad debts of £2,000 and heavy losses on cotton goods, the firm was now in a position to remit sufficient funds to meet their obligations. The turnaround in fortunes, as Ross was willing to admit, was as much the result of good luck as his own financial genius, an additional partner having been found willing to supply capital. The new man was Thomas Harrison, a former partner in the Melbourne firm of Pyne, Harrison, Beath.[16] In the first instance, the new partnership was to run from July 1867 for a period of six years. Of a total capital of £22,590 invested in the enterprise, Harrison was to contribute £2,000, Glendining £8,846, and John Ross the balance of £11,743. Each was entitled to draw £500 per annum for personal expenses and receive interest of 10 per cent on their capital contribution. Harrison was to have an equal share of the profits after the interest had been paid. The warehouse in Stafford St was to remain the property of John Ross and Robert Glendining, with the partnership to pay a rental of £600 per annum for its use.[17]

Although Harrison supplied only a small proportion of the capital, it provided a welcome injection of funds at a most opportune moment. His arrival conferred other benefits too. While Glendining was to 'attend and manage' the stock and Ross's duties were to oversee finance and conduct the firm's 'country house business', Harrison was to 'personally attend to the travelling department in the northern provinces of New Zealand'.[18] In reality, northern provinces simply meant mainly Canterbury and the West Coast, gold production on the Coast now being almost four times that of Otago. With the influx of miners, towns such as Greymouth, Westport, Reefton and Hokitika had all mushroomed. It was the trade of these small towns, still largely in the hands of the Melbourne warehousemen, that Harrison was expected to exploit.[19]

The ability of Ross & Glendining to meet their debts meant that there was no longer any immediate pressure for John Ross to travel to London. Even so, in August he informed Geard that he was still contemplating a brief visit home although, unless an emergency arose, he would not depart until early in 1868 when the summer season had ended.[20] At this stage he did not explain what lay behind his proposed visit. The next few months appear to have produced no new scares and on 4 February, Ross embarked on the coastal steamer *Tararua* bound for Wellington. Once there he boarded the *Kaikoura*, a 1500-ton steamship with auxiliary sail.[21] It was one of two vessels that ran a subsidised monthly mail service between Sydney and Panama, the service having been inaugurated some eighteen months earlier.[22]

## 4. OCEAN TRAVEL BY SAIL AND STEAM

The *Kaikoura* was much better appointed than Ross expected but, being rather narrow in the beam, rolled a lot.[23] Although reasonably large, the vessel had relatively few passengers on board. Certificated for 200 passengers and crew, there were only seventeen passengers in the saloon and another four forward. As luck would have it, three of the seventeen were soft goods men from Sydney, one was from Melbourne, while a fifth was a brother to Kirkcaldie of Kirkcaldie & Stains, the Wellington importers and retail drapers.[24] They were, Ross confided to a friend, the quietest and most sober bunch of shipmates that he had ever sailed with.[25]

Yet again Ross used the opportunity of a long sea voyage to learn how his competitors conducted their business. He became particularly friendly with a Mr Bell, a partner in the Melbourne firm of Banks Brothers & Bell, and had 'sundry conversations' with him concerning business matters. From Bell he learned that the Melbourne firm was capitalised at around £155,000, carried a stock of around £100,000, and dealt mainly in plain goods, avoiding fancy goods as much as possible. Of particular interest to Ross was the way in which Banks Brothers & Bell reduced their buying expenses. Banks, it seems, conducted the United Kingdom buying from his house in Cumberland, the buying expenses not exceeding £350 a year. Their total home buying expenses, including shipping, insurance and freight, came to only 5 per cent. This was in marked contrast to the expenses incurred by Ross & Glendining, who paid for shipping, insurance and freight themselves as well as 2$^1$/$_2$ per cent commission to Geard for buying. Bell also mentioned, in passing, that he had heard that their new partner, Thomas Harrison, was pressing too hard for trade and was likely to make bad debts. Melbourne, it seems, was very familiar with what was going on in the South Island![26]

The *Kaikoura* did not sail directly to Panama but headed south to about 44 degrees in order to pick up southwesterly trade winds. Under sail and steam she averaged ten knots, the passage to Panama, taking twenty-seven days. In addition to discussing business, Ross therefore found plenty of time to sit down and write to family and friends. One particularly entertaining letter was addressed to 'the Cassels household', although it seems likely that the intended recipient of the letter was Margaret Cassels, Robert Glendining's young sister-in-law. After commenting on other passengers, entertainments, and the nature of the meals (Ross only took breakfast at 8.30 and dinner at 4.00), he was able to turn to the subject of cockroaches, rats in bunks, and the ship's solitary cow. The latter, he informed his readers, had been with the ship since she left England two years ago and gave fourteen quarts of milk a day.[27] Perhaps it was just as well that there were so few passengers on board.

The *Kaikoura* arrived in Panama on 5 March. Unfortunately, the New York-bound steamer upon which Ross had intended to sail had left Colon three days earlier. With another steamer not due for a week, he and some fellow passengers decided to travel to Southampton by way of the West Indies. After a day 'sauntering' around Panama – which Ross found expensive even though it was a duty-free port – he took the forty-seven-mile train ride to Colon and boarded a paddle steamer, the RMS *Tyne*.[28] This small vessel took Southampton-bound passengers to Jamaica, where they transferred to the SS *Douro*.

The *Douro*, 3,000 tons, screw driven and very fast, was expected to call briefly at St Thomas in the Virgin Islands to pick up mail and then sail directly to the United Kingdom. Unfortunately two days were lost in St Thomas as the connecting mail steamers had not yet arrived.[29] To make matters worse, there was cholera, smallpox and yellow fever on the hurricane-ravaged island, so passengers were not allowed to go ashore. On 28 March, the *Douro* finally arrived in Plymouth. Rather than sail round to Southampton and experience further delay, Ross disembarked with the mail and caught the train to London.[30]

## 5. CUTTING THE COSTS OF LONDON BUYING

Thomas Geard was still in ignorance of the real purpose of the trip when John Ross arrived. The commission agent must have been aware, though, that Ross & Glendining were not entirely satisfied with the way he had kept them supplied. Certainly they had complained bitterly about delayed shipments, the stock assortment, and the fact that they had lost heavily on certain items. These matters were doubtless on the agenda when the two met in London. The first day was spent reviewing the past two years. It was unpleasant work, Ross told Glendining, 'as I did not mince my words in the least'. The real bone of contention, however, was the $2^1/2$ per cent commission that Geard was paid, with Ross (possibly influenced by Bell) feeling that it was far too high. The canny Scotsman nevertheless felt that it was inappropriate to make a formal proposal at the first meeting. It broke up with Geard still not knowing whether Ross was in the United Kingdom on a permanent or temporary basis.[31]

The next day Ross had a meeting with a friend, a Mr Hannah, and together they discussed what strategy Ross might employ. They concluded that it would be unwise to dispense with Geard's services 'at present' as it would be difficult to find another buyer better suited to the firm's requirements. In the interim, Geard was to be offered $1^1/4$ per cent on all home purchases that Ross made, with the purchases to go through the commission agent's office, and Geard to assist Ross with the London buying.

Geard was not too keen to accept this proposal, especially as he did not know how long Ross was to remain in the United Kingdom. Nor did he take kindly to the suggestion that he might be paid a salary rather than commission. At this Ross relented somewhat, pointing out that he had no wish for a change but the previous arrangement had been made when the agent was expected to purchase £25,000 worth of goods per annum for a retail trade – in which margins were much higher. Geard, too, gave a little ground, suggesting that Ross & Glendining pay the usual commission up to a certain level, then half beyond that figure. Although attractive in principle, Ross was reluctant to close with Geard at this point, particularly as he was uncertain as to how long he was to remain in the United Kingdom. The meeting closed with Geard being assured that if Ross & Glendining were to continue with an agency, then 'he should have the first offer'.[32]

The understanding that Geard would probably continue as agent seems to have cleared the air, for the following week John Ross was invited to stay with the Geard's in the north London suburb of Highgate.[33] Thereafter, the two worked together in the city, leaving home at around eight each morning and returning about twelve hours later.[34] By the middle of April a deal appears to have been struck, with commission agreed at $2^{1}/_{2}$ per cent for the first £30,000 and half the rate thereafter. Ross was not entirely sure whether this was agreeable to Glendining, offering to stay in London on a permanent basis, but his own preference was to return once the winter orders had been placed.[35]

The news from Dunedin was not particularly promising while Ross was away. The sales returns for February and March 1868 were better than expected, but the working out of gold deposits on the West Coast saw a number of diggers leave. Glendining, managing the country trade in his partner's absence, was cautioned to do business 'only where you are certain of being safe'.[36] The question of safety arose in a slightly different context when Glendining took over some of the travelling duties, with Ross highly relieved that his partner had returned unscathed from a journey to North Otago. 'I was afraid you would be attempting the Waitaki River or something equally dangerous'. He was less happy to receive news about the state of trade in Oamaru where a number of accounts 'were sure to come to grief'.[37] Yet it was in places such as Oamaru, rather than the goldfields, that Ross believed that the future lay, having 'much more faith in Otago as an agricultural and pastoral country than a gold producing one'.[38]

As on his previous visit, John Ross frequently bumped into his New Zealand competitors while out buying. His firm, it seems, was not alone when struggling to meet their debts during the downturn of 1867, others also requiring considerable financial assistance. Happily, the credit standing of Ross & Glendining had not been damaged and Ross was able to report that 'our credit is A1 here and we can open accounts with any house in the shipping trade'.[39] The question of prices and credit was often discussed by the Dunedin buyers when they met in London and it was not long before someone proposed an agreement 'respecting terms'. Sargoods, Butterworth Brothers, Watson & Co. and Ross & Glendining were all agreeable, but Bing, Harris & Co. could not be persuaded.[40] Indeed, Harris continued to cut the prices of goods and offer credit in a way that the others deemed both 'suicidal' and 'stupid'.[41] Such action put paid to any notion of a cartel and it was not until the 1880s that an effective warehousemen's association came into being.

## 6. English manufacturers and a Scottish health spa

Ross paid a brief visit to his parents in Caithness towards the end of May, travelling north by steamer and returning from Golspie by railway. Back in London he had another opportunity to observe Geard at work. 'We shall never get a better man than Mr. Geard,' he wrote to Glendining, 'nor a man calculated to give us good standing in the market, or a man more respected and trusted than he is'. Geard's fault, he thought, was expecting too much of human nature and the prestige of certain houses and certain people. This was a doctrine that Ross did not subscribe to, especially in an unsettled market in which prices varied widely. He conceded, however, that buying was an art and knowing where to buy was as important as knowing what type of goods were suited to a particular market. An experienced buyer, such as Geard, clearly held an advantage in this respect.[42]

There was only so much buying that could be done in London. In June, Ross began to tour manufacturing districts, going to Leicester to buy hosiery and to Manchester for cotton goods.[43] By the end of the month he was in Glasgow, where he found that there was still considerable animosity towards Wolf Harris for selling goods in New Zealand at cut-throat prices. Ross had been feeling unwell for some time so he took advantage of the trip to Scotland to spend a week at a 'hydropathic establishment' at Rothesay on the Isle of Bute. Run by a Doctor Patterson, the treatment involved drinking copious amounts of water, hot and cold salt-water showers, incessant bathing, being rubbed with hot towels, a powerful dose of 'galvanism' [electricity] applied to the spine, liver, stomach and feet, and plenty of walks in the fresh air. The day finished with dinner and prayers. While the patients had no complaints about the dinners, they thought that the sermons, at over an hour, were rather too long.[44]

Whether this watery regimen improved the Ross constitution is unclear, but a few weeks later he was back in England visiting manufacturers in

Leicester, Nottingham, Sheffield and Stockport. Most of the purchases he made were for Ross & Glendining but some goods were bought on indent for Brown & Ewing, from whom a small commission was received. While in London he also discharged his fraternal obligations, contacting a hardware shipping house on behalf of his brother, Murdoch. For 7½ per cent commission, the firm was prepared to supply Murdoch Ross and Sandy Gunn, both of whom had finally arrived in New Zealand to set up business.[45]

Ross also began to think about staff who might be needed in Dunedin to cope with the anticipated expansion in the warehouse business. With one of the warehouse staff having recently been fired, a salesman with expertise in manchester was urgently needed. In his travels Ross had received lots of applications from 'hands wishing to go out' to New Zealand but considered none of them suitable. He would, he said, 'endeavour to get Scotchmen'.[46]

### 7. ANOTHER DEPRESSION LOOMS

How much longer John Ross spent in the United Kingdom is not known although, given his intention to buy two seasons' goods when he arrived, he would have been obliged to remain in the country until winter styles appeared in the marketplace.[47] In July 1868 he mentioned to Geard that he would leave on the November mail ship – or the December mail at the very latest – and this, probably, is what happened.[48]

The responsibility of buying for the firm clearly weighed heavily on Ross. Nevertheless, he appears to have been successful for sales rose to over £102,000 for the twelve months up to October 1869. Astute buying doubtless contributed to the increase in business, although firmer agriculture prices and a rise in government expenditure helped to sustain trade. The recovery was short-lived, a sharp fall in prices and a reversal in expenditure by central and local government slashing purchasing power. By the end of the year there was widespread depression, with Dunedin suffering from heavy unemployment.[49]

The depression in trade saw Ross & Glendining's sales fall back to £86,259 for the year to October 1870.[50] The pressure on prices necessarily affected margins and so it can therefore have come as no surprise when the balance sheet for the six months ending in July1870 revealed a loss of £607. Fortunately this did not constitute an actual loss, for the balance was struck after the partners had been paid their £1,690 interest (see Table 3.1).

Thomas Harrison was nevertheless apprehensive about the way the business was turning out. Shortly before the books were balanced, he gave eight months notice that he wished to retire from the firm. He did so, he said, with no ill will, but simply because the arrangement 'ceased to suit'.[51]

TABLE 3.1
SALES, CAPITAL EMPLOYED AND PROFITABILITY, 1870–1872 (£)

| Period ending[a] | Jul 1870 | Jan 1871 | Jul 1871 | Jan 1872 | Jul 1872 |
|---|---|---|---|---|---|
| Total sales | 44,333 | 39,927 | 43,798 | 48,858 | 55,967 |
| Bad debts[b] | 1,280 | 1,308 | [69][b] | 267 | 37 |
| Net profit | -607 | -2,656 | 3,625 | 4,329 | 6,854 |
| Imputed interest | 1,690 | 1,746 | 1,663 | 1,902 | 2,163 |
| Partners' salaries[c] | 750 | 750 | 500 | 500 | 500 |
| Total returns | 1,833 | -160 | 5,788 | 6,731 | 9,517 |
| Estimated average capital employed[d] | 33,816 | 34,921 | 33,255 | 38,056 | 43,267 |
| Return on capital (%) | 10.8 | -1.0 | 34.8 | 35.4 | 44.0 |

Sources: Half-yearly balances, AG 512 15/18.
Notes: (a) Balances struck on the 22nd or 23rd of the month. (b) Bad debts recovered. (c) Salaries are not always included in rates of return calculations but done so in this instance as the partners tended to live out of the business on an ad hoc basis, the salary figure being entirely nominal. (d) Estimated on the basis of imputed interest charged at 10 per cent per annum.

Whether his departure was occasioned by the impending losses, or the fact that John Ross was, in future, to live in London and take care of the buying, is not known. Yet Harrison's time with the firm was hardly wasted. His capital of £2,000 had more than doubled between July 1867 and January 1871 and he had drawn expenses of £500 per annum in the interim.[52]

The exit of Harrison, the principal traveller, did not seem to worry the remaining partners unduly. Indeed, Glendining regarded him as 'an old duffer'. Of greater organisational significance was the decision that Ross should sail to London and set up a buying office there. Why Ross, who found his buying trip in 1868 so extremely stressful, should now agree to take over the London buying is unclear. Maybe it was felt that it was no longer cost effective to rely on Geard, especially when trade was so depressed. In any event, on 1 July, Ross sailed for England. Two hours before departure he married Margaret Cassels, Robert Glendining's sister-in-law.[53] Eight weeks later, the newly married couple set up home in temporary accommodation in Cheapside. Almost immediately, Ross opened an office at 1 Basinghall St and began his long stint as London buyer for Ross & Glendining.[54]

## 8. TRAVELLERS AND THE PUSH FOR NORTHERN BUSINESS

The departure of both Thomas Harrison and John Ross left major gaps in the Dunedin operation that had to be filled. Some time earlier George Hercus, a young Thurso accountant previously employed by J.H. Barr, had been appointed to help John Ross. He now assumed Ross's responsibilities for financial management, acting as accountant and de facto general manager for the next fifty years. A staunch Baptist, he was a useful counterweight to the more entrepreneurial and sometimes reckless Robert Glendining. It was Hercus who prepared the balance sheets every January and July, calculated the key operating ratios used to guide salesmen and travellers, and conducted detailed financial analyses. Ross could not have wished for a more able, diligent and hardworking replacement.

New travellers were also needed to take over the journeys previously undertaken by Harrison and Ross. An attempt was made to persuade the draper J.H. Barr to travel for the firm, but he declined on the grounds that there was too much travelling and too little pay.[55] Over the next year or so three new travellers were recruited: Menzies who covered North Otago, Canterbury and the lower North Island, I.W. McCleod who serviced the West Coast and the top of the South Island, and George Tomes who represented the firm in Otago and Southland. Menzies was almost immediately poached by Arthur & Co. in Christchurch, to be quickly replaced by L.C. Galbraith.[56]

Of the three travellers it was Tomes, an experienced traveller formerly with the Dunedin firm of Butterworth Brothers, who had the most ground to cover. His Southland journey took him as far west as Riverton, going by way of Waihola, Balclutha and Winton before returning via Invercargill. Like Ross before him, he sometimes sailed back from Bluff rather than travel on horseback. His trip around the Otago goldfields was probably even more gruelling, a lack of roads and the harsh winter weather making the going tough. The anti-clockwise circuit took in Hyde, Naseby and St Bathans, before going on to Queenstown and back through Cromwell, Clyde, Lawrence and Waitahuna. Each journey took, on average, 130 days, with Tomes, like the other travellers, spending around 260 days a year on the road.[57]

The Otago goldfields, although less productive than hitherto, remained an importance source of business and, together with Southland, yielded sales in excess of £30,000 per annum in the early seventies. The North Otago and Canterbury journey was of increasing importance, however, especially as Christchurch was growing rapidly. Sales soon exceeded £40,000 and L.C. Galbraith, the principal traveller, occasionally had to be helped out by Tomes and Glendining.[58] Christchurch was also a convenient departure point for the North Island and so Galbraith was required to sail to Wellington and Hawkes' Bay, visiting the growing coastal settlements there. On the

Wellington journey he went up the west coast of the North Island as far as the Rangitikei River, sometimes sailing on to Wanganui, while in Hawkes Bay he served accounts in Napier, Hastings and Waipawa. The amount of business done in these areas was comparatively small, around £12,000 per annum, but with the development of agriculture in Wellington and pastoralism in Hawkes Bay, there was reason for optimism (see Table 4.1).

The third traveller, McLeod, attended to trade in Marlborough, Nelson and the West Coast. The bulk of the accounts served by McLeod were to be found in coastal settlements such as Picton, Nelson and Motueka, with retail outlets further inland left to such locally based merchants as the widely diversified Edwards & Co. There were a number of small craft plying the waters, including the 89-ton paddle steamer owned by Nathaniel Edwards. It was on vessels such as these that travellers like McLeod sailed up and down the West Coast, visiting the major settlements of Westport, Greymouth and Hokitika.

There was considerable competition on the Coast, especially from Melbourne warehousemen and their New Zealand offshoots such as Thompson, Smith & Barclay of Greymouth. As in the case of Nelson, it was the locally based firms that did most of the inland business, their travellers visiting gold mining settlements such as Ahaura, Reefton, and the even more descriptively named, Half Ounce. Thompsons, with branch stores, heavy advertising in papers such as the *Grey River Argus,* and principals who were local dignitaries, proved formidable rivals.[59] Ultimately Ross & Glendining's sales to West Coast customers exceeded £12,000 per annum, although not before Glendining had entertained real doubts about McLeod's ability as a traveller.[60]

### 9. Merchants and other customers
The three travellers were vital to the success of Ross & Glendining, opening new accounts, showing samples, taking orders and collecting outstanding debts. Around 60 per cent of the business, however, was still conducted directly by the warehouse, orders either being sent through the post or received verbally when customers visited to view stock. Goods were delivered using whatever means available although, in later years, Ross & Glendining ran their own express wagon. A small cash business of around £2,000 per annum was done with local traders.

The vast majority of the sales were for less than £100 per customer per season. Nevertheless, there were a number of large accounts, especially in smaller centres where merchants such as Hood & Shennan of Timaru sought to combine wholesaling, retailing and dressmaking operations. Seasonal orders in excess of £1,000 were often placed by these 'big/little' merchants.

Large retailers also ordered extensively, including Hallensteins at Cromwell and Queenstown, William McBeath at Lawrence, Milnes & Duncan of Outram, and H.P. Hjorring of St Bathans, all of whom bought around £500 worth of goods from the warehouse each season.[61]

Less remunerative and extensive than the wholesale trade was an indent business which involved Ross, now in London, buying British and continental goods on commission for a few local merchants and retailers. The amounts involved might be substantial, with Brown, Ewing & Co. receiving over £3,600 worth of goods in the summer of 1871/2. There was also a regular interchange of stock between the Dunedin warehousemen as each sought to serve their customers with a complete and comprehensive range of items as possible. Thus Sargoods, Watson & Co., Butterworth Brothers, and even Bing, Harris & Co., all bought several hundred pounds' worth of goods each year from Ross & Glendining, and vice versa. In total, the partnership served around 250 accounts at the beginning of the 1870s, a figure that was to double during the course of the decade.[62]

The range of goods sold was now quite extensive. Customers regularly received circulars announcing the arrival of the most recent consignments. In March 1871 they were told that the second series of shipments for the season had arrived, with 262 packages per 'Mail Steamer' from Southampton and Marseilles, *Harvest Home* from Liverpool, *Warrior Queen* from London, and *Agnes Muir* from Glasgow. On board the mail steamer came high value fashion items such as kid gloves, satins, silk handkerchiefs, black silk fringes and fancy loops; the slower ships carried more mundane articles including Welsh flannels, Horrocks calicoes, moleskin trousers, ladies wool vests, gaiters, imitation silk handkerchiefs and patent dusters.[63] Yet while advertisements for exotic items might catch the eye, the principal items purchased from Ross & Glendining remained largely the same, with blankets, hosiery, flannels, and moleskin trousers being much in demand. Given the income levels of most settlers and hard conditions in rural New Zealand, this is scarcely surprising.[64]

## 10. FROM LOSS TO PROFIT

The state of the firm's balance sheet in the late 1860s is not known but, with the appointment of George Hercus, regular sets of accounts began to be compiled on the basis of accepted principles. It was Hercus who drew up the six months balance to July 1870 which revealed the loss of £607. The following January total losses, after partners' expenses and interest had been paid, increased to £2,656. Thereafter business improved markedly. Sales rose by around 40 per cent in the six months to July 1872, while losses were transformed into profits of £6,854 – after the payment of £2,163 in interest on partners' capital employed and a further £500 salary and expenses. Profits and interest were immediately ploughed back into the enterprise (see Table 3.1).[65]

The initial phase in the development of the warehouse business had gone well. There was a fine warehouse in Stafford St; Ross had demonstrated himself to be an able buyer in London; and the firm, through their travellers, drove an extensive trade throughout much of the South Island. Since the beginning of their association with Harrison five years previously, the two partners had doubled their net worth to £51,753. While not possessing as much capital as some of their rivals, Ross & Glendining were nevertheless well organised and sufficiently well resourced to take full advantage of the boom that lay ahead.

# Diversification and Consolidation

# 4

# THE 1870s INVESTMENT BOOM AND THE
# GROWTH OF THE FIRM

By the early 1870s, the structure and organisation of Ross & Glendining had caught up with those of their leading rivals. The establishment of the London buying office represented an important step forwards, helping to ensure that a superior range of goods was sourced at lower cost and forwarded more expeditiously than would have been the case had they continued to rely on agents. In New Zealand, too, there were important developments, an expanded sales force, closely monitored by Hercus, providing better coverage of both the South and the lower North Islands. The improvement in capabilities paid off for as the economy grew, sales and market share increased markedly.

## 1. Vogel and the public works programme

The recovery of wheat and wool prices during the course of 1871 helped to lift the economy out of depression. Rather more important in stimulating demand, however, was a sharp rise in government expenditure. Julius Vogel, Colonial Treasurer since 1869, believed that massive investment in transport and communications and large-scale assisted immigration would set New Zealand on the road to rapid economic development. His ideas commanded considerable support, even amongst his political opponents, although not all agreed with his proposal to borrow and spend £8.5 million over ten years. After concessions were made, including agreement to reduce borrowing to £4 million, in 1870 his Immigration and Public Works Bill was finally passed. Specific enabling legislation, containing more detailed proposals, was enacted in 1871.[1]

The benefits of the Vogel programme were not felt immediately for it took time to float loans, arrange contracts for road and rail building, and establish an effective emigration agency in London. Once these matters were settled, construction began to forge ahead. By 1876 when Vogel (he had become premier three years earlier) left office, 718 miles of railway had been opened with a further 427 under construction, 2,000 miles of roads built, and an additional 2,500 miles of telegraph lines added to the network.[2] Assisted migration also helped to swell the population, some 32,000 government migrants landing in 1874 alone. Between 1870 and 1876, the European population of the country rose from around a quarter of a million to almost 400,000. Unfortunately, the small Maori population continued to decline to less than 50,000.[3]

The effects of rising prices, government expenditure and population increase allied to technological improvements had a dramatic effect on the size of gross domestic product (GDP). Over the space of five years it rose by more than 40 per cent in real terms, reaching £18.5 million (at 1911 prices) by 1876. After a brief downturn, the combination of fresh overseas loans, continued government expenditure and a growth in private credit boosted the economy still further. The bubble finally burst towards the end of 1878. By this time real GDP had reached £22.4 million and real per capita incomes had increased by a quarter. More people with more money meant that the demand for most items, including draperies, soared.[4]

John Ross and Robert Glendining had no great love for Julius Vogel. They did not like his approach to finance and, as importers, would certainly have opposed his ideas concerning protective tariffs. Consequently, when a collection was made for Vogel in Dunedin in 1874 they declined to contribute, although Sargood, Son & Ewen were rather more forthcoming.[5] Yet in truth, they had a lot to be grateful to Vogel for. The bulk of the railway expenditure was spent in the South Island where, by January 1879, the main line linked Christchurch with Invercargill. A number of the branch lines were also built, the majority in Canterbury where they struck off west into the interior. In Otago, short spurs connected Port Chalmers and Lawrence to the main line, while in Southland branch lines linked Bluff and Invercargill to Lake Wakatipu in the north and Riverton and Otautau to the west.[6]

The improvement of transport and communications in the South Island conferred quite obvious social and economic benefits. Quite apart from the immediate effects of public works expenditure in the areas where construction took place, lower transportation costs pushed back the margin of cultivation, fostered trade and raised incomes.[7] For Ross & Glendining, heavily dependent upon efficient transportation and communications to market and distribute their goods, the improved networks made life much easier. The telegraph system allowed travellers to place orders and check a customer's credit while still in the field; the railway network meant that they did not have to risk life and limb when trying to cross major natural obstacles such as the Waitaki River. Indeed, Ross & Glendining bought their travellers season tickets so that they might travel safely around the South Island by rail whenever practicable. Only when visiting areas such as the goldfields was the horse and buggy still retained.

Migrants settled principally in the South Island, the unsettled political conditions in the north and the need for construction labour in the south helping to determine their destination. Between 1870 and 1876 the European population of Canterbury, Otago and Southland nearly doubled to reach almost 200,000 inhabitants. Only limited numbers actually went into road and rail construction, while many, although selected because of their agricultural backgrounds, remained in towns.[8] Most seem to have found employment quite easily but accommodation was often a problem. This was certainly the case in Dunedin in the middle of 1874 when nine ships, bearing around 3,500 passengers, arrived within the space of one month. Robert Glendining thought there would be plenty of work for them once the short winter days were over 'but the want of houses for married people to go into with their families is a very serious matter in the meantime'.[9]

Ross & Glendining made the most of the growing domestic market. Annual sales, around £90,000 in the late 1860s, rose to £172,260 in the year to July 1874. Higher interest rates and tighter credit, brought about mainly by financial conditions in Great Britain, slowed trade for a couple of years thereafter and sales fell by almost a fifth. A new peak of £173,081 was reached in the year to July 1878 (see Table 4.1).[10]

## 2. BUYING AND SHIPPING GOODS

While the boom of the 1870s undoubtedly benefited Ross & Glendining, the soft goods trade remained quite competitive. Some firms, such as Sargoods and Bing, Harris & Co., tended to compete right across the board. Others elected to specialise in certain types of goods or customers.[11] Arthur & Co., a British-based firm with warehouses in both Australia and New Zealand, typified those who chose a more focused approach. A relative latecomer to the market, the firm sent out large quantities of plain goods which they sold cheaply. Soon Tomes and other travellers were complaining that Arthur & Co. had spoiled the Southland trade and that it was 'nearly as bad in Christchurch and other places as well'. The only consolation was that Arthur & Co. was doing similar damage in Victoria.[12]

Competition of this nature continued over the next couple of years. Throughout 1873, Hercus complained that Arthur & Co. were playing havoc with the trade in manchester goods. By 1874 they had switched their attention to tweeds.[13] The firm also targeted certain market segments, their travellers going to all the smaller settlements and taking any orders they could get. The 'little tailors', Glendining thought, got all their tweeds from Arthur & Co.[14]

To compete with this type of opposition, it was important that goods were well bought. This involved John Ross making regular visits to the manufacturing districts in the United Kingdom and the Continent where he established close relationships with suppliers. This was essential if keen prices were to be

## TABLE 4.1
## SALES BY REGION, 1871–1879 (£000s)

| July Year | 1872 | 1873 | 1874 | 1875 | 1876 | 1877 | 1878 | 1879 |
|---|---|---|---|---|---|---|---|---|
| Dunedin | 26.9 | 37.5 | 60.6 | 59.2 | 38.3 | 38.0 | 60.2 | 64.8 |
| Southland & South Otago | 14.2 | 16.9 | 20.0 | 21.2 | 18.8 | 19.3 | 24.6 | 25.4 |
| Goldfields | 17.6 | 17.7 | 16.8 | 12.1 | 10.7 | 13.1 | 12.8 | 9.4 |
| North Otago & Canterbury | 26.1 | 33.3 | 42.6 | 41.0 | 45.4 | 46.4 | 52.6 | 53.3 |
| West Coast | 8.5 | 12.6 | 14.7 | 12.8 | 8.5 | 11.2 | 8.5 | 4.2 |
| Marlborough/Nelson & Wellington | 8.3 | 7.0 | 8.5 | 6.2 | 5.5 | 4.2 | 3.7 | 2.5 |
| Hawkes Bay | 3.2 | 5.7 | 8.9 | 10.8 | 7.0 | 6.3 | 10.7 | 8.0 |
| Auckland | – | 0.4 | 0.1 | – | – | – | – | – |
| Total | 104.8 | 131.2 | 172.3 | 162.8 | 134.3 | 138.4 | 173.1 | 167.6 |

## TABLE 4.2
## SALES, CAPITAL EMPLOYED AND PROFITABILITY, 1871–1879 (£000s)

| July Year | 1872 | 1873 | 1874 | 1875 | 1876 | 1877 | 1878 | 1879 |
|---|---|---|---|---|---|---|---|---|
| Total sales | 104.8 | 131.2 | 172.3 | 162.8 | 134.3 | 138.4 | 173.1 | 167.6 |
| Bad debts | 0.3 | 1.4 | 1.3 | 1.4 | 1.9 | 2.3 | 3.1 | 2.8 |
| Net profit | 11.2 | 13.1 | 14.9 | 5.1 | 0.0 | 3.6 | 7.9 | 5.3 |
| Imputed interest | 4.1 | 5.6 | 6.9 | 8.5 | 9.3 | 9.7 | 9.0 | 8.2 |
| Partners' salaries[a] | 1.0 | 1.0 | 1.0 | 1.0 | 1.0 | 1.0 | 1.0 | 1.0 |
| Total returns | 16.3 | 19.6 | 22.7 | 14.6 | 10.3 | 14.3 | 17.9 | 14.5 |
| Estimated average capital employed [b] | 41.0 | 56.0 | 69.0 | 85.0 | 93.0 | 97.0 | 90.0 | 82.0 |
| Return on capital (%) | 39.7 | 35.0 | 32.9 | 17.2 | 11.1 | 14.7 | 19.9 | 17.7 |

Sources: Half-yearly balances, AG 512 15/1, 15/2 & 15/18. Data in this and subsequent tables have been rounded. Entries therefore may not sum to column totals, although the latter are correct.
Notes: (a) Salaries are usually excluded from rate of return calculations but included in this instance to provide comparability with subsequent calculations. (b) Estimated average capital is the capital employed by the warehouse business alone and does not include capital invested in property and the mills.

obtained and requirements promptly met. One of the firm's clothing suppliers, Wathen & Gardiner, even went as far as to deposit funds with the partnership, in addition to supplying goods on credit. Whether this was to take advantage of the higher interest rates on offer in New Zealand or was simply a way of cementing relationships with a valued customer is not clear.[15]

The quantity and nature of goods Ross shipped to New Zealand was determined partly by the demands of the firm's warehouse departments – each of which dealt with a particular range of goods – and partly by the state of trade. He was frequently called upon to exercise his judgement, although Glendining and Hercus provided constant guidance. When, in 1872, Ross intimated that he was going to stick strictly to the orders placed by the heads of departments for the forthcoming season, Glendining replied that while it was wise to be careful, Ross 'should not hesitate buying up job lines that you think cheap as we can always do well with jobs in slops or plain goods'.[16] Job lines – goods that for a variety of reasons might be sold off cheaply – were essential if Ross & Glendining were to compete with the likes of Arthur & Co.

In addition to buying, London office also had to oversee the shipment of goods and sample cards. The low bulk, high value of many goods shipped meant that freight rates were comparatively unimportant. More important in obtaining a competitive advantage was ensuring that both goods and samples were shipped well in advance, on reliable 'sailers', so they arrived prior to the opening of each season's trade. The vagaries of wind and sea meant that even the normally efficient Ross found it difficult to ensure that shipments arrived on time. In September 1872, Glendining complained that the late arrival of sample cards meant that the travellers were unable to get away on time, thereby handing an advantage to the opposition.[17] Ross retorted that the shipping company, Shaw, Savill & Co., did just what they pleased.[18]

The unsatisfactory nature of the service provided by Shaw Savill, the Albion Line and other shipping companies saw leading importers in Otago set up the Otago Freight Association. Formed in 1872, it was a cooperative venture whose object was 'simply to secure A1 fast-sailing vessels, and obtain Freight at the lowest market rate in London, or other ports'.[19] The members of the association believed that, collectively, they imported large enough quantities to ensure that vessels would sail punctually each month, 'and oftener if occasion requires'. The New Zealand Loan & Mercantile Agency Company was appointed agents in London to handle arrangements there. After some success, the Otago Freight Association, together with its Auckland counterpart, the New Zealand Freight Association, was absorbed in 1873 by the newly formed New Zealand Shipping Co.[20] For a short while Ross & Glendining held shares in the Association so that they might obtain a discount on freight rates.[21]

The completion of the Java telegraph cable in the spring of 1872, linking Australia to London, enabled tighter stock control to be exercised. Once the overland link across Australia had been completed Glendining, sending messages in code by way of Australia, was able to transmit urgent orders and issue cancellations when needed.[22] Shipping, nevertheless, remained a problem, with voyages of uncertain length, shipwrecks, and the slow discharge of consignments resulting in the loss of sales.[23] As time went by, Ross became better acquainted with the capabilities of ships and their masters, ultimately managing to ensure that the principal shipments for each season arrived at least as early as those of his rivals.[24] Even so, in 1874 he was being berated by Glendining for sending goods on the *Cordelia*, which arrived from Liverpool after a passage of 132 days. Why didn't he use the *Calypso* that arrived only 80 days after sailing from London?[25]

### 3. THE STRESSES AND STRAINS OF MANAGEMENT

John Ross found the demands of buying extremely stressful, especially as orders from New Zealand grew. Once again he began to complain about his health. Although suffering from little more than indigestion, in April 1872 he began to talk about making a will. He also suggested that he might return to New Zealand. This was quickly rejected by Glendining, whose entire family now lived in Dunedin:

> *from the nature of our business one of us must be in London, and it would have been as well for us if you had remained there when you were home before …. However, you are better suited to manage affairs in London than I would be, and it appears to me that unless your health gives way or some unseen event happens to us here that you will be required to remain in London for some time to come. So take care of your health and do not work too much. If the work you have to do is too much for you, get more assistance.*

The suggestion that a third partner might be taken on also received short shrift from Glendining. While he could see some advantages, the profits would have to be further divided and disagreements might arise. With Ross & Glendining doing a good business and as 'well to do' as any other establishment in Dunedin, he thought another partner unnecessary.[26]

Further exchanges of this nature continued throughout the winter season, with Ross ultimately inviting Glendining to make a trip to London.[27] Whether the reason for the invitation was to discuss buying still further, to acquaint Glendining with the problems faced by London Office, or simply enable his partner to take a break from business affairs and visit old friends, one can only guess. Once again Glendining was not particularly receptive, arguing that in the absence of a third partner or a good warehouse manager

– neither of which he cared for – it was impossible for him to return home. Undeterred, Ross continued to press his partner to make a trip to London. In November 1872, Glendining countered by suggesting that Ross should visit Dunedin instead, saying that it would be beneficial both for reasons of his health and the business. In the interim, Ross should not worry as 'the balance sheet will prove to you that your buying has been a success'.[28]

The strain of running a growing enterprise in a rapidly changing economy was not confined to Ross alone, for Robert Glendining also began to suffer from indigestion, rheumatic pains, and other ailments. He told Ross that he was, 'taking a good deal of horse exercise just now, living on the plainest food and taking good care of myself'.[29] His family was also unwell, suffering from whooping cough, and over Christmas 1872 his infant daughter died.[30]

In spite of exercise and plain living, Glendining's health did not improve. His wife, following her recent confinement and illness, was also unwell. As a result, the prospect of a long sea voyage became ever more appealing.[31] Towards the end of January Mary Glendining announced that she, together with their eldest son John, would visit her sister in the United Kingdom as Margaret Ross was now expecting her first child.[32] On 18 February 1873, Mary, son John and a young relative Jessie Linson, boarded the *May Queen* for the voyage home. After being delayed for three days by adverse winds, the sailing vessel was towed out of Otago harbour and headed for Cape Horn. Glendining was to follow his wife, providing that he could get away.[33]

For the next month or so, Glendining vacillated about whether to return to the United Kingdom or not. Finally, after receiving an encouraging telegram from London and confident that Hercus could manage without him, he informed Ross that, 'all being well, I will leave here on the San Francisco steamer on 5th June'.[34] The collapse of the California, New Zealand and Australia Mail Steam Ship Company in April, however, and the subsequent withdrawal of the heavily subsidised paddle steamer service forced him to revise his plans.[35]

Towards the end of May, Glendining was to be found in Melbourne, waiting for the Suez mail boat. Still feeling unwell, he decided to take a second opinion about his health. The Australian doctor concurred that there was nothing seriously wrong with him but strongly advised against travelling via the overland route on account of the heat in the Red Sea. The alternative was a passage in the *Lord Warden*, 'a comfortable old tub' of 1500 tons sailing via Cape Horn. Hercus was less enthusiastic than his employer about the voyage of around eighty days which, at that time of the year, was likely to include periods of intense cold.[36] By the time his cautionary note arrived in Melbourne, however, Glendining had sailed, the presence of smallpox on the Suez boat convincing him that a passage around the Horn was infinitely preferable.[37]

## 4. Buying out a local competitor

George Hercus, with power of attorney, was now in charge of day-to-day affairs in Dunedin. Important matters were to be referred to Ross in London. Almost immediately, the opportunity arose for Ross & Glendining to acquire the stock of William Watson & Sons, a major competitor with a warehouse in nearby High St. Rumours that Watson & Sons were selling up had been circulating for some months but, when approached by Glendining, Watson had given no firm answer. Once the partners had decided to sell, Hercus wrote to Watson senior expressing an interest in buying their stock – but not their entire business.[38] Having obtained an option over the stock in event of the business not being sold as a going concern, Hercus cabled Ross for permission to proceed.[39]

The cable to Ross, which was telegraphed first to Bluff, taken by steamer to Melbourne, then sent onwards via the Java cable to London, normally took around a week.[40] Before receiving a reply, therefore, Hercus had time to write a lengthy letter to Ross explaining why the purchase made strategic sense:

> *It is certain ... that this colony presents strong inducements to open just now. If this was to take place, and a very strong house took Watson's business besides, the trade would be very much cut up. There was just another matter of the same kind that suggested itself. Brown, Ewing & Co. have been making very ambitious movements of late in the direction of a wholesale business. They have their travellers out and have succeeded in opening accounts in Christchurch ... it appeared to me that to secure Watson's stock would put the capstone on their efforts all at once and it would be worthwhile for us to stop that ...*

He had few doubts that the stock would sell, especially as it looked as though Ross & Glendining were likely to be short of goods in the very near future. However, just to be sure that the prices and assortment of goods were all right, he would have the stock appraised by the heads of the warehouse departments.[41]

Hercus was pretty optimistic that his negotiations would be successful. Watson & Sons had been cutting prices and running down stocks for some time and so he thought it unlikely that the firm would be purchased as a going concern.[42] While a newcomer to the trade might have access to their warehouse, experienced travellers, and established accounts, they might find themselves seriously short of goods for the forthcoming season. Hercus also felt that his approaches had been very 'cordially' received by Mr Watson, although the latter still had to consult with his brother, Edward, and other members of the firm in Melbourne.[43]

Ross encouraged Hercus to continue with his negotiations. He suggested that, as an opening gambit, Watsons should be offered the price that the goods were entered on their stock sheets, less a discount of 33 per cent.[44] This offer was refused. After further negotiations, the stock was secured at a discount of 26¼ per cent.[45] With sales buoyant, the additional £14,000 worth of stock was doubtless sold at a decent profit. More importantly, the purchase also helped to protect the firm's position in the marketplace.

### 5. SAMPLE ROOMS AND MORE INTENSIVE TRAVELLING

Forestalling new entry held obvious advantages for Ross & Glendining but it was equally important to be able to compete with existing warehouse firms. Early in 1873, therefore, Hercus suggested to Glendining that the firm employ yet another traveller 'to take in places that do not yet get looked up until the best of the orders are given away'.[46] Good travellers were extremely hard to come by but by the beginning of March they had secured the services of James Kelly.[47] His territory included Southland and part of Canterbury, although his main responsibility was to push trade up the coast from Wellington to Wanganui and to secure more accounts in Hawke's Bay.[48]

Ross & Glendining were particularly interested in the Hawke's Bay market which, aided by railway building and immigration, was beginning to develop quite rapidly.[49] They already possessed one large account in the area, Blythe & Co. of Napier. Owned by a fellow Dumfries man who Glendining described as 'a fine, decent, fellow', Blythes soon built up a sizeable general business that included wholesale, retail and a dressmaking department.[50] 'Their great outcry', Hercus informed Ross a little later, 'is for new light Fancy-Goods – such as will attract squatters' ladies with too much money to spend – and as they cannot get enough of this class of goods we took an indent from them'. Indenting involved Ross buying in bulk for the Napier firm in return for a commission and interest on any credit advanced. This was not without risks, for customers in developing areas like Hawkes Bay were usually very slow to pay. Hercus nevertheless believed that it was better to advance long credits than to let the trade fall into other hands.[51]

An adequate sales force, both to exploit new markets and cover existing ones more intensively, was essential if the firm was to fend off competitors. Additional travelling, of course, entailed more costs. The very nature of the soft goods business meant that travellers were usually accompanied by trunks full of samples, with Ross & Glendining possessing a stock of over forty such trunks. A more extended trade, therefore, meant not only more travellers but more trunks with greater distances to travel. Transporting all the travellers and their trunks back to the warehouse at the end of each journey seemed a waste of time and money, especially from those areas in which business was growing most rapidly. Opening branch warehouses in the main centres represented one solution to the problem, although a significant volume of business would be required to offset the overhead costs involved. For lower volumes of business, a suite of permanently manned sample rooms – which acted both as a showroom and a base to which travellers might return – was more cost effective.

Ross & Glendining were one of the first firms to open sample rooms. In July 1873, Hercus wrote to Glendining in London that Sargood had come over from Australia and that he and a Mr Tewsley were up in Christchurch. The rumour was that they might open a branch in the city. This was a worrying development for Hercus foresaw that once the main trunk railway was completed both north and south, Canterbury would have 'a very commanding position and the folks there … seem determined to use it'. The flotation of the New Zealand Shipping Company, moreover, was likely to increase the advantage of Christchurch, especially as the new shipping line was principally owned by Canterbury people.[52]

Fortunately, the Canterbury traveller, Galbraith, had just reported that some sample rooms were in the course of construction in Christchurch 'for renting to travellers'. Hercus recommended that Ross & Glendining take one. It would save on freight and result in less money being spent 'uselessly' in the bar. Galbraith, too, was keen, for he thought it would be cheaper both for himself and his employers if he were to live in Christchurch.[53]

The rumour concerning Sargoods opening a branch proved to be unfounded, although the firm did open 'in a large and permanent way' in Auckland. In Christchurch they simply took two large rooms: an office and a sample room. The sample room was to be manned by a salesman, while their traveller was 'constantly' out in the countryside. Hercus was quick to counter this development. By the beginning of August 1873, he had rented two 'excellent' sample rooms at the corner of Cashel St in the 'most convenient place in the city'. What is more, the rooms would be ready before Sargood, Son & Ewen could enter theirs![54] Auckland, however, was a step too far, and it was to be more than a quarter of a century before Ross & Glendining was permanently represented in the north.

## 6. Improving travellers' efficiency

The establishment of sample rooms in Christchurch saved on both travellers' time and the wasteful transportation of trunks full of samples. It also meant that the firm was better placed to serve the rapidly developing Canterbury market. Yet how to monitor travellers in the field remained a problem. In some instances it was quite easy to determine that variations in sales were due to factors beyond their control. Thus, in 1872, small orders from the goldfields traveller, Tomes, were clearly the result of the lack of water for sluicing, it being reported that 'the diggers of Naseby not having been working since November last'. More often than not, though, Glendining and Hercus were left wondering whether greater effort might have yielded better results. Certainly they were constantly complaining about McLeod, the West Coast traveller. Glendining also entertained doubts about the suitability of Galbraith who, although he did 'his best', was not able to secure large orders.[55]

Initially the travellers were paid a fixed wage of around £5 per week, with the firm providing a horse and buggy and paying for expenses such as stabling and accommodation. Daily expenses were closely monitored (and comparisons made by Hercus to several decimal places) but control was exercised simply through exhortation. This arrangement provided little incentive either to work harder or to limit expenses. After long discussions with Ross about how to determine salaries, Glendining decided to introduce a rather more high-powered incentive system.[56] Henceforth each traveller was paid a fixed wage and provided with a sales target for his territory, the target varying according to the nature of the territory and, ultimately, the state of trade. Sales above target were to be rewarded by a commission of 2 per cent. Tomes, whose journeys were the most lucrative, was set the highest sales target of £12,000 per season. The others had targets in the region of £5–6,000.[57]

The new commission-based system was introduced in 1874, but it was not without its pitfalls. The incentive to push sales inevitably carried with it a degree of risk, for the travellers were now inclined to push goods on customers who could not really afford them, notwithstanding strict credit limits imposed by Hercus. When trade turned down later in the year, indiscriminate sales resulted in larger renewals of credit than might otherwise have been the case. A more immediate problem, given the fluctuating nature of trade, was how to establish an appropriate trade-off between commission and expenses. Normally travellers were allowed expenses of up to 4 per cent of total sales, with any excess being deducted from their commission. Unfortunately, expenses did not fall as fast as sales in a downturn, and there was little the travellers could do to rectify the situation.

The first to fall foul of the new system was Galbraith who, in November 1874, was dismissed as his expenses continued to be greater than his commission. He was almost immediately re-employed by Sargoods at a higher wage, though Glendining doubted whether he would ever be much good on the road.[58] By the following January the difficulties of operating the new system had become manifestly evident, with falling sales resulting in all travellers, including the reliable Tomes, having a rapidly falling commission either reduced or completely swamped by their expenses. To offset the downturn, each received a small ex gratia payment on top of their basic salary, an adjustment to targets and commission rates taking place in August 1875 to reflect changing circumstances.[59] The difficulties involved in working the new system nevertheless proved to be insuperable and ultimately the firm was obliged to rely on a simple commission system to encourage the travellers. Expenses were still closely monitored, with targets and commission rates being modified as and when appropriate.[60]

## 7. Enlarging the Dunedin warehouse

The rapid expansion of trade during the early seventies meant that changes were also necessary at the Dunedin warehouse. The lack of space in which to store and display wares became increasingly pressing as the business grew. As 1872 drew to a close Murray, the head of the slops department, suggested that the warehouse be extended.[61] Glendining was not too keen to build, especially in view of the unremitting competition from rivals, but as trade continued to expand he changed his mind. After consultation with Ross, plans were drawn up for a wing to be added to the warehouse. In 1873, Glendining took a set of drawings to London so that the partners might go through the details together.[62] Just before he sailed, the existing warehouse was refurbished and lit by gas for the very first time. 'The pendants are very sightly looking things', Hercus informed Ross, 'and they are quite sufficient to light every corner of the warehouse'.[63]

Towards the end of 1873, a month or so before Glendining returned, Hercus was approached by an agent offering a vacant section, on a short-term tenancy, at the rear of their warehouse. The vacant section fronted on to High St, which Hercus considered a better location than Stafford St as 'there will be more thoroughfare up High St. than Stafford St. from the station'. He thought that if an entrance could be secured from High St, it would be possible to build 'all over the Stafford St. frontage.' A short-term tenancy was unacceptable, however, so the agent promised to refer the matter back to the proprietor who was 'either a minor or lunatic', resident in the Channel Islands.[64]

Glendining and his wife arrived back in New Zealand on the *Mongol*, a steamer with auxiliary sail, on 13 February 1874. The vessel had been procured by the New Zealand Government to reopen the mail service to San Franscisco. On its outward leg to Otago the *Mongol*, together with the New Zealand Shipping Company's *Scimitar*, had been chartered by the Agent-General in London to transport migrants. There were 313 migrants on the *Mongol*, although they mixed little with the Glendinings and other saloon class passengers.

The passage was a memorable one, for three days out from Plymouth scarlet fever broke out, followed by measles amongst the 125 children on board, and then typhoid fever. Health on the vessel was not improved by the fact that the deck of the newly built *Mongol* leaked badly, resulting in damp conditions below. Worse still, the desire of the master to achieve a record-breaking run led to a shortage of water, as coal was diverted from the fresh-water condensers to drive the engines. The passage of fifty-one days to Port Chalmers did indeed break the record, although there were nineteen deaths on the voyage, mainly children.[65] Glendining considered himself ill-used by the New Zealand Shipping Company which had arranged the booking, especially as he and his wife had been charged £73.10.0 each for the experience.[66]

While Glendining had been away, work had continued on adding the wing to the existing warehouse. By April 1874 it was complete.[67] The building, Ross was told, 'looks first rate outside now and is quite a different place altogether'. Inside, a water-powered lift had been installed, while the ceilings of the extension were lined in wood.[68] The additional space was most welcome, for Ross & Glendining had over £75,000 worth of stock under cover in Dunedin and a further £10,000 at the harbour. Of this, £21,000 worth was still in bond as the firm simply had nowhere to store the goods.[69] The extended warehouse comfortably housed the scattered stock, at the same time allowing departments extra room to display their wares. Thus Murray, the head of the slops, now had adequate space for his clothing while the manchester department was divided into two, allowing light and heavy cottons to be shown separately.[70] The hosiery, haberdashery and the fancy goods departments also benefited from better facilities.

Having experimented with incentive schemes for travellers, the way in which heads of warehouse departments were to be paid was also revised. Sargood, Son & Ewen used a method known as the 'stimulation principle' to pay their head salesmen and this was now adopted by Ross & Glendining. In future, payment was to be made on the basis of a fixed salary plus a commission based on the profits made by each department. Linking commission to profits rather than sales, it was hoped, would encourage the salesmen not to wantonly reduce prices or 'slaughter' goods simply in order to shift stock.[71]

## 8. MASS-PRODUCED COLONIAL-MADE CLOTHING

Up to this time, the bulk of the clothing in New Zealand was either imported, made to measure by tailors and dressmakers, produced by the making departments of large retailers and merchants such as Brown, Ewing & Co. or Kirkcaldie & Stains of Wellington, or made at home.[72] Now, as the domestic market expanded and new technology in the shape of the sewing machine was introduced, a number of local entrepreneurs decided to establish clothing factories along the mass production lines used in America and Britain.

Amongst the first to mass-produce clothing was Isaac Hallenstein & Co. Entry into trade was easy. All that was needed was a few hundred pounds' worth of sewing machines, some presses, irons, and workbenches and stools for the hands. Premises might be rented. Sales and distribution was often more challenging. Here Hallensteins were fortunate, for in addition to substantial shops in both Queenstown and Cromwell, in September 1873 they had bought out William McBeath of Lawrence, one of Ross & Glendining's largest customers. The news that Hallensteins were to open their own clothing factory followed shortly, and by December production had started in temporary accommodation over the Provincial Hotel in Dunedin. Isaac Hallenstein's partner, according to Hercus, was Anderson, formerly Sargoods' Melbourne clothing manager and, like Hallenstein, Jewish.[73]

Ross & Glendining were sorry to lose McBeath's trade but with Hallenstein promising to order from them, they were in no hurry to start manufacturing themselves. Other importers evidently did feel threatened for in 1874 Sargood, Son & Ewen bought the old First Church for £1,375, with a view to converting it into a factory.[74] 'Sargood's people are determined to do the trade now,' Glendining informed Ross, 'and are to make-up clothing and manufacture boots so as to cut everybody out of the market – they say they must do so.' Butterworth Brothers also began manufacturing clothing in Dunedin and there was some talk that the Melbourne manufacturers, Scotsberg & Co., were going to start production in Watson's former warehouse.[75]

The emergence of a colonial clothing industry posed fresh challenges for Ross & Glendining. By the middle of 1874, competition in slops was fierce. The main opposition seems not to have come from local manufacturers but from Scotsbergs – still manufacturing in Melbourne. John Ross, having forged strong relationships with 'home' manufacturers, was able to supply clothing that was better made and still price competitive. When it came to style, though, the Australian goods were 'much smarter than home made goods', with the result that customers expressed a strong preference for 'Melbourne made stuff'. Under the circumstances, Hallensteins and other local makers found it hard to make money, though the former were apparently still doing 'a decent trade' and employing a lot of hands.[76]

Trade began to slacken as 1874 wore on, with Glendining quite sure that a reaction to the boom would soon set in.[77] Even so, when the opportunity to acquire permanent title to the section at the rear of the warehouse finally arose, he felt sufficiently confident to press ahead. The section cost £2,050.

Almost immediately Glendining began to think about how the site might be developed, suggesting to Ross that a large packing room might be built onto the rear of the warehouse. Glendining and Hercus also thought that it might be a good idea to build a one-storey building on High St. The walls should be thick enough to bear another two storeys, just in case the firm wished to build a clothing factory at some time in the future.[78]

### 9. COPING WITH A DOWNTURN

Business deteriorated rapidly as Christmas approached, competition being particularly acute in Wellington where a number of firms had recently entered the trade. The largest of these was Thompson & Shannon, Thompson having moved up from the West Coast to the new capital where prospects were greater. Nathans, too, had put up a large new building in Wellington, while Turnbull & Co. were reported to have entered the drapery trade very extensively.[79]

The growth of competition and declining orders meant that by the end of 1874 draperies in the capital were selling 'at any price'. Failures were widely anticipated but Glendining was quite confident Ross & Glendining would be able to compete, especially with Thompson & Shannon who were now supplied by Geard. Indeed, Glendining actually welcomed a year or two of bad trade, 'as it would clear out a lot of the little men and we could make more after it was over'. Nevertheless, he still sent a telegraph to London, reducing a manchester order and cancelling a consignment of slops.[80]

The situation in Christchurch was little better. The traveller, Galbraith, had been temporarily replaced by Saunders, the head of the hosiery and haberdashery department who, the previous year, had married Glendining's sister-in-law, Caroline Cassels. Returning from a short journey just before Christmas 1874, Saunders reported that the city was very much overstocked and there were too many involved in the drapery business. With sales contracting, Bing, Harris & Co. and Butterworth Brothers were selling their goods in Christchurch at the price at which the goods were invoiced to them, while Sargoods had dumped 50,000 yards of dress goods on the market at the knock-down price of 9d a yard. Price cutting also took place in Dunedin, with Ross & Glendining selling all their dress goods at the landed price of 11d a yard.[81]

The economy continued to contract during 1875 and 1876 as the credit squeeze, largely brought about by external factors, led banks in New Zealand to limit advances and raise interest rates. The tightening of credit was too much for some of Ross & Glendining's customers, a number of whom failed, while others restricted their orders to the bare minimum.[82]

It was the more substantial customers who seemed to find themselves in greatest difficulty. One of the largest to fail was Hibberd & Cowan of Timaru, who went bankrupt towards the end of 1875 owing £8,029 to various creditors.[83] Their demise, it seems, was brought about by the bankruptcy of Hibberd himself rather than the business. This being the case, Ross & Glendining took over the drapery business, installing John Cowan as their manager at a salary of £5 per week.[84] He was given a rapid course in financial control by George Hercus.[85] Close attention was also paid to the operations of a number of other large accounts, especially Blythe & Co. of Napier who, by 1877, were also in difficulties. Once again the indomitable Hercus stepped in, carefully going through Blythes' accounts, trimming expenditure, and suggesting how they might trade their way out of trouble.[86]

The downturn in trade had a marked effect on Ross & Glendining's sales, which fell by a fifth in the year to July 1876. By dint of carefully managing struggling accounts, bad debts were not particularly excessive and at no point was the firm in any danger. Even so, the Bank of New South Wales, which supplied the exchange to pay bills in London, began to demand tangible security from Glendining for sterling drafts that might amount to as much as £10,000 each.[87] The bottom of the recession seems to have been reached towards the end of 1876. With the financial situation improving and cheap money from London underpinning the expansion of credit, the economy began to grow once more.[88]

## 10. A DECADE OF PROGRESS

Careful buying in London and tight management control in Dunedin ensured that Ross & Glendining built up a sound and widely spread business during the 1870s. Progress was not uniform. The working out of gold reserves in Central Otago and the West Coast saw sales fall back, while the failure to maintain returns from the Wellington region may have been due to the growth in local competition. Even so, total sales in 1878 were 70 per cent greater than in 1872 and the firm had become the fourth largest importer of soft goods into Otago behind Sargoods, Bing, Harris & Co. and Butterworth Brothers. Ross & Glendining overtook Butterworths in the following year.[89]

The warehouse business was highly profitable, the amount standing to the credit of the partners' capital account increasing from £38,037 in July 1871 to £123,794 by July 1879. In addition they withdrew another £43,000 – much of it towards the end of the period – to fund personal expenditure and investment in land, property and shares.[90] Their net worth would have increased even more had it not been for the recession in 1875 and 1876, which brought bad debts and depressed earnings.

Rates of return on capital which, during the early years of the boom, were in excess of 30 per cent, were largely responsible for their increasing wealth.

At the same time, John Ross and Robert Glendining – aided by George Hercus – made the most of the resources at their disposal. The two partners were personally very frugal, each drawing a salary of only £500 per annum. More than half of the profits – together with the 10 per cent interest they charged themselves on their capital – was ploughed back into the business. Their investment in property was comparatively modest, a bond warehouse apparently being constructed for just over £200 from which rents were received. Albert Buildings in Princes St were also acquired, appearing in the 1878 balance sheet valued at almost £11,000. This was a sizeable property in which space was let to firms requiring offices, work-rooms and storage. In addition, each partner held a modest portfolio of shares, including investments in the National Insurance Company, the Saddle Reef goldmine, and the Colonial Bank of New Zealand – in which Glendining was involved for a short while.[91]

Around the middle of the decade the two men began to spend a little more freely. John Ross moved from London to the countryside, taking up residence in leafy Potters Bar. He also bought building land in Dunedin, signalling to his partner, perhaps, that he ultimately intended to return to New Zealand.[92] Glendining, too, decided to live more in keeping with his new-found status, spending £1,300 in 1875 on the construction of his 24-room residence, *Nithvale*, in North East Valley. Here he was to indulge his passion for gardening.[93]

By this stage, John Ross and Robert Glendining were clearly doing well. As they prospered, their Christian consciences also compelled them to support good causes. They had always contributed to the Presbyterian Church in Dunedin but now they were to be found helping ministers financially, lending money to build a manse, and contributing to the North Dunedin and the Knox churches.[94] Ross, although living in the United Kingdom, also made subscriptions to the Young Men's Christian Association in Dunedin and the Otago Institute.[95]

The combined expenditure by John Ross and Robert Glendining on themselves, their investments in property and shares, and their philanthropic activities absorbed around a third of their resources. They still had funds to spare, however, even after paying cash for the majority of goods they imported. Finding it difficult to source supplies of New Zealand-made woollen cloth, they used their surplus funds to build their own mills on the outskirts of Dunedin. In 1878, construction of the Roslyn Woollen Mills began.

# MILL OWNERS AND MANUFACTURERS

The boom of the 1870s was beneficial not only to importers but to
local manufacturing as well. Between 1867 and 1881, the number
of plants in New Zealand employing more than five persons had expanded
five-fold and, by the time of the 1881 Census, 17,938 hands were
employed in 1,643 factories. One sector to grow noticeably was clothing
manufacturing but, as we have seen, Ross & Glendining initially preferred
to buy rather than manufacture. By the early 1880s, though, the firm was
producing knitted hosiery, shirts and pants as well as men's and boys' outer
garments. This change of heart was brought about, at least in part, by the
need to find an end use for the yarn and cloth produced by their newly
opened woollen mills.

## 1. EARLY WOOLLEN MANUFACTURING IN NEW ZEALAND

Woollen cloth had been manufactured in small quantities in the South Island
since the 1840s but limited scale, primitive methods and high labour costs
meant that local producers were unable to compete with imports. However,
the exhaustion of gold reserves and a fall in agricultural prices in the late 1860s
encouraged the Otago Provincial Government to attempt to foster industry.
To stimulate innovation, prizes were offered for manufacturing, including
£1,500 for the first mill to produce 5,000 yards of woollen cloth. In 1870, this
initiative was followed up by the Joint Committee on Colonial Industry which
proposed, amongst other measures, that a temporary duty be imposed upon
the importation of tweed, cloths, and coarser woollen goods.[1]

The prospect of a bonus and protection was sufficient to encourage
Arthur Burns, politician and flour miller, to return to Scotland in 1870
to raise capital, buy machinery, and recruit hands for a small woollen
mill he planned to open just outside Dunedin. By the following January,
textile machinery – supplied by Platts of Oldham, the leading machinery
maker of the day – had been shipped to New Zealand. Over the next few
months, a brick engine house and 54-foot tall chimney stack were erected
and machinery set up in wooden spinning and weaving sheds. Production
commenced at the Mosgiel Woollen Mills in September 1871. Some 11,424
yards of tweeds, 4,171 yards of plaiding and 352 pairs of blankets, as well as

knitting yarn and hosiery, were produced in the year that followed. Burns was awarded his bonus.[2]

The mills erected by Burns were quite unusual. Whereas British mills tended to specialise in either spinning or weaving, with hosiery the province of an entirely separate industry, Mosgiel undertook all three. Given the limited scale of the domestic market, Burns' decision to combine these activities made excellent sense. Unable to exploit economies of scale, he exploited economies of scope instead, the savings on transactions costs and intermediate profits enabling him to compete with British imports.

Mosgiel woollens were much in demand as the economy boomed, so much so that in November 1873 the firm was reconstituted as the Mosgiel Woollen Factory Co. Ltd. Additional finance was raised and more plant installed. Robert Glendining, observing the popularity of the locally made goods, was keen to obtain a share of this rapidly growing trade. Unfortunately he found that Burns, 'a stupid donkey of a man', insisted on selling to all and sundry from premises in Dunedin.[3] Retailers naturally preferred to buy direct from the mill, believing they got a better deal. As a result, only the more distant and marginal accounts relied on warehousemen to supply them with Mosgiel woollens. Ross & Glendining were naturally dissatisfied with such a restricted trade, and it was only a matter of time before they started to look elsewhere for locally manufactured woollens.[4]

The success of Mosgiel soon encouraged other entrepreneurs to enter the industry. In the middle of 1873 Hercus informed Glendining, now on his way to London, that a new manufactory 'making Bradford goods only' was to be built in the Kaikorai Valley, just south of Dunedin. A Mr Booth had already left for the United Kingdom to buy machinery, the other partners being Alexander Williamson and David Ure, formerly of the grocery firm Jones, Williamson & Ure.[5] Funds were supposed to be supplied by Williamson's brother. When finance was not forthcoming, the partners turned to Dunedin merchants, McLandress Hepburn, who consented to be principal backers of the mills and guarantors for any credit advanced.

Ross & Glendining, realising that here was an opportunity to secure an alternative supply of colonial woollens, also agreed to contribute finance. In 1874 they advanced £4,000 to Williamson, Ure & Booth for a term of seven years, receiving as security the title to five acres of land upon which Kaikorai Woollen Mills were built.[6] Production began in 1875, greatly aided by Ross & Glendining, who advanced working capital to manufacture woollens which they sold on an agency basis.[7]

Kaikorai output continued to be sold through the Stafford St warehouse for the next few years. Woollen manufacturing also commenced at Kaiapoi, just to the north of Christchurch, where a flax mill was converted to make flannels and tweeds. Yet while Mosgiel continued to go from strength to strength, the Kaiapoi and Kaikorai mills struggled. After several years of trading, both concerns found themselves in difficulties, with Kaiapoi being auctioned off in 1877 at 'half its cost or even less'.[8] Meanwhile Williamson and Ure, the two remaining Kaikorai proprietors, were obliged to assign their interests to McLandress, Hepburn & Co., for whom they now worked for a salary. Hercus attributed the failure of the two mills to the fact that both were equipped with old and out-of-date machinery, the direct result of a lack of capital.[9]

## 2. MERCHANTS BECOME MANUFACTURERS

The failure of the Kaikorai mills to supply Ross & Glendining with a competitive product on a regular basis convinced the partners that they could 'greatly increase returns by manufacturing themselves ... with the most modern machinery'.[10] The decision to begin manufacturing was probably taken when Ross returned briefly to New Zealand in 1876 or 1877. The partners prepared their ground carefully, first securing the services of David Ure, who had now fallen out with McLandress Hepburn and was only too pleased to leave Kaikorai and set up new mills. Production at Kaikorai Mills nevertheless continued, thanks to assistance from Mosgiel, which temporarily managed the enterprise.[11]

Initially, Ross & Glendining obtained cost estimates for a relatively modest-sized establishment. Unlike Mosgiel, their mills would begin by producing only yarn and cloth. Hosiery would continue to be sourced from Britain, although provision would be made for the future installation of knitting frames.[12] Ure estimated that two sets of carding engines to straighten wool, two self-acting mules to spin yarn, twenty looms and associated tackle, drying and finishing equipment, steam engine etc., would cost just over £7,000. Land, buildings, and a brick chimney stack would cost a further £3,200, and the total cost of the mills, including working capital, should amount to around £14,000. It would be capable of processing 70,000 pounds of wool per annum, produce a mixture of yarn, blankets, flannels and plaiding, and should yield a net profit of around 10 per cent on capital employed.[13]

These estimates encouraged the partners to continue. In August 1878, Ure took the mail boat home to help Ross buy machinery and recruit hands. If all went well, Ure would not only help set up the new mills but would probably manage them as well.[14]

Until now, the partners had been able to keep their intentions of building their own woollen mills secret. The purchase of fourteen and half acres in the Kaikorai Valley, 'with a long frontage to Kaikorai Rd. and water power running the full length of the property', rather gave the game away and by July

1878, rumours that Ross & Glendining were about to start manufacturing
had become widespread.[15] Glendining, in the meantime, took advantage
of a business trip across the Tasman to discover how woollen textiles were
produced in Australia. There the mills tended to be far more specialised than
in New Zealand and produced only a narrow range of goods. Glendining
commented that the Sydney and Paramatta mills were 'very poor affairs', but
he expected something better in Victoria.[16] Whether the Victorian mills met
his expectations is not known.

Although John Ross and Robert Glendining were now personally wealthy
they had, for some years, accepted deposits from family, friends and others in
Britain to help finance purchases. Paying between 5 and 8 per cent interest,
by 1879 they held over £18,000 in deposits, around half of which was
supplied by the clothing manufacturer, Wathen & Gardiner.[17] While most
of these depositors nominally invested in Ross & Glendining for a short
fixed term, in practice the deposits were allowed to roll over, providing the
partners with a relatively stable source of long term finance. Access to these
deposits, together with their own funds, meant that the partners could afford
to construct a state-of-the-art woollen mill.

With Hercus insisting that 'the very newest and most perfect labour
saving machinery must be the cheapest in the long run', the partners decided
to purchase the latest machinery from Platts. Rather than deal with Platts
directly, John Ross and David Ure dealt with Richard Murray, Platts' agent
in Glasgow. Quite apart from Ross's preference for dealing with 'Scotchmen',
Murray was the obvious man to approach for it was he who had equipped
Mosgiel. As a member of the relatively new profession of consulting engineer,
he not only assisted Ross and Ure in selecting the most appropriate machinery
but also drew up plans and specifications. A local firm of architects, Messrs
Mason, Wales & Stevenson, whose senior partner had been involved in the
design of the 1865 Exhibition buildings, was employed to amend the plans
as necessary, hire local contractors, and supervise construction.[18] The new
mills were to be known as the Roslyn Woollen Mills.

### 3. Building very modern mills

The main mill building, over half an acre in extent, was to be built of brick
throughout, with partly hollow walls bonded with iron and set on massive
foundations to cope with vibration. The front was in two storeys, stretching
165 feet along the Kaikorai Valley Rd, the upstairs containing an office,
warehouse facilities and a design studio. Carding, spinning and weaving
took place at ground level in a single large room with a floor area of around
one third of an acre:

*It is lofty and well lighted, partially by a row of windows along the front, but principally by a series of longitudinal roofs, covered with plate glass, and pitched at an angle that has been found to be the most effective in admitting and diffusing light, without glare, throughout the room. These roofs are fitted with ventilators and are supported by fifty iron columns specially constructed for the purpose.*

The engine room was at the south end of the building with an octagonal chimney stack, eighty feet in height. Elsewhere there was a wool scouring plant, a sulphur house to treat wool, workshops and stables. Coal was delivered to a railway siding. A little way from the mills, on rising ground, land had been set aside for a manager's residence and workers' cottages.[19]

A well-designed plant not only conferred productivity advantages but was also cheaper to insure, not unimportant in a colony where arson was just another strategy employed by local businessmen. Ross & Glendining were nevertheless still concerned about their ability to compete with Mosgiel. In order not to be at a disadvantage with respect to scale, the partners decided to scrap Ure's original plans and increase the spinning capacity of Roslyn Woollen Mills so that it would be roughly equivalent to that of their rivals. Thus the machinery was to consist of not two but three carding engines, while the number of mules was increased from two to six, each running 300 spindles. The weaving capacity was to remain as planned, with twelve blanket and flannel looms and eight Jacquard looms for tweeds, but there was still space in which to install additional looms when required. A 60 h.p. compound steam engine would provide sufficient power for the foreseeable future.[20]

Construction began in late summer and by August 1879 the contractors had used more than 362,000 bricks, 65 casks of cement, and 14 tons of galvanised iron.[21] Apart from a few finishing touches, the mill buildings were now ready to receive the machinery. The installation of the spinning and weaving machinery proceeded smoothly, with testing and commissioning occurring in October. By this stage the total cost of the project amounted to almost £20,000, including land. For insurance purposes, buildings were valued at £7,500 and the machinery at £11,000, with cover split amongst a number of local and overseas insurance companies owing to the large sum involved.[22] On 1 November, with John Ross probably in attendance, Roslyn Woollen Mills commenced production.

The timing was unfortunate, to say the least. The failure of the City of Glasgow Bank, late in 1878, had contributed to a financial crisis in London, with both Australia and New Zealand soon feeling the effects. The repatriation of capital to support activity in the United Kingdom resulted in a loss of deposits by colonial banks, forcing them to restrict lending. In New Zealand, advances and discounts were cut by over £2 million in 1879, plunging the country into deep depression.[23] Ross & Glendining did not escape. In September, with Ross en route to New Zealand, Hercus wired the acting manager in London, 'Refuse late deliveries. Stop everything possible. Trade terribly bad'.[24]

The depression did not appear to interrupt activities at Roslyn Mills. Some £7,814 worth of goods were manufactured in the eight months to June 1880, including over 60,000 yards of flannels, 12,500 yards of plaiding, 1,154 pairs of blankets and 984 lbs of yarn. The costs of manufacturing amounted to £5,882, of which £3,153 was spent on greasy wool and another £2,066 on wages and salaries. To ensure accountability, the mills were to be treated as an independent profit centre, with all products 'sold' to warehouse departments at shadow prices prior to being distributed along with other stock. When the accounts were drawn up in the middle of the year, an operating or gross manufacturing profit of £1,931 was posted.

A more important indicator of the health of the enterprise, however, was the net profit figure, which was calculated by making further deductions from the gross profit figure. These fell under three headings: general expenses, which were principally overhead costs such as rates, insurance etc.; depreciation of land, buildings and machinery; and interest on capital. General expenses came to £301 in this period, but depreciation charges were initially waived. The real burden came in the form of interest charges, since at this time Ross & Glendining imputed a cost of 10 per cent per annum for all capital they personally employed in their enterprise. Thus a manufacturing profit of £1,931 turned into a far more modest profit of £229 for the eight months to June 1880, once general expenses and interest on capital had been deducted.[25] This was acceptable for a new plant at a time of depression, although the question of depreciation had yet to be seriously addressed (see Table 5.1).

### 4. INNOVATION AND COST REDUCTION

The value of goods manufactured at the mills increased steadily thereafter. Depreciation charges were set, for the time being, at a nominal two and half per cent but Hercus remained worried by the burden of fixed costs, especially interest on capital. These seemed to weigh heavily on net profits which, for the second half of 1880, amounted to only £86. In an effort to utilise the mills more effectively, a 'partial night shift' was introduced early in 1881 but this was apparently not cost effective. After some discussion it was decided to increase capacity, installing an additional carding engine and, since yarn by itself returned a loss, another twenty looms. It was also felt that Roslyn, like

## TABLE 5.1
## ROSLYN MILLS OUTPUT AND PROFITABILITY, 1879–1890 (£)

| Nov Year | 1880[a] | 1881 | 1882 | 1883 | 1884 | 1885 | 1886 | 1887 | 1888 | 1889 | 1890 |
|---|---|---|---|---|---|---|---|---|---|---|---|
| Output value | 15,958 | 21,741 | 29,243 | 31,378 | 38,821 | 37,108 | 30,519 | 40,020 | 48,413 | 52,482 | 57,625 |
| Scoured wool used (000 lbs) | 90.8 | 80.2 | 146.6 | 149.4 | 193.7 | 200.2 | 165.0 | 227.4 | 262.8 | 281.9 | 319.4 |
| Manufacturing profit | 3,903 | 5,071 | 5,443 | 8,114 | 10,868 | 9,478 | 9,371 | 9,501 | 13,825 | 15,248 | 12,824 |
| *Deductions* | | | | | | | | | | | |
| General expenses[b] | 486 | 506 | 597 | 721 | 749 | 1038 | 1300 | 890 | 872 | 891 | 1419 |
| Depreciation[c] | 261 | 553 | 999 | 2,690 | 3,056 | 3,963 | 2,028 | 2,730 | 2,610 | 2,919 | 4,322 |
| Interest[d] | 2,840 | 4,363 | 5,505 | 5,780 | 5,948 | 6,271 | 6,533 | 6,720 | 6,477 | 6,150 | 5,791 |
| Net profit[e] | 315 | -351 | -1,658 | -77 | 1,115 | -1,794 | -490 | -839 | 3,866 | 5,288 | 1,291 |
| Net profit + interest (£000s) | 3.2 | 4.0 | 3.8 | 5.7 | 7.1 | 4.5 | 6.0 | 5.9 | 10.3 | 11.4 | 7.1 |
| Estimated average capital employed (£000s) | 28.4 | 43.6 | 55.1 | 57.8 | 67.0 | 78.3 | 81.7 | 84.0 | 81.0 | 87.9 | 82.7 |
| Return on capital (%) | 11.1 | 9.2 | 7.0 | 9.9 | 10.5 | 5.7 | 7.4 | 7.0 | 12.8 | 13.0 | 8.6 |

*Sources: Half-yearly balances, AG 512 15/2–15/4.*
*Notes: (a) November 1879–December 1880. Thereafter balances struck at the end of November. (b) General expenses almost entirely overheads. (c) Wide variations in depreciation due to stock and plant being written down in particular years. (d) Interest rates on partners' capital reduced from 10 to 8 per cent in 1884; and from 8 to 7 per cent in 1889. (e) Goods were transferred to the warehouse at shadow prices. Had the shadow prices been less, then mill profitability would have fallen while warehouse profits would have risen. One can only assume that shadow prices somehow reflected market prices. Net profit figure refers only to manufacturing and excludes wool trading etc.*

Mosgiel, should manufacture hosiery and knitwear. Seven newly patented knitting machines, together with assorted ribbing frames, were therefore ordered from the makers, Griswolds. An extension was added to the main mill building to house the additional machinery.[26]

The patent machines enabled Ross & Glendining to compete in the rapidly growing hosiery and knitwear market. Thus, in addition to men's, women's and children's hose, the Griswold knitters made jerseys, cardigans, pants and shirts, and 'football and cricketing suits'.[27] Hosiery manufacture was also carried out by sub-contractors and outworkers, some of whom purchased Griswold machines from Ross & Glendining, who now held the New Zealand patent rights.[28]

In spite of the arrival of new machinery, Hercus believed that it would still be difficult to earn profits 'on anything except tweeds and flannels, unless the Mill is kept going night and day'. London office was therefore requested to find out what electric lighting systems were available and purchase and ship the most appropriate.[29] Never one to do things by halves, Ross attended evening classes on electricity before inspecting various makes both in London and on the Continent.[30] He chose Joel carbon arc lights to illuminate the main spinning and weaving section of the works, and Swann incandescent globes to light smaller rooms. A Siemens dynamo, connected to the mill engine, was to be used to supply electricity at low tension.[31]

The electric lights were installed early in 1882, a major innovation for New Zealand industry. Shortly afterwards, in a letter to the chairman of a Hokitika committee charged with lighting their township, George Hercus waxed eloquent about the virtues of electricity,

> *The only connections required between the generator and the lamps is an ordinary insulated telegraph wire, which is simply hung along our walls by cloth tacks … They were all fitted up, together with the machine and the lamps, in a day or two…Each of our [carbon] lamps is equal to ten gas jets of the usual 15 candle power. The light is full, constant, steady and free from glare. The lamps are provided with large half-opal globes that diffuse the light very well.*

Not only was the quality of light better, but Hercus thought that electricity was more economical, too. Thus while the carbon rods, which cost 6d each, had to be replaced each day, the lamps saved the equivalent of 4/6d in gas consumption. Given that the overall cost of the plant was under £250, the savings would, in a very short time, 'redeem' the whole cost of installation. Where motive power was freely available – or was sourced from water as was likely to be the case in Hokitika – then Hercus believed that the advantage in favour of electricity over gas was very apparent. However, he advised the committee against the use of a high-tension system, such as that advocated by Sir Julius Vogel's latest company, on the grounds that it was 'apt to be very dangerous'.[32]

The Employment of Females Act (1881) limited the employment of women and young persons to eight hours during the day.[33] Men were not subject to the same restrictions and, with the new lighting system in place, at least part of Roslyn Mills was able to operate from 6.00 a.m. to 9.00 p.m.[34] The extended working hours, in conjunction with the new machinery, meant that it was now possible to achieve significant increases in production.

During the second half of 1882 the value of output rose to over £16,000, almost 30 per cent greater than in the second half of the preceding year. Yet while manufacturing output increased rapidly, it remained difficult to earn profits – even though trade had improved.

There were a number of reasons for the lack of profitability. Expansion necessarily entailed greater capital expenditure. Thus the book value of land, buildings and machinery increased from £18,500 in 1879 to £34,377 at the end of 1882. This, together with the growth in stocks and work in progress, resulted in the interest charges on partners' capital employed increasing by almost 80 per cent. Profits were also hit by the introduction of more realistic depreciation charges, with land and buildings now being written off at the rate of 4 per cent per annum while machinery was written off at seven and a half per cent. As a result of these additional charges, an operating or manufacturing profit of £5,443 in 1882 was transformed into a net loss of £1658 (see Table 5.1).[35]

While the losses may have been purely nominal, it is clear that sales could be made only by accepting margins substantially less than those usually earned on imported goods. To add value and increase revenues still further, a clothing factory was opened in 1883 to manufacture men's and boys' clothing from material supplied by the mills. Capital outlay was less than £300, with the factory set up in leasehold premises opposite the warehouse in Stafford St. Orders were forwarded from the warehouse departments who were then charged for making-up by the factory. Within a couple of years there were over 100 hands at work in the factory, material also being made up into shirts and other garments by outworkers and sub-contractors in the city.[36]

## 5. SUPPORTING THE WAREHOUSE BUSINESS

Increased sales of mill goods helped to offset a decline in Ross & Glendining's traditional warehouse business and by 1883 Roslyn sales accounted for almost a quarter of total turnover. Roslyn Mills, moreover, was now generating a strong positive cash flow, notwithstanding its failure to pay a full 10 per cent interest on partners' capital employed. In spite of nominal losses, it was therefore decided to increase the output of the mills still further. By the beginning of 1884 another carding engine, two additional self-acting mules of 300 spindles each, and ancillary equipment had been installed. The additional outlay was not great, a little over £1,000, but with looms and knitting machinery kept better supplied with yarn, output increased by around a fifth to over £38,000. 1884 proved to be the most profitable year since commencement, the Roslyn balance sheet to November appearing to show a net profit of £2,485 – after overheads, interest and depreciation.[37]

The improvement in Roslyn's fortunes was doubtless welcomed by the partners, although it seems that the balance sheet did not give a true picture of manufacturing profits. For several years Glendining had been shipping wool to the United Kingdom, a sideline that had developed out of buying wool for the mills. A wool store had been built to support this activity where wool, either purchased at the annual wool sales or sent down from the partners' newly acquired sheep runs in Central Otago, was sorted and classed. A fellmongery and tannery had also just been opened at Roslyn, since sheepskins represented a cheap source of fine wool. Once profits from these subsidiary activities had been deducted, a net manufacturing profit of just £1,115 remained. At the same time, the interest charged on the partners' capital used by the mill was reduced from 10 to 8 per cent in order to reflect the changing financial conditions.[38] Had the old rate been applied, Roslyn Mills would have barely made an accounting profit in 1884. Bearing these factors in mind, performance, although still creditable, was not quite as rosy as the balance sheet indicated.[39]

In 1885 the New Zealand economy, which had enjoyed four years of uneven progress, began to falter once more. Primary product prices, which were already modest, fell away still further, wool prices declining almost continuously until the middle of the following decade.[40] With changing economic conditions, private capital ceased to flow in from abroad. Local financial institutions, worried about the values of securities they held, also began to restrict the amount of credit they advanced.[41] Trade was not immediately affected in either Auckland or Wellington, but in the South Island business had become seriously depressed. Particularly hard hit was Canterbury, heavily reliant on wheat and wool, with unemployment showing a sharp increase in Christchurch. The situation was little better further south. Forwarding the six-monthly balance sheets for warehouse operations to Ross, Hercus commented that because of 'the utter collapse of trade in Otago', returns for the half year to January 1886 'were miserable'.[42]

Ross & Glendining were badly hit by the downturn in the economy. Total warehouse sales fell from £145,900 in the financial year to July 1884 to £99,500 in the year to July 1886, the lowest level of sales since 1871. Initially, sales of mill goods held up well. The balance for Roslyn Mills, which was struck in November 1885, told a different story, revealing an overall loss of £4,416. Yet in reality, the situation was not quite so grim. After allowing for huge losses on wool shipments and rather more modest losses at the fellmongery and tannery, only £1,794 was lost through manufacturing. Of this figure, £2,000 was attributable to exceptional losses on wool stocks that had been written down to take into account the collapse in wool prices. Excluding subsidiary businesses and the exceptional losses, manufacturing activities had actually returned a small profit of £206 – plus the 8 per cent interest the partners paid themselves on the capital they had tied up in Roslyn![43]

The strong performance of Roslyn Woollen Mills in adverse circumstances may have been due, at least in some measure, to the appointment in 1885 of a young and energetic manager, James Lillico. A Scotsman who had learnt his trade in the Borders woollen industry, Lillico had emigrated to Victoria, where he had gained experience in colonial manufacturing. It was here he had come to the attention of Glendining. With Lillico now in place and the mills continuing to generate large amounts of free cash, John Ross and Robert Glendining came to the conclusion that they should increase the capacity of Roslyn yet again.

### 6. Pioneering worsted production

Rather than increase woollen production still further, the partners decided to start making worsted yarns and cloth. Although A.J. Burns had supported proposals to build a worsted mill at Timaru in 1881, worsted production had yet to commence in the Southern Hemisphere.[44] In the absence of colonial competition, the introduction of worsteds made excellent sense. Substantial quantities of worsteds were imported into New Zealand each year and so a sizeable market was open to capture by first movers.

There were also strategic advantages in manufacturing worsteds. With the clothing factory specialising in menswear, access to 'fine worsted coatings, costume cloths, and finer dress stuffs' meant that Ross & Glendining would be more likely to win military, volunteer, and railway contracts. They would also be able to develop the quality and more lucrative end of the civilian market for clothing, selling their worsted tweeds under the increasingly well-known 'Roslyn' label. There were benefits for hosiery production too, since worsted was ideal for the manufacture of 'proper stocking and hosiery yarns known as fingering's,' from which imported hosiery was usually made.[45] With the cost savings to be had from a fully integrated business, Glendining was convinced that the new worsted products would be extremely competitive.[46]

Additions to the main mill building were required to accommodate worsted manufacture and by the beginning of 1886 construction had begun. The machinery, which had been selected and purchased by Ross from makers in Yorkshire and Lancashire, arrived shortly afterwards and, over the next few months, it was erected and tested.[47] The spinning section of the new plant included four carding engines, two combing machines, winding and twisting machinery, and spinning frames containing 1,728 spindles. Four of the latest fast looms were also purchased, together with a new and more powerful steam engine of 340 horse power.[48] The cost of the extension and equipment came to well over £12,000.[49]

More hands were now required to work the machinery, the persistent shortage of skilled labour in New Zealand forcing Ross to go on a recruiting drive. For worsted spinners he went to Yorkshire, the employment of 'Yorkies' in a plant full of Scots adding a new and sometimes controversial dimension to labour relations. When worsted production finally commenced in June 1886, there were more than 100 males and 80 females, including boys and girls, employed at Roslyn Mills.[50]

The interruption to the mills while the new equipment was installed meant that the quantity of wool processed in 1886 fell slightly. The value of output, on the other hand, fell much more, a reflection of reduced sales and lower values. Losses, excluding those attributable to ancillary activities, were surprisingly small, a consequence, no doubt, of the savage writing down of wool stocks in the previous year and the added value of worsted production. Thereafter trade showed signs of recovery and soon Roslyn Mills was struggling to keep up with demand for its worsted tweeds.

The new plant, unfortunately, was not operating as well as it should and much of 1887 was spent ironing out problems.[51] A major drawback was that the new steam engine was less powerful than expected, a fact that Ross, who had chosen the machine after consultation with various makers, seemed unwilling to accept.[52] After a sharp exchange between the partners, Ross was persuaded to order a super-heater to raise horse power and economise on fuel, plus a clutch to disengage machinery when idle. In the meantime A. & T. Burt, local plumbers and engineers, did their best to improve the efficiency of the engine. Other problems occurred with the Boyd winding machine, while the twisting machinery was also far too slow. A reluctant Ross ordered additional machinery while Glendining, hampered by the lack of local expertise, was obliged to get an employee to write to an acquaintance in Yorkshire to find out the optimum speed for twisting fine yarns.[53]

The partners also disagreed as to how the weaving might best be undertaken, with Ross suggesting that the new fast looms, operating at sixty shots a minute, might be used instead of slow looms. Glendining demurred, informing Ross that the fast looms, while excellent for weaving strong worsted yarns, cost rather more to tune and frequently cut the weft when weaving woollen blankets and flannels. The slow looms, being wider, were ideal for the latter, even though their speed was only forty-eight shots a minute.[54] Lillico was also of this view. A few months later Glendining ordered another four of Platt's slow looms, together with larger pulleys to bring the existing slow looms up to their rated speed. An additional weft-winding machine was also ordered. Ross was assured that 'this will be all the machinery we want for a long time, at least until we get another building up …'[55]

Slowly the necessary adjustments were made at the mills although adverse weather was still likely to interrupt production. In September 1887, Glendining was complaining about the cold, damp weather:

> ... *everything was cold in the mill. With the cold and damp the wool stuck to the leathers on the machines and Hird says he could scarcely get through it all ... it shows that we will require to do something in the way of heating the room for an hour or so in the cold winter mornings before next winter ... I thought we might get over it without doing any more but from what I know now I fear we will have to face it.*[56]

That it was interruptions to production rather than concern for the workers that encouraged Glendining to heat the mills is, perhaps, a reflection of working conditions at the time. On the other hand, Ross & Glendining were far from poor employers, with sick and injured workers being assisted by the Roslyn Mills Benefit Society to which the firm made a regular contribution. A savings bank, upon which interest was paid, was also started by the firm.[57]

## 7. First mover advantages

In spite of the problems at Roslyn and the difficult trading conditions in New Zealand, Glendining remained remarkably cheerful. In the midst of his troubles he informed his partner that there were sufficient orders on hand to keep the mills going for the next three months, and he was hopeful that there would be more coming in to 'keep us going after that'.[58] Other mills, producing only woollens, were less fortunate, especially those that had come into production since the beginning of the eighties. Undercapitalised and facing a downturn in the market, many sold goods at or below cost in order to maintain liquidity. Some were in desperate straits. Towards the end of June 1887, Ross was told that the Ashburton mill was cutting the prices of 'everything they make', that Oamaru were selling goods 'cheaper than they could make them' and that the Timaru mill was 'on fire the other night'. Lillico thought it was a 'clear case of trying to burn the mill out!' In the North Island things were little better. The Wellington Woollen Mills showed a credit balance of only £34 while the proposed Auckland mills at Onehunga, which had not yet started production, were heavily indebted to the Bank of New Zealand.[59]

Such news, allied to reports in London about the state of the New Zealand economy, concerned the more cautious Ross. He became increasingly worried about the seemingly never-ending investment in Roslyn Mills and questioned the wisdom of throwing good money after bad. Glendining, rather more optimistic by nature than his London-based partner, was obliged to reassure him. 'I have no more wish to increase the machinery account than you do'.[60] As for Ross's rather wishful suggestion of selling up and laying out their money at 6 per cent interest, Glendining was quite blunt, pointing out that such a course of action would result in a substantial loss of capital.[61]

Given the cut-throat competition in woollens, problems in manufacturing worsteds, and the general state of the economy, the performance of Roslyn Mills in 1887 turned out rather better than Ross might have expected. The volume of wool processed rose by a third, the value of manufactured output was up by around 30 per cent, and gross manufacturing profits slightly higher at £9,501. After deductions for overhead costs, interest and depreciation, a net manufacturing loss of £839 was incurred, not a matter for concern given that the partners still received £6,720 interest on capital employed by the mills. The following year, with the profitable worsted tweeds in full production, the balance sheet showed a net profit, excluding ancillaries, of £3,866. Together with the sums deducted for interest and depreciation, this represented a free cash flow of almost £13,000 for the year.[62]

Other mills in New Zealand continued to struggle. When, in 1887, Mosgiel announced that they were to issue debentures to shore up their finances, Glendining took mischievous delight in offering his rivals £5,000 at short call. John Roberts, the chairman of Mosgiel, balked at the idea, but the offer effectively silenced the claims of his manager, Morrison, that Ross & Glendining were only kept afloat by cheap money borrowed from home.[63] In fact, Morrison was so impressed by the production of worsteds at Roslyn Mills that he considered starting production at Mosgiel.[64] As a first step, he installed new hosiery machinery which, using imported worsted yarns, was able to produce goods of better quality than any yet made at Roslyn.[65]

## 8. DEMANDS FOR TARIFF PROTECTION

Deepening depression and rising unemployment throughout New Zealand meant that, as the decade wore on, there were increasing demands for tariff protection, both from manufacturers and the labour movement. Glendining was not wholly in favour of raising duties from the existing 15 per cent, *ad valorem,* especially as the firm was still a major importer and relied on cheap overseas goods to complement Roslyn production, 'Whether it will be good for New Zealand I do not know .... so far as we are concerned the present duty is fair protection but if it was raised 5 or 7 per cent it would be all the better.' At the same time, Glendining thought that increased protection, in so far as it benefited small makers and encouraged new entry, might lead to increased competition – although maybe not for a few years.[66] By April 1888 his opposition to protection had hardened, especially as it looked as though it would probably involve the imposition of duties upon machinery and materials, 'now admitted free'.[67]

Glendining's opposition to tariffs is not surprising. Quite apart from being a major importer, both he and John Ross were philosophically committed to free-trade Liberalism. The tide in New Zealand, however, was setting against them, the failure of the economy to strengthen during the early part of 1888 giving added weight to demands for protection. With the need to service the overseas loans the government was about to raise, the nominally free-trade premier, Sir Harry Atkinson, was persuaded to introduce a tariff bill into Parliament. Glendining, in Lyttelton by the end of May and waiting to sail to London, was kept abreast of its progress through the legislature by Hercus:

> ... although the Bill has passed its second reading, there is still some stonewalling going on to keep it back from the Committee, and as it has yet to be discussed in detail, there is no saying when it will come out, or in what shape, as a finished article. There is little doubt, however, that it will be carried as a whole, though with some alteration in detail.[68]

Hercus proved to be correct. The new tariffs were ultimately agreed at 20 per cent on machinery, clothing, footwear, textiles and on a wide range of other manufactures too.[69] The modest increase resulted in a degree of protection for cheaper manufactures, although the principal beneficiary was undoubtedly the government exchequer.

Why Glendining chose to visit the United Kingdom at this juncture is something of a mystery, although there was a general feeling that he had been working far too hard. His departure was timely, for when the bill was finally passed, Hercus informed Ross:

> ... machinery is exempt until January 4th, and then 20 per cent. All machinery 'ordered' not later than May the 30th and arriving within six months of the passing of the Act, is specially exempted. Mr. Glendining left next morning [31st May] with memoranda of machinery required which had been previously prepared: and I have no doubt his notes will be treated as 'orders' within the meaning of the Act.[70]

Of course, Glendining did not have to go home to place orders for machinery although, given Ross's previous reluctance to spend more money, he may have felt that he needed to explain his plans in person. The sea voyage would also restore his health. In any event, Glendining sailed via Cape Horn, arriving in late summer. He visited machinery makers, personally chose some fast looms, and then took a much-needed holiday with family and friends in Scotland.[71]

Glendining and his wife returned to Dunedin at the end of 1888, travelling back by the faster Australian route. By the time he arrived, the New Zealand economy was beginning to show signs of revival.[72] The new machinery he bought allowed Roslyn Mills to take advantage of the resurgence in demand and, over the next few years, the output of the mill rose by around a quarter. Other mills increased output too, especially the Kaiapoi and Wellington woollen mills, but their concentration on lower quality goods, now shut out by the tariff, allowed Roslyn to dominate the market for quality woollens and worsteds.

## 9. A SUCCESSFUL INVESTMENT

After a dozen years, John Ross and Robert Glendining had every reason to feel that their decision to establish Roslyn Mills was the correct one. Entry into the market for colonial woollens would have been desirable in any case, but it was particularly important given the difficulties faced by the warehousemen in selling more expensive imported goods during the depression. By investing in their own mills, Ross & Glendining were able to secure around a fifth of the growing trade in colonial-made worsteds and woollens, something that would not have been possible had they continued to rely on Mosgiel and the Kaikorai Woollen Mills for supplies.

Quite apart from helping to sustain the business, investment in Roslyn Mills also represented an excellent use of funds when times were hard. True, the enterprise may have barely broken even over the first ten years of its life, earning a profit of only £87 – excluding ancillary activities – to November 1888. However, the partners also received over £50,000 of interest on their capital in this period, Roslyn yielding a rate of return that varied between 5.7 and 12.8 per cent per annum. This was substantially greater than returns elsewhere. The interest that accrued, together with nearly £19,000 written off on account of depreciation, ended up as cash in their pockets. At a time of depression, almost £70,000 of free cash was more than welcome. It meant that John Ross and Robert Glendining were free from the capital constraints that faced many of their rivals.

# BRANCHING OUT

Historians often refer to the period 1879 to 1896 as 'the long depression'. Not all would agree with this description. Although the trend in commodity prices was undoubtedly downwards, real wages for labour, though fluctuating, rose during these years, while unemployment was usually localised and relatively short-lived. Lower prices and periodic financial crises may have slowed investment, but real gross domestic product still grew by almost a half.[1] The 1880s, in particular, was an era of readjustment as a growing population, together with changes in relative prices, encouraged New Zealanders to use their resources in new and different ways.

Perhaps the most fundamental changes occurred on the land, where the production of meat and dairy products provided an additional and vital source of income. Changes also occurred in secondary industries as the country became more self-sufficient. As we have seen, significant developments occurred in the textile and clothing industries, with the emergence of modern, large-scale plants. In commerce, too, there were changes, the sharp downturns of the mid eighties and early nineties encouraging consolidation and the growth of enterprises that aimed to serve a national market.[2] Ross & Glendining were not immune from such forces. By 1890 they had established branches in each of the main cities, except Auckland, as they sought wider markets for both Roslyn Mills and their warehouse business.

## 1. Struggling to maintain sales

The market for soft goods was badly affected by the downturn of 1879. The summer season started poorly and by mid-October Hercus was complaining of 'bad trade, heavy renewals, and bad debts'.[3] The Bank of New South Wales became alarmed that Ross & Glendining continued to extend credit to its customers, only to be reassured that the firm was 'the most conservative house in our line of business in the colony'.[4] But rather than getting better, trade got worse. When the books were balanced in July 1880, annual sales had fallen by over a quarter to just under £122,000.

The slump in sales, together with bad debts of £8,000, resulted in warehouse profits of £4,491 in 1879 being transformed into a loss of £8,313 in the following year. Like Roslyn Mills, the warehouse was debited with interest at 10 per cent on capital the partners had invested in that side of the business. Ignoring interest charges, the warehouse actually returned a tiny profit of £381. This, however, can have been of little consolation to John Ross and Robert Glendining, who still found themselves over £12,800 worse off for the year.

With the exception of the West Coast, sales generally declined (see Table 6.1). Particularly hard hit were what Hercus called the big/little importers, general merchants such as Blythes of Napier, Hood & Shennan of Oamaru and Cowan & Foster of Timaru. These merchants, who generally combined wholesaling, retailing, and dressmaking, often had Ross & Glendining buy for them on commission. As a result, they owed the partners substantial amounts.[5] Situated in the smaller provincial centres, these outlets were progressively squeezed by large competitors. As trade got worse, warehousemen such as Bing, Harris & Co. and Arthur & Co. took advantage of improved communications to send their travellers further afield, capturing the smallest of orders.

Lesser merchants, operating a similar style of business in Dunedin, also struggled, especially the wholesale/retail firm owned by William McBeath and

## TABLE 6.1
## SALES BY REGION, 1880–1890 (£000s)

| July Year | 1880 | 1881 | 1882 | 1883 | 1884 | 1885 | 1886 | 1887 | 1888 | 1889 | 1890 |
|---|---|---|---|---|---|---|---|---|---|---|---|
| Dunedin | 40.7 | 54.8 | 58.8 | 67.8 | 50.3 | 40.6 | 32.6 | 29.8 | 31.5 | 37.3 | 46.7 |
| Southland & South Otago | 20.2 | 25.9 | 26.5 | 24.3 | 23.6 | 25.3 | 15.5 | 15.2 | 15.5 | 24.8 | 25.2 |
| Goldfields | 8.5 | 11.0 | 10.9 | 10.0 | 11.2 | 9.6 | 9.6 | 6.8 | 7.7 | 9.5 | 11.0 |
| North Otago & Canterbury | 38.3 | 40.4 | 40.7 | 27.7 | 30.3 | 32.0 | 18.7 | 24.5 | 27.2 | 40.6 | 51.3 |
| West Coast | 9.0 | 8.8 | 6.2 | 7.9 | 6.4 | 4.7 | 6.0 | 6.1 | 6.3 | 5.8 | 7.5 |
| Marlborough/Nelson & Wellington | 1.3 | 3.3 | 8.7 | 7.1 | 11.1 | 6.3 | 8.6 | 6.7 | 8.8 | 20.7 | 35.0 |
| Hawkes Bay | 3.5 | 2.8 | 3.9 | 2.9 | 4.4 | 4.2 | 3.9 | 2.9 | 3.1 | 5.1 | 8.5 |
| Auckland | 0.4 | 4.3 | 7.0 | 7.0 | 8.2 | 9.5 | 7.7 | 5.0 | 4.7 | 3.8 | 3.0 |
| Other | – | – | 0.6 | 0.5 | 0.4 | 0.5 | 1.1 | 2.6 | 7.8 | 5.0 | 2.6 |
| Total | 121.7 | 151.3 | 163.3 | 155.1 | 145.9 | 132.7 | 103.6 | 99.5 | 112.6 | 152.5 | 190.8 |

*Sources: Half-yearly balances, AG 512 15/2–15/4.*

former employee, Robert Saunders. This recently established business, located in the newly constructed Albert Buildings in Princes St, required substantial financial support from Ross & Glendining in order to survive. That credit was so readily extended was no doubt due to the fact that Saunders was married to the younger sister of Mary Glendining and Margaret Ross.[6] Even so, the cautious Hercus treated Saunders McBeath & Co. like many other large debtors, requiring them to submit their balance sheets and other operating details so that they might benefit from his advice. He came to the opinion that their dressmaking activities should be discontinued, notwithstanding the excellence of their dressmaker, Mrs Smith. The wholesale trade should also be abandoned as margins were very slim.[7]

With large customers struggling, Ross & Glendining decided to copy rivals and sell to a wider geographical spread of smaller retailers. In 1881 a new traveller, Charles Henderson, was appointed, bringing the number of travellers employed by the firm up to five. Henderson was expected to revive sales in Wellington province, which had steadily dwindled following the emergence of Thompson & Shannon and other competitors in the city.

Prospects in the capital now seemed to be promising, especially as Roslyn tweeds and flannels were selling well in the North Island.[8] The proposed construction of a privately financed railway linking Wellington to the Manawatu also gave reason for hope, the new line being expected to lead to substantially greater trade in the lower North Island.[9] Accordingly, Henderson was given a list of established and prospective customers, together with their credit rating, whom he might visit. They stretched from Hawera in the north down to the Wanganui River. He was also expected to revive old accounts in and around Wellington. Thereafter he was to sail up the east coast to Napier, visit a variety of old and new accounts in Hawkes Bay, and then progress northwards to Wairoa and Gisborne, where a little business had been done in the past.[10]

The recovery in trade was well under way by the time Henderson eventually sailed north in the summer of 1881 (see Table 6.1). The results of his journey were quite encouraging, even though summer was not the ideal time to push woollen goods in the North Island. In the meantime Kelly, the senior Christchurch traveller, had begun to sell Roslyn goods in the Auckland region. This journey was soon taken over by another new traveller, John Fothergill. He replaced the other Christchurch traveller, Skeoch, who had been dismissed for persistently cutting prices. Kelly, in turn, resumed his duties in Canterbury.[11]

The costs of travelling in the North Island, which involved coastal shipping as well as horse and buggy, were quite high, often more than double the 3 per cent of sales normally incurred in Otago. Nevertheless, high travelling costs seemed a small price to pay for gaining access to expanding northern markets. Sales in Wellington and Auckland provinces soared, from £1,673 in the year ending in July 1880 to £15,691 two years later. By this time, they amounted to almost 10 per cent of total sales (see Table 6.1).

The recovery in the economy that had begun late in 1880 began to falter in 1883 as the prices of wool and cereals started to fall once more.[12] For Ross & Glendining, it was business in North Otago and Canterbury that began to deteriorate first, sales for 1883 being some 25 per cent less than the preceding year. By 1884 signs of distress were to be found amongst customers in Otago and Southland; in 1885 it was trade in Wellington province that began to weaken; Auckland finally succumbed to depression in 1886 as the property boom there ran its course.[13] By October 1887 things there were so bad that the Bank of New Zealand, heavily involved in the speculative Auckland property market, failed to pay a dividend for the first time since it was founded.[14]

## 2. COPING WITH A DEEP DEPRESSION

Warehouse sales fell continuously from 1883 onwards, notwithstanding a rise in demand for the tweeds, flannels and hosiery produced by Roslyn Mills. The bottom was reached in the year ending in July 1887 when sales amounted to £99,476, the lowest annual total for almost two decades. Part of the decline was attributable to a general reduction in prices but the principal cause was the lack of orders as customers reduced stocks or went out of business. Paradoxically, bad debts peaked early on, although the figure of £14,944 in 1883 was only a few hundred pounds greater than bad debts sustained in 1885 (see Table 6.2).

Amongst the early debtors were a number of the big/little importers, many of whom had been nursed by Ross & Glendining since the downturn in 1879. The largest single debt was that incurred by Hood & Shennan of Oamaru, whose business went into liquidation in February 1883 owing over £16,000. Of this amount, £11,552 was owed to Ross & Glendining, with lesser sums owed to Sargood, Son & Ewen, Saunders McBeath, Brown, Ewing & Co., the Kaiapoi Woollen Co. and others. The creditors agreed to settle for ten shillings in the pound, with bills drawn against Hood over a period of eighteen months.[15] Cowan & Foster and Saunders McBeath also struggled to survive, several attempts being made by Hercus to sell the latter business in an effort to extinguish debt.

When the warehouse balance was struck in July 1883, the loss for the year amounted to a massive £21,523. Not all was the result of bad debts, £4,685 being written off the warehouse and other property to reflect the changing valuations due to the onset of depression. The sum of £1,694 was

TABLE 6.2

SALES, CAPITAL EMPLOYED AND PROFITABILITY: WAREHOUSE
OPERATIONS, 1880–1890 (£000s)

| July Year | 1880 | 1881 | 1882 | 1883 | 1884 | 1885 | 1886 | 1887 | 1888 | 1889 | 1890 |
|---|---|---|---|---|---|---|---|---|---|---|---|
| Total sales | 121.7 | 151.3 | 163.3 | 155.1 | 145.9 | 132.7 | 103.6 | 99.5 | 112.6 | 152.5 | 190.8 |
| Bad debts | 2.8 | 10.6 | 1.6 | 14.9 | 3.1 | 14.5 | 3.3 | 3.3 | 3.7 | 2.3 | 2.7 |
| Net profit | -8.3 | 4.9 | 3.6 | -15.5[a] | -0.5 | -17.9 | -7.4 | -7.5 | -3.3 | 2.5 | 10.1 |
| Imputed interest[b] | 8.7 | 8.3 | 8.8 | 7.5 | 5.2 | 3.7 | 3.1 | 3.0 | 3.6 | 3.0 | 4.4 |
| Partners' salaries | 1.0 | 1.0 | 1.0 | 1.0 | 1.0 | 1.0 | 1.0 | 1.0 | 1.0 | 1.0 | 1.0 |
| Clothing factory profit | – | – | – | 0.6 | 0.9 | 0.9 | 0.4 | 0.7 | 0.7 | 0.7 | 1.7 |
| Total returns | 1.4 | 14.2 | 13.4 | -6.4 | 6.6 | -12.3 | -2.9 | -2.8 | 2.0 | 7.2 | 17.2 |
| Estimated average capital employed | 86.9 | 83.4 | 88.1 | 75.0 | 56.5 | 46.3 | 38.8 | 37.3 | 44.7 | 42.8 | 62.9 |
| Return on capital (%) | 1.6 | 17.0 | 15.2 | - 8.5 | 11.7 | -26.6 | -7.5 | -7.5 | 4.4 | 17.5 | 27.3 |

Sources: Half-yearly balances, AG 512 15/2–15/4.
Notes: (a) Excluding exceptional items – as per text. (b) The rate of interest charged on partners' capital was reduced
from 10 to 8 per cent in January 1884 and from 8 to 7 per cent from July 1888. The interest payments relate only to the
capital employed in the warehouse business and not to capital invested in mills, sheep runs, and other properties.

also written off on account of Roslyn Mills, an unusual occurrence as mill
finance was usually kept entirely separate from that of the warehouse. Again
the warehouse was charged 10 per cent on the partners' capital employed but
even if these charges had been set aside, a loss of over £8,000 would still have
been incurred on warehouse operations.

With sales falling, Ross & Glendining were obliged to consider what
might be done to turn things around. In the autumn of 1883, the firm
finally opened their own clothing factory. Located in a three-storey leasehold
building opposite the Stafford St warehouse, it was initially equipped with
twenty-one new and second-hand sewing machines, including eight Singer
machines, a button-hole machine, presses, benches and stools. The factory
made men's and boys' clothing for the warehouse departments which supplied
most of the materials. Much of the cloth originally came from Roslyn Mills,
while trimmings, buttons and thread were usually bought by Ross in London.
The division of labour and the employment of female machinists helped to
keep costs down.[16]

The factory proved to be a valuable competitive weapon in the battle for scarce orders. Ross & Glendining were now able to enter the chart trade, in which a customer's measurements were recorded by retailers according to a standard chart, details of the order then being forwarded to Stafford St for making up. This allowed small retailers to access the benefits of mass production and wrest part of the trade back from firms such as Hallenstein & Co., Sargood, Son & Ewen and Butterworth Brothers, all of whom owned their own clothing factories. Sales were also enhanced by capitalising on the growing popularity of Roslyn materials, men's clothing being produced in distinctive cuts and styles and marketed under the Roslyn brand.[17]

The ability to buy ready-made clothing clearly appealed to smaller retailers who did not possess the capacity for making-up themselves. Larger outlets may have been less easily persuaded. When Thomson & Beattie of Invercargill were offered clothing as an alternative to Roslyn tweeds that they thought too expensive, agreement foundered over their desire to cut the garments themselves on their own premises.[18] Nevertheless, large orders were regularly secured elsewhere, tenders being successfully submitted to New Zealand Railways, the military, police and other institutions for which low cost, mass production was essential.[19] The contribution of the clothing factory to warehouse sales cannot be quantified, although Glendining thought it important. Whatever the contribution, the factory regularly showed a profit from the charges it levied on the warehouse departments for making-up.

Competitive pressures not only forced Ross & Glendining to diversify, but it also led them to review the functioning of their distribution network. The lack of progress in Canterbury encouraged them to look for fresh premises in Christchurch, both to carry larger stock and to display goods to better advantage. In 1883 an opportunity arose when Thompson, Shannon & Co., the Wellington warehousemen, moved to a new branch warehouse in Lichfield St. Thompson's elegant new warehouse, built of bluestone and brick and 'with pilastered cornices of carved and moulded stone', was opened in March to a grand fanfare.[20] With their old warehouse now vacant, Hercus instructed James Kelly to ascertain whether Ross & Glendining might move in. A lease was quickly secured and, after refurbishment, stock was transferred from the sample rooms to Thompson, Shannon & Co.'s former premises – also in Lichfield St.[21]

While Ross & Glendining may not have enjoyed the promotional advantages of opening a new and showy warehouse, they did use other means to advertise their products. In 1882 it was announced that Christchurch would host a New Zealand Exhibition, similar to that held in Dunedin in the 1860s. Glendining decided that in addition to the usual display of clothing and textiles, his firm might attract considerable interest if they demonstrated one of their Griswold patent knitters. A whole bay was leased in the British Court of the Exhibition in which four machines were installed. A 'Miss Brown, who has come out from Home to superintend our Knitting Department' was to work the machine for a week or two, being replaced thereafter by a 'suitable girl' who was to remain on the stand until the end of the Exhibition.[22] The success of the Exhibition appears to have encouraged a depressed Christchurch to mount a second 'Industrial Exhibition' in 1884, Wellington following suit with its own exhibition in 1885. On each occasion, Ross & Glendining took advantage of the venue to promote Roslyn goods and other wares.[23]

The difficult trading conditions meant that it was important that each and every opportunity was taken to make a sale. Once again the activities of travellers came under scrutiny.[24] In 1884, following complaints about lackadaisical service, Charles Henderson, now serving Auckland, was paid a fixed wage of £6 a week rather than salary plus commission. Closer monitoring followed. In August 1885 he was informed that the firm had decided to:

> adopt a practice that has been found very useful by Home Houses in keeping them well-posted up in everything affecting their business at a distance, viz. that each of their travellers should post every night, from wherever they may be, a short memo of the days events .... Please state shortly each day _where you are: what business has been done or is in progress: any news about customers: or any memo respecting the goods_ that you think will be of use to us etc. Send us also every week statements of cash expenditure, as detailed as possible.[25]

How Henderson received the instructions regarding closer monitoring is not known but James Kelly, the senior Christchurch traveller, decided that they did not apply to him. He was quickly reprimanded for his impertinence, at the same time being instructed 'not to abandon ground where business can be done'.[26] Neither Kelly nor Henderson remained with the firm much longer. William Peters replaced Kelly in Christchurch in February 1886, while Ebenezer Clark, who had previously worked for Sargood, Son & Ewen in their Auckland warehouse, took over the northern journey soon after.[27]

The various initiatives taken by Ross & Glendining offered only limited relief from what turned out to be the worst depression in New Zealand's short history. Bad debts rose again in 1885 while in the following year sales plummeted. In January 1886, Hercus, sending a copy of the half-yearly balance sheet to Ross in London, wrote:

> The result is much worse than I expected, although certainly I did not expect anything other than a loss, owing to the utter collapse of trade for the

*summer season .... We do not think any of our neighbours are doing better, though that is poor consolation. After looking for better days to come, for so long, without avail, one is inclined to give up expecting them. Yet surely things cannot continue as present.*

Even the clothing factory showed a profit of less than half the previous year, having been slack for three or four months.[28]

### 3. MERGERS AND PRICE FIXING

The heavy losses were made worse by the fact that the level of trade was no longer sufficient to support the overhead costs incurred by maintaining a large warehouse in Dunedin, two new Christchurch warehouses, and an army of clerks, travellers and sales staff. Given that other warehousemen were similarly burdened by excess capacity, it was not long before proposals for mergers and rationalisation began to surface. By mid-winter Ross & Glendining were involved in detailed discussions with Sargood, Son & Ewen. Who broached the subject is not clear.

A merger was appealing to both parties. For Ross & Glendining it meant access to Sargood's warehouse in Auckland, enabling them to serve that part of the country far more effectively than hitherto. It also provided them with an outlet for their manufactures in Australia, where Frederick Sargood was senior partner in what was reputedly the largest warehouse company in the Southern Hemisphere. Sargood, Son & Ewen, on the other hand, would be able to draw on Roslyn Mills for the colonial manufactures that all New Zealand warehousemen were now obliged to stock. This would give them an advantage over those competitors still forced to buy in. There would be other cost savings too, the rationalisation of purchasing in London and warehousing in Dunedin enabling surplus properties to be disposed of and warehouse and travelling staff laid off. John Ewen was to remain in London to attend to the buying, while John Ross and Robert Glendining were to manage business in New Zealand. The two partners would retain their sheep runs and other properties while the mill, factories, and warehouses would be taken over by the new firm at valuation.[29]

Discussions between the two parties initially made good progress. Sargood, still resident in Melbourne where he was heavily involved in business, politics and society, was nevertheless concerned about the inclusion of Roslyn Mills. He suggested that the partners should either float the mills as a separate company or guarantee that they would not make losses in the future. His concern was quite understandable since Victorian woollen mills, which produced only a very narrow range of goods, were 'kept at the mercy of the warehouses' and earned only slender profits. Glendining assured

Ewen that things were different in New Zealand where, because of the greater variety of goods produced, it was possible to keep 'moderate stocks and obtain better and more regular prices'. Moreover Roslyn Mills, the 'premier mill in the country', had little to fear from competition from other mills, especially from newer mills, which were under-capitalised, possessed 'imperfect machinery', and lacked skilled direction. Sargood's reservations concerning the acquisition of the clothing factory were similarly dismissed, Glendining pointing to the growing reputation of Roslyn-branded clothing in the marketplace. The advantages of the mill and factory working together when it came to tendering for government contracts were also stressed.[30]

These assurances seem to have satisfied Sargood who arrived in Dunedin to complete negotiations. He brought with him the deeds of partnership of his Australian firm, Sargood, Butler & Nicol, which he used as a guide to draft an agreement. Provisions contained in the draft gave Sargood an absolute veto on 'everything concerning the business'; the sole right to expel a partner at his discretion and to purchase the expelled partner's share; and the ability to veto any attorney who the co-partners might wish to appoint. All powers were to be reserved to Sargood's executors in the event of his death. There were other questionable provisions, too, including the assumption that the goodwill of the new concern would be the property of Sargood alone.

Glendining immediately rejected the draft as too one-sided. Slowly, with the aid of solicitors, points of difference were resolved and an acceptable agreement drawn up. Then, just when it seemed that all outstanding matters had been settled, Frederick Sargood abruptly broke off negotiations and returned to Melbourne.[31]

The ostensible sticking point was who should act as bankers for the new concern, it previously having been agreed that it should be the Bank of New South Wales rather than the Bank of New Zealand. Hercus thought that 'the Colonel', as Sargood was referred to by the partners, had other reasons for the sudden change of mind:

> he was so exasperated at having given in so much on the goodwill and veto points in the forenoon, that his temper got the better of him in the evening and, having once committed himself, he could not go back. He confessed that he did not understand that goodwill involved so much: and possibly he felt annoyed that the arbitrary and absolute effect of the power he held by his other deeds of partnership, should be laid so bare before Mr. Ewen.[32]

Glendining left the way open for negotiations to be resumed but nothing ever eventuated.[33] Ross, back in London, was consoled with the thought that, given the state of the market, the Stafford St warehouse would have been difficult to sell, while the prospects for business in Auckland were far from promising.[34]

Competition, in the interim, continued unabated, especially from Bing, Harris & Co. who continued to cut prices and offer generous credits. What effect this had on their margins is not clear, although the extent of Bing, Harris's bad debts seemed to be no worse than those of their neighbours.[35] Meanwhile, news about the failed merger between Sargoods and Ross & Glendining gradually percolated through to the wider business community. Encouraged by this development, the ever-opportunistic Wolf Harris approached the partners in February 1887 with the suggestion that they might like to buy his firm instead.[36]

The proposal from Harris was not well received for not only was he unable to offer the inducement of an Auckland warehouse, but Glendining thought that he was unlikely to sell out at anything like reasonable terms. Moreover, in view of the cheap prices and long credits that Bing, Harris & Co. offered – a policy that appeared to sacrifice profits for turnover – there were serious questions about the worth of his business.[37] Ross, in London, started negotiations with Harris but he ultimately cabled Dunedin advising them not to proceed. Glendining was not surprised, having doubted whether Harris had ever really wanted to sell his business in the first place.[38]

The keen terms on which Bing, Harris & Co. conducted their business nevertheless continued to be a worry. After discussing the matter with Sargoods, Butterworth Bros. and others, it was decided that the Dunedin warehousemen should adopt a common tariff of four months credit, with no dating forward, and discounts for cash to be strictly controlled. Bing, Harris, it was believed, were tired of heavy price cutting and might just fall in with the terms agreed. Representations were also made to the trade in Christchurch although it was felt that Clarkson, 'an unprincipled scoundrel', would be unlikely to stick to any arrangement.[39] Notwithstanding the lack of complete unanimity amongst warehousemen, William Peters, the traveller in charge of Ross & Glendining's Christchurch operations, and James Simpson, the Southland and South Otago traveller, were instructed to keep to the agreed terms. Not a word was to be said about collusion among the warehousemen 'as the last time the customers seemed to resent this and did their best to upset it …'.[40]

## 4. COMPETING IN AUCKLAND AND AUSTRALIA

Collusion in the south may have helped to reduce pressure on margins but trade remained depressed. Ross & Glendining did not fare any better in the north, especially in Auckland where the new traveller, Ebenezer Clark, was found to be even less satisfactory than his predecessor.[41] His replacement, William Sharples, lasted only a few months before he, too, departed, ostensibly because of ill health.[42] By October 1887, the soft goods trade in the city was reported to be in a state of near collapse, the inability of northern warehousemen to form a price association similar to that down south not helping matters. Not surprisingly, William Mann, Sharples' successor, found it difficult to keep up sales, although whether it was the difficult business conditions or other problems that drove the once sober traveller to drink we will never know. [43] In any event, after 'going on the spree' in Napier and fighting with another traveller, Mann, was also dismissed.[44] John Sheen, formerly of the Kaiapoi Woollen Mills, replaced him.[45]

Ross & Glendining were no more fortunate in their attempts to push sales on the other side of the Tasman. Mosgiel Woollen Mills had been quite successful in selling their manufactures in Australia and now, with trade depressed at home, it was decided that Roslyn Mills should try to emulate their rivals. The omens appeared to be quite promising. The state of Victoria was still in the throes of a boom, while some of the lighter products recently introduced by Roslyn, such as the silk mixtures and worsteds, seemed well suited to the Australian market.[46] In August 1886, Peter Aitken, one of the Dunedin salesmen, was sent to establish an agency business in New South Wales and Victoria. He was to be paid £10 per month travelling expenses and five per cent commission: he might undertake other agency business as long as it did not interfere with the sale of Roslyn goods.[47]

For the next two years Aitken was to travel extensively in Australia; to Rockhampton in the north, inland as far as Wagga Wagga, and back to Sydney to pick up fresh pattern cards. He met with limited success, the uneconomic size of some orders, heavy freights, and problems with uncertain delivery undermining his ability to compete with established manufacturers. On some occasions Roslyn Mills were forced to decline the orders he sent back because they would have lost money on the sale.[48] In August 1888, with sales for the year of £7,350 yielding a loss of 7 per cent after travelling expenses, Aitken was warned that things would have to improve if he was to continue.[49] The collapse of the Victorian boom later that year signalled the end of Ross & Glendining's direct involvement in Australia. In future, distribution on the other side of the Tasman was to be handled by a local agent.[50]

## 5. Competitors sell up as expansion resumes

Slowly the depression began to ease, the first glimmer of hope appearing in Canterbury and North Otago. This area had led the country into depression in 1883 but, by late 1887, the market there seemed to be on the turn. Certainly Ross & Glendining's sales showed a marked improvement, with William Peters complaining that 'he would do better if he had a better place with more stock'.[51] Glendining conveyed these sentiments to Ross early in September, adding, somewhat disingenuously, that he did not feel justified in taking another place in Christchurch given the reservations his partner had expressed about continuing to remain in business.

In fact, Glendining was already negotiating with the struggling Thompson, Shannon & Co. to acquire the lease of their recently opened branch warehouse in Lichfield St.[52] Two weeks later he was rather more forthcoming, confessing to Ross that he was thinking of taking over the lease of Thompson's 'nice little warehouse' as it was better situated than their existing premises, being right next to Sargoods. He added that it had double the room, and there was a chance he might get it at the same rental as their current property.[53] By early October, Glendining had leased the warehouse, initially for one year, for £250.[54]

The decision by Thompson, Shannon & Co. to vacate their new premises was a reflection of the structural changes taking place in the warehouse trade. The depression, which had initially weeded out the big/little importers, now began to take its toll on some of the more substantial importers as well. In the early 1880s, Thompson, Shannon & Co. were doing well and had added to their import business by establishing a clothing factory next to their Wellington warehouse. For a while, all seemed to be proceeding satisfactorily and in May 1885, the firm built a new, enlarged factory, employing 140 hands. At this stage, Shannon seemed unconcerned about the state of trade in the lower North Island, although he was worried about conditions in the South Island where, he conceded, things were 'very bad'.[55]

Their situation deteriorated rapidly over the next year as orders declined and competition increased. By the end of January 1887, Thompson, Shannon & Co. were forced to open their Wellington warehouse to the public, embrace the retail trade and cut prices in order to shift stock. Providentially, perhaps, a disastrous fire swept along Panama and Brandon Streets a month later, destroying the warehouse, factory and much of the contents. This effectively spelt the end of the business. Attempts were made to start again but the decision of a sleeping partner to withdraw, Shannon's poor health, and difficult trading conditions led, in 1888, to liquidation. Thompson acquired some of the stock and continued in retail by himself, finally selling out to Bendix Hallenstein several years later.[56]

Thompson, Shannon & Co. were not the only warehousemen in difficulties. Early in 1888, Glendining noted that Edwards Bennett & Co. were 'slaughtering their goods all over the country in the same style as Thompson Shannon' and wondered whether they would be able to survive. Some of the Wellington firms decided to sell out before they entirely dissipated their capital. Towards the end of January, J.B. Harcourt & Co., whose founder had worked as a warehousemen for Frederick Sargood in Melbourne, sold their stock to Sargoods for 12/9d in the pound. Henceforth Harcourt was to concentrate on auctioneering.[57] Some months later Sargood, Son & Ewen acquired the business of the well-known firm, Turnbull, Smith & Co. and, shortly afterwards, that of Owen and Graham, who reputedly owed the Bank of New Zealand £200,000.[58] The combined stocks of the acquired businesses were disposed of over the next few months, free trips to the Sargoods' warehouses encouraging customers to buy.[59] Thanks to their considerable capital resources and the ability to buy distressed stocks cheaply, Sargood, Son & Ewen were able to trade successfully in Wellington when others could not.

In the South Island, a number of substantial warehousemen also struggled under the weight of reduced trade and bad debts.[60] In 1888, the death of a partner in Butterworth Brothers resulted in a liquidity crisis when £15,000 had to be paid to executors at short notice.[61] Unable to raise this comparatively small amount, their Christchurch warehouse was closed and stock transferred to Dunedin, where it was sold off cheaply. By the end of the year Butterworth Brothers were in the process of being wound up.[62] Shortly afterwards Clarkson & Co., with branches in Christchurch and Dunedin, suspended trading with £180,000 of liabilities. The stoppage was attributed to the Bank of New Zealand refusing to advance any more credit, although matters were probably hastened by the default of Clarks of Wellington, who owed Clarksons £10,000.[63]

Although conditions remained difficult, 1888 saw Ross & Glendining begin to make progress once more. There was still room for improvement, though, and Hercus, running the business while Glendining was overseas, thought it necessary to reorganise the travelling yet again. Having observed how Bing, Harris & Co. conducted operations, he decided to increase the number of travellers from seven to eight to improve coverage of Otago and Southland. 'The orders can only be had little and often now, and the only way to make amounts up is by better working the ground.'[64] This was easier said than done, for good travellers were scarce and Ross & Glendining did not have a reputation for generous salaries.

Difficulties in finding suitable travellers may explain why the new man, Frank Barley, was recruited in Christchurch rather than further south, and employed to travel in Canterbury and North Otago. A judicious reshuffling of journeys, however, enabled southern areas to be covered more intensively.[65] As a result, the proportion of small accounts increased. These customers often required careful monitoring but the greater numbers involved helped spread the risks and provide greater stability.[66]

## 6. OPENING A BRANCH WAREHOUSE IN WELLINGTON

There was still the question as to how the North Island might be worked most effectively. Prior to leaving for the United Kingdom, Glendining had re-appointed former traveller, John Fothergill, who was to serve the top of the South Island, Wellington province and Taranaki. Hercus was very impressed with Fothergill's businesslike attitude when he called to collect his samples in August 1888. He informed Glendining,

> *If we are not too heavily handicapped by distance against the new Wellington houses we ought to do well enough there. He appears to have good connections from Wellington to New Plymouth. He used to do a good boot trade for Turnbull, Smith & Co, and felt that the want of these could put us at a disadvantage against Sargood and Bing, Harris & Co.*

In Glendining's absence, Hercus was not prepared to commit Ross & Glendining to stocking and supplying boots. Nevertheless, he did arrange for Fothergill to carry samples for Tyree, Gavin & Co., a Christchurch boot importer, with orders to be routed through Peters in the Christchurch warehouse.[67]

The movement of population from the South Island to Australia during the depression of the mid-eighties meant that by the end of the decade, the Wellington and lower North Island market seemed to be much more promising.[68] Bing, Harris & Co. were certainly of this view and, having failed to buy the business of J.B. Harcourt & Co., decided to open a warehouse in the capital anyway. With times improving and a lot of competitors having vanished, their opening trade in Wellington exceeded all expectations.[69] Hercus, aware of their success, began to wonder whether Ross & Glendining should open a warehouse there also. In November 1888 he wrote to Glendining, now en route for New Zealand, suggesting that, '… the time has come to see whether we cannot do something [in Wellington] …'.[70]

Glendining was obviously taken by the idea for, upon his return, Hercus was dispatched to Wellington to inspect potential warehouses. Hercus first called on Whittem, Nicholson & Co. who, wishing to leave the trade, had already offered Ross & Glendining both their stock and premises. Their warehouse, a three-storey building on Willis St, turned out to be 'an inconvenient dingy place', while the price they demanded was exorbitant. Hercus then looked at other warehouses, including Harcourt's building which was still empty; a number of upstairs sample rooms; and Sargood, Son & Ewen's old warehouse in Brandon St, behind Kirkcaldie & Stains. The property in Brandon St was 'a neat, two storied warehouse of brick and cement, something like our Christchurch warehouse' but rather small, being only 30 feet by 60 feet. It was, however, available cheaply as Sargoods had temporarily moved into Turnbull, Smith's former warehouse while new premises were being built for them on a waterfront section. When Glendining offered £250 to take over the Brandon St lease, which ran until August 1890, the offer was promptly accepted.[71]

The Brandon St warehouse, although cheap and well appointed, was only ever regarded as a temporary stopgap. Hercus informed Ross,

> *The future situation for wholesale business, will be the new road, Victoria St., on the reclaimed ground fronting the harbour and connecting the town with Te Aro, without the present and narrow inconvenient way through the narrow Willis St. where the Empire Hotel is. This road is also handy to the wharf and central .... If we were intending to build, the best available sites would be those in Hunter St. and Customhouse Quay – corporation leases, 21 years. The rents they ask are 51/- ... to 72/6 per foot frontage'.*

An alternative to building on ground leased from the city corporation was to acquire a freehold site. These were not considered cheap, a recently constructed warehouse on Victoria St costing £10,000, of which the site accounted for £3,000.[72]

Such matters lay in the future, however, the immediate concern for Glendining and Hercus being to arrange for the management and stocking of the Brandon St warehouse. David Jones, formerly a traveller with Owen & Graham, was placed in charge.[73] He had joined the firm in November following the resignation, for a second time, of John Fothergill. Hercus had mixed feelings about Fothergill who, although he was undoubtedly useful in re-opening old ground, 'was inclined to go too fast and we had not the local knowledge to control his credits'. As a result, several bad debts had been incurred. Jones, it was believed, was a far safer man and more likely to win the confidence of customers.[74]

The new Wellington warehouse initially started in a modest way. Travelling in the lower North Island was to be undertaken by Thomas Simpson, currently employed by Clarks, of Auckland, as a traveller for their Wellington branch. He had worked under Jones before. Assisting in the warehouse was W.R. Kirker who came from Turnbull, Smith & Co. with excellent testimonials.[75] The three men made sound progress. By June 1889, £5,000 worth of goods had been sold out of a total stock of £12,700 and more business might have been done had the warehouse been better supplied. The branch was still small in comparison with Sargood's warehouse off Victoria St, which carried a stock of between £50,000 and £70,000. Even so, Hercus was extremely pleased with the outcome and thought that next season they might work up a good business in Wellington. For this a bigger branch warehouse was essential.[76]

The success of the Wellington warehouse was not entirely due to the staff, as business in New Zealand was now improving rapidly. One reason for the improvement was that the affairs of the troubled Bank of New Zealand appeared to have been resolved. In October 1888, a committee of shareholders had investigated the accounts and concluded that in spite of bad debts, the Bank was still solvent. They recommended that £10 shares should be written down by £3 to reflect the depreciated value of securities held.[77] Their somewhat optimistic report helped to revive confidence and, Hercus said, was 'worth millions to the colony'.[78]

## 7. THE 'SWEATING' CONTROVERSY

Recovery was also aided by a rise in commodity prices, wool and wheat prices having increased by some 20 per cent by 1889, and by yet another well-patronised industrial exhibition being held in Dunedin.[79] The effect on demand was dramatic and, before long, Ross & Glendining were experiencing shortages in all classes of goods – 'imported stuff: factory goods: mill goods'. It was estimated that purchases would need to be between £20,000 and £25,000 greater than in previous years.[80]

Mill output was slow to increase for although Glendining had ordered more machinery when in the United Kingdom, it took time to ship and erect. Expanding output at the clothing factory was far easier since less equipment was required, and much of it was available locally. Palmer, the factory manager, had begun to increase capacity in February when he had purchased additional Wheeler & Wilson's sewing machines. Although not as robust as earlier models, they seemed to work well. The new gas irons he bought were less successful, costing too much in the way of gas and annoying workers with the fumes. In spite of these problems, the factory was able to turn out considerably more clothing than hitherto.[81]

While increasing the capacity of the clothing factory was relatively straightforward, the plant was soon beset with labour problems. The catalyst was a sermon 'On the Sin of Cheapness' given by newly arrived Presbyterian minister, the Reverend Rutherford Waddell. Delivered in Dunedin in September 1888, Waddell's sermon criticised the practice of sweating female labour in small clothing workshops. The finger of blame was pointed squarely at the large capitalists, the warehousemen, as it was they who determined what sub-contractors could afford to pay their labour. The press quickly joined in. In an article in the *Evening Star* in February 1889, Bing, Harris & Co. were shown in a particularly poor light, as it was they, apparently, who led the way in forcing rates down.[82]

Largely at Waddell's instigation, a public meeting was held and a committee appointed to consider solutions. After discussions with sub-contractors and small manufacturers, an agreement was reached on a tariff, or 'Log', of minimum piece-work rates. This was promptly rejected by the Dunedin warehousemen, for wage levels were much higher locally than in northern cities. They feared that they would be unable to compete if higher rates were paid. The proposal that they should only patronise sub-contractors who paid minimum rates was also rejected. Hercus, in particular, was incensed that Ross & Glendining might not be allowed to switch from one shirt-maker to another to take advantage of cheaper rates.[83]

Antagonised by the reaction of the warehousemen, a second public meeting was called in June. A committee was quickly formed to establish a union of tailoresses, shirt machinists, finishers and pressers. More than 300 women had joined the Tailoresses Union within a week, rising to 700 by August.[84] In the meantime, Wilson, the Dunedin manager of Bing, Harris & Co. took steps to steal a competitive advantage over his rivals. Perceiving that an agreement would soon be reached between the warehousemen and the union, he arranged for one sub-contractor, Mrs Keales, to do all his work. He also persuaded her to recruit all the finishers in the town by offering higher rates. As a result, Ross & Glendining and the others were left with the 'learners and incompetent finishers' to whom they had to pay the higher rates. Hercus, extremely annoyed, vowed to move all outwork into the factory.[85] This was more easily said than done for, when the 1890 Royal Commission on Sweating reported, Ross & Glendining were still employing subcontractors. The firm was, however, found to be a reasonably good employer.[86]

The formation of the Tailoresses Union in 1889 meant that unionised labour was soon to be found not only in small workshops, but in Roslyn Mills and the clothing factory as well. Occasionally John Millar, the secretary of the union, was taken to task by Hercus for failing to substantiate a worker's claim against the company, or for inadequately monitoring piece rates paid by other employers. Yet thanks to buoyant demand, relations with the union remained reasonably cordial, especially as brisk trade meant that it was relatively easy to pass cost increases on to customers.[87] As a result, higher wages did not seem to reduce sales or cut into profits – at least in the short run.[88]

## 8. Survival of the fittest

The New Zealand economy continued to recover in 1890, sales returns from the firm's warehouses almost doubling between 1887 and 1890. The warehouse balance sheet was transformed, too, a loss of £7,500 being converted into a profit of £10,000 (see Table 6.2). The increase in trade inevitably put pressure on warehouse space in all centres, forcing Ross, Glendining and Hercus to consider when they should start building in Wellington. They also had to think about whether to extend or build new premises in Christchurch and Dunedin.[89] That they should entertain such thoughts is a measure of their success in weathering the depression, and the confidence with which they viewed the future.

The ability of Ross & Glendining to survive the 1880s when others failed is a reflection of the fact that they were well capitalised and well run. This was appreciated by the Bank of New South Wales, always willing to provide working capital, and by depositors both in the United Kingdom and New Zealand who were willing to entrust the firm with their savings. In an age of financial failures, Ross & Glendining & Co. appeared to offer the sort of security that many local banks seemed unable to provide.

Of course, the 1880s were not as profitable as the previous decade, yet the warehouse business still managed to return more than £35,000 in salaries, profits and interest in the eleven years to 1890. This, together with the returns from Roslyn Mills, sheep stations and other property ensured that the sum standing to the partners' capital account rose from £133,518 to £214,117 over this period.[90] The depression had come and gone, and John Ross and Robert Glendining were that much the richer.

# SHEEP FARMING & THE EARLY
# DEVELOPMENT OF LAUDER STATION

The 1870s was a golden age for sheep farming and land speculation in New Zealand. A seemingly inexhaustible demand from British mills saw the price of merino wool increase by around half between 1871 and 1875. After a slight check in 1876, wool prices began to rise once more and, with financial intermediaries offering easy credit, land speculation continued unabated. In 1878, the price of both pastoral and agricultural land doubled.[1] It was against this background that John Ross and Robert Glendining decided that perhaps they, too, should seek to profit by investing surplus capital in sheep farming.

The boom in agriculture of the 1870s saw the Government sell increasing quantities of land, although large tracts – suitable for agricultural or pastoral purposes – were retained by the Crown for future settlement.[2] As a temporary measure, however, and as a means of raising revenue, much of the Crown estate was leased out. In Canterbury and Otago, where the terrain was particularly well suited to sheep farming, land was let on pastoral leases that might run for up to fourteen years. Some blocks or runs were relatively small, although in a country of land abundance and labour scarcity it made sound economic sense to farm on a large scale. As a consequence, many of the early sheep runs were let in blocks in excess of 50,000 acres, with some land companies holding a number of such runs. With annual rentals paid to the Crown being only a few per cent of the freehold value of the land, the major capital expense for the typical run holder was the cost of erecting fences and stocking with sheep. The expenditure required was typically beyond the means of many small farmers and shopkeepers. Wealthier farmers, however, together with the more successful in trade, industry and the professions, found capital no problem, especially as mortgage finance was readily available.[3]

With funds to spare, the costs of entry to large-scale sheep farming were no barrier to Ross and Glendining. In 1878 they acquired their first leasehold property, the 'Romarua' run, a 10,000-acre block some fifty miles from Dunedin. The amount debited to the partners' capital account was £9,836, although whether this constituted the total outlay is not known.[4]

This expenditure probably covered rental for a year, the purchase of sheep, implements and stores, and the value of improvements made by previous leaseholders, such as fencing, yards, etc.

Glendining, responsible for all aspects of New Zealand operations, appointed James Elliott as manager. A 40-year-old Highland shepherd who had arrived in New Zealand in 1862, the well-regarded Elliott had previously managed part of the nearby Cottesbrook Station, a 34,000-acre run to the southeast of Middlemarch.[5] In spite of Elliott's experience and local knowledge, it proved difficult to make money from the 'cold and inhospitable' Romarua. The downturn in wool prices that began towards the end of 1878 doubtless added to the manager's difficulties. In 1880 the partners disposed of the property, with Ross thankful that they had escaped 'at cost'.[6] Yet in common with many others in the South Island, John Ross and Robert Glendining still regarded run holding as a potentially sound investment. Consequently, as soon as wool prices began to improve, they once again started to look around for a suitable leasehold property.

## 1. The creation of Home Hills Station

The early 1880s offered excellent opportunities to acquire pastoral land in Otago. In March 1883, the leases of 71 runs in the province, containing 2.6 million acres of largely unimproved land, expired. Under the terms of the 1877 Land Act, the runs were to be subdivided into smaller blocks of between 5,000 and 10,000 acres, with some larger blocks of up to 30,000 acres being permitted in the more mountainous and remote areas.[7] The leaseholds to the new and smaller runs were to be sold by auction in March 1882, a year prior to entry by the new tenants. Bidders offering the largest annual rentals to the Crown secured the leasehold.

In February, 1882, a letter from Ross & Glendining reached James Elliott who was now working at Garthmyl,

> *We have been speaking to Mr. John Reid about taking advantage of the present opportunity to secure one or two runs; and on consideration, have come to the conclusion that if you are open to join us, we would go into some Leases along with you, we finding the capital and you undertaking the management – salary to be paid you, and interest to be paid us, before dividing profits. Details could no doubt be arranged to our mutual satisfaction afterwards, and the short time at our disposal might be used in looking for suitable runs.*

Reid, an estate agent and partner in the Dunedin firm of Reid & Duncans, had particulars of the runs that Glendining wanted Elliott to look at. It was arranged that Reid and Elliott should meet, either at Garthmyl or on the road from Palmerston, and then travel on together.[8]

Glendining's instructions to the two men were quite explicit. 'Rabbit country' was to be avoided, as was the high country towards the Lakes as it was too distant to manage conveniently. Of those properties closer to hand, Mount Stoker was to be subdivided into two runs of 12,560 and 9,520 acres but the proposed leases – only five and six years respectively – were deemed to be too short. Gladbrook, subdivided into 12,190 and 26,440 acres, was altogether more attractive since the leases were to run for ten years. However, both blocks were adjacent to freehold land and it was thought there might be considerable competition for them. Other subdivisions in the area, including St Buchanans old run and part of Rocklands were also adjacent to freeholds and this, together with the fact that they were accessible to Dunedin, meant that they were likely to command a premium when auctioned. Glendining was prepared to bid for these properties – within limits. More likely subdivisions included several in the Upper Taieri and Mount Ida districts.

Reid and Elliott were unable to view all the runs mentioned by Glendining before the leases were auctioned in March. The two-day sale, held in Dunedin, was far better attended than expected; the prospect of securing one or more of the 170 smaller runs attracting a crowd of over a thousand. A last minute change of venue had to be arranged, with proceedings being switched from the long-room at Watson's Hotel to the Garrison Hall. Bidding was brisk and when the first day of the sales had been completed, there were still more than 400 would-be-purchasers in attendance. All of the runs bar three were ultimately leased, the new aggregate rental totalling £69,000 compared to the £25,000 received by the Government for the original 71 runs. The amount realised was almost twice that anticipated.[9]

The competition for land meant that the leases for runs such as St Buchanans and Rocklands were sold for far more than Ross and Glendining were prepared to pay. Instead, they were obliged to settle for runs some seventy miles inland from Palmerston – close to the mining settlement of Hill's Creek – where both the Hawkdun and Lauder Stations were being subdivided. At the auction the partners were able to secure Hawkdun runs 227 and 227a at an annual rental of £990. Lauder 226a fell to the original lessees of the station, J. Roberts and S.G. Handyside. Pig farmers and butchers, Thomas Keenan and Frederick Morgan, who were based at the nearby gold-mining township of St Bathans, bid successfully for the remaining Lauder blocks.[10]

Although Ross & Glendining did not take possession of their two runs until the following year, towards the end of March it was arranged for Elliott to meet Reid somewhere between Palmerston railway station and Kyeburn. Together the two men were to conduct a thorough inspection of the newly acquired properties. They were also to cast an eye over adjacent runs, including two leased by Dalgety & Co., that portion of Lauder still leased by

Roberts and Handyside, and part of Hawkdun 445 offered to them by the new lessee, Huddlestone. At the same time they should look out for any 'low country' in the vicinity that might be used for lambing.[11]

The report by Reid and Elliott did not comment on either the Lauder or Dalgety runs nor mention any low country that might be available. Their impression of Hawkdun 227 and 227a, however, was generally favourable. They were of the opinion that, except in severe winters, the loss of stock due to bad weather was unlikely to be greater than that of any other run in Central Otago. There were, however, hints of troubles to come:

> Of course, you are aware the eastern boundary is the watershed of the Hawkdun Mountains and Mount Ida at an elevation of from 5,000 to 6,000 feet above sea-level. The faces of the mountain are very steep and naturally are only fit for summer grazing. But the balance and decidedly the major part of the country consists of undulating flats and low downs with an elevation of from 1,800 to about 3,000 feet above sea level and is really capital sound, well grassed, well sheltered sheep country …

Inevitably rabbits were present, but they were particularly invasive only along the banks of the Manuherikia River, which formed part of the boundary.[12]

The combined acreage of the two newly created Hawkdun runs was over 55,000 acres, their relatively large size being a reflection of the limited carrying capacity of each. In the mild winter of 1881, the station manager claimed to have kept 23,000 store sheep on the ground although Reid and Elliott believed that only 20,000 could normally be grazed safely. The planting of turnips and rape, they suggested, would be one way that carrying capacity might be increased. Reid thought that the runs might be operated under the 'comfortably suggestive' name of Home Hills Station. Neither Reid nor Elliott was enthusiastic about the neighbouring Hawkdun 445, which was mountainous, accessible only by pack-horse and would be prohibitively expensive to fence. They believed that Huddlestone was now likely to forfeit the lease and that no matter who subsequently took up the land, the lack of fences meant that stock from Home Hills Station would always be able to graze there.[13]

The location of the runs in a gold mining district, some seven miles from the diggings at St Bathans and seventeen miles from Naseby, was something of a mixed blessing. Both settlements had a telegraph office, a regular wagon service that linked the area via the Dunstan Road with the main railway line at Palmerston, and a twice-weekly stagecoach service from Dunedin.[14] The Central Otago Railway, upon which construction commenced in 1879, promised future improvements in communications if – and when – the line was completed. But the presence of gold miners, whose relationship with the run holders had never been cordial, was problematic, increasing the possibility of stock theft and demands for parcels of land.[15] Indeed, the first petition for fifty acres to be released from Home Hills Station was received by the Otago Land Board even before Ross & Glendining entered the property. A successful objection to the petition was registered with the Commissioner for Crown Lands for Otago, but such demands would grow as the population increased and the diggings were worked out.[16]

The leases of the two new blocks, which were to run for ten years, did not commence until 1 March, 1883. Fortunately, Elliott was able to obtain permission from the existing lessees to erect buildings and yards some months before entry date. He also began to make enquiries concerning the purchase of sheep. Shortly afterwards, Ross & Glendining drew up a memorandum of co-partnership, backdated to the beginning of March. It was to run for eleven years and stipulated that Elliott should receive one third of the profits of Home Hills Station, after interest of 8 per cent had been paid on the capital invested by the two warehousemen. Additionally, he was to receive a salary of £200 per annum 'besides being fully found in House, Furniture, Wages of Domestic Servants, and Household Stores for himself and his family'.[17] This was a generous arrangement, bearing in mind that as an ordinary shepherd Elliott would probably have received in the region of £60 per annum, all found.

## 2. HOME HILLS BECOMES PART OF LAUDER STATION

The interest that Ross & Glendining had shown in securing additional ground, especially that suitable for lambing, did not pass unnoticed. In April 1882, word was received that Roberts and Handyside, who now retained only a small portion of the original Lauder Station, were thinking of selling up.[18] On offer was a flock of 31,000 sheep and the lease to run 226a, comprising 13,600 acres, that they had secured at the March auction. A further 535 acres of freehold land at neighbouring Blackstone Hill was also for sale, including eighty acres in English grass. The freehold, at a relatively low altitude, would be an ideal place from which to work Home Hills since it contained lambing paddocks, mustering yards, woolshed, sheep dip and yards, and stone accommodation for station hands. The right to the registered station brand was to be included.

James Elliott was once again dispatched to join Reid to value 226a, the Blackstone Hill freehold, and the twenty-five miles of fences that had been erected. He was provided with some benchmark values by Hercus, but it was stressed that the partners would be guided by him as to whether they should purchase Lauder – and what price they should pay.[19] Elliott was clearly impressed by what he saw since by June 1882 agreement had been reached with Roberts and Handyside. A total purchase price of £16,000 was settled upon, of which £3,326 was for the Blackstone freehold and £11,000 for 25,000 sheep and 6,000 lambs. The remainder was for the value of improvements to the run and for rentals paid to the Crown by Roberts and Handyside when they had secured their new lease.[20] A deposit of £5,000 was paid in November, at which point Elliott commenced work at Lauder, preparing the way for shearing the flock he was to receive in December.[21]

Elliott, together with his heavily pregnant wife and five children, moved up to the mining settlement of Cambrian, close to Lauder, in November 1882.[22] With the co-partnership agreement stipulating the provision of a house, Hercus immediately placed an advertisement in the *Mt. Ida Chronicle* inviting tenders to construct a suitable residence.[23] The contract was awarded to Charles Lomax, a Dunedin builder who had previously done work for Ross & Glendining. Building supplies, a stove, and furniture were now dispatched from Dunedin to Lauder, along with fencing materials and other station supplies.[24] By March 1883, the partners had sunk £19,267 in Home Hills and Lauder Stations which were now run together.[25]

The purchase of Lauder 226a meant that Ross & Glendining now had around 70,000 acres to farm. Yet they were still in the market for more land, especially if it was easily worked and not too mountainous. In January 1883, Thomas Keenan and his partner, Frederick Morgan, offered to on-sell some of the Lauder leases that they had acquired at auction the previous year.

The willingness of Keenan and Morgan to sell their recently acquired land suggests that, from the very first, they were hoping to make a quick profit. Certainly they were men of modest means who would not have had the wherewithal to fence and stock large properties. They doubtless expected to extract a premium for the leases from Ross & Glendining, but this did not seem to deter Glendining. Indeed, he was quite happy to take over the 16,260 acre Lauder 226b, although he was less sure about taking over Lauder 226c owing to the difficulties in stocking such a large area. There were also concerns as to how the blocks might fare in winter time.[26] However, in April 1883 it was agreed that Ross & Glendining would also take over Lauder 226c, comprising another 8,500 acres, with Keenan and Morgan being paid £1,030 for the leases to both blocks. Finally, in August, after the worst of winter had passed, it appears that 18,500 acres was cut off Lauder 226 and part of it assigned to the partners and part of it to Dalgety.[27] This took the total acreage farmed by Ross & Glendining to around 110,000 acres. Keenan and Morgan were left with a small part of Lauder 226, which may have been incorporated into run 226d.[28] On this they ran pigs and sheep.

## South Island

—N—

Picton
Nelson
Blenheim
Westport
Greymouth
CANTERBURY
Christchurch
Timaru
OTAGO
Lauder Station  Naseby
Cromwell
Oamaru
Middlemarch  Palmerston
SOUTHLAND
Dunedin
Invercargill
Bluff

LEGEND
—— Railway Line Opened
········· Route of Otago
          Central Line
          (under construction)
- - - - Provincial Boundary

Above: Location of
Lauder sheep run
and the South Island
rail network: dotted
line is the Central
Otago Railway under
construction from
1879.

Right: Blackstone Hill
and surrounding runs,
1881. S= subdivided
before 1877. (Source:
J. Cowan, *Down the Years
in the Maniototo*, p. 32.)

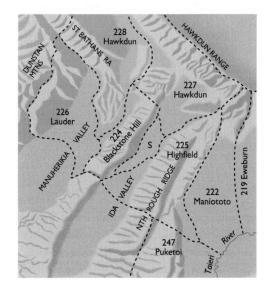

### 3. STOCKING THE RUNS

Even before the Lauder leases were finally secured, Ross & Glendining began to take steps to buy more sheep. Thomas Brydone, a pioneer of the frozen meat trade and local superintendent of the Glasgow-based New Zealand & Australia Land Company, recommended a breeder from whom to buy high quality merino rams. James Johnstone, who worked for the Dunedin stock and station agents, Wright Stephenson & Co., also sought out and bought sheep on their behalf.[29] An additional 9,000 head were ultimately purchased. The bulk of these were two-tooth (one-year-old) wethers, the castrated ram lambs being the most suitable for producing high quality wool. The total stock on the station when mustered at the end of the year amounted to 38,869 ewes, wethers and lambs, valued at £16,338. There were also 160 merino rams worth £480. The partners' total investment at the balance date in February 1884 – in what was now called Lauder Station – amounted to £30,106.[30]

Although the first shipment of refrigerated meat left New Zealand for the United Kingdom in February 1882, the principal output of Lauder Station during its early years was wool. Initially Lauder was entirely stocked with Merinos, a breed which thrived on the native grasses of the high country and was well able to survive the dry, cold conditions of Central Otago. Shearing usually commenced towards the end of November, a little later than runs at a lower elevation. The pieces and locks – that is, wool from around the legs – were scoured on the station but the cleaner, main part of the fleece was left greasy in order to protect the fibre in transit. After classing, the bulk of the clip was taken by bullock wagon to the nearest railway station, initially Palmerston, railed to Port Chalmers, and then shipped to the United Kingdom to be auctioned. Only a small proportion, rarely more than a few per cent, was sufficiently fine to be made into the high quality yarn, cloth and hosiery manufactured at the firm's Roslyn Woollen Mills.

The decision to produce wool rather than meat was a reflection of the fact that high country runs, such as Lauder Station, were not well suited to breeding lambs. With lambing commencing in October when snow might still fall, the shortage of low ground upon which to winter stock and oversee lambing acted as a real constraint. Thus of the flock of over 38,000 sheep mustered at the end of the first year, there were only 18,585 ewes. Most of these were kept solely for their wool, since between them they produced only 3,532 lambs – or at least, that was the number that survived until mustering.[31] The remainder of the flock was made up of wethers, the bulk of which were four-tooth (two-year-old) and above (see Table 7.1).

The acquisition of the Blackstone Hill freehold and the Lauder runs provided Elliott with some lower ground suitable for lambing. Ideally, he

## TABLE 7.1
## FLOCK COMPOSITION EACH FEBRUARY, 1884–1892

| February | 1884 | 1885 | 1886 | 1887 | 1888 | 1889 | 1890 | 1891 | 1892 |
|---|---|---|---|---|---|---|---|---|---|
| Sheep total | 38,869 | 40,736 | 44,069 | 49,386 | 55,759 | 58,193 | 61,125 | 60,721 | 81,372 |
| Wethers (%) | 43 | 41 | 47 | 44 | 42 | 46 | 41 | 43 | 31 |
| Ewes (%) | 48 | 45 | 41 | 39 | 45 | 44 | 43 | 46 | 50 |
| Lambs (%) | 9 | 14 | 12 | 17 | 13 | 10 | 16 | 11 | 19 |
| Bought | 39,631 | 1,444 | 3,000 | 0 | 13,400 | 9,061 | 5,700 | 0 | 27,352 |
| Sold | 1,880 | 1,559 | 2,197 | 1,033 | 9,794 | 6,029 | 7,000 | 3,610 | 17,026 |

Sources: Sheep Accounts, Half-yearly balances, AG 512 15/3 & 15/4.
Note: Wethers' figures include 300–500 rams.

would have been able to breed sufficient lambs not only to replace culls and sheep that had died, but also a surplus to build up his flock and sell off station. Even with the extra land, however, the manager was still not able to breed enough lambs to maintain flock numbers and he was repeatedly obliged to buy in breeding ewes and young wethers. This soon became a major issue for the partners. They quickly realised that as long as they were obliged to buy in sheep, costing up to ten shillings a head, it would be very difficult to run the station at a profit.[32]

## 4. IMPROVING CARRYING CAPACITY

There were a number of measures open to Elliott to improve the carrying capacity of the station. One option was to improve the lower pastures although, since Crown tenants were only supposed to cultivate pastoral lands with permission of the Land Board – and permission was not usually given – improvements were confined largely to the freehold land. This was often done by sowing turnips upon which to winter stock, especially ewes in lamb. Land cleared by turnip cultivation was typically put down to grass with strains imported from the United Kingdom and the United States. Pastures might also be oversown with ryegrass, cocksfoot and white clover, which tended to 'eat out' indigenous vegetation.[33] The nutritional value of these exotic grasses was significantly greater than that of tussock and other native grasses which, with grazing, tended to degenerate. There were costs, for the imported grass seed frequently contained noxious weeds such as the Californian thistle, which got caught up in the fleece and reduced its value.

Furthermore, the rich English grasses did not suit the Merino, which did better on native vegetation.[34]

The benefits of using exotic grasses hugely outweighed the costs, however, particularly after the switch to cross-bred sheep to cater for the freezer trade, with some suggestion that stock capacity might be doubled.[35] In 1884, therefore, James Lush was hired to plough, attend to cultivation, and do general work. His wife was to cook for the ten permanent hands and the twenty or so temporary workers employed for mustering, shearing and other chores.[36] Thereafter scores of acres of turnips were planted each year, although the frequent lack of rainfall meant that conditions were not always ideal. Small quantities of oats were also cultivated which provided feed for the horses, chaff for the sheep in winter and grains to mix with poison for the rabbits.

Good pasture and stock management also involved controlling where the sheep might graze. In addition to the maintenance of boundary fences, runs might be subdivided and, given the huge acreages farmed and the often inclement weather conditions, shepherds' huts constructed at strategic points. During the first year of occupation some twenty-eight tons of number eight wire, two tons of barbed wire and 16,616 iron fence posts or standards were railed and carted up to Lauder Station. These were used in the construction of twenty miles of fences, the total cost of materials, cartage and work done by fencing contractors amounting to £1,442. Thereafter maintenance and replacement was covered by an annual depreciation charge of around £300, the amount being raised when fences were particularly badly damaged by snow. [37]

The inability to fence mountain tops inevitably resulted in the loss of several hundred strays a year but problems were also caused by neighbours who failed to cooperate in the maintenance of boundary fences. In this respect, Ross & Glendining suffered regular losses from the inactivity of Keenan and Morgan. The St Bathans butchers had a particularly cavalier attitude to fencing, allowing their pigs to stray, disputing where true boundaries lay, and failing to take action when they noticed that fences were damaged.

The occupation of land entailed a legal requirement to fence. The Fencing Act of 1881 stipulated that a fence at least four feet high, constructed of seven No. 8 wires and strung on iron posts or standards nine feet apart, be erected along boundaries. An amending act of 1887 allowed the top two strands to be replaced by barbed wire and both acts allowed one party to a dispute to construct fences as and when required.[38] The party constructing the fence might then claim half of the expenses involved, with legitimate claims enforced through the courts. Keenan, who bought out his partner in 1885, became a master of fencing brinkmanship, appearing in court at

St Bathans on numerous occasions. Indeed, so regular were his appearances that in 1889 Hercus commented that fencing disputes must be one of the few pleasures that Keenan had left in life![39]

Control of the rabbit population was also a vital factor in sustaining and raising the carrying capacity of the station. Introduced by early settlers, the hard conditions of Central and North Otago proved an ideal habitat for rabbits and by the 1870s their numbers had exploded. The Rabbit Nuisance Acts of the 1870s represented increasingly strenuous attempts to control the pest, with land divided into rabbit districts, and local boards of trustees and sheep inspectors being empowered to enter land and take action should the occupier fail to discharge rabbiting duties adequately. In 1881, central government became more directly involved, appointing rabbit inspectors to each district and raising a levy on local landowners of up to one farthing per acre to fund rabbit extermination. Failure to control rabbits, when directed, might result in a fine for the occupiers and, in the event of inspectors being obliged to intervene, offenders would be obliged to meet the costs of eradication as well.[40] These measures appear to have checked infestations in old settled areas, but rabbits continued to spread in back country lots, gradually working their way into South Canterbury.[41]

Ross & Glendining, as we have seen, were alive to the rabbit menace and, through Elliott, made every attempt to keep numbers to a minimum. The station was regularly supplied with powder, ammunition, and poisons – principally phosphorus – which was mixed with oats when laid down. In slack periods, it was the job of station hands to lay poison for rabbits.[42] The main method of control, however, was through rabbiting gangs who were paid for their labours by the weight, colour and condition of skins. The skins were baled and, along with wool, shipped to the United Kingdom to be sold at auction. When the first annual balance was struck in February 1884, seven bales of skins had been shipped to London where they realised £254. A further 11,958 skins, with a book value of £70, awaited shipment in the woolshed. The rabbit account for the year revealed a loss of 5/1d, a good result compared to the average deficit of several hundred pounds per annum during the remainder of the eighties.[43]

## 5. FLOCK MANAGEMENT

The judicious purchase and sale of stock was another means by which margins might be improved. Robert Glendining, situated in Dunedin, was rather better placed than James Elliott to keep abreast of the market and hear of what stock was likely to come up for sale. Glendining himself had little experience of sheep although for the past few years he had regularly attended the annual wool sales in Dunedin and Christchurch to buy for

Roslyn Woollen Mills. Many of these sales were held by the stock and station agents, Wright Stephenson, and it was while engaged in wool buying that he had become friendly with one of the rising stars of the agency, James Armour Johnstone.[44] Johnstone, who became a partner in the firm in 1885, was only too happy to pass on information to Glendining about young sheep to be had at advantageous prices. By 1887, Glendining was able to boast to Ross that he was getting quite a name for 'buying sheep cheap'.[45]

Given the need to buy in sheep, buying cheaply had a real bearing on profitability. Important, too, was the ability to cull the flock of less productive sheep and sell them at the best possible price. Glendining's approach to culling was drawn straight from his experience as a warehouseman: 'I feel sure if it will not pay to keep sheep young, it will be worse keeping them when they get old, it is just like keeping old stock in the warehouse, but old sheep are very like old stock just now, it is not so easy getting rid of them.'[46] This comment to Ross was made in 1887, just at a time when the price of wool had slumped to a new low of 8 ½d per pound. Nevertheless, Glendining's philosophy was generally sound since young sheep, especially young wethers, produced more and better wool than old sheep, which tended to lose condition on mountain pastures. Given scarce pasture resources, it made sense to sell off the less productive animals.

Disposing of culls was not easy but, like everything else, it was usually possible to shift stock if the price was low enough. Run holders were generally prepared to accept as little as 1/6d a head rather than boil down the culls or let old sheep die on the runs. Should the latter happen, then rabbiting contractors might be employed to find and skin dead sheep at 1/- per head, with the skin and fleece then being sold. Whether the sheep were quite dead when first found by the contractors was often a matter of dispute.[47]

The depressed nature of the market for culls meant that when, in 1887, some 4,400 ewes and wethers were sold at 1/9d a head, Glendining could scarcely contain himself. He wrote a long letter to Ross, typed out in capitals on an early typewriter that he had started using, very pleased with his achievement

*Before they left the station the ewes were not bad but the wethers were very poor. It is no use trying to fatten old wethers, the ewes will get fat when they are old but the wethers will not. As things go at present it was a good sale. I feel the unfortunate buyer will not think so as they were going away to the Crown Range above the 'Arrow' and it would have paid him better to have their throats cut at the Lauder than take them away there as they will never see the winter through.*

The honest, straightforward Elliott was evidently embarrassed by the deal and became very agitated when the purchaser arrived to collect his sheep. Glendining was highly amused, telling Ross,

> *when [Elliott] gets a little anxious or excited he gets out his pipe and begins to strike matches on the bottom of his trowsers to light it but he never succeeds and I assure you that there were a good many matches struck on his bottom that afternoon as he was frightened that the man would kick up a row about the condition and appearance of the sheep and he was very pleased when he saw the last of them.*

The trouble-free departure of the culls meant that pasturage was freed up for replacements, some Galloway sheep appearing at Lauder Station for the first time.[48] The flock remained principally Merino, however, the large scale movement to half and cross breeds only taking place at Lauder Station in the 1890s.

## 6. THE SEARCH FOR LOW COUNTRY

The improvement of pastures, control of stock through fencing, eradication of rabbits and astute sheep trading all helped to raise returns. But the inability to breed sufficient lambs meant that, despite purchasing young sheep, the Lauder flock progressively aged, with the proportion of full and broken-mouthed sheep rising from 32.6 per cent in February 1884 to 57.2 per cent by February 1887. This inevitably degraded the ability of the flock to produce lambs and wool. The overall result was that even in years when there was a relatively good crop of lambs, such as in 1887, Lauder Station did not come near to covering the imputed 8 per cent interest on capital – let alone make a profit. In 1889, £3,344 of accumulated losses was written off and the imputed rate of interest reduced to 7 per cent.[49] A reduction in overhead costs helped to turn things around and in 1890 Lauder moved into the black for the first time.

The decline in wool prices from 11½d in 1882 to around 9d per lb in 1888 doubtless contributed to the difficulties experienced by the station. The partners were aware, however, that while an upturn in prices might help matters, there was no knowing when the market might recover. Without an upturn in prices, a significant improvement in profitability could only be achieved if Lauder Station had access to more low country for lambing.

There was plenty of high country available. In 1884, Ross & Glendining sent a letter to the Commissioner for Crown Lands for Otago, J.P. Maitland, with a suggestion that they lease Hawkdun 445, the mountain run forfeited by their former neighbour, Huddlestone. The run was presently unfenced, adding to the difficulties Lauder Station faced when mustering stock. They offered to take on the lease of Hawkdun 445 in return for a nominal £10 rental per annum and some fencing.[50] The lease for the 23,000-acre run was granted to the partners from March 1886, taking the total acreage that they leased from the Crown to 133,550 acres.[51] Ross & Glendining had now become one of the largest run holders in New Zealand.

Low country, suitable for breeding lambs, proved much more difficult to secure. Petitions from settlers to have the best land cut off from runs competed with the needs of existing run holders, with the result that low country became increasingly scarce. The periodic expiration of existing Crown leases – and their subsequent re-letting – provided Ross & Glendining with the best opportunity to obtain the land that they required. In 1886, with the pastoral leases of ninety-four runs in Otago and Canterbury coming up for renewal, Elliott was asked to appraise the suitability of those runs soon to be auctioned. The most obvious choice was run 224, Blackstone Hill, which lay on the southeastern boundary of Lauder and where the partners already held their small freehold property. To the east, the run encompassed the 3,000-feet Blackstone Hill range but to the west the land fell away to flats alongside the Manuherikia River, with much land at an elevation of just over 1,000 feet. The run, which was to be auctioned in April 1886 for occupation the following March, was to be split into five smaller runs of around 5,000 acres each.

The existing occupier, Frank Pogson, was an extensive leaseholder and freeholder in the area, owning almost 4,000 acres freehold as well as leasing the 32,000-acre Highfield run (225) to the east of the Blackstone Hill escarpment. He also held properties elsewhere.[52] Glendining was on friendly terms with Pogson, occasionally meeting him out on the runs and sharing a meal with him. As a matter of courtesy, Pogson was informed of the partners' intention to bid for some of the Blackstone Hill runs at the forthcoming auctions. They expressed their regret, but pointed out that 'it is impossible to work our present runs to advantage unless we have some low country for lambing; and for this about 15,000 acres [is] necessary'.[53]

Both parties quickly realised that bidding against each other would run up the annual rental to be paid to the Crown and so they attempted to come to a private arrangement first. Pogson, it seems, was prepared to let Ross & Glendining bid for the properties unopposed, providing they also took over some of the freehold attached to Blackstone Hill Station and paid for improvements. They were not impressed by the terms of his offer,

*The values placed by you on the improvements rather stagger us, especially as most of these would not be of any use, but on the contrary an item of expense only to us: and with the experience of the old Lauder Homestead*

*in our view we do not think anything like your price could be got for the*
*freehold if it were put on the market.*

By way of a counter-offer, they suggested that Pogson alone bid for the runs
up to whatever annual rental he considered reasonable and then, one month
after the auction, they would take the new leases off his hands. They would
also purchase the freehold of 650 acres, including improvements, for the
sum of £2,500, to be paid on entry on 1 March 1887. In the interim, he
should keep the properties free of rabbits and if scab or other infectious
diseases broke out, then they would be at liberty to cancel the purchase.[54]

Further exchanges took place but with Pogson of the opinion that
the terms and conditions offered by the partners were too one-sided, it
was decided that both parties should bid independently.[55] At the ensuing
auction, Ross & Glendining secured contiguous runs 224, 224a and 224c,
comprising some 16,000 acres of the upriver part of the original Blackstone
Hill run. For this they were obliged to pay an annual rental of £461 with the
leases to run until 1897[56]. The runs at a generally lower elevation, 224b and
224d, were retained by Pogson.[57]

The acquisition of part of Blackstone Hill provided the partners with
some, if not all, of the lower ground they needed. Nevertheless, Glendining
was sufficiently encouraged to sell old stock and purchase 10,500 two- and
four-tooth ewes and wethers upon entering their new runs.[58] The lower
altitude of the runs meant that lambing could commence around 1 October,
one week ahead of Lauder, and it was here where the bulk of the new breeding
stock was wintered. When Glendining visited the station during the spring
of 1887, he was able to report to Ross in London that the 10,000 ewes at
Blackstone Hill had produced many lambs. However, he thought the lack
of grass due to a very hard winter and the subsequent return of cold weather
was likely to kill a significant number.

Ross, already anxious about the state of the New Zealand economy, must
have become even more depressed as Glendining continued,

*Blackstone Hill is very good sheep country. If we had been only fortunate*
*enough to have secured the whole of it, but what we have got is all right ...*
*As I have said, it is very good lambing ground [but] it is just too little to*
*keep our high country up with young stock. The 2,000 ewes on the Lauder*
*were not doing so well, the weather was altogether against them and I do*
*not expect very much of a percentage from them. I have almost made up my*
*mind that it is a mistake to try and breed lambs on the Lauder as at the*
*time they come the weather is too cold and stormy for them ... I think if*
*we cannot breed as many on Blackstone Hill to keep the runs stocked with*
*young sheep, we had better take our chance and buy as many as we require*

> *to keep the flock up as it ought to be. So next season I think I will have*
> *nothing but dry sheep on the Lauder.*[59]

As Glendining predicted, the hard weather adversely affected the crop of lambs, a thousand less surviving to shearing in December 1887 compared to the previous year, notwithstanding a younger and larger flock of ewes. Unable to rear sufficient lambs, he was forced to continue buying young stock.[60]

### 7. Settlers' demand for land

The subdivision of runs in 1886 allowed the Government to cut off the better land and dispose of it in much smaller parcels. Some 2,500 acres in the Ida Valley, adjacent to the Blackstone Hill runs, had been reserved for this purpose but it was some time before all the land could be sold or leased to settlers. Glendining, ever alert to opportunities, applied to the Otago Land Board for the right to run sheep over the ground in return for controlling the rabbits. This, together with the grazing rights to another reserve that Glendining had secured, meant that Lauder Station had temporary access to over 5,000 acres of low country, virtually rent free. The settlers around Hill's Creek were infuriated when they found out, petitioning the Land Board against the granting of such rights, but to no avail.[61]

The settlers' demands for land, however, were not so easily dismissed. In June 1888, a group of settlers living in the small settlements of Cambrians, Becks and Tinkers took advantage of provisions in the Land Act of 1885 to petition the Crown to cancel Keenan's lease of Lauder run 226d. They wanted it subdivided into small blocks and re-let to them on perpetual leases at a low rental.[62] As much of the land that the Crown had already put aside at Lauder for closer settlement was now taken up, there were strong grounds for granting the petition for further subdivision. Glendining, fearing the thin end of the wedge, got in touch with Maitland, Commissioner of Crown Lands for Otago and chairman of the local Land Board. The low ground, Glendining argued, was absolutely essential for the operation of the runs.[63] Not surprisingly, the view of a major run holder carried some weight and the settlers' petition was rejected, even though it fell within the purview of the Act.

The Land Act Amendment Act 1888, which saw pastoral leases re-classified if they were deemed suitable for future subdivision, gave fresh hope to small settlers in their battle for more land.[64] Early in 1889, Crown officers visited Otago and reclassified the pastoral runs at Blackstone Hill, Highfield and the Ida Valley as agricultural-pastoral. Much encouraged, the settlers promptly petitioned the Minister of Lands to cancel the leases for the whole of Blackstone run 224c and part of Blackstone 224, some 7,000 acres in all. The nineteen petitioners, which included miners, farmers, storekeepers and labourers, indicated that they wished the land to be subdivided and re-let on perpetual leases.[65]

Upon learning of the petition from the newspapers, Glendining attempted to influence the decision by writing directly to the Minister of Lands. The splitting up of original runs into much smaller blocks in 1882, he contended, was in the nature of an experiment. Under the old system, sheep were able to escape down mountainsides in the event of bad weather. Now this was no longer possible, the reduction in minimum rentals set by government at the 1886 auctions being a tacit recognition of this fact. In the meantime, Lauder Station was still forced to lease lower ground in order to survive. He accepted that land was needed for settlement but pointed out,

> If this low country is taken from us, we shall have to abandon breeding entirely on all these adjacent runs; and they can then only be kept stocked at an enormous loss by purchasing grown sheep every year to make up for the loss by death, and to replace culls for which we can get only a nominal price ...

> We fail to see any urgency for the request of the 19 petitioners, and we think it most probable that if their request were granted, the result would be similar to what followed in other instances of the kind – the land would be used as commonage, and being 'no mans lands' would soon be overrun with rabbits and prove a costly nuisance to the neighbourhood.[66]

These arguments seem to have swayed the Minister of Lands since the petition for subdivision, despite subsequent appeal, was rejected.[67]

A fresh attempt to secure parts of Blackstone Hill was made by a number of the original petitioners in 1890, although this time a mere 2,150 acres was requested. Ross & Glendining's arguments were specious, they claimed, arguing that the whole of the land in the immediate neighbourhood was 'winter country'.[68] A second letter was sent by Glendining to the Minister of Lands, reiterating his previous arguments and claiming that Lauder Station was already struggling to find sufficient feed due to dry conditions.[69] The settlers' petition was again rejected.

## 8. THE SEARCH FOR LOW COUNTRY RESUMES

The general reclassification of land in 1888, although not immediately resulting in the cancellation of the new agricultural-pastoral leases, foreshadowed what might happen to Lauder Station in the future. For the time being, at least, the Blackstone Hill runs seemed to be safe as their leases did not expire until 1897. Of more immediate concern, however, was Home

Hills 227a, where 500 acres were to be resumed (taken back) for settlement upon the expiry of its lease in 1893.[70]

With Lauder Station already suffering from insufficient low ground for lambing, Glendining began to take steps to secure additional acreages to offset anticipated future losses to settlers. Early in 1889, Elliott was sent a list of runs to inspect where the leases were about to expire. The problem was that the most convenient runs, those in the neighbouring Ida Valley, were only to be re-let on one-year leases, and there was always the prospect that the agricultural–pastoral land of other runs might be resumed at short notice if required for settlement.[71] None of the runs proved satisfactory, and the search for additional acreage continued.

Ultimately, a solution to the quest for low ground came from an unexpected quarter. In 1888, Frank Pogson of Blackstone Hill had asked whether Ross & Glendining would be willing to sell him their holdings. Glendining dismissed the idea, stating that he believed times were improving.[72] In 1891 the situation was reversed when Pogson, with his wife now in failing health, decided to sell out. Johnstone, of Wright Stephenson, was to handle the sale and through him, the freehold and leasehold properties at Blackstone Hill, Ida Valley and further afield in the Maniototo were offered to Ross & Glendining for £26,000.[73]

The land on offer, some 5,601 acres freehold and 49,306 acres leasehold, was rather more than Ross & Glendining required. The Maniototo properties, quite apart from being too distant, offered little security as the leaseholds there were due to expire on 1 March 1893. There was also no real requirement for the freeholds, especially those in the Ida Valley, which were 'only cattle country and useless for sheep'. On the other hand, the Blackstone Hill runs, for which Glendining had bid at the 1886 auction and which offered 10,630 acres at just over 1,000 feet, was an attractive proposition even though the leases only ran to 1897. In the Ida Valley the six Highfield runs (225 to 225e) consisted of 32,580 acres at a similar altitude. With the exception of the lease 225d, which expired in 1895, the Highfield leases also ran until 1897.[74]

The advantages of securing the Highfield and remaining Blackstone Hill runs seemed to be compelling, especially as they regularly yielded a crop of lambs equal to one third of the total flock of around 44,000 sheep. Hercus, again in charge of affairs while Glendining was in the United Kingdom, estimated that of the gross profit of nearly 5/6d per sheep received by Pogson between 1882 and 1890, 1/7d came from a breeding surplus and only 3/11d from wool. This stood in stark contrast to Lauder Station, where the sheep breeding account barely broke even from one year to the next. Hercus, ever the careful accountant, concluded,

*It would no doubt be a great advantage to us to have all this country to work along with what we have at present: but there is a good deal to look at on the other side – chiefly the uncertain tenure of the runs and the large amount of money that would be sunk in freeholds and difficult perhaps to realise and that in the meantime are not yielding interest.*

Price also constituted a stumbling block, a valuation indicating that the property and stock was worth only £21,420, rather less than Pogson's demands. Hercus nevertheless conceded that it was the only real chance that Ross & Glendining had of securing convenient lambing ground.[75]

Once again Elliott was dispatched to view the properties while Hercus negotiated with Johnstone and cabled London for advice. After some discussions about whether to include the Maniototo freehold in the purchase, Ross & Glendining offered to buy the freeholds attached to the Blackstone Hill and Highfield runs for £5,500. For the leaseholds of Blackstone Hill and Highfield, amounting to 43,210 acres – together with 25,518 sheep, 189 cattle and 19 horses – they were prepared to offer a further £16,500.[76] This was rather more than the partners wanted to pay but it seems that their hand was forced by the policies of the recently elected Liberal Government.[77]

The Minister of Lands in the new government was Scotsman John McKenzie, an ardent opponent of the clearances in his native land and committed to 'bursting up large estates' in New Zealand. In July 1891, he introduced a land bill into Parliament that included powers to limit leaseholders to 'one-run-per-man'.[78] Although the legislation ran into opposition in the Upper House, Hercus informed Ross he thought it prudent to proceed with the Pogson purchase just in case the bill became law. 'If it is to come, the more runs we can get capable of being worked together the better, for the chances are that as the leases fall in we shall not be able to renew them'.[79] With fresh legislation in the offing and Pogson willing to accept their latest proposal, the purchase was duly completed.

The acquisition of the Blackstone Hill and Highfield runs in September 1891 lifted the carrying capacity of the station considerably. By balance date in February 1892, the size of the Lauder flock had risen by one third to over 81,000 sheep. The bulk of Pogson's sheep were two- and four-tooth ewes and wethers, which allowed Elliott to sell over 17,000 older ewes and wethers from the original Lauder flock. The increase in the number of ewes, a reduction in their average age, and the possession of more suitable lambing ground saw the crop of lambs double, rising to over 15,000 during the spring of 1891. At last, Lauder Station was freed from the necessity of buying in sheep to keep up flock numbers.

## 9. A WISE INVESTMENT?

The difficulties that Elliott faced in farming Lauder Station prior to 1892 are reflected in the profit and loss statements (see Table 7.2). Although income from wool rose, the sheep breeding account rarely turned much in the way of profit, a far cry from the 1/7d per sheep per annum that Pogson earned from his flock in this period. In reality, things were not quite as bleak at Lauder as the accounts showed, for each year profits were calculated after the partners were paid interest on the capital they had invested. Depreciation levels on stock and fencing were also generous. Like Roslyn Mills, therefore, the sheep farming venture generated a positive cash flow throughout the 1880s, providing sufficient funds for Ross & Glendining to develop and extend the scope of Lauder Station.

At the same time, it must be asked whether the partners were entirely wise to continue investing funds in sheep farming in the face of a downward trend in wool prices. Prior to the purchase of Pogson's property in 1891, the rate of return on an average capital of £35,000 invested in Lauder Station was around five cent. This was reasonable given the depressed nature of agriculture in this period but was barely matched by the interest rate that Ross & Glendining offered to those who deposited money with the firm. Had the partners been without capital resources themselves, then Lauder Station, like a number of other large properties in Otago and Canterbury, might have found itself in difficulties.[80]

There were, of course, other less easily quantifiable benefits to be had. The partners made much of the fact that they operated a vertically integrated enterprise, with Lauder wool passing through their mills, hosiery and clothing factories to end up as suits, shirts and stockings in their warehouses. In reality, only a small proportion of the Lauder clip was suitable for Roslyn Mills as it was generally too coarse, with Glendining obliged to buy in finer wool from outside. Such advantages as there were, therefore, lay in the realms of marketing rather than manufacturing.

Probably more important, at least to Glendining, was the fact that in New Zealand, as elsewhere, landed acres represented an important stepping stone to social status and prestige. Clearly he felt at a social disadvantage to others in Dunedin, complaining about 'the leaders of fashion, the elite, the upper society' in the city, many of whom chose to ignore him even after he had become a wealthy man. Whether his emergence as a leading run holder altered the situation is unclear. Possibly it did, for in 1887 he caustically remarked to Ross that people, who 'a few years ago would not think me good enough to walk on the same side of the street as them ... are now happy to share their troubles [with me].[81] What Ross thought about status, Glendining's aspirations, and the workings of Dunedin society one can only guess.

## TABLE 7.2
## SHEEP FARMING SUMMARY PROFIT & LOSS ACCOUNT, 1884–1892 (£)

| Feb Year | 1884 | 1885 | 1886 | 1887 | 1888 | 1889 | 1890 | 1891 | 1892 |
|---|---|---|---|---|---|---|---|---|---|
| **Gross profit** | | | | | | | | | |
| Sale of wool | 5,471 | 5,406 | 6,706 | 7,032 | 8,482 | 9,700 | 8,412 | 7,416 | 9,279 |
| Sheep breeding | 1,729[a] | -722 | 44 | 34 | 56 | -1,304 | 247 | 249 | -798 |
| Cattle/other | 116 | 65 | 35 | 58 | 69 | 30 | 39 | 85 | 134 |
| Total gross profit | 7,316 | 4,749 | 6,785 | 7,124 | 8,607 | 8,426 | 8,698 | 7,750 | 8,615 |
| **Costs** | | | | | | | | | |
| Rents/licenses | 2,704 | 2,686 | 2,703 | 2,715 | 3,178 | 3,186 | 2,713 | 2,083 | 3,015 |
| Interest[b] | 2,182 | 2,350 | 2,669 | 2,836 | 3,092 | 2,854 | 2,591 | 2,267 | 3,020 |
| Charges/deprecn | 1,626[c] | 946 | 1,126 | 1,246 | 1,422 | 978 | 1,034 | 997 | 4,609[c] |
| Wages | 611 | 716 | 827 | 893 | 978 | 976 | 1,017 | 851 | 976 |
| Rabbits | – | 378 | 360 | 99 | -59 | 143 | 368 | 83 | 479 |
| Stores | 431 | 317 | 316 | 261 | 339 | 344 | 261 | 301 | 622 |
| Net profit [loss] | [238] | [2,644] | [1,216] | [925] | [343] | [56] | 714 | 1,168 | [4,106] |
| Profit+ interest | 1,944 | -314 | 1,453 | 1,911 | 2,749 | 2,798 | 3,305 | 3,455 | -1,087 |
| Estimated average capital employed[d] | 27,275 | 29,375 | 33,362 | 35,450 | 38,650 | 40,771 | 37,014 | 32,385 | 43,128 |
| Return on capital (%) | 7.1 | -1.0 | 4.4 | 5.4 | 7.1 | 6.9 | 8.9 | 10.6 | -2.5 |

*Sources. Half-yearly balances, AG 512 15/3 & 15/4.*
*Notes: (a) Profit realised as book values greater than purchase price. (b) Imputed interest on capital invested. (c) Includes stock written down and depreciation of newly acquired freeholds. (d) Estimated from interest payable to partners, Lauder accounts being kept separately to the warehouse business and Roslyn Mills.*

# GAINING A NATIONAL FOOTHOLD

The 1890s proved to be somewhat more prosperous than the preceding decade, in spite of the re-emergence of problems in the banking sector and a renewed fall in commodity prices. Indeed, the growth of real GDP only really faltered in 1894, when both the Bank of New Zealand and the Colonial Bank looked as though they might fail. The steady expansion in the European population, from around 620,000 in 1890 to just over 760,000 ten years later, helped to sustain economic growth. Per capita incomes increased too, especially from 1895 as commodity prices began to recover.[1] By the turn of the century the market facing Ross & Glendining was around 40 per cent larger than it had been in 1890.

The 1890s not only witnessed an upturn in the rate of growth, but the decade also saw a shift in the economic centre of gravity in New Zealand. By 1901 the North Island had become more populous than the South, and it was here that the bulk of the rapidly expanding dairy industry was located. Sheep farming expanded in the north, too, with more freezing works being built in addition to the many dairy factories. The opening up of the North Island saw purchasing power grow in town and country alike, offering new opportunities for business expansion. Not surprisingly, Auckland and Wellington soon outpaced Dunedin, which, after forty years, surrendered its position of economic dominance.

Ross & Glendining, now with a warehouse in Wellington, were well placed to take advantage of economic expansion in the lower North Island. Smaller branch warehouses were also opened in Napier and Invercargill in order to improve market penetration in the regions. Yet while warehouse sales rose by more than half to over £326,000 per annum by 1900, progress was far from even. Thus sales in the Wellington, Nelson and Marlborough territories almost tripled in this period to £92,900, while in the burgeoning Auckland market they remained stagnant at around £5,000 per annum. Ross, in London, must have been concerned by this state of affairs, especially as the overall increase in the warehouse sales was not matched by a similar increase in profits. Indeed, profits were no larger at the end of the decade than the beginning, with losses actually being incurred between 1893 and 1895 (see Tables 8.1 & 8.2).

TABLE 8.1

SALES, CAPITAL EMPLOYED AND PROFITABILTY: WAREHOUSE
OPERATIONS, 1890–1900 (£000s)

| July Year | 1890 | 1891 | 1892 | 1893 | 1894 | 1895 | 1896 | 1897 | 1898 | 1899 | 1900[a] |
|---|---|---|---|---|---|---|---|---|---|---|---|
| Total sales | 190.8 | 180.2 | 191.4 | 207.7 | 197.0 | 213.9 | 258.2 | 274.0 | 275.2 | 300.8 | 154.7 |
| Bad debts | 2.7 | 2.9 | 1.2 | 2.4 | 3.4 | 2.4 | 2.8 | 2.1 | 1.3 | 1.7 | 0.7 |
| Net profit | 10.1 | 3.8 | 4.5 | -4.3 | -6.0 | -0.6 | 6.2 | 5.8 | 5.6 | 6.4 | 4.4 |
| Imputed interest[b] | 4.4 | 5.8 | 4.4 | 5.0 | 5.1 | 4.7 | 6.1 | 5.2 | 6.2 | 6.5 | 3.9 |
| Partners' salaries | 1.0 | nominal salary payment discontinued | | | | | | | | | |
| Clothing factory profit | 1.7 | 0.8 | 0.8 | 0.6 | 0.3 | 0.6 | 0.9 | 0.2 | 0.8 | 1.1 | 0.0 |
| Total returns | 17.2 | 10.4 | 9.7 | 1.3 | -0.6 | 4.7 | 13.2 | 11.2 | 12.5 | 14.0 | 8.3 |
| Estimated average capital employed | 62.9 | 82.9 | 62.9 | 71.4 | 72.9 | 67.1 | 87.1 | 86.7 | 103.3 | 108.3 | [a] |
| Return on capital (%) | 27.3 | 12.5 | 15.4 | 1.8 | -0.8 | 7.0 | 15.2 | 12.9 | 12.1 | 12.9 | |

Sources: Half-yearly balances, AG 512 15/4–15/6, 15/8.
Notes: (a) Half-year to February 1900. Partnership converted to limited liability company thereafter.
(b) Interest charged on partners' capital reduced from 7 to 6 per cent on 31st July, 1896.

In 1890, however, the future looked bright. An improving economy
and the beneficial effects of the New Zealand and South Seas Exhibition in
Dunedin the previous year engendered a spirit of optimism within the firm.
It was in this environment that discussions took place concerning the next
phase of expansion by Ross & Glendining. Space was at a premium in the
three existing warehouses, even in Christchurch where the recent move into
Thompson, Shannon & Co.'s former premises had provided only temporary
relief.

A building programme, either to extend existing warehouses or erect new
premises, seemed unavoidable.

1. BUILDING THE WELLINGTON WAREHOUSE

The most immediate concern was the construction of a new warehouse in
Wellington. At the end of 1889, Hercus had been able to secure a harbour
reclamation site from Wellington Corporation on a 21-year lease; annual
rental £147-10s. It was on a corner section, had a frontage on to Victoria St,

## TABLE 8.2
## SALES BY REGION, 1890–1900 (£000s)

| July Year | 1890 | 1891 | 1892 | 1893 | 1894 | 1895 | 1896 | 1897 | 1898 | 1899 | 1900 |
|---|---|---|---|---|---|---|---|---|---|---|---|
| Dunedin | 46.7 | 34.8 | 34.6 | 36.7 | 32.2 | 30.8 | 38.7 | 42.3 | 39.3 | 38.7 | 46.4 |
| Southland & South Otago | 25.2 | 25.4 | 26.5 | 29.5 | 29.1 | 28.7 | 31.3 | 33.9 | 36.8 | 44.7 | 55.5 |
| Goldfields | 11.1 | 11.3 | 9.3 | 9.0 | 8.1 | 8.0 | 9.3 | 7.2 | 8.1 | 8.5 | 8.8 |
| North Otago & Canterbury | 51.3 | 48.4 | 53.7 | 64.2 | 55.1 | 60.8 | 72.2 | 73.4 | 71.5 | 74.4 | 77.6 |
| West Coast | 7.5 | 7.4 | 5.8 | 5.1 | 5.8 | 5.9 | 8.0 | 11.4 | 10.0 | 8.3 | 8.3 |
| Marlborough/Nelson & Wellington | 35.0 | 38.2 | 46.1 | 50.1 | 52.1 | 56.0 | 68.5 | 73.4 | 78.5 | 88.1 | 92.9 |
| Hawkes Bay | 8.5 | 7.9 | 8.9 | 8.0 | 10.5 | 20.9 | 26.6 | 27.6 | 26.8 | 31.8 | 31.4 |
| Auckland | 3.0 | 4.8 | 5.0 | 4.7 | 3.3 | 2.6 | 3.5 | 4.6 | 4.0 | 5.9 | 5.4 |
| Other | 2.6 | 2.1 | 1.4 | 0.4 | – | – | 0.2 | 0.3 | 0.3 | 0.4 | 0.4 |
| Total | 190.8 | 180.2 | 191.4 | 207.7 | 197.0 | 213.9 | 258.2 | 274.0 | 275.2 | 300.8 | 326.7 |

Sources: Half-yearly balances, AG 512 15/4–15/6, 15/8.

and measured a generous 59 feet wide by 110 feet deep. Hercus was jubilant and informed Ross,

> Our site is in a splendid position. Jervois Quay and Victoria street will be the principal thoroughfare in the city: and as Harbour Street is really a continuation of Lambton Quay the traffic will likely go down that way. The land is all reclaimed to Jervois Quay, but there are no buildings yet on the side of Victoria Street nearest the water: indeed ours is the only site sold on that side.

With Bing, Harris & Co. having bought the site opposite and Sargood, Son & Ewen already building on Victoria St, the new warehouse would be ideally located to conduct trade.[2]

Once again the partners called upon the Dunedin architects, Messrs Mason & Wales, to design a building that, in terms of substance and style, would stand comparison with the warehouse then being built for Sargood, Son & Ewen. Being on a prominent corner site, the warehouse had to be 'sightly' with 'show frontages on both streets'. Construction on the reclaimed land was neither cheap nor easy and Wales, with long experience of Wellington, had his own ideas concerning the nature of the foundations. These, he believed, should consist of longitudinal and transverse iron rails rather than the more common totara posts. The building itself was to be two storeys high with a stone balustrade on top, a corner entrance for customers, large windows on each floor and decorative fluting on upright columns. The walls were to be strengthened against earthquakes. Substance and style did not come cheap, however, with Wales' preliminary estimates indicating that the final outlay was likely to be in the region of £6,500, rather more than had been anticipated.[3]

The need to vacate the temporary Brandon St warehouse towards the end of the year when the lease expired meant that time was now of the essence. At the beginning of April 1890, the Wellington branch manager, David Jones, was instructed to place an advertisement in local newspapers, calling upon builders to submit tenders for the proposed structure. The firm's Inspector of Works, Charles Lomax, would sail up to Wellington on 14 April to look over the tenders with the manager. Their recommendations were then to be forwarded to Dunedin for approval. It was impressed upon Jones that the tender should be awarded to a 'thoroughly substantial man' and that those submitting tenders were to be informed that preference would be given to builders who agreed to do the work quickly.[4]

The tender was soon let but, even with construction going according to plan, it became evident that the warehouse would not be finished in time. From September, therefore, the partners took a short lease on Turnbull's old warehouse, just vacated by Sargood, Son & Ewen. At last, early in 1891, Ross & Glendining moved into their new warehouse on Victoria St.

The final cost of the building was just under £6,500, pretty much what Wales had estimated. This was only a small part of the total outlay, however, for a larger warehouse required additional stock of which a good proportion was sold on credit. By the end of July, the amount absorbed by the new venture amounted to almost £45,000.[5] Not all of this represented fresh money, for considerable progress had already been made by Jones, who now managed the Auckland, Hawkes Bay, Marlborough, Nelson and West Coast sales territories as well.[6] Even so, expansion on this scale forced Hercus to budget very carefully.[7]

There were, nevertheless, a number of advantages to be had by supplying the northern sales territories through Wellington. Most important, perhaps, was the fact that it afforded a considerable saving on insurance and freight costs. Goods might now be shipped from the United Kingdom directly to the capital, removing the need to break bulk, repack, and reship from Dunedin.

The ability to supply directly from Wellington also meant that customers might receive their orders more speedily than before, not unimportant in a trade where fashions changed with the seasons. Being closer to the customer – and the travellers – conferred other advantages too, greater proximity leading to an improvement in information flows and scope for more effective monitoring.

Sales in Wellington and surrounding districts received a considerable boost from the new warehouse, increasing by a third over the next two years. According to Hercus, the old Brandon St warehouse had been regarded by customers as little more than a sample room, the inadequate display facilities and limited stocks placing Ross & Glendining at a disadvantage when compared to rivals. Cramped conditions also constituted a fire risk, making it difficult to insure more than part of the contents.[8] Opening the Victoria St warehouse swept away these obstacles to progress, there being sufficient room in the new premises to introduce a departmental system, each department's goods being laid out for inspection in a manner similar to those of their competitors.

There were initially four departments at the Wellington branch: clothing and woollens, manchester, hosiery and haberdashery, and fancy goods. Each of the departments was run by a head salesman, who was expected to assess market trends, place orders and, in conjunction with Dunedin, set prices. The heads of department, like their counterparts in Dunedin, were paid on the 'stimulation principle', with a commission element based on profits rather than sales. Typically they earned around £300 per annum, of which up to 15 per cent might be commission.[9]

## 2. OPENING IN INVERCARGILL

In spite of the disruption caused by moving from one warehouse to another, the Wellington branch turned in a respectable profit for the year ending in July 1891. This was not the case in the south, where weakening commodity prices and labour unrest curtailed trade. Dunedin was the worst affected, the transfer of accounts to the new Wellington and Christchurch warehouses, together with a drop in sales elsewhere, contributing to a loss of over £1,000 (see Table 8.3).[10] To help resuscitate business, Hercus suggested that the firm follow Sargood, Son & Ewen & others and open a branch warehouse in Invercargill.[11]

Until now it had been cost effective to supply Southland from Dunedin. With trade growing, however, and country customers from Gore and surrounding districts increasingly drawing supplies from Invercargill, the advantages of opening a warehouse in the city were considerable.[12] There were also other considerations to take into account. The recently formed Auckland Warehousemen's Association was now working closely with their

TABLE 8.3
WAREHOUSE SALES AND PROFITABILITY, 1890–1900 (£000s)

| July Year | 1890 | 1891 | 1892 | 1893 | 1894 | 1895 | 1896 | 1897 | 1898 | 1899 | 1900ᵃ |
|---|---|---|---|---|---|---|---|---|---|---|---|
| Dunedin sales | 190.8 | 97.1 | 82.9 | 91.7 | 86.3 | 84.5 | 99.4 | 106.4 | 103.6 | 114.0 | 41.7 |
| Net profit | 10.1 | -1.1 | -0.4 | -4.0 | -3.5 | -1.2 | 0.9 | 0.7 | 0.5 | 0.6 | |
| Invercargill sales | – | 9.0 | 14.5 | [taken through Dunedin books until new warehouse built in 1899] 16.1 17.8 17.5 19.1 21.1 24.6 | | | | | | 30.2 | 21.4 |
| Christchurch sales | – | 34.1 | 42.8 | 48.1 | 38.4 | 43.9 | 54.9 | 55.2 | 56.3 | 58.6 | 30.1 |
| Net profit | – | 1.2 | 2.8 | 0 | -1.5 | 0.3 | 2.5 | 1.7 | 2.6 | 2.0 | |
| Wellington sales | – | 49.1 | 65.8 | 67.9 | 72.3 | 76.5 | 80.6 | 89.6 | 93.7 | 100.4 | 47.2 |
| Net profit | – | 1.5 | 2.1 | -0.3 | -1.0 | 0.1 | 1.0 | 2.4 | 1.4 | 2.7 | |
| Napier sales | – | – | – | – | – | 9.0 | 23.3 | 22.9 | 21.5 | 27.8 | 14.3 |
| Net profit | – | – | – | – | – | 0.2 | 1.7 | 0.9 | 1.1 | 0.1 | |
| Total sales | 190.8 | 180.2 | 191.4 | 207.7 | 197.0 | 213.9 | 258.2 | 274.0 | 275.2 | 300.8 | 154.7 |
| Total net profit | 10.1 | 1.5 | 4.3 | -4.3 | -6.0 | -0.6 | 6.2 | 5.8 | 5.6 | 5.4 | |

Sources: Half-yearly balances, AG 512 15/4–15/6.
Note: (a) Half year to February when limited liability adopted.

Dunedin counterpart, regulating the prices of branded goods and stipulating the terms of credit.[13] The two associations were mainly concerned with monitoring their members although, from time to time, they considered fresh proposals to control competition. One such proposal was to forbid the practice of paying the freight charges involved in supplying far-away customers. This did not suit Ross & Glendining who, in order to compete in remote locations such as Invercargill and Napier, felt obliged to pay the cost of freight on individual orders.

For a while George Hercus, as Secretary of the Dunedin Association, was able to procrastinate.[14] Then, early in 1892, at a conference in Wellington that saw the two associations combine to form a New Zealand Warehousemen's Association, the proposal surfaced again.[15] With the measure likely to be adopted, a branch warehouse in Invercargill was regarded as essential. Shortly afterwards, Ross & Glendining leased modest premises in Tay St staffed by a manager, several assistants, and a traveller.[16] Here bulk consignments from Dunedin might be broken up and sold to local customers. The payment of freight charges on behalf of customers was forbidden by the Association from 1 August.[17]

### 3. THE EXPANSION PROGRAMME CONTINUES

Sales in North Otago and Canterbury had almost doubled between 1888 and 1890. As a result, the small warehouse previously occupied by Thompson & Shannon was soon found to be inadequate. Some thought had been given to purchasing Butterworth Brothers' Christchurch warehouse, but the premises were found to be too narrow and high. After considering a number of alternatives, it was decided that the best way forward in Christchurch was to build.

Freehold land had recently become available in Lichfield St, the main thoroughfare for warehousemen, which Ross & Glendining set about buying. After some delay by the vendors' lawyers, completion took place in June 1891.[18] Almost immediately Charles Lomax was on site, ordering trucks of lime and beginning construction.[19] By the end of the year the work was complete. Apart from having a single street frontage, the Christchurch warehouse was not dissimilar in appearance to the Wellington building. Three storeys high and built of stuccoed brick, it too had a stone balustrade, large windows in the front and side, and ornamented columns. With an extra storey it was somewhat larger than Wellington but, at around £5,400 including land, cost rather less.[20]

The stress involved in running a large, diversified concern was now beginning to take its toll on Robert Glendining. He insisted on continuing to attend wool sales to buy for the mill, managing the warehouse stocks – which he personally inspected twice yearly – and regularly visiting Lauder Station. He had also invested, somewhat unwisely, in the Shag Point coal mine that proved to be both troublesome and time-consuming. Glendining's health, never particularly good, began to deteriorate in the late 1880s when he was again troubled with gastric problems. By 1891 he was suffering from severe headaches as well. With construction about to begin in Christchurch, he sailed to the United States and on to Great Britain, both for the benefit of his health and to seek additional medical opinion.[21] He returned to New Zealand in December 1891, apparently little better and none the wiser. Against the advice of both Ross and Hercus, he plunged immediately into wool buying at the Dunedin and Christchurch sales.[22]

With Glendining back in New Zealand and Ross due to pay a visit later in

1892, the construction of a new Dunedin warehouse took centre stage. When completed in the 1870s, the warehouse in Stafford St had been regarded as the most modern of its time but it was now beginning to look shabby and out-of-date. Certainly it compared unfavourably with the warehouses in both Christchurch and Wellington where, Hercus thought, the goods on display looked far superior. Writing to Ross he complained, 'The effect of being in this place [Dunedin] since it has been behind our rivals in smartness and sightliness, is more against us than perhaps we have been thinking it was'.[23] The declining profitability of the Dunedin warehouse would seem to lend a degree of support to this view. But what should be done with the existing warehouse? Should it be renovated and enlarged, or should new premises be constructed big enough to house the clothing factory, warehouse and bulk store together under one roof? Although Stafford St was no longer ideally located for business, Hercus was of the view that an entirely new warehouse should be erected on the same site as the old one. He disliked the idea of renovation, which, he thought, was tantamount to 'putting new cloth on an old garment'.[24]

After some debate, it was decided to build a completely new warehouse, although not on the original site. Leasehold land had become available in High St in June 1891 and, as the site was one street closer to the centre of town than Stafford St, it was quickly secured.[25] Plans for the new warehouse and offices were drawn up during Glendining's visit to the United Kingdom, enabling construction to be well advanced by the time Ross arrived in Dunedin late the following year.[26] The building, supposedly designed by the partners themselves, was very much in the style of the Wellington and Christchurch warehouses.[27] Consisting of three storeys linked by hydraulic lifts, there were numerous large windows along the front, making the interior light and airy. Outside, ornamentation and balustrading helped to give the warehouse a distinctive and rather elegant appearance. The cost of the building came to £8,104, exclusive of the site for which an additional £2,900 had been paid. The old Stafford St warehouse was retained for storage and other purposes.[28]

The construction of the High St warehouse did not mark the end of the building programme. A smaller section close by in High St had been acquired some time earlier and upon this Lomax began to erect a new clothing factory. By the end of 1893 it was completed for a modest £631, the leasehold of the existing factory in Stafford St being disposed of. Finally, in 1895, Lomax returned to Wellington, where the continued expansion of business had forced the manager to store goods in a shed.[29] An adjoining lot was acquired and a 40- by 60-foot extension built, a further storey also being added to the existing warehouse. These works cost £3,060.[30] Over the space of five years, therefore, Ross & Glendining had spent more than £25,000 on warehouse extensions and additions.[31]

The decision to continue with major building works at a time when the economy was weakening was bold. The impact upon sales revenues was nevertheless positive, even though it was hard to make headway in declining areas such as the Goldfields and along the West Coast. Trade was also difficult in and around Dunedin itself, a recapitalised Butterworth Brothers Ltd adding to the competition, while North Otago seemed to suffer from persistent drought.[32] Further afield, low commodity prices and banking problems also took their toll. Under the circumstances, warehouse sales kept up remarkably well, although heavy discounting and bad debts inevitably ate into returns.[33] The largest single default was that of Hunt & Berry, travelling drapers who went round the South Island in two separate horse-drawn vans. They met twice a year to settle their accounts and place orders. When Berry absconded, Hunt was left owing Ross & Glendining over £2,000.[34] Dunedin was debited with this particular loss, although neither Wellington nor Christchurch escaped unscathed in this period.[35]

## 4. A WAREHOUSE IN NAPIER BUT AUCKLAND NEGLECTED

The atmosphere in Dunedin nevertheless remained positive, the general view being that trade would recover, and that expansion had not been in vain. Underpinning this optimism was a strong belief in the future of New Zealand, especially in the North Island where much land was being opened up. With the trade in frozen meat and dairy produce increasing, Hercus thought that business there promised 'to be brisk for some years to come'.[36]

A chance to expand further afield in the north came in January 1894, when McArthur & Co.'s Napier manager, R.A. Wilson, informed Ross & Glendining that his employers were about to close his branch. Wilson, a former clerk at the Stafford St warehouse, was thanked for the information and urged to stay with his current employers. It was suggested that he might like to provide a little more information.[37]

For the moment little could be done. McArthur & Co., with a buying office in London, branches throughout the North Island and a large warehouse in Auckland, were in the process of winding up as their two resident partners were about to retire to the UK.[38] Matters were finally resolved in April when the bulk of McArthurs' business was sold to Sargood, Son & Ewen. The Napier warehouse was not included, Sargoods opting to work Hawke's Bay and Poverty Bay from their large Wellington warehouse. This being the case, Wilson was given permission by McArthurs to forward trading details of the Napier branch to Ross & Glendining. He also provided particulars concerning the lease of their Emerson St warehouse.[39]

Hercus was very impressed with what he saw. Turnover had increased to £28,200 since Wilson took charge of the branch in 1885, while credit had been tightened up, old overdue accounts reduced significantly, and bad debts for the past four years cut to less than £80. An enthusiastic letter was duly sent to Ross:

> *There can be no doubt that the success is in great measure attributable to Wilson's careful management and thorough knowledge of the district. The business is apt to be scattered now, owing to the break, but I do not think there would be much difficulty gathering it up again .... From the list of accounts you will note that the business is widely spread all over the district, and the customers are not likely to go into Wellington. Most of the names we have never heard of, and they cannot be reached by our travellers in the ordinary way of business. At the same time with the opening up of the railways and the country, we must look to this district for the expansion of our business and this seems one of the most favourable opportunities we could look for to get hold of what is really the wealthiest district in the North Island.*[40]

Given the tenor of this letter, Ross could do little but agree that Wilson should be engaged and that the Emerson St warehouse be taken over.[41] By the end of June, a shipment of goods had been arranged and an account opened with the Bank of New South Wales in Napier.[42] Emerson St opened as a sub-branch of the Wellington warehouse shortly afterwards, becoming an independent profit centre in 1895. For staff, Wilson was supported by one traveller and one junior.[43]

The opening of the small Napier warehouse helped to boost sales. Nevertheless, with the depression still in evidence, trade remained difficult and profits were hard to come by. The most disappointing results occurred in Auckland where, in spite of several changes of personnel, sales remained at a trivial level. Hercus was inclined to blame the 'slow easy ways' of the folks in Auckland for sapping the energies of his travellers but there were other, more potent reasons for the firm's lack of success.[44] For a start, the additional costs of supplying Auckland customers via the Wellington warehouse, together with the increased delivery times, necessarily put Ross & Glendining at a competitive disadvantage in most classes of goods.[45] Moreover, as they had found out in both Christchurch and Wellington, a smart warehouse where customers were able to inspect the latest wares gave local warehousemen a decisive advantage. Only in better quality woollen and worsted goods, often sold under the Roslyn brand, could the firm hope to compete.

In view of the success of the Christchurch and Wellington warehouses, it might be thought that the partners would wish to branch out in Auckland as soon as possible. Certainly it would have put them on an equal footing with Bing, Harris & Co., Sargoods, and other leading warehousemen. For some reason, however, Glendining and Hercus refused to entertain the idea.[46] Instead an agent, Alexander Knight, was engaged in 1895 to handle all future sales.[47] It required the subsequent return of Ross to New Zealand, with an open mind and fresh perspective, to persuade a reluctant Glendining that opening a warehouse in Auckland was absolutely essential. This was not to occur until 1904.

### 4. CONTROLLING BUSINESS 'AT A DISTANCE'

The establishment of a network of branches inevitably gave rise to difficulties in terms of coordination and control. Fortunately, it was possible to apply many of the systems and routines developed in Dunedin in the new warehouses. The departmental system, common amongst most larger warehousemen in the antipodes, was employed in both Christchurch and Wellington branches, although each had fewer departments than Dunedin. Systems for entering and dispatch were also replicated, as were the methods of compiling accounts, with one set of books kept at the branch and a duplicate set at Head Office in Dunedin.[48] This enabled close financial control to be exercised, a task made easier by the fact that safe operating ratios had been established through long experience. Thus the target level for stocks was set at approximately 80 per cent of the previous season's sales, while a gross profit margin of 20 per cent was needed to yield acceptable results.[49] Certain departments were known to show greater profit variation than others, with mundane manchester yielding fairly stable profits whereas fancy goods departments – which dealt in fashion accessories – exhibited greater volatility. Armed with this knowledge and with the performance of each department dissected twice yearly, consistent underperformance was quickly detected.

Yet it was one thing to set key operating ratios and quite another to achieve them. Throughout the early nineties Hercus spent much time instructing the managers and bookkeepers at Wellington and Christchurch on the approved method of casting up accounts, and how to calculate returns.[50] There were also problems when it came to ordering and managing stocks, with salesmen failing to take into account what might be in stock at other branches when placing fresh orders.[51] In an attempt to prevent stock from accumulating, orders from the branches were to be submitted to Dunedin in the first instance. When, due to urgency, this was not possible, duplicates were to be sent to Head Office so that orders might be rescinded by cable if necessary. Thomas Glendining, Robert's younger brother, was given responsibility for coordinating the ordering process.[52]

Inter-branch cooperation nevertheless remained poor, with each branch suspecting the other of receiving favoured treatment. On the basis of no evidence whatsoever, salesmen in the branches imputed the worst of motives to Head Office. Part of the problem was due to the nature of the incentive systems employed, with heads of departments focusing on the profits earned by their individual departments rather than considering the greater good of the enterprise. This attitude exasperated Hercus who wrote to Wellington:

> We have adjusted [discounts] on the most equitable basis we can arrive at, all round, and we are about tired of this constant wrangling. If any errors are made we are always ready to correct them but we will not have this constant snatching and pulling between the warehouses ....

> We feel sure you must recognise that the general interests of the firm should be of the first importance to all connected with it, and that these are not served but thwarted by this spirit of antagonism being allowed to come in between the warehouses ...[53]

Doubtless Hercus conveyed a similar message to his brother, Peter, who in 1891 had become the manager of the Christchurch branch after William Peters had fallen ill.

Gradually control over organisation was tightened up. A schedule of dates by which orders for various classes of goods should be in London was prepared to ensure the timely delivery of consignments.[54] A time clock was also installed in each of the warehouses and a set of 'Rules for Employees' was drawn up. Every existing and new member of staff was obliged to sign and return the rules as a condition of employment.[55] The substitution of formal for informal methods of control was, perhaps, a reflection of the fact that as the organisation grew in size, the gap between management and labour became ever wider.

Yet there still remained areas of weakness, in particular the tendency for heads of departments to cut prices too readily in order to shift slow-selling lines. In August 1893, after an extremely poor set of results, a new and more rational system of pricing was introduced.[56] Hitherto goods had been entered in departmental books at a nominal selling price minus 20 per cent to account for overheads and a profit margin. This worked well when the economy was buoyant as it was possible to realise the full selling price. When times were tough, however, departmental heads, who had no idea of the true extent of overheads, frequently cut prices so that a loss was incurred. Henceforth all goods were to entered in the books in three columns, the original invoice cost, the cost of the goods plus expenses for freight, duty and packing, and the price at which, ideally, the goods should be sold. The salesmen were instructed to return 'a gross profit on sales of 20%' over the cost of goods plus expenses.[57] This did not put an end to price-cutting as prices still had to be reduced to shift otherwise unsaleable stock. Even so, greater accuracy in costing allowed departmental heads to have a better idea of where they were likely to incur a loss.

### 5. UNIONISATION AND SPARE CAPACITY AT THE CLOTHING FACTORY

Trading conditions began to improve towards the end of 1894, after which sales and profits began to grow once more. Fresh attempts were made to source from wider afield and increase the range of products covered, with new articles such as matting from India, oilskins from New York and Levi Strauss' 'denim pants: copper rivetted' being introduced.[58] Special novelty items were sent from time to time, including a consignment of Jubilee handkerchiefs, which sold particularly well. John Ross became an enthusiastic cyclist in his sixties and so bicycles were exported from the United Kingdom to be assembled in Dunedin. This was rapidly discontinued as they could not compete with the 'light and showy' American machines.[59] For the most part, however, expansion was based on those lines in which Ross & Glendining had accumulated a wealth of knowledge and experience.

The clothing factory did not share in the expansion, a state of affairs that gave rise to increasing concern as the decade wore on. It had recovered well towards the end of the eighties depression and in 1890 returned a profit of £1,675. The profits earned, however, were simply from making-up, the factory being paid to make garments 'to order' from materials supplied by the warehouse departments. Labour was a major component of the cost of making-up, in excess of 50 per cent, and might account for as much as 25 per cent of the total cost of a garment. As labour in the north became cheaper relative to that in Dunedin, so making-up at the clothing factory declined, in spite of the construction of new, purpose-built premises.

One of the factors that contributed to the decline of making-up in Dunedin was the unionisation of labour. When the Tailoresses Union was formed in 1889 the impact was negligible, the buoyant economic conditions permitting Ross & Glendining to pass on the advance in wages in the form of higher prices.[60] As the economy began to deteriorate and competition grew more acute, this became increasingly difficult. In November 1891 the secretary of the New Zealand Tailoresses Union, Miss Morrison, was rebuked by George Hercus for allowing her membership in the North Island to work below specified rates. It was pointed out that employment was already being diverted away from the city and that ultimately the whole trade would be transferred to those localities where wages were lowest. The Dunedin manufacturers, for whom Hercus spoke, were prepared to agree to a revised Log of wage rates, but only if it was upheld throughout the entire Colony.[61] Agreement was reached, but not widely enforced.

For a while Ross & Glendining kept their clothing factory fully employed by reducing the charges for making-up, the rationale being that it was better to sacrifice a profit on the clothing factory rather than lose the clothing trade itself. This did not prevent a number of small factories coming into being in other parts of the colony. In February 1892, Hercus informed Ross that it was now possible for the branches to get their clothing made far more cheaply by local makers, 'and between cheap material and cheap making we are being undersold'.[62] Not all Dunedin manufacturers were as scrupulous as Ross & Glendining, with Bing, Harris & Co. getting sub-contractors to work at below 'regulation prices'. One of these, E. Levy, was forced into bankruptcy, arguing that his misfortunes were due to Bing, Harris, who sweated the labour force. As time went by, factories sprang up in northern cities quite independent of the unions, to the further detriment of making in the south.[63]

The inability to compete meant that, apart from seasonal peaks, it was difficult to find enough work to keep the hands employed.[64] In November 1893, a sub-contractor who made up shirts for Ross & Glendining was warned that she would not be receiving as many orders as hitherto due to production being switched to the new High St factory.[65] Making-up declined still further in the following year as the economy deteriorated.

The passage of the radical and much lauded Industrial Conciliation and Arbitration Act in 1895 promised to raise wage rates generally, but it did little to help Dunedin manufacturers. With awards made on a plant-by-plant rather than an industry-wide basis, awards made in one city had virtually no effect on wage rates elsewhere.[66] As a result, the firm's Christchurch and Wellington warehouses continued to send much of their material to local manufacturers to be made up, rather than send their orders to Dunedin.

Hercus was incensed that the branches should patronise other factories when the High St factory was underemployed. In 1897 he wrote to Jones in Wellington:

> we have had the Factory open and all appliances ready for doing all our trade, and the general expenses of running on during the last two months, with only a small proportion of the workers employed – the result being a heavy loss .... During the same time you have paid away about £1,000 to Wellington factories ... It is of no profit to us to make £100 more in Wellington by losing £1,000 in the factory, and seeing that we have both businesses to carry on, the least we can expect is hearty and loyal assistance to the utmost from employees in every department of our service.

The failure by Wellington to order from the factory was attributed by Hercus, at least in his correspondence, to the petty jealousies existing between various parts of the enterprise.[67] Yet he cannot have been blind to the fact that with commission based on profits, the departmental salesmen were always likely to have their clothing made up wherever it was cheapest.

Output at the High St factory appears to have remained at much the same level until 1898, at which point Hercus began to tinker with the system of charging used. Hitherto, the warehouse departments had been charged for making-up garments from material that they supplied, the charge levied being based on cost plus mark-up that guaranteed the factory a profit.[68] Whether the warehouse departments made a profit on the finished goods depended on the nature of the market – and the skill with which they marketed the garments. Such an arrangement seemed to give the factory an undue advantage. In future, the factory would procure and stock the material and charge the departments for garments it supplied.[69] Shifting the balance of risk, it was thought, might encourage greater enterprise on the part of the factory and increased orders from the departments. Additional capacity was subsequently installed in the clothing factory and profits started to rise, although whether this was due to the state of the market or the changed incentive structure is far from clear.[70]

Progress was also made when an arrangement was reached between clothing manufacturers and labour. The improvement in the economy meant that by 1898 the Tailoresses Union had 'been agitating for a higher Log for some time'. The problem for Ross & Glendining and the other manufacturers was that wage differentials between the main cities had not changed very much. Thus wages in Wellington were still lower than Dunedin while the Auckland Log, fixed by the Arbitration Court, was lower still. When, at the beginning of 1898, the Tailoresses Union attempted to introduce a new Log, an association of manufacturers – comprising all members of the clothing trade in Wellington, Christchurch and Dunedin – was formed to frame a response. The outcome was a conference between the association and the union. Faced with the threat that the Auckland Log would be adopted by all manufacturers, the union agreed to accept an advanced Log that put all three places 'on an equal footing'. How this was achieved is not clear, but Hercus believed that it would stop the branches undercutting the High St factory.[71]

Towards the end of the decade the outlook for the factory seemed to be more promising. Indeed, Glendining was sufficiently encouraged to think about building a new factory so that Ross & Glendining might 'keep up' with their neighbours. Given the spare capacity that had hitherto existed at High St, it seems hard to believe that a new building was justified. Such a decision, however, required the agreement of both partners and had to await the arrival of Ross in New Zealand in 1899.

## 6. SLIM MARGINS AND SLACK MANAGEMENT?

While sales, in nominal terms, had grown by more than half during the 1890s, the profitability of the warehouse and clothing manufacturing side of the business was far from outstanding. True, the downturn of the nineties did not result in losses on the scale of the 1880s, but the net warehouse profits at the end of the decade were still less than those of 1890. Given the increase in capital employed in the warehouses and the expanding New Zealand market, this was extremely disappointing.

There were, of course, positive developments. By 1899 the number of accounts served had more than doubled to over 1,600, almost a third of which were located in the North Island.[72] The greatest areas of expansion were Taranaki, Hawkes Bay and Southland, the direct result of the strategy of opening smaller branch warehouses. Indeed, the expansion of trade in Southland was so rapid that towards the end of the decade the firm moved into a larger warehouse in the centre of Invercargill. The firm also incurred fewer bad debts, less than 2 per cent of sales at the depth of the nineties depression compared to around 10 per cent in the mid-1880s. Hercus' policy of spreading risks by selling 'little and often' was clearly bearing fruit.

Yet the fact remains that the margins enjoyed by Ross & Glendining were far lower than those of the halcyon days of the investment boom. Maybe this was because the New Zealand economy was simply becoming more efficient, with abnormally high profits rapidly being eroded by the normal processes of competition. The degree of risk involved in the warehouse trade may also have declined, warehousemen now being prepared to accept lower margins than before.

At the same time, the decline in margins appears to have been indicative of more deep-seated problems at Ross & Glendining, for Roslyn Mills was also struggling to make profits. After thirty years of progress, the quality of management in Dunedin was, perhaps, not all that it once was. John Ross certainly began to harbour doubts, becoming increasingly resistant to Robert Glendining's suggestions to invest still more capital in various parts of their enterprise. Glendining, now quite unwell, was most aggrieved.[73] After more than thirty years, their once-harmonious working relationship was beginning to break down.

SECTION THREE
# Expansion Against the Odds

# CONFLICT,
# 1889–1900

The problems facing Roslyn Mills were altogether more fundamental than those of the warehouse business or clothing factory. Like the rest of the enterprise, the mill benefited from the recovery of the late eighties, the annual value of output increasing to reach a peak of £65,527 by the end of 1892. The downturn that followed saw production cut back but, in spite of significant additions to capacity thereafter, it was not until the very end of the decade that the value of output recovered. Worse still, a failure to offer an acceptable product range at competitive prices meant that it was not possible to sell all that was produced. By 1898, stocks on hand exceeded annual output.[1] Meanwhile, the rest of the woollen and worsted industry prospered. A new mill, the Bruce Woollen Mills at Milton, came into production and existing mills added to capacity. As a result, the output of industry as a whole increased in value by almost 30 per cent in the ten years to 1901.[2]

## 1. A FOCUS ON QUALITY PRODUCTS

Roslyn Mills had started the decade well. The erection of additional spinning mules and looms, purchased by Glendining on his visit to Britain in 1888, added significantly to capacity, and the volume of wool processed increased by around 50 per cent in the five years that followed. The increase in the value of output was rather more modest, the growth in competition resulting in a squeeze on margins, especially on staple products such as flannels and tweeds.

To restore profitability, Lillico, the mill manager, gradually shifted the product range up market where it was easier to extract a price premium. Thus, in addition to worsted tweeds, a line of dress tweeds was introduced, more hosiery was manufactured, and better quality knitted pants and shirts were turned out.[3] The strategy made a lot of sense, the ability of Roslyn Mills to spin fine worsted yarns enabling it to compete at the more expensive end of the market. Indeed, quality products, marketed under the Roslyn brand, were increasingly in demand, although it was the lighter and cheaper makes that were preferred in the rapidly expanding northern markets. In the short run, however, such weaknesses in Roslyn Mills' product range were not evident and, with wool prices beginning to fall, profits rose to a record £6,053 (see Table 9.1).

TABLE 9.1
ROSLYN MILLS OUTPUT AND PROFITABILITY, 1890–1900 (£)

| Nov Year | 1890 | 1891 | 1892 | 1893 | 1894 | 1895 | 1896 | 1897 | 1898 | 1899 | 1900[a] |
|---|---|---|---|---|---|---|---|---|---|---|---|
| Output value | 57,625 | 60,275 | 65,527 | 62,559 | 48,424 | 53,640 | 59,034 | 59,854 | 59,260 | 60,136 | 72,036 |
| Scoured wool used (000 lbs) | 319.4 | 352.8 | 387.9 | 400.2 | 303.8 | 316.7 | 362.9 | 380.2 | 362.1 | 387.2 | 383.4 |
| Manufacturing profit | 12,824 | 14,629 | 17,318 | 16,544 | 8,165 | 18,629 | 16,096 | 14,565 | 11,267 | 18,949 | 2,799[f] |
| *Deductions* | | | | | | | | | | | |
| General expenses | 1,419[a] | 1,220 | 1,322 | 1,111 | 866 | 916 | 783 | 1,192 | 1,289 | 1,054 | [f] |
| Depreciation | 4,322[b] | 2,612 | 4,041[c] | 3,772 | 3,515 | 3,278 | 4,262[d] | 3,280 | 3,165 | 2,980 | [f] |
| Interest | 5,791 | 5,805 | 5,901 | 6,395 | 7,049 | 7,063 | 6,515[e] | 6,691 | 6,956 | 7,165 | [f] |
| Net profit | 1,291 | 4,491 | 6,053 | 5,266 | -3,266 | 7,371 | 4,537 | 3,401 | -143 | 7,750 | [f] |
| Net profit + interest (£000s) | 7.1 | 10.3 | 12.0 | 11.7 | 3.8 | 14.4 | 11.1 | 10.1 | 6.8 | 14.9 | [f] |
| Estimated average capital employed (£000s) | 82.7 | 82.9 | 84.3 | 91.4 | 100.7 | 100.9 | 98.0 | 111.5 | 115.9 | 119.4 | [f] |
| Return on capital (%) | 8.6 | 12.4 | 14.2 | 12.8 | 3.8 | 14.3 | 11.3 | 9.1 | 5.9 | 2.5 | [f] |

Sources: Half-yearly balances, AG 512 15/4–15/7.
Notes: (a) Includes £107 subscription to New Zealand & South Seas Exhibition. (b) Additional £1,599 on goods written down. (c) Following introduction of income tax in 1891, rate of depreciation on land & buildings was increased from 4 to 7.5 per cent, machinery increased from 7.5 to 10 per cent. This was in excess of that allowed by the taxation authorities. (d) Additional £766 on goods written down. (e) Imputed rate of interest reduced from 7 to 6 per cent at the end of July. (f) Basis of accounts change with adoption of limited liability in March 1900.

The buoyant economic conditions of the early 1890s allowed other woollen mills to make progress, too. The most successful were the Kaiapoi Woollen Manufacturing Company Ltd, just outside Christchurch, and the Wellington Woollen Manufacturing Company Ltd, located at Petone. Both were well capitalised joint stock concerns, with Kaiapoi having a fully paid-up capital of £100,000 in 1890, while the Wellington mills were partly paid to £38,650. Kaiapoi was somewhat larger in terms of the scale of its plant and machinery than Wellington, and it also operated a clothing factory in Christchurch. The capacity of Roslyn Mills probably fell somewhere between the two.[4]

Kaiapoi and Wellington manufactured a wide range of woollen goods although they did not, as yet, possess worsted spinning machinery. Consequently, when it came to producing cloth or knitted goods with a worsted content, they were obliged to buy in worsted yarns either from Roslyn Mills or overseas. Both mills tended to focus on lighter and less expensive goods, although why this should be the case is not entirely clear. Maybe they found it hard to compete with Roslyn in quality goods, or it might be that, following the recent tariff increases, they felt that this sector of the market offered greater opportunities. There was also the matter of access to raw materials. Hercus, who visited the mills at Petone in 1889, marvelled that they were able to make their cheap tweeds pay. The manager of the Wellington mills told Hercus that they would never have been able to show a profit with the sort of wool used by Roslyn. He bought wool up country, 'a very cheap, low class of rough wool such as we never see here.'[5]

With this sort of advantage, the Wellington Woollen Mills were able to make money from lower-quality cloths. In 1891, for example, the firm was happy to enter a contract with Bing, Harris & Co. to supply them with cheap flannels, blankets and tweeds – at a preferential discount of 15 per cent.[6] Shortly afterwards, Kaiapoi Woollen Mills contracted with Sargood, Son & Ewen to supply them with flannels bearing their own brand. These goods Sargoods threatened to sell 'at net cost to ruin Bing, Harris & Co.' Butterworth Brothers Ltd also began selling cheap flannels.[7]

Ross & Glendining were not to be drawn into this price war, their Christchurch and Wellington warehouses being instructed not to push low-priced flannels as the firm would lose money. Roslyn was, in any case, struggling to meet existing orders, leading Hercus to suggest to Ross that maybe additional buildings and machinery were called for.[8] Ross was clearly alarmed by this thought and Hercus was obliged to backtrack, replying that his comment was 'not intended to be a suggestion for present action'. Nevertheless, he did point out that there was an acute shortage of worsteds due to a want of producing power, and that orders for dress goods for delivery prior to May 1892 had to be declined. Tactfully, he suggested that Ross might want to consider the question of increasing mill capacity when he arrived later in the year[9]

## 2. STRUGGLING THROUGH A DEPRESSION

The year ending in November 1892 proved to be the high point of the decade for Roslyn Mills, with the downturn in trade beginning to bite thereafter. Matters were made incomparably worse when Lillico, who had played a vital role in transforming the scale and scope of the plant, departed in October to join a syndicate about to purchase the defunct South Canterbury Woollen

Manufacturing Company. Here he became managing director, successfully bringing the company back into production after years of neglect.[10] Meanwhile, the day-to-day management of Roslyn Mills was entrusted to Glendining's younger son, Robert Cassels Glendining. In his early twenties and with little experience, Bob Glendining was now called upon to steer the mill through the looming depression.

Economic conditions began to deteriorate towards the end of 1892 when commodity prices, already down from the peak of 1889, began to fall sharply once more. The situation became progressively worse thereafter. In 1893, an international financial crisis, occasioned by the collapse of Barings in London, saw capital flow back to the United Kingdom with a consequent tightening of local credit conditions. A run occurred on the Auckland Savings Bank, while the Colonial Bank of New Zealand, a largely South Island institution, experienced a sharp drop in deposits.

The troubles that beset the Bank of New Zealand in the eighties now resurfaced once again, hastened by a financial crisis in Australia that left the bank badly exposed. When, in 1894, the bank's associated loan company, the New Zealand Loan & Mercantile Agency, was obliged to suspend payment, failure seemed to be just around the corner. Such a calamity was unthinkable and, in order to save both the bank and the credit of the colony, the government was obliged to intervene. In June 1894, legislation was passed allowing the government to provide a guarantee of £2 million so that the Bank of New Zealand might continue trading.[11] This afforded temporary relief, a thoroughgoing reorganisation and capital reconstruction taking place the following year.

The depression was felt everywhere. The worst affected areas, however, appear to have been in the South Island, particularly Southland and Otago, where Ross & Glendining saw their sales decline continuously from 1893 onwards. Canterbury, too, experienced a sharp decline, especially in 1894, the Christchurch warehouse manager, W.S. Angus, being dismissed as sales and profits collapsed.

While trade in general suffered, Roslyn Mills was doubly unfortunate since the incidence of depression was most acute in precisely those areas in which mill sales were greatest. Not that the northern mills escaped the depression, the Wellington Woollen Manufacturing Company slashing the price of tweeds towards the end of 1893 in a fresh bout of price cutting. Shortly afterwards, the firm wrote to Ross & Glendining, inviting them to join in the formation of a New Zealand Woollen Manufacturers Association in order to fix prices. The invitation was declined. Whether this was due to the fact Roslyn could not afford to go down to Wellington and Kaiapoi prices or Glendining had no wish to cut the prices of branded goods, or merely reflected his suspicions concerning the durability and effectiveness of price associations, is unclear.[12]

In spite of the depression, the value of Roslyn Mills output fell only slightly during the course of 1893 while net profits, after payment of interest to partners, remained remarkably buoyant at £5,266 (see Table 9.1). This result was something of a mirage, for profits were calculated on the basis of revenues received from goods delivered to warehouse departments at purely nominal transfer prices. Once in the warehouses, prices might subsequently be reduced so as to clear stocks, reductions being taken through departmental accounts in the year in which they occurred.

Warehouse prices were indeed cut during the course of 1894 although, on this occasion, the reductions did little to reduce the level of stocks. When William Doughty, the firm's leading traveller, wrote from Wellington requesting lower prices on flannels and blankets, he received short shrift from Hercus:

> *The last reductions made bring the prices down to bed-rock, and we could not allow any concessions on all we sell of these lines, without leaving a loss instead of a profit at the end of the year. The difficulty in fixing these low net prices is that a few of the largest semi-wholesale buyers consider themselves entitled to some little concession in consideration of their larger purchases, and as the Kaiapoi people have been specially running after this class of customer offering any terms to secure orders we fixed the present discounts ... The goods cannot be produced and sold to any advantage to us under present prices, and any further concession such as you suggest would simply mean so much loss.*[13]

Whether the Kaiapoi Woollen Manufacturing Company was making money on such goods is not known – but Ross & Glendining most definitely were not. Gross margins on both blankets and flannels were only about 18 per cent, more than ten points lower than normal, while margins on all classes of goods barely averaged 20 per cent.[14] The combination of falling output, slim margins and rising inventory costs led to Roslyn Mills posting a loss of £3,266 in 1894.

The economy began to grow again in 1895, although commodity prices showed little signs of improvement. The capital reconstruction of the Bank of New Zealand in the middle of the year clearly helped matters. As usual, it fell to Hercus to keep Ross in London abreast with the financial affairs of the colony. Writing in September, his letter was suitably caustic:

> *Demands for renewals this month are unusually heavy. What it would have been if the Bank of New Zealand loss had not been staved off, as it has*

*been, we cannot imagine. Parliament seems to have made the best of a very bad job, but it is bad enough at best. The assets for which bonds of £2¾ million with interest are to be given, will not likely realise one third of that amount: and there will no doubt be further loss of the globo assets [dubious assets transferred off balance-sheet], about which they are judiciously silent. It is not too much to expect a loss of 3 million to the country, beside the shareholders' loss, before everything is settled. The London capitalists, who were so plastic in Mr. Ward's hands, will no doubt be disillusioned by this time, and they will not be so ready to lend at 3% to the next New Zealand Treasurer!*

Even so, Hercus thought that the forced realisation of some of the locked-up assets would come as a welcome relief to the country. Indeed, it might even encourage fresh enterprise.[15]

### 3. ROSLYN MILLS FALLS BEHIND

The market for woollen and worsteds began to improve even before banking affairs were settled. Wholesalers and retailers, after several years of depression, appear to have started to replenish their inventories and the lift in demand, in conjunction with low wool prices, allowed the mill-owners to rebuild their margins. The rapid improvement in trading conditions encouraged fresh investment to take place. Kaiapoi, with orders flooding in, made further extensions to their clothing factory in Christchurch so as to handle the additional business. They also opened a warehouse in Wellington to support their already extensive North Island clothing trade.[16] Later in the year, the Wellington Woollen Manufacturing Co. also opened a clothing factory in Wellington, close to the wharf, in order to capture a share of this growing trade.[17]

Robert Glendining had been extremely fortunate the previous year in his wool buying. With substantial stocks of wool on hand at very low prices, Roslyn Mills was now in a position to compete in virtually all types of goods. Young Bob Glendining, however, seems to have been incapable of restoring output to former levels. Thus in March 1895, Ross & Glendining were obliged to supply a customer with No. 1 quality blankets at a discount because the mill was unable to manufacture No. 2 quality fast enough. Nor did the possession of almost a year's output in stocks help matters much, the stock assortment being so poor that certain types of goods had to be sold at bargain basement prices to clear them out.[18] Even then, stocks remained stubbornly high.

In spite of the opportunities afforded by rapidly improving trade, Roslyn Mills continued to lag behind the market for the rest of 1895. By the November balance date, the total amount of wool processed during the year amounted to only 316,000 lbs, barely 5 per cent more than 1894. Profits were excellent, some £7,371, but the results were extremely flattering. Hercus, in the absence of Glendining senior who usually provided a commentary on the mill balance, pointed out to Ross that the good result was almost entirely the result of an exceptional profit made on the extra large wool purchases bought at extremely low prices. The profits derived from the sale of surplus wool had virtually halved the cost of wool actually used in manufacturing. Pure manufacturing profits, on the other hand, had only marginally improved, mainly because of a small increase in prices.

Clearly unhappy at this state of affairs, Hercus proceeded to paint a dim picture of what was actually going on at Roslyn Mills:

> It is satisfactory that the wool has carried us through so well this time: but we must do more manufacturing to make regular profits. What we turn out now is only three quarters of what we have turned out in former years with less machinery, and I am sure that the other mills are producing very much more in proportion to their plant than we are. The general expenses, interest and depreciation alone are costing us at present £5 per working hour. This goes on whether the machines are running or not. It takes about our regular profit on 350,000 lbs of goods to meet this. The surplus pays very well: but the profit is in the surplus: and we have been below that out-turn the last two years. What we want is a much larger output of tweeds, and a much larger factory: and we want the branches to take as full an interest in pushing Roslyn goods as imported goods.[19]

The inability to rack up output and take full advantage of the improvement in trade was almost certainly a reflection of young Glendining's lack of experience and limited managerial skills. At the same time, a decision appears to have been taken to accelerate the switch away from woollens towards worsteds and, in particular, worsted hosiery. Whether this was due to the fact the firm was simply unable to compete in many categories of woollens, or merely chose not to, is far from clear. In all probability, the decision would have been taken not by Bob Glendining, but by his father. After working closely with Lillico, Robert Glendining now considered himself to be an expert on all matters relating to woollen and worsted manufacturing in New Zealand. Whatever lay behind his thinking, the strategy led to machinery lying idle – 34 looms being broken up[20] – and a loom tuner being dismissed 'on account of our not requiring the same number of tuners' as hitherto.[21]

To help raise capacity, additional carding machinery was shipped out by Ross towards the end of 1895. Somewhat surprisingly, it was not pressed into immediate use, with Hercus making the pointed observation that there was little likelihood of it coming into service until the end of the following year. An additional £2,000 or so was also spent on hosiery and knitting machinery, including several '12-at-once' rib machines, two '6-at-once' pants machines, Rothwell automatic knitters and Hague seaming equipment.[22] The mills were reconfigured and the new equipment installed during the first half of 1896. Crucially, little provision was made for increasing combing and spinning capacity, the inability to produce sufficient yarns being the Achilles heel of the expanded enterprise.

The bottleneck in yarn production, previously noticed when the mills were running at full capacity four years earlier, began to bite towards the end of 1896. Manufacturing profits for the year were somewhat improved, with the return on capital employed equal to 11.3 per cent. Even so, results were still not as good as they should have been, often due to goods not being ready in time.[23] Some orders were refused outright. In November, a request from the Wellington Woollen Manufacturing Company to supply worsted yarn was declined, not because they were competitors, but because Roslyn Mills was unable to meet the needs of its own hosiery department.[24] A few days later, an apologetic letter was sent to an Invercargill customer for the non-delivery of tweeds. They were, he was told, a great favourite in the colony, and he would have the next piece as soon as it came off the loom.[25]

Capacity constraints also influenced the type of goods that Roslyn Mills produced. In the middle of 1897, Macky, Logan, Steen & Co., one of the leading warehouse firms in Auckland, was informed that Ross & Glendining had almost completely withdrawn from producing lower quality makes of flannels 'as it will take up our working capacity to produce other goods'. That being the case, they were unable to quote for such goods in advance.[26]

## 4. WAREHOUSES OFFERED GREATER INCENTIVES

Shortages of stock, an unwillingness to produce some of the lower quality goods, and Robert Glendining's failure to price as keenly as he might, meant that warehouse departments were obliged to buy in from outside. This was only to be expected on occasions but when, in 1897, the Wellington warehouse purchased yet another consignment from the Onehunga Woollen Mills, the manager, Jones, received a sharp letter from Hercus. In defence of his head salesmen, Jones pointed out that some customers had complained about the Roslyn range. Hercus was unmoved, arguing that taking the mill goods all round, 'they will hold their own with anything in the market'.[27] This was of little comfort to either Jones or his staff who were obliged to compete on price, quality and style for each and every sale they made.

This latest disagreement between Hercus and the warehouses was part of an ongoing conflict that had lasted for some years. At the heart of the matter lay the nature of incentives offered to head salesmen to sell mill goods, with commission being paid not on the basis of sales revenues, but on the profitability of each individual department. Robert Glendining, for reasons that had always puzzled Ross, transferred goods from the mill to the warehouse departments at prices close to those paid by retailers.[28] The departments were reimbursed for any costs they incurred in handling mill goods, but their ability to earn profits was dependent on the nature of the market and whether they were able to sell the goods at more than their transfer prices. This convoluted incentive system meant that the rewards salesmen received for selling Roslyn products were far less generous than those on goods bought in, especially imports. As a result, salesmen and travellers preferred the latter and had to be constantly urged to push mill goods.

In earlier years, when Roslyn goods were keenly priced and demand was increasing, the system seems to have worked well. Indeed, when dissecting departmental returns in 1888, Hercus commented that mill goods enabled the shirt department to earn good profits and they actually constituted 'the best spoke' in the haberdashery department's wheel.[29] By 1893, this was no longer the case. As part of the accounting reforms taking place at that time, attempts were made to encourage the warehouses to push mill goods by introducing a new charging system. Instead of each department charging Roslyn an arbitrary $12^{1}/_{2}$ per cent commission to cover the expenses involved in handling mill goods, they were now allowed to charge the actual costs incurred – usually in the region of 14 per cent. This, Hercus argued, was more equitable all round, especially as Roslyn Mills received double profit in that it received the full retail purchase price for many of their products.[30]

The new commission regime may have been more equitable than hitherto, but it still did not provide departmental salesmen with much of an incentive to sell. In March 1895, with sales of mill goods paltry compared to those of their rivals in the North Island, Hercus called upon warehouse staff and travellers to double their efforts so that Roslyn Mills might do more than simply cover its costs.[31] Such exhortations were to little avail. Apart from hosiery, the price, range and quality of many of the Roslyn goods were such that they simply did not sell themselves, especially in the North Island where the lighter wares of Kaiapoi and the Wellington Woollen Manufacturing Company were generally preferred. Improving economic conditions gradually enabled the branch warehouses to sell more mill goods, but Roslyn products still fell as a proportion of warehouse sales.[32]

The worst performing warehouse was Wellington, where sales of mill goods as a proportion of total business shrank from a third in the winter season of 1893 to less than a fifth by 1897. Convinced there was an irrational prejudice amongst the salesmen to articles produced at Roslyn, Hercus arranged for the person responsible for mill goods to be replaced. A new manager, formerly with Thompson, Shannon & Co., was appointed to head the Woollens and Clothing Department. It was therefore with some surprise that when Thomas Glendining visited Wellington in 1898, he found that the new man, a Mr Henry, was making no effort whatsoever to push Roslyn serges. Upon being questioned, Henry alleged that the branch manager had told him that he got no credit in his department for selling mill goods. How, therefore, was he to be compensated for pushing these goods?

Hercus was apoplectic, writing to Jones: 'We have had too much of this thing in the past …. We engage and pay men to sell the goods that it suits us best to sell, and expect them to do as they are told'. He was instructed to put things right with the veiled threat that things might change if he didn't.[33]

Hercus was clearly outraged by the attitude of the new departmental head and annoyed that Jones had not explained the incentive system in a more constructive way.[34] Nevertheless, there seems little doubt that he was well aware that the system of rewards still left a lot to be desired. In an attempt to circumvent the lack of enthusiasm exhibited by the warehouse staff, it was agreed that the top Wellington traveller, William Doughty, should be paid an enhanced commission on all Roslyn products sold.[35] This did not completely satisfy Doughty who had been expecting an increase in salary. Writing to Head Office, the traveller pointed out that what was really needed were cheaper and lighter mill goods so that he might meet the competition. His suggestions were passed to Robert Glendining for consideration but Hercus was unable to offer any promises as to the future, merely repeating that the firm could not make a profit on such goods.[36]

Yet something had to be done about prices and products because, although annual output of Roslyn Mills had remained roughly constant since 1896, stocks had risen while profits had steadily fallen (see Table 9.1). With trade deteriorating sharply in the middle of 1898, Robert Glendining was at last forced to act, cutting prices on a wide range of goods. He did so with great reluctance, complaining to Ross in a long, and increasingly extravagant letter,

> it does not put me in a good humour … going over every line that we make at the Mill to see how much we can reduce the _price_ of each article, this is not very nice work but it has to be done and done by myself … there is nothing that we make now but somebody trys and cuts the price below ours and although I say it myself, I can make cheaper at Roslyn than they can be made anywhere else in New Zealand, as in the first place the Mill

*is written down to a very much less sum than any of the other mills in the Colony, then the Roslyn Mill has only one <u>director</u> and he does not get any <u>screw</u>, then the Mill Manager does not get £500, £600 or £700 as other Mill Managers get, then we have no Engineers that go about in Black Coats and White Shirts as they have in the other Mills, then we do not pay any commission to Wool Buyers for buying the wool as other Mills do, and other things. With all this difference in working expenses you would think that we ought to be making our fortune very fast. The warehouse charges in Mill Goods sold is what sticks in my throat when I am making up cost, but for this I am tempted to say that I will make other Mills sell at a loss and the end of them would soon come, and no doubt it would.*

He continued to ramble on for several more pages, inviting Ross to run the mill at a loss for two years in order to bankrupt the opposition, and closing with the observation that the financier, Larnach, had just shot himself dead.[37]

### 5. DISAGREEMENTS BETWEEN THE PARTNERS MULTIPLY

Glendining's letters to Ross had always been on the discursive and rather colourful side. This letter, however, left Ross concerned. It is evident that the two had not seen eye-to-eye for some time, the original points of difference being Glendining's involvement in wool buying and his propensity to spend money on the mill. Increasingly, Ross called into question proposals made by Glendining, especially after the fiasco of the Shag Point coal mine.

Shag Point mine, about thirty miles north of Dunedin, had been bought by Glendining, together with a New Zealand partner, Hazlett, in 1889. It had been established in 1863 as a dip mine driven into the side of a hill, the workings subsequently going down under the sea as they followed a coal seam. By 1885 some 35 men were employed and over 170,000 tons of coal had been extracted.[38] Glendining and Hazlett had run into problems almost as soon as they bought the mine, with labour problems and flooding hampering production.[39] An opportunity to sell Shag Point arose when Glendining was in London in 1891 but, despite being advised by Hercus to get rid of the property, he remained bent on developing it himself.[40]

Further problems arose while Glendining was still out of the country and Hercus again urged him to sell:

*The ground is very broken and uncertain – even the seam you are going for is not extra thick or solid and the cost of working it has yet to be found out. Even the market is not very certain if you had an unlimited supply. Before you get down to the new seam, a great many expenses that cannot be foreseen must be met, and it is not unlikely the cost will be very much more than the estimate. And after that you would have to face much stronger competition than you have at present. Besides all of which, if you do succeed, the worry and trouble of it makes it not worth your while.*[41]

Glendining was unmoved, even persuading Ross to take over Hazlett's share of the concern. Whether Ross ever saw Hercus' careful analysis of the prospects for the mine seems doubtful. In any event, he must have regretted his decision to join his partner for, in addition to an initial outlay of £2,540, he was required to advance another £14,232 between 1892 and 1896 to buy pumps, pipes and other equipment and to pay for development work.[42] The mine hardly ever made a profit, being abandoned in 1902 after serious flooding.[43]

The Shag Point venture can only have made Ross more wary of his partner's schemes. Consequently when, in 1898, Glendining informed Ross that a larger wool store was needed – the implication being that he was going to increase the firm's involvement in the highly speculative wool trade – Ross replied that he thought the wool stores were large enough already. There was also the question of extending the hosiery factory and trebling the size of the clothing factory in Dunedin. Ross cannot have expressed much enthusiasm for these plans either, because Glendining, in high dudgeon, subsequently insisted that his partner should come out to New Zealand to see for himself what was really wanted. He, himself, had absolutely no intention of going to London, either for the benefit of his health or to explain his plans![44]

The conflict between the two partners got worse in 1899. Ross was prepared to relent over the extension to the hosiery plant, but only after visiting Nottinghamshire in February and talking to machinery makers and others in the trade. While there, he discovered a new and superior machine with an arrangement that allowed knitted woollen garments to be narrowed and widened. Capable of making pants, shirts and ladies' dresses, it would add 'very materially to mill plant' and should provide the firm with a strong competitive advantage in that area of business.[45] Having satisfied himself that the new machinery was worthwhile, Ross agreed that orders should be placed. Nevertheless, he warned Glendining the plant would have to be kept going if the investment was to pay.[46]

Glendining was also taken to task over the size of the bank overdraft. Apart from Shag Point mine, the other parts of the enterprise had returned substantial interest and profits since 1895. On top of the capital generated internally, the firm also continued to take in deposits from outside investors, upon which it paid 4 or 5 per cent interest. Much of the capital had originally come from the United Kingdom but in the 1890s, and probably not unconnected with problems experienced by New Zealand banks, many in the local community now chose to place their surplus funds with Ross & Glendining. Depositors included established business such as Wright Stephenson, numerous newly floated gold-mining companies, the Presbyterian Church, other institutions, and local worthies such as ship-owner Sir James Mills. At the beginning of 1899, deposits accepted by the firm amounted to more than £80,000.[47] Given the size of these deposits and the capital generated internally, Ross wondered why Glendining still had to rely on a bank overdraft.[48]

### 6. The adoption of Joint Stock Limited Liability

Although Ross was persuaded that additional hosiery machinery was needed, he refused to give way over the construction of a larger wool store. In the meantime, he pressed Glendining to consider whether or not it might be advantageous for the pair to convert the partnership into a joint stock limited liability company.

The adoption of joint stock limited liability by hitherto privately owned firms was very much in vogue in the United Kingdom at this time, with limited liability no longer regarded as a probable precursor to fraud. The advantages of incorporation must have become quickly apparent to John Ross. Both partners were now quite elderly, with Ross suffering from headaches and Glendining patently unwell. It therefore made excellent sense to adopt an ownership form in which the firm possessed its own corporate identity. This meant that in the event of the death of one or both of the partners, the firm would not be wound up and capital withdrawn. Instead, shares belonging to the deceased would simply be placed in the hands of executors. These shares might then be used to satisfy legacies, it being up to the beneficiaries as to whether they held or sold the shares. In the meantime, the day-to-day running of the firm would go on as normal, there being no need for executors to become involved in the practicalities of the business.

Quite apart from the ease of dividing and transferring property, there were other advantages to be had from adopting joint stock limited liability. Shares in the company might be gifted to members of the family or other legatees prior to death, thereby avoiding death duties. Capital might also be conserved by paying dividends in the form of shares. The disadvantages were minimal, for as long as there was no appeal to the general public for capital, there was no need to publish an annual balance sheet. All that was required was registration under the Companies Act of 1882.

Glendining seemed quite unwilling to discuss the question of joint stock limited liability, although one can only speculate why this should be the case.[49] Possibly his autocratic style did not take kindly to the appointment of a local board of directors which might constrain his freedom of action. Maybe he thought Ross was trying to seize control of Ross & Glendining to the detriment of Glendining family interests. What is evident, though, is that his behaviour had now become both irrational and extremely disagreeable; he had even managed to fall out with his long-time friend, James Johnstone, of Wright Stephenson.[50] In May 1899, and in all probability under the influence of drink, he wrote an unpleasant letter to Ross insisting that a bigger wool store be built and demanding that his partner should come out to New Zealand straight away.[51]

Ross was quite taken aback by the tone of this letter and made his feelings known. By this stage, however, he had already decided that the only way to move things forward was to return to New Zealand.[52] During the next few months he visited the hosiery machinery makers in the Midlands, discussing the dimensions and technical requirements of the new equipment, and liaising with Dunedin. This resulted in a more powerful steam engine being ordered, together with pulleys and shafting to drive the machinery. In November the bulk of the machinery was shipped.[53]

Just before Christmas, with all outstanding business completed, John Ross sailed from Marseilles.[54] He was accompanied by his eldest son, John Sutherland Ross. Known as 'Sutherland' in order to avoid confusion, the young man had been educated at an English public school, spent time at the University of Leipzig, and had served an apprenticeship with a retail draper in London. He was now coming out to New Zealand to learn the business.

The reception that awaited Ross senior and junior in Dunedin was not exactly cordial. Glendining took an instant dislike to Sutherland Ross, who was summarily dispatched to Wellington to learn the warehouse trade under the tutelage of the manager, David Jones. This was not at all what Ross senior had in mind, since he really wanted his son to study the clothing manufacturing business in Dunedin. Fortunately, Sutherland Ross got on well with Jones, even if the latter did not approve of the young man's 'German learned' notions of religion.[55] After a while, Jones suggested to Ross senior that it might be advantageous for Sutherland to work his way around the firm to gain further experience. Naturally Ross concurred, but Glendining was adamant that Sutherland should stay in Wellington, even suggesting that he might study book-keeping.[56] This refusal to allow Sutherland Ross to gain experience in clothing manufacturing was to have fatal consequences for Ross & Glendining Ltd.

The main task facing John Ross on arrival, however, was the conversion of Ross & Glendining into a joint stock limited liability company. Glendining was soon persuaded that conversion was in his interest. With agreement reached as to how the company should be structured, instructions were given to solicitors to draw up a memorandum of association. Ross & Glendining

Ltd was to be registered with a nominal capital of £500,000, divided into 15,000 preference and 35,000 ordinary shares of £10 each. The seven original subscribers, as required by law, were the two partners, Glendining's two sons John Ross Glendining and Robert Cassels Glendining, his brother Thomas Glendining, John Sutherland Ross and George Robertson Hercus.[57] The company was duly incorporated on 5 March 1900.[58]

The next step was to complete a valuation of those assets that the partners wished to transfer to Ross & Glendining Ltd. These were to include the land, buildings, machinery and stocks at Roslyn Mills, the clothing factory, and the five warehouses. The partners' sheep runs and other properties were not included. The valuation finally arrived at was £263,520, the value of the properties being based on government assessment values, while plant and stocks were taken in at book values as per the final balance. The existence of goodwill was recognised but not included in the valuation. The new firm commenced trading on 19 March 1900 although the formal transfer of assets had yet to occur.[59]

Final settlement took place at the beginning of April when Ross & Glendining Ltd purchased the assets of the firm by issuing 15,000 preference shares and 11,352 ordinary shares, fully paid to £10.[60] A further 6,148 ordinary shares were issued later in the month, taking the total paid-up capital of the new concern up to £325,500. The preference shares were held solely by John Ross and Robert Glendining. The ordinary shares they divided between themselves, their families, and senior managers in New Zealand and London.[61] Strict conditions were attached to share ownership, with all shareholders being obliged to offer their shares to the board for reallocation should they wish to sell. This ensured that although Ross & Glendining Ltd had now adopted joint stock limited liability, it remained essentially a family firm.

With Ross & Glendining Ltd safely floated and Robert Glendining installed as chairman of the board, John Ross sailed for the United Kingdom once more. He did so with some misgivings, for he was privately dismayed by the conduct of Robert and Bob Glendining, both in their attention to business and by their overindulgence in alcohol. There was the consolation that, at Head Office, Ross had Hercus on his side: in Wellington, he had become quite friendly with Jones. Both were happy to keep him informed about what was really happening in Dunedin, writing to him confidentially when the occasion arose. Nevertheless, Ross felt that it would not be long before he was forced to return to New Zealand.[62]

## TABLE 9.2
## ROSS & GLENDINING LTD. SHARE ALLOCATION APRIL 1900

**£10 Preference Shares**

| | | | |
|---|---|---|---|
| John Ross | 7,500 | Robert Glendining | 7,500 |

**£10 Ordinary Shares – Family**

| | | | |
|---|---|---|---|
| John Ross | 7,500 | Robert Glendining | 5,700 |
| Mrs Margaret W. Ross | 900 | Mary Glendining | 500 |
| John Sutherland Ross | 100 | John Ross Glendining | 500 |
| Thomas Cassels Ross | 100 | Robert Cassels Glendining | 500 |
| Walter Alexander Ross | 100 | Miss Nancy Isabella Glendining | 100 |
| Miss Jessie Linson Ross | 50 | Miss Margaret Linson Glendining | 100 |
| Miss Mary Cassels Ross | 50 | | |
| Miss Margaret Zealandia Ross | 50 | Thomas Glendining (brother) | 600 |

**£10 Ordinary Shares – Management**

| | | | |
|---|---|---|---|
| George Hercus (Dun) | 200 | David Jones (Wgtn) | 50 |
| Bedo Boys (UK) | 100 | Alexander Henderson (Ch) | 50 |
| James Gibson (UK) | 100 | Samuel Strain (Ch) | 50 |
| Percy Brodie (Inv) | 50 | Robert Wilson (Napier) | 50 |

*Source: Directors Meeting – Fair Minutes 23.04.1900, AG 512 8/1.*

# GOVERNMENT LAND POLICY AND THE RETREAT FROM SHEEP FARMING

The general improvement in trading conditions from the mid-nineties onwards was associated with the global upturn in primary product prices. The market for wool and lamb began to recover in 1895 and over the next ten years prices rose by around one third. Dairy farming also experienced an upturn in prices, the expansion of dairying, together with productivity gains across agriculture, contributing to a rise in per capita incomes.[1] Lauder Station benefited from the upturn in prices, returning substantial and increasing profits from 1898 onwards. Yet management of the sheep runs was far from straightforward, the demands for land by settlers leading to the introduction of legislation that saw leases of pastoral runs revoked and better land being reserved for closer settlement. Faced with the progressive loss of low country, by 1905 both John Ross and Robert Glendining were ready to throw in their leases and abandon sheep farming altogether.

### 1. RUNHOLDERS AND LAND REFORM

The architect of the major pieces of land legislation was the Liberal Minister of Lands and Agriculture, John McKenzie. His 1891 bill, which contained the one-run-per-man clause, failed to pass the Upper House but in the following year a modified bill became law. The Land Act of 1892 effectively spelt the end of large runs based on pastoral leases. Henceforth, no runs leased by the Crown were to be larger than was sufficient to carry twenty thousand sheep, except under special circumstances. Land classified as suitable for both pastoral and agricultural use was to be subdivided into runs of no more than 5,000 acres, and no person or company was to hold more than one run. An earlier, if largely ignored provision of land legislation, that pastoral lessees might have their leases cancelled at twelve months' notice should the Government require land for closer settlement, was carried over and applied to Class 2 pastoral-agricultural leases. To placate large leaseholders, McKenzie agreed to provide security of tenure for up to twenty-one years for lessees of purely pastoral land, now classified as Class 1 pastoral lands. They were also supposed to have sufficient low country for working their stations, but how this was to operate in practice was nowhere stipulated.[2]

The strategies employed by Ross & Glendining in 1891 to secure low country and protect Lauder Station from the legislation proposed by McKenzie proved to be only partially successful. Their speedy acquisition from Frank Pogson of remnants of the Blackstone Hill and Highfield runs did indeed enable them to pre-empt the restrictions relating to one-run-per-man. But their actions in grabbing land ahead of McKenzie's new bill aroused fierce resentment amongst the settler population.

A letter to the *Mt. Ida Chronicle* in October 1891 gave expression to popular feelings in Otago:

> *Sir, – You had a local the other week in your paper that should have had a black border round it. It referred to the sale of Mr. F.G. Pogson's property .... How is it possible for our business people to prosper, or the district to survive, if men such as Ross & Glendining and the Mt. Ida Pastoral Co. are allowed to hold nearly half a million acres between them .... Witness the sections that were sold the other day – no less than 30 applicants for each of them! Should any poor devil want 50 acres, a lawyer is employed to make all sorts of protest that it should not be granted to him. If there is one place more than another where the Hon. J. McKenzie's Land Bill is required, it is here.*[3]

The situation was further inflamed when it was learnt that Ross & Glendining had also secured temporary rights to graze sheep over Government reserves in the Maniototo, courtesy of their old friend Maitland, the Commissioner of Crown Lands for Otago.[4]

Given the growing pressure from settlers, it is not surprising that the Liberal Government should take steps to release land for closer settlement even before their Land Act became law. In February 1892, a number of run holders in Otago were given the statutory twelve months' notice that their fourteen-year pastoral leases were to be cancelled. Ross & Glendining, surprised that this hitherto ignored provision of Crown pastoral leases was now to be enforced, received notice that a 'large portion of Highfield and Blackstone Hill' was to be taken.[5] Through Maitland it was agreed that as from 1 March 1893, the government would resume some 10,000 acres at Blackstone Hill and a further 20,000 acres at Highfield. The remains of the two subdivided runs were to be re-let to Ross & Glendining on secure leases for a term of three years. At the same time, a further 2,185 acres was cut from Lauder block 224d and re-let for one year.[6] At a stroke, therefore, the expanded Lauder Station lost approximately one fifth of its acreage, with a further fifth now subject to short leases. That which remained on long pastoral leases tended to be the more mountainous stretches of the Home Hills, Lauder, and Hawkdun runs.

The loss of 30,000 acres of mainly low land to the Government necessarily forced Elliott to reduce the size of the Lauder flock. The ability to lease back parcels of land until required for settlement helped to ease matters, but sheep numbers fell from a peak of over 87,000 in February 1893 to around 60,000 head in the late 1890s. The reduction in sheep numbers slashed the returns derived from the wool clip. Unfortunately, lower returns from wool were not immediately offset by a surplus on the sheep account, the forced sales of surplus stock at below book value producing a deficit. The balance sheet took further hits from losses due to rabbits and by the conservative accounting policies of Hercus, who progressively reduced the book value of sheep to reflect the decline in wool and mutton prices.

## 2. SNOWSTORMS AND STOCK LOSSES

With surplus stock disposed of, book values written down to a minimum and lamb production up, Elliott may have been forgiven for thinking that the station might soon return to profitability. Certainly he would have hoped so, given that he had a one third share in any profits earned. Fate decreed otherwise, for agricultural prices continued to fall while the winter of 1895 in the South Island produced the worst snowstorms in living memory.

Snow began to fall in Otago and Canterbury in May, further falls and severe frosts ensuring that in the high country snow lay on the ground for up to three months. The low temperatures and lack of feed spelt disaster for many high country stations, in some instances an almost total loss of stock being recorded. At Morven Hills, 10,000 wethers were snowed in and offered free to anyone who cared to rescue them.[7] In the Ida Valley, snow was level with the tops of fences while at Blackstone Hill the ground was covered for several months before a slow thaw commenced. Despite Elliott's best efforts to save sheep by creating tracks for them to reach shelter, many died of exposure, starvation or the effects of eating each others' ears and wool.[8] The annual loss at Lauder amounted to 33,322 sheep or 49.8 per cent of the total flock, compared to normal losses of around 5 per cent.[9] Worse still, many of the sheep that survived were in very poor condition and had to be culled, adding to the cost of replacing the flock. In total, losses were estimated at £12,000.[10]

The stock losses bore particularly heavily upon tenants of crown pastoral leases who farmed the bulk of the high country. After representation from run holders and the Otago Agricultural & Pastoral Society, the government tabled a bill in late September 1895 with a view to providing relief. Glendining lost no time trying to influence the outcome by writing to the Minister of Lands. Once again he condemned the 'dangerous experiment' of attempting to work high country runs without sufficient low country. The remains of runs

224 and 225 left in the partners' hands after the 1892 cancellation of leases, he told the Minister, were 'quite inadequate for the purpose'. The leases to these runs expired in 1896 and 1897, but even if they were renewed to fall in line with the expiry date of the other Lauder leases, stock levels would have to be reduced to avoid further disasters. Glendining concluded by arguing that rents were far too high, having only been offered on the understanding that the government would continue 'the practice invariably pursued until 1892, of allowing the leases to run their course ...' [11]

The Liberal Government, while sympathetic to the problems of crown tenants, was not prepared to take steps that might slow the process of settlement. Consequently the Pastoral Tenants Relief Act, which rapidly became law, contained provisions that provided merely for a remission of rent, the extension of existing leases or the surrender and re-issue of new ones, and the remission of sheep tax of £1 per thousand sheep levied under the Stock Act of 1893. The Relief Act was to be administered by the local Land Board, which would consider applications for relief.[12] The policy towards low country remained unchanged, with Class 2 agricultural-pastoral runs continuing to be let on the basis that they might be resumed for settlement at any time.

The legislation clearly did not satisfy Glendining's major demand, namely, that secure access be provided to low country. Nevertheless, the provision that allowed for the surrender and re-issue of leases did allow scope for negotiation. The partners' first gambit was to offer to surrender all their leases, the runs then to be combined and re-let to them as a Class 1 run under a single license for a term of fourteen years. The Minister, through the Land Board, was perfectly happy to issue a Class 1 license to cover the pastoral runs of Lauder, Home Hills, and Hawkdun, all of which might then be let to Ross & Glendining on a secure 14-year tenancy at £900 per annum. The agricultural–pastoral land at Blackstone Hill and Highfield was a different matter. McKenzie was only prepared to lease this land as a Class 2 run, with the Government reserving the right to give twelve months notice at any time throughout a 14-year lease. Highfield blocks 225c and 225e were to be resumed on the expiry of their leases in 1896, with the latter re-let on a yearly basis until required for settlement. A remission of sheep tax on 29,054 sheep, amounting to £30, was also to be granted.[13]

The offer to lease the whole of Lauder, Home Hills, and Hawkdun as a Class 1 run at approximately half the previous rental was welcomed by Ross & Glendining. The uncertainty of tenure that arose from the designation of Blackstone Hill and Highfield as Class 2 runs, and the loss of 225e from the latter, nevertheless gave rise for concern:

> *To accept a long lease of the mountain runs with an uncertain tenure of even the small remnant of low country now left to work with, would involve very much greater risk of loss to us than that which we protested against when the other portion of lower lands was resumed .... Unless the Board can see its way to grant us a fixed tenure over the whole country, we regret that we do not feel justified in attempting any longer to carry on the mountain runs.*[14]

Given the strong pressures for settlement from Central Otago, McKenzie was not prepared to change his mind over Blackstone Hill and Highfield. He was, however, prepared to offer the Class 2 runs on a three-year lease, after which time the question of land for settlement might be revisited. In addition, some 2,000 acres of low country adjacent to Lauder 226b, previously held on a temporary license, might now be included as part of the Class 1 run.[15] When Glendining learnt that the Class 2 lease might still be interrupted at any time, the compromise was rejected and the intention to surrender all leases reiterated.[16]

The threat by a major run holder to abandon sheep farming appears to have provoked an immediate response from McKenzie. In a telegram to Maitland, full of nods and winks, he stated,

> *The modifications of the original proposition of the Board, which Mr. Glendining now wants, seem already agreed upon, excepting the rent for the high runs which I left to the Board to settle. The only question remaining is the low country which can be leased as previously proposed by the Board for 14 years ... I could not however give a guarantee that the land will not be resumed at any time, as such a guarantee would be illegal: but Mr. Glendining could be informed that unless there are strong and urgent demands for settlement he will not be disturbed in his leases. The question will depend on a bona fide demand for land for settlement being found in the district after enquiry.*[17]

The possibility that the low country at Blackstone Hill and Highfield might be resumed at any time, notwithstanding the assurances of the Minister, still worried Glendining. After protracted negotiations, in which the Land Board chaired by Maitland decided to reduce rents still further, he nevertheless agreed to take up both the Class 1 and Class 2 runs for fourteen years.[18]

Despite their failure to gain secure tenancies for the lower ground, there seems little doubt that Ross & Glendining secured substantial benefits by exploiting the provisions of the Pastoral Tenants Relief Act. First, their ability to renegotiate their leases enabled them to circumvent the provisions of the Land Act of 1892, which prohibited a single person or company from holding more than one run. Second, although they were unable to lease Blackstone Hill and Highfield on secure tenancies, they were able to have over 2,000 acres of lower ground adjacent to Lauder included in their Class 1 run. Furthermore, run 225c, which was to be surrendered, was now included in the Class 2 run. Finally, a significant reduction in rentals was obtained as compensation for the risks born, the rentals and license fees falling from £2,821 in 1896 to £1,454 in 1897.

Ross & Glendining were not alone in obtaining such comprehensive relief from the Government, with crown tenants of all descriptions obtaining remissions and reductions valued at over £50,000. However, they were clearly major beneficiaries, their annual rent reductions amounting to almost one fifth of the reduction of £7,090 granted to all pastoral lessees who, together, farmed over 3.2 million acres in Otago and Canterbury.[19]

## 3. The introduction of new breeds

The mid-nineties marked the nadir in the fortunes of sheep farming in New Zealand, after which profitability began to improve. For run holders such as Ross & Glendining, the reduction in rents made a healthy contribution to finances. Of greater importance was the fact that on international markets the prices of wool and meat both began to trend upwards once more. Prices were still subject to short-term fluctuations due to seasonal variations, the state of the British economy, and other external factors such as the Boer War in South Africa, but they continued to rise until 1914. Profitability was also aided by the fact that following the disasters at the Bank of New Zealand and the Colonial Bank in the early nineties, the nation's financial institutions were now on a firm footing. This, together with prudence in government expenditure, helped to ensure that the rise in sheep returns over these years was real rather than the result of inflation.[20]

The Merino sheep at Lauder, while excellent for the production of wool, had neither the carcass weight nor conformity required for the frozen meat trade. This was well understood by Elliott who, in the late 1880s, had crossed several hundred Merino ewes with Leicester rams to supply the station hands with better quality mutton. Yet while a few hundred half-bred sheep continued to be kept at Blackstone Hill, the lack of low ground meant that Elliott was hard pushed to breed sufficient lambs to maintain stock levels, let alone generate a surplus of fat lambs to sell off station. When, following the acquisition of Pogson's land in the early nineties, it was finally decided to increase the production of half-bred sheep, Glendining opted for a Merino/Cheviot cross. Although not as widely used as Leicesters, Cheviots were particularly well suited to cold mountainous conditions and were not prone to difficult lambing. Some 1,696 half-bred lambs were produced at Lauder in 1894.[21]

Given that a premium of upwards of 2/- per head was paid for young half-bred and cross-bred sheep sold off the station, there was every incentive to modify the flock composition still further. The heavy losses incurred during the big snow of 1895 provided an ideal opportunity for change, for extensive restocking had to take place in order to bring the station up to its normal carrying capacity. McKenzie's comments concerning the future resumption of the Class 2 runs were also reassuring. Believing that they effectively had security of tenure over their low country, Ross & Glendining now began to produce sheep more suitable for the freezer trade.

### 4. THE ACQUISITION OF BAREWOOD ESTATE

In 1895, the partners acquired a 14-year lease to the 30,000 acre Barewood Estate from the University of Otago. This run, part of a government endowment used to fund the University, came onto the market in 1894 when the tenant indicated that he could no longer pay the rent of £1,200 per annum.[22] The partners took it up at an annual rental of £900 per annum, the University being paid a further £750 for improvements that had been made to the property. Additional expenditure of £941 was incurred as alterations and repairs were made to buildings, gates replaced and new fencing erected.[23]

Barewood Estate was located just south of Middlemarch, half-way to Dunedin. Glendining had considered taking up the lease back in 1880 when Elliott, in conjunction with Reid, the estate agent, had reported, 'It is composed of comparatively low-lying well-grassed hills and downs (no swamps) and is situate in the forks of the Taieri and Sutton rivers on the one hand, and the Deep Stream on the other, forming as they do, almost unequalled natural boundaries'. The stock levels at Barewood were much higher than those of Lauder and carried a flock of 18,000 Cheviot cross-bred sheep. Elliott thought this number of sheep too high and their condition would suffer.[24] George Maider, appointed to manage Barewood at £100 per annum, all found, evidently took a similar view, for stock levels rarely exceeded 16,000 thereafter.

With an eye to accountability, Barewood and Lauder were worked as independent profit centres, an annual balance sheet being drawn up for each every February. Nevertheless, there was close cooperation between Elliott and Maider, with a regular traffic of sheep occurring between the two properties.[25]

Typically, Cheviot cross-breds were sent up to Lauder while Merino moved in the opposite direction.

## 5. MAKING MONEY FROM BREEDING

At the heart of the breeding programme at Lauder Station was a small pure-bred Cheviot flock. By 1897, a flock of 179 ewes and rams had been assembled, including a pedigree ram – the 'Auctioneer'. The sole purpose of the flock was to produce pure-bred Cheviot rams to put across Merino and half-bred ewes. There was also a smaller flock of ninety two-tooth Romneys, including forty-one rams, and sixty-three full-mouthed Leicester rams.[26] Later that year, Elliott entered his sheep at the Naseby Show, receiving prizes for all including 'best-in-show' for a Leicester ram.[27] The Lauder flock, nevertheless, remained about 60 per cent pure Merino, the ewes providing the basis for the production of half-bred and cross-bred lambs that yielded an ideal combination of meat and wool.

The decision to introduce Cheviots to Lauder doubtless seemed reasonable given the nature of much of the terrain, but after several years Elliott began to doubt their suitability. The fleeces of the Leicester cross-breds, he told Glendining, were far superior to the Cheviot cross-breds, both in terms of quantity and quality.[28] These concerns were later conveyed to Ross by Glendining:

> The Cheviots are a fine handy sheep and are doing very well but they don't give much weight of wool … there is so much (coarse wool) grown now owing to so many sheep being bred for freezing that it is bound to be a low price for many years to come …. I am beginning to think that it was a mistake on our part to go into Cheviots or long-woolled sheep at all, but we did not see that three years ago'.[29]

Cheviots nevertheless continued to be used at the station, albeit with Romney, Leicester and Merino sheep in the production of cross-bred stock.[30]

In spite of Glendining's misgivings, from 1897 onwards Lauder Station turned out to be extremely profitable. Gross profits from breeding were much improved, running at over £2,000 per annum in the late nineties. At first, most of the young stock was retained on station, helping to rebuild the flock, which had fallen to just over 43,000 head following the snows of 1895. After a couple of years, flock numbers had recovered and sheep sales resumed. Initially sales were of culls, still only fetching around 2/- per head. From 1900 onwards, however, a regular surplus of young half-bred and cross-bred stock was being produced, with some 3,000 to 5,000 wethers sold annually. These generally made a minimum of 12/- each, the cash generated by such sales together with the production of replacement stock lifting the gross profit on breeding account to over £3,000 per annum.[31]

Returns from wool also improved, wool production from the mixed flock averaging sixteen bales per 1000 sheep, compared to just over fourteen bales for the pure Merino flock.[32] Coarser wools, as Glendining observed, generally made lower prices than pure Merino, yet this did not prevent the average price per bale of Lauder wool sold in London increasing from around £10 in 1895 to £17 in 1906. The combination of increased fleece weights and an upward trend in wool prices saw gross profits on the wool account rise from £6,815 to £11,625 over the same period. By the latter date, the total net profit of Lauder Station had soared to £13,147 per annum, even though flock numbers had fallen by around a fifth to just over 51,000 sheep (see Table 10.1).

## 6. STRUGGLES AT BAREWOOD

Barewood Estate was altogether less profitable than Lauder Station, Ross & Glendining incurring losses in all but three of the first ten years the property was in their possession (Table 10.2). Part of the problem was that they had agreed to make £1,500 worth of improvements. Of course, in the long run improvements yielded benefits in terms of increased output. In the meantime, however, the expenditure of between £200 and £300 per annum was incurred as a cost in the profit and loss accounts, depressing the results accordingly. Barewood, like Lauder Station, also had to pay interest on capital employed but while the imputed rate of interest fell from 7 to 6 per cent in 1900, charges of up to £500 per annum still weighed heavily on profits.

Yet even if one ignores the cost of improvements and imputed interest charges, it is clear that in most years the rate of return on capital was only in the region of a few per cent. Heavy stock losses in the winter of 1903 wiped out even these slender gains, with Hercus informing Ross that over a period of nine years the estate had incurred a loss of £373, plus the interest on capital foregone for the whole period.[33]

A number of factors contributed to the relatively poor performance of Barewood. For a start, rents were proportionately greater than those at Lauder Station, the average rental per sheep being as much as nine pence per head higher. It was also more heavily committed to obtaining returns from sheep breeding than Lauder. To aid the Barewood breeding programme, two pedigree Cheviot rams and fifty-five ewes had been imported from Scotland during the course of 1895.[34] This was an expensive departure, for the sheep had to be accompanied all the way by a shepherd, while fodder on the voyage alone cost £63. All in all, the expenditure on the purchase and importation of fifty-seven pedigree sheep amounted to £647. Given the uncertainty regarding the suitability of Cheviots, it would appear that this outlay constituted a poor investment – unless cups at agricultural shows were a consideration!

The main problem at Barewood, however, seems to have been that George Maider was not a very effective manager. Glendining had first expressed his

# TABLE 10.1
## LAUDER STATION: SUMMARY PROFIT & LOSS ACCOUNTS, 1893–1907 (£)

| Feb Year | 1893 | 1894 | 1895 | 1896 | 1897 | 1898 | 1899 | 1900 | 1901 | 1902 | 1903 | 1904 | 1905 | 1906 | 1907 |
|---|---|---|---|---|---|---|---|---|---|---|---|---|---|---|---|
| **Gross profit** | | | | | | | | | | | | | | | |
| Sale of wool | 9,542 | 7,531 | 6,815 | 4,124 | 5,111 | 7,153 | 8,445 | 5,323 | 6,037 | 7,642 | 8,143 | 6,447 | 10,717 | 11,625 | 11,331 |
| Sheep breeding | 878 | -217 | -792 | -4,338 | 2,394 | 2,248 | 2,489 | 2,584 | 3,335 | 3,136 | 2,379 | -429 | 3,205 | 6,313 | 18,376 |
| Cattle/other | 34 | 800 | 110 | 708 | 344 | 78 | 84 | 435 | 431 | 664 | 680 | 726 | 824 | 1,167 | 2,066 |
| Total gross profit | 10,454 | 8,114 | 6,133 | 494 | 7,869 | 9,479 | 11,018 | 8,342 | 9,803 | 11,442 | 11,202 | 6,744 | 14,746 | 19,105 | 31,773 |
| **Costs** | | | | | | | | | | | | | | | |
| Rents/licences | 3,370 | 2,980 | 2,848 | 2,821 | 1,454 | 1,363 | 1,363 | 1,363 | 1,363 | 1,363 | 1,362 | 1,700 | 1,700 | 1,700 | 1,762 |
| Interest | 3,614 | 2,629 | 2,423 | 2,302 | 1,861 | 1,537 | 1,544 | 1,540 | 1,426 | 1,460 | 1,487 | 1,450 | 1,586 | 1,325 | 1,158 |
| Depreciation etc. | 1,992 | 1,661 | 941 | 887 | 1,467 | 1,105 | 891 | 844 | 769 | 935 | 807 | 760 | 1,154 | 858 | 892 |
| Salaries/wages | 1,236 | 1,258 | 1,149 | 1,188 | 1,297 | 1,300 | 1,742 | 1,582 | 1,994 | 1,563 | 1,691 | 1,649 | 1,524 | 1,490 | 1,922 |
| Rabbits | 851 | 1,007 | 1,152 | 369 | 450 | 600 | 475 | -7 | 179 | 205 | 243 | 136 | 161 | 154 | 99 |
| Stores | 398 | 296 | 297 | 385 | 332 | 473 | 848 | 390 | 536 | 458 | 133 | 856 | 509 | 431 | 299 |
| Net profit [loss] | [1,007] | [1,716] | [2,678] | [7,459] | 988 | 3,102 | 4,156 | 2,630 | 3,536 | 5,458[a] | 5,479 | 192 | 8,113 | 13,147 | 25,641[b] |
| Profit + interest | 2,607 | 913 | -255 | -5,157 | 2,849 | 4,639 | 5,700 | 4,170 | 4,961 | 6,918 | 6,966 | 1,642 | 9,699 | 13,136 | – |
| Estimated average capital employed | 51,628 | 37,557 | 34,614 | 32,888 | 31,017 | 25,617 | 25,733 | 25,666 | 23,750 | 24,333 | 24,783 | 24,166 | 26,433 | 22,083 | – |
| Return on capital (%) | 5.0 | 2.4 | -0.1 | -15.7 | 9.2 | 18.1 | 22.1 | 16.2 | 20.9 | 28.4 28.1 | 6.8 | 36.7 | 59.5 | – | – |

Sources: Half-yearly balances, AG 512 15/4–15/7. Notes: (a) Profit includes 10% paid to Elliott and subsequently Armour between 1902 and 1906. (b) In 1907 Lauder Station was resumed and hence the profit includes operating profit for the year and surplus over book value when stock, implements and effects were sold.

TABLE 10.2
BAREWOOD ESTATE: SUMMARY PROFIT AND LOSS ACCOUNTS, 1896–1909 (£)

| Feb Year | 1896 | 1897 | 1898 | 1899 | 1900 | 1901 | 1902 | 1903 | 1904 | 1905 | 1906 | 1907 | 1908 | 1909 |
|---|---|---|---|---|---|---|---|---|---|---|---|---|---|---|
| **Gross profit** | | | | | | | | | | | | | | |
| Sale of wool | 1,466 | 1,324 | 1,305 | 1,504 | 1,369 | 781 | 787 | 1,181 | 738 | 1,580 | 2,163 | 2,703 | 2,330 | 2,391 |
| Sheep breeding | 1,192 | 834 | 706 | 1,170 | 1,707 | 1,295 | 1,037 | 830 | -358 | 924 | 1,193 | 1,312 | 939 | 5,066 |
| Cattle/other | 10 | 15 | 23 | 94 | 56 | 115 | 60 | 111 | 24 | 27 | 42 | 117 | 63 | 357 |
| Burnt grass | | | | | | | | | | | | | 516 | |
| Total gross profit | 2,668 | 2,173 | 2,034 | 2,768 | 3,312 | 2,191 | 1,884 | 2,122 | 404 | 2,531 | 3,398 | 4,132 | 3,848 | 7,818 |
| **Costs** | | | | | | | | | | | | | | |
| Rents/licences | 1,050 | 900 | 900 | 900 | 900 | 872 | 894 | 894 | 894 | 894 | 894 | 894 | 894 | 965 |
| Interest | 582 | 790 | 609 | 579 | 495 | 465 | 499 | 535 | 497 | 339 | 368 | 374 | 322 | 317 |
| Depreciation etc.[a] | 602 | 774 | 542 | 597 | 641 | 657 | 538 | 443 | 640 | 578 | 658 | 613 | 456 | 180 |
| Salaries/wages | 276 | 322 | 359 | 387 | 383 | 408 | 442 | 355 | 455 | 419 | 535 | 559 | 654 | 681 |
| Rabbits | 352 | 131 | 185 | 81 | 6 | -109 | -17 | -40 | 199 | 173 | 136 | 73 | 76 | 50 |
| Stores | 321 | 390 | 145 | 179 | 178 | 119 | 221 | 158 | 177 | 117 | 169 | 217 | 230 | 187 |
| Net profit [loss] | [516] | [1,134] | [705] | 45 | 530 | [219] | [695] | [223] | [2,456] | 11 | 637 | 1,400 | 1,215 | 5,435[b] |
| Profit + interest | -66 | -344 | -96 | 624 | 1,025 | 246 | -196 | 312 | -1,959 | 350 | 1,005 | 1,774 | 1,537 | |
| Estimated average capital employed | 8,314 | 13,167 | 10,160 | 9,650 | 8,250 | 7,750 | 8,316 | 8,917 | 8,283 | 5,650 | 6,133 | 6,233 | 5,367 | |
| Return on capital % | -0.8 | -2.6 | -0.9 | 6.4 | 12.4 | 3.1 | -2.3 | 3.5 | -23.6 | 6.2 | 16.4 | 28.5 | 28.6 | |

Sources: Half-yearly balances, AG 512 15/4–15/7. Notes: (a) Depreciation includes sundry charges, cultivation, and improvements. (b) In 1909 Barewood passed back into the hands of Otago University. Profits includes operating profit for the year and surplus over book value when stock, implements and effects were sold.

concern to James Elliott who, in 1897, had to reassure him that the way Maider was managing the flocks was not necessarily wrong.[35] A continued flow of poor results finally led to Maider being moved. In 1903 it was decided that James Elliott should move down and manage the Barewood Estate, along with his own adjacent property, Mount Ross, which he had purchased many years earlier.[36] Maider was to move up to Lauder Station and act as working manager under the supervision of a neighbouring run holder, Alexander Armour of Closeburn Station. This arrangement was eminently practicable, as the steady resumption of Lauder land for settlement had led to part of the Lauder flock being grazed at Closeburn.[37] In addition to payment for grazing, Armour was now to receive a salary of £150 per annum and 10 per cent of any profits earned by Lauder Station.[38]

## 7. FRESH PRESSURES FOR CLOSER SETTLEMENT

The resumption of parts of Blackstone Hill and Highfield in the mid-nineties had been taken by Elliott in his stride. Commenting on Highfield in 1897, he informed Glendining that, while 'most of the cockies who have taken up land there have their blocks fenced in', there were still substantial areas unoccupied. As on previous occasions, Ross & Glendining applied to the Land Board for temporary grazing rights, with Elliott turning out sheep and poisoning rabbits on the unoccupied land pending a decision. This, it was hoped, would forestall any other claimants for the grazing rights. Relationships with the settlers nevertheless appeared to be amicable and a number of them chose to purchase their stock from Lauder Station.[39]

The slow occupation of the surrendered runs by settlers might indicate that the pent-up demand for land was temporarily satisfied. At the same time, it seems clear that unusual weather patterns and the consequential hardship for the farming community may have deterred the more risk-averse from taking up land. Thus the snows of 1895 were followed by hot dry conditions during the late spring of 1896, the occasional cold snap often proving fatal for lambs. The dry weather continued well into 1897, affecting much of Otago including the Barewood Estate.[40]

Lauder was better able to cope with the dry conditions than the smaller subdivided blocks, Elliott being able to shift his flock to cooler mountain pastures where the vegetation continued to grow.[41] Nevertheless, the failure of the turnip crop at lower levels meant that even he was obliged to reduce the number of ewes put to the rams in 1897, owing to the lack of feed.[42] Those farming smaller blocks at lower altitudes suffered badly, some of whom Elliott believed to be worse off than during the snows of 1895.[43] Glendining, naturally, felt vindicated, writing to Ross, 'The season means ruin to a number of small men and some will learn to their cost the folly of taking up country like Blackstone in small blocks'.[44]

Although the progress of settlement may have been slowed by the adverse weather conditions, it was by no means halted. Access to the region was improved by the progress of the Central Otago Railway, which reached Middlemarch in 1891, Hyde in 1894, Ranfurly in 1898, and the Ida Valley in 1901.[45] The railway, it was hoped, would promote closer settlement and in 1898 a special train was run to take people to Ranfurly, where town sections were being sold. With only James Elliott and the property developer on the train, the outlook for Ranfurly did not seem to be particularly promising![46]

While the construction of a railway may not have led to the influx of population that the projectors had envisaged, it certainly conferred benefits on the farmers of Central Otago. Wool, previously carted by wagon to Palmerston, might now be sent directly and more cheaply to the annual wool sales, or Port Chalmers for shipment, and stock could be railed to market or freezing works without losing condition. More crops were now grown in the Maniototo, the railway providing an outlet for oats and chaff not used as winter feed for horses and sheep.[47] A quick and regular passenger service to Dunedin, with its wide range of shops, made life easier for the farming community as well. When in town, farmers – and their wives – naturally visited the warehouses of stock and station agents such as Wright Stephenson, the National Mortgage & Agency Co. and Donald Reid Farmers. This led to a number of agents being increasingly drawn into the supply of general household goods, in addition to agricultural items.[48]

## 8. FURTHER LOSSES OF LAND

It was the level of prices and profitability, however, that primarily determined the rate at which settlers spread into the interior. A softening in agricultural prices in the late nineties, together with the competing claims of gold-mining as the industry underwent a brief renaissance, resulted in a temporary slackening in the demand for land.[49] After 1900, with prices rising once again, there was a fresh clamour for small blocks for settlement. Ross & Glendining, alert as ever, sought to profit from the opportunities presented by an active land market. Together with other investors, in 1902 they bought the 50,000-acre freehold of Castle Rock Station in Southland for £80,000, for the purposes of subdivision and resale to small farmers.[50] Unfortunately, the demand for land also led to the unoccupied blocks at Blackstone Hill and Highfield being steadily taken up and by 1902 there were virtually none left. Under pressure from the local community, the Government now gave notice that it wished to resume the Highfield runs 225b and 225c.

The resumption of the two runs hit at the heart of Lauder operations for they consisted of 13,000 acres of prime lambing country.[51] Temporary relief was afforded by the grazing secured at Closeburn Station but there was little chance of securing land elsewhere. As Hercus explained to a Mr Rex who was looking for a job as a station manager,

> *The policy of the New Zealand government has for some years been to cut up every available run into small holdings which are let as small grazing runs. There are only a few large runs left and their leases will be cancelled … Existing runs are managed either by their owners or by shepherds or cadets.*[52]

It was in the winter of 1903, however, that the full import of the Government's land policy became evident. Heavy snow in July, a month of severe frost, and a cold snap in the spring resulted in heavy stock losses throughout Otago.[53] Lauder Station was badly affected. Although Alexander Armour had taken the precaution of moving sheep below the normal snow-line fence, the lack of adequate low ground meant that 14,693 sheep, or over 35 per cent of the flock, perished. The chief losses were in the young flock and breeding ewes, with about 5,000 lambs dying. This was particularly serious, for it undermined the ability of Lauder Station to sustain flock numbers.[54]

As in 1895, Ross & Glendining turned to the Government for redress. Hercus put the case to D. Barron, Maitland's successor as Commissioner of Crown Lands for Otago, most forcibly:

> *Our present position is this. Being left with many miles of wrecked fences, and with the mere remnants of flocks, we must face very heavy expenditure in reinstating both …. It will take at least two years, even in the most favourable circumstances, to bring our stock into workable condition and for that time there would be the risk of all our fresh outlay being lost as in the past. We are also met by the possibility of the Blackstone Hill runs containing the only winter country left being dealt with as was done with the Highfield country; as we had the same assurance regarding both.*
>
> *Under all circumstances, we think we have very strong claims upon the consideration of the Government and the Land Board: and we shall be glad if in any way these claims can be recognised, whether by remission of rent, or by improved conditions of tenure, and of compensation for improvements. Failing these, we have to request that in any case, no further encroachment be made on the country left to us, until the expiry of the leases. Without some certainty on this point, it would be suicidal to expend fresh capital again in re-instating the runs at the present juncture.*[55]

The profitability of agriculture at this time and the fact there was now little Crown land left in Otago suitable for subdivision and settlement meant that Hercus' plea fell on deaf ears. The Government did, however, set up a Royal Commission on Land Tenure in 1905 to consider, amongst other things, the position of pastoral tenants. Both Alexander Armour and James Elliott's nephew, Robert, now manager at Blackstone Hill, gave evidence on behalf of Ross & Glendining. Although both were questioned on the sustainability of high country runs, it seems that the members of the commission were mainly concerned with raising carrying capacity. Recommendations thus focused on improved pasture management, the use of artificial grasses, and irrigation. Almost inevitably, the now well-worn comments about incentives, the need for greater security of tenure and the provision of adequate low country made their appearance. The commission also suggested, somewhat unrealistically, that the government might, in future, consider buying back low country for the use of high country runs.[56]

## 9. The decision to abandon sheep farming

Ross had no illusions as to what might happen in future. Concerned about the agitation in New Zealand newspapers for cutting up runs and worried that the Government might resume Blackstone Hill, he suggested to Glendining that they should take advantage of high wool and stock prices and exit the industry.[57] Glendining concurred, the Land Board being approached concerning the surrender of all leases ahead of their expiry date in 1910. It was also suggested that the Government might purchase some or all of the freeholds.

In 1905, Ross returned permanently to New Zealand and, with Glendining failing in health, took charge of negotiations with the Government. After meeting the Minister of Lands, a figure of £8,700 was agreed upon to compensate Ross & Glendining for the value of improvements to the leaseholds.[58] The Government was also to pay a further £9,000 to secure the freeholds at Lauder and Blackstone Hill. Together, these properties comprised over 1,100 acres. Of the remaining freehold, Alexander Armour agreed to take over 1,600 acres at Highfield for £3,385 while 440 acres of freehold in the Ida Valley was sold to James Wilson for a further £1,813. This left 2,000 acres unsold. Some sheep were disposed of ahead of shearing, but most were sold early in 1907. A drought during the summer meant that prices were not as good as Ross expected but the sheep, cattle, and horses still realised £35,687. All told, the partners received over £58,000 from the proceeds of their sales.[59] Shortly afterwards, 16,354 acres of Crown land at Blackstone Hill were subdivided for closer settlement.[60]

There was still the question as to what should be done with the Barewood estate. Sheep losses during the snows of 1903 had contributed to a deficit of £2,457 in the year to February 1904. Thereafter, the change in management and improving agricultural prices saw the station move into surplus. With prospects for agriculture generally looking brighter, Hercus urged Ross to sell.[61] The help of Johnstone of Wright Stephenson was enlisted and early in 1905 he took a potential buyer up to view Barewood. No sale resulted, the expiry of the lease in a couple of years' time – there being no prospect of renewal on favourable terms – proving to be 'a fatal objection'. Ross was consoled by the fact that Elliott hoped to make good profits for the rest of the lease.[62]

Over the next few years the profits returned by Barewood did improve markedly, possibly aided by the increased use of Leicester and Corriedale rams.[63] In 1907, a record profit of £1,400 was recorded, the £1,215 returned in the following year being inflated by £516 compensation for 'burnt grass' after an exploding shell set fire to tussock during army manoeuvres.[64] Even so, Ross was still anxious to give up the property, writing to his son that he would be quite happy to surrender his half to Glendining. Nor did he wish to take on another lease elsewhere, even if land were available. He concluded, 'The days of squatting in New Zealand are nearly at an end and only the distant mountainous leases will be renewed, all the big blocks being cut up as leases expire for closer settlement'.[65] In March, 1909, Ross & Glendining finally vacated Barewood. The sale of stock, implements and wool realised £12,698. A surplus over book value of £5,423 was obtained from the sale of stock and implements, while wool yielded a gross profit of £2,391.[66] The land was subsequently subdivided and re-let by the University of Otago.

In the end, both Lauder Station and Barewood succumbed to popular demands for 'lands for the people'. Changes in technology, especially the introduction of refrigeration, meant that it was now possible to make a living from sheep on far smaller acreages than hitherto. The New Zealand Government bowed to pressures from those of modest means, resuming Crown leases and splitting up the larger runs for closer settlement. Unable to renew their leases from the Crown, John Ross and Robert Glendining chose to leave sheep farming to concentrate on their business as warehousemen and manufacturers.

# THE STRUGGLE FOR EXPANSION:
# ROSLYN MILLS, 1900–1914

The economic upswing that got under way in New Zealand in the mid-1890s continued without serious interruption until 1907, when a long spell of dry weather and financial problems in London brought expansion to a halt. The reduction in output and weaker export prices saw the balance of trade deteriorate sharply, the ensuing depression affecting all parts of the country. Recovery got under way during the course of 1909 and by 1910 the economy was booming once more. Thereafter growth was constrained by labour unrest and recurring financial difficulties. Even so, in 1914 real GDP was still more than 50 per cent greater than at the turn of the century.[1]

An expanding European population, which increased by around one third to over a million, was the main factor driving the growth in GDP. Improvements in the terms of trade and technological change, both in agriculture and industry, contributed to a growth in real per capita incomes. By the outbreak of World War I therefore, the population of New Zealand was both more numerous and more prosperous than ever before.

Ross & Glendining Ltd, with their focus on the quality end of the market, took advantage of the growing affluence of consumers. Between 1901 and 1914, their total sales rose from £325,220 to £782,360, with straw and felt hats, women's clothing, boots and shoes being added to the men's clothing, hosiery and textiles already manufactured in Dunedin. The distribution network was also strengthened, a large warehouse being built in Auckland while sample rooms and smaller warehouses were opened elsewhere.

Expansion did not come without a struggle. In 1904, the growing hostility that existed between the former partners burst into the open, when Bob Glendining was reprimanded for his intemperate habits and inefficient mill management. Thereafter, Glendining senior, unwell and also drinking heavily, became increasingly irrational and autocratic in the way that he behaved. Alarmed by the behaviour of the two Glendinings, in 1905 John Ross took up permanent residence in Dunedin in order to institute management reforms and oversee the daily running of the concern.

The cantankerous tone of Glendining's letters during the late 1890s suggests that he was already finding it difficult to manage the business effectively. Whether John Ross appreciated that his partner was no longer in good health prior to his arrival in Dunedin in 1900 is not clear. During his short stay, though, it became quite evident that all was not well and that too much alcohol was being imbibed. The latitude that Glendining gave his incompetent son at Roslyn Mills, the disorganised state of the Dunedin warehouse and clothing factory, and the condition of the stocks at branch warehouses all concerned Ross.[2] When he sailed back to London after a stay of a few months, Hercus was instructed to write to him privately if matters got out of hand.

## 1. Ross increasingly concerned about Roslyn Mills

It was the operation of Roslyn Mills, which constituted around half the assets of the newly converted company, which worried Ross most. Almost as soon as he arrived back in London he was told that work on an extension that was to house new hosiery machinery was lagging behind, with the frames that he had ordered yet to be erected.[3] Worse was to follow. By October 1900, it became apparent that there was not enough room in the extension for all the hosiery machinery, some frames having to remain in their original location. Ross, with commendable restraint, wrote to Glendining suggesting that it might be a good idea to have the new building extended so that all the machines might be worked together. He added, cheerfully, that he had just been to Leicestershire and for £450 had arranged to buy the exclusive New Zealand rights to the Delta process by which knitted goods might be made unshrinkable. The process, he assured Glendining, was the only reliable one and the machinery was not very expensive.[4]

The emollient tone of Ross's letter disguised the fact that he was, in reality, extremely alarmed by the state of affairs in Dunedin. On the same day he wrote a private and confidential letter to Hercus:

> I will be glad to hear from you on a subject which you know gives me great concern. I am under the impression there is some improvement but I don't know. If things are no better than when I was in Dunedin you can word your reply by recommending me to pay you a visit – or vice-versa. I see, with concern, that Dunedin has fallen behind Wellington both in returns and profits; surely this should not be the case if we are holding our own.[5]

A letter was also sent by Ross, in strictest confidence, to David Jones and Sutherland Ross in Wellington. It contained a copy of branch warehouse returns for their comments and the lament that there was 'a lack of push in Dunedin'.[6]

Hercus seems to have allayed some of Ross's worst fears, for there was no immediate talk of another visit to New Zealand. In the meantime, John Ross continued to chip away at both Glendining senior and junior, urging them to ensure that customers' complaints about the non-delivery of goods did not re-occur.[7]

It was not long, however, before the vexed question of mill wool buying surfaced once again. High prices paid for wool at the beginning of 1900 had resulted in a loss of £4,000 on surplus wool shipped to the UK and 120,000 bales still remained unsold when the mill balance was struck in November. Ross wondered whether it might not be possible for Roslyn Mills to use more fine wool from the partners' sheep stations. This, he suggested to Glendining, would relieve him of the trouble and anxiety of buying wool at the auctions and would probably be more profitable than sending the surplus home as in the past.[8] A similar letter was sent to Hercus.[9]

Hercus' reply was hardly reassuring. Some station wool was used, he told Ross, but according to 'Mr. Glendining', much of it was not fine enough for the quality goods that Roslyn Mills now produced. This necessitated buying in wool which, after sorting, yielded only a third to a fifth suitable for processing. The problem, moreover, would get worse as consumption of fine wools grew, for with the switch to mutton production local supplies of fine wool were declining. Some wool had been obtained from Canterbury, as it was generally of better quality, and a small amount purchased from Australia. Even then, the hosiery plant had still been held up for the want of fine wools. The result of the lost production, on top of the losses incurred on wool shipments, meant that the mills now looked as though they were heading for a record deficit.[10]

Ross received the news with a degree of scepticism. 'Is the great back of the Merino not suitable for our purpose – or what?' he enquired. He also wondered how it was, given the high wool prices, that the Kaiapoi and Wellington woollen mills had managed to do so well.[11] Hercus was unable to enlighten him, although he thought it might have been due to the fact that Kaiapoi required less fine wool than Roslyn and was more fortunate in buying forward. He warned Ross that the quantities of wool shipped to the United Kingdom were unlikely to change in the near future. As hosiery sales rose and more capacity was installed, Glendining's wool purchases were bound to increase.[12]

The argument over wool sourcing continued to rumble on for some months, a sample of fine Australian merino wool sent out by London Office being rejected by Glendining as unsuitable.[13] When an Australian wool vessel was subsequently forced into Dunedin on its way to the United Kingdom, Glendining was congratulated – possibly with a touch of irony – on his purchase of a number of bales. At the same time, Ross was aware that his old partner was not at all well. With this in mind, he suggested to Glendining that he might benefit from a long sea voyage back home. The Glasgow Exhibition was being held – Ross was on the committee – and there would be a lot of New Zealanders there. Glendining turned down the invitation on the grounds that there was too much building going on.[14]

A temporary decline in sales towards the end of 1900 led to another area of disagreement being revisited, namely, the prices at which mill goods were transferred to the warehouses. In a long letter to Thomas Glendining, Ross complained,

> *I do not understand Mr. G's attitude. The departments will not push them unless they get as good a profit on them as imported goods, in fact, several of the hands made the admission to me and this has been abundantly proved. The goods should be invoiced to the departments at such prices as will leave departments in the warehouses a profit corresponding to that on imported goods .... Mr. G. makes a point of the mill having as much profit as possible but I do not see that it makes any difference whether the profits are shown in the mill or the warehouse.*[15]

Ross appears to have won this particular argument and, by the beginning of April 1901, a new list of transfer prices had been agreed. It was not long before Glendining was complaining that he did not like the new system of charging.[16]

## 2. EXPANSION PROPOSALS SEES ROSS RETURN TO DUNEDIN

Demand for high quality Roslyn hosiery, already brisk prior to the change in the charging regime, soared thereafter. Ross, once again, turned his attention to buying additional machinery, investigating a new type of hosiery frame in the process.[17] A large combination frame was shipped in June with a further three frames sent out in July. Still, he was unwilling to go in much deeper at this stage, suggesting to Thomas Glendining that it was perhaps wise to 'ca canny' as New Zealand would not always be booming.[18] Moreover, the success of the hosiery plant brought other problems in its wake, the most important being the pressures that it placed on the spinning department, which did not have enough room to expand.[19] There was also the question as to whether the existing boilers could generate sufficient steam.[20]

For Bob Glendining the answer was obvious, a new mill should be built in the paddock next to the existing plant. Ross was not so sure. He was now sixty-seven and was thinking that he would like to be able to give some money away in his lifetime. This, he felt, was not possible with the large amount of indebtedness that always seemed to be hanging over their heads. Besides, the current prosperity of New Zealand would not continue indefinitely, so they ought to move forward with caution lest they be left with a big plant and little work. Ross also wondered whether 'Bob and the others who are urging such rapid and extensive [additions] are aware that the Mill only turns over its capital once in two years'. He was not averse to a cautious and reasonable increase in capacity, but was not prepared to embark on a second mill.[21]

Whether John Ross was really averse to building a second mill, or simply did not wish to build another mill to be run by Bob Glendining, we will never know. At this juncture he began to suffer from severe headaches, a condition that was probably not helped by Glendining senior's announcement that it had been decided that the worsted plant must be doubled in size if the firm was to stay ahead. Ross was not to be drawn, merely replying that he would consider any plans that might be submitted. He also indicated that Glendining's plans for a new hat factory should remain in abeyance.[22] In August, with his headaches no better, Ross visited a specialist in Hindhead. Apparently there was nothing seriously wrong with him; all that was needed was a rest and a change of air. That being the case, he informed Glendining that he was off to Scotland for a month – or more.[23]

Feeling somewhat better, Ross returned to London in mid-September with the thought that a voyage to New Zealand might completely restore his health. In the meantime, it had been decided in Dunedin that not only would the firm start manufacturing hats, but it ought to enter the boot making trade as well. Ross remained sceptical, pointing out that, as Sargood, Son & Ewen and Butterworth Brothers had just erected hat factories, he scarcely thought there was room in the city for a third. However, as the rest of the board was all agreed, he felt obliged to fall in with their decision. As for boot making, he knew nothing about the trade but would make enquiries. The proposal to enter two new industries nevertheless concerned him – especially as Glendining was also entertaining the idea of manufacturing dress shirts and collars as well.[24]

While Ross had been in Scotland, Robert Glendining had occasion to speak to Sutherland Ross quite sharply. If Ross senior was annoyed, it was not evident in his reply:

> I am much obliged to you for speaking to John [Sutherland]. His manner has always been too bouncing and we have told him of it many a time and perhaps a word from one interested in him outside his family will cause him to think of what he has often been told at home. Neither do I approve of so much going out to dances – I am glad you spoke of that too.[25]

What motivated Glendining's censure is not clear. Still, his open criticism of Sutherland Ross, together with his refusal to let the young man work around the business, suggests that the question of the future control of Ross & Glendining Ltd was beginning to occupy his thoughts.

For the next few weeks, John Ross busied himself visiting various hat machinery makers in the United Kingdom. To his dismay, he found that the industry was largely in the hands of one firm, Turner Atherton & Co., with no other maker capable of supplying a complete plant. This being the case, he placed three quarters of the order with them, the remainder being spread between three smaller makers. His view of hat-making and the prospects for its success in Dunedin was not improved by closer acquaintance. Hatters, he thought, were not a very satisfactory lot and he anticipated considerable difficulty in finding good men to go out to New Zealand at reasonable wages.[26]

With his health still not good, the question of a new mill up in the air, and the firm about to branch out into hat and boot making, Ross became increasingly inclined to return to New Zealand. Glendining, too, could see the advantages of having Ross in Dunedin and suggested that he and his family should pay them a visit. There were, however, easier and more pleasant options open to Ross, he and his wife being attracted by the prospect of a trip to Morocco and Tangier with some friends. Naturally the views of Margaret Ross had to be considered and in October Ross wrote: 'I think the longer trip to New Zealand would do me more good and I am disposed to it, but Maggie does not see her way to go and I don't care to go without her. We shall decide, however, one of these days.'[27]

Over the next few weeks Margaret Ross appears to have changed her mind, for early in November a Dr Fergus was informed that the two were to leave 'in a fortnight hence'. They left on a German steamer, arriving back in New Zealand at the end of January 1902.[28]

### 3. ROSS OVERSEES CONSTRUCTION OF SECOND MILL

When Ross left London he intended to stay away for only two or three months but, once in Dunedin, he soon changed his mind. Writing to Thomas Brown, head of an Anglo-Australian warehouse firm for whom Ross acted as a director, he explained,

> *I have been busy assisting to make plans for an extension of the mill – or rather we are building a new mill to house the worsted hosiery departments. This had been rendered necessary by the pressure of orders for the latter class of goods. We are deficient in spinning power for yarns to begin with, and then for machinery to make the garments. Under the circumstances I have decided to prolong my stay here until the new mill and hat factory are started. We have also arranged to start straw hat making as you will no doubt guess from the orders for plait by current mail.*[29]

The new mill was to be built in the small paddock to the right of the existing buildings, long designated the site for any major expansion. The original mill was to concentrate on the production of woollen yarns and cloth.

A letter Ross received from Hercus the previous year probably explains why Ross was now in favour of a second mill. The Roslyn Mills balance date had been shifted from November to July to fall in with the warehouse balance dates. In August 1901, the balance sheet for the eight-month period to 19 July had become available. Dissected by Hercus, it did not make for pleasant reading:

> *The annual output is not so much as it reached ten years ago, whereas the capital account has been loaded in the meantime with £25,000 machinery and plant extra with about £8,000 revaluation of Land & Buildings and with £10,000 reserve withdrawn. The net cost of goods for the eight months was under £35,000 while the capital is four times as much. To enable 6% to be returned on the capital, the goods would have to yield 16% besides 12% depreciation and expenses, or 28% altogether …. The most serious thing to consider now is how to restore the balance of the producing power lost by having to use the whole plant feeding the hosiery department, leaving other departments of the mill short of yarns for their purposes. To add spinning power now raises the demand for more light and more steam, all of which are barely sufficient already. The cure may be in getting swifter spinning machinery to replace some of what we have. In any case, the difficulty will have to be met and overcome as soon as possible.*[30]

Given the force of Hercus' argument, it is scarcely surprising that John Ross now agreed that a new mill was necessary.

The designs for the new mill were soon completed, but bad weather delayed progress. By May 1902, the foundations had still not been laid. Ross, in the interim, began to send orders for mill machinery to his long-serving deputy, James Gibson, now acting manager in London. He also wrote directly to a number of textile machinery makers in the U.K., many of which he had dealt with personally.[31] Through Gibson, worsted plant was ordered from the Huddersfield firm, J. Sykes & Sons, while additional carding machinery was supplied by Platts of Oldham. Hosiery machinery was obtained from a variety of sources in the Midlands, with Gibson told to play off frame manufacturers Moses Mellor and Cotton & Co. against each other.[32]

By the following July, much of the machinery had arrived but the re-arrangement of Roslyn Mills was a tedious process. Spinning frames had to be dismantled, overhauled and re-erected, as did sixteen large hosiery frames, each of which took between two and three weeks to take down, remove, and set going once more.[33] At the same time the plant had to be kept working as hard as possible in order to meet the growing demand for hosiery. This was achieved, with the weight of wool processed increasing by around 15 per cent between 1902 and 1904. The value of output went up even more as the proportion of hosiery and knitwear manufacture increased and, by the latter date, it accounted for nearly half of Roslyn Mills' annual production (see Table 11.1).[34]

The bulk of the work connected with the second mill was completed by the middle of 1904. Carding, combing, twisting and spinning took place on the ground floor of the new building, yarn capacity being increased by adding another 1296 spindles to those already in operation. Hosiery manufacturing was accommodated on the first floor, many of the original Griswold knitters being replaced by modern automatic knitting machinery. There were also additional frames, seaming machines and sewing machines. The whole was powered by a 200-horsepower Corliss compound steam engine. The old mill, which housed the woollen carding, spinning and weaving machinery, was also refurbished and re-equipped with an additional 2000 spindles installed.[35]

## TABLE 11.1
## ROSLYN MILLS OUTPUT AND PROFITABILITY, 1901–1914 (£000s)

| July Year 1901[a] | 1902 | 1903 | 1904 | 1905 | 1906 | 1907 | 1908 | 1909 | 1910 | 1911 | 1912 | 1913 | 1914 |
|---|---|---|---|---|---|---|---|---|---|---|---|---|---|
| **Output value** | | | | | | | | | | | | | |
| 34.9 | 71.1 | 82.6 | 100.0 | 118.4 | 103.1 | 123.5 | 130.9 | 115.2 | 122.7 | 135.1 | 135.7 | 137.7 | 147.3 |
| **Scoured wool used (000 lbs)** | | | | | | | | | | | | | |
| 279.7 | 593.4 | 600.1 | 683.7 | 868.8 | 633.7 | 727.2 | 736.5 | 720.2 | 712.0 | 743.4 | 792.8 | 819.4 | 822.9 |
| **Sales[b]** | | | | | | | | | | | | | |
| 47.3 | 74.6 | 78.5 | 93.1 | 100.6 | 100.3 | 113.4 | 113.8 | 117.3 | 123.9 | 128.7 | 139.0 | 144.8 | 137.5 |
| **Gross profit** | | | | | | | | | | | | | |
| 8.2 | 15.7 | 8.7 | 9.3 | 13.3 | 3.2 | 2.4 | 2.8 | 19.7 | 21.7 | 12.8 | 19.3 | 18.4 | 16.6 |
| **Net profit** | | | | | | | | | | | | | |
| 3.1 | 9.2 | 1.9 | -0.4 | 4.5 | -5.9 | -6.4 | -5.1 | 9.9 | 14.1 | 4.1 | 10.5 | 9.5 | 8.0 |
| **Total mill assets** | | | | | | | | | | | | | |
| 134.0 | 142.2 | 181.6 | 195.5 | 195.6 | 190.6 | 176.9 | 187.6 | 175.5 | 183.2 | 192.6 | 186.4 | 188.5 | 205.4 |

*Sources: Half-yearly balances, AG 512 15/7–15/10.*
*Notes: (a) Eight months to July. (b) After warehouse charges.*

### 4. FINANCING EXPANSION

The cost of expansion was substantial. More than £11,200 had been spent on the new mill building to July 1904, with a further £20,000 on additional machinery. Expansion also entailed larger inventories of raw materials and finished goods, the total assets tied up in Roslyn Mills increasing by almost £61,000 to over £195,000 within the space of three years.

Under any circumstances, expenditure on this scale would have placed a strain on resources. As it happened, it occurred at a time when Ross & Glendining Ltd were expanding in other directions too. Thus in addition to the construction of a larger clothing factory, capital was being sunk into the new hat factory, the refurbishment and extension of the Dunedin and Wellington warehouses, new premises in Christchurch, and the purchase of a prime warehouse site in Auckland. All in all, the total amount invested in mills, factories, warehouses and stocks, together with working capital, rose from £458,998 in July 1901 to £630,057 by July 1904.[36]

The enterprise as a whole was reasonably profitable during this period, profits for the three years to 1904 amounting to £76,920 in total. Yet while the bulk of the profits were retained by paying out dividends as shares rather than cash, internal cash flow was nowhere near enough to fund the capital expenditure required. One option would have been for capital to be raised through the issue of additional shares but, with commitments elsewhere, neither John Ross nor Robert Glendining were in a position to contribute personally. As Ross explained to his London friend, the warehouseman Thomas Brown,

> .... since coming out here I have got into several things, two or three of the biggest I may mention to let you see that I have got involved as deep as prudence will admit. First, I became one of a syndicate of seven who bought a bankrupt [Dunedin & Roslyn] tram car line, each member to contribute £4,300 ... Then we bought a property called Castle Rock Station for £80,000, Glendining and I taking £30,000 each in the concern ... We have had the land surveyed and mapped in moderate blocks to sell to farmers but it means we have to find the money for three years at least; and lastly I have promised a sum of £2,000 a year for five years to start a Presbyterian Theological College in Dunedin ...

These commitments meant that Ross was already personally overdrawn at the bank and unable to accede to his friend's request to put money into T.H. Brown & Sons Ltd.[37]

Fortunately, Ross & Glendining Ltd had a very good relationship with the Dunedin branch of the Bank of New South Wales, which, for many years, had granted generous overdraft facilities. This was invaluable given the seasonal nature of the warehouse and woollen manufacturing businesses, both of which ran heavily into stock at various times of the year. Yet although happy to finance stocks, the bank was not willing to tie up capital in illiquid assets such as plant and machinery, especially after the banking debacles of the 1890s. For additional funds, therefore, Ross & Glendining Ltd were forced to rely heavily on their depositors.[38]

During the nineteenth century a substantial proportion of the firm's deposits came from overseas. Now, with the growing maturity of the New Zealand economy, it was possible to obtain more funds domestically. Given the competitive rate of interest offered by Ross & Glendining Ltd, usually around 4.5 per cent per annum, institutions and individuals were only too happy to invest.[39] Total deposits increased by around £60,000 to over £165,000 between 1901 and 1904, with the cream of local society placing their funds at the firm's disposal.[40] This was invaluable in financing expansion.

### 5. Ross and Glendining at odds over mill management

The presence of John Ross in New Zealand, able to take charge of ordering machinery and generally push things ahead, ensured that good progress was made. By early 1904, with the new building complete and virtually all the hosiery frames erected, he booked a passage home. Suddenly, at short notice, the booking was cancelled. Writing to a London friend in strictest confidence, he confessed,

> *The reason for this change is that relations are rather strained at present owing to my taking exception to the intemperate habits of my partners' younger son who has been managing the mill for several years. I have endeavoured for some time to get him into better ways but not succeeding, at last brought the matter before his father who, instead of investigating, accused me of making false charges against his son. Under all the circumstance surrounding the case, I deemed it advisable to continue here some time longer with a view to endeavouring to put things on a better footing, generally, and particularly to get rid of – if possible – the drinking element among the employees.*[41]

A quest for efficiency rather than a renewed interest in temperance was, undoubtedly, the main reason why Ross raised the issue. At the same time, he was certainly no lover of alcohol, the Ross Institute that he erected in his home town of Halkirk, a few years later, being purposely opened to counter drunkenness amongst youngsters in Caithness.[42]

The refusal of Glendining to acknowledge his son's failings did little to deter Ross and, with the support of the rest of the directors, Bob Glendining was taken to task. The young man immediately offered his resignation as mill manager, but this was declined. Instead, the board encouraged him to continue as manager, providing that he co-operate with them in an investigation of the workings of the mill, and that he faithfully carried out their instructions to check irregularities. Unnecessary employees were to be removed – especially those of intemperate habits – and conditions of working were to be generally improved.[43] Robert Glendining, it seems, was prepared to go along with his fellow directors and support their demands for reform, as was his son who withdrew his resignation.

With the question of mill management apparently addressed, John Ross felt able to return to the United Kingdom. He arrived back in London on 12 June, accompanied by his wife, Sutherland Ross and his youngest son, Walter. Sutherland was to assist his father both in the counting house and as a buyer, a welcome step since the acting manager, Gibson, had died a year earlier. Walter, who had spent a short time in Roslyn Mills learning the woollen and worsted trades, was sent to Leeds University to receive a more formal grounding in textile manufacturing.[44]

Within a short time of his arrival Ross received a letter from Hercus, only to learn that there had been little improvement at Roslyn Mills. He was nevertheless reassured by the fact that both George Hercus and Thomas Glendining had spoken firmly to Bob about the need to implement the board's recommendations.[45] Their words appear to have had little effect, and it was not long before the exchanges between Ross and Glendining began to become a little more acerbic. Thus when Glendining complained about shortages of labour at the mill, Ross tartly replied, 'If you had the Roslyn Tramcar running down the valley in the vicinity of the mill as I suggested, you would get this class of labour from town.'[46] Ross was also annoyed by Glendining's unwillingness to provide information regarding mill operations when cabling balance sheet details. From the results, however, it was clear that it was the poor performance of Roslyn Mills, and not the warehouses, which was depressing profits. With other mills paying seven per cent, Ross caustically observed that 'we are not as clever as we would like people to give us credit for'.[47]

Exasperated by the continued failure of the 'slack and useless' Bob Glendining, John Ross did what he could from England to improve matters. Articles and advertisements concerning the latest sweater and pants machines were forwarded to Dunedin, together with copies of the *Hosiery Trade Journal*. On a visit to Leeds, he called in at the university to discuss some of the latest technical advances in the textile industry. Having discovered that all the home worsted manufacturers were using backwashing, he duly recommended that Roslyn Mills adopt the process, only to have it rejected out of hand.[48] He also came across a book, 'how to make woollen mills pay', which dealt with the practical aspects of manufacturing starting with

John Ross and parents, 1854.
'The March of Time' (pamphlet), p. 10, Hocken Collections S09-533a.

Princes Street, Dunedin, in 1860, shortly before John Ross arrived in the settlement. Hocken Collections S04-098

Stafford Street, Dunedin, in 1862. Hocken Collections S06-443c

Early advertising by Ross & Glendining Ltd. *Otago Witness*, 5 March 1864, p. 12, 4 June 1864. Courtesy of the Heritage Collections, Dunedin Public Libraries.

WINTER GOODS.

LARGE ARRIVALS OF FASHIONABLE DRAPERY

AT

ROSS & GLENDINING'S,

CONSISTING OF—

SILKS IN ALL THE NEW SHADES AND PATTERNS.
SHAWLS & MANTLES, THE FINEST LOT EVER IMPORTED INTO OTAGO.
WINCEYS. CLAN AND FANCY TARTANS. FURS AND STAYS.
FRENCH MERINOS. HOSIERY AND GLOVES.
FANCY DRESSES. HATS AND BONNETS. FLOWERS, FEATHERS, &c.

ROSS & GLENDINNING'S ENTIRE SHIPMENTS OF WINTER GOODS HAVING COME TO HAND TWO MONTHS LATER THAN THEY HAD ANTICIPATED, OWING TO THE UNUSUALLY LONG PASSAGES MADE BY THE LATE ARRIVALS FROM LONDON AND GLASGOW, HAVE BEEN MARKED AT THE LOWEST REMUNERATIVE PRICES, AS THEY MUST ALL BE CLEARED OUT PREVIOUS TO STOCK-TAKING.

R. & G. WOULD RESPECTFULLY INVITE THEIR FRIENDS AND THE PUBLIC, TO GIVE THEM A CALL AND SEE FOR THEMSELVES THE GREAT BARGAINS GIVEN, BEING CONFIDENT THAT FOR STYLE, QUALITY, AND PRICE, THE GOODS THEY ARE NOW SHOWING CANNOT BE SURPASSED.

ROSS & GLENDINING,

PRINCES-STREET & MANSE-STREET.

---

ROSS & GLENDINING'S,

PRINCES & MANSE-STREETS.

WE beg to announce that our SECOND ANNUAL CHEAP SALE of SUMMER

GOODS commenced on

FRIDAY, THE 4TH INSTANT.

It is unnecessary for us to assure parties who have patronised our former Cheap Sale, that ours is a genuine one, the object of it being to clear out the remainder of our SUMMER STOCK before our shipments of WINTER GOODS (already advised) arrive. Those whose requirements did not then lead them to favor us with a call, we especially invite now, and are certain they will be satisfied of the reality of the REDUCTION announced, and of the advantages to be obtained by making their purchases while our SALE lasts.

N.B.—An equal REDUCTION made in all the Departments, including a Lot of

NEW GOODS

of the latest designs, just landed, ex the Ethereal and Brechin Castle.

We are,

Your most obedient servants,

ROSS & GLENDINING.

Dunedin, 5th March, 1864.

Original Ross & Glendining retail store (right) in Princes Street, opened 1862. R & G Annual Report 1962, Hocken Collections S09-529k.

Ross & Glendining's first warehouse (left) in Stafford Street, opened 1866. R & G Annual Report 1962, Hocken Collections S09-529j.

Dunedin in 1865, showing the New Zealand & South Seas Exhibition building under construction, centre, left. Hocken Collections S09-529d.

The exhibition building viewed from London Street, *c.* 1868.
Hocken Collections S07-062e.

Main road three miles north of Invercargill, 1860s. Hocken Collections S09-202h.

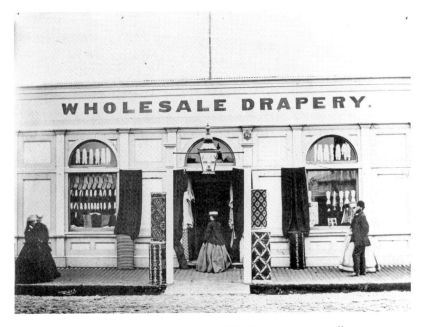

One of Ross & Glendining's customers, Esk Street, Invercargill. Hocken Collections S09-202f.

Gold rush town: Lawrence in the late 1860s. Hocken Collections S09-202g.

Blackstone Hill from across the Ida Valley, Hawkdun Range to the right.
Author photograph.

Lauder Station in 1873. Pen and ink wash by 'A.R.' National Library of Australia. 2904347.

Men working on the Central Otago railway, c. 1903. Hocken Collections S09-362g.

Blackstone Hill Station homestead. *Otago Witness*, 24 May 1905.

Telling the age of sheep, Blackstone Hill Station. *Otago Witness*, 24 May 1905.

From top: Blackstone Hill Station woolshed; a general view of the station buildings; the woolscouring paddock. *Otago Witness*, 24 May 1905

The Ross and Glendining families, about 1888. 'March of Time' (pamphlet), p. 26, Hocken Collections S09-533b.

Winter Garden, Dunedin Botanical Gardens, gifted to the city by Robert Glendining. Hocken Collections S09-202d.

The Glendining residence, 'Nithvale', North East Valley, Dunedin. *Otago Witness*, 24 September 1902, p. 35. Hocken Collections S09-281a

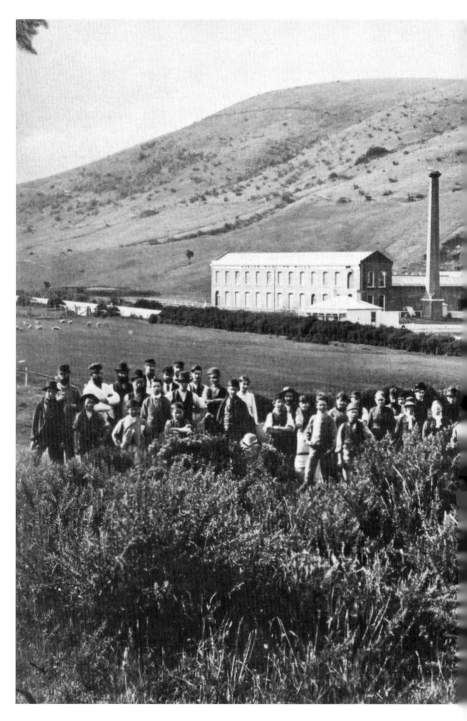

Roslyn Mills and workers, early 1880s. Hocken Collections S06-152b.

Knox College, endowed by John Ross. Hocken Collections S09-202c.

Ross Institute, Halkirk, Caithness, Scotland, funded by John Ross.
Author photograph.

mixing wool. Two copies were forwarded to Dunedin, one for Hercus and the other for the mill engineer.[49] Whether the latter made use of the book is not known, but Hercus certainly found it helpful.

Glendining, for his part, continued to withhold information regarding operations at the mills. Early in December, a very anxious Ross invited Hercus to send him a private letter bringing him up to date:

> I am wondering what is going on at the mill as I have not had any information about it since I left. Is RCG keeping straight and have the other topers been dispensed with? Has the mill office been moved to the gate as suggested? Is all the machinery all right? Are the goods we are turning out giving perfect satisfaction? I have no time to say more except that I rely on you to keep things straight and give me all the information.[50]

Hercus did his best to get rid of 'the topers' and obtain the information that was required. However, with little support from Thomas Glendining and constant obstruction from Glendining senior, Hercus found life very difficult. He complained to Ross that he felt 'oppressed' and was advised not to take things 'to heart too much'.[51]

The goods produced by the new machinery evidently did give customer satisfaction, for output in the year to July 1905 reached a new record. The quality of the products appears to have been the key, for a number of other mills were obliged to shorten hours.[52] In August 1904, the Oamaru and Onehunga woollen mills went as far as to propose a tariff conference with a view to checking the importation of shoddy products.[53] Ross & Glendining Ltd did not warm to the idea, nor was much enthusiasm shown when some months later it was suggested that they might like to buy the Onehunga mills. The Onehunga manager was assured that, as his goods were complementary to Roslyn products, Ross & Glendining would continue to buy Onehunga woollens to supply the branches. But running a mill 'at a distance' was quite a different matter to operating branch warehouses, apart from which the company had just made 'extensive additions'. In view of the slump that had befallen the industry, they just wanted to feel their way for a while.[54] A similar proposal from the proprietors of the Rosedale Mill, Invercargill, was also politely declined.[55]

## 6. ROSS RETURNS TO NEW ZEALAND AND TAKES CONTROL

John Ross had always intended to return to New Zealand once his Highgate house had been sold and he was satisfied that the London Office, now managed by Charles Netting, was running smoothly. His family, it seems, had different ideas and were 'dead set against an early departure'.[56] Nor, given the unpleasantness experienced on his previous visit, was Ross in any hurry to leave, and in March 1905 he opted for a trip to the south of France rather than return to New Zealand. Yet with the mills still barely scraping a profit, even when they were running at full tilt, he accepted that it was only a matter of time before he left.[57] Early in September 1905, he and his wife arrived back in Dunedin, a few days before the sixth annual general meeting of Ross & Glendining Ltd.

The meeting was held on 12 September with John Ross in the chair. The report to shareholders was mixed. The mill had been kept running 'day and night' – even though other mills in the colony had been obliged to shorten hours – and output was at record levels. The hat and clothing factories, on the other hand, had fared less well and the margins on both mill and factory goods were not regarded as adequate. The most significant announcement, however, was that John Sutherland Ross, still in London, had been elected to the board of directors.[58] There had been some talk earlier in the year of Bob Glendining taking the fifth and last vacant seat on the board and, not surprisingly, Ross had expected some opposition from that quarter.[59] In the event, Robert Glendining was happy to support the election of Sutherland Ross who, he thought, 'had always taken an interest in the business'.[60]

For the rest of the year the two former partners remained on reasonably amicable terms, even though a good deal of the newly installed worsted machinery was now standing idle. Ross charitably attributed the lack of demand to a mild winter and not to competition. This had recently increased since Wellington and a number of the other mills now spun their own worsted yarn, but Ross thought they could not yet match Roslyn for quality.[61] Harmony was not to prevail for much longer. Early in 1906, relations became 'very strained' after Ross tried to prevent Glendining from going to Christchurch to buy wool. The question of Glendining's retirement was discussed, but as Ross explained to his eldest son, 'In the state of mind and body Mr. G is there is no knowing what he might do but I think that it is quite evident that I must remain here at present'.[62] Shortly afterwards Glendining went up to Blackstone Hill, ostensibly for a long holiday, but he only remained ten days, returning to Dunedin to continue his previous 'kind of life'.[63]

With Robert Glendining clearly in no fit state to attend to business affairs and Bob frequently absent from the mill, John Ross decided to try to implement some much-needed reforms. In a long memorandum that might have been drawn straight from the pages of a book by F.W. Taylor, the father of scientific management, he outlined his philosophy on manufacturing. Paragraphs dealt with what he expected of senior staff, the need for systematic organisation, and how costs were to be attributed. He was keen that foremen should be confided in and encouraged to put forward their suggestions for product and process improvement; for piece workers to share in the proceeds if they increased their output 'beyond expectations'; and for all workers to be rewarded for any useful ideas they might have. Yet Ross realised that incentives did not, by themselves, eliminate opportunistic behaviour and that labour worked not from choice 'but from necessity'. Accordingly, he recommended that a Bundy Time Recorder be installed.[64]

Unfortunately, the scope for altering the culture, customs and practices at the mill was limited by the fact that it was Bob Glendining and 'the topers' who still controlled what went on. This was about to change. Towards the end of May, the young Glendining was 'laid up again', his troubles apparently being indigestion and muscular rheumatism. After a few weeks he returned to work, but in August his illness returned, attributed by Ross to 'imbibing more than is good for him'. It soon became clear, however, that Bob was seriously ill. Robert Glendining had no doubt as to who was to blame, as Ross wrote to his son,

> His father told me the other day that I had killed Bob by worrying him and that I was killing him too. He is in a most unsettled state of mind and does not know what to do with himself. His friends advise him to take a long holiday and go home but he is most stubborn and will not take anyone's advice.[65]

Ultimately, Bob was diagnosed as having lead poisoning. After several months he began to show signs of recovery and his father took him to Blackstone Hill to recuperate.[66]

The absence of Bob Glendining allowed Ross, with the backing of Hercus and Thomas Glendining, to insist that an assistant mill manager be appointed.[67] Applicants for the post proved to be disappointing, so in late August Ross began to assume control of the Roslyn Mills himself. His first task was to identify and sack a few of the more idle hands.[68] Several weeks later he decided to appoint one of the cotton spinners, Henry Beesley, as acting mill manager. Glendining senior was furious. There was also opposition from Bob Glendining's cronies in the mill, some of whom told Ross that he had 'made the worst appointment possible.'[69] Complaints from this group continued for some weeks, confirming Ross in his view that he had made the best appointment possible.[70]

The mill under Beesley was soon working smoothly, allowing Ross to test the accuracy of costing methods. It was found that goods were costed too low and so a new standard of wool costing was introduced. Time management in various departments was also improved, with 'no lounging around in corners and more stuff coming through the machines'.[71] This happy situation was not to last much longer. At the end of November, Robert Glendining decided to take up the reins again, putting the half-fit Bob Glendining back in charge of the mill and turning the existing arrangements 'topsy-turvy'. Ross took legal advice but found himself powerless to act, votes at the directors' meetings being cast by heads rather than shares. He promptly acquired powers of attorney, to be exercised on behalf of the other shareholding members of his family, so that he might carry the day at annual general meetings if necessary.[72]

## 7. IMPROVEMENTS CONTINUE AT ROSLYN MILLS

The return of Bob Glendining proved to be not such a disaster. After several months, two or three of the most troublesome staff had left to start their own mill in Invercargill and, with plenty of work on hand, Roslyn was 'going on quietly under Bob's jurisdiction'.[73] Nevertheless, Glendining senior continued to interfere, taking advantage of a visit by Ross to Auckland to sack the hapless Beesley.[74] Yet with continued pressure from Ross, improvements continued. By the time of the annual general meeting in September 1907, he was confident that the mill, although still making a loss, was working on much better lines than hitherto. The losses were attributed to the high price of wool and unresolved problems with costing, not a lack of effort.[75]

Bob Glendining suffered a fresh bout of lead poisoning towards the end of 1907. In April the following year, accompanied by his sisters, he took a trip 'home', not having fully recovered the power in his hands.[76] Ross, with greater freedom of action, began to push forward with improvements once again, asking the Dunedin Town Clerk for quotations for the supply of municipal electricity to Roslyn Mills at 3,000 and 400 volts, and for various periods of time during the day. His aim, he said, was to reduce the load on the steam engine from 357 to 300 horsepower.[77] This time, electricity was to be used not only to light the mill, but drive a variety of electric motors as well, principally in the hosiery department. After some haggling with the Town Clerk, a price was agreed upon and, by the end of the year, twelve motors had been installed.[78] Glendining, now barely on speaking terms with Ross, was very dismissive about the full electrification of the mill. The advantages, however, were undeniable, with electricity costing £3 a day, saving ten tons of coal at 15/- a ton.[79]

The output of Roslyn Mills continued to rise thereafter, in spite of a lack of cooperation from Glendining, but margins were adversely affected by the depression that now gripped the country. Some relief was afforded during 1907 when tariffs were raised on a number of goods, including hosiery, but it was not until 1909 that the economy began to recover.[80] 1910 was a boom year and once again Ross & Glendining Ltd were unable to meet the demand for high quality hosiery and knitted goods. Additional machinery was installed on a regular basis, a further £14,000 being spent between 1908 and World War I.[81]

The period leading up to the war was not entirely trouble free, problems regarding the supply of fine wool, delays in the delivery of machinery, a lack of spinning power, and a shortage of hands all resulting in lost production.[82] There were several short strikes, one in 1911 the result of the mill engineer bestowing his favours on two of the female hands. Presbyterian values were offended and the engineer was subsequently discharged for immorality.[83] The mill also suffered from the general labour unrest and the wave of strikes that occurred in 1913.[84] The management of the mill, back in the hands of Bob Glendining after he had returned to New Zealand, was scarcely dynamic either, while his father continued to oppose change.[85] Even so, by 1914, the value of goods produced amounted to £147,300, ten per cent up on 1908 and twice as much as that produced prior to building the second mill. Profitability was also much improved, notwithstanding the breakup of a mill owners' association in 1910 which, from 1907 onwards, had helped to keep prices up.[86]

The expansion that took place after 1900 meant that by World War I, Roslyn Mills was the leading textile mill in the country. Indeed, over the first decade of the twentieth century, the increase in Roslyn production represented half of that achieved by the industry as a whole. In 1910, it accounted for more than one fifth of the New Zealand's total output of woollens, worsteds and hosiery.[87] The hosiery and knitted underwear produced was often of the highest quality, mixed yarns of Indian gauze, pure silk, and the finest Merino being pioneered at the mills.[88] These were just the sorts of goods demanded by an increasingly affluent New Zealand society.

The credit for initiating the expansion must go to Robert and Bob Glendining who saw what possibilities lay ahead, especially in the area of high quality knitted goods. Yet their contribution largely ended with conception, their ability to carry out good ideas being impaired by an attachment to alcohol. From 1908 onwards they managed to get their drinking problems under control, with Bob going 'pretty straight'[89] and Robert Glendining giving up his previous excesses in favour of 'a glass of champagne a day'.[90] Even as reformed characters, however, they contributed little to mill development. In fact, by 1912 Ross had become so exasperated with the obstructive and increasingly senile Glendining that he offered to buy the latter's shares in Ross & Glendining Ltd. Nothing ever eventuated.[91]

Had the two Glendinings been left to their own devices, then the story of Roslyn Mills might have been quite different. Fortunately John Ross, in his late sixties, remained as vigorous and as astute as ever. It was he who presided over the successful completion of the new mill, took charge of the hat and boot factories, and managed the growing and increasingly profitable warehouse business. Without the latter, Roslyn Mills would have found itself short of both capital and an efficient distribution network.

# THE STRUGGLE FOR EXPANSION: THE FACTORIES, 1900–1914

The increasing size and affluence of the population in New Zealand meant that the market for clothing, footwear and textiles both widened and deepened before World War I. Imports from the United Kingdom and, increasingly, from the United States, still supplied the greater part of the market, with leading makes often asked for by name. Thus cotton thread manufactured by J. & P. Coats of Paisley, Horrocks' flannelette, floral prints from Hoyles of Manchester, and Clark's shoes all commanded a loyal following. When it came to more modern and stylish dress, particularly for the female form, then it was to American manufacturers such as Warner Brothers that local customers often turned.

Warehousemen eagerly sought agencies with well-known foreign manufacturers for the exclusive right to distribute their goods within New Zealand. At the same time, they began to manufacture a wider range of goods themselves as they attempted to capture a larger share of the growing domestic market. They increasingly developed their own registered trademarks and brands, not only to differentiate their own products from those of importers and local competitors, but also to persuade the public that they were now capable of manufacturing good quality clothing and footwear. Greater attention was paid to advertising such goods, especially in newspapers and periodicals, with some firms enlisting the assistance of New Zealand-based agencies to produce attractive and appealing copy.[1]

Ross & Glendining Ltd, with their own supplies of worsted yarn and the latest machinery from the United Kingdom, possessed a first-mover advantage in the market for quality hosiery and fully-fashioned knitwear. Often marketed under the Roslyn brand, such goods commanded a ready sale. The firm did not possess the same advantage in the production of clothing, hats and footwear, and for much of the period leading up to World War I their clothing and hat factories struggled to meet the competition.

## I. A NEW MENSWEAR CLOTHING FACTORY

As the new century dawned, the question as to how the firm should expand was a source of constant discussion between John Ross, Robert Glendining and George Hercus. Quite apart from the obvious need for greater hosiery capacity, it was agreed that a new clothing factory should be built as well. A site was obtained in High Street, to the rear of the old Stafford Street warehouse. Back in London, it fell to Ross to order the iron columns, glass and guttering that was needed. Everything was dear, he complained, as coal was a third more expensive than a year previously. Iron and steel manufacturers were also busy, with the Boer War placing additional demands on industry, and it was November 1900 before the ironwork was ready to be shipped.[2]

Not everyone in the firm was convinced that a new clothing factory was necessary. The Wellington branch manager, Jones, made his views quite plain, criticising the manager of the existing factory, the construction of a new and larger plant, and the extensions that were being made to the Dunedin warehouse. While Ross accepted that the factory manager, Palmer, had become quite slack, he was quick to defend the building programme:

> You are certainly wrong in your idea that the Buildings which are in the course of erection in Dunedin are more for show than money making. I assure you that as far as I am concerned such is not the case. When in New Zealand ... I found the Mill Stock scattered about, partly in the present warehouse, partly in Stafford St. and partly in the High St. store while the waterproof stock, besides being scattered in the aforementioned places, was lying about in every corner of the Clothing Factory as well. The Factory, as you know, is an old building, too small, inconvenient and having a poor appearance, while the ground on which it stands is not utilized to the best advantage. My idea, therefore, was to have an up-to-date Factory with sufficient room to enable us to add shirt and mantle making to our present activities ....

He added that had he not thought the building programme necessary, he would not have sanctioned a single brick.[3]

The delay in shipping the iron columns, together with an unusually long spell of wet weather, held up building work. By March 1901, however, good progress had been made, and it was anticipated that the premises would be ready in time for the spring trade.[4] Costs had long since passed the figure that Glendining had estimated but Ross was not in the least surprised, commenting that he would still consider the factory wonderfully cheap if the building came in at less than £5,000.[5] Additional plant added to the costs and by January 1902, after operating for six months, plant and stocks at the new factory had a book value in excess of £12,000.[6]

The new High St factory was quite sizeable, measuring 66 feet by 115 feet deep, the basement and three storeys providing some 30,000 square feet of working space.[7] Motive power was supplied by a nine horsepower Campbell oil engine, replacing the three-horsepower Otto gas engine used in the old factory. More power enabled the number of sewing machines to be increased, there being over sixty Wilson & Wheeler and almost thirty Singer machines of various types installed in the factory by January 1902. There were also button-making machines, riveting machines, pressing blocks and irons, sundry other items and 146 stools and twenty-two forms.[8] A new machine that automatically sewed on buttons was added a little later, with other sewing machines to follow. The extra capacity of the new plant increased potential output by approximately one half.

The report to the annual general meeting in September 1902 noted that after the first year of full working, the clothing factory had performed satisfactorily. Output had risen by around £3,000 to £25,207 and profits on manufacturing amounted to £1,916. The next year saw output continue to rise, but the factory was prevented from expanding more rapidly by a shortage of female labour. Only 127 hands were at work at the end of March and, with 146 stools and twenty-two forms on the premises, there was plenty of room for more. Attempts were made to obtain additional machinists by enlisting the assistance of the Tailoresses Union but, after making enquiries in other centres, the secretary informed Hercus that all union members in New Zealand were employed. Learning that trade was slack in Victoria, Hercus then placed advertisements for three coat machinists and three experienced trouser machinists in leading Melbourne newspapers. Wages were to be 22/6d per week, although a 'girl' who could regularly make more than six dozen trousers a week might expect 25/-. Prospective employees were offered a twelve-month contract, with passage money to be advanced and repaid from wages.[9] Extra labour was evidently obtained from somewhere, for output increased over the next two years to reach a peak of £30,219.

Increased output did not lead to greater profitability. A loss of £717 was made in the year to July 1905, forcing the factory to slash prices in order to compete. The reduction, however, was still insufficient to offset competition from the northern factories where, in spite of wages being lifted by arbitration awards, the costs of making were significantly cheaper than in the south.[10] With their salaries linked to profitability, the departmental heads in the branch warehouses once again began to patronise cheaper, local suppliers of clothing.[11] As on previous occasions, the Wellington manager, Jones, was summoned to Head Office and instructed to source more clothing from Dunedin.[12] An improvement in the economy over the next eighteen months resulted in an increase in orders, but losses continued (see Table 12.1).

In spite of underperformance, there was no question of abandoning making clothes in-house since the Dunedin factory was regarded as an indispensable adjunct to the warehouse departments. As Ross explained to a critical Sutherland in London,

TABLE 12.1

FACTORY OUTPUT AND PROFITABILITY,[a] 1901–1914 (£000s)

| July Year | 1901 | 1902 | 1903 | 1904 | 1905 | 1906 | 1907 | 1908 | 1909 | 1910 | 1911 | 1912 | 1913[b] | 1914 |
|---|---|---|---|---|---|---|---|---|---|---|---|---|---|---|
| **Clothing** | | | | | | | | | | | | | | |
| Output | 22.5 | 25.2 | 28.4 | 29.1 | 30.2 | 26.9 | 26.9 | 26.2 | 24.5 | 23.3 | 22.8 | 22.4 | 20.4 | 16.6 |
| Net profit | 1.3 | 1.9 | 1.2 | 0.6 | -0.7 | 0.0 | -0.2 | 0.4 | -1.0 | 0.2 | -0.2 | -1.2 | -0.8 | -1.3 |
| **Hats** | | | | | | | | | | | | | | |
| Output | – | – | 3.5 | 8.5 | 10.6 | 12.0 | 11.7 | 10.6 | 9.2 | 9.7 | 10.2 | 10.0 | 9.2 | 9.2 |
| Net profit | – | – | -2.3 | -2.5 | -2.3 | -1.3 | 0.9 | 0.8 | 0.3 | 0.6 | 0.3 | 0.4 | 0.2 | -0.1 |
| **Boots** | | | | | | | | | | | | | | |
| Output | – | – | – | – | – | – | – | 1.1 | 11.1 | 19.7 | 29.5 | 29.0 | 37.4 | 32.3 |
| Gross profit | | | | | | | | -0.2 | 0.3 | 0.2 | 0.8 | 0.9 | -1.4 | -13.2 |
| **Mantles** | | | | | | | | | | | | | | |
| Output | – | – | – | – | – | – | – | 5.7 | 8.9 | 13.7 | 13.0 | 12.7 | 12.8 | 10.1 |
| Gross profit | – | – | – | – | – | – | – | | n.a. | n.a. | n.a. 0.9 | 1.2 | 1.1 | 0.6 |
| Total output | 22.5 | 25.2 | 31.9 | 37.6 | 40.8 | 38.9 | 38.6 | 43.6 | 53.7 | 66.4 | 75.5 | 74.1 | 79.8 | 68.2 |

Sources: Half-yearly balances, AG 512 15/7–15/10.

Notes: (a) Profits in all cases are based on prices at which goods are transferred to the warehouses, not final selling prices. Trade charges for Boots and Mantles apparently deducted in warehouses to produce a net profit figure. (b) From 1913 onwards, output values based on goods actually dispatched to warehouses instead of factory output x transfer prices.

*A clothing department of any magnitude could not be run here at present without a factory. We could not work on government contracts or the chart trade without one and both are considerable. All the warehouses have something of the sort. Sargood, Son and Ewen tried to get along by getting outsiders to make up for them but did not find it a success and started a factory of their own about a year ago. The prices, you may be aware, are fixed by the arbitration court, as are the hours of labour, and we get as much as possible done, piecework.*

The laws and regulations, he pointed out, did not leave much of a margin for profit.[13]

By 1911, the clothing factory was still struggling to break even. Hercus, writing to the Government Statistician, tended to blame the scarcity of labour, high wages, 'and other legal charges and restrictions'.[14] What restrictions he had in mind we do not know although immigration policy, which offered assisted passages only to domestic servants and would-be farmers, may have been one of them.[15] Changes in the law also meant that employers no longer had the right to recover advances in passage money from employees' wages.[16] In 1912, Hercus raised the question of labour shortages with the Dunedin Expansion League and the New Zealand Woollen Manufacturers Association.[17] He also wrote to the Minister of Immigration on several occasions, requesting assisted passages for nominated workers for both the factories and the mill.[18]

## 2. A BELATED MOVE INTO LADIES' CLOTHING

The clothing factory had always concentrated on making menswear. A limited quantity of ladies' clothing was produced but, until the turn of the century, Ross & Glendining had imported most of their ladies' mantles and costumes from Europe. As real incomes rose, however, the market changed, with growing informality of dress, rising hemlines, and a penchant for brighter colours being readily embraced by increasingly fashion conscious consumers.[19] With style appealing to New Zealand women almost as much as price, it became easier to extract a price premium for well-designed and well-made clothes. Local producers, better able to pass on high labour costs on more fashionable lines, found that it was now possible to earn good profits in this sector of the trade. They were aided by the tariff amendments of 1907, in which items commonly used in making up, such as crepes, silks and laces, benefited from a 5 per cent reduction in duties.[20]

Changes in fashion rather than amendments in the tariff were probably what prompted John Ross to start manufacturing women's garments. Some months before the reduction in duties took place, he decided to convert the top floor of the old Stafford St warehouse into a mantle and costume factory. Thirty or so sewing machines and other dressmaking tools were installed, and 'a smart working man' by the name of Pratt was employed to manage operations. 'I think we made a mistake not going into this line years ago', Ross told his son, 'as Butterworth Brothers have got a strong hold now and we will have difficulty wresting the trade from them'.[21] He need not have worried. Within a few years the output of mantles and costumes had risen to over £13,000 per annum, more than half that of the clothing factory. The unit apparently traded profitably (see Table 12.1).[22]

### 3. STRAW BOATERS

Until Sargood, Son & Ewen started making hats in Dunedin in 1901, there were no large-scale factories in New Zealand, the bulk of hats sold being imported from abroad. Encouraged by Wellington hatter John Stafford, and the fact that contemporary fashion dictated that everybody – adults and children – wore hats, Glendining felt compelled to emulate Sargoods.[23] The venture, as far as fur and woollen hats were concerned, proved to be as disastrous as Ross had originally feared. Only in the production of panama hats and straw boaters was the firm ever able to compete.

By comparison with the clothing and mantle factories, the costs of establishing the hat factory were not trivial. The expenditure on plant and machinery alone came to almost £5,500, with stocks of raw materials and finished goods after four months' work accounting for a further £8,000. The largest single outlay was in providing motive power and steam to the factory, the steam engine, boiler, steam pipe connections, belting and gearing having a landed cost of £1,423.[24] As the factory was to occupy part of the old Stafford St warehouse, extensive alterations had to be made, including the erection of a 60-foot chimney at the back of the building.[25] This further added to the costs, although these were subsequently offset when the engine was used to supply electricity to the clothing and mantle factories. The work was finally completed in August 1902, and on 22 August an application was made to the Inspector of Factories for the premises to be registered. Known as 'Ross & Glendining's Hat Factory', the motive power was recorded as steam, the maximum number to be employed was 150, and work was to start the following Monday.[26]

The firm was fortunate in that it was able to obtain experienced hands for straw hat making without too much difficulty. Early in 1902, a Mr and Mrs Brown approached the Christchurch branch manager, offering to staff the Dunedin factory. After establishing how much the couple, their son-in-law, two machinists, a finisher and apprentice could produce in 'legal working hours', the family was engaged.[27] The manufacturing process, it seems, was equally relatively straightforward, with straw plait imported from China, Japan and elsewhere being rolled, shaped and formed by a succession of machines. The company soon boasted that it could produce any colour and any conceivable shape that might be required to meet the needs of the marketplace.[28] More importantly, perhaps, it was able to do so quite economically and, by 1905, straw hat sales of around £2,400 yielded a modest profit.[29]

Thereafter, straw hat production returned a regular profit, the Edwardian craze for boaters ensuring a ready sale for the firm's products each summer. Like the clothing factory, the straw hat factory also found it difficult to hire additional hands and so, in 1907, Sutherland Ross was allowed to investigate a new patent process. Ross senior admitted that he was 'not sweet' on patents and impressed upon his son that he did not want straw hats that would wash or last too long.[30] Increasing affluence, it seems, had ushered in the throwaway society! Nothing more was heard of the new technology and, even without it, the value of straw hats manufactured slowly crept up. In 1912, annual output exceeded £5,000 for the first time.

## 4. FELT HATS

By comparison, hat making using felted fur and wool was far more complicated. The fur hats were made from rabbit fur, expensive blending, blowing and forming machines being employed to produce a cone-shaped object. After felting, the cone was soaked in shellac and methylated spirits, dried in a steam chest, formed over a wooden block, then sanded, styled and finished – one at a time. Woollen hat making commenced with the production of a felt hood – or rough hat shape – from carded wool. After dyeing at the mill, the hoods were next formed, stretched and curled on a variety of machines. Finally they were lined, trimmed, labelled and boxed.[31]

Such work required considerable expertise and it was Ross & Glendining's misfortune that John Stafford, who had been appointed as the hat factory manager, turned out to be 'a duffer'.[32] Having ordered large quantities of fur, rabbit skins and hoods, expensive hat leathers, a vast assortment of feathers, 240 gallons of methylated spirits, four hundredweights of glue and sundry other items, by Christmas 1902 he had turned only a very small proportion of the huge stock into hats.[33] Stafford was promptly dismissed. In February, John C. Ross, formerly of the Denton Hat Mills, was put in overall charge of the hat factory and sent home to England with instructions to 'engage and bring out half a dozen working hatters'. En route he was to visit leading hat manufacturers in Italy, Germany and America, acquaint himself with the latest methods, and buy such additional machinery as he saw fit.[34]

Some fourteen hands were employed in felt hat making by end of March. The first year of fur and woollen hat production, however, turned out to be a fiasco. Up until July 1903, losses of £1,231 were sustained on an output of less than £2,400, and that was even before overheads were deducted. A special charge of £370 to cover the salary and travelling expenses of J.C. Ross was also excluded. The next year, 1904, proved to be a little better, with output increasing to over £6,300, but losses still remained high, some £645 before overheads were taken into account. The latter were swollen by high inventory charges due to the manager having 'too rosy expectations of the quantity he might turn out'. There was also a heavy overhang of useless trimmings and so forth ordered by Stafford that nobody knew what to do with. Some of these were sent back to the United Kingdom in 1905 in the hope that they might be resold, but the rest were ruthlessly depreciated by Hercus.[35] Output rose still further, to £8,249, but poor trading and inventory write-downs resulted in a massive loss of £1,727, again before overheads were deducted.[36]

The return of John Ross to New Zealand saw closer attention paid to hat manufacturing and, early in 1906, he conducted a detailed appraisal of the plant. He found that the quality of the labour force left much to be desired. The felt hat manager, Harrison, was in poor health, a number of the hands were incompetent, too many possessed only a limited range of skills, and the plant was overmanned. To remedy these deficiencies, he recommended that several of the hands not be re-engaged when their contracts expired and that Mrs Newton, the head of trimming, be discharged as her work was 'disgraceful'. Two of her fellow workers, Ross thought, could quite easily take her place. An additional finisher should also be sought from Melbourne, preferably one who could shape hats as well as finish. Other recommendations were that only a restricted number of qualities should be kept in stock; small, low quality hoods should be dispensed with as they entailed too much work; colours should be carefully controlled; and several different-shaped blocks be acquired.[37]

The recommendations were slow to be put into effect and so, in August 1906, Ross stepped in and fired Mrs Newton and her husband.[38] The new regime was evidently not to the liking of John C. Ross, who also decided to leave, much to the relief of Ross senior who thought his namesake had cost the firm 'thousands of pounds'.[39] Improvements in quality and value took place thereafter, but in spite of pressuring the warehouses to send more orders to Dunedin, sales of felt hats gradually fell away. In 1909, the felt hat section of the factory was still making losses, even though the hats were now sold at what was thought to be a competitive price. 'The trade does not appear to have got over the prejudice created by the bad quality hats put on the market by other makers', Ross mused, 'and then there are two or three small concerns who cut prices very keenly but I suppose we must persevere until success comes around.'[40] Some progress was made, contracts for caps being secured from New Zealand Railways and from several tramway companies. Profits nevertheless remained modest and in 1911, having decided to use only imported hoods, surplus machinery was sold to a buyer in Auckland.[41] When the felt hat manager, Harrison, died in 1913, Ross contemplated selling off the rest.[42]

## 5. BOOTS AND SHOES

Ross & Glendining Ltd had never done much in the way of boots and shoes, having left the trade to large-scale makers such as R. Hannah & Co. and W. & J. Staples of Wellington, and specialist importers. Amongst the warehousemen, Sargood, Son & Ewen had begun making boots in Dunedin in the 1890s.

The market for both leather and rubber footwear had grown substantially thereafter and, by the early twentieth century, Glendining felt that his firm, too, ought to start manufacturing, lest they be left behind. Ross was not convinced and with considerable building taking place elsewhere, the decision to set up a boot factory was deferred. Instead, the Dunedin warehouse set up a boot department and an experienced salesman, a Mr E.W. Roy, was appointed to buy footwear and manage sales. He started on 1 January 1903.[43]

The sales of boots expanded steadily thereafter, with rubber boots imported from the United States and boots and shoes from a variety of makers in the United Kingdom.[44] Salmon Brothers, who had a factory in Filleul Street, Dunedin, supplied a large proportion of the firm's special orders. When, in April 1908, the factory closed, Ross & Glendining promptly acquired it 'at a low price'. Shareholders were informed that: 'The plant is modern and in every respect suitable for the purpose, and there is good reason to believe the factory will prove a valuable adjunct to the Boot Department of our business'. The Filleul Street factory went back into production almost immediately, presumably taking on hands who had previously worked for Salmon Brothers. Some thirty men and women were initially employed, doubtless glad to be back in work during a time of depression. By July 1908, £1,100 worth of boots had been produced and a small loss incurred.[45]

The cost of entry into the boot industry was relatively modest, with the premises leased and the plant and machinery purchased for £600.[46] There were evidently advantages in having a factory up and running for, by July 1909, annual output was already in excess of £11,000. Unlike the clothing and hat factories, the boot factory found little difficulty in disposing of all that it made. The fact that Roy was now given the responsibility for managing the sales of boots in all branches, whether manufactured or bought in, undoubtedly helped, as did the appointment of a traveller specialising in footwear.[47] Demand was also bolstered by the tariff changes of 1907, which helped to cut out cheaper imports.[48] The combination of tariff protection and a recovering economy saw sales and profitability rise sharply, the former peaking at over £37,000 in 1913.[49]

The rapid expansion, although welcome, brought its own problems when, towards the end of 1909, Ross & Glendining were informed by the local factory inspector that conditions were too cramped in Filleul St. A new and larger building, with a 54-foot frontage, was acquired at the south end of Princes St.[50] With room to expand, additional workers were recruited just as fast as they could be hired. This caused some friction with Sargood, Son & Ewen as a number of their employees, attracted by better working conditions and the more convenient location of Princes St, left to work there. By the middle of the year, 130 workers were employed in the new factory.[51]

The need for a large number of workers is a reflection of the labour-intensive and capital-light nature of the New Zealand boot and shoe trade at the time. Thus of the £1,905 sunk in plant and machinery in July 1910, the largest single item was a back blocking machine which cost £343, followed by 135 sets of uppers patterns valued at £337 and thirty-four sewing machines and benches with a book value of £234. The sewing machines were mechanically driven, motive power being supplied, via a system of gearing, by a 25-horsepower Westinghouse motor. The gearing and electric motor cost £221, the latter replacing the 9-horsepower gas engine used in the previous factory.[52] Electricity, it seems, was now being adopted as a cheap, clean and flexible power source in most of the company's factories.

The annual report for 1910 stated that the firm now had a splendidly planned and equipped up-to-date factory with 'the latest machinery and appliances, fully manned and in full work'.[53] This was something of an overstatement, given that the machinery and appliances were still clearly rudimentary. Over the next two years the situation was to change, with an extra £1,500 invested in modernising the plant. Additions included an outsole stitching machine, screwing and pegging machinery, self-feeding eyelet machines and more – as well as another twelve sewing machines, benches and stools.[54] The substitution of capital for labour made excellent sense, given the state of the local labour market, and it seems likely that there were productivity advantages as well. Even so, still more labour was required and, by the beginning of 1912, some 150 men and women were at work in the factory. Operations were small compared to Hannahs' large factory in Wellington but, as Ross told his son, the boot factory was growing rapidly and did a much better trade 'than you seem to give us credit for'.[55]

The continued growth in output meant that it was not long before there was need for still more space. In the middle of 1912, the property adjoining the Princes St boot factory was acquired, enabling it to be enlarged. Additional equipment was installed, with Roy travelling to the United Kingdom in the middle of 1913 to visit shoe suppliers, secure new agencies, and inspect the latest machinery. The best machines, according to Robert Hannah, were to be found in Melbourne and Sydney, but Ross encouraged Roy to make up his own mind.[56] A few months later, with the prospect of a new and higher tariff, Roy was instructed to buy the British machinery without delay.[57] Additional machinery was purchased and over the next eighteen months the book value of the boot factory and plant rose by nearly a half to almost £12,500.[58]

The timing of the expansion was unfortunate, to say the least, coinciding as it did with growing labour unrest and the watersiders' strike, a sharp rise in material costs, and a downturn in the economy. In 1913, boot manufacturers in Christchurch were reported to be working half time. Ross & Glendining's sales kept up reasonably well, but the boot factory recorded its first loss since 1908. This was not as bad as it seemed, since the prices at which boots were transferred to the warehouses enabled the latter to earn an unusually high net profit of 22 per cent.[59] The situation continued to deteriorate over the following six months, however, and in January 1914, for reasons that were not entirely clear to Ross, the Princes St factory recorded an even greater loss.[60] Shortly afterwards the manager was sacked. A new man Rae, recruited in Glasgow, was put in charge.[61] This did not prevent a 'terrible' loss of over £11,000 being sustained in the second half of the year.[62] With the outbreak of war, fortunes at the factory rapidly revived.

## 6. NEW PRODUCTS AND NEW BRANDS

The decision by Ross & Glendining Ltd to increase both the scale and scope of their manufacturing business was part of a general trend in New Zealand in this era. A growing and increasingly affluent population meant that between 1900 and 1914 the size of the domestic market had grown substantially. This, in conjunction with adjustments to the tariff, meant that more factories were able to survive – providing they were able to operate at a reasonably efficient scale.

As new opportunities arose, it was perhaps inevitable that leading warehousemen in New Zealand should integrate backwards into manufacturing. Already importing and distributing large quantities of clothing, footwear and textiles, their ability to draw on reserves of capital and leverage off existing capabilities often gave them a competitive advantage. By 1914, Sargood, Son & Ewen were to be found manufacturing clothing, hats and boots; Butterworth Brothers Ltd had widened their clothing horizons to embrace costumes and mantles; and Bing, Harris now manufactured their own clothing which they sold under the 'Arrow' brand. In the north, too, a similar picture prevailed, with Macky, Logan, Steen & Co. of Auckland possessing extensive manufacturing facilities in the city.

The development of mass markets on a national scale meant that it was perhaps inevitable that domestic manufacturers, like their counterparts overseas, should attempt to capture the attention of consumers by developing their own brands and logos. Ross & Glendining, of course, had long sold Roslyn goods by name and the achievements of Roslyn Mills were well publicised through copy placed in newspapers and publications such as the *New Zealand Cyclopaedia*. The firm also tended to support exhibitions where a stand might be taken to show off both their own manufactures and goods they imported. After 1900, advertisements for mill goods were increasingly found in daily and weekly newspapers incorporating the distinctive Roslyn logo. Often these advertisements were taken out in conjunction with leading retailers, such as John Court of Queen St, Auckland, the cost of plates being shared.[63]

Even so, evidence suggests that Ross & Glendining Ltd may have been followers rather than leaders in the field of advertising. Certainly they lagged behind both Bing, Harris and Sargood, Son & Ewen in adopting registered trade marks. When it came to parting with money for advertising, a degree of caution was evident. Hercus's letter to Jones in 1905 epitomised this attitude:

*We must do something in advertising, now. We have arranged for one or two contracts; but it takes money we find and while spending it, we must see that we scatter the seed in likely soil. We are pleased that you did not make a 'poor mouth' to the interviewers. The Kaiapoi people have made a sad mess of it by their appeals to the charitable instincts of the community.*[64]

Gradually outlays increased. In 1912 the firm spent over £2000 on advertising as well as exhibiting a range of goods at the Dunedin Industrial Exhibition, boasting in the souvenir programme that it provided everything from 'the crown of the head to the sole of the foot'.[65] By this stage, Ross & Glendining was not only using its Roslyn brand, but had also adopted and registered the name 'Defiance' in order to differentiate the hats and caps it produced from other makes. This brand was extended to cover shirts, hosiery, boots and other goods.[66] Suddenly, brands had become important to the clothing, footwear and textile industries. Indeed, Sargoods took strong exception to Ross & Glendining's use of the phrase 'standard screwed' to describe their boots. 'Standard', it was pointed out, was the registered brand name of Sargood, Son & Ewen.[67]

## 7. MARKETING LADIES' UNDERWEAR

The increase in time and money spent on advertising was partly forced on Ross & Glendining by their competitors. They were also persuaded to spend more by one of their travellers, the Auckland-based Thomas Finlay. In 1910 he paid a visit to Dunedin to discuss the methods he used. He was, according to Ross, a bit of a character, and picked up a lot of trade by placing 'paragraph ads' in papers in the areas he visited.[68] Suitably impressed, Ross decided to give Finlay a bigger role in organising the advertising within the firm, and he was ultimately made responsible for arranging contracts, placing copy, and managing the agency the firm held for corsets made by Warner Brothers of New York.[69] Advertising was co-ordinated from Auckland, with Finlay working under the supervision of the warehouse manager, Alexander Snedden.

Sales of Warner's corsets only amounted to around £10,000, a small proportion of Ross & Glendining's total sales. Yet corsetry and other foundation garments could not be ignored since they represented the height of fashion at the time. Rising incomes meant that these goods now fell within the reach of many, and female customers were offered a variety of exotic sounding brands including 'Ortiz', 'Zantor' and 'P.D.' – the latter thoughtfully adapted for the 'fuller figure'. Warner's, though, were probably the best known. Guaranteed never to break, rust or tear, replacement free of charge was offered should any defect occur.[70]

The Warner Brothers corset agency was not entirely straightforward. Early in 1904, Ross & Glendining had accepted the sole New Zealand agency for a full line of corsets and specialities after correspondence with the main Australian agents, J.P. Richardson & Co. of Melbourne.[71] For the remainder of the decade corsets were obtained via the Australian agents, but it appears that neither the supply of goods nor the promotional support was all that it might have been. In 1912, the costs of advertising were greatly in excess of the £462 'subsidy' allowed by the makers, and there were still excess stocks of corsets held in the Auckland warehouse.[72] Dissatisfied with the existing arrangements, Finlay was sent on a 'secret' mission to New York in September to negotiate a separate agreement with Warner Brothers.[73] In a letter of introduction, Ross explained that direct relations between the two firms would enable Warner's corsets to be advertised in New Zealand far more effectively than at present. As a result, 'the good results already achieved could be greatly extended.'[74] The letter, together with Finlay's powers of persuasion, evidently had some effect. While complete agreement was not reached, Ross & Glendining now sent orders straight to Warner Brothers and received an improved allowance to cover the cost of advertising and other promotional expenses.[75]

In January 1913, Thomas Finlay was engaged for a further year as manager of the advertising department in Auckland. He was to be paid a salary of £400 per annum, together with a commission of 1¹/₄ per cent on sales of all American agency lines. In addition to dealing with Warner Brothers and other American suppliers, he was expected to make, 'Personal visits throughout the dominion for the purpose of selling special agency lines, together with any special lines of our own manufactures or importations that may be placed in your hands for the purpose.' Finlay's approach to advertising did not always go down well with the more staid warehouse managers, and his new contract stipulated that no fresh material was to be issued without their consent. Some existing advertisements were also to be withdrawn.[76]

The new method of working appears to have made little difference to corset sales and in 1914 it was decided to close the advertising department. All future arrangements regarding Warner Brothers' goods and advertising were to be made in Wellington, where the Australian agents now had an office. As Hercus explained to Snedden, given the difficulties that Ross & Glendining were experiencing in supplying orders for Roslyn goods, it was decided that there was no need to spend so much money on advertising. He was instructed to tell Finlay to wind up his department in time for the July balance, and provide suggestions as to what to do about any outstanding advertising contracts.[77]

### 8. WAS FACTORY EXPANSION JUSTIFIED?

The use of the Defiance brand and increased advertising expenditure appears to have done little for the firm's new factories. Excluding the losses incurred by the boot factory in 1914, the four factories probably just about broke even in this period although, in the absence of net profitability data for the mantle and boot factories, it is difficult to be sure.[78] Poor management was partly to blame, but labour shortages and persistent wage differentials between Dunedin and northern cities also made life difficult.

While the factories themselves may not have yielded much of a profit, the warehouses that they supplied were, on the whole, quite profitable and therein lay the factories' justification. Between 1901 and 1914, the annual value of goods supplied by the factories to the warehouses increased by around £50,000, the bulk of which were then sold to retailers with a decent margin added on. Had the warehouses been obliged to buy in, then prices would generally have been higher, quality and scheduling problems greater, and profits correspondingly reduced.

# THE STRUGGLE FOR EXPANSION: THE WAREHOUSES, 1900–1914

The relationship between the factories and the warehouses was symbiotic. Just as the warehouses relied on the factories to supply them with locally made goods at competitive prices, so the factories relied upon the network of warehouses to market and distribute their goods efficiently. As the New Zealand market was growing rapidly, especially in the north, efficient distribution called for both the extension of the branch network and the enlargement and reorganisation of existing warehouses. With Glendining insisting that he should oversee mill activities, John Ross largely undertook the job of developing the warehouse side of the business. He was extremely successful, warehouse sales more than doubling to over £780,000 by the time of World War I.

## 1. MORE WAREHOUSE EXTENSIONS

The rapid expansion of trade in the late 1890s meant that by 1900 the existing warehouses at Dunedin, Wellington and Christchurch were once again pressed for space. A massive building programme ensued. Work started on extending and modernising the Dunedin warehouse as soon as the clothing factory was finished and by the middle of 1902 it was ready for occupation. The refurbished building was an imposing structure, with a frontage on High St of 133 feet and a depth of 100 feet, and consisted of three floors and a basement. This doubled the warehouse space available and allowed stocks to be transferred from the old Stafford St warehouse and from a store further along High St. The company's own products were displayed in the new part of the building, which was still lit by gas.[1] Indeed, as late as 1914, the only electricity used in the High St warehouse was for John Ross's foot warmers and a newly arrived calculating machine – somewhat surprising in view of the pioneering step taken to light Roslyn Mills by electricity.[2]

As soon as the Dunedin warehouse was completed, Charles Lomax, the Inspector of Works, moved on to Roslyn Mills to superintend the construction of the second mill. His work was not to stop there, for in 1903 the Directors had purchased the lease of the premises adjoining the Wellington warehouse. Before that site could be cleared and an extension built, the busy Lomax was sent to the Christchurch branch, which was also being enlarged.[3] In November he moved on to Wellington where, by the middle of 1904, a three-storey extension measuring 50 feet by 110 had been constructed for just under £6,000. This effectively increased the space available by two thirds.[4] Then, it was back to Christchurch, where Ross & Glendining had agreed to exchange their recently enlarged warehouse for one to be built for them by their neighbours, W. Strange & Co. The new warehouse, on the opposite side of Lichfield St and directly across from Sargood, Son and Ewen, was to cost around £8,400. At 120 feet by 60, it was to be about the same size as their old premises.[5] After Hercus had demanded changes to the cornices and ornamentation, building got under way. When completed early in 1905, he thought it was 'in every way suitable, being one of the most handsome and up-to-date warehouses in the colony'.[6]

The increased capacity of the three principal warehouses was extremely welcome, for between 1901 and 1905 their combined sales rose by half to almost £400,000 (see Table 13.1). The Christchurch branch registered the lowest increase, poor management and fierce competition from local importers tending to hold back sales. Wellington, on the other hand, did very well, sales being swollen by the acquisition of two new sub-branches, one in Nelson and the other in Wanganui.[7]

The two sub-branches had previously been owned by a small firm of general merchants, Scandler & Co., based in Nelson. In 1902 their business was taken over by Levin & Co. Ltd, an old established firm of Wellington merchants which had just begun to expand into the South Island. Levins were principally provision merchants, grain brokers, and stock and station agents, and had little interest in carrying on the clothing, footwear and textile side of Scandlers' business. When Ross & Glendining's Wellington manager Jones heard of this, he immediately alerted Dunedin. A deal was quickly struck, even though Ross & Glendining had recently opened a small sample room in Nelson. Possession of the stock of around £20,000, together with occupancy of two leased warehouse properties, took place in December 1903.[8] Henceforth both branches were administered from Wellington, which already did a considerable business in both areas.

## 2. Opening a warehouse in Auckland

There was still one region, however, in which Ross & Glendining were not properly represented, namely, Auckland. Ross had first drawn attention to the desirability of opening a warehouse in Auckland when he had visited New Zealand in 1900. Towards the end of 1902, with the planned expansion of the mills, factories and warehouses well under way, he once again turned his attention to the Auckland market.

TABLE 13.1
WAREHOUSE SALES AND PROFITABILITY, 1901–1914 (£000s)

| July Year | 1901 | 1902 | 1903 | 1904 | 1905 | 1906 | 1907 | 1908 | 1909 | 1910 | 1911 | 1912 | 1913 | 1914 |
|---|---|---|---|---|---|---|---|---|---|---|---|---|---|---|
| **Dunedin** | | | | | | | | | | | | | | |
| Sales | 99.4 | 101.2 | 115.2 | 136.0 | 146.0 | 152.6 | 176.5 | 153.1 | 162.8 | 167.8 | 168.5 | 176.1 | 182.4 | 170.5 |
| Net profit | 6.7 | 3.4 | 3.9 | 5.6 | 6.1 | 7.1 | 8.2 | 6.9 | 10.3 | 11.9 | 10.0 | 9.4 | 11.3 | 9.1 |
| **Invercargill** | | | | | | | | | | | | | | |
| Sales | 46.7 | 46.7 | 52.0 | 53.0 | 56.8 | 53.7 | 55.7 | 51.8 | 52.5 | 56.7 | 55.3 | 57.1 | 62.1 | 58.3 |
| Net profit | 3.1 | 2.2 | 3.3 | 2.7 | 3.0 | 2.9 | 3.9 | 2.6 | 2.8 | 4.4 | 3.3 | 3.0 | 4.2 | 3.9 |
| **Christchurch** | | | | | | | | | | | | | | |
| Sales | 62.2 | 62.7 | 70.4 | 72.0 | 68.6 | 72.2 | 83.7 | 78.3 | 77.3 | 78.2 | 80.4 | 88.1 | 89.2 | 91.4 |
| Net profit | 4.3 | 4.0 | 5.1 | 4.4 | 3.1 | 2.9 | 5.6 | 3.7 | 1.7 | 1.9 | 2.5 | 6.0 | 4.5 | 4.5 |
| **Wellington** | | | | | | | | | | | | | | |
| Sales | 108.2 | 110.1 | 135.6 | 157.4 | 174.2 | 188.1 | 207.3 | 208.4 | 203.3 | 210.1 | 219.2 | 219.7 | 218.4 | 217.3 |
| Net profit | 8.7 | 7.2 | 10.2 | 10.6 | 10.9 | 13.4 | 14.7 | 12.1 | 6.3 | 10.5 | 9.2 | 9.5 | 11.1 | 8.1 |
| **Napier** | | | | | | | | | | | | | | |
| Sales | 28.3 | 29.3 | 30.1 | 33.9 | 37.6 | 41.6 | 49.2 | 54.6 | 52.7 | 52.0 | 55.2 | 53.3 | 51.3 | 53.7 |
| Net profit | 1.8 | 1.4 | 1.9 | 1.6 | 2.4 | 3.3 | 3.5 | 5.3 | 2.9 | 2.4 | 4.3 | 2.8 | 3.8 | 2.0 |
| **Auckland** | | | | | | | | | | | | | | |
| Sales | taken through Dunedin books until 1908 | | | | | | | 71.4 | 119.8 | 134.4 | 163.9 | 179.3 | 180.1 | 189.1 |
| Net profit | – | – | – | – | – | – | – | 1.5 | 1.0 | 5.3 | 8.0 | 9.6 | 7.8 | 8.3 |
| Other sales [a] | – | – | – | 1.6 | 3.3 | 2.7 | 2.2 | 1.8 | 1.0 | 1.2 | 1.1 | 0.7 | 0.6 | 2.1 |
| Total sales | 344.7 | 350.1 | 403.2 | 453.8 | 486.5 | 511.0 | 574.5 | 619.4 | 669.4 | 700.5 | 743.7 | 774.3 | 783.9 | 782.4 |
| Total net profit | 24.6 | 18.2 | 24.3 | 24.9 | 25.6 | 29.7 | 35.9 | 32.2 | 25.0 | 36.4 | 37.4 | 40.4 | 42.6 | 35.7 |

Sources: Half-yearly balances, AG 512 15/8–15/10. There are discrepancies between this data set and other sales series but gross returns, from which profits are calculated, is regarded as the most reliable. Notes: (a) Includes sales direct to customers from Dunedin factories. Profits taken through factory accounts.

A firm of solicitors, Hanna & Co., was given sole authority to search for suitable properties in Auckland city.[9] Ross was very particular. He wanted a property with a frontage of at least 60 feet, a minimum depth of 100 feet, and ideally it would be located in Elliott St, which was in the centre of the warehouse and clothing district.[10] Over the next nine months, premises in a variety of locations were put forward – and rejected – until in August an Elliott St property was secured. After some haggling, the owners, New Zealand Insurance Co., accepted an offer of £7,500 in cash.[11]

The property, which was to be demolished and rebuilt, was tenanted until 1905, but it was not thought that building would start before then.[12] In September 1903, Ross went north to survey his new purchases, sailing first to Nelson and Wanganui and then onwards to Auckland, to arrange payment for the Elliott St property. As he explained to his London friend, George,

> We have had an agent and sample room there [Auckland] for some years but our representation is very inadequate and quite out of keeping with the show we make at headquarters. That part of the country has gone on wonderfully of late years, impelled by the dairy factories which are very numerous thanks to the generous support given to them by the [Bank of] New South Wales. Our view is to erect a decent building there and to start a branch there by and by, say by the time the trunk line of railway gets through from Wellington.

His trip north, which involved meeting staff and customers at the new sub-branches, was a success, although it was somewhat overshadowed by the sudden death of the firm's London manager, Gibson. Ross was greatly upset, having worked 'for half a lifetime' alongside the man.[13]

The delay in erecting a 'decent building' was not ideal, given the rapid economic growth then taking place in the Auckland region. The poor performance of Roslyn Mills, however, together with the extensive programme of factory and warehouse development taking place, meant that resources were exceedingly stretched.[14] In the interim, more sample rooms were leased in Auckland until the firm could afford to build.

Construction was delayed a lot longer than Ross had anticipated.[15] One of the stumbling blocks was Glendining, who had little good to say about the Auckland venture. Thus he criticised the quality of the sample rooms that Ross had leased, complained about the high price paid for the Elliott St property, and repeatedly procrastinated when the question of building in Auckland arose.[16] The main constraint, though, was the continued shortage of funds. After balancing the books in July 1904, Hercus concluded that it would be some years before the firm could prudently spend another £80,000 to £100,000 on branching out in Auckland.[17] Ross, now back in London, profoundly disagreed. He insisted that a start be made, and shortly afterwards the first steps were taken towards opening a branch in the city.

The choice of branch manager was absolutely crucial. Ross & Glendining were therefore extremely fortunate when, towards the end of October, Hercus was able to secure the services of Alexander Snedden, apparently 'one of the best warehousemen in the colony'.[18] Snedden, who had previously worked for the large Auckland firm of Macky, Logan, Steen & Co., visited Dunedin shortly after his appointment. He brought with him details of warehouses available on short-term leases.[19] One of the properties, a small warehouse in Durham St, was secured and, by the middle of December, arrangements had been made to start trading from the new premises.

Ross approved of the arrangements made. Nevertheless, he couldn't resist pointing out to Hercus that a warehouse should have been opened in Auckland long ago, adding,

> the difficulty was and is that Mr. G likes to take the initiative in everything himself and does not favour suggestions from others. There is no doubt that the opportunities for trade are greater in Auckland than in any other centre in the colony, and it is unfortunate that it is such a long time to look ahead before we are in a position we should occupy there.[20]

Shortly afterwards, Hercus went up to view the Durham St warehouse, a visit that gave him a far better appreciation of the scope for increasing sales in the Auckland region.[21]

The next couple of months were spent by Snedden in assembling stock, making up samples and hiring staff for the winter season. Thomas Finlay, the future advertising manager, was engaged and offered a 7.5 per cent commission to sell to outlets throughout the northern part of Auckland province.[22] These he was to visit in a horse-drawn van, at the same time selling goods supplied by the Auckland Co-op. Boot Co. and Messrs Entrican & Co. The connections with the latter two companies satisfied the suspicious Hercus that Finlay was reputable, even if his *modus operandi* did resemble that of a hawker.[23] There was also an extensive town trade to be done; this was handled by Snedden and his assistant, Holt, who had previously been in charge of the sample rooms.[24]

## 3. BUILDING A NEW WAREHOUSE IN ELLIOTT ST
The Auckland branch initially made sound if unspectacular progress, the turnover of almost £20,000 for the calendar year 1905 being some 40 per cent greater than that achieved in 1904. Sales, however, were still only a fraction of those made in the other main cities although, given the limited

nature of Auckland operations, this was only to be expected. Only after a new warehouse had been built – and staffed by a full complement of departmental salesmen and travellers – could serious inroads be made into the burgeoning Auckland market.

The return of Ross to New Zealand in the middle of 1905 provided a fresh impetus to the business, although funds remained tight after Roslyn Mills had been forced to pay high prices for wool.[25] Even so, Ross was keen to start building as soon as possible. Early in 1906 he and Charles Lomax, the Inspector of Works, began to draw up plans for the new warehouse. Before building work began, Lomax was to pay a brief personal visit to the United Kingdom, where Sutherland Ross was to take advantage of his presence and 'show him any new warehouses and anything worth copying for use in the future Auckland warehouse'.[26] At the annual general meeting in September it was announced that work on the Elliott St warehouse was about to start. Completion was due twelve months hence – in time for the 1907 spring season.[27]

Complications arose almost immediately when Lomax, visiting Blackburn, died suddenly. Unfortunately, his death deprived Ross & Glendining not only of their Inspector of Works, but also of his plans for their warehouse, no trace of which could be found. A fresh set of plans was commissioned from John Currie, the noted Auckland architect.[28] These were drawn up under close supervision from Hercus and Ross.

The building was an imposing affair and was designed to be 'visible and prominent from Queen Street', the main Auckland thoroughfare.[29] Four storeys high with an 81-foot frontage on Elliott St, it incorporated large plate glass windows and the usual ornamentation. Internally there were two rows of supporting columns to cope with the heavy bolts of cloth, a passenger lift for visiting customers and a lift for stock, both of which were to be supplied and installed by Messrs Turnbull & Jones. The interior was to be plastered in Auckland hydraulic lime, as it was superior to ordinary lime and would prevent the spoilage of goods.[30] To the rear an additional section, with a 40-foot frontage on Albert St, had been purchased to provide goods access.

Conditions in the construction industry were not particularly favourable when building began. Two other warehouses were then being built in Elliott St and this, in conjunction with the emigration of bricklayers to rebuild earthquake-shattered San Francisco, resulted in a shortage of labour. Raw material prices were inflated, too.[31] There were also delays owing to a 'scarcity of cement to make concrete foundations and in getting trucks to carry the sand and bricks'. When Ross paid a visit to the site in April 1907 to arrange for lifts and lighting, he found that the builders had only just started the third storey.[32] Wet and stormy weather retarded progress still further so that by the time of the annual general meeting in September, the warehouse was only partially occupied.[33]

Building work continued into November, with painters and decorators yet to finish.[34] By this stage, however, the temporary warehouse in Durham St had been disposed of and Elliott St was open for business with a full complement of staff.[35] Early in 1908, Snedden appointed the first of the company's 'typistes', quite an innovation in an age in which business letters were still largely handwritten.[36]

Although Ross had found it a struggle to persuade Glendining and Hercus to branch out in Auckland, the outcome vindicated his persistence. The transition from agency to branch warehouse enabled the firm to drive a far more substantial trade than hitherto, the combination of heavier stocks and five full-time travellers resulting in far greater market penetration. Henceforth, the warehouse was able to serve customers in an area that extended from Gisborne in the east, down through the Waikato and up into Northland. Sales increased dramatically, from £16,330 in the year ending in July 1905 to £134,403 by 1910, approximately one third of the sales being made by the travellers.[37] Poor transport facilities in Auckland province meant that travelling was both difficult and relatively costly. All the same, profits rose to £5,267 by the end of the decade, one tenth of the profits earned by the entire enterprise.[38]

The success of the Auckland venture left Robert Glendining profoundly unmoved and he refused to re-invest any of the money he received from the disposal of Lauder Station back into the business. Ross was not totally surprised, even though in 1907 his former partner had agreed that the nominal capital of the company should be raised from £500,000 to £750,000 to accommodate extra investment. Glendining's 'unfriendly action' nevertheless left the firm short of funds, and it was necessary to economise on capital by keeping a tight control over warehouse stocks.[39] Ross himself sank another £30,900 into the company and this, it seems, was sufficient to support the growth in business at the new warehouse.[40]

## 4. MORE SAMPLE ROOMS

The establishment of the Auckland branch meant that Ross & Glendining were able to supply most areas of New Zealand without too much difficulty. Yet there were still some remote regions, especially on the West Coast of the South Island, where it was felt that service might be improved. Sample rooms had been leased in Greymouth for some years but the accommodation provided there was pretty 'miserable'.[41] Early in 1908, therefore, Ross ventured over to the West Coast and spent three days in Hokitika and Greymouth looking for larger and more attractive premises. None being suitable, Ross purchased some Maori leasehold land in Greymouth upon which to build. The purchase price of the land was £2,000, and it was estimated that a small warehouse would cost a further £500.[42] In February, tenders were invited for the construction of two-storey premises, 45 feet by 80 feet deep, preferably to be completed before the onset of winter.[43] Building took longer than anticipated and it was not until the end of the year that Ross & Glendining were able to move in. With room to spare, the rear part of the warehouse was let to the New Zealand Railways Traffic Department.[44]

The Greymouth warehouse was a sub-branch of Wellington, which, until July 1908, also controlled sales in Gisborne and the Poverty Bay area of the North Island. The successful establishment of the Elliott St warehouse, however, saw this northern territory transferred to the Auckland branch. Jones, in Wellington, was not at all pleased, claiming that his staff had long experience in dealing with the special needs of customers in Poverty Bay. But Hercus was adamant, 'The Auckland warehouse cannot be expected to pay until all its territory is taken up and the East Coast, including Gisborne, is an important part of the field they are depending on. If Gisborne were left out, they could not work the East Coast at all.'[45] In fact, Gisborne was central to operations, poor transport and communications in the East Cape area making sample rooms in the town absolutely essential if the firm was to compete. A set of rooms was quickly leased from which the traveller could set out with his samples, firstly on a motor bike and later in a Buick motor car.[46]

The expansion of the warehouse network meant that by World War I Ross & Glendining Ltd could claim to be a truly national enterprise. Sales between 1901 and the year ending in July 1914 more than doubled to almost £800,000, nearly a quarter of which was accounted for by the new Auckland warehouse. The growth in sales, which included many new products, placed an added burden both on the branches and on Hercus and his staff at Head Office. Fortunately, the firm was well organised, with its established systems and routines enabling additional business to be accommodated with a minimum of effort. Indeed, warehouse operations were almost mechanical in nature. As Hercus told W.R. Wilson of the Onehunga Woollen Mills, it was much easier to manage a warehouse at a distance than a manufacturing enterprise.[47]

## 5. CONTROLLING WAREHOUSE ACTIVITIES

A departmental system, which was common to all soft goods warehouses in New Zealand, was the key to effective management. From the very first, Ross & Glendining had grouped their product lines together to be sold in separate departments. Specialisation enabled departmental salesmen to gain familiarity both with the nature of the products sold and the different needs of their customers. Moreover, with a limited range of goods in their care, heads of department were better able to keep abreast of changes in fashion, order more precisely, and exercise tighter stock control. In addition to reducing the task of selling to manageable proportions, the adoption of a departmental system made it easier for Head Office to determine the returns yielded by various classes of goods, and the costs involved in supporting a particular type of trade.

The number of departments in each warehouse varied according to the scale of the business conducted. In smaller warehouses, such as those at Invercargill and Napier, products were nominally separated on a departmental basis, although a single warehouseman took charge of a number of product groups. Christchurch and Wellington, on the other hand, had seven departments at the beginning of the twentieth century, while Dunedin had eight, each with their own manager. Entry into the boot trade saw specialist boot departments established in several of the larger warehouses. It was also decided to sell mill goods in separate departments in order to overcome the tendency for salesmen to push imported goods where margins were greater. When Auckland opened in 1908 it had eight departments, including a mill department. Another department was subsequently opened to handle sales of clothing produced by a local sub-contractor.[48]

Control over the departments was made easier by virtue of the fact that each warehouse was obliged to operate according to a set formula. Accounts were to be drawn up according to rules specified by Hercus, and there were key operating ratios to which departmental managers were expected to adhere.[49] Long experience had shown that gross profits of 20 per cent on sales were needed to yield acceptable margins and while the increasingly competitive nature of the New Zealand economy made this figure ever more difficult to achieve, 20 per cent gross profit remained the target right up until World War I. To help managers meet their targets, there were also other operating ratios to guide them in their actions. Stocks, on which Hercus charged each warehouse interest, were to be maintained at around 80 per cent of each season's sales, with the entire stock to be turned over at least once a season. To achieve this, orders for each season were normally expected to be no more than four fifths of quantities ordered the previous year, with additional purchases made as and when required. Branch managers and heads of department were constantly reminded to guard against excessive stock holding, Hercus' pet refrain being that in Australia stocks were turned over, on average, at least four times a year.[50]

Each warehouse was obliged to report to Head Office at the end of the summer and winter seasons, with accounts forwarded to Dunedin every January and July for incorporation in the company balance sheet. The branch managers provided information on sales, departmental gross profits and reasons for over- or underperformance, stocks held, travellers' sales and expenses, details of current balances owing, and comments concerning bad or doubtful debts. They also made recommendations concerning advances in salary and performance bonuses that they felt that their staff merited. Occasionally a plea was made for an increase in their own salaries.

Once the warehouse accounts had been received by Head Office, it was possible to attribute interest, trade and other charges so that net profits for each branch and each department might be calculated. These results, together with the managers' reports, were reviewed by the board. When the gross profit figure was less than the 20 per cent demanded, the accounts were minutely dissected in order to discover the source of 'the leakage'. On occasions, when stocks were high or warehouse and travelling expenses were large relative to sales, it was relatively easy to pinpoint why profits were down. A fall in gross profits when trading conditions seemed good was less easy to explain. Strong competition might be to blame, but underperformance was frequently attributed to departmental managers and their tendency to 'slaughter' slow moving stock. Alternatively, travellers were accused of wantonly granting unauthorised discounts. With the review complete, Hercus wrote to each branch manager with the board's recommendations. The tone of his letters was usually one of encouragement, instruction, admonition, sometimes disappointment and, very occasionally, faint praise.

## 6. THE WELLINGTON WAREHOUSE MANAGER SECURES A SEAT ON THE BOARD

Of all the warehouses, Wellington gave Head Office the least cause for concern. David Jones, the manager, had a wealth of experience in serving the lower North Island and he was ably supported by the branch accountant, William Greig, and his chief warehouseman, Andrew Blacklock. Late in 1901 the leading salesman at the branch, William Doughty, was poached by commission agents, Herbert Thompson & Co., who offered him a salary of £600 per annum, equal to that of Jones.[51] Although Ross felt that a traveller of Doughty's calibre only came along 'once a blue moon', his replacements appear to have performed well.[52] Thereafter Jones shuffled his travellers around, adjusted their territories, fired some and hired others. Between 1900 and 1910, the number of travellers working out of the Wellington warehouse increased from four to eight, one of whom was devoted to serving the town trade in the rapidly growing suburbs.[53]

By 1910, annual sales by the Wellington branch had doubled to over £210,000, notwithstanding the loss of territory to Auckland, but industrial unrest prior to World War I and the effects of the waterside workers' strike in 1913 checked further progress (see Table 13.1, p. 214).[54] Profitability did not increase to the same extent, the downturn in the economy in 1908 and 1909 depressing margins, while local economic problems in Wellington district in 1910 resulted in a build-up of dead stock in some departments. These were subsequently cleared at low prices, to the detriment of margins.[55] Usually, though, Wellington returned around 20 per cent gross profit and a net profit of between 5 and 6 per cent on sales.

Apart from the occasional reprimand for buying-in from local factories, Jones was left to run Wellington pretty much as he pleased. Being in the capital, he proved to be extremely useful in keeping Head Office abreast of proposed changes in legislation. What measures he was to support, and why he was to support them, was carefully spelt out by Dunedin. In 1906, for example, Jones enquired what action he should take over a government report concerned with increases in the tariff. Hercus' reply was quite explicit,

> we have come to the conclusion – which we believe is generally adopted by the leading traders and manufacturers – that it would not be advisable at present to press for any serious changes in the tariff. To attempt to secure increased duties on woollens would be injudicious in the present state of politics. It would afford another pretext for the 'poor working man' to cry out, and lend weight to the very strong and determined crusade against employers that labour agitators are working up for the coming session. Mr. Seddon has indicated reductions on the necessities of life and customs will either be reduced or made exempt …. So long as importers all pay the same duty at each port, it matters little to us what duty is payable.
>
> In view of the very determined movement of the labour party now in preparation, the southern employers feel the importance of pulling together to resist the attack, and are trying to combine with the Farmers' Unions on this subject. The farmers are against protection, and if increased duties were mooted by the manufacturers, there would be no hope of securing support from agriculturalists.[56]

The equanimity with which Ross & Glendining approached the issue reflected the fact that they were importers as well as manufacturers. John Ross and Robert Glendining, of course, were long-standing and committed free-traders.

The importance of Jones to the firm was recognised by the fact that his salary, at £600, was the same as Thomas Glendining's and larger than that of any of the other branch managers. He was still not entirely satisfied, and in 1905 asked for an increase. Jones also suggested that he and Bedo Boys – the chief buyer in London with whom he was very friendly – be placed on the board. Ross, still in London at this stage, was not persuaded. If Jones' salary was to be increased, then Thomas Glendining would also expect more. Nor was he anxious to put Jones or Boys on the board, for the company was still essentially a family business. As he explained to Hercus, since the articles of association stipulated that there should be only five directors, he thought the last vacant position should go to Sutherland Ross. This would ensure that the Ross family had an adequate voice in running the concern.[57]

Yet Ross clearly valued Jones and appreciated that he was underpaid compared to his counterpart at the Drapery and General Importing Company (DIC) in Wellington. He therefore suggested to Robert Glendining that Jones' salary might be augmented by paying him, and other branch managers, a percentage of the profits of the entire company. This system of incentives he felt, would encourage branch managers to consider the welfare of Ross & Glendining as a whole, not just their particular branch.[58] It was some years before this forward-looking incentive scheme was introduced. In the interim, Jones continued to draw his salary of £600 until a trip to Dunedin, later in the year, saw him offered a bonus of £250 on the basis of the preceding year's profit.

The Wellington manager nevertheless remained anxious to secure a seat on the board and, in 1907, pointed out that all the other managers of Wellington soft goods houses were on the boards of their respective companies.[59] As Jones was now suffering from very poor health, Ross finally relented.[60] At the annual general meeting in September, the Articles of Association were amended with the nominal capital of the company being raised from £500,000 to £750,000, and the directorate increased to seven in number.[61] Jones was duly appointed, his salary increased to £800 per annum, and he was sent on a voyage to London for the benefit of his health. By the end of the decade, and still far from well, Jones was earning £994 per annum in salary and bonuses.[62]

## 7. PERFORMANCE OF THE SMALLER WAREHOUSES

The warehouses in Invercargill and Napier were never able to return gross profits of 20 per cent. Their small scale meant that they often found it difficult to shift slow-moving lines and consequently were unable to turn over their stock as quickly as some of the larger warehouses.[63] On the other hand, their overheads were lower and so both were able to return net profits of between 5 and 7 per cent on sales between 1900 and 1914.[64]

Sales grew more rapidly in Napier than Invercargill, the completion of the rail link between Hawkes' Bay and Wellington in 1898 helping to open up the region. For the Napier manager, Robert Wilson, this was something of a mixed blessing, with some of his larger customers now going to the capital to place their main orders rather than buy locally.[65] Business in Invercargill was altogether slower, although matters were not helped by problems that Percy Brodie, the manager, had with some of his warehouse staff.[66] Even so, sales rose, with both the Invercargill and Napier warehouses requiring extensions to accommodate larger warehouse stocks.[67] Neither Wilson nor Brodie were in good health as the decade drew to a close. In 1911 Brodie, aged 42, died. The Invercargill traveller, Dunlop, replaced him.[68]

The performance of the Christchurch warehouse was disappointing when compared to Auckland and Wellington, with turnover slow to increase and profitability declining as time wore on. The population of the city itself grew rapidly during the early 1900s, the urban population of over 80,000 in 1911 being some 10,000 larger than that of Wellington and over 15,000 greater than Dunedin. In spite of the growth in the market, competition was apparently keen, with a number of the larger retailers importing soft goods directly from overseas suppliers.[69] Even so, it is evident that the branch was not managed as well as it might have been, with tension between the branch manager, Alexander Henderson, and his accountant, Samuel Strain, preventing either from doing their job properly. As Ross was later to observe, the two men did 'not pull well together'.[70] Their dislike of each other went back to the mid-nineties when Henderson, a salesman, was appointed branch manager rather than the long-serving accountant. Only after direct instructions from Hercus was Strain prepared to show the books to his new manager.[71] Even then, cooperation was only half-hearted.

Ross thought he detected problems at the branch when he visited New Zealand at the turn of the century, but the trade boom of the early 1900s seems to have masked the extent of the deficiencies.[72] Certain departments, it was evident, were performing badly, and attention was drawn to their shortcomings in half-yearly balance reviews of both 1902 and 1903. Strain was apt to blame a shortage of staff for any underperformance, but Hercus roundly rejected this. What was required was better staff supervision and he reprimanded the accountant for keeping irregular hours. 'How can you know what they do, or when they start, if you are not there yourself until 10.00 or after?' Some allowance was made for disruption due to building work, with Hercus expressing the hope that when the new warehouse was complete, results might improve.[73]

Towards the end of 1903 it was Henderson's turn to be criticised, especially when he replaced the manager of the haberdashery department with a young and inexperienced warehouseman.[74] Hercus counselled Henderson against such a course of action, but to no avail. The young man was sacked barely a year later for inattention to business and other misdemeanours.[75] Meanwhile, sales and profits began to fall, partly the result of a panic that seems to have gripped Canterbury in the middle of 1904, but it was evident that all was not well at the branch.[76] When, in February 1906, gross profits for the preceding half year fell to 13.8 per cent and net profits virtually to zero, it was decided to draft in one of the firm's bright young prospects, James Evans, to sort things out.

Evans' speciality was manchester goods, a major contributor to both sales and profits in all branches, and he promptly took charge of the manchester departments and clothing as well. To his surprise, he found that a number of fictitious stock entries had been made and that there were serious accounting problems.[77] He soon turned things round, with the branch returning a gross profit of 19.24 per cent for the half-year ending in July 1906 and the manchester department posting outstanding results.[78] The New Zealand International Exhibition, which opened in Christchurch in November 1906, helped to sustain trade, and profits for the year ending in July 1907 were the highest on record.

James Evans remained in Christchurch for almost a year before leaving to take charge of manchester at the new Auckland warehouse. Problems began to resurface almost as soon as he left. In 1909, with gross profits back down to just over just over 15 per cent and the result from D department – fancy goods – the worst in the history of the company, it was decided that Hercus should subject the branch to a thorough investigation.[79] He soon discovered what was amiss. 'Sam Strain has taken to the whisky' Ross told his son. 'Hercus found out he had been drinking deeply for six months in consequence of the troubles with his wife. She is apparently quite mad and worries the life out of him.'[80] Strain, in fact, had been drinking for at least three years, but as he had been working for the company since 1873, he was pensioned off at £3 a week rather than fired. Glendining also gave the accountant £100 out of his own pocket.[81] On the next visit, Ross presented Strain with a cheque for his services, at the same time dismissing the latest haberdashery department manager because of 'irregularities'.[82]

Alexander Henderson was treated rather less generously. Following an argument with Glendining at the Christchurch sheep sales a month later, he resigned. Whether the resignation was forced on him is not clear, but Ross was not entirely sorry as the man 'had no control of the hands'. He was replaced by Peter Davidson, formerly of Sargood, Son and Ewen in Christchurch.[83] After struggling for several years, clearing out dead stock and replacing members of staff, Davidson finally put the branch on a sound footing.[84]

## 8. ELLIOTT ST GETS OFF TO A GOOD START
Once the Elliott St warehouse had opened, few problems were encountered with the Auckland branch. Sales increased rapidly, from £71,400 in the year

ending in July 1908 to £189,100 by 1914, an excellent performance given the 1908 downturn and the union unrest that followed. Net profits were slower to increase, the downturn seeing all departments run up excessive stocks, which, at the end of February 1909, stood at almost 150 per cent of sales. Even the admirable Evans carried more stock in his department than necessary, though he still managed to return a gross profit of over 20 per cent. Snedden was urged to see that his departmental heads did not buy too much, and ensure they adhered to the operating ratios laid down by Head Office.[85]

The main worry, though, was the clothing department where, with gross profits barely 1 per cent of sales, a net loss was incurred. This appears to have been brought about by employing a local sub-contractor, Greenough, to make up garments for the branch. Hercus could not understand why so much had been ordered or how a loss had been made,

> *Materials, trimmings etc. were charged at cost price, and yet on the year's work the factory loss on the £6,240 goods charged to us is £716 – or 11.5%. From the new season's returns to March 19th, just to hand, there appears to be large cash advances and small returns in the way of sales to the warehouse. Possibly there is an increasing stock being made and still undelivered, or perhaps some making is going on for other branches and not yet charged … but on the face of it, it looks like a loss to Greenhough is going on.*

What made matters worse, from Hercus' point of view, was that the clothing factory in Dunedin was 'starving' for work. If the arrangement with Greenough could not produce acceptable margins, then it might be better to shut up the Auckland factory and source elsewhere.[86] How Snedden resolved this problem is unclear, but over the next year or so excess stock was worked off and sales driven up. By September 1910 the department was operating profitably. Hercus declared the recovery to be 'phenomenal'.[87]

Gradually overall margins at Auckland branch improved, with Snedden taking prompt action when necessary. For example, when it was pointed out that travellers' expenses in Auckland province were rather high, Snedden himself rode out to see what improvements might be made in working the territories. Expenses duly fell, while sales increased.[88] Not all problems were so easily solved. Disagreement between Auckland warehousemen over the list price for manchester goods resulted in 'guerilla warfare' amongst firms in the form of selective price cutting. Even so, branch profits as a whole continued to increase. By 1912 they had risen to £9,617, some £200 greater than those generated in Dunedin.

## 9. THE WAREHOUSE BUSINESS GENERALLY SUCCESSFUL

The profitability of the Dunedin warehouse was comparatively modest, with margins generally lower than Wellington. The slender profits earned on the small quantities of goods sent overseas to the Chatham Islands, Australia and elsewhere, depressed returns, as did the management of Auckland affairs until 1908. Perhaps it was no coincidence that once the Auckland warehouse became self-supporting, margins in Dunedin improved.[89]

There is little doubt that, in the period leading up to World War I, it was the traditional warehouse business – not Roslyn Mills or the newly established factories – that was primarily responsible for driving the enterprise forwards. Expansion of existing warehouses and the establishment of a national network of branches enabled the firm to increase its share of an ever more wealthy New Zealand market. Of total profits of around half a million pounds earned between 1901 and 1914, more than 90 per cent was derived from the distribution of imported and locally produced goods by the warehouses. Yet the development of manufacturing capacity was not in vain, the popularity of Roslyn hosiery, in particular, helping to raise market awareness of the firm. It was not until after World War I, however, that Roslyn Mills became the mainstay of Ross & Glendining Ltd.

# LONDON OFFICE,
# 1900–1914

When Ross senior returned to New Zealand in 1905, he left Sutherland Ross behind to oversee United Kingdom operations. This was an important position because much of what Ross & Glendining sold in New Zealand was still sourced in Europe. London Office, recently moved to larger premises at 119 Finsbury Pavement, was therefore vital to the success of the enterprise. Although buying well and shipping efficiently still remained a key factor in sustaining a competitive advantage, the rise of mass advertising meant that time now had to be spent securing agencies for leading brands. Orders for machinery, building materials and other items were also routed through London Office, with senior members of staff expected to acquire the necessary technical expertise to deal with suppliers. Perhaps it was just as well that Sutherland Ross was able to rely on Charles Netting, the manager, and the chief buyer, Bedo Boys, both of whom had considerable experience in the warehouse trade.

## 1. DIFFICULTIES WITH THE CHIEF BUYER

First-hand knowledge of the colonial market was regarded as an advantage for staff at London Office and, in 1902, Boys had been brought out to New Zealand to better acquaint himself with local conditions.[1] While in Dunedin, he agreed to a fresh contract of employment with the firm. Hitherto, Boys had bought for both Ross & Glendining and Thomas Brown & Sons Ltd, the Anglo-Australian warehouse firm of which John Ross was a director. With Ross remaining in Dunedin until the new mill was finished and with the volume of goods to be bought likely to grow, it was decided that this arrangement now had to cease. Henceforth, Boys was required to spend his time buying solely for Ross & Glendining. By way of compensation, his salary was to be raised to £1,000 per annum, he was given full control of the buying department and, should a vacancy occur in the buying department, then the job would go to his son.[2]

The death of the London manager, Gibson, shortly after Boys' visit, raised the question as to whether Charles Netting, the assistant manager, might assume charge in London. Boys was consulted and, it seems, wholeheartedly supported Netting's appointment.[3] By 1905, however, it is evident that he was no longer satisfied with his position in the company. The amount of work had increased substantially and he found it particularly irksome that contracts had to be signed by Netting. After corresponding with Jones in Wellington, he pressed for an increase in salary and a place on the board. Hercus was incandescent, and with good reason,

> You recall the proposal made many years ago, for a junior partnership. It is more than probable that if that proposal had been carried out you would by this time have gained a considerable share of the prosperity that has attended the firm: but it was through your own choice that the proposal was shelved, and unfortunately for the present writer, _he_ had to share the same fate in consequence of your decision, and thus failed to reap the results that appeared likely at that time to accrue to him.

Hercus went on to point out that there was no need to have contracts signed by Netting. If any difficulty arose, it would be quite easy to arrange for Boys to have power of attorney, which, owing to his unwillingness to take on more responsibility, he had previously refused.[4]

With Boys threatening to resign, some concession had to be made if his services were to be retained. In a separate letter to Ross, back in England, Hercus noted that, given the growth in business, what was really needed in London Office was a colonial expert in fancy goods. There was still 'a need for Mr. Boys', however, and he suggested that the chief buyer be offered temporary assistance until a fancy buyer was appointed. The question of a place on the board and an increase in salary should be deferred to a later date. At the annual general meeting in September 1905, Bedo Boys' salary was increased to £1,500 and he was promised a directorship 'when practicable'. Still far from happy, he agreed to continue to buy for the firm. From 1907, James Smith, formerly in charge of the fancy department at Wellington warehouse, assisted him.[5]

## 2. SUTHERLAND ROSS UNHAPPY IN LONDON
Given that the day-to-day management of London Office was undertaken by Netting and that buying was largely in the hands of Bedo Boys, the role of Sutherland Ross was very much that of executive director. He authorised financial dealings on behalf of the company in the United Kingdom, oversaw the activities of Netting and Boys and, in regular correspondence with his father, commented on the operational and strategic options facing Ross & Glendining Ltd at home and abroad. He also attended to John Ross' personal affairs.

Although New Zealand firms often retained a London director to oversee affairs, it was a post that Sutherland Ross did not find particularly fulfilling.

Almost from the beginning, he seems to have hankered for a return to Dunedin so that he might take a more active role in running the company. Ross senior was not at all keen, insisting that Sutherland remain in London to perform the job that was asked of him.

The first of Sutherland's letters enquiring whether it might not be better if he were to return to New Zealand arrived in April 1906, less than a year after his father had left London. Whether he felt that John Ross needed assistance in his battles with Robert Glendining, or he feared that the firm might be left to the tender mercies of cousin Bob, is not clear. John Ross, well able to look after himself, offered his son no encouragement;

> *You need not say any more about this. You can surely have patience and wait. You will get your proper place all right when I am gone and nobody can keep you out of it. I have done all I can for you in the meantime, and I have no doubt you will be able to hold your own when your time comes. I don't know what more I can do for you at present.*[6]

Sutherland Ross pleaded to be allowed to return to New Zealand on numerous occasions thereafter but his father, notwithstanding his advancing years, remained unmoved.

The refusal to have Sutherland back in Dunedin may have been a reflection of the fact that Ross senior felt that his son, only twenty-nine years old, still had a lot to learn. Certainly there is little evidence to suggest that the young man was particularly astute, while his carelessness with money was largely what one might expect from an English public schoolboy born into a privileged position. In 1906 his salary was raised to £850 per annum, with instructions from his father that he should save.[7] The following year he was called to task for allowing items of personal expenditure to be passed through the London accounts. When he complained that he had insufficient money to 'commit matrimony', Ross tartly pointed out that with salary and dividend income, his son was not badly off at all. He would, in any case, give Sutherland a cash sum to enable him to set up house when he got married.[8]

The bickering between the two men about the amount of income needed to support a wife continued into 1908. When the young man complained that he did not understand his father, John Ross could only agree![9] He also wished to know what Sutherland Ross was doing for his salary,

> *I would like more information than you give about what work you do in the office. For instance, I would like to know what work you do yourself, whether you take the responsibility for anything special in the buying round. You will recollect that when Mr. Boys resigned it was decided*

*that you should qualify yourself in his place if he should think again of*
*leaving us. Kindly enlighten me on this subject and tell me what you do,*
*day by day.*[10]

In March 1908, Sutherland Ross finally got married, the event being greeted
by his father more with relief than joy. Ross expressed the hope that now
that the 'turtledoving' was over, his son would pay rather more attention to
business than he had done for some time past.[11]

### 3. DISSATISFACTION WITH THE BUYING DEPARTMENT

Sutherland spent his honeymoon visiting New Zealand, where he introduced
his bride, Muriel, to his parents. While he was absent from London Office,
his father attempted to instil greater discipline into the buying department
there. In a letter home, which would have been read by both Netting and
Boys, Ross drew attention to the fact that the branch warehouses had
repeatedly complained about the excessive quantities of goods shipped. In
the case of Christchurch, a very large consignment of ties had been followed
by another shipment that had not been ordered at all. Nor was the quality
of goods all that might be desired. High-quality linoleum had been sent to
Auckland, which, owing to the low qualities required by the market there,
was quite unsaleable. Conversely, the quality of clothing sent to Dunedin
was so low as to be totally unsuitable. While Ross understood that it was
necessary to have samples of new lines sent out, it was important that orders
should not be exceeded by more than 10 per cent. In the case of fancy goods,
where fashions might change overnight, 10 per cent was to be taken as a hard
and fast rule.[12]

Much of this was doubtless repeated to Sutherland while he was in New
Zealand and the visit does seem to have led to an improvement in relations
between father and son. Indeed, Sutherland was complimented shortly after
returning home for preventing Smith, the fancy buyer, from going to France
to see what was on offer. French goods, his father told him, did not sell well
in the New Zealand market.[13] Even so, Ross senior continued to maintain a
careful watch over what was going on in London. In 1910, with buying costs
escalating to more than $2^{1}/_{2}$ per cent of purchases, Sutherland was instructed
to economise. No increases in salary were to be allowed, while the possibility
of moving premises to cut costs should be considered.[14]

To reinforce this message, Ross took advantage of news of Bedo Boys'
remarriage to write a long letter to the chief buyer making the same point.
After a friendly preamble, in which he offered his compliments, commented
on the Roslyn tram company, and mentioned his involvement with Dr
Hocken's collection of books and paintings, Ross turned to business,

*You have no doubt observed the changes that have taken place in buying, that many lines we used to order from home are now bought in the colony, and that the tendency in that direction is on the increase. As shown at stocktaking, a large proportion of the various stocks are colonial bought. This reduces the home buying and tends to increase the percentage of cost of the home office.*

Ross may have overstated the importance of colonial bought goods, but rising costs clearly were a problem. One solution under discussion was the adoption of standard lines for many types of goods. Purchasing in bulk would cut costs through greater buying power, the ability to transfer standard stocks between branches also reducing the need to buy small lots at greater cost to fill customers' orders. Further details of the standard line scheme would be sent to Boys in due course. In the interim, he was urged to do his best to economise by buying manchester in larger quantities.[15]

The system of standard lines and stock transfers was introduced by the end of 1910, followed a year later by the first of a series of bi-annual conferences of warehouse buyers, as attempts were made to coordinate ordering.[16] More systematic ordering may have limited the extent to which London Office was likely to exceed orders, but the problem did not go away. Nor did Ross's concern that his son might not have been spending as much time at work as he ought. When reports filtered through to Dunedin that Sutherland was playing billiards during the day, he suggested that in view of constant fault-finding by Robert Glendining, it might be better if the young man were to confine his billiards playing to outside business hours.[17]

How much time Sutherland spent playing billiards is not clear, although the very fact that he regularly spent time away from the office suggests that he had either too little work to do, or that he found the nature of work unrewarding. Whatever the case, early in 1911 he once again asked his father if he might come out to Dunedin. John Ross, now 76, still felt able to cope and told Sutherland that with relations between himself and the Glendinings very strained at present, it was pointless for him to return.[18]

### 4. OVERBUYING CONTINUES

The growth in business meant that in spite of more goods being sourced from within the Dominion, the work at London Office still increased.[19] With such a vast and diverse assortment of goods being shipped, it was perhaps inevitable that overbuying continued. Sometimes goods were sent out because it was thought that an order had been omitted, at other times because the London buyers felt that what was in fashion at home might easily become fashionable in New Zealand.[20] At the beginning of 1912, it was the unexpected arrival of

Swiss embroidered robes that upset salesmen in the warehouses. The garments shipped were wide, flounced and in dark colours, whereas the fashions that sold in New Zealand were narrow skirts with panel backs made of altogether lighter materials. As a result, the consignment had to be jobbed off at a loss.[21] There were also problems with the quality and workmanship of some of the goods. Sutherland Ross responded by suggesting that a packing room be opened at London Office so that purchases might be monitored. Ross senior thought it was pretty pointless re-packing manchester goods in London, and doubted whether it would be cost effective for the firm to do its own packing.[22]

Many of the problems that arose were laid at the feet of the buyers, especially the fancy buyer Smith who, for a long period of time, John Ross was inclined to fire.[23] Gradually Boys brought Smith under control and, as he did so, the quality and assortment of goods appeared to improve.[24] Another buyer, Thomson, was also appointed. To provide continuity in buying, Bedo Boys, who had intimated that he would retire at the end of 1911, agreed to continue on a part-time basis at a reduced salary of £1,000 per annum.[25]

The continued presence of Boys at London Office meant that towards the end of 1912 it was possible for Sutherland Ross, together with his wife and new-born son, to visit New Zealand.[26] Whether Sutherland thought that he might be able to persuade his father that he should remain in Dunedin is not clear. If so, he was to be disappointed. On 27 March, he and his family boarded the SS *Ruahine*, which was to take them back to London via Cape Horn and Montevideo.[27] Despite one further request to be allowed to return, he was to remain in London until after World War I.[28]

Once back in London, all seemed to go well for a while, with Sutherland Ross apparently doing rather more of the buying than before. This development seems to have alarmed Bedo Boys, who thought he was about to be 'set adrift'. He was rapidly reassured that this was not the case. By the end of 1913, though, complaints about the buying began to occur again, both with respect to the excessive quantities sent and the nature of some of the goods selected.

Since Netting was visiting New Zealand, Sutherland decided to tackle the problems in the buying room himself. He was therefore greatly upset to receive more letters of complaint from his father, especially as they appear to have been written after Ross had discussed the London reforms with Netting.[29] Ross, unusually, wrote a long letter to placate his son:

> ... I am sorry that I distressed you so much by my remarks re. the buying in my letter of the 21ˢᵗ January. I had just been hearing the oft repeated complaints of inattention to instructions by the buyers and in view of the many remonstrances made by me from time to time without any result, I

*felt desperate. Of course, I was not reflecting on you personally, but when we wrote season after season not to send certain lines, and they continued to come to be continually discounted heavily, in some cases their value being nil, I don't think that my remonstrances were too strong. Then, if one branch places an order for a special line, then the buyers seem to think it would be suitable for all the branches forgetting the difference in latitude and requirements between one end of New Zealand and another. Also the overbuying. As I told you in a late letter we are left this season with very heavy stocks, and consequently a big overdraft. This is not altogether the result of overbuying but there is too much of it .... S.S.E. [Sargood, Son & Ewen] only allow a margin of 5 per cent for extra over orders. I have been more liberal allowing up to 10 per cent and if the overbuying did not exceed that the ratio of loss would be much less.*

To guide London in future, a list of goods discounted was compiled, showing which lines were especially bad and those to be avoided. Sutherland was also asked to investigate whether the buyers were too friendly with suppliers and, if so, whether they received greater favours than was desirable.[30]

Over the next few months buying seems to have been gradually brought under control and in June 1914, Sutherland was complimented on the fact that his plans for reforming the buying room seemed to be working.[31] The outbreak of World War I in August, however, meant that for the next four years it was the scarcity of goods, rather than overbuying, that was the main cause for concern.

### 5. Ross & Glendining Ltd generally makes sound progress

The number of complaints concerning the quantities and nature of the goods bought might lead one to suppose that London Office operated less efficiently under Sutherland Ross than his father. Maybe this was the case. The loss of Ross senior's expertise, greater reliance upon the skill of relatively new and untested buyers, and growing disharmony in the buying room as an aging Boys became increasingly bad-tempered, were all bound to affect performance.[32] At the same time, buying was a difficult art and Glendining had raised similar complaints when Ross senior had done the bulk of the buying. Trade, too, was not as generally buoyant after 1908, and hence slow-moving lines were necessarily more difficult to shift. Given the scale and diversity of the business conducted by this time, errors were bound to be made by London Office. Even so, this did not prevent the warehouse business from driving Ross & Glendining Ltd forward, high-margin imports being more than sufficient to offset low returns from goods made in New Zealand (see Table 14.1).

## TABLE 14.1
### NET PROFITS, CAPITAL AND RETURN ON CAPITAL EMPLOYED, 1901–1914 (£000s)

| July Year | 1901 | 1902 | 1903 | 1904 | 1905 | 1906 | 1907 | 1908 | 1909 | 1910 | 1911 | 1912 | 1913 | 1914 |
|---|---|---|---|---|---|---|---|---|---|---|---|---|---|---|
| *Profit Source* | | | | | | | | | | | | | | |
| Roslyn Mills | 3.1[a] | 9.2 | 1.9 | -0.4 | 4.5 | -5.9 | -6.4 | -5.1 | 9.9 | 14.1 | 4.1 | 10.5 | 9.5 | 8.0 |
| Clothing factory | 1.4 | 1.9 | 1.2 | 0.6 | -0.7 | 0 | -0.2 | 0.4 | -1.0 | 0.2 | -0.2 | -1.2 | -0.8 | -1.3 |
| Hat factories | – | – | -2.3 | -2.5 | -2.3 | -1.3 | 0.9 | 0.8. | 0.3 | 0.6 | 0.3 | 0.4 | 0.2 | -0.1 |
| Boot factory | – | – | – | – | – | – | – | n/a | n/a | n/a | n/a | n/a | n/a | -13.4 |
| Warehouses | 24.6 | 18.2 | 24.3 | 24.9 | 25.6 | 29.7 | 35.9 | 32.2 | 25.0 | 36.4 | 37.4 | 40.4 | 42.6 | 35.7 |
| Total profits as per balance sheet | n/a | 29.2 | 25.1 | 22.6 | 27.2 | 22.6 | 30.2 | 28.3 | 34.1 | 51.3 | 41.6 | 50.1 | 51.5 | 28.9 |
| Paid-up capital | 335.9 | 352.0 | 379.4 | 404.5 | 427.3 | 451.8 | 500.0 | 550.0 | 571.2 | 580.0 | 597.0 | 615.7 | 615.7 | 656.2 |
| Shareholders' funds[b] | 353.6 | 374.9 | 400.5 | 420.9 | 446.3 | 467.4 | 523.0 | 572.9 | 600.7 | 631.9 | 655.4 | 688.2 | 700.7 | 732.0 |
| Net tangible assets per share (£-s) | 10-10 | 10-13 | 10-11 | 10-8 | 10-9 | 10-7 | 10-9 | 10-8 | 10-10 | 10-18 | 10-19 | 11-3 | 11-8 | 11-3 |
| Return on capital (%) | 7.5 | 7.8 | 6.2 | 5.4 | 6.1 | 4.8 | 5.8 | 4.9 | 5.7 | 7.8 | 6.3 | 7.3 | 7.3 | 3.9 |
| Dividend paid (%) | 7.5 | 7.0 | 7.0 | 6.5 | 6.0 | 5.5 | 5.5 | 5.0 | 5.0 | 5.5 | 6.0 | 6.0 | 6.5 | 6.0 |

Sources. Half-yearly balances AG 512 15/8–15/10; Share Values as per Article 18, AG 512 15/4.
Notes: (a) 8 months only. (b) Shareholders' funds = capital plus undivided profits and reserves.

While not all parts of Ross & Glendining Ltd operated as efficiently as they might, the enterprise generally made sound progress during the early years of the twentieth century. By 1914 the firm was pre-eminent in New Zealand in the manufacture of high-class hosiery, was rapidly gaining a name for itself in the production of footwear and ladies' clothing, held valuable agencies for leading overseas brands, and had consolidated its position as one of the Dominion's three leading soft goods warehousemen. Dividends of between 5 and 7 per cent were regularly paid to shareholders, funds written to reserves, and undistributed profits ploughed back into the enterprise. In the process, the asset backing of £10 shares rose to over £11, in spite of an increase in the number of shares issued. Of course, in the absence of differences between John Ross and Robert Glendining, the performance of the firm may have been rather better. As it was, Ross & Glendining Ltd continued to expand and diversify while at the same time remaining consistently profitable.

SECTION FOUR
# Wartime and After

# MAKING MONEY IN WARTIME

Business was quite slack and the economy scarcely growing when, on 4 August 1914, Great Britain declared that a state of war existed between herself and Germany. A similar declaration by the Dominion Government was read from the steps of Parliament on the following day. By the end of the month, New Zealand forces had occupied Western Samoa.[1] John Ross 'had no idea that anything quite so disastrous was about to happen' and for a brief period was in a quandary about what to do. His immediate concern was about the future course of wool prices. He recalled that during the Franco-Prussian war of 1870 there had been a great fall in values, a particular worry now as the firm had more than £60,000 worth of wool on hand. Nevertheless, he consoled himself with the thought that while demand was likely to be small, customers would still continue to buy.[2]

Ross need not have worried, for the period between 1914 and 1918 was one of unparalleled prosperity. Although Ross & Glendining experienced restrictions on imports and difficulties in maintaining mill and factory output, the firm reaped handsome profits from selling into a market in which goods were scarce and inflation rampant. Sales virtually doubled to over £1.4 million while net profits soared. Even after allowing for inflation of around 50 per cent, the increase was substantial (see Tables 15.1 & 15.3).

## 1. THE EFFECTS OF WAR INCREASINGLY FELT IN NEW ZEALAND

The most immediate sign that the European powers and their allies were at war was the disruption caused to shipping. Straightaway, the New Zealand Government decided to commandeer six 'home' steamers, together with several of the Union Steamship Company's large overseas trading vessels. As a result, the service to the outside world became expensive, 'uncertain and intermittent'.[3] Insurance premiums also went up, the branch warehouses being instructed by Hercus to add '3 ½ to 4 ½%' for war risks, a further one per cent being added for the increased cost of sterling exchange.[4] The overall effect was to increase final invoice prices by approximately 5 per cent. The inability to replace existing stocks at current prices meant that departmental salesmen were to offer no discounts whatsoever. While this might result in some loss of sales, Hercus was insistent that margins be maintained.[5]

TABLE 15.1
WAREHOUSE SALES AND PROFITABILITY, 1914–1920 (£000s)

| July Year | 1914 | 1915 | 1916 | 1917 | 1918 | 1919 | 1920 |
|---|---|---|---|---|---|---|---|
| **Dunedin** | | | | | | | |
| Sales | 170.5 | 193.8 | 293.5 | 285.8 | 390.9 | 321.7 | 483.1 |
| Net profit | 9.1 | 8.7 | 18.0 | 16.3 | 35.4 | 19.5 | 47.8 |
| **Invercargill** | | | | | | | |
| Sales | 58.3 | 63.5 | 67.6 | 75.0 | 95.4 | 129.2 | 155.2 |
| Net profit | 3.9 | 3.8 | 4.8 | 4.1 | 6.5 | 10.0 | 12.9 |
| **Christchurch** | | | | | | | |
| Sales | 91.4 | 92.5 | 97.7 | 102.2 | 150.5 | 151.8 | 231.3 |
| Net profit | 4.5 | 5.3 | 5.0 | 4.4 | 14.0 | 9.2 | 26.0 |
| **Wellington** | | | | | | | |
| Sales | 217.3 | 245.7 | 271.3 | 284.7 | 376.4 | 395.0 | 581.8 |
| Net profit | 8.1 | 13.1 | 16.8 | 11.2 | 31.9 | 28.6 | 59.1 |
| **Napier** | | | | | | | |
| Sales | 53.7 | 56.8 | 60.2 | 64.9 | 87.8 | 95.9 | 147.2 |
| Net profit | 2.0 | 3.8 | 3.9 | 2.2 | 5.7 | 7.0 | 12.1 |
| **Auckland** | | | | | | | |
| Sales | 189.1 | 195.9 | 210.0 | 198.6 | 302.8 | 348.1 | 584.1 |
| Net profit | 8.3 | 5.3 | 12.2 | 8.4 | 23.5 | 27.8 | 46.0[a] |
| Other[b] sales | 2.1 | 3.3 | 8.9 | 28.3 | 43.3 | 20.7 | 9.0 |
| Total sales | 782.4 | 851.7 | 1,009.3 | 1,039.2 | 1,447.2 | 1,462.5 | 2,191.7 |
| Total net profit | 35.7 | 40.0 | 60.7 | 46.7 | 117.0 | 102.1 | 203.9 |

Sources: Half-yearly balances, AG 512 15/10.
Notes: (a) After £12,500 held back in reserves from Auckland profits. (b) Includes direct sales by factories. Profits taken through individual factory accounts.

For the remainder of 1914 it seemed to be 'business as usual'. Sales continued relatively flat, the inability to clear stocks at a time of uncertainty encouraging retailers to ask Ross & Glendining for an extension of credit.[6] As it was, the lack of civilian demand was made up for partly by the requirements of the military, Ross paying a visit to Roslyn Mills early in September to see what progress was being made on a New Zealand Expeditionary Force order. Not that many government orders seemed to find their way south, the Dunedin business community being enraged by the rumour that Wellington manufacturers were bribing the 'man in authority'.[7] When orders did arrive, the additional work was both welcome and remunerative. During the first year of the war the quantity of wool processed at Roslyn Mills increased by around 7 per cent, while mill profits more than doubled to a record £17,914 (see Tables 15.2 & 15.3).

TABLE 15.2
ROSLYN MILLS OUTPUT AND FACTORY SALES, 1914–1920 (£000S)

| July Year | 1914 | 1915 | 1916 | 1917 | 1918 | 1919 | 1920 |
|---|---|---|---|---|---|---|---|
| **Roslyn Mills** | | | | | | | |
| Output value | 137.8 | 155.2 | 202.4 | 202.8 | 265.5 | 207.9 | 284.6 |
| Scoured wool used (000lbs) | 822.9 | 803.6 | 987.8 | 959.1 | 958.5 | 771.6 | 851.2 |
| **Dunedin factories** | | | | | | | |
| Clothing | 16.6 | 16.9 | 18.4 | 33.7 | 46.1 | 29.1 | 27.6 |
| Hats | 9.2 | 10.5 | 11.7 | 13.5 | 32.5 | 33.8 | 42.1 |
| Boots | 32.3 | 35.6 | 41.9 | 50.3 | 56.1 | 48.7 | 69.4 |
| Mantles | 10.1 | 9.3 | 12.7 | 18.5 | 29.7 | 35.1 | 45.1 |
| Total sales | 68.2 | 72.4 | 84.6 | 116.1 | 164.5 | 146.7 | 184.3 |

Sources: Half-yearly Balances, AG 512 15/10.
Notes: (a) Auckland factory produces an additional £3,700 worth of shirts.

At first, the outbreak of war appears to have been largely ignored by ordinary New Zealanders, much to the annoyance of Sutherland Ross who was struggling to source goods at reasonable prices. His father sympathised, 'Personally we quite realise the seriousness of the war situation but many people in New Zealand do not seem to be much affected by it. Last week, for instance, was carnival week in Christchurch and gambling and racing went on all week'.[8] Nor, it seems, did the average customer worry about where the goods came from, being perfectly happy to buy German manufactures. Slowly, however, imports from central Europe began to disappear and, by the end of the year, Roslyn Mills was beginning to experience a shortage of German dyestuffs.[9]

The mild depression that affected business during the closing months of 1914 soon vanished, the demand for clothing and blankets by the belligerents leading to an increase in wool prices around the world. In New Zealand, the 'great requirements of the army for clothing' led to record prices realised at the annual wool sales.[10] Other markets were similarly affected, with the Germans, no longer able to source supplies from Australia and New Zealand, forcing up prices in Montevideo to unprecedented levels.[11] Ross, who had been expecting the wool market to fall, was quite surprised. Luckily,

## TABLE 15.3
## NET PROFIT, CAPITAL AND RETURN ON CAPITAL EMPLOYED,
## 1914–1920 (£000s)

| July Year | 1914 | 1915 | 1916 | 1917 | 1918 | 1919 | 1920 |
|---|---|---|---|---|---|---|---|
| **Profit source** | | | | | | | |
| Roslyn Mills | 8.0 | 17.9 | 18.5 | 20.3 | 12.5 | 14.3 | 26.4 |
| Clothing factory | -1.3 | -0.9 | 0.1 | 2.2 | 3.0 | 1.2 | 1.3 |
| Hat factories | -0.1 | 0.3 | 0.0 | 0.1 | 2.1 | 1.5 | 6.7 |
| Boot factory | -13.4 | 0.9 | 1.0 | 4.3 | 3.7 | 3.8 | 7.9 |
| Mantles | – | – | – | – | – | – | 2.6 |
| Auckland factories | – | – | – | – | – | – | 0.2 |
| Warehouses | 35.7 | 40.0 | 60.7 | 46.6 | 117.0 | 102.1 | 203.9 |
| Total profit as per net returns | 28.9 | 58.3 | 80.2 | 73.5 | 138.4 | 122.9[a] | 249.0[b] |
| Profit & loss a/c entry | 28.9 | 58.3 | 80.2 | 73.5 | 138.4 | 100.0 | 178.6 |
| Paid-up capital | 656.2 | 656.2 | 677.0 | 701.0 | 701.0 | 741.6 | 750.0 |
| Shareholders' funds[c] | 732.0 | 754.3 | 808.6 | 857.9 | 932.2 | 1,000.5 | 1,130.0 |
| Net tangible assets per share (£-s) | 11-3 | 11-10 | 11-19 | 12-5 | 13-6 | 13-5 | 15-1 |
| Return on capital (%) | 3.9 | 7.7 | 9.9 | 8.6 | 14.9 | 12.3 | 22.0 |
| Dividend paid (%) | 6.0 | 6.0 | 7.0 | 7.0 | 8.0 | 7.5 | 9.0 |

*Sources: Half-yearly balances, AG 512 1/10; Share values, 1901–1925, AG 512 15/14; Annual Reports and Balance Sheets, AG 512 8/6.*
*Notes: (a) Before deduction of staff bonuses. (b) Before deduction of staff bonuses, war-loan and £5,000 building charge written off. (c) Shareholders' funds includes capital, undivided profits and reserves.*

Roslyn Mills had been able to buy wool supplies relatively cheaply and this undoubtedly contributed to the record profits recorded in July 1915.

## 2. SHORTAGES OF LABOUR AND A SCARCITY OF IMPORTS
The demand for goods quickly overwhelmed Roslyn Mills and it was soon struggling to meet the requirements of domestic customers. Orders that now began to flood in from Australia and Latin America were disregarded.

The expansion in output was partly held up by the poor quality of mill management, but there was also a growing shortage of inputs. In the short run, the main constraint was the loss of workers who now began to enlist in some numbers.[12]

Particularly critical was the loss of skilled men, whose absence could have unexpected and quite far-reaching consequences. Thus, when a worsted spinner left to join the army it was found that the quality of the yarn deteriorated significantly, uneven and poorly spun threads resulting in a sharp increase in the number of hosiery machine needle breakages. The needles became increasingly difficult to replace, especially as Germany had been a major supplier. By October 1915, the yarn situation had become so bad that a cable was sent to the Hon. Arthur Myers, the Minister of Munitions, requesting that he secure the release of worsted spinner Lance Corporal Adam Dobson from Tauherenikau Camp.[13] When asked by the Commanding Officer how long Dobson's services might be required, Ross & Glendining replied that Roslyn Mills would be unable to do without him as long as the large government contract for 1916 was outstanding. The firm appreciated that Dobson wished to enter active service and would release him as soon as practicable 'consistently with the Government demands'.[14] Appeals against the enlistment of hands rose as the war progressed.

The warehouses, in the meantime, were registering a record level of sales, although part of the increase was due to higher prices rather than greater volumes. Certain goods were in short supply, especially hosiery, a considerable proportion of which had previously been imported from Germany. In London, Sutherland Ross tried to make good the shortfall by purchasing from Leicester, but he found that prices were very high.[15] Matters were not helped by the New Zealand consumer, who, as yet, was unwilling to pay the higher wartime prices. Salesmen and managers in the warehouses were also of the same mindset and complained bitterly about the quality and prices of the goods supplied by London. As stocks began to run down, they started to look to alternative sources of supply, Auckland obtaining fabric gloves and cheap hosiery underclothing from Japan.[16]

The warehouses, too, began to suffer as members of staff enlisted to fight overseas. The most serious loss was that of James Evans, the outstanding manchester department manager who had moved to join Snedden at the new Auckland warehouse. Hercus was scarcely overjoyed when he received a letter from Evans announcing his appointment as Lieutenant in the 6th Reinforcements. He replied, 'We appreciate very highly the loyalty and devotion to your country that has prompted you to make this sacrifice of private interests in this her time of trouble, and we trust that you will have no cause to regret the step that you have taken'. Evans was assured that his job would remain open for him until his return and that an allowance would be made 'on account of salary'.[17] Almost inevitably, a row erupted between John Ross and Robert Glendining about how much this rising star of the warehouse business should be paid. Later in the war, senior staff were put on half-pay while they were away at the front, but at this stage Robert Glendining was prepared to give nothing. Thomas Glendining, very much in dread of his elder brother, was equally reluctant. In the end, Ross and Hercus dipped into their own pockets and sent Evans £300 in the hope that they might retain his services.[18]

Congestion at British docks, the shortage of shipping space, the inability to source from Central Europe and the competing demands from wartime governments meant that London Office found it ever more difficult to procure goods. In the six months to May 1915, the value of goods shipped to the warehouses amounted to just over £80,000, barely 60 per cent of that sent in the corresponding period in the previous year.[19] Given disruptions to the supply chain, Sutherland Ross felt inclined to use his discretion and buy and ship goods as and when he could. Ultimately this turned out to be a wise policy, with Ross & Glendining benefiting from rising prices and growing scarcity. In the middle of 1915, however, John Ross was worried that the warehouses were being loaded up with expensive stock that might have to be sold at a loss if the war ended suddenly. The warehouse managers also complained about unsaleable stock being sent and, as a result, Sutherland was once again told to stick to orders.[20]

By the end of the year, Ross senior appears to have become a little more philosophical about the activities of London Office, writing to Charles Netting, 'I note the difficulties you experience in getting and shipping goods and think you do wonderfully well considering all the obstacles in your way. I have reason to believe we are as well supplied as anybody and better than most.'[21] Even so, a month later the buyers were told to stick to instructions 'as near as possible', an exhortation that was repeated at regular intervals thereafter.[22]

There is little doubt that Sutherland Ross was becoming increasingly irked by the failure of the warehouse managers to appreciate the extent of inflation and the procurement problems that he faced. In the middle of 1915 he suggested that he should return to New Zealand, although whether it was to inject some realism into the warehouse ordering process or because he thought that his father, now in his eighties, should not work so hard, is far from clear. John Ross was not to be moved: his son should not contemplate coming home until after the end of the war. Sutherland Ross stayed on in London and, while he had an exemption from military service, it was not long before he was spending a day a week in exercises such as digging trenches.[23]

### 3. WOOL BUYING, GOVERNMENT CONTROLS AND MILL MANAGEMENT

The long-drawn-out nature of the conflict and the heavy demands of total war meant that governments were increasingly drawn into managing key sectors of the economy. Towards the end of 1915, it was decided that woollen and worsted mills in New Zealand should be placed under central control. At a meeting between Government and mill representatives in November, the latter were told that their mills had, in effect, been commandeered, and that each had to make certain quantities and garments until the end of 1916. This output was to be reserved purely for the military. Ross observed that woollen goods for civilian use, already scarce, were likely to 'become scarcer as the season advances'.[24]

To safeguard essential supplies, the Government now intervened in the wool market, instructing mill buyers on which lots they might bid for at the annual wool sales. At the first of the controlled sales, Bob Glendining created chaos by bidding freely for many of the lots that were put up. Shortly afterwards, a letter arrived from the Minister complaining that Ross & Glendining were not working cordially with the Government buyer. At the second sale in Christchurch, Bob Glendining again ignored orders and 'bid for lots he shouldn't have'.[25] This was explained away as sheer inadvertence and unfamiliarity with the new buying procedures. When, at the Dunedin sale that followed, Glendining yet again failed to 'adhere to the terms of arrangement for the purchase of wool', Hercus was obliged to dispatch an emollient letter to the enraged Government buyer, Walter Hill. He was assured that it had been impressed upon Bob Glendining that he should cooperate more fully and had been instructed to clarify matters with Hill personally before the next Christchurch sale.[26]

What happened at Christchurch is not known, but it appears that Glendining's wayward behaviour may have been due more to an excess of alcohol than a lack of understanding. Shortly afterwards he entered a private hospital for treatment, emerging at the beginning of March a somewhat chastened man. With Robert Glendining now very frail and incapable of taking business decisions, it fell to John Ross to make the necessary changes in mill management. Sutherland Ross was kept abreast of events:

> Bob ... came out a few days ago and has not been doing anything since as we have told him that the mill is in charge of Miller who managed it before when Bob was in England and that he must not interfere with him. I advised him to go on a long holiday. He told me he was going to Mt. Cook for a few days. He went very much to the bad a short time ago and behaved very badly during the wool buying season. He came to me today and promised amendment.[27]

When he returned to work a few weeks later, Bob was told that he was now manager in name only. He was warned that if he was ever found to be the worse for drink again, he would be 'set adrift'.[28]

The new manager, Miller, did not take over at a particularly opportune moment. Labour unrest in New Zealand mills saw workers at the Wellington Woollen Mills at Petone come out on strike, demanding a 10 per cent increase in wages. Shortly afterwards, a group of agitators from Timaru came down to Dunedin but although a resolution was passed by Roslyn workers in support of the Petone strikers, there was little enthusiasm for action. Ultimately it was agreed, through the Arbitration Court, that the mills would pay a 10 per cent war bonus on basic rates, backdated to February 1916, and the situation was defused.[29] Regular increases in wages took place thereafter to keep pace with inflation.[30]

Miller soon had Roslyn Mills working smoothly and by the May it was turning out 'as much stuff as is practicable'.[31] With the Government taking most of the output, however, there were few woollen and worsted goods to spare. Yarns, in particular, were in short supply, apparently because knitting for soldiers had become a 'great craze'.[32] There was also a shortage of hosiery and with machinery out-of-date and inefficient, orders were sent to London for replacements.[33] More crucially, the hosiery section was rapidly running out of machine needles. In September, Ross wrote

> I was up at the mill this morning and found most of the machines standing idle, and in a few days all of them will have to stop and we will lose the hands. We were hoping that the parcel on the Tongariro would help and now she is wrecked that hope is gone. The loss of the Tongariro on top of the Rangatira and the want of millinery and season's lines generally is rather serious and the only consolation we have is that all are in the same boat.[34]

## 4. FUTURE PLANS FRUSTRATED BY THE INABILITY TO IMPORT MACHINERY

In spite of the day-to-day problems that he faced, John Ross still had time to engage in long-run strategic planning. While he accepted that there was likely to be a slump sometime after the end of the war, he considered that 'as sellers of what everybody wants', the future of New Zealand should be bright.[35] During the course of 1916, therefore, he began to think about the scale and scope of the firm in the post-war years.

Ross's first thoughts were concerned with increasing the size of the boot factory and equipping it with the latest machinery. Orders for more boot-making machines were promptly sent to London.[36] His mind then turned to

Roslyn Mills. Sutherland was warned that big expenditure lay ahead, both to renew worn-out machinery and bring things up to date. Additional buildings would also be needed to house new machinery.[37]

Given the legal constitution of the company, an investment programme of such magnitude required the acquiescence of the board of directors. With Robert Glendining now incapable of business and Ross in control of the board, agreement was easily secured. Indeed, the board was even prepared to go further than Ross had envisaged. He wrote to Sutherland Ross in November,

> *We have decided on extensive alterations to the mills. The order for boilers has been given to the agents of Babcock & Wilcox, their tender being £12,500 exclusive of buildings. Then probably some machinery orders will be sent shortly, especially for a wool drying machine and a wool dyeing machine … I always found it advantageous to go and see the suppliers of machinery as you can always get greater advantages seeing men face to face than by correspondence. I have an idea that it will be difficult to get the machines when the war ends as there will be a great demand and the man who gets in first will have an advantage … there are more extensive alterations in view for the greater efficiency of labour which must stand over for present.[38]*

The plans involved a virtual reconstruction of the old mill at a total expenditure of between £25,000 and £30,000.[39]

The orders for boilers seemed to go through without any difficulty. At the suggestion of Babcock & Wilcox's agent in New Zealand, the Minister of Munitions in Wellington was asked to support a request to the British Government for an A or B priority certificate. The existing boilers, the Minister was informed, were more than thirty years old and if, as was likely, the government inspector insisted on working pressures being reduced, then the completion of government contracts would be delayed.[40] A cable to the High Commission was duly sent and the appropriate certificates were granted.

At this point, things started to go wrong. In July 1917, the boilermakers informed Ross & Glendining that their order had been delayed due to the lack of raw materials.[41] Work commenced thereafter, but it was not until February 1918 that two of the three boilers on order finally arrived in Glasgow for shipment. The diversion of shipping to the trans-Atlantic food trade then delayed the boilers still further. At last, in the middle of 1918, the two boilers arrived in New Zealand. This was hardly a cause for celebration, especially as all three boilers had been designed to work together.[42]

In the meantime, with prices rising rapidly, it was decided to push ahead and renew the rest of the plant.[43] Early in 1917, orders for spinning, weaving, dyeing and drying machinery were placed. Sutherland Ross was urged not to ignore his father's advice, as he had with the hosiery machines, but follow up the orders with a personal visit to Platts of Oldham.[44] He was quite stung by this comment,

> I quite appreciate your remarks as to the advisability of going down personally, I shall do so as soon as we receive a reply from Platts. You have not yet grasped the difficulty of getting metal goods manufactured unless they are proved to be for war work in some shape or form. To begin with, manufacturers cannot obtain the steel without a certificate stating exactly the purpose for which the same is required. Certificates are in 3 grades with sub-divisions. 'A' certificate is for war work pure and simple. 'B' one is for machinery and parts wanted by those who are engaged in making goods for war purposes, and on only three occasions have we succeeded in getting a 'B'. 'C' grade is of very little use at the present time, as many firms are compelled to devote 0 to 95% of their labour and output on war work. I have asked on several occasions for you to give us the numbers of any contracts you have with the New Zealand Government, with such details of same as you think advisable. Without being able to give chapter and verse, we find it difficult to get any consideration on the score of being contractors to the New Zealand Government.[45]

Sutherland followed up this letter with one to his younger brother Tom who, after dabbling with accountancy, was at last applying the engineering knowledge he had gained at Cambridge University to Roslyn Mills. The point concerning priority certificates was reiterated and the suggestion made that, as in the case of the boilers, details of the contracts should be cabled or transmitted through the New Zealand High Commission in London.[46]

A quotation from Platts to manufacture carding and spinning machinery was received at London Office in April. The news was not good. Delivery could not be undertaken for another eighteen months to two years. Thought was given to placing the orders elsewhere, but it was ultimately decided to persevere with the Oldham firm. Prince Smith & Co. of Keighley, worsted machinery makers, were rather more accommodating. They would start work on the spinning frames immediately if Ross & Glendining were able to supply an A or B priority certificate. This was out of the question, and Sutherland Ross was still waiting for the certificates in May when he paid a visit to both makers. Fortunately, the B certificates were obtained – just before export restrictions were imposed on future orders for textile machinery.

In November 1917 an invoice was received from Prince Smith for two spinning frames. The following January, Platts asked for instructions for shipping 45 cases of machinery.[47] If John Ross thought that, at long last, the new machinery was about to be dispatched, he was mistaken. Ships to New Zealand, irregular since the beginning of the war, had become increasingly scarce as the British Government commandeered more tonnage. Whereas there had been two steamers a month at the beginning of the war, by the end of 1917 there was one every five or six weeks at best.[48] These might leave at the shortest notice, the Royal Navy dictating when ships might sail owing to the German submarine menace. The result was that many vessels arrived in New Zealand only partially laden. This was of little concern to the shipping companies, since the Government paid them on the basis of gross register tonnage of their vessels rather than of the cargoes they carried.[49]

To add to shipping difficulties, export permits were now required before goods might be shipped. An application for permission to export forty-five cases of Platts' machinery had been made immediately news of the restrictions came through but, by the beginning of May 1918, nothing had been heard from the authorities.[50] The permit was finally forwarded to Liverpool in August and the machinery shipped on the SS *Remuera* in September.[51] The consignment, containing mules, arrived in November. While Ross was pleased to receive the mules he noted, with a degree of resignation, that they were useless without the carding engines ordered at the same time.[52] Another year passed before most of the machinery on order from Platts had been delivered.[53]

The difficulties encountered in sourcing supplies, retaining staff, replacing worn-out machinery, and enlarging the plant meant that it was not easy to increase output at Roslyn Mills. Notwithstanding these difficulties, the quantity of wool processed at the mills rose from just over 800,000 lbs in the year ending July 1914 to just under 900,000 lbs in 1916, before falling back as constraints began to bite. A reduction in the quantity of wool processed and an increase in costs made it difficult to increase profits thereafter, although the value of output peaked at £265,481 in 1918 (Table 15.2).

## 5. BUYING SUFFERS AS STAFF ARE CALLED UP

The growing shortages of both shipping space and manufactured goods meant that keeping the warehouses well supplied was a never-ending struggle. In an environment in which prices were rising rapidly and the supply chain subject to frequent interruption, Sutherland Ross and his staff continued to snap up new lines and buy freely when goods became available. The confused conditions led to inevitable mistakes, and it was John Ross who bore the brunt of complaints when he inspected the branches. After visiting Wellington and Auckland in August 1916, he supplied his son with a catalogue of sins apparently committed by the buyers,

*I would especially direct your attention to the system adopted when lines are cabled for by one of the branches, of sending a supply all round overlooking, as you know, that there is as great a difference in the different parts of N.Z. as there is between Scotland and Italy and that many lines that suit Auckland and Napier are no use in Dunedin or Invercargill. Then there is another bad system into which the buyers have fallen, viz, sending large quantities of new lines instead of simply enough to test the market ... The amount of loss being made as the result of overbuying and bad stock is neither as small nor unimportant as you imagine, the loss will amount to many hundreds if not thousands but the money loss does not matter so much as the loss of prestige in the minds of the public and the warehouse hands. I fear it is having a bad effect on the latter.*

Ross suggested that the London manager, Netting, be put in charge of the buying room to scrutinise orders. Alternatively, one of the New Zealand warehousemen might be sent home to supervise and help buy or, failing that, somebody might be recruited in London.[54] None of the suggestions was taken up.

Some of the problems in buying, it seems, was due to the fact that London Office was losing staff. At the beginning of the war there had been seventeen employed but their numbers fell steadily. Two book-keepers and several juniors were called up fairly quickly and several more left when offered higher wages. Bedo Boys, who had bought for Ross & Glendining for many years, also retired in 1916. By the end of the year the shortage of staff had become extremely serious, with three clerks leaving within a short space of time. With all the additional work that had to be done because of hostilities, Sutherland Ross admitted that he now found it difficult to keep an eye on the buying.[55]

The staffing situation at London Office was already bad by 1916 but worse was to follow, the huge losses of men on the Western Front forcing the British Government to trawl more widely for recruits. Existing exemptions on medical grounds were therefore reviewed, and the upper age limit for recruitment raised. As a result, a number of the senior staff now found themselves eligible for military service.

The first to be called for medical examination was Thomson, the hosiery and boot buyer. Passed fit, he joined the Queen's Westminster Rifles in February. With some firms in the city paying full wages to enlisted staff while others paid nothing, it was agreed that Thomson should be retained on half pay until the end of the war.[56] Before he left for camp, he sent a large consignment of hosiery, unordered, to the Wellington warehouse. David Jones, the manager, duly complained. He got little sympathy from Sutherland

Ross who told him that given the difficulties faced by manufacturing in the United Kingdom, he should be thankful that he was overstocked.[57]

The next to be examined was James Smith, the fancy buyer. Born in Otago in 1875 and in the employment of Ross & Glendining since 1901, he, too, was passed A1 – fit for service abroad. Although neither John nor Sutherland Ross cared much for the man, his expertise in fancy goods in general and millinery in particular was not to be denied. They therefore lobbied the High Commission very hard to ensure that his exemption be continued. A conditional exemption was granted until July 1917 and, although appealed against by the Military Authorities, it was sustained by the City of London Appeals Tribunal. His exemption was later extended to March 1918.[58]

Finally, in March 1917, Sutherland Ross was called to Kingston Barracks for a medical examination. Poor eyesight meant that he was classified as only suitable for garrison duty, which, in the short run, meant that he, like Smith, had simply to turn up for training on a regular basis. He proudly told his father that he had become an expert in the use of a Hotchkiss machine gun.[59]

With the threat of military service removed, Sutherland Ross immediately began to reorganise buying to cover for the absent Thomson. He himself was to look after boots, Sidney Boys would buy hosiery as well as light manchester and haberdashery, and Smith, the fancy buyer, was to take over heavy manchester. A little earlier John Ross had suggested sending a female buyer from New Zealand to help purchases dresses and female millinery. The notion that a female buyer should enter this all-male preserve was, however, too radical for London Office – even in wartime. While Sutherland Ross was prepared to do his best 'with anyone you send', Smith and Boys were not at all enthusiastic.[60] The lady buyer never appeared, even though there were loud complaints about Boys' lamentable lack of taste.[61]

Amidst all this turmoil, Ross & Glendining Ltd were required to move their London offices as the lease had expired. New premises were obtained a few doors along at No. 24, Ropemaker St. Although somewhat larger than needed for the moment, they provided better facilities for inspection and re-packing.[62] On four floors, the building also possessed a basement. Here staff were able to shelter during a bombing raid in the middle of June.[63] With further raids reported in the New Zealand press, Ross anxiously cabled his son. A few weeks later Sutherland replied, 'I am glad to state that up to this date Fritz has not done us any injury. As I told you in a recent letter, during the moonlight nights we are closing the office at about four o'clock in company with many other city firms'. The possibility of censorship prevented him from providing further details but he promised to enlighten his father in due course.[64]

## 6. Rising prices and delays in shipping add to difficulties

As the war progressed, buying in Great Britain became ever more difficult. Government demands and the disruption of shipping led to severe shortages, contributing to a sharp rise in prices. Worried that the warehouse staff in New Zealand did not appreciate the nature of changes in the international marketplace, a circular letter was sent from London Office in July. It was pointed out that woollen goods were rationed, and that exports to friendly neutrals took precedence to overseas Dominions; that the price of linen goods had more than doubled since the beginning of the war; and that nobody had the least idea what the cotton market was going to do. The circular concluded,

> It is very disheartening to the London buyers to read of stuff being slaughtered, with the knowledge that it cannot be replaced under an advance of at least 25%. Horrock's list has gone up nearly 20% in the course of the last month, Finlay's list has been withdrawn, but we know that the new one is at least 20% higher.

> The orders for Cotton piece goods at or about 4½ d. which we have seen in recent order sheets, are mere waste paper, and we would ask you in all seriousness to grasp the fact that the low prices are gone, never to return. We could say much more in the same strain, but realize that the more that is written, the less there is read.

> We have been more closely in touch with our competitors in the past two years than heretofore, and we know that all London buying houses are regarded as trying to make excuses for bad buying, but you must give us credit for a modicum of intelligence, and take heed of the fact that we are nearer the markets than yourselves.[65]

To drive home the point, a detailed list of price increases that had occurred since 1914 was sent to New Zealand, broken down by departments and principal manufacturers.[66]

The situation in the cotton textile industry deteriorated almost as soon as the list had been sent. In August 1917, the warehouses were cabled that a large number of looms in Lancashire were shutting down owing to a shortage of raw materials. The supply of cotton and woollen goods became even more restricted after America entered the war, especially as Britain appeared to be 'undertaking the outfit of the whole American army'. In November, a contract for 13 million yards of wool was placed in Bradford, while the price of cotton, already 22d per lb, was limited by the British Government to an increase of no more than 1d per day.

To secure whatever supplies were available, Sidney Boys was sent to Manchester with instructions to buy for early delivery only – later delivery being considered too risky.[67] For the next few weeks it proved impossible to get a bedroom in any of the Bradford or Manchester hotels. Foden, the Kaiapoi buyer, was obliged to sleep in a hotel bathroom – and he was offered that only because he was a customer of twenty years' standing. The only way to get supplies, Foden told Sutherland Ross, was to sit on the manufacturer's doorstep.[68]

## 7. LONDON OFFICE AND THE NEW ZEALAND EXPEDITIONARY FORCE

In addition to coping with the extra work brought about by wartime conditions, London Office also fulfilled an important role in supporting workers and others who had enlisted in the forces. In November 1917, news came through that James Evans, promoted to Captain and awarded the Military Cross, had been gassed in France. Shortly afterwards he was moved to a hospital in Hampshire where he was visited by Sutherland Ross. Other members of staff were also 'badly knocked about' by gas attacks in Northern France, including Thomas Glendining's son, Herbert, who was hospitalised in Chelsea.[69]

Members of the New Zealand Expeditionary Force frequently dropped in at Ropemaker St. On a few days' leave from the front and with no friends in London, they sometimes requested a cash advance and frequently asked for good quality Roslyn blankets and underwear to replace army issue. The power of the brand, it seems, had percolated through even to the Western Front! Usually, however, they just wished to have some contact with home. The firm therefore acted as a clearing-house for information, with cables passing to and fro between London and Dunedin. Evans, somewhat typically, complained about the lack of efficiency in their dispatch. By the end of 1917, the weekly average of 'visitors in khaki' was about twenty.[70]

## 8. KEEPING THE WAREHOUSES SUPPLIED

The difficulties in keeping the New Zealand warehouses well supplied saw the level of stocks reduced. Part of the shortfall was made up by Japanese imports, and at one stage Ross & Glendining considered appointing a buyer in Japan.[71] By the middle of 1918 it was reported that a considerable quantity of towels and flannelette was flooding in from Japan.[72] Sutherland Ross was not impressed, complaining to Jones about Japanese business morality. 'I believe that a large amount of their manufacturing is done by child labour, and under conditions that amount to temporal slavery, and I do not see the benefit of encouraging their goods in our market unduly.'[73] The quality of goods, moreover, was suspect, although this was less of a concern for the Auckland market where the demand for cheaper draperies was proportionately greater.

The shortfall in imports was also filled by New Zealand manufactures, with Ross & Glendining's own factories increasing their output in both monetary and real terms. The boot factory, re-equipped in 1914, produced over £56,000 worth of goods in 1918, while the much maligned hat factory managed to treble the value of its output to £32,510 (see Table 15.2, p. 242). Increased labour and raw material costs nevertheless meant that profits remained slim, with the perennial arguments about warehouse transfer prices – and how profits should be apportioned – occurring yet again.[74]

In spite of the many difficulties, John Ross was much encouraged by the factories' performance and came to the conclusion that, after the war, more goods should be made in-house. The prospects for blouse making, he thought, looked particularly promising, while the manufacture of underclothing, already undertaken in Auckland, ought to be adopted in Dunedin. In view of the likelihood of a higher tariff to pay for the war loan, he considered 'the chances are much more favourable for local production'.[75]

The immediate problem, though, was to decide on what quantity of goods London should order for the rest of 1918. As with machinery, the lack of shipping space complicated matters. With the railways refusing to take consignments to the docks without the guarantee of a vessel, London Office did not wish to order goods if it was then obliged to store them at considerable expense. There were dangers, too, in ordering goods in advance, for with the market still rising, firms were now taking orders to be priced 'at the date of delivery'. Given rampant inflation, there was no knowing how much the goods would cost when delivered – or how the bills were to be met.[76]

### 9. ATTEMPTS TO INTRODUCE ORDER INTO CHAOS

The lack of consistent information about the quantity of goods already in stock added to the uncertainty, as did the desperate efforts of the branches to secure supplies by dealing directly with manufacturers' agents rather than London.[77] It was therefore with some relief that Sutherland Ross learned that, following his repeated suggestions, somebody had finally been appointed to coordinate ordering.[78] The job of David Hogg, designated Inspector General, was to see that warehouses' demands for stock were matched by the supply of goods from the mills, factories and London. Hogg also relieved John Ross from his winter stock-taking trips around the branches, which the old man sometimes found 'a little trying'.[79]

Yet even with improved systems, Sutherland Ross was still unsure as to the quantity of goods to be ordered, given that the war might end suddenly.

In 1917, he entertained hopes that the conflict might soon be over. Towards the end of August 1918 he was altogether more confident. Using a metaphor that would doubtless have appealed to his father, he wrote, 'Things are looking a bit brighter nowadays, and I think one makes a mistake in viewing the War from the point of view of Maps, as my own impression is that Fritz has got most of his goods in the shop window, and there is not a very great deal of manpower behind.' By the middle of October the general expectation in London was that peace was about to be declared. On 13 November, news reached New Zealand that the Armistice had been signed.

The closing months of the war saw continued bickering between father and son. The bone of contention, as ever, remained the failure of London Office to stick to orders, with Sutherland Ross complaining that his father's comments were rather 'pungent'. Relationships deteriorated still further after John Ross took umbrage when he thought his son was suggesting that he was too old for the job,

> I cannot admit that my age has stood in the way of any possible improvement or extensions as the work that is going on and the amount of money spent in those directions will show. Besides, I have reason to believe that we have been doing the biggest softgoods business in the colony since the beginning of the war in consequence of ordering goods and having stock when our contemporaries held back and lost their chance.[80]

The fact that Sutherland Ross, by exceeding orders, had helped to ensure that the branches were well stocked seemed to escape Ross senior. Sutherland had no wish to pursue the matter further, however, and assured his father that he had not intended to offend him. Indeed, he thought that John Ross possessed 'the youngest brain in the whole concern'.[81]

### 10. WARTIME FINANCE

The increase in the cost of everything between 1914 and 1918 meant that substantial additional funds were still needed to finance stocks, work in progress, and capital works.[82] Wool purchases at the annual sales, together with expenditure on the forthcoming season's stocks, had always placed a strain on the firm's resources during the early months of the year. This continued to be the case in wartime, the need for funds growing as the price of wool increased. During the early years, Ross & Glendining seemed to manage quite well but by April 1917, the overdraft at the Bank of New South Wales had risen to over £100,000. Fortunately, help was available in the shape of deposits from local institutions, with £30,000 placed by Wright Stephenson and £20,000 by Dalgety & Co. allowing the overdraft to be settled a few months later. Substantial sums were also invested by employees, the total owed to private and institutional depositors increasing from £154,430 in 1914 to £250,432 in 1918.[83]

The death of Robert Glendining on 23 June 1917 brought fresh financial complications. The need to pay death duties of over £60,000 raised the possibility that Ross & Glendining would not only have to repay the executors some £40,000 that Glendining had on deposit with the firm, but would also have to buy back some of his shares as well. This concerned Ross, especially as a further £20,000 was earmarked for mill extensions and another £100,000 for wool. On top of this, there was the prospect of being forced to subscribe to a Government War Loan.[84] He need not have worried. With net profits for the year at over £73,000 and cash flowing in as stocks were run down, by November 1917 the firm was sufficiently 'flush with money' for Dunedin to send £38,000 to London.[85] As for the War Loan, the Bank of New South Wales was happy to advance £40,000 at 5½ per cent, while the Government paid Ross & Glendining interest of 4½ per cent, tax free.

It was the middle of 1918 before the Glendining estate was finally wound up, huge profits enabling the executors to be paid without difficulty. As there was no need for any shares to be bought back to help defray death duties, Robert Glendining's holding in the company was divided between his wife and children.[86]

## 11. A PROFITABLE WAR

There is little doubt that in spite of the loss of staff, interruptions to shipping, and widespread shortages, Ross & Glendining Ltd had a very profitable war. Clearly the firm benefited from inflation, so that while some items were virtually unobtainable, the purchase of warehouse stock on a rising market proved to be an almost foolproof way to make money. The factories and mills were also able to benefit from rising prices, although with inadequate supplies of raw materials and machinery difficult to replace, there were limits to what they were able to produce.

In the face of these constraints, the virtual doubling of warehouse sales to more than £1.4 million during the course of the war, together with the increase in output of the mills and factories, was an impressive achievement. The increase in profits was even more impressive, soaring from £28,877 to £138,358 by 1918. This rendered the firm liable to excess profits tax from 1916 onwards, with the firm being obliged to pay 40 per cent on the annual surplus over the average profits of the three previous years.[87] Their first tax bill amounted to £9,235. Yet even after excess profits tax, the policy of paying modest dividends – often in the form of additional shares – meant that a considerable amount of capital was ploughed back into the firm. Thus the paid-up capital of the firm increased from £656,200 to £701,100 between

1914 and 1918, while shareholders funds rose from £732,000 to £932,000. The worth of the warehouses, factories and mills also increased, although it was not until 1922 that values were written up.

The fact that this complex, multi-plant enterprise was not only very profitable but also able to grow relative to other soft goods firms suggests that, for the most part, it was extremely well managed. John Ross was clearly the driving force. At eighty-four, the old man was still walking to work every day although, by the end of the war, he was ready to step down. Just before Christmas 1918, he cabled Sutherland Ross to return to New Zealand 'as soon as possible'.[88]

# READJUSTMENT AND RETRENCHMENT, 1919–1926

The end of World War I, although greeted with much enthusiasm by the general population, left New Zealand farmers and businessmen wondering what the future had in store. The price of exports and imports had increased by almost fifty per cent between 1914 and 1918, driven up by belligerent governments that had abandoned the gold standard and printed money to buy the materials of war. Now, with the readjustment from war to peace, the future course of global prices was far from clear. If they fell, as many thought likely, what effect would this have on the general level of business activity?

The fear of a sudden fall in prices had haunted John Ross throughout the entire war. It was this that had led him to admonish his son repeatedly about the tendency of London Office to buy unordered stock at inflated values. He was also sure that when prices fell – of which he was certain – then the New Zealand economy would experience a period of depression. As it happened, the fall in prices and ensuing depression took rather longer to materialise than Ross had thought likely. The continuation of budget deficits, together with the easy money policies adopted by overseas governments after the war, fuelled a world-wide re-stocking boom and a further surge in prices. By the middle of 1921, however, supply began to outstrip demand, especially in primary products. Thereafter prices fell alarmingly, exacerbated by governments that now attempted to revert to balanced budgets as depression loomed.

As a small open economy, New Zealand could not escape this transition from boom to bust. The price of wool fell by half in 1921 and, in the following year, dairy prices fell by a third. The situation was not helped by a British Government that ended its wartime schemes for purchasing wool, meat and dairy produce from the Dominion.[1] A similar collapse in import prices averted a balance of payments crisis but it did not prevent per capita incomes from falling by around twenty per cent between 1920 and 1922.[2] Export prices of primary products recovered somewhat thereafter, and farmers quickly adopted the latest technology in an attempt to restore incomes. Yet while farm output rose and there were occasional good years, such as 1925, the level of prices was insufficient to ensure that a heavily indebted agricultural sector was restored to prosperity. Inevitably this meant that New Zealand as a whole did not prosper, while per capita incomes remained fairly static. In 1926 prices, incomes and unemployment began to deteriorate once more.

Sutherland Ross did not take control of Ross & Glendining Ltd until his permanent return to New Zealand in July 1920. Like his father he, too, thought that a depression was inevitable, although given the sentiment prevailing in London he believed that the post-war boom had a little further to run. He was proved to be correct, the downturn occurring just after he had arrived back in Dunedin. For the rest of the nineteen-twenties, Sutherland and fellow members of the board focused on retrenchment.

## 1. REORGANISATION IN UNCERTAIN TIMES

The restrictions that had hampered trade during World War I started to be lifted soon after the armistice was signed in November 1918. Indeed, the Post Office in London began to publish daily shipping lists of mail inwards and outwards almost immediately.[3] Business as a whole was slower to return to normal, with continuing uncertainty hampering readjustment. Under the circumstances, little could be said about future prospects, although in London the immediate effect of the cessation of hostilities was to 'beat down the price' of fashion goods for the forthcoming season.[4]

Business was also affected by the influenza pandemic that swept around the globe in the closing months of 1918. Sutherland Ross was unaffected by the virus, although his wife and children were confined to bed for a short while.[5] In New Zealand, things were altogether more serious. Towards the end of November there were 150 hands off sick from the mills and a hosiery man, 'a drinker' according to John Ross, was in a hopeless condition.[6] The North Island was also ravaged by the epidemic and by mid-December the situation there was even worse than in the south.[7] Writing to Netting, the London manager, early in the New Year, Tom Ross lamented, 'Business here the last three months have been very much upset owing to the epidemic, and peace celebrations and the cessation of hostilities led many people to expect a speedy fall in prices and it is taking time to readjust their perspective. In the month of November and December our sales fell away by £46,000.'[8] In the medium term, the situation looked a little brighter. There seemed to be 'plenty of money about' in New Zealand and as the British Government was going to take wool, meat and cheese for at least another year, the prospects for the agrarian sector appeared 'fairly stable'.[9]

John Ross, along with many others in New Zealand, was nevertheless convinced that a slump was imminent, even though in the United Kingdom it was generally believed that prices were likely to be higher for some time to come.[10] He was also worried about rising stocks and the huge financial commitments that had been entered into by his firm, which amounted to £265,000 for the first three months of 1919.[11] Early in January, a directive was sent to warehouse managers to cancel all the orders they were not bound to accept.[12]

Sutherland Ross, still in London, was exasperated by such caution as he saw good opportunities for trade in the year ahead. Writing to his father he argued, 'If a slump had been coming it is only reasonable to suppose that we should have felt the full effect of it within three months of the armistice. You will see from the cables that the present time is full of industrial unrest and outcry for less production at higher wages and I consider you have nothing to fear in 1919.'[13] In a circular letter to New Zealand branches shortly afterwards, it was pointed out that London Office had been in touch with many suppliers in the U.K. and all believed prices would remain firm until September/October. There was a divergence of opinion as to what was to happen thereafter – although the general consensus was to expect lower values.[14]

There were other matters that Sutherland wished to discuss with his father in person, including who was to take charge in London in future, what more might be done to streamline warehouse ordering and stock transfer processes, and how London Office could best be re-organised. In March 1919, with his father not very well, he paid a short visit to New Zealand, leaving his family in Wimbledon.

Who was to take charge of London Office was not settled immediately. For some time past Ross senior had been pressing his son, Tom, to go to England to work with Sutherland, gain experience, and then take over as director at London Office. Tom was not at all keen. His expertise was in machinery, not soft goods and, as he explained to Sutherland, there were a number of large questions concerning the future of the company that needed to be discussed in front of a full board.[15] His brother claimed that the idea that the two were supposed to swap places came as a complete surprise to him.

Sutherland, for his part, was trying to arrange for James Evans to stay on in London in some capacity or other.[16] When it transpired that the best that could be offered was the position of chief buyer, Evans elected to return to New Zealand.[17] A year later, Netting was still being informed by Hercus that Tom Ross was to assume control in London.[18] Ultimately, Charles Netting took over from Sutherland Ross when the latter finally returned to New Zealand. Netting was appointed London Director in 1923.[19]

The warehouse ordering and stock transfer processes were the responsibility of David Hogg, appointed in 1918 to sort out the wartime chaos. It soon became evident that Hogg was struggling. Part of the problem was that with many of the more experienced hands serving in the forces, the warehouses were staffed by a 'swarm of boys', while there were 'girls in the entering room and counting house'.[20] The situation was eased somewhat by the return of servicemen the following year. Jones, the Wellington branch manager, was inclined to re-employ only the more able, a suggestion that outraged Sutherland Ross. He was instructed that soldiers must be rehired for at least three months, 'if only as a matter of good business!' It was unthinkable that the firm's good name should be 'dragged through the mud' by turning away servicemen.[21]

The principal obstacle to reforming warehouse systems, however, was the lack of cooperation received by Hogg. He had met with considerable resistance from the heads of departments, a situation made worse by an absence of support from Head Office. Thomas Glendining, upset by the fact that Hogg was reporting directly to John Ross, refused to pass on information to the 'Inspector General', while the elderly Hercus, who Tom Ross thought a bit out of touch, was also unsupportive.[22] After battling on until the middle of 1919 Hogg resigned, citing reasons that were 'partly personal and partly domestic'. He left to go into the agency business in the North Island, his final act being to recommend as his replacement Major James Evans, MC and bar.[23]

The appointment of Evans satisfied all concerned. He got on well with Sutherland Ross and was doubtless acceptable to the warehouse fraternity, who were well aware of his outstanding abilities as warehouseman and soldier. It would have been a brave man indeed who chose to trifle with this veteran of the Western Front. To ensure a smooth transition, Sutherland Ross worked through the issues with an unhappy Thomas Glendining.[24] Glendining, suitably mollified, offered no opposition to Evans when he arrived to take up his duties.

The powers of the new Inspector General were set out in a circular sent by Hercus to all branches and factories. It was quite unequivocal. Evans was to control all transactions between branches, mills and factories. He was to receive and transmit all orders, conduct all correspondence, and arrange for the transfers of stock. In times of excess demand, it was he who was to determine how resources were to be allocated.[25] Evans was soon into his work, introducing a new purchasing scheme for mill hosiery, and putting in place an improved stock transfer system. Tom Ross thoroughly approved of the latter, commenting that if the system worked properly, 'we should be able to carry on with smaller stocks and smaller capital'. Moreover, everybody seemed to be happy, the annual meeting of branch managers in November proving to be a huge success. Indeed, some even suggested that more regular meetings might be held.[26]

The centralisation of ordering was of considerable assistance to London Office, as was the decision to indicate the season for which particular goods were required. This allowed the buyers to place fewer orders, prioritise their work, and improve the scheduling of shipments. They also benefited from the stock transfer system. Henceforth, new lines and unordered consignments were no longer held as dead stock in inappropriate branches but were transferred to where they were most likely to command a sale.[27] At the same time, changes were made in the buying staff at London Office, the hapless Sidney Boys' employment being terminated after thirty years service.[28] After a locally appointed replacement turned out to be a disaster, Amos was sent from Wellington to buy hosiery while Scott, the Napier manager, was transferred to London to buy manchester.[29]

## 2. Expansion in an era of acquisitions

Contrary to the expectations of those in New Zealand, both sales and prices continued to rise. Profits at £100,054 for the year ending in July 1919 were some £38,000 less than the previous year although, as Ross explained to Sutherland, 'in view of what we are giving away, £20,000 odd to returned soldiers and £22,000 [bonus] to employees there is much to be thankful for. The overdraft has been coming down steadily and stands at about £65,000 today. The fly in the ointment is the enormous stocks …'[30] The bonus payment marked the beginning of a short-lived profit-sharing scheme which, during the course of the following year, saw over £60,000 added to wages of workers of twelve months standing – providing they were of good character and had not threatened to strike. Given Ross's worries about the future, the initial award of fifteen per cent of wages, payable in cash at Christmas, was a generous act.[31] Maybe, as a good Presbyterian, he was somewhat embarrassed by the huge profits now being earned. Shareholders were not neglected. They received a handsome dividend of 7½ per cent, a further £40,000 being added to reserves and another £29,000 carried over in undistributed profits.[32]

Sales continued to increase for the remainder of the year, the early months of 1920 also being extremely busy. The 'enormous stocks' were soon run down. Even so, Sutherland Ross saw problems ahead, writing to his father in February,

> As I said to you when out in New Zealand, I consider this year will be one of the biggest in the firm's history but I am seriously concerned about 1920/21. My own feeling is that prices are now near the top of the wave, and I have instructed buyers to buy nothing for delivery later than say November next, as while I feel confident that prices will hold till the end

*of this year, I do not consider that data are sufficient to express an opinion regarding 1921, especially as regards woollens.*

As for purchasing elsewhere, he thought American goods should be avoided until the rate of exchange improved. Shoddy Japanese goods should be avoided at all costs.[33]

The shortages of clothing at the end of the war meant that there was a ready market for locally made goods. In 1918, Ross had opened a blouse-making factory in the Stafford St building with the intention that an even greater proportion of clothing would be made in-house in future.[34] During the first half of 1919, with wages lower in Auckland, it was decided to expand factory operations there, the idea being to sub-contract work more extensively than hitherto. Arrangements were duly made with Messrs Smith, the firm's shirt suppliers, and Fowler & Co., who made blouses and boys' clothing, to manufacture exclusively for Ross & Glendining in return for financial support.[35]

An increase in output that required only limited capital and no managerial responsibilities held obvious attractions. Before the new contracts came into effect, however, the clothing trade in New Zealand was thrown into turmoil by Macky, Logan, Caldwell Ltd, the Auckland warehousemen, who embarked on a massive acquisition spree. With this firm 'taking over all the factories they could lay their hands on in Auckland', the branch manager, Snedden, and his accountant, Jeavons, were summoned to Dunedin to discuss how supplies might be protected. It was decided that Ross & Glendining should open their own factories in Auckland, with Snedden to look for suitable properties.[36]

By early December a site had been found, with Ross informing Sutherland,

*We had a letter from them this morning telling us the best site they can find is a corner one in Grey St [Avenue] near the town hall – 66 feet frontage and 100 feet deep. The site is sloping so part of the building will be four floors, the rest three. The price is £1,452, they consider it cheap compared to similar sections in Queen St .... The men who have been making for us will find the necessary machinery and will pay us a rental of 10 per cent on the outlay, confining their output to us.[37]*

The purchase went through rapidly. Shirt manufacturing commenced at the Greys Avenue factory shortly afterwards, although by then the notion of employing inside contractors had been rejected in favour of outright ownership and control.[38] Early in 1920 another property was secured in nearby Wellesley St, where blouses and other clothing were to be made.[39]

The Wellesley St factory entered production in 1921.[40]

While the two factory properties were being purchased, it was learnt that the elderly owner of E. Le Roy & Co., a major supplier of tents, waterproof coats, stock covers and tarpaulins was to cease manufacturing to concentrate on retail. With Le Roy having a virtual monopoly on waterproof coats in the country, it was quickly agreed that Ross & Glendining Ltd should acquire the manufacturing side of the business, together with associated patent rights.[41] The existing coat and covers factory in Queen St was not included in the deal, so the firm had to acquire yet another factory property. Once again Ross elected to build, securing a site on Sale St for around £3,500. Construction costs were estimated at £20,000 and the total costs of the venture at £55,000.[42] When costs started to balloon out of control Herbert Glendining, who was given responsibility for Auckland factories, was instructed to ask Le Roy if a top floor was essential. Ultimately, the firm's Dunedin builder was sent to Auckland to make the necessary economies.[43] It was 1921 before the machinery, stocks and hands were transferred and the new coat and covers factory commenced production.[44]

In 1920, the Auckland warehouse began to source boot supplies from the locally based New Zealand Boot Company, the firm's Dunedin factory being inundated with orders. The proprietors of the boot company, doubtless aware that Ross & Glendining had been buying up suppliers, very soon offered to sell them their business. Given the heavy capital outlays already undertaken, the board were reluctant to purchase yet another firm. Tom Ross nevertheless encouraged Snedden to contract for the entire output of the N.Z. Boot Co., subject to suitable systems to control costs, quality and product lines being put in place.[45]

While the majority of the new factories were located in Auckland, the other main centres were not neglected. A three-storey building was purchased early in 1920 in Marion St, Wellington, the upper two floors being used as a clothing and shirt factory while the ground floor was let as a bulk store.[46] Production here appears to have been undertaken by inside contractors. Capacity was also increased in Dunedin as soon as the war was over, a four-storey factory being erected behind the Stafford St premises, there also being access to High St. The bottom two floors were devoted to hat making, with blouses made on the third floor and mantles on the fourth.[47] The following year, space in the building was partitioned off for making boys' clothing.

The expansion of output during the middle of a boom proved to be far from easy, with seamstresses and raw materials difficult to procure.[48] The shortage of woollen and worsted cloth was a reflection of the fact that Roslyn Mills, like most other mills in New Zealand, was still awaiting the delivery of new machinery. Mill hours had also been reduced from forty-eight to forty-five per week, as had the amount of overtime that might be worked. These factors, in conjunction with the demands of a civilian population starved of woollen and worsteds, meant that an informal system of rationing imposed by the mills during wartime was continued well into the post-war period. Even with rationing, Ross & Glendining still struggled to meet a backlog of orders, some of which were almost two years old.[49]

With a shortage of capacity, mill owners wishing to sell their businesses were in a strong position. In April 1919, John Ross was asked yet again if he wished to buy the Onehunga Woollen Mills. Onehunga had been supplying Ross & Glendining for many years, their focus on cheaper woollen goods complementing Roslyn Mills' better quality lines. While Ross was 'not anxious at the present time to launch out into new ventures', he still inquired about their machinery and current output, and what price the vendors had in mind. In the interim, he was happy to take their entire output.[50]

Difficulties in obtaining woollen and worsted cloth also affected other warehousemen. During the course of 1919, Macky, Logan, Caldwell Ltd attempted to buy the relatively small Ashburton Woollen Mills. When their approaches were rebuffed they bought the Oamaru Woollen and Worsted Mills, paying 55/- for each £1 share. This helped them secure raw material supplies for the factories that they were about to acquire in Auckland.[51]

### 3. EXPANSION HELD UP BY CONTINUED SHORTAGES OF MACHINERY AND LABOUR

Meanwhile, the reconstruction of Roslyn Mills continued to be held back by the slow delivery of machinery.[52] The most serious delays occurred in the supply of spinning machinery as Platts of Oldham, having shipped poorly constructed mules towards the end of 1918, showed no signs of sending the carding engines and tape condensers that prepared wool for the mules. Throughout 1919 and 1920, London Office continued to press them for action, but to no avail.[53] Platts continued to offer a variety of excuses until finally, in May 1921, it was revealed that they had been instructed by the British Government to supply no machinery until the French had got all they needed to make good wartime losses.[54] Ross estimated that the delays had cost Roslyn one third in mill profits foregone, in spite of running double shifts on the existing carding engines.[55]

Roslyn Mills did no better when it came to the supply of looms. The makers, Hutchinson Hollingsworth, had promised to deliver the Dobson looms at the beginning of 1919 but by the middle of 1920 they had still not arrived.[56] Tom Ross, who was now heavily involved in mill affairs, thought that by this stage another fifteen looms were required. If Netting was unable to get satisfaction from Hutchinson Hollingsworth, then he should approach another maker, even if this meant running two different types of loom in the same shed.[57] In the interim, an unsuccessful attempt was made to purchase looms from the small Rosedale Mill in Invercargill.[58] The first of the Hutchinson Hollingsworth looms finally arrived in the middle of 1921.[59]

Building works were completed at Roslyn Mills by Christmas 1920, but another year was to elapse before all the machinery on order was delivered.[60] This did not mark the end of the expansion programme, the continued demand for locally made woollens and worsteds resulting in additional orders being placed for the latest textile machinery. Platts, as the leading makers, were once again asked to quote for tape condensers and worsted carding machinery. Not surprisingly, London Office was told that they should not hesitate to place orders elsewhere if better delivery dates were offered.[61] An American 'Northrop' loom, relatively new to New Zealand, was also ordered on a trial basis and an attempt was made to secure surplus looms and carding engines from the still-born woollen mills at Masterton.[62]

Expansion after the war was also bedevilled by labour shortages. A larger hat factory meant that another twenty-one workers, male and female, were required, the request being passed on to London Office late in 1919. Unfortunately, New Zealand was no longer as attractive as hitherto since wages in the United Kingdom were now 'practically on a par'.[63] Sutherland Ross nevertheless did his best, 'As a first step, I went along to New Zealand offices to find out what prospects there were of shipping them, if we had hands to send. In a nutshell, there are five thousand people today trying to get out to New Zealand who must be sent in rotation'.[64] Passages gradually became easier to obtain, but recruitment problems remained.[65]

The greatest need for labour occurred at Roslyn Mills. In June 1919, Tom Ross wrote to Netting in London telling him that mature workers were urgently required. In particular, there was a need for four darners, four pickers and a loom tuner, all to be recruited from the Scottish borders. Whether, like his father, Tom Ross had a personal preference for 'Scotchmen' is unclear, but it made good sense to recruit Scottish textile workers as Roslyn Mills worked to the Galashiels' cut. Hosiery was another matter, with Netting instructed to procure four hosiery knitters from the Leicester hosiery district, which also supplied most of the machinery. In addition, a newspaper advertisement was to be placed for a worsted spinner, presumably in the Bradford papers.[66]

Labour continued to be recruited locally and early in 1920 a further 35 hands were taken on.[67] This took the total employed at Roslyn Mills to around 540 hands, but still shortages persisted. In May, three female hosiery workers were nominated for assisted passages to New Zealand on the grounds that the mills were 'experiencing great difficulty in finding sufficient female labour'.[68] The following month, the firm's hosiery mechanic retired to the United Kingdom with a brief to purchase needles, inspect hosiery machinery, and recruit labour. Over twenty hosiery workers were still needed, including machinists, menders, darners and a cutter. To push things along, London Office was told that they should encourage both shipping companies and the New Zealand High Commission to tell migrants about employment opportunities at Roslyn Mills. Arrangements would then be made to meet the migrants at their first New Zealand port.[69]

Even more serious, perhaps, than shortages of experienced labour was the departure of key workers from Roslyn Mills, either to retire or to work elsewhere. A programme for training up future mechanics and foremen had been put in place a couple of years earlier but 'the policy was not initiated early enough to provide fully trained men for our present needs'.[70] In 1919, therefore, London Office was asked to recruit a foreman worsted spinner and a mechanic to service the hosiery frames. Attempts were also made to replace the designer at the mills who, at least according to John Ross, was devoid of initiative.[71] Scottish friends played their part, with Alexander Trotter, a prominent Galashiels wool broker, making enquiries about skilled textile workers willing to emigrate.[72] With British labour markets extremely tight, contacts in Australia were also asked to search for spinners, dyers and finishers.[73] Each of these sources yielded a few hands, as did the local labour market due to frequent movement between the mills.

The complement of hands at Roslyn Mills slowly built up and, by the middle of 1922, Tom Ross was able to report to London Office that the mill was fairly well staffed with 662 persons employed. Many, though, were young and not very dependable, often girls just having left school. There were also some older hands that Ross said he would discharge, providing suitable replacements were available. Once again it was suggested that advertisements be placed in hosiery districts' newspapers for mechanics and machinists, in the hope that some might take advantage of assisted passages and emigrate.[74]

The increase in the size and number of factories, the expansion programme at Roslyn Mills, and the rising cost of inventories necessarily raised the amount of capital required by Ross & Glendining Ltd. Much of the capital sunk in plant and equipment came from ploughed-back profits, although the firm still relied on the Bank of New South Wales for working capital.[75] With prices soaring after the war, the amount tied up in stocks necessarily increased. Yet as long as money rolled in from sales, there seemed to be little pressure on finance. In 1919, Hercus was even talking about paying off depositors.[76]

## 4. Boom gives way to bust

The financial situation remained comfortable during early 1920 but, with a 'check to demand' bound to occur soon, Netting was urged to be cautious.[77] Sales, nevertheless, continued to boom and profits for the year to July, after paying a soldier-employee war bonus of almost £10,000 and a further worker bonus of £60,493, were a record £178,644.[78] By the time of the annual general meeting in October, however, it was a different story. Writing to Dunlop, the Invercargill branch manager, Hercus explained,

> *There has been during the past month a very marked change in the financial matters in the Dominion that calls for our most serious attention …. The stocks which had run down to moderate amounts in August have suddenly been swamped with huge shipments from Home and Foreign Markets which we cannot hope to make use of this season. These, added to the more that are coming on in the next few months for winter will keep us overstocked for the next nine months: and we must do everything in our power, not only to bring the amount down by pushing sales but by stopping all orders from Home or other markets, except such as cannot be avoided.*[79]

Similar letters were sent to other branch managers with instructions to cut or cancel orders where possible.

The expectation of a slump saw sales ease off in July but it was the end of the Imperial Government wool purchases in August, together with a weakening of the British economy, that probably triggered the downturn. By October all export prices were down, except butter, the slide continuing into the following year.[80] George Hercus, as company secretary, applied to Bank of New South Wales for support. Reduced sales and the delay of shipments, the bank was told, meant that the firm was likely to accumulate a whole year's stocks over the next six months. Could it therefore increase its overdraft limit to £500,000? The bank was assured that Ross & Glendining Ltd. proposed to strengthen its balance sheet by increasing the nominal capital of the firm to £1,250,000; a number of deposits, currently held by shareholders, might also be converted into shares.[81] Further shares would be issued to the public if necessary although the chairman was not keen to go outside for finance.[82] On 4 November 1920, 15,000 bonus shares, fully paid to £10, were created from reserves and issued to family and management.[83]

The next few months proved to be extremely difficult. Large depositors, such as Dalgety and the National Insurance Company, withdrew their funds from Ross & Glendining Ltd while sales continued to fall. There was also another Government loan to which the firm was obliged to subscribe. Early in 1921, Thomas Glendining and James Evans went round the branches, ruthlessly cutting prices in order to shift surplus stocks.[84] Stock was discounted by a fifth to £1¼ million, £100,000 worth of goods having already been sacrificed at cost the previous November. Other warehousemen, worse off than Ross & Glendining, cut prices even more. Macky, Logan, Caldwell Ltd were reported as 'pitching away stuff', while Sargoods were 'selling stuff at any price offered'. Tom Ross wondered whether it did much good as in many cases the retailers were too short of cash to buy.[85]

Fierce competition and the continued deterioration in trade meant that the estimates of the firm's overdraft requirements proved to be woefully inadequate. By 11 March 1921, the Bank of New South Wales was owed £686,000. George Hercus was obliged to offer the Bank an explanation as to why the October figures were so inaccurate,

*We were not then aware that both in London and America, there were orders that had been given during the war-years and were held as still pending execution; and our warehousemen in sending fresh orders, had reckoned on them as cancelled. The English Manufacturers' Association took concerted action last year to refuse cancellations, and as time of delivery was not made a condition of the contract, we could not demand the annulment of our orders. Since November last, we have had to receive, and pay for, goods to the value of from £350,000 to £400,000 worth above the estimate then made, partly owing to increased values, but principally owing to these back orders.*

Drafts of £50,000 in March, £40,000 in April, and £30,000 thereafter were required to settle outstanding debts and it was anticipated that the total overdraft would fall to £472,000 by the end of the year.[86] Following an interview between Sutherland Ross, James Evans and the Chief Inspector of the Bank of New South Wales in Wellington, further support was granted – providing that Ross & Glendining maintained sales at sixty per cent of the previous year's figure.[87]

Sales for the year to July 1921 were surprisingly robust, at £1.77m only eighteen per cent down, although they fell to £1.38m the following year. Discounting, it seems, had helped to shift stock but the lower prices – plus high inventory costs – played havoc with profits (see Table 16.1). The biggest losses occurred in Auckland, where a lack of caution in ordering necessitated massive discounting to turn otherwise dead stock into cash. John Ross was not amused and the manager, Snedden, although unwell, received a sharp reprimand for incurring losses of almost £100,000.[88] Napier also experienced heavy losses but all centres were affected to some degree, the total warehouse losses amounting to £261,500 in 1921 and £52,400 in 1922.

With the factories also losing money and Roslyn Mills' profits dwarfed by the warehouse losses, Hercus was called upon to 'shake his sleeve' in order

## TABLE 16.1
### WAREHOUSE SALES AND PROFITABILITY, 1919–1927 (£000s)

| July Year | 1919 | 1920 | 1921 | 1922 | 1923 | 1924 | 1925 | 1926 | 1927 |
|---|---|---|---|---|---|---|---|---|---|
| **Dunedin[a]** | | | | | | | | | |
| Sales | 342.4 | 492.2 | 356.5 | 322.8 | 285.3 | 239.3 | 226.2 | 220.3 | 200.8 |
| Net profit | 19.5 | 47.8 | -45.0 | -4.8 | 12.6 | 3.8 | 5.8 | 7.3 | -0.2 |
| **Invercargill** | | | | | | | | | |
| Sales | 129.2 | 155.2 | 136.8 | 107.8 | 110.7 | 97.3 | 90.5 | 85.3 | 81.4 |
| Net profit | 10.0 | 12.9 | -4.8 | -2.2 | 4.7 | 3.2 | 1.5 | 3.4 | -0.1 |
| **Christchurch** | | | | | | | | | |
| Sales | 151.8 | 231.3 | 181.4 | 144.9 | 140.7 | 129.2 | 129.0 | 124.4 | 117.8 |
| Net profit | 9.2 | 26.0 | -12.3 | -0.8 | 6.7 | 4.0 | 4.2 | 1.8 | -0.6 |
| **Wellington** | | | | | | | | | |
| Sales | 395.0 | 581.8 | 479.4 | 383.0 | 391.8 | 367.1 | 365.7 | 343.4 | 315.4 |
| Net profit | 28.6 | 59.1 | -55.1 | -8.9 | 13.4 | 9.0 | 3.2 | -0.2 | -1.3 |
| **Napier** | | | | | | | | | |
| Sales | 95.9 | 147.2 | 122.2 | 95.1 | 100.6 | 98.5 | 101.9 | 96.5 | 90.0 |
| Net profit | 7.0 | 12.1 | -47.8 | -7.0 | 3.1 | 0.6 | 1.2 | 1.8 | -1.0 |
| **Auckland** | | | | | | | | | |
| Sales | 348.1 | 584.1 | 494.1 | 337.1 | 374.8 | 334.1 | 324.2 | 318.0 | 288.4 |
| Net profit | 27.8 | 46.0 | -96.5 | -28.7 | 1.1 | -1.5 | -2.7 | -4.9 | -9.0 |
| Total sales | 1,462.5 | 2,191.7 | 1,770.4 | 1,390.7 | 1,403.9 | 2,65.5 | 1,237.4 | 1,187.8 | 1,093.8 |
| Total net profit | 102.1 | 203.9 | -261.5 | -52.4 | 41.6 | 19.0 | 13.2 | 9.2 | -12.2 |

Sources: Half-yearly balances, AG 512 15/10 to 1921, then Half-yearly analysis of results 1911–1933, AG 512 15/12.
Note: (a) Includes direct sales to customers in all territories.

to post a profit. Property values, written down in 1920 so as to reduce tax liabilities, were promptly written up again and reserves, already called upon to finance £150,000 worth of bonus shares, were raided yet again, a further £42,500 brought forward to balance the books. After this financial sleight of hand, a profit of £837-17-2d was posted in the 1921 profit and loss accounts followed by £1,681 in 1922. No dividends were paid (see Table 16.4).[89]

### 5. A HALTING RECOVERY
Conditions stabilised around the middle of 1922 and, with sales beginning to increase, stocks were slowly brought back to normal proportions.[90] The following year the warehouses returned to profitability but, with sales starting to slide once more, profits slowly dwindled until in 1927 Ross & Glendining returned a loss. Sales revenues were not helped by falling prices, although the situation was made worse by continued competition. British manufacturers, now with lower wages and surplus capacity, flooded New Zealand with cheap

## TABLE 16.2
### SUMMARY PROFIT AND BALANCE SHEET, 1919–1927 (£000s)

| July Year | 1919 | 1920 | 1921 | 1922 | 1923 | 1924 | 1925 | 1926 | 1927 |
|---|---|---|---|---|---|---|---|---|---|
| **Net profit** | | | | | | | | | |
| Warehouses | 102.1 | 203.9 | -261.5 | -52.4 | 41.6 | 19.0 | 13.2 | 9.2 | -12.2 |
| Roslyn Mills | 14.3 | 26.4 | 73.0 | 61.7 | 32.9 | 31.5 | 19.5 | 24.7 | 9.7 |
| Dunedin factories | 6.5 | 18.3 | 3.4 | 2.7 | -3.5 | 10.0 | 6.4 | 8.3 | 6.5 |
| Auckland factories | | 0.2 | -6.4 | -6.5 | -4.6 | 2.9 | 3.2 | 4.1 | -0.8 |
| Total net profit as per half-yearly analysis | 122.9 | 249.0 | -191.5 | 5.5 | 66.4 | 63.4 | 42.3 | 46.3 | 3.2 |
| Profit & loss a/c return | 100.1[a] | 178.6[b] | 0.8[c] | 1.7 | 41.8 | n.a | n.a | 30.7 | 4.2 |
| Paid-up capital | 741.6 | 750.0 | 900.0 | 900.0 | 900.0 | 900.0 | 900.0 | 900.0 | 900.0 |
| Shareholders' funds | 1,000.5 | 1,130.0 | 900.8 | 902.5 | 946.2 | 945.9 | 928.3 | n.a | n.a |

*Sources: Half-yearly balances 1914-1921, AG 512 15/10, Half-yearly analysis of results 1911–1933, AG 512 15/12, Letterbook, AG 512 4/10; Share values, AG 512 15/4; Government Returns, 1922–33, AG 512 15/11.*
*Notes: (a) After deduction of staff bonus. (b) After deduction of staff bonus, loss on war loan and £5,000 building charges written off. (c) After property values written up and other 'creative accounting' by Hercus.*

goods, 'the agents of the home houses chasing almost into the back blocks' to secure orders. Large retailers, who had been forced back into the hands of the soft goods warehouses during the war, also returned to direct importing.[91] Some of these deliberately boycotted warehousemen who were believed to favour smaller customers.[92]

Macky, Logan, Caldwell Ltd, with heavy fixed costs following their acquisition of mills and factories at inflated post-war prices, soon found themselves in difficulty. Early in 1924, T.H. Macky wrote to Ross & Glendining suggesting that all might benefit if firms could agree to close a number of smaller branch warehouses.[93] The savings to be made by closing sub-branches were already being considered in Dunedin, with reports commissioned on the economic viability of Gisborne, Wanganui and New Plymouth. Before any closures might take place, however, the matter had to be put before the New Zealand Warehousemen's Association. Paradoxically, the Association's permission was not required when opening a branch. Thus at the same board meeting that Macky's suggestions for closures were being received, Ross & Glendining's directors resolved to upgrade the company's sample room in Greymouth to a branch, in order to 'meet the competition'.[94]

The opportunity to cut costs without sacrificing a competitive advantage was nevertheless too good to miss. At a specially convened meeting of the Warehousemen's Association, it was agreed that all members' branches in Gisborne were to be closed from 19 August 1925.[95] Subsequently Ross & Glendining were represented in the area by Auckland-based travellers, who made regular visits in one of the company's many Buick motor cars. A sample room was also retained in the town, to which a youth with 'four or five years' experience' was sent to replace the five warehouse staff. How the area was to be worked was left to the discretion of the new Auckland branch manager.[96] Sample rooms were also opened at other smaller provincial centres, including Palmerston North and Timaru, presumably in order to compete with home agents who were now selling so aggressively in the countryside.

Further attempts to retrench and restructure followed, including a proposal that a number of warehouse firms should amalgamate. These initiatives came to nothing, the general unwillingness of Sargood, Son & Ewen to cooperate, together with concerns about the solvency of Macky, Logan, Caldwell Ltd, posing insurmountable barriers.[97]

The difficult trading environment of the 1920s proved a real challenge for the newly opened Auckland factories. After peaking at £135,536 in 1923, sales to the warehouses began to fall (see Table 16.2). A tariff increase in 1921 on non-British goods provided a limited measure of protection from America, Europe and Japan, with further increases occurring in 1927, but competition from the United Kingdom remained fierce. The shirt factory in Greys Avenue proved to be the most successful and, in 1924, it was decided that the company's entire shirt production would be concentrated there.[98] The waterproof coat and covers factory, which also produced a limited quantity of denim clothing, was also reasonably successful. Production at the latter factory declined after 1925, however, as the agricultural sector, the major purchaser of covers for cows and horses and tarpaulins for stacks, suffered from falling commodity prices. As a result, the Sale St factory soon became far too big for the business it conducted and in 1926 an unsuccessful attempt was made to sell the property.[99]

The underclothing and clothing factories, located in Wellesley St, were distinctly less profitable. The former, facing stiff overseas competition, made horrendous losses until it was closed in 1925. The clothing factory also found it difficult to make money, even though the value of sales was substantial. Slim margins may have been partly the result of high transfer prices charged by Roslyn Mill for materials, although the somewhat larger Dunedin clothing

## TABLE 16.3
## ROSLYN MILLS AND FACTORY SALES, 1919–1927 (£000s)

| July Year | 1919 | 1920 | 1921 | 1922 | 1923 | 1924 | 1925 | 1926 | 1927 |
|---|---|---|---|---|---|---|---|---|---|
| **Roslyn Mills** | | | | | | | | | |
| Sales[a] | 207.9 | 284.6 | 309.2 | 290.1 | 349.3 | 349.8 | 311.7 | 243.3 | 226.9 |
| **Dunedin factories[b]** | | | | | | | | | |
| Clothing | 29.1 | 27.6 | 95.6 | 68.0 | 58.8 | 45.2 | 44.5 | 34.4 | 36.4 |
| Hats | 33.8 | 42.1 | 54.5 | 35.6 | 46.7 | 42.8 | 47.2 | 46.6 | 45.5 |
| Boots | 48.7 | 69.4 | 62.9 | 45.0 | 42.3 | 37.1 | 42.3 | 46.0 | 43.9 |
| Mantles | 35.1 | 45.1 | 72.9 | 62.0 | 47.6 | 33.3 | 27.0 | 27.6 | 22.6 |
| Total | 146.7 | 184.3 | 285.9 | 210.6 | 195.4 | 158.4 | 161.0 | 154.6 | 148.4 |
| **Auckland factories[b]** | | | | | | | | | |
| Shirts | – | 3.7 | 6.0 | 22.0 | 32.0 | 33.4 | 37.9 | 33.0 | 29.0 |
| Clothing | – | – | – | 14.0 | 39.6 | 38.3 | 36.6 | 33.5 | 27.2 |
| Underclothing | – | – | 2.2 | 20.1 | 23.5 | 13.5 | 3.7 | closed | |
| Coat, cover & denim | – | – | 38.2 | 29.6 | 40.5 | 44.7 | 55.3 | 45.1 | 25.8 |
| Total | – | 3.7 | 46.4 | 85.7 | 135.6 | 130.0 | 133.5 | 111.6 | 82.0 |

*Sources: Half-yearly balances, AG 512 15/10, Half-yearly analysis of results 1911–1933, AG 512 15/12.*
*Notes: (a) Sales to factories and warehouses. (b) Sales to warehouses.*

factory, facing similar prices, was rather more prosperous. To provide for 'more economical working', it was decided in 1924 to concentrate all the Auckland clothing manufacturing in Greys Avenue and sell the Wellesley St factory.[100] Unfortunately, profits did not improve while the growing popularity of Anzac Avenue and Beach Rd as locations for manufacturing meant that the Wellesley St property remained unsold.[101]

The Dunedin factories fared marginally better than those in Auckland, although sales declined steadily for most of the 1920s. Profits were more robust but while mantles initially did well, none of the plants was consistently profitable. A major departure occurred towards the end of 1922: webs of knitted material, made at the mill, were sent to the High St factory to be cut

## TABLE 16.4
## ROSLYN MILLS AND FACTORY PROFITABILITY, 1919–1927 (£000s)

| July Year | 1919 | 1920 | 1921 | 1922 | 1923 | 1924 | 1925 | 1926 | 1927 |
|---|---|---|---|---|---|---|---|---|---|
| **Roslyn Mills** | | | | | | | | | |
| Net profit | 14.3 | 26.4 | 73.0 | 61.7 | 32.9 | 31.5 | 19.5 | 24.7 | 9.7 |
| **Dunedin factories** | | | | | | | | | |
| Clothing | 1.2 | 1.3 | 1.4 | 3.5 | -2.3 | 5.3 | 1.6 | 1.2 | 1.6 |
| Hats | 1.5 | 6.7 | -2.4 | -2.4 | 3.7 | 4.2 | 4.3 | 4.7 | 3.6 |
| Boots | 3.8 | 7.9 | -2.6 | -3.7 | -3.6 | -2.2 | 1.3 | 2.3 | 2.7 |
| Mantles | n/a | 2.6 | 7.0 | 5.3 | -1.3 | 2.7 | -0.8 | 0.1 | -1.4 |
| Net profit | 6.5 | 18.5 | 3.4 | 2.7 | -3.5 | 10.0 | 6.4 | 8.3 | 6.5 |
| **Auckland factories** | | | | | | | | | |
| Shirts | – | 0.2 | 0.3 | 0.9 | 1.9 | 1.7 | 1.9 | 1.2 | 0.8 |
| Clothing | – | – | – | -2.7 | -0.3 | 0.4 | -1.1 | 0.3 | -1.2 |
| Underclothing | – | – | -0.3 | -2.6 | -7.0 | -0.4 | -1.0 | closed | |
| Coat, cover & denim | – | – | -6.4 | -2.1 | 0.8 | 1.2 | 3.4 | 2.6 | -0.4 |
| Net profit | – | 0.2 | -6.4 | -6.5 | -4.6 | 2.9 | 3.2 | 4.1 | -0.8 |

Sources: Half-yearly balances, AG 512 15/10, Half-yearly analysis of results 1911–1933, AG 512 15/12.

up and made into garments.[102] The adoption of cut-wear, regarded by the trade as an inferior line, suggests that Ross & Glendining had at last decided to compete at the cheaper end of the market. Certainly it proved a success, with capacity being increased in 1925.

## 6. PROGRESS AT ROSLYN MILLS
Roslyn Mills did a lot better than the factories, sales peaking at £349,846 in 1924 before falling sharply two years later. Profits were regularly returned, even when a spike in wool prices occurred in the middle of the decade. Yet operations were far from trouble free. In 1922, the newly knighted Sir John Ross, still chairman of the company at almost 90, became dissatisfied with

the performance of the manager, Miller, calling for his dismissal. George Hercus was given the delicate task of writing to Ross to explain why the board chose not to adopt the 'drastic' changes he proposed,

> *Already, owing to prevailing conditions at the Mill, our returns are showing reduced figures and the prospect of greatly curtailed orders for the coming season.*
>
> *These adverse conditions are not in the management directly, but are owing to the want of competent heads in the designing, dyeing and finishing departments which has prevented the production of many leading lines. Until the positions are filled, and are in good working order, we are absolutely dependent on the manager for carrying on the work that is being done. With all his faults, he had proved himself capable of keeping the work going, with good results …*

Instead, it was suggested that Tom Ross should move from Head Office to the mills and devote his entire time to mill affairs. This would bring him into contact with the manager, foremen, and employees, enable him to gain invaluable technical knowledge, and pave the way for any future changes with the minimum of disruption. It would also raise morale and check the 'idle gossip and slander' that was making the position of the manager more difficult.[103]

Tom Ross was joined at Roslyn Mills by his younger brother Walter, recently married and newly arrived in New Zealand. Walter was appointed assistant manager and given responsibility for monitoring internal transactions. The decision to re-deploy Tom Ross was fortunate, for within six months Miller had resigned. This seems to have had little to do with the arrival of the Ross brothers, his departure being the result of an offer to manage Onehunga Mills at a one third increase in salary, a free house, and removal expenses of £100.[104]

The resignation of Miller coincided with the departure of the engineer and the carder. Once again, the help of the Galashiels wool broker, Trotter, was enlisted to search for replacements. Trotter was able to recruit a first-class carder but the new mill manager, Gosling, came from Foy & Gibson Ltd, Melbourne. Here Gosling had been in charge of a mill, which, like Roslyn, turned out a variety of worsted and woollen goods. He arrived in August 1923. When the new manager found his feet, Tom Ross proposed to experiment with wool blending, so as to reduce the costs of wool without compromising the quality of Roslyn goods.[105]

Shortly after arriving, Gosling was called upon to report on the condition of the mills and make recommendations for alterations and additions. His immediate requirements, which included two new drying machines, a dyeing machine and a variety of hosiery machines, costing around £10,000, were approved. A proposal that a new dye house be erected was rejected, however, and future plans for the installation of ring spinning and the purchase of Hattersley flannel and blanket looms were quietly shelved. The refusal to accept all the recommendations may have been partly due to a change in trading conditions, a sharp increase in the cost of wool suddenly placing an acute strain on funds. The firm's overdraft, £181,610 in September 1923, had mushroomed to £407,636 by the following March, necessitating yet another visit, cap in hand, to the Bank of New South Wales. With deposits amounting to almost £400,000, short-term indebtedness – including the overdraft – now came to around £800,000.[106]

The high price of wool made it difficult to sell locally made goods. With pressure on prices, the New Zealand Wool Manufacturers Association met in July 1924 to agree a new list of prices. The list lasted barely a month before financially strapped competitors began to discount. With trade increasingly difficult, Gosling was asked to make plans to reduce mill staff.[107]

Wool prices remained buoyant for another year but while farming and the general economy may have benefited, mill owners continued to struggle. As Tom Ross explained to Netting,

> the public will not pay the high prices the retail ask for and the retail are full of imported goods so it looks as though we will have to go back to our pre-war ideas about profit on mill lines. Kaiapoi is in a pretty rocky state and the impression in the trade is that they will sooner or later have to reconstruct. In the meantime they are reported to have two years stocks around their necks which must be unloaded somehow. The Wanganui mill is also scratching hard for business; all these things make business hard for Roslyn.

Under the impression that the retail trade was not pushing Roslyn goods, an advertisement was placed in newspapers inviting customers to write to the firm directly if they were unable to obtain certain lines. Tom Ross also continued with his blending experiments, mixing artificial silk [rayon] with wool in an effort to push down costs.[108]

## 7. THE FIRM BENEFITS FROM BETTER MANAGEMENT

The brief resurgence in wool and meat prices came to an end in 1926 and, while mill owners benefited from lower input costs, these advantages were more than outweighed by the adverse effects that falling prices had on general economic activity. The slump in incomes was not as great as that in 1921, although Ross & Glendining still suffered. The worst affected was Roslyn

Mills, where returns fell by a fifth. The unfortunate Gosling was given six months notice, his major failing apparently being an inability to get the specialists in the mills to work harmoniously together. Warehouse sales and profits held up surprisingly well, notwithstanding a decline in the sales of Roslyn goods.[109]

In spite of the trading difficulties of the 1920s, Ross & Glendining Ltd was never in any danger of failing. Unlike Macky, Logan, Caldwell Ltd, the firm was well capitalised and had not become too financially stretched when it embarked on expansion. This cautious approach enhanced the firm's reputation for conservatism, allowing it to rely on the Bank of New South Wales and a host of depositors to see it through. The ease with which the firm survived also reflected an improvement in management, with stock control tightened up, production reorganised as circumstances dictated, and spare capacity eliminated.

Leading the way was James Evans, who proved to be far more effective in warehouse supervision and inventory management than Thomas Glendining. By 1921 he had already been appointed to the board.[110] Tom Ross, too, confounded his father's expectations and used his technical expertise to become a very effective director of Roslyn Mills. Well educated and open-minded, he was instrumental in modernising the mills and its products and improving the quality of the labour force. Sutherland Ross relied heavily on both men, especially from 1923 onwards when he became chairman of the company organising the New Zealand and South Seas Exhibition in Dunedin. Their experience was to prove vital in meeting the challenges that lay ahead.

# THE END OF AN ERA

The conversion of Ross & Glendining to a joint stock limited liability company in 1900 had been undertaken by the partners so that the firm might continue as a going concern in the event of the illness or death of one or both of them. The adoption of a modern governance structure meant that henceforth major decisions were taken by a board of directors which, as a rule, met monthly. The constitution of the company provided for John Ross and Robert Glendining to be permanent board members, with the remaining members elected at the annual general meeting. Held in September or October, it was at this meeting that the chairman presented his report to shareholders, who might then question him or the other directors on the performance of the company. As well as providing for continuity of governance, incorporation also enabled the erstwhile partners to pass on ownership of the company more easily, the steady transfer of their shares to family members having the added advantage of reducing liability for death duties.[1] In 1925, a little over a year before the death of John Ross, he and the executors of Robert Glendining held less than 40 per cent of the shares in the limited company.[2]

## 1. CONTROL OF THE FIRM GRADUALLY PASSES TO ROSS

While the new governance structure provided, at least in theory, a mechanism that provided for change, it was extremely difficult to persuade Robert Glendining to cede power to the board of directors. When John Ross finally returned to New Zealand in 1905, Glendining attempted to retain exclusive control of wool buying and mill management. The extent to which Glendining personally participated in these activities appears to have declined as time went on, although he still insisted that he approve of any decision taken. Obtaining agreement was not always easy as he frequently refused to speak to Ross, and did not always attend board and annual general meetings.[3] At other times he was too ill or simply did not comprehend what was going on.[4] In 1911, Ross was surprised when Glendining advanced plans for more buildings at Roslyn Mills but it turned out to be nothing more than an additional wool store.[5]

On a number of occasions, Glendining said that he would like to retire from the firm. He first threatened to retire in 1907 when Ross, without consulting him, had installed Beesley as acting mill manager. He very soon changed his mind but repeated the threat regularly thereafter – often after an argument – although he usually set terms and conditions that he knew Ross would be unable to meet.[6] In 1912 the situation arose yet again after Ross had reinstated a warehouseman that Glendining had just fired. For once, Ross decided to call Glendining's bluff, arranging with the bank for an overdraft to buy out the latter's shareholding in the company. After a dispute as to whether Glendining would be free to set up in opposition to Ross & Glendining Ltd, the matter was quietly forgotten.[7] Towards the end of 1913, Glendining was reported to be shaky and confused and, although he recovered somewhat, he became increasingly frail. When he died in June, 1917, he had not left his room for over a year. He was seventy-five years old.[8]

Ross, by comparison, remained involved in the company until an illness in 1922 forced him to assume a largely nominal role. An inveterate traveller, upon his return to New Zealand he spent several months each year visiting the branches and inspecting stocks, sailing around the coast in steamers belonging to the New Zealand Shipping Company. This lifestyle, he told Sutherland, seemed to suit him 'better than anything else'.[9] Occasionally this routine might be broken, such as in 1913 when the waterside workers' strike led to a breakdown of law and order in Wellington. With the warehouse having to be guarded to prevent fire-raising and window breaking, Ross decided to spend no more than four hours ashore.[10] The outbreak of war in 1914 meant travelling became far less comfortable than hitherto, with 'steamers fewer, more crowded, old, and often inferior'.[11] He finally gave up his tours of inspection in 1918.

Although working with the increasingly senile Robert Glendining was not particularly pleasant, once Ross had made changes to the factories and curbed Bob Glendining's worst excesses at the mill, he began to enjoy living in Dunedin.[12] His headaches had disappeared and, apart from increasing deafness, his health was generally good. Ross initially lived in a hotel and then in rented property. In December 1907, he bought a three-acre site in Newington upon which to build a house.[13] Shortly afterwards, he asked for his woodworking tools and books to be sent out from England.[14] The latter reflected his strong Christian faith and included a French Bible, a Gaelic testament, and a dictionary that accompanied each.

Ross was extremely proud of what he had achieved once he had taken up the reins in Dunedin. Writing to Sutherland Ross in 1910, he pointed out that sales had risen every year since putting his 'shoulder to the wheel, from £345,454 for the year ending in December 1901 to £673,844 for last year'.[15]

He was therefore a little disappointed when his contribution to commerce was not recognised in the 1911 Birthday Honours List.[16] Undeterred, Ross continued to push forward with his vision for the firm, investigating the possibility of securing new sample rooms in Gisborne, doubling the floor space in Napier, and making plans for alterations to the Wanganui warehouse. Once this work was done, he told Sutherland, the warehouses will 'be complete for my time'.[17]

## 2. THE SECOND GENERATION DO NOT LIVE UP TO EXPECTATIONS

By comparison, Robert Glendining enjoyed little happiness in his declining years. He evidently cared little for his eldest son, Jack [John Ross Glendining] who was employed as a lowly warehouseman in the High St premises.[18] He clearly had higher hopes for Bob, and it was his failure to see any fault in his younger son that led to so much acrimony between himself and Ross. As we have seen, Bob's fondness for alcohol made him increasingly unfit for business.[19] The warning for excessive drinking in 1904 and the subsequent bout of lead poisoning appears to have had a sobering effect upon him, for he managed to lead a reasonably temperate life for a while. When Walter Ross commented on Bob's lack of sobriety in 1911, Ross was able to reply, 'I have not seen him under the influence of drink since his illness and only once heard of him being in such a state. I know that he frequents public houses but think he keeps within bounds'.[20]

Slowly, however, Bob reverted to his old intemperate ways and towards the end of 1915 he was drinking heavily once more.[21] He seems to have sobered up after a spell in the private hospital in 1916 and for some months was back at work, even attending the wool sales towards the end of the year.[22] He began drinking heavily again during 1917, especially after his father died. In November, he was sent with a minder to spend time in the resort town of Rotorua to continue his battle with alcoholism. He never arrived, vanishing while in Wellington. After this episode, Bob was banned from entering the mills and his career with Ross & Glendining Ltd came to a rather sad end.[23] Thereafter, he spent his time fishing in Central Otago until his early death in 1921.[24]

John Ross, likewise, did not have all his ambitions realised through his sons. Sutherland, as we have seen, was not the most diligent of workers when left in charge of London Office, and his repeated requests for permission to return to Dunedin and become more involved with running the business were constantly turned down. Tom Ross, after reading for a degree in engineering in Cambridge and gaining work experience with the renowned diesel engine firm, Sulzer & Co., took a position as an engineer with a firm in Bombay.[25] His contract of employment was to run for five years but, after being there for a short while, he and another ex-patriot engineer resigned owing to the unexpected demand that they should undertake 'strenuous work'.[26] Ross urged his son to return to Cambridge to take his final examinations and continue his profession as an engineer, but to no avail.[27] Early in 1907, Tom Ross came out to New Zealand to work in the counting house in Dunedin and to study for a qualification in accountancy.[28] Once again he failed to complete his studies, much to his father's disgust.[29]

Walter, the youngest son, followed an even more chequered path. He worked briefly in Roslyn Mills while his father was in Dunedin, returning to the United Kingdom in 1904 to study woollen manufacturing in Leeds. He spent some time at the University before working for a local textile machinery maker.[30] Unfortunately, ill health and depression forced him to abandon his studies.[31] After a period recuperating in Highgate, he returned to New Zealand to a 973-acre farm bought for him by his father at Pukepito, near Balclutha.[32] When Walter abandoned Pukepito to farm in the United Kingdom, John Ross took over the property himself – installing a manager to run it on his behalf. Ross spent many happy hours there in his declining years, painting barns and hanging gates.[33] Walter finally returned to New Zealand in 1922.

### 3. SUTHERLAND ROSS PRESSES FOR HIS BROTHER TO BE ON THE BOARD

Sutherland Ross clearly thought more highly of Tom Ross than his father. The two brothers were very close, with Tom even volunteering to take Sutherland's place in the British army should the latter be called up for active service.[34] In the event neither saw action, Tom's military service being limited to six weeks towards the end of 1918. He spent his time emptying latrines and digging graves when influenza swept through the camp at which he was supposed to be doing his basic training.[35]

At the beginning of 1917, however, Sutherland Ross started to press his father to give Tom a greater say in the running of the business,

> He is the only one of either family with technical knowledge of the mechanical portion as you do not want to be bothered with details of it now and he has had a good opportunity of learning the organization of the company as a whole during the past ten years. I would urge you to find a seat for him on the board and do not suppose there would be any serious objection to such a step now.[36]

Sutherland Ross was probably being optimistic when he believed that the Glendining family would mount no objections. The real opposition, though, came from John Ross himself. There was, he thought, little possibility of

Tom being appointed to the board while Robert Glendining was still alive. The fact that his son had thrown over his chosen profession of engineer and then, after ignoring repeated advice, had failed to complete his accountancy degree, was also a bone of contention. Those in the counting house should be able to look up to him, his father maintained, rather than down upon him. While he accepted that Tom was kind and considerate, Ross felt that he 'lacked the push and perseverance that has characterised the business hitherto'. Instead, it would be better for Sutherland to return to New Zealand as soon as practicable and take charge himself. Nevertheless, he did agree to put Tom's name forward at the next annual general meeting.[37]

Why Sutherland should have asked for Tom to be placed on the board at this juncture is unclear, although it is evident that by this stage he was beginning to think about how the firm should be run after the war. Who should represent the firm in London when he finally returned to New Zealand was a vexed question, especially as he thought that Charles Netting, the manager, was not the man for the job. As he explained to his brother, 'I do not say it snobbishly, it is to a great extent who and what you are that counts, equally with what you do'. It seems that Sutherland Ross, the English public schoolboy, had fully assimilated the mores and values of the middle classes who now dominated life in the City of London! With Tom Ross unwilling to return to the United Kingdom, Netting took charge by default.

The competing claims of the Ross and Glendining families necessarily had to be considered when the question of board appointments arose. Sutherland Ross did his best to be fair. 'We are honest men,' Sutherland wrote to Tom, 'and we have no wish to dispossess them of what is theirs'. He also expressed the hope that better feeling might exist between the two families in future.[38] Meanwhile, Tom should be less easy-going and exhibit a bit more drive. In an oblique reference to Robert's brother, Thomas Glendining, Tom was told that what the company did not need at this stage was another man on the board 'without guts'.[39]

## 4. The composition of the board following the death of Glendining

Sutherland's schemes concerning board appointments and future management were brought to an abrupt halt by the death of Robert Glendining in 1917. Now the question became who, amongst the Glendining clan, should represent that family's interest on the board. Sutherland was kept up to date with developments by his father,

*It would, of course, be quite right that one of the other family should have a seat on the board, but the difficulty is that neither can give any useful*

*service. Bob is simply impossible and Jack's case has monopolised my thoughts the past two days. I went down to the valley [Robert Glendining's home] by request the day before yesterday – your aunt [Mary Glendining] suggested that we should give Jack an interest in the business by giving him a seat on the board to which I replied I would see about it. She then began to speak about mill affairs, saying that Mr Miller was unpopular and unsuitable, that Bob was ignored and suggested that he should be reinstated when I told her it could not be done. Hercus, Thomas Glendining and I had a talk about these matters when we practically came to the conclusion that although Jack would be comparatively harmless on the board when sober, we must make a proviso that he must abate from drink if he is to become a board member and your mother agrees with the idea.*[40]

Unfortunately, Jack Glendining's subsequent behaviour proved to be 'rather troublesome and sometimes insulting', with the result it was decided not to offer him a place on the board. At another stormy meeting, Mary Glendining was told that she was free to appoint any sober businessman she wished to represent her but Ross refused to accept a drinking man on the board. In the interim, Mr. Park, the company's auditor and manager of the Trustee Company, would act on her behalf.[41]

The arrangement appears to have suited Mary Glendining well for, after a short while, she nominated Park to be her permanent representative on the board. This was perfectly acceptable to Ross, who believed Park to be a reasonable man. With the relations between the two families beginning to thaw, he told Sutherland that the time was not right to push for Tom's election to the board. Moreover, an additional Ross vote was not essential as the family controlled the board anyway.[42] Tom Ross was elected to the board the following year and although Jack Glendining appeared to be less than happy with this development, there were no further recriminations.[43] When Sutherland Ross briefly visited New Zealand in 1919, he was able to mend fences still further. Following his return to London in August, the annual general meeting – attended by members of both families – passed off very pleasantly, with 'no jarring note'.[44]

## 5. PHILANTHROPIC ACTIVITIES

By the early twentieth century, John Ross and Robert Glendining, although at odds with one another, decided that now was the time to increase the amount of money that they gave away to charitable causes. Glendining, although very difficult in his later years, was at heart a public-spirited and generous man. A staunch Presbyterian all his life, for many years he was an elder of the Knox Church. He played a leading part in the erection of the church, was a member of the Presbyterian Board of Property, and built the Knox Church Sunday School buildings on the corner of King St.[45] He had few political ambitions, although in 1901 he was elected to the Dunedin Drainage Board. Shortly afterwards, London Office was called upon to purchase and ship diesel engines and pumping machinery to New Zealand.[46] Glendining resigned from the board in 1905 although, two years later, London Office was still involved in securing spare parts for the pumps.[47]

Glendining was also a keen horticulturalist who, since the 1870s, had developed splendid gardens at his home, *Nithvale*, in North East Valley. At one stage he had asked Ross to purchase a copy of *The Ligurian Bee* and was regularly in receipt of gardening journals from the United Kingdom. When, in 1907, the local community was struggling to fund the construction of a winter garden in the city's botanical gardens, he gave £4,000 to aid completion of what was the first public conservatory in Australasia.[48] London Office once again provided assistance by purchasing the boilers, pipes, glass and other materials required by Messrs Mason & Wales, the supervising architects.[49]

Glendining's last major gift to the community was that of the Anderson's Bay Orphans' Home, which opened in 1913 with places for seventy young children. When he died in 1917, his estate was entered for probate at £363,000, which included the value of shares transferred and other gifts made in the preceding three years.[50] Shortly after his death, his wife made an anonymous donation of £8,000 to help fund a second chair of medicine at the University of Otago.[51] A bequest of £3,000 was also made to Knox College, Mary Glendining subsequently contributing £600 each year for the upkeep of the college while she was alive. The college received a further endowment of £12,000 upon her death in 1936.[52]

John Ross had contributed to a number of charitable causes in Dunedin while still resident in London but, when he returned to New Zealand, the scale of his giving increased significantly. Like Glendining, he took a practical interest in the Presbyterian ministry. Consequently when, in 1902, the Reverend Cameron had an article published in a local Presbyterian magazine, *The Outlook,* calling for 'a college in which to house all our Presbyterian students attending the University, in all faculties', Ross was sympathetic. After they met at a garden party, Cameron was invited to the company offices in High St, where Ross agreed to contribute towards the £25,000 building programme. Shortly afterwards, *The Outlook* was able to announce that an anonymous donor had promised to give a sum of £10,000 over a period of five years. Encouraged by this act of generosity, other subscriptions soon began to roll in.

Knox College opened, unfinished, in 1909, with half of the forty-two residents being divinity students.[53] Inevitably, perhaps, London Office became involved in supplying what was needed, with bedding, crockery and other items being purchased for the college.[54] Further financial assistance from Ross was to follow, a south wing and chapel being added in 1913, by which time he had contributed over £20,000. The next year attic rooms were built, taking the total number of students in residence to ninety-three, and once again Ross bore the cost. In 1918, he undertook to provide £500 per annum to support a tutorial fund. Finally, in 1925, he donated a further £3,000 to a building extension scheme.[55]

Ross held a particularly enlightened attitude to women, as evidenced by the support he provided for his sisters' education and his willingness to countenance a 'lady buyer' working at London Office. When approached by a suitor wishing to marry his youngest daughter, he insisted that Zeala (Margaret Caroline Zealandia Ross), should be free to marry the man of her choice. Not surprisingly, he supported his wife in her efforts to establish St Margaret's College, a residential college for women at Otago University. He also contributed financially. Ross served on the University Council as well as on the Board of Governors of Otago Boys High School. He retired from both in 1920 on the grounds that he had become too deaf to listen to proceedings.[56]

John Ross, although committed to the welfare of the young in his adopted country, never ever forgot his Scottish roots. In 1901 he had been pressed by the Reverend McBeath of Halkirk to surrender feudal rights over land in the village so that a church might be erected. Ross, who had inherited the rights from his parents, had other ideas, explaining that he intended 'to erect a building for the use of the community on the site at the end of the bridge where I spent some of my schooldays'. He invited the reverend gentleman to help him to secure full title to the site but help, it seems, was not forthcoming.[57] It was not until 1908 that Ross made a fresh attempt to acquire the site of his old school. Writing to William Black he stated, 'If it can be acquired now I am ready to give a reasonable price for it and erect such a building as will be suitable for the social and educational requirements of the inhabitants'.[58] He also contacted his brother Donald, who lived in Halkirk, presumably asking him to push things along. Unfortunately Donald died soon after.[59]

The following year saw negotiations for the purchase of the site continuing, although the price was rather more than Ross had in mind.[60] Finally the sale was completed and, towards the end of the year, plans began to be drawn up in Scotland for the Ross Institute. They turned out to be a bit too ornamental for Ross's taste, although he went along with the residents' suggestion that they pay for a tower with an electric clock – the first of its kind in Scotland. In spite of his reservations about the design, Ross agreed to sanction the plans. He was adamant, however, about what the rules for the Institute should include. He told his niece, Ella, that they would,

> *certainly provide for barring all intoxicants, as one of my reasons for providing the institute is to keep people from the temptations connected with public houses.*[61]

His deceased cousin William Ross, the former Right Worthy Chief Templar of the World, would have greatly approved. In 1910, Sutherland Ross paid a visit to Halkirk to preside over the opening of the institute.[62]

Ross was constantly called upon for donations. For many years he supported both the YWCA. and the YMCA. in Dunedin. In 1909 he helped pay for a building for the latter institution, at the same time becoming a trustee.[63] Ross also gave £5,000 for the establishment of a Presbyterian home in North East Valley for the aged and destitute. At the time of his death in 1927, there were over fifty people resident in the Ross Home.[64]

John Ross was far less keen to let the government have his money. In 1913, at the behest of his family, he made arrangements to give away a sizeable amount of his fortune. Providing he lived for three years, gifts would only incur a five per cent duty as opposed to death duties, which were levied at seventeen per cent on bequests to immediate family, and at a greater rate when the beneficiaries were not so closely related. Writing to Sutherland, he outlined his plans for his shares:

> *The amount transferred is £150,000, say £30,000 to your mother, £18,750 to each of the family, and £7,500 to your aunt Mrs. Thomson … as your mother and each of the family have a sufficient income from the shares already given them, it is my wish during my lifetime at least that the income from the shares now transferred be left in the business and additional shares be bought with the dividends accruing from them from time to time. In view of the continued enlargement and expansion of the business and owing to the large amount owed to depositors, I consider this necessary if the business is to continue and progress.*

Once this transfer was complete, 7,900 £10 shares were left in his own name, some £50,000 of which was to be set aside to meet bequests, including sums to be given to Knox College and the Ross Institute. Death duties would be waived on the latter two bequests as they were for charitable purposes. Should he die within three years, then the sale of his Pukepito farm should realise £12,000 and his investments in the Roslyn Tramway, Wright Stephenson, the Brisbane Telegraph and other shares a further £24,500 or so. This, he felt, would be sufficient to meet any death duties incurred in the event of his early demise.[65]

Ross was to live for another 13 years, long enough to receive his well-merited knighthood in 1922. He continued as chairman of Ross & Glendining Ltd until February 1925, when he stepped down in favour of Sutherland Ross.[66] He retained a seat on the board until his death early in January, 1927. His estate was entered for probate at £267,004.[67]

## 6. Complementary talents

John Ross and Robert Glendining were both outstanding businessmen. They were very fortunate, however, that their accountant, general manager and company secretary, George Robertson Hercus, was not only extremely able but also blessed with considerable longevity. Like John Ross, Hercus continued to work well into old age, his last major task being to massage the accounts in 1921 and 1922 so that profits might be announced during the depths of the depression. He resigned as company secretary in August 1922, being replaced by the Auckland accountant, Alfred Jeavons. Hercus continued to oversee the preparation of accounts until August 1925, at which point he finally retired. A kindly and helpful man, he was asked to remain on the board on whatever basis he chose. George Hercus died a year later, aged eighty-two, after fifty-six years in the service of Ross & Glendining. He had pre-deceased Sir John Ross by five months.[68]

While John Ross and Robert Glendining had operated successfully prior to Hercus joining them, the subsequent history of their enterprise might have been rather different had they not been able to rely on his considerable talents. It was he who developed the routines and systems vital to the successful operation of the Dunedin warehouse and the branches, providing a degree of control that was patently lacking in the company after World War II. His mastery of financial detail was second to none, his dissection of accounts helping to identify and eradicate loss-making activities in all areas of the business. More generally, Hercus acted as a useful foil to the thrusting Glendining, even if he found this role increasingly difficult as alcoholism and illness made the latter ever more irascible and autocratic. The two men were very different, with Hercus meticulous and careful in what he did while Glendining, with huge ambition and energy, tended to concentrate on the bigger picture. Despite their differences, the two men worked well together for many years.

Ross, too, was ambitious. Yet his was an ambition that was tempered with caution, and he was always prepared to put in the necessary intellectual effort to work through problems in a systematic and thorough manner. He was a passable linguist, did his best to obtain a good technical knowledge of the woollen, worsted and hosiery industries, and was even prepared to study in the evenings in order to gain an elementary understanding of electricity. He was, without doubt, open minded and forward looking, always searching for the latest innovation so that his firm might gain a competitive advantage

Together, John Ross, Robert Glendining and George Hercus ensured that, by 1920, their firm enjoyed a position of pre-eminence in the New Zealand business world. Their demise, just as the world economy was about to face a downturn of unparalleled proportions, was unfortunate, especially as Sutherland Ross seemed not possess the business acumen of his father.

SECTION FIVE
# Second Generation

# DEPRESSION AND RECOVERY, 1926–1939

The downturn that began in 1926 continued into 1927, resulting in a sharp rise in unemployment.[1] With protectionism on the rise around the world, it was not long before both manufacturers and labour began to lobby Government for changes in the tariff. John Ross and Robert Glendining had always been committed free traders, but now both were dead. Sutherland Ross, with factories to keep going, saw things differently and was persuaded to support protection, petitioning the Government 'for an increase in the tariff on lines manufactured by us'. His firm also agreed to display some of their New Zealand and South Seas Exhibition material, on show in Dunedin in 1925–6, at the New Zealand Protection League exposition held in Auckland.[2]

The Government set up a tariff commission and, in March 1927, the commissioners took a break from 'sifting evidence all day' to visit Roslyn Mills. While there, Tom Ross showed them looms standing idle and pointedly commented that since 1923 the number of employees had fallen from 700 to 525.[3] Small changes in the tariff followed, with rates raised by five per cent on some non-British goods and lowered on certain items used by New Zealand manufacturers. The changes, Ross thought, were of no benefit at all, apart from 'removing the 4d per lb on raw cotton and cotton yarns'.[4]

In 1928 a fresh initiative was undertaken when the Government convened a National Industrial Conference that brought together economists and representatives of employers, farmers and employees' organisations. There was little agreement on what needed to be done. The economists and farmers ruled out further tariff protection and all, bar the employees' organisations, sought to improve wage flexibility by abolishing the Arbitration Act. Only in this way, they argued, would costs be reduced and the nation's purchasing power restored.[5]

The real problem, as they all admitted, was the fact that export prices had fallen dramatically since 1920. An upturn in prices in 1928 saw business improve for a short while, but unemployment remained stubbornly high. The onset of the Great Depression in 1929, brought about by a combination of worldwide agricultural surpluses, misguided monetary and fiscal policies, and the collapse of international institutions, engulfed New Zealand.

Between 1929 and 1932, export prices fell by almost a half, while GDP shrank by around a quarter in money terms.[6] The collapse in monetary values resulted in widespread business failures, soaring unemployment, and distress in town and country alike.[7] Ross & Glendining Ltd were hard hit by the depression. Aggregate warehouse sales fell by over a fifth, although losses remained relatively small (see Tables 18.1 & 18.5).

Economic recovery began in 1933, set in train by a gradual improvement in export prices and devaluation of the New Zealand currency. The election of a Labour Government in 1935 and their pursuit of expansionary policies cemented the recovery in place.[8] Sutherland Ross, although not a supporter of Labour or its policies, was quick to take advantage of the opportunities offered by economic expansion. New factories were opened, production increased and, between 1933 and 1939, warehouse sales increased from £858,756 to £1,285,402.

## I. PRESSURES TO REDUCE COSTS

While Ross & Glendining were better off than many of their competitors during the late twenties, the reduction in profitability, lower dividends and frequent delays in their payment soon began to cause some unease amongst shareholders. Although still essentially a family company, marriage and bequests meant that people who knew little about the enterprise now held a considerable number of the shares. The first stirrings of discontent surfaced early in 1926, when seven shareholders requisitioned an extraordinary general meeting to discuss ways of improving profitability. They also requested the appointment of a general manager, maybe because Sutherland Ross had spent so much time as chairman of the New Zealand and South Seas Exhibition Company. When Ross agreed to go through the concerns of shareholders with Frank Mitchell, a son-in-law of Robert Glendining, the request for an extraordinary meeting was withdrawn.[9]

During the course of subsequent discussions, Mitchell was told that it was inappropriate to compare the performance of Ross & Glendining Ltd with ordinary woollen mills, as their business was quite different. Nor was it opportune to convert the company from a private to a public company, although it was a subject that could be revisited in the future. However, the mill manager was certainly going to be replaced and as for half-yearly meetings requested by shareholders, the board would be only too happy to oblige.[10]

These limited concessions do not seem to have pleased everybody. In March 1927, the first half-yearly meeting of shareholders took place. With Sutherland Ross in London, both Thomas Glendining and Tom Ross braced themselves for trouble. They need not have worried. Mitchell, after

## TABLE 18.1
### WAREHOUSE SALES AND PROFITABILITY, 1927–1939 (£000s)

| July Year | 1927 | 1928 | 1929 | 1930 | 1931 | 1932 | 1933 | 1934 | 1935 | 1936 | 1937 | 1938 | 1939 |
|---|---|---|---|---|---|---|---|---|---|---|---|---|---|
| **Dunedin** | | | | | | | | | | | | | |
| Sales | 200.8 | 196.6 | 188.4 | 184.6 | 167.3 | 164.4 | 192.2 | 205.4 | 213.2 | 221.1 | 248.5 | 216.2 | 248.5 |
| Net profit | -0.2 | 1.7 | 0.1 | 0.6 | -5.5 | n/a | n/a | n/a | n/a | 4.7 | 7.3 | 5.5 | n/a |
| **Invercargill** | | | | | | | | | | | | | |
| Sales | 81.4 | 83.5 | 76.3 | 71.5 | 60.0 | 57.5 | 23.8[a] | branch closed | | | | | |
| Net profit | -0.1 | 2.0 | -2.8 | -0.3 | -2.4 | n/a | n/a | | | | | | |
| **Christchurch** | | | | | | | | | | | | | |
| Sales | 117.8 | 121.1 | 112.2 | 113.9 | 94.3 | 95.9 | 101.5 | 106.6 | 120.8 | 137.5 | 155.3 | 140.1 | 154.7 |
| Net profit | -0.6 | -0.1 | 1.1 | 1.5 | -4.2 | n/a | n/a | n/a | n/a | 2.7 | 4.7 | 2.4 | n/a |
| **Wellington** | | | | | | | | | | | | | |
| Sales | 315.4 | 323.1 | 319.7 | 321.7 | 284.2 | 299.2 | 284.5 | 292.8 | 288.5 | 323.3 | 387.3 | 353.3 | 415.2 |
| Net profit | -1.3 | -2.0 | -4.0 | -2.8 | -9.6 | n/a | n/a | n/a | n/a | 3.1 | 7.5 | 3.6 | n/a |
| **Napier** | | | | | | | | | | | | | |
| Sales | 90.0 | 95.2 | 89.6 | 85.7 | 35.3 | branch closed following earthquake | | | | | | | |
| Net profit | -1.0 | 1.7 | -0.6 | 0.1 | -1.7 | | | | | | | | |
| **Auckland** | | | | | | | | | | | | | |
| Sales | 288.4 | 303.7 | 320.4 | 334.5 | 264.3 | 264.9 | 256.7 | 267.7 | 293.4 | 360.6 | 441.5 | 403.9 | 467.1 |
| Net profit | -9.0 | -13.7 | -3.8 | 5.6 | -11.4 | n/a | n/a | n/a | n/a | 9.6 | 13.3 | 7.0 | n/a |
| Total sales | 1,093.8 | 1,123.2 | 1,106.6 | 1,111.9 | 905.3 | 881.8 | 858.8 | 872.4 | 915.8 | 1,042.4 | 1,232.6 | 1,113.5 | 1,285.4 |
| Net profit | -12.2 | -10.4 | -10.0 | 4.7 | -34.8 | n/a | n/a | n/a | n/a | 20.1 | 32.8 | 18.5 | n/a |

*Sources: Half-yearly analysis of results, 1911–1933, AG 512 15/12; Half-yearly balances/Government Returns Ledger, AG 512 15/11.*
*Notes: (a) Half-year.*

commenting on the lack of financial data, merely read 'a long and rambling resolution about bringing in outside businessmen of experience and turning the business into a public company'. Stuart Glendining [Jack Glendining's son] then stood up, 'primed with a speech to second it', but after a few sentences 'lost his thread' and sat down. After others stated that 'steps would have to be taken' if things did not improve, and Mitchell obliquely hinted that he would accept a seat on the board if pressed, the meeting closed.[11] Mitchell was subsequently invited to nominate an outsider to sit on the board. After several nominees had been rejected, Edgar Hazlett, a director of a number of companies including Standard Insurance and the Westport Coal Company, was appointed to the board. It was not until 1934 that capital reconstruction took place, with new shares issued and provisions made for wider ownership.[12]

By the time of the 1927 meeting, Ross & Glendining Ltd had already taken steps to reduce costs and so it seems unlikely that the additional pressure from shareholders made any difference. As it was, management continued to seek economies wherever they could. Their main focus was the warehouse business, which was yielding negligible returns on an annual turnover in excess of a million pounds. Following a review of senior staff in October 1926, seven warehousemen were dismissed from the larger branches.[13] Other cost-cutting measures saw the Invercargill warehouse purchased outright and spare land disposed of, the Napier warehouse sold after the firm moved to more modest premises, and fresh attempts made to sell the surplus Auckland factories. At the same time, a small sample room was opened in Thames.[14]

These measures all helped to improve profitability but the main problem remained surplus capacity in the warehouse trade. During the first half of 1927 an approach had been made by the Auckland firm, Clark & Co., who had offered to sell out to Ross & Glendining Ltd. This was followed in October by a similar proposal from longstanding Dunedin competitors, Butterworth Brothers. In an age of excess capacity and with rationalisation very much in vogue around the world, these proposals held a certain appeal. As Tom Ross explained to Netting,

> Our idea is that a good scheme would be that the three big firms, Sargood, Son & Ewen, Macky, Logan, Caldwell & Co. and ourselves might take over the stocks of Clark's, Butterworth's and Bing's. But there are two unknown factors in this, these are: Can Macky, Logan & Caldwell stand any further extension? They might even be sellers; Bing's may not be anxious to sell, and if they are agreeable to do so, I do not think they are up against it like the other two. My personal feeling is that a reduction in branches would relieve us all, and if B.B's and Clarks go out in addition, so much the better.[15]

Shortly afterwards, a meeting was held by the Warehousemen's Association to discuss the possibility of mergers and branch closures.[16] In spite of the fact that smaller branches were generally losing money no agreement was reached, with Sargood, Son and Ewen refusing to cooperate with the rest of the trade in any shape or form.[17]

In the meantime, Ross & Glendining Ltd continued to pursue other measures to improve performance and cut costs. The worst performing warehouse in the 1920s was undoubtedly Auckland, with 1923 the only year in which it was able to return a profit. Part of the problem was that the far-flung nature of the territory, poor roads and lack of rail transport all contributed to high travelling costs. Stocks and credit required by customers also tended to be heavier than elsewhere.[18] At the same time, it appears that some departments were not particularly well run, especially the fancy department where rapid changes in fashion taxed the ingenuity of even the most able warehousemen. Towards the end of 1927, three new heads of department were appointed which, the Auckland branch manager assured Head Office, 'will improve our staff considerably'.[19] The improvement in profitability was far from immediate, however, and with fancy departments in all branches 'a bottomless pit', the London buyer of fancy goods was told that his performance must also improve. He was ultimately discharged.[20]

An alternative to improving margins by conducting existing trade more efficiently was to do slightly less trade at significantly lower cost. With complete closure of smaller warehouses out of the question, it was decided to restructure and cut back operations instead. Early in 1928, Sutherland Ross and James Evans asked Atkinson, the manager of the Wanganui sub-branch, to submit plans that would reduce costs without unduly sacrificing turnover. Atkinson duly obliged, 'By eliminating the lesser wanted lines it should be possibly to carry on all departments on one floor downstairs. The better wanted lines together with a more intensive "forward order" business should provide a turnover within 25 per cent of present takings and the figures should gradually rise to normal as the customers get used to new conditions'. Providing Wellington branch was able to take over travelling along the Main Trunk line, it would be possible to cut the number of staff from twelve to eight – at a saving of £900 per annum.[21] Inventory costs would also be reduced and vacated space might be leased.

A subsequent board meeting saw Atkinson's plans adopted in their entirety, with stock carried at the sub-branch reduced significantly. To ensure that the Taranaki region continued to be well supplied, the amount of stock held at the New Plymouth sample rooms was to be raised to £10,000. Fresh premises were also leased in the town at a cost of £300 per annum.[22] Other measures designed to cut costs included re-organising travelling throughout the branches and placing a limit of £2,000 per annum on advertising. In Dunedin, the 'Sentinel' steam lorries that carried goods between the warehouse and the mills were sold to their drivers, the work being contracted out to them instead. Amidst all this pruning, the firm still had sufficient funds to subscribe £150 to the anti-labour Reform Party.[23]

The steps taken did little to stem the losses sustained by the warehouses, although a slight rise in export prices in 1928 seems to have helped sales stabilise. Additional goods were also bought by some of the larger retailers who, anxious to manage inventories more effectively, reduced their own imports and bought from warehousemen instead. Auckland branch appears to have benefited from this trend, increased sales and a profit of £5,620 in 1930 offsetting losses incurred by other warehouses. Yet welcome though this was, it could not mask the fact that Ross & Glendining's warehouses were no longer the driving force in the business that they once had been.

## 2. ROSLYN MILLS, THE MAINSTAY OF THE COMPANY

The main source of profit, as in the early twenties, continued to be Roslyn Mills. At the beginning of 1927, James Porteous, fifty-two years old and recently resigned from Wanganui Mills, replaced Gosling as manager. Porteous had been considered for the post in 1923, striking Tom Ross as 'a good sound man who knew both his business and his own mind', but rumours of excessive drinking seem to have counted against him.[24] Now, with these rumours laid to rest, he was appointed at £1,000 per annum, with three months' notice on either side. He was, in many respects, an ideal choice, having had experience of working in the Scottish woollen industry as well as managing a comparatively unruly colonial labour force.[25]

Tom Ross appears to have been well satisfied with his latest appointment. In March 1927, he was able to inform Sutherland that Porteous was 'shaping up well' and it looked as though the new manager was going to be able to deliver economies in both labour and materials.[26] Porteous soon began to tighten up systems and improve the flow of work through the plant. In April, a progress book was installed in the hosiery section; in June, he insisted that scoured wool be weighed for stock-taking rather than estimated; later that month, a small night shift was set to work on the cards and mules in order to improve delivery times and hosiery mechanics were shuffled around in order to keep the machines going. Slowly but surely he 'straightened things up' and improved the general working of the mills.[27]

In spite of the economic gloom, orders for mill goods kept up reasonably well, with sales for the first half of 1927 well ahead of those for 1926. The demand for worsted goods was quite brisk, Roslyn swimming costumes being extremely popular with the general public.[28] Yet although Porteous continued to make progress, the outcome for the year to July 1927 was disappointing, with declining incomes contributing to a fall in sales. Mill profits, at only £9,734, were the lowest for the decade (see Table 18.3).

The fall in profits was partly the result of heavy discounting, but there were other factors that tended to hold back the mills.[29] Somewhat surprisingly, in view of unemployment levels in New Zealand, Roslyn Mills continued to suffer from shortages of skilled labour. The greatest need was for darners to rectify flaws that occurred in worsted cloth. Early in 1927, London Office nominated two young women for assisted passages. The two darners arrived several months later but they were unable to cope with the backlog of work.[30] Additional workers were sought but, unfortunately, would-be migrants were generally not robust enough to satisfy the High Commission in London. Writing to London Office in 1928, Tom Ross commented, 'it is unfortunate that the applicants have been such a weedy lot, we trust that some healthier workers will apply. In the meantime, we are impressing on the worsted spinner the necessity of turning out better yarns which will reduce the amount of darning required.'[31] Healthier workers, it seems, did not apply, for worsted production continued to be held up by a shortage of darners. In 1929, Porteous put his darners on piecework to raise productivity. Greater output resulted but it was insufficient to overcome the shortage of staff.[32]

Roslyn Mills also found it difficult to recruit and retain competent dyers. This was a perennial problem in New Zealand, with most mills having inadequately staffed dyeing shops. At one stage Tom Ross had suggested to Sargood, Son & Ewen that the Mill Owners Association might offer a scholarship at one of New Zealand's universities 'with a view to maintaining a supply of educated and competent dyers in the colony'.[33] Whether the suggestion was taken forward is not known, but Ross & Glendining continued to hire and fire dyers at regular intervals.

Scots, as ever, were preferred, and in 1927 London Office was instructed to place advertisements in *The Scotsman* and *The Glasgow Herald* for an assistant dyer with experience in silk, artificial silk and hosiery dying. They seem to have been unsuccessful, for the following year Ross told London,

*we want a man who has had some scientific training which he will not display unduly as the very practical rule of thumb experts are very suspicious. Any man engaged should be prepared to have his various recipes recorded in a book along with a sample of the shade produced. Our present dyer has refused positively, saying such knowledge is his capital'.*[34]

Again London Office appears to have been unsuccessful. A little later they were informed that Roslyn Mills had hired a new arrival to New Zealand who said he had dyed hosiery, including artificial silk, at Messrs. Cash & Co. of Leicester. He was given a trial and, when a week had passed with 'no damage' done, he was kept on. Soon he was dyeing silk, artificial silk and wool quite successfully.[35]

The economy, which had shown a brief resurgence in 1928, began to slow down in 1929. Again, trends in primary produce prices were responsible, with Roslyn Mills paying ten per cent less for a bale of wool than a year previously. The first two months' trading, Netting was informed, came out 'badly', a worrying feature being that when Evans and Sutherland Ross went round the warehouses, sales of mill goods seemed rather slow. A sudden surge in orders for Roslyn worsteds improved matters but confidence as a whole was lacking, people preferring to deposit money with the banks rather than spend it on consumption or investment.[36] Trade in the South Island was especially slack, and Tom Ross wondered whether it might be appropriate to reduce the price of woollens and worsteds, in line with the reduction in wool prices. This was not a step to be rushed, however, for it would mean discounting prices at the July stocktaking – and all it then needed was two months of cold weather and stocks would vanish completely.[37]

### 3. A COLLAPSE IN TRADE MADE WORSE BY THE NAPIER EARTHQUAKE

Auckland appears to have propped up Ross & Glendining towards the end of the decade, with warehouse and factories doing better than for several years past (see Tables 18.1 & 18.2). The situation was not to last. The world price of agricultural products, already showing signs of weakness, began to collapse in 1930. As ever, the response of the New Zealand farmer to falling prices was to increase output, a reaction that simply added to surpluses and pushed down prices still further. To make matters worse, farmers' costs did not fall as fast as the prices they were paid, so that gross farm incomes actually fell by 40 per cent. The rest of New Zealand, heavily dependent on the farming sector, inevitably suffered. As incomes dropped, so businesses failed and unemployment soared. How many workers were actually unemployed is unknown, since women and Maori males were not allowed to register for relief. For 1931 and 1932, however, estimates suggest that the actual number unemployed was in excess of 100,000 – somewhere between sixteen and twenty per cent of the working population.[38]

The massive reduction in purchasing power inevitably wreaked havoc on the warehouse trade. The first major casualty was Macky, Logan, Caldwell Ltd. Halfway through 1930, the firm closed all their South Island warehouses and tried to sell their Timaru woollen mill. A meeting of the Warehousemen's Association was promptly convened in an attempt to prevent cut-throat

## TABLE 18.2
## ROSLYN MILLS AND FACTORY SALES, 1927–1933 (£000s)

| July Year | 1927 | 1928 | 1929 | 1930 | 1931 | 1932 | 1933 |
|---|---|---|---|---|---|---|---|
| **Roslyn Mills[a]** | | | | | | | |
| Sales | 226.9 | 260.2 | 268.8 | 231.7 | 222.0 | n.a | n.a |
| **Dunedin factories[b]** | | | | | | | |
| Clothing | 36.4 | 31.8 | 34.5 | 32.5 | 29.1 | 26.9 | 30.3 |
| Hats | 45.5 | 43.7 | 48.4 | 38.4 | 29.6 | 30.7 | 31.1 |
| Boots | 43.9 | 45.7 | 45.2 | 60.8 | 44.1 | 41.4 | 44.6 |
| Mantles | 22.6 | 23.7 | 23.2 | 22.9 | 26.1 | 46.0 | 40.0 |
| Total | 148.4 | 144.9 | 151.3 | 154.6 | 128.9 | 145.0 | 146.0 |
| **Auckland factories[b]** | | | | | | | |
| Shirts | 29.0 | 35.6 | 41.3 | 41.5 | 29.1 | 24.2 | 21.3 |
| Clothing | 27.2 | 28.0 | 40.7 | 34.9 | 20.7 | 15.9 | 20.1 |
| Coat, cover & denim | 25.8 | 29.5 | 35.2 | 39.3 | 20.2 | 18.7 | 20.8 |
| Total | 82.0 | 93.1 | 117.1 | 115.7 | 70.0 | 58.8 | 62.2 |

Source: Half-yearly analysis of results 1911–1933, AG 512 15/12.
Notes: (a) Sales to factories and warehouses. (b) Sales to warehouses.

competition. Sargood, Son & Ewen, recently recapitalised and possibly with a view to driving competitors to the wall, refused to cooperate. Six months later Butterworth Brothers were forced into liquidation. In the meantime Macky, Logan, Caldwell continued to struggle, resigning from the New Zealand Warehousemen's Association in September 1931. Later that year, Sutherland Ross also gave notice of his firm's intention to withdraw from the Association, due to 'depleted membership and altered conditions'.[39]

Ross & Glendining were comparatively well placed to meet the depression. During the previous decade, improved inventory management had resulted in a significant reduction in the level of stocks carried. This, along with modest group profits and the disposal of unwanted assets, meant that by 1930 their once-large overdraft had all but disappeared.[40] Retrenchment continued through the depression, with the boot factory being relocated in the factory complex behind Stafford St, and the empty factory disposed of. Early in 1932, it was decided to dispose of unwanted properties as a matter of policy – at a loss if necessary. Later that year the Invercargill warehouse was downgraded to a sub-branch of Dunedin and part of the building converted to flats.[41]

While a sound financial position meant that the firm was able to continue to support creditworthy customers, it did not insulate them from the collapse in trade. Annual sales fell from £1,111,858 in the year to July 1930 to £905,264 the following year, a trough of £858,754 being reached in 1933. All areas appear to have been equally affected, the exception being Napier where, early in February 1931, a massive earthquake practically flattened the town. The warehouse in Emerson St was one of many properties destroyed, being completely wrecked and then burnt out. Fortunately, staff were able to escape from the building unharmed, three by means of a 'blanket rope' just before the back wall fell in.[42]

The destruction of the warehouse resulted in many thousands of pounds worth of stock being lost. A week later, a bulk store the firm owned in the town was broken into by the army, who took tents and loose blankets – with promises of reparations.[43] The main concern, however, lay with the customers, for most owed Ross & Glendining money and many had lost both their premises and their livelihoods.

With business at a standstill and little immediate hope of improvement, thirteen of the warehouse staff were given six weeks pay and discharged. The accountant, Ashcroft, was retained, and it fell to him to reconstitute the Napier branch books, which had been destroyed. Towards the end of February he wrote to Dunedin from temporary headquarters in the Havelock Hotel, his own house having been severely damaged,

> I am sorry that our book debt list did not get away before the earthquake. It is a fact that the list was actually completely finished five minutes before the quake. ... For some time it was absolutely impossible to even broach the subject [of debts] to our customers, some of them were dead; Perry Wright of Napier, killed in the Kaiapoi Building, J. Leaming of Hastings, H. Williamson of Napier (it is thought he ran out of his shop under our falling front), many were more or less injured and in a great number of cases unable to save a record of any kind ...

> I have called on every customer in Te Awanga, Haumoana, Waipawa, Waipukurau [small settlements] and with the exception of a few who were away have obtained a copy of the January 19th statement and amounts of invoice from them.

*In Hastings I have only got a few so far. Here it is difficult to find customers as many of them are carrying on in their own homes. When the temporary shops are erected it will be easier.*

*As regards Napier, it is a puzzle to know what to do, so many lost everything, stock, books, everything but the clothes they had on. Still, I shall get some of them. I am taking the suburbs first as there the fire did not reach; at the same time some of the customers will be unable to pay but that question can be left until later.*[44]

By May, 80 per cent of book debts had been established 'by rule of thumb'. Where customers had suffered serious losses no interest was charged on the overdue accounts, although very few debts were written down or immediately written off.[45] All in all, the losses sustained by the firm due to the earthquake came to £55,336. This amount was written off when the firm was restructured in 1934.[46]

While Ashcroft was busy establishing indebtedness and collecting sums owing, arrangements were being made to recommence business in Napier. With James Fletcher & Co. being awarded a government contract to build temporary premises for retailers, Stuart Glendining recommended that the firm 'move at once' to open a small sample room with stock supplied from Wellington.[47] At first it was hoped to build a corrugated iron shed on the Emerson St site but, when permission was refused, a temporary site was obtained from Napier Borough Council. As Sargoods were soon going full swing and Kaiapoi Woollen Mills were putting stock into Hastings, a private house was used as sample rooms until a makeshift building could be erected on the council site.[48]

For the next few months the board debated what was to be done in Napier, initially rejecting and then accepting an offer of £9,500 for the now cleared Emerson St site. In August, Ashcroft, no longer required now that operations were so much scaled down, was discharged – with an extra month's pay, thanks, and a good reference.[49] Once the sale of the Emerson St site was finally completed, the Napier manager was instructed to secure a fresh site and obtain building estimates. Henceforth Napier was to operate as a sub-branch controlled by Wellington.[50] Sales, over £85,000 in the year before the earthquake, were much reduced.

### 4. The depression deepens

Charles Netting, the London Office director, kept those in New Zealand abreast of business conditions in the United Kingdom. He, too, faced problems as the collapse of international institutions meant that sourcing goods from Europe became less straightforward. Matters got worse as the depression deepened, with the depreciation of the New Zealand pound against sterling from 1929 onwards, exchange rate instability in Europe in the early 1930s, and changes in tariffs making it progressively more difficult for him to buy goods that would show a profit. Ever the optimist, Netting observed that these factors would allow Ross & Glendining to obtain a bigger margin on those goods they manufactured at home![51]

The difficulty in sourcing goods from Europe on competitive terms may well have helped Roslyn Mills a little. In January 1931, Tom Ross informed Netting,

> *The mill has kept going wonderfully well although on the textile side there has been an unduly large proportion of the less profitable stuff made ... On the hosiery side bathing costumes, lumber jackets, cardigans and fancy outerwear have had a good run, the new circular machines being kept hard at it. We have now bought the greater part of our wool, the lowest price we paid was 1/- for a bale of merino wool. I wish we had been paying more, as cheap wool means less money in the country to buy our products.[52]*

The demand for hosiery products doubtless contributed to improved mill profits, although by April some of the hands were working short time.[53]

The lack of purchasing power at home, as Ross correctly observed, was the major problem facing manufacturers. Sadly the Government, wedded to the economic orthodoxy of the time, did little to help matters. Anxious to check a growing budget deficit, in 1931 a Finance Act was introduced that proposed a ten per cent reduction in wages and an increase in taxes on earned and unearned income.[54] Tom Ross, writing again to Netting, was unimpressed,

> *Trade continues bad and sales still drop. As soon as the government puts through its financial proposals we shall all have our salaries reduced and as compensation our income tax will be raised – if things do not improve in the next few months some of us will be getting pretty hungry.[55]*

The problem with deflation, as Ross explained in a subsequent letter, was that the reduction in business was greater than the fall in values, with little opportunity being afforded to cut expenses.[56]

Reductions in public service wages and salaries were followed in May 1931 by a cut in arbitration award rates of ten per cent for private sector workers.[57] These actions further depressed demand in an already depressed economy and, as a result, competition in the warehouse trade became even worse. Macky, Logan, Caldwell Ltd, having disposed of their South Island warehouses, now decided to conduct a retail trade from their wholesale warehouses and sell at wholesale prices from their factories.[58] This did little to ease their predicament and in November 1932, with accumulated losses amounting to £172,632, it was decided that the firm should be wound up. Some months later their Wellington and Christchurch warehouses were offered to Ross & Glendining by the liquidator, but the offer was declined.[59] At the beginning of 1933, Sargood, Son & Ewen also admitted to feeling the pinch, cutting staff in their Dunedin warehouse by ten and Auckland by twenty. Shortly afterwards they at last agreed to proposals for setting prices, possibly satisfied that their weaker competitors had by now been driven to the wall.[60]

Meanwhile, Ross & Glendining had returned to profitability, largely due to the activities of Roslyn Mills, which continued to employ over 550 hands. Even in 1932, when other mills were struggling, Roslyn remained profitable, sales of fingering yarn increasing fivefold as an impoverished nation took to knitting at home. The demand for manufactured knitwear fell accordingly.[61] The factories, too, managed to keep up sales, the appointment of a dynamic new mantle factory manager – recruited by Netting in 1931 – boosting returns (see Tables 18.2 & 18.3).[62]

The increase in the proportion of goods sourced in-house meant that it was only a matter of time before the role of London Office was called into question. At the annual general meeting in September 1932, Stuart Glendining suggested that, 'the London Office was an unnecessary luxury and might be cut out, the buying to be done more economically by one of the big buying houses'. Sutherland Ross disagreed, pointing out that London Office expenses were little, if anything, greater than a buying commission. The outside director, Hazlett, was also in favour of keeping London Office, since the buyers there bought exclusively for Ross & Glendining, unlike buying agents who bought in bulk and resold to all and sundry.[63] There were other advantages, too, for London kept Dunedin up-to-date with trends in the fashion world, as well as monitoring developments in textile machinery. Yet with the buying costing somewhat more than the 2½ per cent on invoice that Sutherland Ross believed to be the case, London operations were scarcely cost effective. When, in 1933, annual shipments fell to £182,000, Netting was forced to start cutting staff.[64]

## 5. GOVERNMENT POLICY AND ECONOMIC RECOVERY

As 1933 drew to a close, business began to recover. Auckland branch led the way, with sales increasing by ten per cent over the next twelve months. The recovery, like the depression, reflected movements in the international economy, an improvement in export prices gathering momentum in the second half of the year. By 1935 export prices were twenty-five per cent greater than they had been two years earlier.[65]

## TABLE 18.3
## ROSLYN MILLS AND FACTORY PROFITABILITY, 1927–1933 (£000S)

| July Year | 1927 | 1928 | 1929 | 1930 | 1931 | 1932 | 1933 |
|---|---|---|---|---|---|---|---|
| **Roslyn Mills** | | | | | | | |
| Net profit | 9.7 | 32.1 | 31.2 | 13.7 | 28.0 | 37.2 | n.a |
| **Dunedin factories** | | | | | | | |
| Clothing | 1.6 | 1.2 | 2.1 | 1.1 | 1.6 | 3.0 | 3.4 |
| Hats | 3.6 | 3.1 | 5.3 | -0.2 | -0.3 | 0.8 | 1.2 |
| Boots | 2.7 | 4.0 | 1.6 | 5.5 | 2.7 | 3.0 | 3.0 |
| Mantles | -1.4 | 0.6 | 0.1 | 0.4 | 1.5 | 5.6 | 4.0 |
| Net profit | 6.5 | 8.9 | 9.1 | 6.8 | 5.5 | 12.4 | 11.6 |
| **Auckland factories** | | | | | | | |
| Shirts | 0.8 | 1.7 | 2.0 | 2.1 | 0.7 | 0.9 | 0.9 |
| Clothing | -1.2 | -0.3 | -0.2 | 0.3 | -2.4 | -1.4 | -2.4 |
| Coat, cover & denim | -0.4 | 0.0 | 1.5 | 3.2 | -0.7 | -0.2 | 0.2 |
| Net profit | -0.8 | 1.4 | 3.3 | 5.6 | -2.4 | -0.7 | -1.3 |

*Source: Half-yearly analysis of results 1911–1933, AG 512 15/12.*

The recovery was also aided by the devaluation of the currency. Since the mid-nineteenth century the New Zealand currency had been loosely tied to sterling, the rate of exchange being determined by the supply and demand of New Zealand and Australian banks for British pounds. When the worsening depression led to an increase in the combined external deficit of the two countries, so the demands of their banks for sterling exceeded supply, initially forcing the cost of exchange to £1.10 in local currency for every £1 sterling bought. The New Zealand economy suffered from its close banking links with Australia, especially as the acute Australian deficit pushed up local interest rates. Towards the end of 1932, therefore, the New Zealand Government decided to separate the monetary systems of the two countries so that it might control both domestic interest rates and the rate of exchange. Early in 1933, foreign exchange transactions were channelled through the Bank of New Zealand, now an agent of the Government, and the New Zealand currency was devalued from £1.10 to £1.25.[66] The newly constituted Reserve Bank took over central bank functions a year later. The combination of a lower exchange rate and improving prices meant that returns to farmers were much improved.

Ross & Glendining had lobbied strenuously against the decision to devalue, which they saw purely as an attempt to help agriculture.[67] After all, the depreciation of the New Zealand pound prior to devaluation had already pushed up the costs of importing soft goods, raw materials and machinery, with seemingly few corresponding benefits for the wider economy. Yet apart from a few items of soft goods, their fears concerning devaluation proved to be largely groundless. Roslyn Mills, as we have seen, did comparatively well during the Depression, while the company's factories also began to recover ahead of the general economy. Other mills and factories began to recover, too.[68] It seems that the progressive devaluation of the currency, an additional impost on imports in 1931 in the form of a three per cent primage duty, and the maintenance of tariff protection, was sufficient to encourage import substitution.

The tariff, like devaluation, constituted a battleground between free-trade primary producers and manufacturing interests. The conflict was not restricted to New Zealand, the Ottawa Conference in 1932 resulting in an imperial consensus that gave ex-colonial primary producers unfettered access to British markets in return for the imposition of relatively low tariffs on Britain's manufactured exports. The immediate outcome of Ottawa for New Zealand manufacturers was a slight fall in tariff protection, a reduction in duty from 32.5 to 27.5 per cent on ready-made clothing and hosiery being amongst a number of changes.[69] These reductions were almost immediately negated by the devaluation of the currency.

While in Ottawa, New Zealand Government representatives had agreed to conduct a review of tariffs on manufactures with a view to making better targeted reductions in future. In 1933, a Tariff Commission was established with a remit to report within one year. Ross & Glendining Ltd immediately became involved, drafting submissions on behalf of the apparel, hat and boot-making industries for presentation by the New Zealand Manufacturers' Federation. The firm also made submissions to the Commission through the New Zealand Mill Owners Association. The general thrust of these submissions was that, given higher labour costs in New Zealand due to the payment of award rates, higher interest rates, and the tendency for English manufacturers to dump surplus stocks abroad at the end of each season, existing rates of duty should at least be maintained. The New Zealand Farmers' Union, in their submission, advocated the abolition of all duties – apart from those required to raise revenue.[70]

Wellington and harbour, *c.* 1890, shortly after Ross & Glendining Ltd established a branch in the city. Hocken Collections S09-202e.

Auckland, Queen Street wharf, 1904. Three years later, Ross & Glendining established a branch and bought a clothing factory in the city. Photograph by Henry Winkelmann. Special Collections, Auckland City Libraries (N.Z.) 1-W1089.

Stafford Street warehouse, following its conversion to a costume and felt hat factory in 1902. Hocken Collections S09-529c.

The four main warehouses, all completed by 1908. R & G Annual Report, 1953, Hocken Collections S09-529l.

Roslyn Mills workroom, *c.* 1921. Hocken Collections S07-270a.

'Sentinel' steam wagon en route with bales of wool to Roslyn Mills. *Otago Daily Times*, 13 May 1908.

An expanded Roslyn Mills, *c.* 1921. Hocken Collections S09-202b.

Hasting Street, Napier, before the 1931 earthquake. Hocken Collections S09-202a.

Emerson Street Warehouse after the 1931 earthquake. Hocken Collections S09-529a, S09-529b.

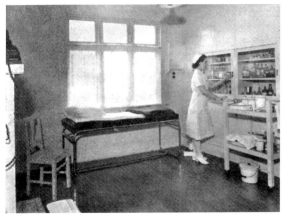

Above: Hostel for Country Girls. 'Ross & Glendining Ltd Annual Report 1951. Hocken Collections AG-512/65 S09-534a.

Left and below left: Clinic and rest rooms, Roslyn Mills. 'Saga of a Woollen Mill' (pamphlet) undated, Hocken Collections S09-533d, S09-533c.

Opposite: Original partners and Members of the Board, 1952. R & G Annual Report 1952, Hocken Collections S09-529e.

SIR JOHN ROSS

# ORIGINAL PARTNERS
## 1862

In 1862 two young men, Mr. John Ross (later Sir John) and Mr. Robert Glendining, who had recently arrived from Scotland, formed a partnership from which the present Company of Ross & Glendining Ltd. has developed.

This year marks the 90th Anniversary of the commencement of the business which was then set up, and it is due to the sound principles of trading laid down by the partners and faithfully observed through the succeeding years that the present success of the Company can be attributed.

ROBT. GLENDINING

# COMPANY DIRECTORATE
## 1952

A. W. JEAVONS
Appointed 1932

J. SUTHERLAND ROSS, C.M.G.
CHAIRMAN
Appointed 1905

T. C. ROSS
Appointed 1918

The partnership was formed into a Company in 1900, the first Directors being the two original partners, Mr. John Ross and Mr. Robert Glendining, together with Mr. Thos. Glendining (Dunedin Branch Manager) and Mr. Geo. R. Hercus (Finance and Accounts). This original Board of four has since been increased to seven.

E. C. HAZLETT
Appointed 1928

L. C. MILLER
Appointed 1939

J. McKEE
GENERAL MANAGER

E. O. HUNTER
SECRETARY

R. S. GLENDINING
Appointed 1949

J. H. EDMOND
Appointed 1949

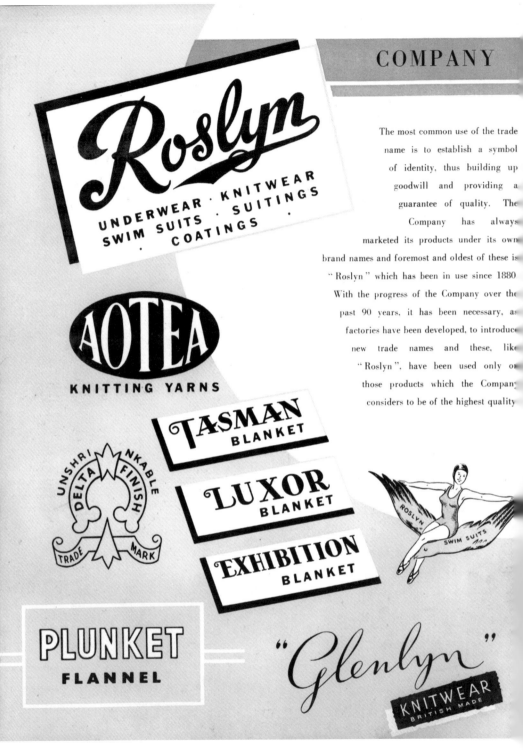

COMPANY

The most common use of the trade name is to establish a symbol of identity, thus building up goodwill and providing a guarantee of quality. The Company has always marketed its products under its own brand names and foremost and oldest of these is "Roslyn" which has been in use since 1880. With the progress of the Company over the past 90 years, it has been necessary, as factories have been developed, to introduce new trade names and these, like "Roslyn", have been used only on those products which the Company considers to be of the highest quality.

A diversified enterprise: company trade marks, 1952. R & G Annual Report 1952, Hocken Collections S09-529f.

TRADE MARKS

CHRISTYS'
*London*
HATS
(UNDER LICENSE)

# Mimosa
*Lingerie*

*Mayfair*
*Shoes*

*Regent*
FOOTWEAR

*Glenross*
MILLINERY

Footeeze
COMFORT SHOE

*Wellesley*
HATS - SHOES - SHIRTS - SOCKS

*Glenar*
GOWNS

CATHEDRAL
FINE SHOES
(UNDER LICENSE)

*Ranelagh*
INTERLOCK UNDERWEAR

*Le Roy*
*Excelsior*
OILSKINS

CORONATION
HATS

Ross & Glendining Ltd enter the fashion market, 1959. R & G Annual Report 1959, Hocken Collections S09-529g.

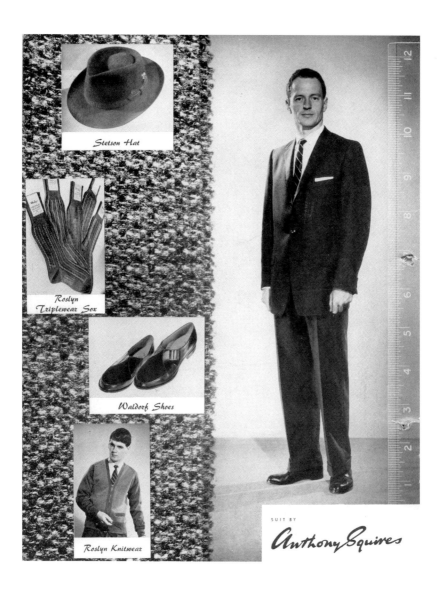

Stetson Hat

Roslyn
Triplewear Sox

Waldorf Shoes

Roslyn Knitwear

SUIT BY
*Anthony Squires*

Male fashions, too. R & G Annual Report 1959, Hocken Collections S09-529h.

Roslyn Mills in 1959. R & G Annual Report 1959, Hocken Collections S09-529i.

Clifton Knitwear Ltd, Sumner, *c.* 1930s. Hocken Collections S09-526b.

Auckland Factory, Sale Street, *c.* 1938. Hocken Collections S09-526a.

When delivered in July 1934, the Tariff Commission report did not satisfy either manufacturers or farmers. While it proposed modest reductions in some rates of duty, the vast majority were to remain unchanged. The Customs Act Amendment Act that followed broadly adopted these proposals, with British preferential duties being reduced from twenty-five to twenty per cent on a number of items manufactured by Ross & Glendining.

Sutherland Ross, who had declined to serve as a delegate for mill owners at the Ottawa Conference, greeted the outcome with some relief.[71] At the annual general meeting in 1934 he was able to report that, while some of the changes made were to the firm's detriment, they were not of a serious nature and would 'not unduly hamper our future manufacturing operations'. More importantly, now that the tariff question had been settled for the foreseeable future, it was possible to plan for the future expansion of manufacturing with some degree of certainty.[72]

## 6. RESTRUCTURING, REFURBISHMENT AND CAPITAL RECONSTRUCTION

The recovery of the economy continued apace throughout 1934 and 1935 and, with trade improving, Ross & Glendining began to restructure manufacturing operations. For some time it had been intended to move straw hat and millinery manufacture from Dunedin to Auckland and this was finally accomplished. In exchange, some clothing manufacturing was transferred to Dunedin, which was beginning to specialise in mantles and frocks. Spare capacity in Auckland was taken up by the manufacture of denim clothing, the output of which began to expand dramatically.[73]

Early in 1934 a representative of the Yorkshire firm of Prince, Smith & Sells had visited Roslyn Mills and recommended 'bringing the worsted plant up to date'. With modernisation costing over £10,000, only two urgently needed gill boxes – used for combing – were ordered. There was also the question of loom replacement, it being twelve years since the last looms were purchased, but this was also left over for the time being.[74] Once the Tariff Report had been submitted, the Roslyn manager, Porteous, began to scrutinise the manufacturers' catalogues and quotations. The suggestion by the Tariff Commission that New Zealand mills ought to consider serving the lower end of the market, using cotton and wool mixes, also led Tom Ross to ask London Office to obtain quotations for Sea Island cotton sliver.[75]

The two new gill boxes had been installed by early September, but a decision on precisely what type of loom should be installed still had to be taken. The nature of the problem facing Ross and Porteous was explained to Netting,

*Porteous would like to get six new Dobson looms as they are most useful for general purposes and he does not see our being able to specialise much. Hattersley looms he says are too light and would not stand up to heavy weaving. Northrops might suit us for flannels and absolutely plain work but again the variety that we turn out makes them a doubtful proposition. Evans is anxious to go in for narrow width high class flannels but these would require narrow looms if they are to have a decent selvedge, also we would have to work several looms per weaver to make them a paying proposition.[76]*

Ultimately it was decided to order seven Dobson looms rather than a combination of Hattersley and Northrops, there being the added advantage that there were a number of old Dobson looms in the weaving shed which were used to train young weavers.[77]

With the economy improving, the board agreed that the time was now ripe to grasp the nettle of capital reconstruction. In 1932, following a special meeting held to announce that a dividend would not be paid, Sutherland Ross had suggested that it might help certain shareholders if some share capital was converted to fixed interest debentures and preference shares written down by half. Netting agreed, especially as he thought that, following the issue of bonus shares to repair the balance sheet in 1920, the firm was overcapitalised. The position of depositors would, of course, have to be protected, particularly Lady Ross who was a major investor, but the changes should certainly appeal to older shareholders. They would also be acceptable to trustees who administered shareholdings on behalf of institutions and deceased estates.[78]

The Bank of New South Wales, though, was less enthusiastic about the planned reconstruction. By this stage Ross & Glendining had wiped out their huge overdraft, reduced their level of indebtedness to depositors, and were actually depositing surplus funds with institutions such as Auckland City Council. Nevertheless, the firm still relied on the bank for occasional accommodation, especially for wool purchases. In May 1932 their overdraft limit had been set at £200,000, with property as security. But in spite of the fact that their overdraft stood at no more than £5,276 by mid-November, the Bank of New South Wales could not be persuaded to support capital reconstruction. Sutherland Ross reluctantly agreed to defer the matter until better times.[79]

In July 1934, with a surplus of £20,590 in the bank and deposits reduced still further, reconstruction finally took place. Preference shares were dispensed with, debentures issued to the value of £203,600 and 75,000 ordinary shares of £10 each written down to 593,750 shares of £1 each.[80] Scope for future share issues was made with the new nominal capital of Ross & Glendining Ltd being set at £1 million.

## 7. Taking advantage of Labour's largesse

The 1935 elections saw a Labour Government returned for the first time, a result that was viewed as a mixed blessing by manufacturers. On the one hand, Labour was committed to the development of the manufacturing industry and the reduction of unemployment in New Zealand; on the other, it regarded a rise in wage rates from depression levels as absolutely essential. A major step was taken in the latter direction in 1936, when the Finance Act fully restored the cuts to wages and salaries made in 1931. The Industrial Conciliation and Arbitration Amendment Act of the same year also empowered the Arbitration Court to make wage awards that were sufficient to 'maintain a man, wife and three children in a fair and reasonable standard of comfort'. To limit potential inflation, price controls were extended to cover bread and dairy produce.[81]

The stimulus imparted to the economy by Labour policies clearly benefited Ross & Glendining Ltd. At the annual general meeting in September 1936, shareholders were told that it was 'the most successful trading period for some years'. Sutherland Ross nevertheless expressed concern about the higher labour costs entailed by the new legislation, although it did not prevent the board from sanctioning further re-equipment of the mills and factories.[82] In spite of Ross's reservations, the New Zealand economy boomed for the next couple of years, with real per capita incomes soaring by almost a third between the beginning of 1936 and the end of 1938. At the annual general meeting in 1937, he was able to report that all manufacturing units were working 'at top pressure'.[83]

To cope with the additional demand, both the clothing and boot manufacturing units in Dunedin were reorganised and extended. In Auckland, all units benefited from an expansion in capacity, none more so than the denim factory, which saw its sales virtually double by the advent of World War II. The Wellesley St factory, still unsold, was re-commissioned for hat making.[84] Roslyn Mills was also extended, with Tom and Sutherland Ross travelling to Great Britain to visit a hosiery machinery exhibition at Leicester and attend to other business. Additional hosiery frames were purchased, together with spinning and dyeing machinery.[85] On his return to Dunedin in April 1937, Tom Ross wrote to his brother, still in London: 'The mill is still very busy, all the looms are going at top speed and I have never seen the hosiery department so busy, all the machines except the very old frames going ... Peter Paterson, the hosiery mechanic, was complaining of overwork so has been given an assistant'.[86] The expansion in output saw additional labour taken on. By the time of the firm's 75th anniversary in August, there were 2016 people employed by Ross & Glendining at various locations. A bonus of a week's pay was given to each worker.[87]

The growth in business saw warehouse sales increase markedly, from £872,441 in the year to July 1934 to £1,232,570 in the corresponding period in 1937. Profits at £54,275 were the highest since 1924. Around seventy per cent of goods sold were now sourced from within New Zealand, most of which came from the firm's own mills and factories. Thus sales of Roslyn goods by the warehouses increased by a quarter between 1934 and 1937, while sales of factory goods rose by around two thirds. Auckland was particularly important in supporting this growth, with an expanding local population and a relatively elastic labour supply helping to drive the provincial economy (see Tables 18.1 & 18.4).

The revival in fortunes in this period was partly a reflection of rising prices, although a surge in per capita incomes contributed to real increases in activity. Growth, however, could not be expected to continue at this rate indefinitely. Towards the end of 1937, a dip in the prices of primary exports administered a slight check to farming incomes, which drifted downwards for the next two years.[88] The reversal in farm incomes was almost immediately felt by Ross & Glendining, who saw their sales fall by almost ten per cent. Sutherland Ross was also worried by other developments when he spoke at the annual general meeting in September 1938. Shorter working hours meant that labour costs were continuing to rise, as were capital costs due to additions to capacity and the need for larger inventories. Profits, as a consequence, were being squeezed, though Ross still felt reasonably confident as to the future.[89]

The future, unfortunately, was not as bright as Ross imagined. Like Ross & Glendining, other manufacturers had also modernised plant and increased capacity in their attempts to profit from the government-induced boom. As a result, orders placed abroad for iron, steel, machinery and motor vehicles rose significantly from 1936 onwards. This, together with a growth in consumption, meant that imports to New Zealand increased by more than fifty per cent over the next two years.[90] The increase in imports was not initially regarded as a problem. When export prices began to head downwards in 1938, however, it became apparent that the country was heading for an acute balance of payments crisis.

## 8. The beginnings of a controlled economy

Matters came to a head shortly after the re-election of the Labour Government in November of that year. To protect foreign exchange reserves, the new Government immediately implemented a system of import licensing and foreign exchange control. Henceforth, those wishing to import were obliged to apply to the government both for licenses to bring goods into New Zealand, and for the foreign exchange with which to pay for those goods.

## TABLE 18.4
## ROSLYN MILLS AND FACTORY SALES, 1932–1939 (£000s)

| July Year | 1932 | 1933 | 1934 | 1935 | 1936 | 1937 | 1938 | 1939 |
|---|---|---|---|---|---|---|---|---|
| **Roslyn Mills** | | | | | | | | |
| Sales[a] | 176.5 | 194.6 | 210.6 | 199.2 | 211.7 | 257.7 | 209.8 | 178.2 |
| **Dunedin factories[b]** | | | | | | | | |
| Clothing | 25.4 | 28.8 | 33.3 | 57.9 | 60.6 | 79.5 | 96.7 | 86.9 |
| Straw hats/millinery | 13.4 | 13.6 | 9.1 | moves to Auckland | | | | |
| Felt hats | 14.5 | 14.7 | 14.9 | 19.4 | 18.4 | 17.5 | 15.2 | 25.5 |
| Boots | 37.3 | 40.1 | 36.5 | 36.0 | 47.9 | 56.6 | 40.1 | 52.1 |
| Mantles | 45.6 | 39.1 | 40.4 | 39.0 | 29.8 | 42.3 | 34.2 | 29.9 |
| Frocks | moves from Auckland | | | 4.1[c] | 6.2 | 6.7 | 8.1 | 11.6 |
| Underwear | | | | 1.3[c] | 5.8 | 8.6 | 8.3 | 5.3 |
| Total | 136.2 | 136.3 | 134.2 | 157.7 | 168.7 | 211.2 | 202.6 | 211.3 |
| **Auckland factories[b]** | | | | | | | | |
| Shirts | 23.8 | 21.3 | 24.6 | 30.7 | 31.1 | 33.5 | 36.7 | 32.8 |
| Clothing | 11.2 | 16.0 | 14.4 | 7.3 | 11.8 | 18.3 | 16.6 | 17.1 |
| Coats | 9.4 | 9.3 | 13.4 | 16.9 | 18.2 | 23.7 | 23.1 | 16.5 |
| Covers | 1.4 | 1.2 | 1.4 | 1.8 | 2.2 | 3.4 | 2.3 | 3.3 |
| Denim | 7.3 | 9.6 | 15.6 | 18.8 | 20.7 | 32.3 | 36.9 | 36.7 |
| Millinery | moves from Dunedin | | | 19.6 | 26.0 | 26.4 | 21.3 | 29.1 |
| Total | 53.1 | 57.4 | 69.4 | 95.1 | 110.0 | 137.6 | 136.9 | 135.5 |

Source: Factory Returns 1922–1946, AG 512 19/9.
Notes: (a) In addition to goods sold through the warehouses, Roslyn Mills also sold goods to the factories and, like the factories, may have engaged in direct sales. (b) Sales to warehouses and direct sales. (c) Half year only.

## TABLE 18.5
### SUMMARY PROFIT AND PROFIT & LOSS ACCOUNT, 1927–1939 (£000S)

| July Year | 1927 | 1928 | 1929 | 1930 | 1931 | 1932 | 1933 | 1934 | 1935 | 1936 | 1937 | 1938 | 1939 |
|---|---|---|---|---|---|---|---|---|---|---|---|---|---|
| **Net profit** | | | | | | | | | | | | | |
| Warehouses | -12.2 | -10.4 | -10.0 | 4.7 | -34.8 | n/a | n/a | n/a | n/a | 20.1 | 32.8 | 18.5 | n/a |
| Roslyn Mills | 9.7 | 32.1 | 31.2 | 13.7 | 28.0 | 37.2 | n/a | n/a | n/a | n/a | n/a | n/a | n/a |
| Dunedin factories | 6.5 | 8.9 | 9.1 | 6.8 | 5.5 | 12.4 | 11.6 | n/a | n/a | n/a | n/a | n/a | n/a |
| Auckland factories | -0.8 | 1.4 | 3.3 | 5.6 | -2.4 | -0.7 | -1.3 | n/a | n/a | n/a | n/a | n/a | n/a |
| Total net profit as per Half-yearly analysis | 3.2 | 32.0 | 33.6 | 30.8 | -3.7 | n/a | n/a | n/a | n/a | n/a | n/a | n/a | n/a |
| Profit & loss a/c return | 4.2 | 30.5 | 33.7 | 27.6 | -12.8 | 11.5 | 34.9 | 23.8 | 28.3 | 34.6 | 54.3 | 34.0 | 38.3 |

Sources: Half-yearly analysis of results 1911–1933, AG 512 15/12; Half-yearly balances/Government Returns Ledger, AG 512 15/11, AG 512 8/8. The lack of data prevents reconciliation between the two sets of profit figures.

Import licensing was supposed to be temporary, with quotas granted to firms based on the quantities they imported in 1938.[91]

The new regime of import licensing and foreign exchange controls inevitably made life more difficult for Ross & Glendining. Not only did the firm import manchester, silks, laces, clothing and a wide range of fancy goods that it did not manufacture itself, but both Roslyn Mills and the factories were reliant upon overseas suppliers for machinery, semi-finished goods and raw materials. Reliance on imported materials was particularly great in Auckland, where cotton fabrics, silk, artificial silk, buttons and thread were imported for use in the shirt and denim factories; the principal item used in the coat and cover factory was imported canvas.

Despite the inconvenience and loss of time involved in applying for import licences and foreign exchange, the firm does not appear to have suffered unduly from the introduction of controls. As established importers, Ross & Glendining Ltd were able to obtain licences that covered around eighty per cent of their normal import requirements. Through the careful use of their licenses and by dint of running down stocks, both the warehouses and the factories recovered from the setback they had received in 1938 and even managed to increase returns. Indeed, by the time of the annual meeting in 1939, all manufacturing units were reported to be fully employed. The only problem, and one shared by other manufacturers, was that of a growing shortage of labour.[92]

The firm was just coming to terms with import controls when, on 3 September, the Government followed Great Britain by declaring war on Germany. Controls over the economy were quickly extended. By the early 1940s, Ross & Glendining Ltd found themselves working under the close direction of government, with labour subject to manpower planning, rationing applied to raw materials, prices of manufactures fixed, and production almost totally dictated by the needs of the armed forces. Even so, the entry of Japan into the war in December 1941 was to stretch resources to their utmost.

# GOVERNMENT CONTROLS IN
# WAR AND PEACE

Unlike the outbreak of World War I, the commencement of hostilities in 1939 took nobody in New Zealand by surprise. Hitler's annexation of Austria and part of Czechoslovakia in 1938 led to increasing alarm in the capitals of Europe and, by early 1939, the *Otago Daily Times* and other newspapers were regularly reporting bellicose speeches by Lord Halifax, Anthony Eden, Winston Churchill and others. The Labour Government in New Zealand was pacifist in nature, with former conscientious objectors in its ranks, and it made little attempt to stockpile the materials of war. Nevertheless, from 1937 onwards, contingency plans were drawn up, providing for the control of supplies in the event of hostilities. To this end, a list of factories for the supply of essential commodities was prepared. In addition, a Manpower Committee was appointed to work out a schedule of reserved occupations, and make provision for the general enlistment of all males and females over the age of seventeen.[1]

The outbreak of war at the beginning of September 1939 saw emergency regulations come into effect that gave the Ministry of Supply wide powers over the use and movement of goods. At the same time, recruitment commenced for the creation of the 2nd New Zealand Expeditionary Force, recruits being enlisted on a voluntary basis until the middle of 1940. Thereafter, service became compulsory, although those in essential occupations could be compelled to stay at work.[2] With the entry of Japan into the war in December 1941, general mobilisation took place, and by September 1942 there were 50,000 men and women serving overseas and in excess of 100,000 in New Zealand. Powers were also taken to conscript workers for industrial purposes, such workers being allocated amongst employers by District Manpower Officers.[3]

The transition to a wartime footing was made a lot easier by virtue of the fact that the New Zealand economy was already subject to a number of government controls. The prices of bread, fertiliser, and motor spirits were already subject to fixation by the time the Labour Government came to power in 1935, with butter, cheese, eggs, onions and other foodstuffs being added thereafter. The advisory board that administered prices became the Price Investigation Tribunal in June 1939, that body being replaced in

December 1939 by the Price Tribunal.[4] Applications to increase prices of goods and services above those ruling at the outbreak of war were only to be allowed if it could be proved that costs had increased.

In addition to price controls, the policy of import selection in 1938 meant that businessmen had become used to – if not happy with – the Government influencing what they might produce. Import licences and foreign exchange controls proved effective instruments in determining what was manufactured in New Zealand in the years ahead. Workers, too, had become accustomed to direction by the Government, a State Placement service having been in operation prior to the war. Suitably strengthened, it proved extremely useful in allocating scarce manpower.[5]

The controls introduced were undoubtedly helpful in ensuring that industrial production, already stretched at the beginning of the war, was increased still further. At Roslyn Mills, longer hours, labour dilution, more flexible working practices and compulsory night shifts – where men might perform work normally reserved for women – all helped to boost output.[6] Yet there were limits to what might be achieved. The demands of the armed forces during the first year of the war for 100,000 pairs of blankets, over a quarter of a million socks, almost half a million yards of shirt material, underpants, vests, and countless trousers and battledresses put an immense strain on New Zealand's mills. With one pair of army underpants alone consuming three miles of spun yarn, civilian clothing was soon in short supply.[7]

Shortages inevitably led to price increases, with the result that government sought to limit demand by using general wage orders to award small pay increases every six months. By itself this measure proved ineffective and so a policy of price stabilisation was introduced. In September 1941 the prices of seventeen items of foodstuffs, sixteen items of clothing and footwear, gas, coal and coke, electric lighting and tram fares were fixed by the Price Tribunal.[8] Roslyn underwear was included, with a list of prices published in the *New Zealand Gazette*.[9] Problems of equitable distribution nevertheless remained, and in 1942 a comprehensive system of clothing rationing was introduced.[10]

The combination of small general wage orders, price controls and rationing, together with an attempt by the Labour Government to finance the war out of taxation, meant that inflation was kept in check. Popular expectations that controls might end with the coming of peace, however, were only partially realised. Rather more generous wage orders were made from 1945 onwards, manpower controls gradually relaxed and rationing was ultimately abandoned. The Acting Prime Minister, Walter Nash, nevertheless made it abundantly clear during the Hamilton by-election of 1945 that it was the intention of the Government to maintain the policies of import selection and exchange control. The reason given was that shortages of foreign exchange meant that such policies were essential – probably a genuine concern at this time.[11] Yet with prices of primary products soaring in the post-war world and New Zealand soon running a healthy balance of payments' surplus, it rapidly became evident that the continuation of controls had more to do with the Labour Government's desire to promote domestic industry, generate self-sufficiency and maintain full employment.

For manufacturing businesses such as Ross & Glendining, the immediate post-war era was one of prosperity. Yet Labour's management of the economy had its drawbacks. The promotion of industry resulted in acute labour shortages, exchange controls often left firms without the funds required to buy vital supplies from abroad, and import selection based on government priorities frequently meant that goods most needed were simply not purchased. With farm incomes rising and full employment at home, pressures in both goods and labour markets were considerable. The inevitable outcome was that wage and price controls were retained, with manufacturers having to supply the Price Tribunal with detailed costings every time they wished to raise the price of an existing product or introduce a new one.

The New Zealand population, after a long period of wartime and post-war austerity, finally tired of the tight controls imposed by Labour. At the general election of 1949, a National Government was returned that was committed to opening up markets. The road to economic liberalisation proved to be far from smooth, however, and in 1952 the country was gripped by a fresh balance of payments crisis. Foreign exchange restrictions were put in place once more, while falling export prices together with a credit squeeze precipitated a sharp recession.

## 1. Struggling to increase output

The outbreak of war in September 1939 occurred when Ross & Glendining Ltd was already struggling to increase output at its manufacturing units. Restrictions on the importation of raw materials undoubtedly hampered efforts, but the principal problem was a shortage of labour.[12] Faced with the prospect of even more severe disruption, a flyer was immediately sent round to customers warning them that, 'with respect to present or future orders, we cannot accept responsibility for delays in delivery, non-delivery or price increases occasioned by war, strikes, finance and import restrictions or any other causes beyond the seller's control'.[13] During the ensuing year, sales increased by almost a quarter to nearly £1.6 million and although price inflation accounted for some of the rise, this still represented a real increase in goods delivered.

Much of Roslyn Mills' output was absorbed by the armed forces and since imports were also restricted, the firm's civilian customers soon began to complain of shortages. Ross & Glendining would probably have preferred to have served the civilian market, margins on military work generally being slim, but 'immense volumes' and 'comparatively few sizes' ensured that such work remained remunerative. As a result, after-tax profits rose from £38,348 in 1939 to £96,879 in the following year, notwithstanding a rise in company and other taxation to over 12/- in the pound.[14]

A considerable increase in production initially came from the Auckland-based factories, where the value of output soared from £149,254 in the year ending in July 1939 to £214,496 two years later. Denim production accounted for more than half of this increase, a good proportion of which may have been destined for the forces. Manufacturing in Auckland was also boosted during the course of 1940 by the transfer of the underwear manufacturing unit – and its valuable import licences – from Dunedin. While labour appears to have been relatively abundant in Auckland, the commencement of underwear manufacturing led to growing congestion at Grey's Avenue, even though the factory had been built out to the limits of its existing site. The following year an adjoining site – 66 feet by 100 feet – was purchased, a new extension adding significantly to the space available.[15] By July 1945, underwear production had quadrupled to £70,614 per annum and accounted for around one third of all factory output in the city.[16]

The other major departure in Auckland was for Ross & Glendining to become involved in the production of clothing for children and teenagers. Prior to the war, stiff competition from imports had meant that their attempts to manufacture children's clothing had been unsuccessful. The introduction of import licensing in 1938, with its ensuing shortages, altered matters. Almost immediately a number of small clothing firms were set up to fill the void, including Childswear Ltd, founded by the future mayor of Auckland, Dove-Myer Robinson. Commencing in 1939, the firm started with six employees and operated from a small workroom in Albert St, close to the Elliott St warehouse. Regular orders from Ross & Glendining meant that output grew rapidly and within two years there were 126 employees at work. Increasing scale saw the firm switch to modern mass production methods.

A growing reliance on Childswear led Sutherland Ross to forge a closer relationship with the firm. During the course of 1941 he acquired a small parcel of their shares – with an option to purchase the remainder in the future. Working capital was also provided and, in return, Childswear agreed to manufacture exclusively for Ross & Glendining, an arrangement that benefited both parties. Employment at the Auckland clothing factory increased to around 250 by 1943, while Roslyn Mills found a steady outlet for types of cloth used in school clothing. The growing supply of Childswear products also enabled the warehouses to capture a sizeable share of the juvenile market, helping them to maintain returns at a time when their traditional business was severely restricted.[17]

Increasing output at Roslyn Mills proved to be altogether more difficult. The total employed at Roslyn rose from just over 600 pre-war to 818 by August 1940, almost a quarter of all those employed in New Zealand's mills. Thereafter, additional workers were hard to find.[18] As the shortage of labour was general, the Industrial Emergency Council sought to alleviate the situation by ordering shift work in mills to be rotated, double shifts to be worked to make the best use of machinery, and additional rates to be paid to those on night shifts.

The order was not well received. Workers were resistant to additional shifts and longer hours, while employers were alarmed at the extra costs involved and the fact that they might be liable for back pay. A test case was taken against Ross & Glendining for non-compliance. The order, the firm complained, would cost them between £17,000 and £18,000 per annum, and it was not clear precisely who should be paid for what. There were also practical difficulties. Labour was strategically deployed within the mills to take account of differing degrees of skill involved, with apprentices and the unskilled engaged in the production of flannels and cheap cloths, while skilled workers were reserved for more technically complicated work such as military and air-force cloths. This, together with the fact that only 200 or so employees worked at Roslyn Mills on the night shift, meant that it was extremely difficult to increase plant utilisation.[19]

## 2. Labour shortages and Manpower Planning

The steady mobilisation of the New Zealand population – and the fact that it took 35¼ miles of spun yarn to equip each soldier with a minimum of one suit, two pairs of vests and pants, two pairs of socks, one jersey, one overcoat and two shirts – nevertheless required that output be increased somehow.[20] Rather than dictate to the industry how they should run their mills, the Government now decided to establish quotas. This they did on the basis of standard timings for the production of various items, together with estimates of the capacity of each mill. With the knowledge that it typically took 60 minutes to manufacture one pair of blankets, 20 minutes to produce one yard of tunic cloth, 13 minutes to make one yard of great coating and 4.8 minutes to make a yard of flannel, plant hours were allocated amongst the different mills so that the desired quantity of defence textiles might be produced. In August 1941, for example, it was estimated that Roslyn Mills, with seventy-seven looms working forty hours per week, was capable of producing 9356 yards of cloth weekly. The machine hours were divided up so as to provide specific quantities of blankets and clothing for the armed forces, and material to satisfy railway and police contracts. Civilians were allocated a mere fourteen per cent of the yardage.[21]

The growth in production since the beginning of the war meant that by September 1941, Ross & Glendining Ltd, employing more than 2,300 staff, was the largest non-governmental enterprise in New Zealand. Yet still more production was required in order to meet the war effort. With Sutherland Ross confident that industry was likely to enjoy protection for the foreseeable future, the firm applied for permission to erect an extension at Roslyn Mills.[22] The new building was designed to accommodate 250 extra hands. By the time it was finished, the outbreak of war with Japan had led to general mobilisation and, unable to obtain sufficient labour, the extension was never fully utilised.

The early part of 1942 saw 45,000 men withdrawn from industry to bolster home defence forces, the number of men and women in the armed forces at home and overseas building up to a peak of 157,000 by September.[23] All required uniforms. At the beginning of 1942, the Factory Controller at the Ministry of Supply sent the following telegram to all mills: 'The result of recent events compels a significant increase in output from each mill in the woollen industry both for internal and external calls for clothing'.[24] The Bruce Woollen Mills at Milton was among the first to reply, asking for some clear definition as to what constituted military and civilian work. They also pointed out that past experience showed that while it was possible to speed up output using existing staff, after a short spurt lasting two or three weeks, output began fall back once more. What was needed was more staff – including skilled staff – for the present working shifts were carefully balanced. Roslyn replied in a similar vein, while at Timaru they complained that they could not work an extra shift without additional loom tuners. Millers, of Invercargill, stated that the lack of skilled labour was 'restricting our maximum productive effort'.[25]

The Government had already relaxed some employment regulations, including those relating to shift working and the employment of apprentices. The war with Japan saw these regulations relaxed still further, with employers being allowed to extend hours and postpone holidays.[26] Yet greater labour flexibility could not obscure the fact that there were simply not enough workers to meet the demands of industry. To ensure that the pool of scarce workers was used effectively, the Government amended the National Service Emergency Regulations and gave themselves powers to conscript workers for industrial purposes. From the beginning of March 1942 the civilian population was obliged to register for work, the ages of those required to register being progressively extended as the war progressed. Skilled workers up to the age of seventy in the metal and engineering trades were immediately expected to register, as were other males between the ages of forty-six and forty-nine. By the end of the year the male age limit had risen to fifty-nine, younger women also being required to register. They were directed to essential war work by District Manpower Officers and could not leave, be fired, or laid off without reference to the authorities.[27]

The introduction of Manpower Planning undoubtedly aided the woollen and worsted industry and, in the ensuing year, the numbers employed at Roslyn Mills rose from around 800 to 932.[28] The majority entering the plant were young females but older skilled hands were also recruited, in one instance a retired gold dredge engineer being summoned from Central Otago to operate the stationary engines at the mill.[29] Even so, with the demands from the Government continuing to grow, the industry struggled to keep up supply. In November 1942, the Controller of Textiles informed the Factory Controller that the mills were only able to accept ninety per cent of orders placed. The main problem was the lack of skilled hands – too many having left to fight – while those who remained were often elderly and infirm. Age and infirmity had already led to Roslyn and Mosgiel losing skilled hands. Such men, the Controller of Textiles added, were not easily replaced, for they had to have been trained in the industry and, as a rule, could not be co-opted from elsewhere.[30]

The situation progressively got worse, with shortages of unskilled labour also becoming prevalent. In November 1943, Ross & Glendining wrote to the Factory Controller stating that they were alarmed at their staffing position, Roslyn Mills having lost sixty workers since the beginning of the year. Production had fallen by 12½ per cent in the last six months and, while this was due partly to changes in the product mix, at least half was due to staff shortages. They had appealed against staff leaving, but most appeals had been unsuccessful. The clothing factories were also affected, the 'recent intensive call for land girls' making matters worse.[31] Shortly afterwards, the Woollen Mill Owners Association sent a sharp memorandum to the Factory Controller, complaining that the manpower authorities had done little to meet their members' needs for 350 additional female workers.

To make matters worse, production at Roslyn Mills was hit by the insistence of the military authorities that male workers should present themselves for one month's training. Castigating the Factory Controller for not having responded to their letter concerning the loss of staff, Ross & Glendining pointed out that of the thirty-seven male workers instructed to report for duty, a large number were key men and included five foremen, six spinners and four loom tuners. This, they understood, was just the first batch of male workers required for training.[32] The outburst seems to have prompted both a sympathetic reply and some action. In January 1944, the Controller of Manpower informed the Factory Controller that 26 girls had been directed to take up work at Roslyn after the Christmas holidays.[33] Manpower direction continued for the duration. By July 1945, some 90 males and 181 females had been directed to work at Roslyn Mills – over one third of those subject to direction in the woollen and worsted industry.[34]

### 3. CLOTHING SHORTAGES, STANDARD DESIGNS AND RATIONING

Although the labour situation was a little easier in Auckland, the clothing factories owned by Ross & Glendining found it particularly difficult to maintain output throughout 1942 and 1943. A destructive fire in the Wellesley St factory in 1944 also hampered production.[35] To aid the efficient use of scarce resources, the New Zealand Standards Institute prepared standard designs for many of the items produced, including shirts and pyjamas, outerwear, and women's and girls' underwear. This, unfortunately, did little to curb shortages and frustrated members of the Hawkes' Bay branch of the Association of Retailers by suggesting that the Minister be petitioned to allow pyjama cloth to be released by the piece, thereby allowing people to make up pyjamas at home.[36]

Clothing and footwear rationing was introduced in 1942 but its implementation left a lot to be desired, especially as it was up to individual firms to see that each retail customer received their 'fair share'. The number of ration coupons presented over the counter supposedly determined what each retailer might sell. The illegal trading of coupons, however, and the fact that the retailers operated an 'honesty system' – where coupons were not checked against goods sold – meant that rationing did not always work as envisaged. Audits were threatened but apparently never implemented.[37]

Throughout the war, supplies from overseas augmented the domestic production of clothing, footwear and textiles. As in peacetime, Ross & Glendining continued to send orders to London Office. At the end of 1940, operations were temporarily brought to a halt when an incendiary bomb destroyed Ropemaker St, 'the building being left a tangled wreck'. Fortunately, no staff were killed in this attack. After working out of a teashop for a short while, staff obtained fresh premises in Eastcheap.[38]

Shipping problems and shortages of supplies in the United Kingdom interrupted the flow of goods, while the system of import licensing was subject to bureaucratic confusion and delay. Not surprisingly, machinery of all descriptions proved difficult to procure, even when the necessary certificates of essentiality issued by the New Zealand Government had been forwarded to the United Kingdom. Thus of the twenty Dobcross looms ordered by London Office from Hollingsworth Hutchinson in 1944, none had arrived by the beginning of 1947.[39]

Obtaining licences for goods that were not habitually handled proved to be virtually impossible. In 1941, Ross & Glendining informed London Office that their Dunedin clothing factory was not interested in manufacturing army chevrons and badges as they did not possess the necessary licences to import the materials required.[40] Greater enterprise, it seems, existed in the Auckland underwear factory. When told that knicker elastic was virtually unprocurable, the attention of London Office was drawn to the fact that a UK trade magazine had pointed out that elastic was absolutely essential for the manufacture of army bloomers. In any event, the factory wished to be sent samples of underwear in the latest styles and kept up to date with trimmings and the machinery used in their manufacture.[41]

Difficulties experienced in obtaining labour, procuring raw materials and replacing machinery that was rapidly wearing out, meant that from the middle of 1943, the output of clothing, footwear and textiles in New Zealand began to decline. It was just as well that the demands of the armed forces were beginning to decline too, with Roslyn Mills able to offer 86 per cent of its piece good production to the civilian sector in the second half of 1943, compared to 32 per cent in the preceding six months.[42] As winter approached, Ross & Glendining felt able to advertise that increasing supplies of piece goods, underwear and outerwear would now be available for their customers.[43] The following year, advertisements appeared in the *New Zealand Draper & Allied Retailer* featuring 'Childswear Children', inviting retailers to apply to their nearest branch warehouse for supplies of clothing for 'tots, toddlers and teens'.[44]

Even though war demands were easing off, supplies of civilian clothing remained in desperately short supply. Government subsidies were offered to the makers of flannel and cotton shirts, working trousers and boys' and men's pyjamas in an effort to offset the high cost of imported raw materials. While the scheme was portrayed as a means of keeping prices down, there seems little doubt that authorities also hoped that it might lead to an increase in supply of those goods most needed by the general public.[45] The situation deteriorated as the war drew to a close, with woollen mills and clothing factories haemorrhaging labour as female staff left work to marry returning servicemen. By July 1945, Roslyn Mills reported there were seven looms idle on the day shift and only twenty looms working on the night shift compared to forty previously. The second largest mill in the country, Kaiapoi, was even worse off, having abandoned weaving at night at the end of 1944. Other mills were in a similar position. By the end of the war, it was estimated that the country needed an additional two million yards of cloth.[46]

## 4. PRICE CONTROLS CURB EXCESS PROFITS

Ross & Glendining Ltd clearly made a significant contribution to the war effort, especially their mills. Between 1940 and the end of 1944, Roslyn Mills supplied, on average, nearly ten per cent of all blankets, almost a fifth of piece goods, and around a quarter of yarns and flannels.[47] Throughout the war most goods continued to be distributed via the warehouses, although some direct contracting occurred. The value of mill sales recorded by the warehouses remained fairly static at around £300,000, a testimony perhaps to tight price controls, hard bargaining over military contracts, and the Government subsidy on wool. Only in 1945 did values increase as Roslyn began to make better quality goods for the civilian market. By way of contrast, the value of factory goods passing through the warehouses doubled to almost £600,000 per annum during the war, again the bulk of the increase coming in 1944 and 1945. The real increase was somewhat less, part of the growth being a reflection of domestic inflation and the higher prices paid for imported raw materials (see Table 19.1).[48]

Tight price controls and the imposition of excess profits duty, which rose to almost 19/- in the £, ensured that woollen and clothing manufacturers did not profit unduly from wartime shortages. How Ross & Glendining fared is not entirely clear as few balance sheets have survived. Apart from the first year of the war, however, when controls were fairly lax, it seems that profits were held in check. Thus, after nearly trebling to £96,578 in 1940, they appear to have drifted down to £85,734 in 1944, in spite of turnover rising by one third to £2.1 million. Even so, dividends appear to have been maintained at eight per cent per annum, with substantial sums regularly written to reserves. Profits improved during the final year of the war as production switched to civilian goods, the recorded balance sheet profit of £70,221 subsequently being augmented by a further £69,000 when it was found that provisions made for taxation had been overly generous. While there was not the profiteering of World War I, World War II was clearly good for business (see Table 19.2).

## 5. CONTROLS RETAINED AND SHORTAGES CONTINUE

The shortages that characterised the war years continued for the rest of the decade. While this was not a peculiarly New Zealand phenomenon, the retention of import controls to protect domestic industry and develop a more balanced economy was a major contributory factor.[49] In October 1945, *The New Zealand Draper* complained,

> *In effect, this means the continued lockout of numerous lines not at present economically produced in the Dominion, as well as protection of some industries in the tender stage of just getting on their feet. In the range*

## TABLE 19.1
### MILL AND FACTORY OUTPUT, 1939–1953 (£000s)[a]

| July Year | 1939 | 1940 | 1941 | 1942 | 1943 | 1944 | 1945 | 1946 | 1947 | 1948 | 1949 | 1950 | 1951 | 1952 | 1953 |
|---|---|---|---|---|---|---|---|---|---|---|---|---|---|---|---|
| Roslyn Mills | 178.2 | 238.7 | 246.6 | 243.9 | 231.2 | 260.8 | 300.3 | 461.1 | 424.5 | 447.7 | 424.3 | 454.5 | 705.5 | 803.0 | 888.2 |
| Dunedin factories | 211.3 | 253.6 | 272.9 | 253.9 | 246.4 | 328.8 | 367.3 | 375.1 | 381.8 | 427.9 | 422.3 | 511.4 | 593.3 | 625.8 | 607.6 |
| Auckland factories | 135.5 | 184.1 | 214.4 | 197.3 | 213.1 | 243.9 | 223.5 | 219.8 | n/a | n/a | n/a | n/a | 397.8 | 446.4 | 369.3 |
| Total output | 525.0 | 676.4 | 733.9 | 695.1 | 690.7 | 833.5 | 891.1 | 1,056.0 | n/a | n/a | n/a | n/a | 1,696.6 | 1,875.2 | 1,865.1 |
| Total turnover | 1,285 | 1,594 | 1,644 | 1,809 | 1,824 | 2,102 | 2,330 | 2,464 | 2,675 | 3,570 | 3,107 | 3,733 | 4,482 | 4,457 | 4,136 |

Sources: Aggregate Factory Returns 1922–1946, AG 512 19/9; Half-yearly sales AG 512 15/13; Report on Annual Accounts, 1947–1953; Directors' Reports and Annual Accounts AG 512 8/8.

Notes: (a) Data for 1939–1945 relates only to values recorded passing through warehouses. Data from 1946–1951 onwards has been estimated from gross profits and recorded margins. The estimates provide a more accurate picture of total output than recorded warehouse values which do not capture direct sales. Actual factory data used for 1952 & 1953.

# TABLE 19.2
## SUMMARY BALANCE SHEETS, 1939–1953 (£000s)

| July Year | 1939 | 1940 | 1941 | 1942 | 1943 | 1944 | 1945 | 1946 | 1947 | 1948 | 1949 | 1950 | 1951 | 1952 | 1953 |
|---|---|---|---|---|---|---|---|---|---|---|---|---|---|---|---|
| Turnover | 1,286 | 1,594 | 1,644 | 1,809 | 1,824 | 2,102 | 2,330 | 2,464 | 2,675 | 3,570 | 3,107 | 3,733 | 4,565 | 4,597 | 4,136 |
| Net profit | 38.3 | 96.6 | n/a | n/a | n/a | 85.7 | 139.2[a] | 134.8 | 130.0 | 146.0 | 136.4 | 146.8 | 175.3 | 152.6 | 40.8 |
| Share capital | 593.8 | 593.8 | 593.8 | 593.8 | 593.8 | 593.8 | 593.8 | 593.8 | 593.8 | 593.8 | 593.8 | 593.8 | 950.0 | 950.0 | 950.0 |
| Dividends paid | n/a | n/a | n/a | n/a | 47.5 | 47.5 | 47.5 | 47.5 | 47.5 | 47.5 | 47.5 | 47.5 | 90.5 | 95.0 | 95.0 |
| Expenditure[b] | n/a | n/a | n/a | n/a | n/a | n/a | n/a | n/a | n/a | 26.8 | 56.2 | 60.3 | 100.0 | 184.0 | 83.4 |
| Current assets | n/a | n/a | n/a | n/a | n/a | 1,085.2 | 1,107.1 | 1,061.9 | 1,322.7 | 1,446.7 | 1,479.4 | 1,621.6 | 2,265.4 | 3,136.1 | 2,679.9 |
| Shareholders' funds | n/a | n/a | n/a | n/a | n/a | n/a | 923.3 | 1,079.6 | 1,162 | 1,260.1 | 1,316.7 | 1,416 | 2,124.3 | 2,185.9 | 2,221.4 |
| Shareholders (no.) | n/a | n/a | n/a | n/a | n/a | n/a | n/a | n/a | 443 | 463 | 471 | 508 | 1115 | 1258 | 1304 |
| Employees (no.) | n/a | n/a | n/a | n/a | n/a | n/a | n/a | n/a | 1,441 | 1,493 | 1,525 | 1,525 | 1,634 | 1,702 | 1,689 |

Sources: Directors' Reports and Annual Accounts; Reports on Annual Accounts, AG 512 8/8.
Notes: (a) Tax credit of £69,000 added to reported net profit. (b) Plant, machinery, etc.

*of banned imports are electric lamps, carpet sweepers, aluminium ware,*
*manufactured apparel, radios, cordage, rope, twine, combs, bicycle tyres,*
*domestic gas cookers, electric ranges, refrigerators, washing machines,*
*brushware, woodenware, and many other domestic requirements.*

The retail trade found these restrictions particularly irksome, especially as Britain had just freed a number of goods from export control in order to overcome a squeeze on foreign exchange reserves.[50]

For the clothing and textile industries, the most immediate problem was how to supply 35,000 demobilisation suits to returning service personnel during the second half of 1945. Given that the total annual domestic output ran to only a little more than twice that figure, such demands would have placed a strain on resources at the best of times. Matters were made far worse, however, by the fact that female labour continued to abandon the workplace to settle down to family life – even though Manpower Controls were still in place.[51] Addressing the Canterbury Manufacturers Association, the Controller of Manpower, H.L. Bockett, indicated that the direction of labour 'would not be revoked for some time yet and then it would be taken off gradually'. He was of the opinion that if controls were removed, one third of the employees in the clothing industry would walk out to seek more congenial occupations.[52]

Ross & Glendining were badly affected by the shortage of labour, with the number of employees at Roslyn Mills falling from a peak of 953 in 1943 to 816 by June 1945.[53] Numbers continued to fall thereafter, with the wholesale value of output at the mills falling by a sixth in the following year, in spite of a ten per cent rise in the prices of woollens.[54] The factories were less badly affected although they, too, saw output fall back somewhat. Fortunately, the firm still possessed valuable import licences and although the import schedules for 1946 were revised three times before finally being released, London Office was able to send enough goods to make up for the shortfall of in-house production. As a result, turnover for 1946 reached a record £2.4 million while profits, at £134,818, were roughly equivalent to that of the preceding year.[55]

The comfortable financial situation in 1946 meant that Ross & Glendining Ltd was able to pay dividends of eight per cent, and carry a further £150,000 to reserves. A generous staff superannuation scheme for white-collar workers was also put in place. Administered by the Government Life Insurance Office, the scheme entailed joint employer/employee contributions. To fund the past service of existing employees, the firm agreed to pay around £7,500 per annum for the next twenty years or so. By the end of the decade there were 330 contributing members plus another twenty-four on superannuation, the scheme being extended to all workers in 1953.[56]

## 6. Expansion hindered by underinvestment and a lack of staff

The growth in both the volume and value of exports after the war encouraged the Government to partially relax import controls, the result being that between 1946 and 1947 imports of apparel, textiles, fibres and yarns doubled.[57] The remaining restrictions nevertheless ensured that while manufacturers now enjoyed better access to raw materials and machinery, for the most part they continued to be protected from foreign competition. In the meantime, domestic demand continued to grow strongly and, with labour shortages and ageing plant, Roslyn Mills struggled to meet orders. In 1946 the Roslyn manager, Frank Taylor, was sent to Great Britain to visit machinery makers. He returned full of ideas and produced 'a detailed report on new machines offering'.[58]

If Taylor had expected major investment in his worn-out mill, he was sadly mistaken. Part of the problem was that few of the board members had little direct experience of manufacturing. Thus Alfred Jeavons, who had taken over as General Manager in 1940 when James Evans died, was an accountant by training and had spent most of his life in the warehouses. Sutherland Ross, forbidden to enter the mills or factories by Robert Glendining, was also a warehouseman, as was L.C. Miller. Only Tom Ross understood manufacturing and he, like his fellow board members, was now rather elderly. Conservative and cautious, they decided that with looms already on order from Hollingsworth Hutchinson and the American makers, Northrop, 'no great expenditure should be incurred until it was absolutely necessary'.[59]

The decision not to engage in a major re-equipment had serious repercussions. Within a few years, Roslyn had been left behind by other mills which, possessing the latest machinery, were able to make a superior range of products at lower cost. By the mid-fifties, Ross & Glendining was struggling to compete both in blankets and hosiery, the latter being a sector in which it had once been a dominant force.[60] Yet the board's reluctance to replace machinery is understandable. After all, following the war the firm could sell all the mill goods it produced and, since Roslyn Mills was pretty much fully depreciated, costs were low. In addition, there were still acute shortages of labour in Dunedin. This meant that a considerable proportion of the existing plant and machinery already lay idle.

The pressing need for manpower in 1945 was partially met by demobilisation. Practical politics, however, soon spelt the end of the Government direction of labour, and manpower controls were finally swept away in 1946.[61] The woollen textile industry was badly affected. Full employment after the war meant that there were plenty of employment choices for those women who wished to work. Few, it seems, wanted to work in the hot and noisy mills.[62] Roslyn, already suffering from a lack of female hands at the end of the war, saw its labour force steadily dwindle. From over 850 workers in 1945, by May of the following year the numbers had shrunk to 602, falling to 445 in April 1949. All mills were short of labour but the situation at Roslyn was particularly dire, there being vacancies for 302 females and 55 males. By way of comparison, Kaiapoi had vacancies for only 121 females and 14 males.[63]

With the female vacancy rate in the Dunedin employment area in excess of 20 per cent, Ross & Glendining tried to circumvent the shortage of labour by having work done elsewhere. Premises were opened in Invercargill and, some miles away, in decidedly rural Winton. Attempts were also made to improve conditions of service. A health clinic had been opened at Roslyn in 1943, which expanded until it consisted of a unit of four rooms supervised by a qualified nursing sister. In the twelve months to July 1949, some 1,633 cases were treated at a cost of £460. As the clinic seemed to contribute to a significant reduction in absenteeism, the investment was considered well worthwhile. [64]

Considerable effort was also put into attracting labour to work at the mill. A free bus service was provided to overcome the fact that the plant was located 'so far from the city', and a property purchased for £2,600 to act as a hostel 'for country girls'.[65] The firm was drawn further into the housing market when, owing to a shortage of accommodation, the Department of Labour refused to issue a travel permit for a technician recruited in England until Ross & Glendining Ltd provided a house.[66] Early in 1950 Jeavons wrote to the Dunedin Drainage Board, 'At the present time we are suffering in the Mill from a very great shortage of staff and in endeavouring to rectify this, we are seriously considering proposals to erect anything up to 30 houses in the Kaikorai Valley, which we hoped would be of help.'[67] Neither the Drainage Board nor Dunedin City Council proved to be particularly helpful, with Jeavons accusing the latter of 'refusing reasonable cooperation'.[68] Ultimately permission to build was granted and over the course of the next three years, the firm spent around £40,000 on buying and building houses.[69]

The labour shortages experienced by Roslyn Mills and the factories meant that the total directly employed by Ross & Glendining fell from a wartime peak of around 2,500 to 1,523 by 1949. By concentrating on the quality end of the market, the firm tried to make best use of both scarce labour and a wool subsidy, which, in 1947, amounted to £47,000. Yet manufacturing output continued to fall in real terms, even in Auckland where the shirt and millinery factories operated in a somewhat easier labour market.[70]

## 7. ASSOCIATE COMPANIES INCREASE OUTPUT BUT PROFITS SQUEEZED

While labour was rather more plentiful in Auckland than Dunedin, the female vacancy rate there was still in the region of ten per cent.[71] Faced with difficulties in obtaining sufficient hands for its central city factories, Ross & Glendining decided to relocate its rapidly expanding underwear factory in the township of Henderson, on the outskirts of Auckland. Opened in January 1948 and situated close to the suburban railway station, the new factory was able to draw on the growing population of West Auckland for the much-needed female labour. Childswear Ltd also began to look further afield for labour, establishing cut, make and trim operations in Te Awamutu and Whangarei.[72] By 1952 it employed around 400 staff including, for the first time, a significant number of Maori seamstresses.[73]

With problems of increasing output in its own factories, Ross & Glendining were only too happy to offer financial support to associate companies. At balance date in 1949, total advances to Childswear Ltd for stock and working capital amounted to £148,000 while Clifton Knitwear, a Christchurch-based company that produced knitted outerwear, accounted for a further £44,000. A decision was also made to buy the Christchurch-based Regent Sports Footwear business when the owners decided to discontinue making sandals. The cost was trivial, a mere £10,000 for factory and plant. After an initial loss, in 1950 the sandal factory earned a gross profit of over ten per cent on an annual turnover of around £60,000.[74]

The easing of overseas supply restrictions meant that the shortfall in mill and factory output was, to some extent, offset by an increase in the quantity of goods sent by London Office. Yet although total turnover rose from £2.9 million in 1946 to over £3.6 million two years later, importing from London was not entirely trouble free. In 1948, the appreciation of the New Zealand currency by 25 per cent after sterling was devalued meant that existing stocks had to be written down. Shipping problems also held up consignments, while bureaucratic delays in both the issue of import licenses, and the annual schedule of goods that might be imported, made it very difficult to order in time.

Rising labour costs due to generous wage orders and the progressive squeezing of margins by the Price Tribunal also cut into profits. Thus at the relatively profitable Dunedin clothing factory, gross profits fell from around ten per cent of turnover in 1946 to six per cent in 1949. Imports, too, were squeezed, gross profits on total warehouse sales falling from over 20 per cent to around 14½ per cent over the same period. Company profits of £136,364 in July 1949 were little more than those returned four years earlier (see Table 19.2).[75]

While Ross & Glendining were quick to blame the Price Tribunal for the pressure on margins, it is clear that by the end of the 1940s they were aware that competition in the New Zealand economy was beginning to increase. 'With the state of the trade today', Sutherland Ross told shareholders at the ordinary general meeting in September 1949, 'one has got to go and look for the business and not wait for it to come'. The sales force was therefore expanded and the comparatively large sum of £5,000 spent on new vehicles, almost half as much as that invested in new machinery at Roslyn Mills. As the chairman explained, 'to cover the ground we had to get a decent fleet of cars'. Sutherland Ross also gave up responsibility for advertising, appointing a warehouseman from the Christchurch branch to head up a new advertising department. Advertising expenditure was to grow rapidly over the next few years as the firm sought to appeal to the new post-war generation of consumers.[76]

Sutherland Ross announced other changes at the September meeting. Alfred Jeavons, who 'had been trying to burn the candle at both ends' for many years, was to step down as General Manager, although he was to retain the post of Managing Director. He was to be replaced by James McKee, a Scotsman who had spent the greater part of his working life in Melbourne. Thought had been given to appointing a new General Manager from within the firm, but nobody had been deemed suitable. What Stuart Glendining, the founder's grandson and manager of the Dunedin warehouse with thirty-five years' service thought about this can only be imagined. In any event, he was happy to be voted on to the board, the first Glendining in such a position for many years.[77]

## 8. FROM BOOM TO BUST WITH THE NATIONAL GOVERNMENT

The 1950s began with major changes in the economic environment facing Ross & Glendining Ltd. At the general election held in November 1949, the National Government was swept to power after promising freedom from the controls and regulations of the preceding decade. Eight months later the Korean War erupted, hostilities lasting for another three years. The effect on commodity prices was dramatic. The export price of wool – already rising – more than doubled over the next eighteen months. Import prices rose too, although this did not prevent the terms of trade from moving sharply in New Zealand's favour.[78]

The sharp increase in inflation that ensued meant that any thought that the National Government might have had about further relaxing price controls had to be abandoned for the time being. Indeed, the amount of subsidy paid to food producers in order to keep down the cost of living was increased, while wool subsidies – which had been in the process of being phased out – were restored on condition that woollen manufacturers reduced factory gate prices.[79] Yet because the balance of payments was improving rapidly, the Government still felt able to continue with its plans to remove import controls. In 1950, 326 items were freed from licensing control, a further 700 items being removed from a schedule of 990 items the following year. Exchange controls were also relaxed, with importers now able to buy the necessary foreign exchange without restriction.[80]

The commodity price boom brought about by the Korean War saw nominal GNP grow by more than one third, and private income increasing exceptionally rapidly during 1950–51, especially in farming. Retail prices rose, too, but people were still better off in real terms and they began to spend more freely. The relaxation in import and exchange controls meant that some of the additional purchasing power was spent on goods from overseas. Imports into the country soared.[81] It was not until the beginning of 1952, however, that the full effects were felt, as shipments had been delayed by striking waterside workers, New Zealand ports being at a standstill for a good part of the preceding year.[82]

Ross & Glendining Ltd, like other manufacturers, benefited greatly from the interruption to imports. Between 1950 and 1952, turnover at the Dunedin factories increased by almost a quarter, peaking at over £625,000, while in Auckland the value of goods produced rose to £450,000. At Roslyn Mills, output virtually doubled to £803,000, though much of the growth was accounted for by the rising price of wool. Real output nevertheless increased, and total sales by the firm, including imported goods, rose from £3.1 million to £4.6 million. With margins generally holding up, profits of £175,362 were announced in 1951 – a post-war record (see Tables 19.1 & 19.2).[83]

Although the firm had regularly reinvested the bulk of its profits since the end of the war, soaring prices could not help but strain resources. Capital tied up in warehouse stocks increased by one fifth in the year to July 1950, while the value of raw materials and work in progress also rose. In addition, funds had to be found to finance the expansion that was taking place in associate companies – Childswear alone absorbed almost £250,000 in 1950. Then there was the continued expenditure on plant and machinery at the manufacturing units, not to mention the proposed investment in workers' houses.

While Ross & Glendining Ltd had maintained cordial relations with the Bank of New South Wales, it was decided to rely on equity rather than debt to fund the expansion. Additional shares were offered to the general public, thereby significantly broadening the ownership of the company. By the time of the annual meeting in September 1951, the new issue had been virtually fully subscribed with the capital of the firm being lifted from £593,750 to £950,000. The number of shareholders more than doubled to 1,115.[84]

The end of the watersiders' strike in the middle of 1951 saw imports begin to flow back into the country once more. Ross & Glendining, hitherto short of stock, was suddenly inundated with goods:

*after the settlement of the dispute, deliveries from the United Kingdom began to arrive at a much accelerated rate. The movement of cargoes was also pushed forward by the increasing ability of U.K. suppliers to make early delivery, owing to the restrictions placed by certain overseas countries on United Kingdom imports. This meant that during the six months ended 19ᵗʰ January 1952, shipments were made to the extent of £900,443, against the previous twelve months deliveries of £1,087,941. The increasing value of cargo was maintained during February and March to the extent of £315,069, making a total for the first eight months of £1,215,512.*

Alarmed by rapidly rising stocks and slowing sales, warehouse buyers were instructed to cut back purchases to a minimum. Even so, imports for the year to July still rose to over £1½ million, while the amount of stock on hand ballooned by more than £1 million to £2½ million.[85]

The flood of imports was not confined to Ross & Glendining. Other wholesale and retail importers, taking advantage of the relaxation of import controls, had also ordered heavily from overseas and their goods were now arriving. At this juncture wool prices began to moderate, and it soon became evident that New Zealand was heading for a massive balance of payments crisis. Alarmed by these developments, in March 1952 the Government began to tighten foreign exchange controls in order to cut back on imports. The Reserve Bank of New Zealand reinforced these measures in August, with a credit squeeze.[86]

The tightening of exchange controls came too late, as excessive importing had already resulted in a glut of stocks. The credit squeeze, coming on top of falling wool prices, simply flattened an economy that was already in decline. By discounting heavily, Ross & Glendining managed to maintain turnover at £4.6 millions in the year to July 1952. Sales dropped sharply thereafter, while profits plummeted from £156,602 to £40,783 in 1953, a post-war low (see Table 19.2).[87] For the first time in many years, the firm began to struggle.

# TOO LITTLE, TOO LATE

The difficult trading conditions that began early in 1952 were to last for another eighteen months, with tighter credit and the check to incomes making it difficult for retailers to work off the surplus stocks they had accumulated. Business began to improve thereafter, but for Ross & Glendining the years of easy profits were over.[1] Henceforth the firm faced fierce competition, both from old-established firms such as Lane Walker Rudkin Ltd, owners of the Ashburton Woollen Mills with their popular 'Canterbury' clothing brand, and from new entrants such as Holeproof Industries Ltd, which operated a modern hosiery factory in Auckland. The relaxation of import licensing also led to growing competition from abroad, with large city stores often buying directly from overseas suppliers. These outlets took an increasing share of the retail trade as rising real incomes and the spread of car ownership encouraged country customers to shop in town for high fashion imports.[2]

The principal threat to the company, however, came from the many small clothing manufacturers that had emerged following the introduction of import controls. Rather than compete across the board, these firms chose to specialise, often in better quality fashion garments in the style of Dior, Balmain, Hartnell and other leading couturiers.[3] The latest materials such as rayon and nylon were used, while the styles were often loose and billowing, the lightness of materials being increasingly acceptable in an age of electricity and the heated motor car.[4] Distribution costs were kept down by selling directly to a limited number of select outlets. By way of contrast, Ross & Glendining's own factories were still firmly rooted in the austere years of the 1940s, producing garments that were rather old-fashioned and often made of wool. Their products, moreover, were indiscriminantly supplied to the trade at large through the relatively costly system of branch warehouses.

During the 1950s, attempts were made to upgrade plant, introduce modern product lines, and overhaul methods of distribution. Unfortunately, repeated crises in the domestic economy, combined with a lack of capital and poor management, saw Ross & Glendining Ltd continue to lose ground.

## 1. ROSLYN MILLS AND MOST FACTORIES FOUND TO BE GROSSLY INEFFICIENT

The flood of imports that had arrived in the country in 1952 was slowly worked off and by the first half of 1953 there were signs of revival in the retail trade. Yet in spite of heavy discounting, Ross & Glendining still found it difficult to shift stock, with total sales for the year to July falling by around half a million pounds to just over £4.1 million. Profits plummeted to £40,783, although a ten per cent dividend was still paid, notwithstanding the recent issue of additional shares. This may have pleased some but it did mean that, for the first time in many years, dividends were being paid out of capital. Sutherland Ross nevertheless remained upbeat. The reduction in profits, he stated in the annual report, 'had been occasioned entirely by the movement of the market against the value of imported stocks'. Sales from manufacturing units, on the other hand, 'were very satisfactory'.[5]

The picture painted by Sutherland Ross was optimistic, to say the least, for there were clear signs that all was not well. During the course of 1953, W.D. Scott & Co., management consultants of Sydney, had been employed, 'not only to install a modern costing system but also to examine in detail the efficiency of the various processes throughout the mill'. What they found at Roslyn Mills shocked them. Ross & Glendining were advised that unless Taylor, the mill manager, was dismissed without delay, there was every chance that the plant would be forced to close. He was duly fired, J.F. Ross being appointed acting manager until someone more experienced could be found.[6]

The state of Roslyn Mills when J.F. Ross assumed control was far worse than McKee, the general manager, had envisaged. Efficiency in the mills was low, discipline poor and organisation weak. 'Machines making goods in short supply were allowed to be idle and major items of plant were purchased without proper investigation and planning for their efficient deployment'. The staff position was 'unsound' and the individual wages paid were based on 'an alleged productive bonus' which bore no relationship whatsoever to the output of the various units.[7]

Yorkshire-trained Harry Hall, the new mill manager, was appointed at the end of 1955. His report to the board a few months later doubtless confirmed their worst fears. A very great percentage of the plant was out of date and, due to it having operated under considerable pressure during two world wars, was in no fit state to produce goods comparable to those coming out of opposition mills. This was particularly true of the hosiery section, which had been allowed 'to go down hill very fast.' Ross & Glendining had once dominated the hosiery trade but, 'the new specialist manufacturers who had commenced operations after the war had left this section of the Mill far behind'. The condition of the buildings also gave rise to concern. A report by the mill engineer at the end of 1956 estimated that simply in order to carry out urgent maintenance to the roofs and floors, an expenditure of £86,864 would have to be incurred.[8]

The factories, too, struggled to survive in an increasingly competitive market environment. The value of a strong brand had long been recognised by the firm and in 1949 a department had been established to coordinate advertising and promotions. By 1952 considerable progress had been made in differentiating the products of some of the newer factories. Following the acquisition of the Christchurch footwear factory, the 'Cathedral' brand now supplemented the well-established 'Regent' and 'Footeeze' range, while 'Mimosa' lingerie and 'Ranelagh' interlock underwear were amongst the labels produced in Henderson. Greater use was also made of the 'Roslyn' trademark and it was extended to cover a range of products made by the company.[9]

Some of the factories were reasonably successful. In 1952, the hitherto loss-making felt hat factory was re-equipped with the latest machinery and rapidly moved into profit. Elsewhere the picture was not so bright. The Dunedin clothing factory was obliged to discount heavily in order to make sales, the mantle factory barely broke even, while the gown factory – operating at the premium end of the market – was an unmitigated disaster. In Auckland, things were little better. The millinery workroom, unable to attract sufficient staff, regularly returned a loss, while the once-profitable Henderson underwear factory, faced with a slump in orders from the warehouses, saw losses soar. The shirt factory in Grey's Avenue seemed incapable of making a profit.[10]

The initial response to increasing competition was to increase the resources devoted to sales and advertising. In the 1953 annual report, much was made of the service provided by the sales representatives – and their seventy-eight cars. The advertising budget also rose sharply until by 1954 expenditure stood at £41,000, rather more than the after-tax profits earned in the preceding year.[11] Yet all the sales representatives and advertising in the world could not hide the fact that the factories were producing goods that were overpriced and poorly styled.

Part of the problem appears to have been the unwillingness of factory managers to move with the times. During the 1940s, the shortage of goods had meant that the factories had been able to sell virtually everything they made. This appears to have led to the development of a production orientation within the company where, 'it was generally recognised that the factories had to be free to produce to capacity, and the warehouses would have to sell within reason whatever products were supplied'. Not surprisingly, with outlets for their products practically guaranteed, factory managers had little incentive to keep in touch with the latest fashions or the demands of the company's retail customers. Regular conferences of buyers and factory managers went some way to ensuring that certain unprofitable lines were not 'foisted on to the warehouses'. Over the years, however, the inability of the factories to produce a satisfactory range of products had led to considerable antagonism between factory managers and the warehouse departments. With discounting necessary to clear stock, both factories and warehouses often found it difficult to recover costs.[12]

## 2. MANAGEMENT STRUGGLE TO RESUSCITATE THE COMPANY

The deteriorating situation in Roslyn Mills and the factories led to an executive committee of McKee, company secretary Hunter and the vice-chairman, Jeavons, being set up to improve coordination within the company. Yet apart from organising a visit by the Queen to Roslyn Mills during her tour of New Zealand early in 1954, the triumvirate appear to have done very little. Profits, it is true, recovered somewhat during the year, in spite of the progressive relaxation of import licensing by the National Government, but they were still lower than the halcyon years of the late 1940s. Somewhat surprisingly, dividends continued to be maintained at ten per cent, even though Ross & Glendining Ltd found itself short of capital. This was to be remedied by issuing new shares, which would 'provide the necessary finance and enable full advantage to be taken of the increasing business available to the company', the shareholders were told.[13] No mention was made of the fact that radical restructuring and major expenditure on the mills and factories was urgently required.

The annual general meeting in October 1954 saw the departure of James McKee. He was to return to the United Kingdom to replace the retiring Charles Netting as buying office manager and London Director. E.O. Hunter was promoted to general manager in Dunedin in his stead. Before Hunter took over, he was encouraged by W.D. Scott & Co. to spend some time in Australia studying modern methods of warehousing and retail distribution. By the time he returned, he had formulated his ideas as to what needed to be done to resuscitate the company.[14]

Hunter, who became managing director in 1957, believed that the major threat came from small niche-market producers supplying fashion goods. Early on he proposed to the board that Ross & Glendining should attempt to 'outspecialise the specialists' by entering the fashion trade themselves. This involved manufacturing selected overseas brands under license, acquiring a number of specialist producers who were to sell directly to the retail trade, and re-organising a number of existing factory units so that they, too, were able to offer a range of fashion items. A more cost-efficient system of distribution was also to be introduced. Direct selling was to be adopted by the mill and factory units wherever possible, with the branch warehouses being relegated to the role of bulk distribution centres.[15]

The new share issue of 1954 increased the paid-up capital of the firm by a massive £712,500 to £1,662,500. A good proportion of the shares were bought by existing investors, presumably in the belief that it was going to be used to finance the expansion alluded to by Sutherland Ross at the annual general meeting. Unfortunately, much of the additional capital raised had to be used to fund current business, a fresh credit squeeze in 1955 seeing retailers turning to Ross & Glendining for relief instead of their bankers. With sales reaching a record £5 million and extensive credit given, there was little scope for reducing the overdraft at the Bank of New South Wales, let alone finance the major changes that Hunter and his mentors at W.D. Scott & Co. had in mind.

Some progress was made. The poorly performing Clifton Knitwear Ltd, hitherto partly owned, was bought out in its entirety and the management replaced. In Dunedin, the clothing factory manager was sacked and the plant reorganised. Improvements were also evident in Auckland. The underwear factory increased output by a third and posted excellent results, while the struggling shirt factory at last returned a profit. The following year the Dunedin gown and mantle factories were closed, with some production moved to Childswear Ltd in Auckland. The move to the more fashionable Auckland, it was hoped, would help the designers keep up to date with 'modern trends'. Distribution charges would also be lower since the greatest concentration of population now lived in the north.[16]

The improvements taking place at the factories were not immediately mirrored by group profits, which fell back to just under £120,000 for the year to July 1955. Margins at Roslyn Mills benefited from improved efficiency, but the warehouses were still finding it hard to push sales of Roslyn piece goods due to growing competition from imports. Other New Zealand mills were similarly affected and, following representations to the Government, piece goods once again became subject to import licensing.[17] Foreign competition was also beginning to play havoc with the clothing industry. At the annual general meeting in October, Sutherland Ross told shareholders, 'The importation of many lines manufactured in countries where a much lower standard of living than ours exists has created further difficulties.'[18] With both the textile and clothing industries suffering from acute competition, turnover fell once more.

### 3. DETERIORATING TRADING CONDITIONS FORCE ROSS & GLENDINING TO CHANGE

Some of the difficulties mentioned by Sutherland Ross in his speech were of Ross & Glendining's own making. The National Government, however, was far from blameless. Excess demand was ever-present in the New Zealand economy during the post-war years, with the result that the government clung on to price and wage controls in their attempts to curb inflation. Wages, therefore, continued to be set by general wage orders, a succession of which pushed up unit labour costs until they were significantly higher than those prevailing in the United Kingdom. Even with the twenty per cent British preferential tariff and the costs of shipping, New Zealand manufacturers were frequently unable to compete with their U.K. counterparts.[19] At the same time, the maintenance of price controls by the government did not make life any easier for local businesses. Price fixation, which resulted in narrow margins, meant that Ross & Glendining were unable to generate a surplus 'to offset the losses which must, of necessity, be incurred in a business handling many fashion and seasonal lines'.[20] This inevitably hit profits and the ability to re-invest.

Trading conditions deteriorated still further in 1956, the delay in re-introducing import licences for piece goods forcing Roslyn Mills to lay off staff and operate well below full capacity. As a consequence, the board now began to contemplate the unthinkable – supplying rival manufacturers with yarn and materials directly from their mills.

The argument as to whether New Zealand mills should sell directly to the wider trade was one that had concerned their owners for some years. Traditionally, most woollen mills and their associated factories had sold their output through warehouses, with mills such as Roslyn, Kaiapoi and Wellington having their own warehouses through which they sold yarn, cloth, clothing, and knitted goods. This meant that mill owners received the profits of both manufacturing and making up, the latter activities guaranteeing them an end use for cloth and yarn. Vertical integration of textile production with garment making also conferred substantial transaction cost savings, while the refusal to supply competitors with raw materials, except through the warehouses, was believed to yield strategic benefits. The main disadvantage, however, was that independent hosiery and garment manufacturers were often unwilling to patronise mills such as Roslyn and Kaiapoi. They felt, not unreasonably, that it would be cheaper to buy directly from those mills, domestic or foreign, which did not distribute through their own warehouses and conducted few or no downstream operations.

The ferocious nature of competition meant that by the mid-1950s, mill owners had to rethink their refusal to sell directly to the growing number of independents. After a fierce internal battle, Hunter persuaded his fellow directors to make 'a certain proportion' of mill output directly available to other clothing and mantle manufacturers. In 1956, the Auckland firm of Garth Ledgard Ltd was appointed Roslyn Mills' sales representatives for the entire country. Although mill profits were not immediately turned around, the scheme was regarded as an 'outstanding success'. Within a few years Mosgiel and other mills also started to sell directly to independent manufacturers.[21]

There were other aspects of the way Ross & Glendining did business that Hunter believed needed attention. Hitherto, forty-eight buyers, based in the various branch warehouses, had placed orders on the basis of their personal estimates of demand. In spite of buying conferences and improved communications between warehouses, this system frequently left large stocks unsold at the end of the season, which were then marked down and sold off cheaply. 'Jobbing off' surplus stocks in this fashion had always taken place, but serious losses now seemed to be more frequent. In one year, they amounted to £161,524. To reduce over-ordering, twelve 'dominion buyers' were appointed to purchase for all departments, subject to budgets set by Head Office. Each dominion buyer was responsible for a particular category of merchandise and had the power to override warehouse buyers. It was also intended that they should maintain close contact with manufacturing units so that a more 'satisfactory range' of goods might be produced.[22]

The New Zealand economy, in the meantime, was beginning to run into fresh balance of payments problems. In 1955, the responsibility for foreign exchange control had passed from the Reserve Bank to the Department of Industries & Commerce. Overseas funds were made more readily available and with so many items no longer subject to import licensing, the flow of goods to New Zealand increased. Exports, too, continued to grow, but as commodity prices began to deteriorate, so a fresh balance of payments crisis developed. When a Labour Government was returned to office in November 1957, it was found that overseas currency reserves had been reduced to £50 million, sufficient to pay for only six weeks' worth of imports. By Christmas, import licensing had been re-introduced on a wide range of goods.[23]

The re-introduction of import licensing was doubtless welcomed by Hunter. At the annual general meeting in 1957, he pointed out to shareholders that the firm's own mills and factories now supplied half of all goods sold by the warehouses. Manufacturing, he argued, was already an important part of the business and would become even more prominent in future. Government policy, of course, was of paramount importance in this regard but he felt that, 'both major political parties fully appreciate the value to this country of healthy and expanding secondary industries and will always give the necessary protection'. Sutherland Ross also seemed to believe that some degree of protection was likely to continue – although he preferred tariffs to quotas. However, with New Zealand tied by international agreements, he accepted that a system of import controls was the only feasible option.[24]

## 4. DEVELOPING A NEW STRATEGY

Given the belief that manufacturing business was likely to remain protected – whatever party was in power – Hunter sought to offset the gradual loss of warehouse sales by investing in 'the better class fashion field'.[25] Manufacturing under license was common in New Zealand by the 1950s, with well-known overseas brands such as Jantzen swimwear, Berlei foundation garments, and Polly Peck frocks all being produced by local makers.[26] In 1955, Ross & Glendining began manufacturing Stetson hats under license, a further five licensing agreements being concluded during the course of 1957. These included the rights to produce Town Talk ties, Anthony Squires suits, Country Club shirts and Osti lingerie – all licensed from Australia – and Sacony (NY) fashions.[27]

Most of the licensed production took place in existing manufacturing units, with lingerie made at Henderson, ties in Auckland and hats in Dunedin. Ross & Glendining did not itself possess the capacity for producing high-quality gentlemen's suits of the sort to be sold under the Anthony Squires label. It therefore purchased a controlling interest in one of its menswear suppliers, J.A. Wilkinson & Son Ltd, located at Frankton Junction, near Hamilton.[28]

Re-branded as the International Style Co. Ltd, the Frankton operation would not only manufacture Anthony Squires' suits but market and distribute them as well. Upgrading the Wilkinson factory so that it was able to produce reasonable quantities of high quality suits proved to be far from straightforward. Skilled labour was both expensive and hard to come by, there were difficulties in obtaining imported raw materials – paradoxically because of the reintroduction of import controls – while promotional costs were extremely high.[29] To make matters worse, the whole factory was destroyed by a fire in 1958 that set International Style back 'at least two years'. Production started again after some delay and thereafter sales of the by-now popular suits soared. Unfortunately, the remote location of the plant (relative to Dunedin) meant that expansion could not be closely monitored, to the ultimate detriment of both Ross & Glendining Ltd and Hunter himself.[30]

The increasing sale of mill and factory goods direct to retailers inevitably reduced the quantity of business flowing through the warehouses. As a consequence, in 1958 a thorough review was conducted of their operations. It was decided that warehouse salesmen should not call regularly on all customers in future, since the size of many accounts did not warrant the expense. Sub-branches in New Plymouth, Wanganui, Napier and Invercargill were also to be closed, staff being either retired, dismissed or transferred to the remaining warehouses. This would yield annual savings of between £80,000 and £90,000 without detracting from the sales effort of the company to 'any extent'.[31]

Thought was also given as to how the remaining four branch warehouses might operate more efficiently. A bulk store had already been purchased in central Auckland towards the end of 1956 to assemble and dispatch goods ordered in advance from local factories.[32] Eighteen months later, an indent division was established in Dunedin to handle all forward orders for southern factories. By 1960, separate indent divisions had also been set up in Auckland and Christchurch.[33]

There was, however, concern as to whether the more fashionable items could be sold effectively using the old-fashioned warehouse format. To handle some of the leading lines, in 1958 two separate companies were set up to sell fashion goods to specialist stores. Fleur Fashions was to promote the new Osti range of fashion lingerie manufactured in Henderson, while a second company, Sacony (NZ), was established to market and distribute dresses made under license with designs and materials supplied by S. Augstein & Co., New York. Special up-to-date showrooms were created in the warehouses so that the goods might be properly displayed.[34]

The strategy developed by Hunter to reduce warehouse operations and concentrate on manufacturing was endorsed by his fellow board members, any reservations that they may still have entertained being dispelled by the re-introduction of import licensing. A change in heart may also have been brought about by the retirement and death of some of the old stalwarts on the board. In 1956 the elderly Tom Ross decided not to stand for re-election, as did Stuart Glendining, manager of the Dunedin warehouse and past-president of the New Zealand Warehousemen's Association. Hunter and C.J. Wood replaced them.[35] Two years later the vice-chairman and former managing director, A.W. Jeavons, died after being unwell for several years. Finally, in February 1959, Sir John Sutherland Ross died, aged eighty-two, having served the company for sixty years – the last thirty-six years as chairman.[36] The break with the past was complete.

## 5. Positive developments in spite of an economic downturn

The changes that Hunter now sought to push through could not have occurred at a worse time. Upon taking office in November 1957, the Labour Government was not only confronted by a balance of payments crisis, but a blow-out in the domestic budget as well, the budget deficit of £99 millions being ten times that of three years earlier. Far from being able to introduce the generous welfare measures that had been promised in Labour's election manifesto, the new Minister of Finance, Arnold Nordmeyer, was obliged to bring down his notorious 'black budget'. This increased direct and indirect taxes by a massive eighteen per cent.[37] The effect on the New Zealand economy was dramatic.

Hunter, who had now become chairman of Ross & Glendining Ltd, explained the situation in the annual report for 1959: 'Shareholders are fully aware of the many disturbing economic factors that have affected trade in the financial year, and these have been most seriously felt in warehouse turnover. The general slowing down of trade in the retail field, largely because of the restriction of buying power, has resulted in decreased sales and a consequent reduction in gross profits.' There were, however, positive developments to report. The new selling methods had contributed to an 'outstanding' expansion in turnover at Roslyn Mills. Manufacturing units, apart from fire-wracked International Style, were also showing encouraging progress. As a result, total production and sales for the year to July reached record levels, while net profits, at £129,698 were the highest since the early 1950s.[38]

The growth in profitability allowed an increased dividend to be paid, up from four to five per cent, but with capital still in short supply, undistributed profits of almost £50,000 were ploughed back into the business. The most pressing need for capital was at Roslyn Mills where, in addition to the renovation and extension of buildings, much money needed to be spent on replacing old and obsolete machinery. Although the first air-conditioned 'worsted white spinning room' in New Zealand was installed, the shortage of funds restricted building works to the dye-house roof and the refurbishment of the hosiery block. Instead, money was spent on machinery, the worsted spinning section being re-equipped so that the hosiery section might be supplied economically with high-quality yarns. The replacement programme was so effective that in 1961 an agent was appointed to sell surplus machine knitting yarns to other knitting manufacturers. Wool for hand knitting was also produced and, within a short space of time, 'Aotea' knitting wools became the market leader.[39]

Rather less progress was made with hosiery manufacturing itself. The fact that previous mill managers had not been 'hosiery minded' meant that much of the hosiery machinery was out of date. As a result, Holeproof Industries Ltd had stolen a march on Roslyn Mills so that by 1960 it produced thirty per cent of all men's socks made in New Zealand and seventy-five per cent of children's ankle socks.[40] With £20,000 needed to renew hosiery plant and no certainty that Ross & Glendining would be able to recapture lost markets, it was decided to exit the market for half-hose. Henceforth hosiery was bought in to complement goods produced in-house.[41]

A similar story of lost opportunities existed in blanket manufacturing, where looms purchased after the war proved unable to cope with the demand for new patterns and styles. In 1961, Onehunga Woollen Mills was contracted to produce a proportion of the blankets required, with thought being given to vacating this sector of the market completely. Investments continued to be made in knitwear production, with more than £20,000 spent on installing a Bentley Cotton Fully Fashioned Machine, which 'was the most modern in the Southern Hemisphere' at the time. The decision to focus on what Roslyn Mills could still do well appears to have paid off. Net mill profits before tax, which had been no more than £14,704 in 1958, recovered to reach £162,156 in 1962. As such, Roslyn made a major contribution to the health of the company.[42]

## 6. A FOCUS ON FASHION

Ross & Glendining also started to make a name for itself in the fashion industry. In January 1960, the hitherto staid firm stunned trade buyers with an innovative fashion show in Auckland at which they displayed their latest spring and summer creations. Held at the Winter Garden of the Great Northern Hotel, the show ran for 106 minutes, employed a three-piece orchestra and used ten models – including two children – to display 140 garments. 'Organising brain behind the scenes, the man who dreamed up the whole idea, was Mr. Ian Couldrey, Ross and Glendining's on-the-ball sales promotion controller, a well known identity in New Zealand's publicity and marketing circles'. After two further nights in Auckland, the entourage and props were airlifted to Wellington, Christchurch and Dunedin, a motion picture being made of the show for distribution in small-town cinemas. The fashion show, E.O. Hunter promised the Auckland audience, was the first of many bigger and brighter displays in the future.[43]

In the meantime, there was still work to be done rationalising and reorganising existing manufacturing facilities. During the course of the year, Ross & Glendining had been obliged to purchase the remainder of the shares in Childswear Ltd from Dove-Myer Robinson under the terms of an agreement entered into in 1946. The sum involved, a 'very substantial' £112,745, represented a real drain on scarce capital resources, with further outlays required, since much of the plant needed to be replaced. It was also necessary to 'carry out a complete overhaul of the management, general staff, and the production planning, and also to integrate this operation with our parent company.' As in the case of the Christchurch knitwear factory, the organisation had to be rebuilt so as to provide for direct selling. Thought was also given to moving the unit from its dilapidated factory in the centre of

Auckland to more suitable premises elsewhere. Before long, a considerable amount of production had been transferred to a factory unit on the new industrial estate of Panmure, to the south of Auckland.[44]

Further rationalisation took place in 1961, when it was decided to terminate the Sacony (N.Z.) license agreement with Augstein & Co. of New York and stop manufacturing their garments. While the re-imposition of import licences in 1957 had helped certain sectors of the clothing trade, for those obliged to import materials from America the difficulties proved to be 'almost insurmountable'. No such difficulties existed with the Osti lingerie franchise, secured in 1958, where the garments were well styled and the service provided by the Australian franchise owners was found to be excellent. Production initially took place at the Henderson underwear factory, with the goods merchandised by Fleur Fashions Ltd through the Auckland warehouse showroom. The acquisition of specialist lingerie producers R.W. Saunders Ltd of Christchurch in 1961 saw the production of the 'Osti' range relocated. Henceforth, the Christchurch subsidiary was to produce and merchandise the Osti range, along with its own 'Adrian' and 'Lisbet' lingerie. It was, Hunter claimed, the perfect example of vertical integration, with a specialist manufacturer engaged in direct selling.[45]

The product range that Ross & Glendining offered to the public at the beginning of the 'sixties was vastly different to that available only five years previously. Nevertheless, there were still gaps to be filled. In January 1963, the company acquired Sportscraft Sportswear (NZ) Ltd. This firm had been formed in 1960 by a leading Australian women's sportswear house, Sportscraft Pty Ltd of Melbourne, in conjunction with Elgan Enterprises Auckland. The joint venture, which used Australian designs, had been set up to produce a complete range of casual fashion wear for women that included slacks, suits, blouses, and a 'most exciting range' of pleated skirts. Hunter saw the Sportscraft acquisition as 'a further step on the road of developing a specialist women's outerwear company'. It was intended that the garments it produced would replace many of the slow-selling and low-profit warehouse items in the women's outerwear field.[46]

## 7. STRUCTURAL CHANGE SEES THE ABANDONMENT OF THE WAREHOUSE BUSINESS

The refurbishment of the mill, the reorganisation of the factories and the establishment of subsidiary companies to operate overseas franchise agreements for the production of fashion goods represented the first part of Hunter's plan for the re-invigoration of Ross & Glendining. Nevertheless, the vexed question of what to do with the warehouses still remained.

The closure of sub-branches in 1958, with the subsequent disposal of properties and streamlining of sales and distribution, had undoubtedly helped to economise on capital and reduce warehouse costs. Sadly, these measures were insufficient to ensure that the warehouses remained economically viable. Warehouse volumes had inevitably been reduced by the expansion of direct selling, a situation rendered much worse by the re-introduction of import controls in 1957. Between 1955 and 1962, the value of warehouse importations from London had fallen from £1,075,000 to £263,000 per annum. Since warehouse sales over the same period fell from just over £5 million to just around £4 million, the loss of £812,000 of high margin business proved to be absolutely critical. Warehouse profits before tax plunged – from almost £159,000 to £8,308 in 1962 – representing a mere 0.47 per cent return on a capital employed of £1.75 million. By way of contrast, the rate of return at Roslyn Mills had risen to 13.2 per cent, the factories managed 5.3 per cent, and the subsidiaries 8.6 per cent – excluding exceptional costs.[47]

With little hope for a revival in the fortunes of the warehouses and virtually all the profits coming from the mills, factories and subsidiaries, Hunter decided that the time had come for Ross & Glendining to abandon the warehouse business. In a very full report to the board in May 1963, he bluntly stated the position:

> *There is definitely no future in general warehouse operation, largely because of the extension of local manufacturing and the development of import licensing, and even a substantial turnover increase could not offer a sufficient return for the time and expense involved … Warehouses, as constituted today, are not profitable against specialists, and our subsidiary companies are taking care, very largely, by direct selling, of many of the items handled by the warehouse sections selling our own or locally manufactured goods.*

He therefore recommended a complete re-organisation of the enterprise, with warehouses transformed into bulk distribution centres and a structure put in place that properly supported the growing number of manufacturing units.

Head Office control over the increasingly far-flung enterprise had been strengthened in 1961 when two new directors, one in Auckland and one in Christchurch, together with two associate directors, had been drafted onto the board. Head Office had also been reinforced by the appointment of additional management staff. Further measures were now proposed so that lines of communication, responsibility and control in the ramshackle organisation might be simplified. To aid this process, the multifarious activities of Ross & Glendining were to be concentrated in a number of separate operating divisions that individually reported back to Head Office.

Since the greater part of manufacturing and selling was centred on Auckland province, Hunter thought it would probably be better in the long run if Head Office moved there also.

In future, each of the major product areas such as Roslyn Mills, Clifton Knitwear, shirt production, and underwear was to constitute a division, as was International Style Co. Ltd, R.W. Saunders Ltd, and the House of Sportscraft (NZ) Ltd. Childswear Ltd was also to operate as a separate division, although the production of schoolwear might be abandoned 'because of the low mark-up and intense competition'. The continuation of footwear manufacturing in Dunedin and Christchurch was also to be reviewed.[48]

At the unit level, a number of inner-city factories were to be closed and the buildings disposed of, including the Dunedin factories in High St and Stafford St and the Greys Avenue and Albert St factories in Auckland. Where appropriate, production was to be located in modern buildings in the suburbs, with the factories selling direct to their customers. Most of the warehouse departments were to be closed and their selling functions assumed by manufacturing units, with just four merchandising departments retained. These were to have divisional status and distribute manchester, piece goods, haberdashery and millinery, most of which were still largely imported. There would be little use for the vast Wellington warehouse, which was to be sold off, smaller leased premises being employed instead. London Office was to be replaced by agents.[49]

The effect of restructuring, Hunter calculated, would be to reduce funds employed from £5.1 million to £3.9 million. The amount realised by the disposal of surplus properties and the reduction in stocks would not only enable Ross & Glendining to pay off their £900,000 overdraft, but it would also release a further £325,000 to modernise existing plant and extend operations where advisable. The net additional profit after tax was estimated at £84,100, lifting total profits to well over £200,000 per annum.[50] The prospect of enhanced profits evidently appealed to the board who, upon receiving his report in May 1963, promptly adopted the restructuring proposals. They were also fully endorsed by local accountants Barr, Burgess, Stewart and by W.D. Scott & Co., in Sydney.[51]

## 8. HUNTER'S PLANS RUN INTO TROUBLE

A number of shareholders, especially those who worked for Ross & Glendining, viewed the changes with misgivings. Others probably accepted that the switch from warehousing to manufacturing was inevitable, especially as Bing, Harris & Co. and Sargood, Son & Ewen were also going down this route. They would also have been encouraged by the fact that, under extremely difficult circumstances, Hunter's grand strategy seemed to be yielding an improvement in profitability. Yet in August 1963, just after he had sent out a circular to shareholders outlining the progress made and plans for the future, things started to go badly wrong.[52]

The main problem lay in the operations of the International Style Co. Ltd, which unexpectedly returned a heavy loss. It transpired that the board had known that the subsidiary had been struggling for several years. In August 1961, an inquiry had been instituted when International Style failed to meet its targets. Unfortunately, the budgets and assurances of the then managing director of the subsidiary were accepted somewhat uncritically, a further fourteen months elapsing before control of the firm was placed in the hands of its newly appointed company secretary. By March 1963, the board,

> having lost the confidence in the then Managing Director, requested his resignation, and immediately appointed a Head Office executive committee under the chairmanship of our ex-Company Secretary to carry out a management audit. The order of reference was very complete. This was duly completed and confirmed that the stock of cloth and garments was out of all proportion to the business done.

Even so, the committee felt that there was every indication International Style would trade profitably in the second half of the year, although it accepted that some discounting would have to take place.[53]

The assessment of the executive committee proved to be hopelessly optimistic. Trading in Anthony Squires suits to July 1963 returned a loss of £12,000, while stock discounts cost a further £7,500. On 17 August, Ross & Glendining's auditors were instructed to carry out a detailed investigation of the books. When they reported back on 7 September, the outcome was far worse than anyone had anticipated. On an examination of the stocks, it was clear that a further provision of £109,000 would have to be made for materials purchased and garments manufactured in earlier years. When the audit report was finally signed off on 19 September, the loss provision had climbed to £133,000.[54]

Losses on a rather smaller scale were also incurred at the House of Sportscraft (NZ) Ltd, which had been acquired on 1 January 1963. At the first annual balance in July, a profit of around £6,000 had been forecast – with a few provisions for stock and book debts to be made. On 21 August, Head Office was informed that the accounts were not all that they should be. Once again, the auditors were sent in. Their report received on 19 September revealed that provisions for losses of £23,000 would have to be made.[55]

The need to provide for unforeseen losses and stock discounts of £156,000 came as rather a shock to shareholders, especially as a circular sent out by

Hunter on 8 August had dwelt on the record £6.25 million turnover and a satisfactory trading position. Indeed, Ross & Glendining Ltd's shares had risen from 21/3d to 23/3d on the basis of Hunter's comments, only to fall back to 20/- when news of the losses leaked out. What particularly outraged shareholders and other interested parties, however, was the decision to treat the £156,000 as non-recurring and exceptional losses, to be covered in the accounts by a transfer from General Reserves. Given that it was clear that the firm had, in reality, made a loss of over £4,000, why did Hunter continue to maintain the fiction that a profit of £151,403 had been made? Why was a final dividend of 3½ per cent still to be paid?[56]

These views were thoroughly ventilated in the press in advance of the annual general meeting in October, with the result that Hunter received a most hostile reception. He attempted to explain that when he had sent out the circular in August, his statement had been made in the utmost good faith. The magnitude of the losses subsequently revealed, he said, had shocked everyone. It was to no avail. Hunter's failure to allude to the difficulties at International Style rather earlier than he did was criticised, as was the decision to pay a dividend.

Criticism was also levelled at his strategy. What was the rate of return yielded by the subsidiaries? Wouldn't it be better to cut out the subsidiaries and rely on the profits from Roslyn Mills? A long term opponent of Hunter, a Mr R. Dwyer, said that seven years previously he had warned that the policy of the board 'could bring nothing but trouble, and the present policy would wreck the entire organisation'. The branch warehouses should be set up as independent units to see if they could make money.[57]

Hunter may have survived the storm of criticism had he received the unequivocal backing of the board of directors. He did not. Before discussion of the annual report passed to the floor of the meeting, one of the more recently appointed directors, R.S. Brittain, announced that since Mr Hunter had been doing far too much lately, it had been agreed that,

> he should have an extended break, leaving the next stages of the plan of re-organisation to be carried on by other executives, with outside assistance ... Mr. B.E. Woodhams, our new Director, who is widely experienced in our activities, has agreed, that, if you will elect him today, he will carry on the duties of Chairman during Mr. Hunter's absence.

With the board distancing themselves from the policies that they had all adopted, Hunter was doomed. When it was proposed that he should be re-elected to the board, several speakers, including H.S. Ross and I.C. Glendining, insisted that the proposal be put to a vote. The result was that shareholders holding two-thirds of the equity in the company opposed Hunter's re-election.[58]

TABLE 20.1
SUMMARY BALANCE SHEETS, 1951–1965 (£000s)

| July Year | 1951 | 1952 | 1953 | 1954 | 1955 | 1956 | 1957 | 1958 | 1959 | 1960 | 1961 | 1962 | 1963 | 1964 | 1965 |
|---|---|---|---|---|---|---|---|---|---|---|---|---|---|---|---|
| Turnover | 4,565 | 4,597 | 4,136 | 4,896 | 5,024 | 4,634[a] | 4,355[a] | n/a | n/a | n/a | n/a | 5,982 | 6,248[a] | 6,500 | n/a |
| Net profit | 175.4 | 156.6 | 40.8 | 129.3 | 119.4 | 59.8 | 76.6 | 72.1 | 129.7 | 140.8 | 113.2 | 138.7 | -4.2 | 131.1 | 106.7 |
| Share capital | 950.0 | 950.0 | 950.0 | 950.0 | 1,543.8 | 1,662.5 | 1,662.5 | 1,662.5 | 1,662.5 | 1,662.5 | 1,662.5 | 1,662.5 | 1,662.5 | 1,662.5 | 1,662.5 |
| Dividends paid | 90.5 | 95.0 | 95.0 | 95.0 | 118.7 | 99.8 | 99.8 | 66.5 | 83.2 | 99.8 | 99.8 | 99.8 | 99.8 | 58.2 | 58.2 |
| Additions[b] | 100.0 | 184.0 | 83.4 | 71.3 | 57.9 | 69.4 | 128.7 | n/a | n/a | n/a | n/a | n/a | n/a | n/a | n/a |
| Current assets | 2,265 | 3,136 | 2,680 | 3,134 | 3,696 | 3,235 | 3,225 | 3,493 | 3,414 | 3,618 | 3,850 | 3,973 | 3,972 | 3,485 | 3,410 |
| Shareholders' funds | 2,124 | 2,186 | 2,221 | 2,258 | 2,795 | 2,933 | 2,913 | 2,919 | 2,993 | 3,065 | 3,103 | 3,109 | 3,010 | 3,119 | 3,230 |
| Shareholders (no.) | 1,115 | 1,258 | 1,304 | 1,370 | 1,957 | 2,103 | 2,157 | 2,281 | 2,300 | 2,430 | 2,530 | 2,574 | 2,637 | 2,695 | 2,818 |
| Employees (no.) | 1,634 | 1,702 | 1,689 | 1,796 | 1,873 | 1,578 | 1,531 | 1,823 | 1,794 | 2,112 | 2,292 | 2,520 | 2,307 | 2,157 | 2,009 |

Sources: Directors' Reports and Annual Accounts; Report on Annual Accounts, AG 512 8/8. Board Report May 1963, AG 512 19/1; R & G Reporter, Vol 1, No. 1, September 1964.
Notes: (a) Approximations based on chairman's comments. (b) Plant, machinery, etc.

The new chairman, B.E. Woodhams MBE, was a retailer and local councillor from Hamilton, who had left school at fifteen and worked his way up. Far more personable than the somewhat reserved Hunter, he held a number of directorships in commercial companies, although he had no direct knowledge of manufacturing. What he did know, however, was that while the strategy implemented by his predecessor may have been basically sound, he had no wish for Hunter to remain employed by Ross & Glendining Ltd. Early in 1964, Hunter was dismissed. A case was brought for wrongful dismissal but it was settled out of court. For the next eighteen months, Woodhams and his executives struggled to refine the strategy that the much-maligned Hunter had worked so hard to put in place.[59]

# ENDGAME,
# 1963–1966

The economic environment facing Ross & Glendining when B.E. Woodhams became chairman in 1963 was relatively prosperous. Rising export prices and an increase in productivity saw national income growing strongly, with farm receipts up and companies generally doing well. The balance of payments, too, was improving, although with imports also rising rapidly there was always the possibility that another foreign exchange crisis might loom over the horizon.[1] A National Government had been returned to office in 1960, but this did not fundamentally alter the situation for those firms reliant on continued protection. Employment in the manufacturing industry was now quite substantial and so import licensing was maintained, though the new government did attempt to make the system more flexible. Thus licensing codes were simplified, and manufacturers were allowed to substitute and amalgamate various licenses so that their requirements might be better met.[2]

The National Government, it is true, did not lose sight of their policy to move to a more open economy, gradually increasing import license entitlements and exemptions as the balance of payments allowed. More immediately, however, there was a focus on the need to stimulate industrial growth and development, with particular emphasis placed on the need to expand manufactured exports. In 1962 a Trade and Development Board was created to foster development. As an interim measure, manufacturers were granted replacement import licenses to the value of the licensed content of goods that they exported. An Export Development Conference held in June 1963 also led to the creation of an export guarantee scheme.[3]

Ross & Glendining had periodically considered re-entering export markets. In 1962, with Roslyn Mills now largely modernised, Hunter expressed the hope that 'more definitive steps' could now be taken in exporting mill goods. Donald Ross, the younger son of Sutherland Ross and now part of the management team, was sent to investigate North American markets.[4] Yet for the most part, attention was directed almost entirely towards the domestic market. This remained Woodhams' main preoccupation and both he and Neil Sinclair, the newly promoted general manager, spent much of their time refining and implementing the structural reforms conceived by E.O. Hunter.

At the same time, Woodhams, ex-local government politician and director on the board of a number of national companies, was not entirely oblivious to government exhortations to export more.

One suggestion that he explored was the proposal that domestic mills might expand their production of woollen 'tops'. It was envisaged that local wool, instead of being exported greasy, should be scoured and combed first, thereby enabling New Zealand to capture the value added. The development of a tops industry had been mooted in the late 1940s and again in the 1950s. Labour shortages, however, together with the need for economies of scale, had meant that even large mills, such as Roslyn, simply concentrated on producing enough tops for their own use.[5] In 1964, Woodhams deemed the time was now ripe to take this proposal forward and began negotiations with other parties to set up a joint venture to manufacture and export tops.[6] His efforts were unsuccessful. When the share price of Ross & Glendining began to slide once more, other large players in the industry, also with an eye on expanding tops production, saw the possibility of acquiring the company's assets, including Roslyn Mills and its tops capacity, on the cheap.[7]

## I. A HALF-HEARTED APPROACH TO STRUCTURAL REFORM

The first task that Woodhams faced upon becoming chairman in 1963, however, was to ensure that Head Office exercised greater control over the various operating units. The divisional structure that Hunter had proposed was quickly adopted. It had much to commend it, being very much in line with modern management thinking and increasingly utilised by large and diffuse corporations overseas. The idea was that each division should be responsible for its own administration, product development, production planning, material purchases, manufacturing and marketing. Overall control was to be exercised by Head Office, which would determine strategy, allocate funds, and coordinate activities.

Head Office was moved to Auckland in 1964. As Woodhams explained to shareholders,

> *A general should be where the fighting is thickest and with 70 per cent of our business being done in the North Island – and 40 per cent in Auckland province – that's where our top management belongs. Our roots will always be in Dunedin but we are no longer a Dunedin company – we're a New Zealand company. Controlling the company from Dunedin would be like trying to drive a motor car from the back seat.*[8]

This move was not welcomed by all. To help mollify antagonised shareholders and to keep staff both informed and involved, a group magazine, the *R & G Reporter,* was to be published six times a year.[9]

An executive committee was established to ensure coordination between the divisions and to supply special management services as required.[10] A key figure was the group finance controller who, in addition to forecasting expenditure up to five years in advance, also established a system of monthly financial reporting. An 'aggressive, long-term and co-ordinated marketing programme' was to be developed by the head of marketing, while planning and development was the responsibility of former marine engineer, J.G. Glendining, a great-grandson of the founder. The committee was to be led by Neil Sinclair, who also became a director after he replaced Hunter as general manager.[11]

Before implementing structural changes, further thought was given as to how many divisions there should be and which units fitted into what division. Roslyn Mills, with over 800 workers and the firm's most profitable manufacturing unit, had been treated as an independent profit centre for many years. It was therefore appropriate that it should continue as a separate division. Clifton Knitwear, which employed a mere sixty people, was also included within this division, presumably because it drew most of its yarn from the mills. Roslyn Mills was to sell Clifton knitted garments alongside the piece goods, hosiery and men's underwear that it produced – even though Hunter's original plan envisaged knitwear sold through separate agencies. The fact that fashionable female knitwear was now to be sold through the same channels as men's underpants did not seem to concern anybody.[12]

In an attempt to simplify the organisational structure still further, the Childswear and Sportscraft subsidiaries were incorporated in a Womenswear Division. With five main factories in Auckland province, a staff of 500 and a turnover of almost £1 million per annum, this constituted the company's second largest division. Some rationalisation took place, although a scheme proposed by the Henderson factory management to rename their unit 'Glendining Productions', move upmarket, and produce and sell quality lingerie and frocks direct to retailers never saw the light of day.[13] Instead, Henderson was to produce the new 'Hi-Fi' range of dresses, costumes, coats and lingerie which, together with 'Sportscraft' women's outerwear, was sold through 'Fashion House', the grand name given to divisional headquarters in the old Childswear factory in Albert St. Henderson continued to make 'Mimosa' lingerie and 'Lyndene' coats and dresses, while the Childswear unit persevered with low-margin 'Teenswear' and 'Maidswear' clothing. These more mundane labels continued to be sold through the four warehouses. The Christchurch subsidiary, R.W. Saunders Ltd, which was to operate as a separate division, manufactured and marketed the 'Osti' and 'Adrian' lingerie range as before.

Hunter had suggested that International Style Ltd, which employed around 180, might also be accorded divisional status, although it should retain its identity as a wholly owned subsidiary. This suggestion was adopted and, by the time of the 1964 annual general meeting, much effort had been expended in turning around the struggling Frankton Junction operation. With the concept of well-styled men's suits rapidly gaining ground in New Zealand, tight financial control and operational reforms saw stock levels fall by £128,000 and indebtedness to the parent company reduced by almost £200,000. Distribution facilities for suits and slacks, hitherto located at the Grey's Avenue factory in the centre of Auckland, were now concentrated in rural Frankton. Capital reconstruction the following year, which included the injection of £150,000 in share capital, enabled International Style to return a profit by 1965. With demand buoyant, the plant was extended and the production of 'Sax Altman' slacks, which had previously taken place in rented premises in Hamilton, was brought on site.[14]

The production of all other menswear was nominally grouped together in a single division. The division was quite diverse in nature, encompassing the shirt factory, recently moved from Grey's Avenue to a new building on the Panmure industrial estate, the Sale St factory in Auckland city – which produced industrial clothing, neckwear, dressing gowns, sports jackets and blazers, and the hat factory in High St, Dunedin, where the 'Stetson' and 'Wellesley' brands were produced. The units were relatively small, but together they employed over 150 hands. Hunter had envisaged closing the clothing and hat factories, probably on account of their small scale and relatively slim margins. Under Woodhams and Sinclair, the factories were granted a stay of execution and a new manager, formerly clothing manager for Bing, Harris & Co., was appointed to head the division.[15]

Footwear production also survived under the new regime, being reconstituted as the Regent Footwear Division. To cut costs, both the Dunedin footwear factory and the Barbados St factory in Christchurch were closed, production being relocated in new and larger premises in Christchurch. Technical support for the move, which took place in May 1964, was provided by the British United Shoe Machinery Company Ltd, which also installed a transporter and conveyor belt system. Although the plant made all types of shoes except those in canvas, rubber and plastic, the main focus was on 'children's summer sandals, school and college shoes, men's shoes and matron's footwear'. The plant employed about 140 men and women and there was plenty of room for further expansion. As the sale of footwear had always been a highly specialised activity, a dedicated sales team was formed to represent the division throughout the country.[16]

The failure to restructure and rationalise in a way that Hunter had envisaged meant that many of the clothing factories continued to rely on the four warehouses to market and distribute what were often very ordinary goods. In an attempt to improve the efficiency of this outmoded form of distribution, a 'Wholesale Division' was created, which would be administered from Auckland. Although emphasis was placed on forward ordering and the speedy dispatch of goods by the warehouses closest to the point of manufacture, many elements of the old departmental system were in evidence. Thus there were sections to handle men's and boys' wear, women's underwear, frocks and outerwear, school clothing, piece goods, mill goods, as well as haberdashery and manchester imported from overseas. All were retained in stock. With fifty sales representatives, the Wholesale Division boasted 'one of the biggest field forces in New Zealand' which called 'on more than 5,000 shops, ranging from small country general stores to the largest big city departments'. The travellers not only took orders but, in a major advertising campaign, also supplied point of sale advertising that might involve dedicated radio scripts and slides for local cinemas. A further 170 men and women were retained in the four centres to serve customers and dispatch goods.[17]

The restructuring and rationalisation programme implemented by Woodhams and Sinclair allowed some savings to be made. By the time of the annual general meeting in October 1964, the Grey's Avenue shirt factory in Auckland and the old footwear factory in Christchurch had been disposed of, the company cafeteria in Dunedin sold, and some knitwear and garment making transferred to the now-vacant footwear factory. Millinery production in Auckland was to end shortly. The retention of a number of factories that Hunter had earmarked for disposal, however, together with the continued use of warehouses for distribution, necessarily limited the amount of capital that could be released. Worse still, in spite of the creation of a new wholesale division, the costs of distribution remained stubbornly high. Stocks, it is true, fell by almost half a million pounds but this was less than half the reduction that Hunter had originally planned. In the year to July the company posted a profit of £131,113, an improvement over the loss of £4,245 sustained in 1963, but hardly startling progress. At the annual general meeting, Woodhams warned shareholders, 'We have a long, hard haul in front of us to reach levels of profitability which we feel are adequate and, indeed, essential'. To maintain liquidity, the dividend was reduced from 6 to 3½ per cent (see Table 20).[18]

## 2. RESTRUCTURING COMPLETED AND NEW INITIATIVES PROPOSED
The drawbacks of the half-hearted approach to restructuring became evident in 1965, when profits fell to £106,000. Slowly but surely, Woodhams and Sinclair found themselves adopting the remainder of Hunter's proposals. In

a costly change of heart, they announced the closure of the Christchurch footwear factory. Shareholders were told that the board, 'had been giving serious consideration to the poor net return on footwear for some time but it had hoped that consolidation of the manufacturing unit in Christchurch would make overall investment more profitable. A study of developments overseas convinced your directors that further heavy capital outlay would be necessary in the near future if we wished to remain competitive.'[19] The Auckland menswear clothing factory in Sale St was also closed, many lines discontinued, and staff redeployed elsewhere.[20] By Christmas 1965 the Menswear Division had ceased to exist, with shirts, hats and the remnants of menswear production falling within the ambit of the Wholesale Division.[21]

The Womenswear Division was not left unscathed in the drive for efficiency. In an attempt to stem losses, the low-margin Childswear products were finally axed, with Fashion House concentrating on upmarket labels. The most significant change, however, occurred in the Wholesale Division, where only the Auckland and Christchurch warehouses were retained as distribution centres. Henceforth, Wellington and Dunedin were simply to maintain 'sales and service stock offices'.

How the closure of the Dunedin warehouse was received in the city can only be imagined, but there was some logic behind these developments. With Roslyn Mills engaged in direct selling, it made sense to have the main distribution centres located closer to their markets. The sale of the Dunedin and Wellington warehouses would also release capital. Whether it made sense for Ross & Glendining to continue wholesaling in any shape or form, however, is debatable.[22]

Woodhams, needless to say, continued to put a brave face on the changes taking place when he addressed the annual general meeting in November 1965. While net profits had fallen, the sale of the Auckland and Christchurch factory units for more than book value had boosted capital reserves by some £75,000. The board, he said, was looking for 'new opportunities for profitable operation'. To that end, a joint venture had been formed with the Australian Osti Holdings to enter the warp-knitting field. Speaking in support of the chairman was a recently appointed director, Dr G.A. Lau, a well known financial consultant who had assisted the rapidly growing and highly successful United Empire Box (UEB) Ltd. He told shareholders that the financial situation was sound, but profitability would improve only gradually. He also stated that the company would now seek more profitable activities.[23]

By early summer the warp-knitting project was well under way. A site had been purchased at Rosebank Rd on the Avondale industrial estate in West Auckland, a manager had been appointed, and a 48,000 sq. ft building was in the course of construction. The warp-knitting process, which could use both natural yarn and the nylon that was now being manufactured in New Zealand, produced a very close-knitted fabric that resembled woven cloth. Most deniers and gauges could be made, ranging from 'fabric for the lightest, filmiest lingerie' to cloths able to 'compete with woven fabrics in suitings and upholstery material'. It was hoped that the plant would supply not only group needs but the trade at large.[24]

These developments and others were written up in the most glowing terms in the *R & G Reporter*. There were reports of the installation of modern high speed twisting machines at Roslyn Mills, the latest printing techniques used for newspaper copy when advertising 'Anthony Squires' suits, and a preview of designs to be offered by 'Hi-Fi' for the 1967 summer season. Sports and casual wear for men was to be sold under the new 'Simon Dare' label, and in April and May 1966, 'Aotea' knitting wool was to be advertised nationally on television.[25]

### 3. A WEAKNESS IN SHARE PRICE PROMPTS A TAKEOVER BID

The share market was not impressed by these activities. £1 shares, which had been converted to 10/- in anticipation of decimalisation, began to slide. By the end of March 1966, they stood at 7/3d, having sunk to as low as 6/6d a little earlier.[26] On the evening of 29 March, Dr Lau received a telephone call from James Doig, chairman and managing director of UEB Ltd, who was endeavouring to get in touch with Woodhams. When Doig finally contacted Woodhams, he informed him that the UEB board were considering making an offer for Ross & Glendining Ltd. He also alerted Woodhams to the fact that his board's intentions appeared to have leaked out, since Ross & Glendining's share prices in the south had already started to rise. The following day Doig confirmed that UEB would indeed make a formal offer. The Stock Exchange was immediately informed and a 'Don't Sell' warning issued by Woodhams. [27]

Woodhams can have been under no illusions about the seriousness of the offer from UEB. The limits to organic growth in the small New Zealand market meant that, by the 1960s, ambitious firms were increasingly turning to growth through acquisition, a process aided by a more widely dispersed share ownership and the willingness of target companies to accept payment in shares as well as cash.[28] UEB were leading exemplars of this trend, having moved beyond their origins in box making and packaging to diversify into textiles. In the previous five years their net assets had increased from £2.5 to £5 million, partly the result of acquiring combing and spinning capacity at Napier, together with two leading carpet manufacturers. In so doing, their shares had risen and they had become a sought-after stock amongst New Zealand investors.[29]

Since rejecting the approach from UEB out-of-hand might have upset shareholders, Woodhams convened a board meeting in Hamilton on 4 April to discuss the bid. All members of the board claimed that they had no prior knowledge of the offer, including Lau who, given his close association with UEB, said he would retire from the meeting. After a short discussion, he was invited back. The details of the offer were then examined. It transpired that Doig was prepared to offer one UEB Ltd ordinary 5/- share plus 3/- in cash for every single Ross & Glendining share. As UEB shares were then trading around 12/-, the offer represented around 15/- value in exchange for each Ross & Glendining share, which had been trading at 7/3d at the close of market.[30]

Woodhams seemed to be in favour of the bid. He thought the board would bear a heavy responsibility if the offer was rejected, for it represented a considerable increase in cash value for shareholders. The consensus view, however, was that at 19/6d, the book value for each Ross & Glendining share was substantially greater than Doig's offer. Attempts should therefore be made to get UEB to raise their bid by 2/- a share. Concern was also expressed about the future of the firm's employees. James Doig was invited into the meeting for a short while but declined to improve his offer. This stance was confirmed after he had conferred with the UEB board, although he did provide nebulous assurances regarding the future of employees. After further discussions, the board of Ross & Glendining decided to make a qualified recommendation to shareholders for acceptance, 'the qualification to be based on the higher asset backing for R & G shares in relation to the monetary value of the offer'. The qualification, it transpired, was that the board would not sell their own shareholdings until the offer had been accepted by 75 per cent of the remaining shareholders.[31]

Not everyone was impressed by the feeble response by the board. On 5 April, Donald Ross, now a director, received a letter from an elderly accountant, C.R. Grey. Grey had carried out an investigation into South Island woollen mills for the Department of Industries & Commerce during the war, had been well known to Sutherland Ross and others in the company, and had paid close attention to developments ever since Hunter's dismissal. He had also quite recently interviewed Lau for the position of finance controller in Ross & Glendining Ltd! Grey was unequivocal in his views. Putting the value of the UEB bid at £2 ½ million, he considered this to be, 'a very meagre sum for the purchase of such substantial assets. Your Company's 1965 Balance Sheet disclosed assets of approximately £5 million but no doubt on market values, the true valuation is nearer £8 million. Therefore shareholders funds are in the region of £6 million. This attempted market valuation indicates a value nearer 35/- than 14/9d a share.' He suggested that a fresh policy of more effective investment and return to shareholders was long overdue. For a start, attempts should be made to extract the inherent value from the warehouses by selling them off and reducing stocks. This alone would raise between £1 ½ and £2 million which might be ploughed into a new venture – a policy likely to be followed by UEB in any case. Ross & Glendining should place themselves in a position to make takeovers, rather than be 'the golden peach for someone else to pick'.[32]

## 4. Ross & Glendining Ltd acquired very cheaply

Donald Ross certainly had a vested interest in enhancing the value of the UEB bid. He held 43,000 shares, whereas most of the other directors, including J.G. Glendining, only held 1,000. Moreover, in his reply to Grey, it was obvious that he, too, thought the bid considerably undervalued the company, especially as he was personally confident about the future prospects for Ross & Glendining. Others may also have expressed doubts about the adequacy of the bid since in an attempt to persuade wavering shareholders to accept UEB's offer, James Doig announced that his company's dividend was to be raised from 10 to 11 per cent. He also publicly talked up the 'brilliant' prospects afforded by the proposed acquisition in an effort to arrest a dip in the UEB share price. [33]

On 28 April, Grey wrote once more to Donald Ross in an attempt to galvanise opposition from the Ross and Glendining families who, together, still held around 20 per cent of the shares. Again he reiterated his view that the UEB bid was inadequate, suggested that Ross & Glendining make a bonus share issue to reflect value tied up in property, and that thought should be given to diversifying forward into retailing where margins were greater. He also pointed out that when overseas companies such as Courtaulds and International Computers made takeover bids in New Zealand, they usually offered something for goodwill. Wasn't New Zealand's premier mill and leading men's suits company worth anything in terms of goodwill? Grey concluded that shareholders had a right to expect a hardening in the stand taken by the board, and fresh leadership and direction.[34]

Yet again Ross agreed that the 'takeover offer was too low in view of the assets involved', but that the law prevented the board from allowing the offer simply to lapse. He was confident that an improvement in earnings was on the way but could not give any assurances to shareholders because of imponderables such as fashion, weather, and that ever-present variable in the New Zealand economy, the price of wool. Shareholders, he wrote, were more interested in earnings now than the underlying asset value of the company.[35]

Ross, without doubt, was unhappy about the takeover, although whether he raised any of Grey's concerns with family shareholders or his fellow board members is not known. Doig, though, may have been alerted to continued murmurings of discontent, for on 16 May 1966, UEB announced that it was increasing its bid for Ross & Glendining by 2/- per share, payable in cash on 30 June 1967. This was sufficient to overcome any resistance. Shortly afterwards, it was announced that Ross & Glendining's shareholders 'had overwhelmingly agreed' to accept UEB's offer to take over the century-old woollen textile and garment firm. By the middle of July, the once-proud New Zealand institution had been incorporated into the United Empire Box group of companies.[36]

### 5. ASSET STRIPPING AND EXIT

The chairman and managing director of UEB Industries Ltd, James Doig, welcomed the staff of Ross & Glendining to his company with a typically bullish statement. He was convinced that within a short space of time, New Zealand would become an exporter of substantial quantities of processed woollen goods, 'from tops right through to finished piecegoods and garments'.[37] UEB would be a major contributor to those developments. It was not long, though, before Doig began to dispose of those parts of the Ross & Glendining that he regarded as peripheral to his company's core business. First to go was the wholesale division. In August 1966, customers were advised that while their summer orders would be delivered, the men's and boy's clothing stocks would be sold to the retailers, Hallensteins.[38] The warehouses themselves were subsequently sold off, with Bing, Harris & Co. purchasing the Wellington warehouse occupied by Ross & Glendining since 1891.

Slowly but surely, other parts of the Ross & Glendining operation were sold off. Early disposals included the Auckland manufacturing units, followed by Clifton Knitwear in 1968, R.W. Saunders in 1969 and International Style Co. Ltd in 1970.[39] For a while it seemed that Roslyn Mills were safe since it constituted a key part of the UEB's recently formed textile division. A considerable amount of machinery had been installed in the mills in recent years and, under the stewardship of its new owners, this process continued for a while.[40]

Yet while UEB may have profited by asset-stripping Ross & Glendining, making money from the New Zealand woollen industry proved altogether more difficult. In November 1966, close neighbours Mosgiel Woollens Ltd, with the assistance of the New Zealand Wool Board, pre-empted UEB by opening the country's first woollen tops factory.[41] Competition in other sectors also increased as the Tariff & Development Board abolished duties on lightweight fabrics, at the same time allowing additional quantities of heavier-weight woollen piece goods to be imported.[42] As the industry sank deeper into depression, James Doig was forced to amend his strategy.

The need to secure efficiency gains through rationalisation and the exploitation of economies of scale was, by this stage, acknowledged both by Mosgiel Woollens and UEB. A government committee on woollen industry rationalisation in 1966 merely confirmed the point. With both parties agreed that a merger was in their best interests, it was only a matter of time before they came to an arrangement. In December 1968 it was announced that Mosgiel Woollens Ltd would acquire the assets of the Roslyn Mills division of UEB for $4,463,000, with UEB holding 50 per cent of the shares in the enlarged company. Management and control would remain with Mosgiel. The new combined operation commenced in April 1969 and within a few months major items of plant, especially those relating to tops production, started to be transferred from the Roslyn Mills site to Mosgiel.[43]

The difficulties experienced by the woollen textile industry saw other mergers take place, with Kaiapoi and the Wellington Woollen Company combining forces in 1963. A decade later, worsted combing and carding activities were transferred from Kaiapoi to Mosgiel, but it did little to transform the fortunes of either company. In May 1975, UEB decided to end its interest in Mosgiel Woollens Ltd, incurring a loss of $984,000 when it disposed of its shares.[44] Roslyn Mills finally closed in 1980 when Mosgiel went into receivership.[45]

# EPILOGUE

The story of Ross & Glendining exemplifies the progress of many merchant houses around the world during the course of the nineteenth century, which began manufacturing goods themselves as the countries in which they were based experienced economic growth.[1] In New Zealand, Ross & Glendining were not alone; as we have seen, competitors Sargood, Son and Ewen and Bing, Harris & Co. also developed manufacturing capacity. Other merchants in the colony made a similar transition, including chemists Kempthorne, Prosser & Co., coffee and spice merchants W. Gregg & Co., and shoe importers and retailers R. Hannah & Co. This process continued into the twentieth century, with electrical appliance suppliers, Fisher & Paykel Ltd, and Skellerup Industries Ltd, makers of rubber-based products, being just two of a number of New Zealand companies that moved back along the supply chain and became manufacturers.

John Ross and Robert Glendining were undoubtedly lucky as the Otago gold rush was just getting under way when they started out in business, the substantial profits that accrued providing the capital base the two partners needed to become large-scale importers of soft goods. Even so, they made the most of their opportunities: Ross's willingness to return to London to buy goods and Glendining's expert management of the warehouse trade in New Zealand made it possible for them to reap the benefits of the Vogel boom of the 1870s. It was this combination of good luck, favourable economic conditions and entrepreneurial flair that enabled them to amass sizeable fortunes, large enough to allow them to diversify into property, sheep farming and woollen manufacturing.

The period between the late 1870s and the mid-1890s has been referred to by historians as 'The Long Depression', with Michael King suggesting that 'the New Zealand economy did not grow for around sixteen years'.[2] Yet it seems doubtful whether either partner would have recognised this description of the economic environment that confronted them. True, there were cyclical downturns – that of the mid-eighties was particularly severe – and the price of wool tended to fall. At the same time, the value of exports soared, population expanded, the cities grew – especially Wellington and Auckland – and the real value of Gross Domestic Product increased by

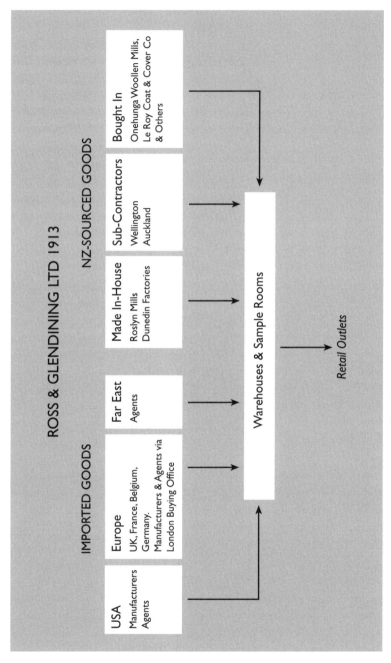

Ross & Glendining Ltd supply network, 1913.

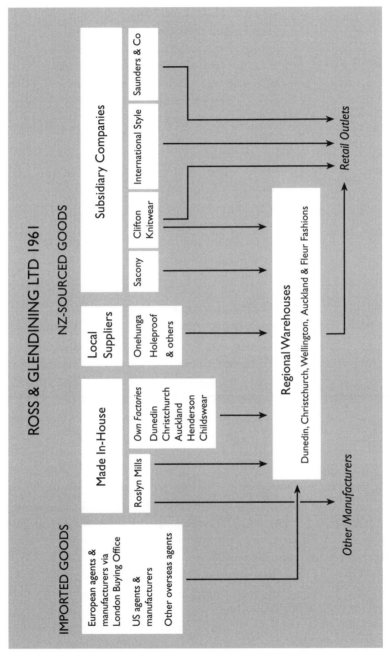

Ross & Glendining Ltd supply network, 1961.

around 70 per cent. This was the New Zealand that Ross & Glendining & Co. sought to exploit, opening branch warehouses, expanding their sales force, adding worsted capacity to woollens at Roslyn Mills, and equipping a clothing factory geared up to serve an expanding chart trade. Indeed, the experience of Ross & Glendining – and that of their rivals – supports the notion that the so-called 'Long Depression' was, in fact, a period of substantial growth, entailing both structural change and organisational and technical innovation.

The expansion of Ross & Glendining Ltd during the early years of the twentieth century was partly a reflection of the general prosperity enjoyed by New Zealand as commodity prices recovered. Once again, the firm made the most of its opportunities, the powerful ambition of Robert Glendining and the boundless energy and talents of John Ross ensuring that, by the end of World War I, Ross & Glendining Ltd stood pre-eminent amongst New Zealand manufacturers. For the two Scots, the Protestant ethic was a reality: frugal, focused, hard-working and honest, it seems that they saw their application to business as just another part of their Christian duty. Ross was possibly more driven than Glendining, but there is little doubt that both men viewed their worldly success as a sign of God's grace. Having done well, the desire to do good became overpowering, their generous charitable bequests being a necessary closing chapter to their lives as devout Presbyterians.

The second generation of both the Ross and Glendining families were by no means as capable – and certainly not as driven – as their fathers. Fortunately, by the time John Ross relinquished control in 1922, Ross & Glendining Ltd was both diversified enough and sufficiently well-capitalised to withstand the economic collapse that followed. Tom Ross, it must be said, ensured that Roslyn Mills was kept up to date between the wars, while James Evans, the general manager until 1940, cast a watchful eye over warehouse operations. Yet the entrepreneurial spirit that ran through the firm in the nineteenth century seems to have been lacking, especially after World War II, when a failure to develop new products and processes saw the firm lose market share to aggressive and innovative rivals.

The 1950s, according to conventional wisdom, was a period in which tight economic controls ensured that competition was moribund and a cost-plus mentality ruled.[3] This may have been true of some sectors, but competition in the clothing, textile and footwear industries was ferocious. General manager E.O. Hunter was alive to the challenges that Ross & Glendining Ltd faced, but he found it difficult to make progress against the entrenched opposition of the board, a staff frightened of change, and a corporate culture that was, by now, inflexible and backward looking. He believed that a major change in policy should have been made 'as soon as the post-war boom had ended in

1951'; the failure to develop specialist manufacturing units selling directly to retailers lay at the root of many of the company's subsequent problems.[4]

Whether a change in strategy and structure in the early 1950s would have allowed Ross & Glendining Ltd to survive is open to question. Certainly Lane Walker Rudkin Ltd, whose founders had worked in Roslyn Mills, not only survived but prospered, their Canterbury clothing brand becoming an icon in international sportswear and activewear markets. Holeproof Industries Ltd also experienced considerable success, their hosiery and men's underwear capturing a sizeable share of the New Zealand market. Bendon Ltd, a small specialist firm producing ladies' lingerie, not only extended its manufacturing capacity on the basis of its own and licensed designs, but also developed a number of retail outlets to sell its fashion products. These were market segments hitherto served by Ross & Glendining.

Yet it would seem that the old warehouse firms found it difficult to develop the capabilities necessary to meet the challenges of the post-war world, with Bing, Harris & Co. and Sargood, Son and Ewen faring only a little better than Ross & Glendining. The former was the more successful of the two. Under the leadership of Jack Harris, the firm opened and acquired a number of specialist clothing factories in the 1950s. They also bought out fellow warehousemen, Macky Logan. By the 1960s, Bing, Harris were making and distributing a wide variety of clothing, including 'Rainster' children's outerwear and upmarket 'Guardsmen' sports jackets. In the early 1970s, merger talks took place with loss-making Sargood, Son & Ewen – who now owned Onehunga Woollen Mills – and whose principals were eager to dispose of their business. The resulting creation, Bing, Harris, Sargood & Co., was left as the sole survivor of the once-important warehouse trade. In 1981, Bing, Harris, Sargood was acquired by Brierley Investments Ltd, and in 1984 it was broken up.[5]

Nowadays, there is little to remind New Zealanders of the three large warehouse firms that dominated the clothing and textile industries for almost a century. Some of the warehouse buildings still in existence are protected, while Roslyn Mills has been converted to industrial units. For visitors to the Botanical Garden in Dunedin, the winter garden paid for by Robert Glendining still survives as an abiding memorial both to his generous nature and to his love of gardening. Similarly, Knox College is a reminder of the belief that John Ross had in the improving effects of education, and his desire to further the Presbyterian ministry in New Zealand. At his birthplace in Scotland, the Ross Institute, Halkirk, lives on as a community resource, just across the road from the local hostelry. Sadly, the original Glendining Home for Children in Anderson's Bay was demolished in 1976. The Ross Home for the elderly in North East Valley, however, continues to provide care, albeit as part of a broader range of services offered by Presbyterian Support in Otago.

# BIBLIOGRAPHY

## I. PRIMARY SOURCES

### A. MANUSCRIPT SOURCES

Ross & Glendining archive, Hocken Collections (previously known as the Hocken Library), University of Otago, Dunedin. General reference number ARC-0145; bulk accession number AG 512.

The extensive Ross & Glendining archive in the Hocken Library covers letter books & correspondence 1865–1966; minute books, 1900–1935; annual reports 1935–1965 (broken); half-annual reports 1870-1922; half-yearly analysis results, 1911–1932; factory returns 1922–1946; cash books and financial ledgers 1861–1928; wages and salary books, 1885–1961 (broken); articles of partnership; share records 1900–1951; United Empire Box take-over documents, 1966; photographs. A short, typed manuscript outlining the early life of John Ross and subsequent history of the company exists, probably the basis for a 36-page booklet written by Norah Ross, *The March of Time: One Hundred Years with Ross & Glendining Ltd.*

Census Enumerators Returns for Scotland, 1841, 1851 & 1861.

A.T. Inglis Minute Books, Hocken Library, Miss. MS 0711-00.

Otago Runs Register, Archives New Zealand, Dunedin, Acc. D84 776b.

Industry & Commerce Files, Archives New Zealand, Wellington, IC 1 54/7/3; IC 1 9/13.

### B. OFFICIAL PRINTED PAPERS

*Appendices to the Journal of the House of Representatives*, 1870 Vol. IV; 1890, Vol. III; 1896, C. 1; 1900, C.1; 1904, C. 1;1905, C. 4; 1906, C; 1928, H35: 1940, H. 19.

*Statistics of New Zealand,* 1861, 1865.

*Statutes of New Zealand,* No. 6 & No. 23, 45 Victoria; No. 28, 46 Victoria; No 56, 49 Victoria; No 17, 52 Victoria; No. 27, 56 Victoria; No. 44, 59 Victoria.

### C. NEWSPAPERS AND PERIODICALS

*Auckland Weekly News,* 1911.

*Dominion,* 1963.

Edinburgh & Leith Post Office Directories, 1850–51, 1854–55, 1859–60.

*Mackay's Otago Provincial and Goldfields Almanac*, 1865, 1866.

*Mount Ida Chronicle*, 1891,1892, 1895.

*New Zealand Draper & Allied Retailer*, 1943, 1944, 1945, 1953, 1956, 1958, 1959, 1960.

*New Zealand Financial Times*, 1957.

*New Zealand Herald*, 1912.

*Otago Daily Times*, 1863, 1917, 1927, 1959.

*Otago Witness*, 1860, 1864, 1907, 1926, 1927.

*R & G Reporter*, 1964, 1965, 1966.

*The Southern Provinces Almanac, Directory & Year Book for 1864*, Christchurch.

*Unibox*, 1966.

Wise's New Zealand Post Office Directory, 1894/5.

### D. Contemporary books & pamphlets

*The Cyclopedia of New Zealand*, Volume 4, Otago & Southland (Christchurch, 1905).

Eccles, Alfred, 'The First New Zealand Exhibition and Dunedin in 1865', *Otago Witness*, reprint (1905).

Hastings, D.I.H., *A Plea for Protection* (Dunedin, 1888).

Hocken, T.M., *Contributions to the Early History of New Zealand* (London, 1898).

Jenkins, W. Emlyn, *John Alexander Ewen: A Memoir* (1902).

*New Zealand Official Yearbook*, 1892, 1894, 1910, 1907, 1913, 1937, 1940, 1942, 1946, 1947, 1948, 1949, 1956.

Ross, Norah, *The March of Time: One Hundred Years with Ross & Glendining Ltd* (Dunedin, 1967).

*Official Catalogue of the New Zealand Exhibition 1865* (Dunedin, 1865).

*Roslyn: The Saga of a Woollen Mill* (Dunedin, u.d.).

*Souvenir Catalogue, Industrial Exhibition and Art Union* (Dunedin, 1912).

*They Came From Caithness*, pamphlet (Inverness u.d.).

## II SECONDARY SOURCES

### A. Published books and articles

Anderson, Len, *Throughout the East Coast. The Story of Williams & Kettle* (Hastings, 1974).

Arnold, Rollo, *The Farthest Promised Land* (Wellington, 1981).

Baker, J.V.T., *The New Zealand People at War, 1939–1945* (Wellington, 1945).

Belich, James, *The New Zealand Wars* (Auckland, 1988).

Bott, Alan, *The Sailing Ships of the New Zealand Shipping Company* (London, 1972).

Brooking, Tom, *Lands for the People? The Highland Clearances and the Colonisation of New Zealand* (Dunedin, 1996).

Brooking, Tom, 'Economic Transformation', in G.W. Rice, ed., *The Oxford History of New Zealand*, second edition (Auckland, 2000).

Chapman, R., 'From Labour to National', in G.W. Rice, ed., *The Oxford History of New Zealand,* second edition (Auckland, 2000).

Chappell, N.M., *New Zealand Banker's Hundred: A History of the Bank of New Zealand, 1861–1961* (Wellington, 1961).

Condliffe, J.B., *New Zealand in the Making* (London, 1936).

Cowan, J., *Down the Years in the Maniototo* (Christchurch, 1978).

Croot, Charles, *Otago Before Department Store Days* (Otago Settlers Museum, 1995).

Dalziel, Raewyn, *Julius Vogel: Business Politician* (Auckland, 1986).

Devine, T.M, *Scotland's Empire, 1600–1815* (London, 2004).

Dunlop, Jean, 'Pultneytown and the Planned Villages of Caithness', in John R. Baldwin, ed., *Caithness: A Cultural Crossroads* (Edinburgh, 1982).

Forrest, James, 'Population and Settlement on the Otago Goldfields', *New Zealand Geographer*, Vol. 17, No. 1 (1961).

Forrest, James, 'Otago During the Goldrushes', in R.F. Watters, ed., *Land & Society in New Zealand* (Wellington, 1965).

Gould, J.D., 'Pasture Formation and Improvement', *Australian Economic History Review*, 16 (1976).

Greasley, David, and Oxley, Les, 'Measuring New Zealand's GDP, 1865–1933: a Cointegration-Based Approach', *Review of Income & Wealth,* Series 46, No. 3 (September 2000).

Greasley, David, and Oxley, Les, 'Globalization and Real Wages in New Zealand, 1873–1913', *Explorations in Economic History*, Vol. 41.1 (January 2004).

Harris, Sir Jack, *Memoirs of a Century* (Wellington, 2007).

Hawke, G.R., *The Making of New Zealand* (Cambridge, 1985).

Hearn, Terry, 'Scots Miners on the Goldfields, 1861–1870', in Tom Brooking & Jennie Coleman, eds, *The Heather and the Fern* (Otago, 2003).

Herman, Arthur, *The Scottish Enlightenment: The Scots Invention of the Modern World* (London, 2001).

Hodgson, T., *The Heart of Colonial Auckland* (Auckland, 1992).

Hunter, E.O., *'Productivity of Distribution'*, Background Paper 15, Industrial Development Conference (June 1960).

Ilott, Jack, *Creating Customers: The Story of Advertising New Zealand: 1892–1982* (1985).

Jones, Geoffrey, *Merchants to Multinationals: British Trading Companies in the Nineteenth and Twentieth Centuries* (Oxford, 2002).

Jones, Steve, 'The Establishment and Operation of European Business', in John Deeks & Peter Enderwick, eds, *Business and New Zealand Society* (Auckland, 1994).

Jones, S.R.H., 'Government Policy and Industry Structure in New Zealand', *Australian Economic History Review*, Vol. 39 (1999).

Jourdain, W.R., *History of Land Legislation and Settlement in New Zealand* (Wellington, 1925).

King, Michael, 'Between Two Worlds', in G.W. Rice ed., *The Oxford History of New Zealand* (Auckland, 2000).

— *The Penguin History of New Zealand* (Auckland, 2003).

Leitch, D.B., *Railways of New Zealand* (Newton Abbot, 1972).

Mackenzie, John N., 'A Scottish Empire' in Tom Brooking & Jennie Coleman, eds, *The Heather and the Fern* (Otago, 2003).

McAloon, Jim, *No Idle Rich: The Wealthy in Canterbury & Otago, 1840–1914* (Otago, 2002).

— 'Long, Slow Boom: Manufacturing in New Zealand, 1945–1970', *Australian Economic History Review*, Vol. 46, No. 1 (2006).

McDonald, K.C., *City of Dunedin: A Century of Civic Enterprise* (Dunedin, 1965).

McGraw, John, *Harbour Horror* (Dunedin, 2001).

McKinnon, Malcolm, *Treasury: The New Zealand Treasury 1840–2000* (Auckland, 2003).

McLean, Gavin, *The Southern Octopus: The Rise of a Shipping Empire* (Wellington, 1990).

McLean, G.J., *Spinning Yarns: A Centennial History of Alliance Textiles and its Predecessor* (Dunedin, 1981).

Malthus, Jane, & Brickell, Chris, 'Producing and Consuming Gender: The Case of Clothing' in Barbara Brookes, Annabel Cooper & Robin Law, eds, *Sites of Gender: Women, Men and Modernity in Southern Dunedin* (Auckland, 2003).

Marwick, W.H., *Economic Developments in Victorian Scotland* (London, 1936).

May, P.R., *The West Coast Gold Rushes* (Christchurch, 1967).

Millen, Julia, *Kirkcaldie & Stains: A Wellington Story* (Wellington, 2000).

Morrell, W.P., *The University of Otago: A Centennial History* (Dunedin, 1969).

Olssen, Erik, *A History of Otago* (Dunedin, 1984).

Parry, Gordon, *National Mortgage and Agency Co. of NZ Ltd: The Story of its First Century* (Dunedin, 1964).

Lloyd Prichard, M.F., *An Economic History of New Zealand to 1939* (Auckland, 1970).

Reed, A.W., *Two Hundred Years in New Zealand* (Wellington, 1979).

Reed, P., 'The Victorian Suburb' in P. Reed, ed., *Glasgow: The Forming of a City* (Edinburgh, 1999).

Simkin, C.G.F., *The Instability of a Dependent Economy: Economic Fluctuations in New Zealand, 1840–1914* (Oxford, 1951).

Simpson, Tony, *The Slump: The Thirties Depression – It's Origins and Aftermath* (Auckland, 1990).

Singleton, John, & Robertson, Paul L., *Economic Relations Between Britain and Australasia, 1945–1970* (Basingstoke, 2002).

Singleton, John, 'Auckland Business: The National and International Context', in Ian Hunter & Diana Morrow, eds, *City of Enterprise: Perspectives on Auckland Business History* (Auckland, 2006).

Stewart, Peter J., *Patterns on the Plain: A Centennial History of Mosgiel Woollens Limited* (Dunedin, 1975).

Stone, R.C.J., *Young Logan Campbell* (Auckland, 1982).

Sumpter, D.J., & Lewis, J.J., *Faith and Toil: The Story of the Tokomairiro* (Christchurch, 1978).

Sutch, W.H.B., *The Quest for Security in New Zealand* (Wellington, 1966).

Ville, S., *The Rural Entrepreneurs: A History of the Stock and Station Agent Industry in Australia and New Zealand* (Cambridge, 2000).

Wright Stephenson, *A Century's Challenge: Wright Stephenson & Co. Ltd, 1861–1961* (Wellington, 1961).

Yonge, J., *New Zealand Railway and Tramway Atlas* (Exeter, 1993).


## B. PUBLISHED ON THE INTERNET

Davis, Richard & Marianne, 'Two Ulster Entrepreneurs in New Zealand and Victoria: The Multifaceted Careers of J.S.M. Thompson and G.V. Shannon'.


## C. UNPUBLISHED THESES AND RESEARCH ESSAYS

Kuzma, J., 'The 1895 Snowstorm' (B.A., University of Otago, 1999).

Robertson, R.T., 'Sweating in Dunedin, 1888–1890' (Postgraduate Diploma in History, University of Otago, 1974).

Timms, Hilda A., 'The Development of the Woollen Industry in Otago to 1900' (University of New Zealand M.A., 1947).

# NOTES

**INTRODUCTION**

1   T.M. Devine, *Scotland's Empire, 1600–1815* (London, 2004), pp. 330–39.
2   John N. Mackenzie, 'A Scottish Empire', in Tom Brooking & Jennie Coleman, eds, *The Heather and the Fern* (Otago, 2003), p. 27.
3   Arthur Herman, *The Scottish Enlightenment: The Scots Invention of the Modern World* (London, 2001), pp. 20–23.
4   R.C.J. Stone, *Young Logan Campbell* (Auckland, 1982), p. 86.
5   *Ibid.*, pp. 108, 132–3.
6   Stone, p. 83.
7   K.C. McDonald, *City of Dunedin* (Dunedin, 1965), pp. 3–4, 17.
8   Jim McAloon, *No Idle Rich: The Wealthy in Canterbury & Otago, 1840–1914* (Otago, 2002).

**1 SCOTTISH FOUNDATIONS**
**CHAPTER 1**

1   Personal Reminiscences of John Ross, MS, AG 512, Box 10, Ross & Glendining Archives, Hocken Library, University of Otago, New Zealand. (Hereafter referred to by deposit number AG 512.)
2   Obituary, Sir John Ross, *Otago Daily Times*, 6.1.1927.
3   Personal Reminiscences of John Ross, AG 512 Box 10.
4   *Ibid.*, AG 512 Box 10.
5   *They Came From Caithness*, pamphlet (Inverness u.d.), pp. 16–17, AG 512 Box 8.
6   Unpublished MS, p. iii, AG 512 Box 10.
7   Personal Reminiscences, AG 512 Box 10.
8   *Ibid.*

9   Jean Dunlop, 'Pultneytown and the Planned Villages of Caithness', in John R. Baldwin, ed., *Caithness: A Cultural Crossroads* (Edinburgh, 1982), pp. 145–7.
10  Unpublished MS, p. iii, AG 512 Box 10.
11  Personal Reminiscences, AG 512 Box 10. W.H. Marwick, *Economic Developments in Victorian Scotland* (London, 1936), pp. 135–6.
12  Dunlop, *op. cit.*, p. 131.
13  Personal Reminiscences, AG 512 Box 10.
14  Erik Olssen, *A History of Otago* (Dunedin, 1984) pp. 44–5.
15  P. Reed, 'The Victorian Suburb' in P. Reed, ed., *Glasgow: The Forming of a City* (Edinburgh, 1999), p. 74.
16  Edinburgh & Leith Post Office Directories, 1850–51, 1854–5, 1859–60.
17  John Ross to Robert Glendining, 19.4.1865, AG 512 1/1.
18  Personal Reminiscences, AG 512 Box 10.
19  *Ibid.*
20  *Ibid.*
21  *Ibid.*
22  *Ibid.*
23  Unpublished MS, AG 512 Box 10.
24  *Ibid.*
25  Personal Reminiscences, AG 512 Box 10.
26  T.M. Hocken, *Contributions to the Early History of New Zealand* (London, 1898), pp. 198–9.

**CHAPTER 2**

1   Hocken, *op. cit.*, p. 175.
2   Olssen, *op. cit.*, pp. 50–51.
3   *Statistics of New Zealand*, 1861, Table 1.

4   Hocken, *op. cit.*, p. 199.
5   Terry Hearn, 'Scots Miners on the Goldfields, 1861–1870', in Brooking & Coleman, *op. cit.*, pp. 72–5.
6   M.F. Lloyd Prichard, *An Economic History of New Zealand to 1939* (Auckland, 1970), pp. 84, 94–5.
7   Charles Croot, *Otago Before Department Store Days* (Otago Settlers Museum, 1995), p. 21.
8   Reminiscences, AG 512 Box 10.
9   Unpublished MS, pp. iv–v, AG 512 Box 10.
10  Unedited version of unpublished MS, p. 7, AG 512 Box 10.
11  Hocken, *op. cit.*, p. 308; Croot, *op. cit.*, p. 24.
12  *The Southern Provinces Almanac, Directory & Year Book for 1864* (Christchurch, 1863), pp. 53–4.
13  *Mackay's Otago Provincial and Goldfields Almanac* (Dunedin, 1866), p. 83.
14  W. Emlyn Jenkins, *John Alexander Ewen: A Memoir* (1902), pp. 30–32.
15  *Mackay's Almanac, op. cit.,* pp. 163–71.
16  Unpublished MS, AG 512 Box 10, p. v.
17  *Otago Witness*, 20.10.1860.
18  Scottish Census Returns, 1841, 1851 & 1861.
19  Unedited MS, AG 512 Box 10, p. 7.
20  Ledger No. 1, 1862–66, AG 512 11/15; *Otago Witness*, 15.10.1864.
21  Unedited MS, p. 7, AG 512 Box 10.
22  Ledger No. 1, 1862–66, AG 512 11/15.
23  *New Zealand Draper & Allied Retailer*, 22.4.1958, p. 19.
24  Unedited MS, AG 512 Box 10, p. 8.
25  D.J. Sumpter & J.J. Lewis, *Faith and Toil: The Story of the Tokomairiro* (Christchurch, 1978), pp. 111–15.
26  *Ibid.*, p. 102.
27  J. Cowan, *Down the Years in the Maniototo* (Christchurch, 1978), p. 37.
28  James Forrest, 'Population and Settlement on the Otago Goldfields', *New Zealand Geographer*, Vol. 17, No. 1 (1961), p. 69.
29  *Statistics of New Zealand* (1865), Table 1.
30  James Forrest, 'Otago during the Goldrushes', in R.F. Watters, *Land &*

31  *Society in New Zealand* (Wellington, 1965), pp. 94–5; *Goldfields Almanac* (1866), pp. 163–71.
31  *Otago Witness*, 5.3.1864, p. 12; 15.10.1864, p. 24.
32  Unedited MS, AG 512 Box 10, p. 8.
33  *Goldfields Almanac* (Dunedin, 1865), unpaginated.
34  Unedited MS, AG 512 Box 10, p. 8.
35  John McGraw, *Harbour Horror* (Dunedin, 2001), pp. 19–48; *Otago Daily Times*, 6.7.1863, Hocken, *op. cit.*, p. 309.
36  J. Ross to T. Geard, 16.9.1865, AG 512 1/1; Unedited MS, AG 512 Box 10, p. 8.
37  P.R. May, *The West Coast Gold Rushes* (Christchurch, 1967), p. 464.
38  *Otago Witness*, 4.6.1864, p. 24.
39  Alfred Eccles, 'The First New Zealand Exhibition and Dunedin in 1865', *Otago Witness*, reprint 17.10.1905.
40  *Ibid.*, pp. 5–15; *Official Catalogue of the New Zealand Exhibition 1865* (Dunedin, 1865).
41  J. Ross to R. Glendining, 27.3.1865, AG 512 1/1.
42  *Ibid.*
43  *Ibid.*
44  *Ibid.*
45  *Ibid.*
46  J. Ross to R. Glendining, 19.4.1865, AG 512 1/1.
47  *Ibid.*
48  Hocken, *op. cit.*, p. 311.
49  J. Ross to R. Glendining, 19.4.1865, AG 512 1/1.
50  *Ibid.*
51  J. Ross to R. Glendining, 8.5.1865, AG 512 1/1.
52  J. Ross to R. Glendining, 19.5.1865, AG 512 1/1.
53  J. Ross to R. Glendining, 27.3.1865, AG 512 1/1.
54  J. Ross to James Arthur, 12.6.1865, AG 512 1/1.
55  J. Ross to Miss Geard, 7.7.1865, AG 512 1/1.
56  J. Ross to 'Charles', 19.7.1865, AG 512 1/1.
57  J. Ross to T. Geard, 16.9.1865, AG 512 1/1.
58  J. Ross to M. Ross, 16.12.1865, AG 512 1/1.

59 J. Ross to T. Geard, 17.3.1866, AG 512 1/1.
60 *Ibid.*
61 *Ibid.*
62 Title Abstract, 28, Stafford St., 4.9.1866, AG 512 Box 10.
63 J. Ross to T. Geard, 5.11.1866, AG 512 1/1.

CHAPTER 3
1 Unedited MS, AG 512 Box 10, p. 9.
2 J. Ross to T. Geard, 5.11.1866, AG 512 1/1.
3 J. Ross to T. Geard, 5.11.1866, 8.6.1867, AG 512 1/1.
4 J. Ross to T. Geard, 5.11.1866, AG 5122 1/1.
5 Ledger No. 1, AG 512 11/15, AG 512 Box 10.
6 J.S. Ross, speech in 1941, Miscellaneous Papers, AG 512 Box 8.
7 J. Ross to T. Geard, 5.11.1866, AG 512 1/1.
8 J. Ross to Miss Reid, 15.12.1866, AG 512 1/1.
9 James Belich, *The New Zealand Wars* (Auckland, 1988), p. 206.
10 C.G.F. Simkin, *The Instability of a Dependent Economy: Economic Fluctuations in New Zealand, 1840– 1914* (Oxford, 1951), pp. 141–3.
11 J. Ross to T. Geard, 5.11.1866, AG 512 1/1; Raewyn Dalziel, *Julius Vogel: Business Politician* (Auckland, 1986), chapter V.
12 Simkin, *op. cit.*, p. 142.
13 J. Ross to T. Geard, 19.7.1867, AG 512 1/1.
14 J. Ross to T. Geard, 6.8.1867, AG 512 1/1.
15 J. Ross to T. Geard, 19.7.1867, AG 512 1/1.
16 J. Ross to T. Geard, 6.8.1867, AG 512 1/1.
17 Partnership agreement 27.8.1867, back-dated to 23.7.1867, AG 512 Box 10.
18 *Ibid.*
19 Richard & Marianne Davis, 'Two Ulster Entrepreneurs in New Zealand and Victoria: The Multifaceted Careers of J.S.M. Thompson and G.V. Shannon'. (Unpublished MS – subsequently published on the Internet). Chapter 2 provides an

excellent survey of the growth of the early soft goods trade on the West Coast.
20 J. Ross to T. Geard, 6.8.1867, AG 512 1/1.
21 J. Ross to Henry Geard, London, 29.2.1868, AG 512 1/2.
22 A.W. Reed, *Two Hundred Years in New Zealand* (Wellington, 1979), p. 136.
23 J. Ross to James Smith, Dunedin, 3.3.1868, AG 512 1/2.
24 J. Ross to R. Glendining, 3.3.1868, AG 512 1/2
25 J. Ross to J. Mitchell, 2.3.1868, AG 512 1/2.
26 J. Ross to R. Glendining, 3.3.1868, AG 512 1/2.
27 J. Ross to the Cassels household, Dunedin, 4.3.1868, AG 512 1/2.
28 J. Ross to R. Glendining, 6.3.1868; J. Ross to Rev. John Ross, 7.3.1868, AG 512 1/2.
29 J. Ross to R.L. Begg, Dunedin, 14.3.1868, AG 512 1/2.
30 J. Ross to Mr & Mrs J. Ross, Westerdale, 28.3.1868, AG 512 1/2
31 J. Ross to R. Glendining, 1.4.1868, AG 512 1/2.
32 *Ibid.*
33 J. Ross to R. Glendining, 24.4.1868, AG 512 1/3.
34 J. Ross to T. Harrison, 16.5.1868, AG 512 1/3.
35 J. Ross to R. Glendining, 24.4.1868, AG 512 1/3.
36 *Ibid.*
37 J. Ross to R. Glendining, 21.5.1868, AG 512 1/3.
38 J. Ross to T. Harrison, 1.6.1868, AG 512 1/3.
39 J. Ross to R. Glendining, 24.4.1868, AG 512 1/3.
40 J. Ross to R. Glendining, 21.5.1868, AG 512 1/3.
41 J. Ross to T. Harrison, 1.6.1868, AG 512 1/3.
42 J. Ross to R. Glendining, 21.5.1868, AG 512 1/3.
43 J. Ross to R. Glendining, 16.6.1868, AG 512 1/4.
44 J. Ross to Mrs R. Glendining, 27.6.1868, AG 512 1/4.
45 J. Ross to R. Glendining, 16.7.1868, AG 512 1/4.

46  J. Ross to R. Glendining, 1.7.1868, AG 512 1/4.

47  J. Ross to J. Mitchell, 2.3.1868, AG 512 1/2.

48  J. Ross to H. Geard, 17.7.1868, AG 512 1/4.

49  Simkin, *op. cit.*, pp. 142–3.

50  Small Memorandum Book, AG 512 Box 10.

51  T. Harrison to Ross & Glendining, 21.5.1870, AG 512 5/1.

52  Ledger, 22.7.1879, AG 512 12/18.

53  Telegram, George Hercus to Mr & Mrs J. Ross, 1.7.1870, AG 512 5/1; Unedited MS, AG 512 Box 10, p. 11.

54  Receipts, AG 512 5/1.

55  J.H. Barr to Ross & Glendining, 28.6.1870, AG 512 5/1.

56  R. Glendining to J. Ross, 18.1.1872, 17.2.1872, 18.3.1872, AG 512 5/5.

57  Half-yearly balances 1871, AG 512 15/18.

58  R. Glendining to J. Ross, 15.4.1872, AG 512 5/5.

59  Details of the West Coast trade is largely drawn from Davis & Davis, *op. cit.*, chapter 2.

60  Glendining to Ross, 9.5.1872, AG 512 5/5.

61  Half-yearly balances, 1871 & 1872, AG 512 15/18.

62  *Ibid.*

63  Circular, 8.3.1871, AG 512 Box 8.

64  Small Memorandum Book, AG 512 Box 10.

65  Half-yearly balances, 1872, AG 512 15/18.

**CHAPTER 4**

1  Lloyd Prichard, *op. cit.*, pp. 125–8; Dalziel, pp. 106–8.

2  Lloyd Prichard, *op. cit.*, p. 132.

3  Michael King, 'Between Two Worlds', in G.W. Rice, ed., *The Oxford History of New Zealand* (Auckland, 2000), pp. 285–6.

4  Estimated from David Greasley & Les Oxley, 'Measuring New Zealand's GDP, 1865–1933: A Cointegration-Based Approach', *Review of Income & Wealth,* Series 46, Number 3, September 2000, Appendix, Table 1A.

5  Hercus to Ross, March 1874, AG 512 15/1.

6  D.B. Leitch, *Railways of New Zealand,* (Newton Abbot, 1972), p. 34.

7  J.B. Condliffe, *New Zealand in the Making* (London, 1936), p. 38.

8  Rollo Arnold, *The Farthest Promised Land* (Wellington, 1981), pp. 2–17.

9  Glendining to Ross, 31.7.1874, AG 512 5/7.

10  Notebook, AG 512 Box 10; Half-yearly balances, AG 512 15/1.

11  Glendining to Ross, 15.1.1873, AG 512 5/6.

12  Glendining to Ross, 9.5.1872, AG 512 5/5.

13  Hercus to Ross, 20.2.1873, AG 512 15/1; Hercus to Ross 1.10.1873, AG 512 1/5.

14  Glendining to Ross, 11.4.1873, AG 512 5/7.

15  Half-yearly balances, 1872–78, AG 512 15/1.

16  Glendining to Ross, 17.2.1872, AG 512 5/5.

17  Glendining to Ross, 24.9.1872, AG 512 5/5.

18  Glendining to Ross, 14.12.1872, AG 512 5/5.

19  Freight Association Circular, 2.9.1872, AG 512 Box 8.

20  Alan Bott, *The Sailing Ships of the New Zealand Shipping Company* (London, 1972), pp. 12–13.

21  Hercus to Ross, 24.12.1873, AG 512 1/5.

22  Glendining to Ross, 20.11.1872, AG 512 5/5.

23  Glendining to Ross, 1.6.1874, 31.7.1874, AG 512 5/7.

24  Draperies imported into Otago, AG 512 Box 8.

25  Glendining to Ross, 27.10.1874, AG 512 5/7.

26  Glendining to Ross, 15.4.1872, AG 512 5/5.

27  Glendining to Ross, 5.5.1872, 5.6.1872, AG 512 5/5.

28  Glendining to Ross, 22.10.1872, AG 512 5/5.

29  Glendining to Ross, 14.12.1872, AG 512 5/5.

30  Glendining to Ross,14.12.1872, 27.12.1872, AG 512 5/5.

31  Glendining to Ross, 15.1.1873, AG 512 5/6.

32  Glendining to Ross, 24.1.1873, AG 512 5/6.

33  Glendining to Ross, 24.1.1873, 12.2.1873, 21.2.1873, AG 512 5/6.

34  Glendining to Ross, 12.3.1873, AG 512 5/6.

35  Gavin McLean, *The Southern Octopus: The Rise of a Shipping Empire* (Wellington, 1990), p. 69.

36  Hercus to Glendining, 31.5.1873, AG 512 1/5.

37  Glendining to Ross, 1.6.1873, AG 512 5/6.

38  Ross & Glendining to William Watson & Sons, 6.6.1873, AG 512 1/5.

39  Hercus to Ross, 7.6.1873, AG 512 1/5.

40  Glendining to Ross, 30.10.1872, AG 512 5/5.

41  Hercus to Ross, 11.6.1873, AG 512 1/5.

42  Glendining to Ross, 5.7.1872, AG 512 5/5.

43  Hercus to Ross, 11.6.1873, AG 512 1/5.

44  Ross & Glendining to William Watson & Sons, 30.7.1873, AG 512 1/5.

45  Ross & Glendining to William Watson & Sons, 31.6.1873; 1.8.1873, AG 512 1/5.

46  Glendining to Ross, 15.1.1873, AG 512 5/6.

47  Glendining to Ross, 12.3.1873, AG 512 5/6.

48  Half-yearly balances, January 1873, AG 512 15/1.

49  Leitch, *op. cit.*, pp. 45–6; Len Anderson, *Throughout the East Coast. The Story of Williams & Kettle* (Hastings, 1974), pp. 21–4.

50  Glendining to Ross, 24.9.1872, AG 512 5/5; Hercus to Messrs Blyth & Co., 21.3.1879, AG 512 1/6.

51  Glendining to Ross, 22.2.1873, Half-yearly balances, AG 512 15/1.

52  Hercus to Glendining, 8.7.1873, AG 512 5/1; Alan Bott, *op. cit.*, pp. 11–21.

53  Hercus to Glendining, 8.7.1873, AG 512 1/5.

54  Hercus to Ross, 5.8.1873, AG 512 1/5.

55  Glendining to Ross, 15.1.1873, AG 512 5/6.

56  Glendining to Ross, 7.6.1872, 22.1.0.1872, AG 512 5/5.

57  Half-yearly balances, July 1874, AG 512 15/1.

58  Glendining to Ross, 28.8.1874, AG 512 5/7.

59  Hercus to Ross, 30.1.1875, 10.8.1875, AG 512 1/5.

60  Glendining to Ross, 10.8.1875, AG 512 1/5; Bonuses paid, August 1877, AG 512 1/6.

61  Glendining to Ross, 22.1.1872, AG 512 5/5.

62  Glendining to Ross, 12.3.1873, AG 512 5/6.

63  Hercus to Ross, 14.5.1873, AG 512 1/5.

64  Hercus to Ross, 24.12.1873, AG 512 1/5.

65  Arnold, *op. cit.*, pp. 49–59.

66  Glendining to Ross, 17.2.1874, AG 512 5/7; Bott, *op. cit.*, p. 53.

67  Glendining to Ross, 10.3.1874, 7.4.1874 AG 512 5/7.

68  Glendining to Ross, 11.4.1874, 31.7.1874, AG 512 5/7.

69  Half-yearly balances, AG 512 15/1.

70  Half-yearly balances, AG 512 15/1.

71  Hercus to Ross, 5.8.1873. AG 512 1/5; Glendining to Ross, 28.8.1874, AG 512 5/7.

72  Julia Millen, *Kirkcaldie & Stains: A Wellington Story* (Wellington, 2000), p. 18.

73  Hercus to Ross, 1.10.1873, 24.12.187, AG 512 1/5.

74  Hercus to Ross, 1.10.1873, 10.2.1874, AG 512 1/5.

75  Glendining to Ross, 11.4.1874, 8.8.1874, AG 512 5/7.

76  Glendining to Ross, 9.5.1874, 29.9.1874, AG 512 5/7.

77  Glendining to Ross, 29.9.1874, AG 512 5/7.

78  Glendining to Ross, 24.11.1874, AG 512 5/7.

79  Glendining to Ross, 11.4.1874, AG 512 5/7.

80  Glendining to Ross, 24.11.1875; 25.11.1875, AG 512 5/7.

81  Glendining to Ross, 23.12.1874, AG 512 5/7.

82  Memorandum, balance papers, July 1875, AG 512 15/1.

83  Glendining to Ross, 16.101875, AG 512 1/5.

84 Hercus to J.G. Cowan, 8.12.1875, AG 512 1/5.

85 Hercus to Cowan, 24.12.1875, 24.12.1875, AG 512 1/5.

86 Memorandum, balance papers, 1877; Accounts 1878, Blyth & Co., Napier; Accounts 1879, Blyth & Co., Napier, Ross & Glendining to Blyth & Co., 21.3.1879, AG 512 1/6.

87 Bank of New South Wales, Dunedin to Ross & Glendining, 15.2.1876, AG 512 5/1.

88 Simkin, *op. cit.*, p. 159.

89 Draperies imported into Otago, AG 512 Box 8.

90 Half-yearly balances, AG 512 15/1, 15/18.

91 Memorandum, 1875, Half-yearly balances, AG 512 15/1; Glendining to Ross, 9.5.1874, AG 512 5/7; 1878 Abstract Balance Sheet, Half-yearly balances, AG 512 15/1.

92 Glendining to Ross, 9.5.1874, AG 512 5/7; Half-yearly balances, AG 512 15/1.

93 Memorandum, Half-yearly balances, AG 512 15/1.

94 Glendining to Ross, 14.12.1872, AG 512 5/5; Glendining to Ross, 17.3.1874, AG 512 5/7.

95 Half-yearly balances, AG 512 15/1.

## CHAPTER 5

1 Joint Committee on Colonial Industries, *Appendices to the Journal of the House of Representatives* (hereafter *AJHR*), Vol. 4, 1870.

2 Peter J. Stewart, *Patterns on the Plain: A Centennial History of Mosgiel Woollens Limited* (Dunedin, 1975), pp. 25–30.

3 Glendining to Ross, 12.12.1872, AG 512 5/5.

4 General Ledger No. 1, 1877/87, AG 512 11/1.

5 Hercus to Glendining, 31.5.1873, AG 512 1/5.

6 Memorandum, 5.3.1874, AG 512 1/5.

7 Half-yearly balances, July 1875, AG 512 15/1.

8 Hercus to Ross, 29.7.1878, AG 512 1/6.

9 Hercus to Ross, 18.7.1878, AG 512 1/6.

10 Memorandum, April 1888, AG 512 1/10.

11 Hercus to Ross, 18.7.1878, 29.7.1878, AG 512 1/6.

12 Description, Roslyn Woollen Mills, 1879, AG 512 1/6.

13 Memorandum, u.d. (probably July 1878), AG 512 1/6.

14 Hercus to Ross, 18.1.1878, AG 512 1/6.

15 Balance commentary, July 1878, Half-yearly balances, AG 512 15/1; Hercus to Glendining, 12.7.1878, AG 512 1/6.

16 Hercus to Ross, 18.7.1878, AG 512 1/6.

17 Interest, Discount and Exchange Account, July 1879, Half-yearly balances, AG 512 15/2.

18 Ross & Glendining to Mason, Wales & Stevenson, 10.1.1879, AG 512 1/6.

19 Description, Roslyn Woollen Mills, 1879, AG 512 1/6.

20 *Ibid.*

21 Analysis, Roslyn Woollen Mill Account, August 1879, AG 512 1/6.

22 Roslyn Woollen Mills Manufacturing Accounts, 1879/80, Half-yearly balances, AG 512 15/2.

23 Simkin, *op. cit.*, p. 161.

24 Hercus to Ross, 16.10.1879, AG 512 1/6.

25 Hercus to Ross, July 1880, AG 512 1/7.

26 Hercus to Ross, 12.8.1881, AG 512 1/7.

27 Ross & Glendining to Collector of Customs, Dunedin, 1.6.1886, AG 512 1/8.

28 Memorandum, February 1886, AG 512 1/9.

29 Memorandum, Febuary 1886, AG 512 1/9.

30 'Tribute to Sir John Ross', *Otago Witness*, 19.4.1927, p. 5.

31 Ross & Glendining to Paterson, Hokitika, 22.7.1882, AG 512 1/7.

32 *Ibid.*

33 Employment of Females and Others in Workrooms and Factories, Statutes of New Zealand, No. 23, 45, Victoria, 1881.

34 Instructions to Nightwatchman, 29.4.1884, AG 512 1/8.

35   Roslyn Mills, Profit and Loss Account
     and Abstract Balance Sheet, December
     1883, AG 512 15/3.
36   Half-yearly balances, AG 512 15/3,
     15/4; Memorandum, June 1886, AG
     512 1/9; Memorandum, April 1888,
     AG 512 1/10.
37   Roslyn Mills Machinery Account,
     1884; Profit and Loss Account 1884,
     AG 512 15/3.
38   Lloyd Prichard, *op. cit.*, pp. 157–8.
39   Roslyn Mills Profit and Loss Account
     and Abstract Balance Sheet, 1884, AG
     512 15/3.
40   Lloyd Prichard, *op. cit.*, p. 161.
41   Simkin, *op. cit.*, pp. 164–5.
42   Hercus to Ross, 29.1.1886, AG 512
     1/9.
43   Roslyn Mills Balance Sheet and Profit
     and Loss Account, November 1885;
     Manufacturing Account 1885, AG 512
     15/3.
44   Hercus to Ross, 19.8.1881, AG 512
     1/7.
45   Memorandum, February 1886, AG
     512 1/9; Memorandum, April 1888,
     AG 512 1/10.
46   Glendining to Ewen, 14.9.1886, AG
     512 1/9.
47   Memorandum, February 1886, AG
     512 1/9.
48   Memorandum, April 1888, AG 512
     1/10.
49   Roslyn Mill Abstract Balance Sheets
     1884–1886, AG 512 15/3.
50   Employment Returns, June 1886, AG
     512 1/9.
51   Glendining to Ross, 21.4.1887,
     16.6.1887, AG 512 5/8.
52   Glendining to Ross, 5.3.1887,
     8.9.1887, AG 512 5/8.
53   Glendining to Ross, 21.4.1887,
     3.5.1887, 19.5.1887, 16.6.1887, AG
     512 5/8.
54   Glendining to Ross, 3.5.1887, AG 512
     5/8.
55   Glendining to Ross, 6.10.1887, AG
     512 5/8.
56   Glendining to Ross, 20.9.1887, AG
     512 5/8.
57   Roslyn Mills Abstract Balance
     Sheet, 1886, AG 512 15/3: Hilda A.
     Timms, 'The Development of the
     Woollen Industry in Otago to 1900',
     (University of New Zealand M.A.,
     1947, unpublished) p. 98.
58   Glendining to Ross, 16.6.1887, AG
     512 5/8.
59   Glendining to Ross, 29.6.1887, AG
     512 5/8.
60   Glendining to Ross, 20.9.1887, AG
     512 5/8.
61   Glendining to Ross, 8.9.1887, AG 512
     5/8.
62   Roslyn Mills, Profit and Loss
     Accounts, Abstract Balance Sheets,
     and Manufacturing Accounts, 1887 &
     1888. AG 512 15/4.
63   Glendining to Ross, 1.12.1887, AG
     512 5/8.
64   Glendining to Ross, 26.1.1888, AG
     512 5/9.
65   Glendining to Ross, 19.5.1887, AG
     512 5/8.
66   Glendining to Ross, 16.6.1887,
     6.10.1887, AG 512 5/8.
67   Memorandum, April 1888, AG 512
     1/10.
68   Hercus to Glendining, 14.6.188, AG
     512 1/10.
69   Gardner, *op. cit.*, p. 83.
70   Hercus to Ross, 12.7.1888, AG 512
     1/10.
71   Hercus to Glendining, 8.11.1888, AG
     512 1/10.
72   *Ibid.*

**CHAPTER 6**
1   David Greasley & Les Oxley,
    'Globalization and real wages in New
    Zealand, 1873–1913', *Explorations in
    Economic History*, Vol. 41.1, (January
    2004), Appendix A; Estimated
    from Greasley & Oxley, 'Measuring
    New Zealand's GDP 1865–1933:
    A Cointegration-Based Approach',
    *Review of Income & Wealth*, Series 46,
    No. 3, (September 2000), Appendix,
    Table 1A; G.R. Hawke, *The Making of
    New Zealand* (Cambridge, 1985), p.
    55.
2   Steve Jones, 'The Establishment and
    Operation of European Business', in
    John Deeks and Peter Enderwick,
    eds, *Business and New Zealand Society*
    (Auckland, 1994), pp. 48–51.
3   Hercus to Ross, 16.10.1879, AG 512
    1/6.

4    Ross & Glendining to Bank of New South Wales, Dunedin, 23.9.1879, AG 5112 1/6.

5    Hercus to Ross, July balance 1880, AG 512 1/7.

6    Glendining to Ross, 12.2.1873, AG 512 5/6.

7    Hercus to Ross, 26.8.1880, 19.8.1881, AG 512 1/7.

8    Hercus to Ross, 12.8.1881, AG 512 1/7.

9    Davis and Davis, *op. cit.*, chapter 4, pp. 7–9.

10   Memorandum for Henderson, 3.8.1881, AG 512/ 1/7.

11   Hercus to Skeoch, 20.1.1881, AG 512 1/7. Travelling returns, Half-yearly balances, 1881–83, AG 512 15/2.

12   Lloyd Prichard, *op. cit.*, p. 161.

13   Half-yearly balances, AG 512 15/2, 15/3.

14   Stone, *op. cit.*, p. 66.

15   Memorandum, estate of John Hood, Oamaru, April 1883, AG 512 1/7.

16   Ross & Glendining to Thomson & Beattie, 21.9.1883, AG 512 1/8.

17   Memorandum to Mr Ewen, 16.9.1886, AG 512 1/9.

18   Ross & Glendining to Thomson & Beattie, 17.8.1883, 21.9.1883, AG 512 1/8.

19   Ross & Glendining to Collector of Customs, Dunedin, 14.6.1885, AG 512 1/8; Memorandum for Mr Ewen, 14.9.1886, AG 512 1/9.

20   Davis and Davis, *op. cit.*, chapter 6, p. 35.

21   Hercus to Kelly, 25.6.1883, 30.6.1883, AG 512 1/8; Hercus to Ross, 1.2.1884, AG 512 1/8.

22   Hercus to Kelly, 4.2.1882, AG 512 1/7.

23   Hercus to Kelly, 6.12.1883, AG 512 1/8.

24   Hercus to Ross, 14.9.1883, AG 512 1/8.

25   Hercus to Henderson, 5.8.1885, AG 512 1/8.

26   Hercus to Kelly, 10.9.1885, AG 512 1/8.

27   Ross & Glendining to Peters, 1.2.1886, AG 512 1/9; Half-yearly balances, 1886, AG 512 15/3.

28   Hercus to Ross, 29.1.1886, AG 512 1/9.

29   Memorandum for Mr Ewen, 14.9.1886, AG 512 1/9.

30   *Ibid.*

31   Hercus to Ross, 5.11.1886, AG 512 1/9.

32   *Ibid.*

33   Hercus to Ross, 16.11.1886, AG 512 1/9.

34   Hercus to Ross, 5.11.1886, AG 512 1/9

35   *Ibid.*

36   Hercus to Ross, 22.2.1887, AG 512 1/9.

37   Glendining to Ross, 5.3.1887, AG 512 5/8.

38   Glendining to Ross, 21.4.1887, AG 512 5/8.

39   *Ibid.*

40   Hercus to Peters, 21.4.1887; Hercus to Simpson, 30.4.1887, AG 512 1/9.

41   Half-yearly balances, AG 512 15/3.

42   Hercus to Sharples, 3.5.1887, AG 512 1/9.

43   Hercus to Ross, 18.10.1887, AG 512 1/9.

44   Hercus to Ross, 6.9.1888, AG 512 1/10.

45   Hercus to Peters, 17.12.1888, AG 512 1/10.

46   Roslyn Mills advertising copy, February 1886, AG 512 1/9.

47   Hercus to Aitken, 3.8.1886, AG 512 1/9.

48   Hercus to Ross, 10.11.1886, 29.9.1887; AG 512 1/9; Hercus to Aitken, 3.5.1887, 14.10.1887, AG 512 1/9; Hercus to Aitken, 31.5.1888, AG 512 1/10.

49   Hercus to Aitken, 8.8.1888, AG 512 1/10.

50   Hercus to Glendining, 23.11.1888, AG 512 1/10; Hercus to Aitken, 3.1.1889, AG 512 1/10; Hercus to Ross, 4.3.1889, AG 512 1/10.

51   Glendining to Ross, 8.9.1887, AG 512 5/8.

52   Davis and Davis, *op. cit.*, chapter 6, p. 35.

53   Glendining to Ross, 20.9.1887, AG 512 5/8.

54   Glendining to Ross, 6.10.1887, AG 512 5/8.

55   Davis and Davis, *op. cit.*, chapter 6, p. 39.

56 Hercus to Ross, 12.7.1888, AG 512 1/10. Much of this account of Thompson, Shannon & Co's demise is drawn from Davis and Davis, *op. cit.*, chapter 6.

57 Glendining to Ross, 26.1.1888, AG 512 5/9; Davis and Davis, *op. cit.*, chapter 6, p. 45.

58 Hercus to Ross, 12.7.1888, 9.8.1888, AG 512 1/10.

59 Hercus to Ross, 6.9.1888, AG 512 1/10.

60 List of Soft Goods Houses in N.Z. Creditors in Bankrupt Estates, 8.8.1888, AG 512 1/10.

61 Hercus to Glendining, 14.1.1888, AG 512 1/10.

62 Hercus to Ross, 8.11.1889, AG 512 1/10.

63 Hercus to Ross, 8.1.1889, AG 512 1/10.

64 Hercus to Ross, 9.8.1888, AG 512 1/10.

65 Hercus to Ross, 6.9.1888, AG 512 1/10.

66 Hercus to Ross, 21.2.1889, AG 512 1/10.

67 Hercus to Ross, 9.8.1888, AG 512 1/10.

68 Hercus to Ross, 6.9.1888, 1.11.1888; Hercus to Glendining, 8.11.1888, AG 512 1/10.

69 Hercus to Ross, 4.10.1888, AG 512 1/10.

70 Hercus to Glendining, 8.11.1888, AG 512 1/10.

71 Hercus to Ross, 4.3.1889, AG 512 1/10.

72 *Ibid.*

73 Hercus to Peters, 17.9.1888, AG 512 1/10.

74 Hercus to Ross, 21.2.1889, AG 512 1/10.

75 *Ibid.*

76 Hercus to Ross, 13.6.1889, AG 512 1/10.

77 N.M. Chappell, *New Zealand Banker's Hundred: A History of the Bank of New Zealand, 1861–1961* (Wellington, 1961), pp. 116–7.

78 Hercus to Glendining, 8.11.1888, AG 512 5/10.

79 Olssen, *op. cit.*, p. 102; Lloyd Prichard, *op. cit.*, p. 161.

80 Hercus to Ross, 13.6.1889, AG 512 1/10.

81 Hercus to Ross, 20.8.1889, AG 512 1/11.

82 This account is largely drawn from R.T. Robertson, 'Sweating in Dunedin, 1888–1890' (Unpublished dissertation, Department of History, University of Otago, 1974).

83 Hercus to Ross, 13.6.1888, AG 512 1/10.

84 Robertson, *op. cit.*, p. 32.

85 Hercus to Ross, 13.6.1888, AG 512 1/10.

86 Report of Sweating Commission, *AJHR* 1890, Vol. III, H5, pp. 1–99.

87 Ross & Glendining to Millar, 2.1.1889, 5.11.1889, AG 512 1/11.

88 Hercus to Ross, 20.2.1890, AG 512 1/11.

89 Hercus to Ross, 26.12.1889, AG 512 1/11.

90 Half-yearly balances, AG 512 15/3, 15/4.

**CHAPTER 7**

1 Simkin, *op. cit.*, pp. 158–61.

2 McAloon, *op. cit.*, pp. 41–3.

3 *Ibid.*, pp. 44–5.

4 Half-yearly balances, 15.7.1878, AG 512 15/1.

5 Mrs Janet Thomson, Elliott family history, unpublished MS.

6 Ross to Johnstone, 6.5.1899, AG 512 4/13.

7 *AJHR*, 1877 C1.

8 Ross & Glendining to Elliott, 16.2.1882, AG 512 1/7.

9 Gordon Parry, *National Mortgage and Agency Co. of NZ Ltd: The story of its First Century* (Dunedin, 1964), p. 49–50.

10 Otago Runs Register, Archives New Zealand, Dunedin, Acc. D84 776b.

11 Ross & Glendining to Elliott, 29.2.1882, AG 512 1/7.

12 Reid and Elliott to Ross & Glendining, 2.4.1882, AG 512 1/7.

13 Reid and Elliott to Ross & Glendining, 6.4.1882, AG 512 1/7.

14 *Ibid.*

15 Cowan, *op. cit.*, pp. 31, 66–71.

16 Ross & Glendining to J.P. Maitland, Commissioner for Crown Lands for Otago, 10.5.1882, AG 512 1/7.

17  Memorandum of Agreement, 12.5.1882, AG 512 1/7.
18  Ross & Glendining to Elliott, 20.4.1882, AG 512 1/7.
19  Ross & Glendining to Elliott, 4.5.1882, AG 512 1/7.
20  Lauder Balance Sheet, 29.4.1884, Half-yearly balances, AG 512 15/3.
21  Ross & Glendining to Elliott, 22.12.1882, AG 512 1/7.
22  Ross & Glendining to Elliott, 25.11.1882, AG 512 1/7; Elliott family history MS.
23  Ross & Glendining to the Manager, *Mt Ida Chronicle*, Naseby, 5.12.1892, AG 512 1/7.
24  Ross & Glendining to Elliott, 4.1.1883, AG 512 1/7.
25  Cash Account, 28.2.1883, AG 512 1/7.
26  Ross & Glendining to Elliott, 18.1.1882, AG 512 1/7.
27  Otago Runs Register, Acc. D84 776B; Ross & Glendining to Keenan & Morgan, April 1883; Ross & Glendining to Elliott 16.8.1883, AG 512 1/8.
28  The Otago Runs Register is not clear as to how 226 was subdivided.
29  Ross & Glendining, 25.1.1883, AG 512 1/7.
30  Lauder Balance Sheet, 29.2.1884, Half-yearly balances, AG 512 15/3.
31  Sheep Account, Half-yearly balances, AG 512 15/3.
32  Ross & Glendining to the Minister of Lands 16.9.1889, AG 512 1/11.
33  Alexander Armour; evidence to Royal Commission on Land Tenure, 1905, *AJHR*, C. 4, p. 184.
34  J.D. Gould, 'Pasture formation and improvement', *Australian Economic History Review*, 16 (1976), pp. 1–22.
35  Robert Elliott; evidence to Royal Commission on Land Tenure, 1905, *AJHR*, 1905, C. p. 203.
36  Hercus to Elliott, 22.5.1884, AG 512 1/8.
37  Half-yearly balances, AG 512 15/3, 15/4.
38  Fencing Act 1881, Statutes of New Zealand, 46 Victoria, No. 28; Fencing Act 1887, Statutes of New Zealand, 56 Victoria, No. 27.
39  Hercus to Elliott, 19.10.1889, AG 512 1/11.
40  Rabbit Nuisance Act, 1881, Statutes of NZ, 45 Victoria, No. 6.
41  *AJHR*, C. 1, p. 4.
42  Glendining to Ross, 3.5.1887, AG 512 5/8.
43  Half-yearly balances, AG 512 15/3, 15/4, 15/5.
44  Wright Stephenson, *A Century's Challenge: Wright Stephenson & Co. Ltd, 1861–1961* (Wellington, 1961), p. 35.
45  Glendining to Ross, 3.4.1887, 21.4.1887, AG 512 15/8.
46  Glendining to Ross, 21.4.1887, AG 512 5/8.
47  Glendining to Ross, 25.5.1888, AG 512 5/9.
48  Glendining to Ross, 21.4.1887, AG 512 5/8.
49  Half-yearly balances, AG 512 15/3, 15/4.
50  Ross & Glendining to J.P. Maitland, 16.10.1884, AG 512 1/8.
51  Otago Runs Register, Acc. D84 776B; Ross & Glendining to Elliott, 27.3.1886, AG 512 1/9.
52  Ross & Glendining to F.G. Pogson, 10.8.1891, AG 512 1/12.
53  Ross & Glendining to Pogson, 4.2.1886, AG 512 1/9.
54  Ross & Glendining to Pogson, 18.3.1886, AG 512 1/9.
55  Ross & Glendining, 1.4.1886, AG 512 1/9.
56  Half-yearly balances, AG 512 15/4.
57  Ross & Glendining to Elliott, 4.6.1891, AG 512 15/11.
58  Sheep Account, Half-yearly balances, AG 512 15/3.
59  Glendining to Ross, 3.11.1887, AG 512 8/8.
60  Sheep Account, Half-yearly balances, AG 512 15/3.
61  Glendining to Ross, 21.4.1887, AG 512 8/8.
62  Statutes of New Zealand, 49 Victoria, No. 56, Cl. 142.
63  Glendining to Elliott, 16.6.1888, AG 512 1/8.
64  Land Act Amendment Act 1888, Statutes of New Zealand, 52 Victoria, No. 17, Section 9.

65  Hercus to Elliott, 5.9.1889; Copy of Appeal to Minister of Lands, u.d., AG 512 1/11.
66  Ross & Glendining to Minister of Lands, 16.9.1889, AG 512 1/11.
67  Appeal to Minister of Lands, u.d., AG 512 5/11.
68  Copy of Petition, u.d., AG 512 1/11.
69  Ross & Glendining to Minister of Lands, 3.6.1890, AG 512 1/11.
70  Hercus to Elliott, 16.2.1889, AG 512 1/10.
71  *Ibid.*
72  Hercus to Pogson, 1.10.1888, AG 512 1/10.
73  J.A. Johnstone to Ross & Glendining, 2.6.1891, AG 512 1/12.
74  Hercus to Elliott, 4.6.1891, AG 512 1/12.
75  *Ibid.*
76  Memorandum of Agreement, 8.8.1891, AG 512 1/12.
77  Hercus to Ross, 8.9.1891, AG 512 1/12.
78  Tom Brooking, *Lands for the People? The Highland Clearances and the Colonisation of New Zealand* (Dunedin, 1996), p. 102.
79  Hercus to Ross, 11.8.1891, AG 512 1/12.
80  McAloon, *op. cit.*, pp. 46–7.
81  Glendining to Ross, 16.6.1887, AG 512 5/8.

**CHAPTER 8**
1  Greasley & Oxley, (2000), *op. cit.*, Table 1A.
2  *Ibid.*
3  *Ibid.*
4  Hercus to Jones, 5.4.1890, AG 512 1/11.
5  Half-yearly balances, 1891, AG 512 15/4.
6  Hercus to Ross & Glendining, Wellington, 16.3.1891, AG 512 1/12.
7  Hercus to Ross, 17.4.1890, AG 512 1/11.
8  Hercus to Ross, 20.8.1889, AG 512 1/11.
9  Half-yearly balances, AG 512 15/4.
10  Hercus to Ross, 24.2.1891, AG 512 1/12.
11  Hercus to Ross, 17.9.1891, AG 512 1/11.

12  Hercus to Ross, 17.9.1891, AG 512 1/12.
13  Hercus to Messrs Sclanders & Co., Nelson, 30.1.1891, AG 512 1/12.
14  Hercus to Ross, 20.8.1889, AG 512 1/11.
15  Hercus to Ross, 26.2.1892, AG 512 1/13.
16  Hercus to Ross, 17.2.1892, AG 512 1/13.
17  Hercus to Ross, 17.8.1892, AG 512 1/13.
18  Hercus to Ross, 25.5.1891, AG 512 1/12.
19  Hercus to Glendining, 25.6.1891, AG 512 1/13.
20  Hercus to Ross, 24.1.1892, AG 512 1/13.
21  Hercus to Ross, 28.5.1891, AG 512 1/12.
22  Hercus to Ross, 15.10.1891, 24.1.1892, AG 512 1/13.
23  *Ibid.*
24  Hercus to Ross, 26.12.1889, AG 512 1/11.
25  Hercus to Ross, 16.6.1891, AG 512 1/12.
26  Half-yearly balances, AG 512 15/4.
27  *The Cyclopedia of New Zealand,* Vol. 4, Otago & Southland (Christchurch 1905), p. 337.
28  Half-yearly balances, AG 512 15/5.
29  Hercus to Jones, 13.11.1894, AG 512 1/15.
30  Hercus to J.S. Ross, 15.3.1907, AG 512 2/5.
31  Half-yearly balances, AG 512 15/4, 15/5.
32  Hercus to Ross, 23.2.1892, 17.8.1892, AG 512 1/13.
33  Hercus to Ross, 5.12.1893, AG 512 1/14.
34  Ross & Glendining to Hunt, 20.3.1894, AG 512 1/15.
35  Hercus to Ross, 5.9.1893, AG 512 1/14.
36  Hercus to Ross, 17.8.1892, AG 512 1/13.
37  Hercus to Ross, 23.1.1894, AG 512 1/15.
38  *Wise's New Zealand Post Office Directory, 1894/5* (Auckland), p. 1604.
39  Wilson to Ross & Glendining, 6.4.1894, AG 512 1/15.

40  Hercus to Ross, 16.1.1894, AG 512 1/15.
41  Hercus to Wilson, 25.6.1894, AG 512 1/16.
42  Hercus to Wellington Branch, 19.6.1894, AG 512 1/16.
43  Hercus to Wilson, 31.8.1895, AG 512 1/17.
44  Hercus to Ross, 27.2.1889, AG 512 1/10.
45  Hercus to Ross, 20.8.1889, AG 512 1/11.
46  Hercus to Peters, 9.5.1894, AG 512 1/15.
47  Ross & Glendining to Messrs A. Knight & Co., Auckland, 28.5.1895, AG 512 1/16.
48  Hercus to Ross & Glendining, 30.1.1891, AG 512 1/12.
49  Hercus to Jones, 25.8.1893, AG 512 1/14; Hercus to Henderson, 1.3.1897, AG 512 1/18.
50  Hercus to Ross & Glendining, 30.1.1891; Hercus to Jones, 19.8.1891, 2.9.1891, AG 512 1/12; Hercus to Walter Smith, Wellington, 2.3.1892, AG 512 1/13; Hercus to Christchurch Branch, 22.6.1893, AG 512 1/14.
51  Hercus to Wellington Branch, 7.3.1891, AG 512 1/12.
52  Hercus to Jones, 19.1.1891, AG 512 1/12.
53  Memorandum to Wellington Branch, 26.9.1891, AG 512 1/12.
54  Hercus to Ross, 28.5.1891, AG 512 1/12.
55  Rules for Employees, 18.5.1893, AG 512 1/14.
56  Hercus to Jones, 25.8.1893; Hercus to Angus, 26.8.1892, AG 512 1/14.
57  Memorandum for Wellington Branch, 25.8.1893; Hercus to Angus, 26.8.1893, AG 512 1/13.
58  Hercus to Jones, 19.4.1894; Ross & Glendining to Levi Strauss 15.5.1894, AG 512 1/15.
59  Jones to Ross, 25.1.1897, AG 512 5/10.
60  Hercus to Ross, 20.2.1890, AG 512 1/11.
61  Hercus to Miss H. Morrison, 21.11.1891, AG 512 1/13.
62  Hercus to Ross, 23.2.1892, AG 512 1/13.
63  Hercus to Ross, 17.8.1892, AG 512 1/13.
64  Ross & Glendining to Alex. Garden, 7.11.1893, AG 512 1/14.
65  Ross & Glendining to Mrs E. Mayer, 7.11.1893, AG 512 1/14.
66  Hercus to Ross, 7.6.1898, AG 512 5/11.
67  Hercus to Jones, 8.4.1897 AG 512 1/18.
68  Although the factory supplied materials such as linings and trimmings. Half-yearly balances, AG 512 15/3 to 15/5.
69  Hercus to Ross, 28.2.1899, AG 512 1/19.
70  Clothing Factory Plant, January 1898–January 1900, AG 512 15/7.
71  Hercus to Ross, 7.6.1898, AG 512 5/11.
72  Half-yearly balances, AG 512 15/4, 15/6.
73  Glendining to Ross, 20.10.1898, AG 512 5/11.

**CHAPTER 9**

1  Roslyn Mills Balance Sheets and Manufacturing Accounts, Half-yearly balances, AG 512 15/4 to 15/6.
2  *New Zealand Official Yearbook,* 1892, p. 105; 1902, pp. 141–2; G.J. McLean, *Spinning Yarns: A Centennial History of Alliance Textiles and its predecessors* (Dunedin, 1981), pp. 84–90.
3  Roslyn Mills Manufacturing Accounts, Half-yearly balances, AG 512 15/3, 15/4.
4  Wellington Woollen Manufacturing Co. Ltd, Balance Sheet 3.5.1890; Kaiapoi Woollen Manufacturing Co. Ltd, Balance Sheet 30.9.1890, AG 512 1/11. Roslyn Worsted & Woollen Mills Balance Sheet, 30.11.1890, Half-yearly balances, AG 512 15/4.
5  Hercus to Ross, 13.6.1889, AG 512 1/10.
6  Hercus to Ross, 17.9.1891, AG 512 1/12.
7  Hercus to Ross, 3.11.1891, AG 512 1/13.
8  Hercus to Ross, 24.9.1891, AG 512 1/12.
9  Hercus to Ross, 26.2.1892, AG 512 1/13.
10  McLean, *op. cit.,* pp. 62–3.

11 Simkin, *op. cit.*, pp. 167–8; Chappell, *op. cit.*, p. 153.

12 Ross & Glendining to the Wellington Woollen Manufacturing Co., 27.9.1894, AG 512 1/15.

13 Hercus to Doughty, Wellington, 14.4.1894, AG 512 1/16.

14 Half-yearly balances, AG 512 15/5.

15 Hercus to Ross, 2.9.1895, AG 512 15/5.

16 Hercus to Ross, 19.3.1895, AG 512 1/16.

17 Hercus to Ross, 17.3.1896, AG 512 1/17.

18 Hercus to T. Glendining, 14.3.1895, AG 512 1/16.

19 Hercus to Ross, 24.12.1895, AG 512 1/17.

20 Hercus to Ross, 19.1.1897, AG 512 1/18.

21 Ross & Glendining to Bennet, 14.10.1895, AG 512 1/17.

22 Machinery Accounts, Half-yearly balances AG 512 15/5.

23 Hercus to Ross, 19.1.1897, AG 512 1/18.

24 Ross & Glendining to Wellington Woollen Manufacturing Company, 16.11.1896, AG 512 1/16.

25 Ross & Glendining to Geddes, Invercargill, 21.11.1896, AG 512 1/18.

26 Ross & Glendining to Macky, Logan, Steen & Co., Auckland, 6.7.1897, AG 512 1/17.

27 Hercus to Jones, 8.4.1897, AG 512 1/18.

28 Ross to T. Glendining, 22.12.1900, AG 512 4/13.

29 Hercus to Ross, 9.8.1888, AG 512 1/10.

30 Hercus to Ross, 5.9.1893, AG 512 1/14.

31 Hercus to Jones, 14.3.1895, AG 512 1/16.

32 Departmental Returns, Half-yearly balances, AG 512 15/5, 15/6.

33 Hercus to Jones, 17.3.1898, AG 512 1/18.

34 Hercus to Jones, 25.3.1898, AG 512 1/18.

35 Hercus to Doughty, 19.3.1898, AG 512 1/18.

36 Hercus to Doughty, 16.4.1898, AG 512 1/18.

37 Glendining to Ross, 25.10.1898, AG 512 5/11.

38 D.I.H. Hastings, *A Plea for Protection* (Dunedin, 1888).

39 Hazlett & Glendining to Williams, Shag Point, 6.10.1890, AG 512 1/11.

40 Hercus to Glendining, 25.6.1891, AG 512 1/12.

41 Hercus to Glendining, 8.9.1891, AG 512 1/12.

42 Half-yearly balances, AG 512 15/4–15/6.

43 Unpublished MS, AG 512 Box 10.

44 Glendining to Ross, 25.2.1898, AG 512 5/11.

45 Ross to Ross & Glendining, Dunedin, 10.2.1899; Ross to Glendining, 11.2.1899, AG 512 4/13.

46 Ross to Glendining, 2.6.1899, AG 512 4/13.

47 Deposit Account, Half-yearly balances, AG 512 15/6.

48 Ross to Glendining, 2.6.1899, AG 512 4/13.

49 Ross to Glendining, 2.6.1899, AG 512 4/13.

50 Ross to Johnstone, 30.6.1899, AG 512 4/13.

51 Ross to Glendining, 2.6.1899, AG 512 4/13.

52 Ross to Johnstone, 6.5.1899, AG 512 4/13.

53 Ross to Glendining, 26.8.1899, 6.10.1899, 21.10.1899, AG 512 4/13.

54 Ross to Glendining, 6.10.1899, AG 512 4/13.

55 Ross to Jones, 27.7.1900, AG 512 4/13.

56 Ross to J.S. Ross, 14.3.1901; Ross to Glendining, 15.3.1901, Ross to T. Glendining, 18.5.1901, Ross to Glendining, 20.9.1901, AG 512 4/13.

57 Ross & Glendining to Payne, Solicitor, 1.3.1900, AG 512 1/19.

58 Minutes, Directors Meeting, Ross & Glendining Ltd, 20.6.1900, AG 512 8/1.

59 *Ibid.*

60 Ross & Glendining to Ross & Glendining Ltd, 29.3.1900. AG 512 1/19.

61 Ross to Ross & Glendining Ltd, 23.4.1900; Glendining to Ross & Glendining Ltd, 23.4.1900, AG 512 1/19.

62    Ross to Hercus, 5.10.1900; Ross to
      Jones, 19.10.1900, AG 512 4/13.

**Chapter 10**

1     J.B. Condliffe, *op. cit.*, p. 244.
2     W.R. Jourdain, *History of Land
      Legislation and Settlement in New
      Zealand* (Wellington, 1925), pp. 116–
      25. For the politics of the land reform
      movement, see Tom Brooking, *op. cit.*
3     *Mt Ida Chronicle,* 1.10.1891, p. 3.
4     Hercus to Elliott, 16.7.1892, AG 512
      1/13.
5     Hercus to Ross, 3.3.1892, AG 512
      1/13.
6     Ross & Glendining to Commissioner
      for Crown Lands for Otago, 3.3.1892,
      AG 512 1/13; Half-yearly balances,
      AG 512 15/5, 15/6.
7     *Mt Ida Chronicle,* 12.7.1895.
8     J. Kuzma, 'The 1895 Snowstorm', B.A.
      Otago University, Long Essay 1999.
9     Half-yearly balances, AG 512 15/4.
10    Ross & Glendining to Minister
      of Lands, 14.10.1895; Ross &
      Glendining to Chairman of Otago
      Land Board, November 1895, AG 512
      1/17.
11    Ross & Glendining to Minister of
      Lands, 14.10.1895, AG 512 1/17.
12    Statutes of New Zealand, Pastoral
      Tenants Relief Act 1895, 59 Victoria,
      No. 44.
13    Commissioner to Ross & Glendining,
      8.2.1896, AG 512 1/17.
14    Ross & Glendining to Chairman of
      Otago Land Board, 17.2.1896, AG
      512 1/17.
15    Under-Secretary, Ministry of Lands to
      Commissioner, 27.2.1896, AG 512
      1/17.
16    Ross & Glendining to Chairman,
      Otago Land Board, 21.2.1896, AG
      512 1/17.
17    McKenzie to Commissioner, 2.3.1896,
      AG 512 1/17.
18    Commissioner to Ross & Glendining,
      10.3.1896, AG 512 1/17.
19    *AJHR* 1896, C. 1, p. 28.
20    Simkin, *op. cit.*, pp. 180–83.
21    Sheep Account, Half-yearly balances
      1895, AG 512 15/5; J.A. Johnstone,
      *NZOYB* 1894, pp. 302–3.
22    W.P. Morrell, *The University of Otago:*
      *A Centennial History* (Dunedin, 1969),
      p. 81.
23    Ross & Glendining to Smith,
      Chapman, Sinclair & White,
      Solicitors, 17.12.1894, AG 512 1/16;
      Barewood Improvements Account,
      February 1896, AG 512 15/5.
24    Reid & Duncans to Ross &
      Glendining, 24.12.1880, AG 512
      1/16.
25    Sheep Accounts, Half-yearly balances,
      AG 512 15/4, 15/5, 15/6.
26    Sheep Account, Half-yearly balances,
      AG 512 15/6; Elliott to Glendining,
      22.12.1897, AG 512 5/10.
27    Elliott to Glendining, 20.12.1897, AG
      512 5/10.
28    *Ibid.*
29    Glendining to Ross, 30.8.1999, AG
      512 5/11.
30    Sheep Accounts, Half-yearly balances,
      AG 512 15/6, 15/7.
31    Sheep Accounts, Half-yearly balances,
      AG 512 15/6, 15/7.
32    Wool and Sheep Accounts, Half-yearly
      balances, AG 512 15/6, 15/7.
33    Hercus to Ross, 2.7.1904, AG 512
      2/3.
34    Cheviot Flock Account, 29.2.1896,
      AG 512 15/5.
35    Elliott to Glendining, 28.5.1897, AG
      512 5/10.
36    Ross to Thomson, Highgate, 4.5.1903,
      AG 512 4/5.
37    Hercus to A. Armour, 31.1.1903, AG
      512 2/3.
38    Half-yearly balances, AG 512 15/7.
39    Elliott to Glendining, 16.7.1897, AG
      512 5/10.
40    Elliott to Glendining, 18.1.1897, AG
      51 5/10.
41    Glendining to Ross, 16.2.1897, AG
      512 5/10.
42    Elliott to Glendining, 12.3.1897;
      Glendining to Ross, 6.7.1897, AG 512
      5/10.
43    Elliott to Glendining, 25.1.1897, AG
      512 5/10.
44    Elliott to Glendining 25.1.1897, AG
      512 5/10.
45    J. Yonge, *New Zealand Railway and
      Tramway Atlas* (Exeter, 1993), Map 26.
46    Elliott to Glendining, 10.6.1898, AG
      512 5/11.

47 Cowan, *op. cit.*, pp. 81–2.

48 S. Ville, *The Rural Entrepreneurs: A History of the Stock and Station Agent Industry in Australia and New Zealand* (Cambridge, 2000), p. 116.

49 *AJHR* 1900, C. 1, p. 27.

50 Ross to T. Brown, 28.2.1903, AG 512 4/5.

51 Ross & Glendining to Commissioner of Crown Lands for Otago, 16.2.1904, AG 512 2/3.

52 Hercus to Rex, New Norfolk, Tasmania.

53 *AJHR* 1904, C. 1, p. 59.

54 Evidence of Armour, *AJHR*, Royal Commission on Land Tenure 1905; C. 4, p. 184.

55 Ross & Glendining to Commissioner, 16.2.1904, AG 512 2/3.

56 *AJHR*, Royal Commission on Land Tenure 1905, C. 4, xxiv–v.

57 Ross to Glendining, 15.4.1905, AG 512 4/13.

58 Ross to J.S. Ross, 9.6.1906; 23.7.1906, AG 512 4/5.

59 Ross to J.S. Ross, 20.2.1907, AG 512 4/5; Half-yearly balances AG 512 15/7.

60 *AJHR* 1906, C, p. 40.

61 Hercus to Ross, 3.12.1904, AG 512 2/3.

62 Hercus to Ross, 23.1.1905, AG 512 2/3.

63 Sheep Accounts, Barewood Station, Half-yearly balances, AG 512 15/7.

64 *Otago Witness*, 13.2.1907.

65 Ross to J.S. Ross, 1.6.1907, AG 512 4/5.

66 Barewood Station, Final Balance 31.3.1909, Half-yearly balances, AG 512 1/7.

#### Chapter 11

1 Simkin, *op. cit.*, pp. 180–88; GDP estimates based on Oxley & Greasley (2000) *op. cit*, Table 1A.

2 Ross to Jones, 12.1.1901, AG 512 4/13.

3 Ross to Glendining, 13.7.1900, AG 512 4/13.

4 Ross to Glendining, 5.10.1900, Ross to Jones 22.12.1900, AG 512 4/13.

5 Ross to Hercus, 5.10.1900, AG 512 4/13.

6 Ross to Jones, 19.10.1900, AG 512 4/13.

7 Ross to R.C. Glendining, 1.11.1900; Ross to Glendining, 2.11.1900, AG 512 4/13.

8 *Ibid.*

9 Ross to Hercus, 9.11.1900, AG 512 4/13.

10 Hercus to Ross, 22.12.1900, AG 512 4/13.

11 Ross to Hercus, 1.2.1901, AG 512 4/13.

12 Hercus to Ross, 18.3.1901, AG 512 2/1.

13 Ross to Glendining, 27.4.1901, AG 512 4/13.

14 Ross to Glendining, 19.5.1901, AG 512 4/13.

15 Ross to T. Glendining, 22.12.1900, AG 512 4/13.

16 Ross to Hercus, 4.4.1901; Ross to Glendining, 27.4.1901, AG 512 4/13.

17 Ross to R.C. Glendining, 26.4.1901, AG 512 4/13.

18 Ross to T. Glendining, 28.5.1901, AG 512 4/13.

19 Ross to Jones, 26.6.1901, AG 512 4/13.

20 Ross to Glendining, 28.6.1901, AG 512 4/13.

21 *Ibid.*

22 Ross to Glendining, 19.7.1901, AG 512 4/13.

23 Ross to Glendining, 7.8.1901, AG 512 4/13.

24 Ross to Glendining, 20.9.1901, AG 512 4/13.

25 *Ibid.*

26 Ross to Glendining, 11.10.1901, AG 512 4/13.

27 *Ibid.*

28 Ross to Dr Fergus, 2.11.1901, AG 512 4/13.

29 Ross to Brown, London, 29.2.1905, AG 512 4/5.

30 Hercus to Ross, 17.8.1901, AG 512 2/1.

31 Ross to J.F. Gibson, London, 12.5.1902; Ross to T. Woodward, Nottingham, 1.5.1902; Ross to Messrs. Spiers & Grieve, Leicester, 19.3.1903, AG 512 4/5.

32 Ross to Gibson, 12.5.1902, 24.1.1903, 19.3.1903, 25.5.1903, 6.7.1903, AG 512 4/5.

33  Ross to Gibson, 6.7.1903, AG 512 4/5.
34  Manufacturing Accounts, 1901–1905, AG 512 15/8.
35  Machinery Accounts 1901–1905, AG 512 15/8.
36  Annual Report & Balance Sheets, AG 512 8/6.
37  Ross to Brown, London, 28.2.1903, AG 512 4/5.
38  Hercus to Ross, 3.9.1904 AG 512 2/3.
39  Hercus to Ross, 11.5.1905, AG 512 2/3.
40  Half-yearly balances, 1901–1904, AG 512 15/8.
41  Ross to D. George, 14.4.1904, AG 512 4/5.
42  Ross to niece Ella, 7.12.1909, AG 512 4/6.
43  Ross & Glendining Ltd to R.C. Glendining, 8.3.1904, AG 512 2/3.
44  Ross to T. Glendining, 18.11.1904, AG 512 4/13.
45  Ross to Hercus, 25.6.1904, AG 512 4/13.
46  Ross to Glendining, 22.8.1904, AG 512 4/13.
47  Ross to Glendining, 6.10.1904, AG 512 4/13.
48  Ross to Ross & Glendining Ltd, 28.10.1904, 21.1.1905, AG 512 4/13.
49  Ross to Hercus, 29.10.1904, AG 512 4/13.
50  Ross to Hercus, 10.12.1904, AG 512 4/13.
51  Ross to Hercus, 4.3.1905, AG 512 4/13.
52  Ordinary General Meeting, 12.9.1905, AG 512 8/6.
53  Hercus to Oamaru Woollen Mills, 6.8.1904, AG 512 2/3.
54  Ross & Glendining to W.R. Wilson, Onehunga Woollen Mills, 29.3.1905, AG 512 2/3.
55  Hercus to J. Cruickshank, Rosedale Mills, 2.5.1905, AG 512 2/3.
56  Ross to Hercus, 30.12.1904, AG 512 4/13.
57  Ross to Glendining, 15.4.1905; Ross to Johnstone, 26.6.1905, AG 512 4/13.
58  Report of Ross & Glendining Ltd, 12.9.1905, AG 512 4/6.
59  Ross to Hercus, 11.2.1905; 25.3.1905, AG 512 4/13.
60  Ross to J.S. Ross, 12.9.1905, AG 512 4/5.
61  Ross to J.S. Ross, 2.12.1905, AG 512 4/5.
62  Ross to J.S. Ross, 19.3.1906, AG 512 4/5.
63  Ross to J.S. Ross, 18.4.1906, AG 512 4/5.
64  Memorandum, May 1906, AG 512 4/5.
65  Ross to J.S. Ross, 7.9.1906, AG 512 4/5.
66  Ross to W.S. Ross, 3.11.1906, AG 512 4/5.
67  Ross to J.S. Ross, 13.8.1906, AG 512 4/5.
68  Ross to J.S. Ross, 27.8.1906, AG 512 4/5.
69  Ross to J.S. Ross, 7.9.1906, AG 512 4/5.
70  Ross to J.S. Ross, 24.9.1906, AG 512 4/5.
71  Ross to W.S. Ross, 3.11.1906, AG 512 4/5.
72  Ross to J.S. Ross, 27.11.1906, AG 512 4/5.
73  Ross to J.S. Ross, 20.2.1907, AG 512 4/5.
74  Ross to J.S. Ross, 15.5.1907, AG 512 4/5.
75  Ross to J.S. Ross, 18.9.1907, AG 512 4/6.
76  Ross to J.S. Ross, 1.4.1908, AG 512 4/6.
77  Ross & Glendining Ltd to Town Clerk, Dunedin, 30.3.1908, AG 512 4/6.
78  Ross & Glendining Ltd to Town Clerk, Dunedin, 27.4.1908; Ross to J.S. Ross, 2.12.1908, AG 512 4/6.
79  Ross to J.S. Ross, 55.1909, AG 512 4/6.
80  Ross to J.S. Ross, 18.9.1907, AG 512 4/6.
81  Reports to Ordinary General Meeting, 1908–1914, AG 512 8/6; Ross to J.S. Ross, 7.6.1911, AG 512 4/14; Roslyn Mills Machinery Accounts, 1908 to 1914, AG 512 15/9, 15/10.
82  Ross to J.S. Ross, 15.9.1909, 6.4.1910, AG 512 4/6; 23.4.1913, 3.6.1913, AG 512 4/14.
83  Ross to J.S. Ross, 12.7.1911, 1.11.1911, AG 512 4/14.

84  Ross to J.S. Ross, 3.9.1913, 19.11.1913, 26.11.1913, AG 512 4/14.
85  Ross to J.S. Ross, 14.8.1912, AG 512 4/14.
86  Ordinary General Meeting, 24.9.1907, AG 512 8/6; Ross to J.S. Ross, 7.9.1910, AG 512 4/6.
87  *NZOYB*, 1913, p. 627.
88  Ross to D. Henderson, Montevideo, 9.4.1913, AG 512 14/4.
89  Ross to J.S. Ross, 31.5.1911, AG 512 4/14.
90  Ross to J.S. Ross, 9.12.1908, AG 512 4/6.
91  Ross to J.S. Ross, 27.3.1912, AG 512 14/4.

CHAPTER 12

1  Hercus to Jones, 12.6.1905, AG 512 2/3; Jack Ilott, *Creating Customers: The Story of Advertising New Zealand: 1892–1982* (1985).
2  Ross to Glendining, 13.7.1900; 2.10.1900, AG 512 4/13.
3  Ross to Jones, 12.1.1901, AG 512 4/13.
4  Report, Ordinary General Meeting, 4.3.1901, AG 512 8/6.
5  Ross to Glendining, 28.6.1901, AG 512 4/13. The final cost is not recorded.
6  Clothing Factory Accounts, 19.1.1902, AG 512 15/8.
7  *Cyclopedia*, Vol. 4, p. 337.
8  Clothing Factory Plant, Half-yearly balance, 19.1.1902, AG 512 15/8.
9  Hercus to Messrs Groin, Gibson & Co., Melbourne, 25.4.1903, AG 512 2/2.
10  Ross to Hercus, 30.12.1904, AG 512 4/13.
11  Report to Ordinary General Meeting, 12.9.1905, AG 512 8/6.
12  Hercus to Ross, 27.6.1904, AG 512 2/3.
13  Ross to J.S. Ross, 11.6.1907, AG 512 4/5
14  Hercus to Government Statistician, 30.11.1911, AG 512 2/6.
15  *NZOYB*, 1910, pp. 110–11 and insert.
16  Ross to J.S. Ross, 14.8.1907, AG 512 4/6.
17  Hercus to Secretary of New Zealand Woollen Manufacturers Association;

18  Hercus to Dunedin Expansion League, 19.9.1912; AG 512 2/6.
    Hercus to Ministry of Internal Affairs, 22.1.1912; Hercus to Minister of Immigration, 30.1.1913, AG 512 2/6.
19  Jane Malthus & Chris Brickell, 'Producing and Consuming Gender: The Case of Clothing', in Barbara Brookes, Annabel Cooper & Robin Law, *Sites of Gender, Women, Men and Modernity in Southern Dunedin* (Auckland University Press, 2003), pp. 134–7.
20  *NZOYB*, 1907, p. 843.
21  Ross to J.S. Ross, 1.4.1907, AG 512 4/5.
22  Half-yearly balances, AG 512, 15/9.
23  Unpublished MS, p. 20, AG 512 Box 10.
24  Hat Factory Plant, Half-yearly balances 1902–3, AG 512 15/8.
25  Ross & Glendining Ltd to Town Clerk, Dunedin, 5.3.1902, AG 512 2/2.
26  Ross & Glendining Ltd to Inspector of Factories, 22.8.1902, AG 512 2/2.
27  Hercus to A. Henderson, Christchurch Branch, 11.2.1902, AG 512 2/2.
28  *Cyclopedia, op. cit.*, p. 338.
29  Half-yearly balances, AG 512 5/8.
30  Ross to J.S. Ross, 17.4.1907, AG 512 4/5.
31  *Cyclopedia, op. cit.*, pp. 337–8.
32  Ross to Brown, 28.2.1903, AG 512 4/5.
33  Hat Factory Stock, 19.9.1902, AG 512 2/2.
34  Ross to Brown, 28.3.1903, AG 512 4/5, *Cyclopedia, op cit.*, p. 338.
35  Hercus to Ross, 23.1.1905, AG 512 2/3.
36  Factory Returns, Half-yearly balances, AG 512 15/8.
37  Hat Factory Memorandum, April 1906, AG 512 4/5.
38  Ross to J.S. Ross, 27.8.1908, AG 512 4/5.
39  Ross to J.S. Ross, 13.8.1906, AG 512 4/5.
40  Ross to J.S. Ross, 29.9.1909, AG 512 4/6.
41  Ross to J.S. Ross, 5.4.1911, AG 512 4/14. *Souvenir Catalogue, Industrial Exhibition and Art Union, Dunedin 1912,* p. 8.

42  Ross to J.S. Ross, 23.4.1913, AG 512 4/4.

43  Hercus to E.W. Roy, 20.11.1902, AG 512 2/2.

44  Hercus to Hartenbody, New York, 17.8.1903, AG 512 2/2; Ross to J.S. Ross, 23.2.1908, AG 512 4/5.

45  Factory Returns, Half-yearly balances, AG 512 15/9.

46  Hercus to Commercial Property & Finance Co., 22.4.1908, AG 512 2/5.

47  Ross to Jones, 22.12.1908, AG 512 4/6.

48  Ross to J.S. Ross, 20.6.1910, AG 512 4/6, *NZOYB*, 1907, p. 843.

49  Factory Returns, Half-yearly balances, AG 512 15/9, 15/10; Half-yearly analysis of results, 1911–33, AG 512 15/14; Report to Ordinary General Meeting, 17.9.1914, AG 512 8/6.

50  Ross to J.S. Ross, 29.12.1909, AG 512 4/6.

51  Ross to J.S. Ross, 17.8.1910, AG 512 4/6.

52  Boot Factory Plant, Half-yearly balances, AG 512 15/9.

53  Report to Ordinary General Meeting, 14.9.1910, AG 512 8/6.

54  Boot Factory Plant, 19.7.1912, AG 512 15/9.

55  Ross to J.S. Ross, 13.12.1911, AG 512 4/14.

56  Ross to Roy, 20.8.1913, AG 512 4/14.

57  Ross to J.S. Ross, 5.11.1913, AG 512 4/14.

58  Half-yearly balance sheets, 19.1.1914 & 19.7.1915, AG 512 5/10.

59  Ross to J.S. Ross, 10.9.1913, AG 512 4/14.

60  Ross to J.S. Ross, 19.3.1914, AG 512 4/14.

61  Ross to J.S. Ross, 17.6.1914, AG 512 4/14.

62  Ross to J.S. Ross, 3.9.1914, AG 512 4/14.

63  *Auckland Weekly News,* 30.11.1911, p. 53.

64  Hercus to Jones, 12.6.1905, AG 512 2/3.

65  Hercus to T. Finlay, 6.6.1912, AG 512 2/6.

66  Ross to J.S. Ross, 15.1.1911, 10.5.1911, 21.2.1912, AG 512 4/14.

67  Ross to Percy Sargood, 18.12.1912, AG 12 4/14.

68  Ross to J.S. Ross, 15.5.1910, AG 512 4/6.

69  Hercus to Thomas Finlay, 6.6.1912, AG 512 2/6.

70  *New Zealand Herald,* 4.11.1912.

71  Hercus to Richardson & Co., Melbourne, 29.1.1904, AG 512 2/3.

72  Hercus to Snedden, AG 512 2/6.

73  Ross to Snedden, 26.9.1912, AG 512 2/6.

74  Ross & Glendining to Messrs Warner Brothers, New York, 7.10.1912, AG 512 2/6.

75  Hercus to Finlay, 78.1913, AG 512 2/6.

76  Hercus to Finlay, 12.2.1913, AG 512 2/6.

77  Hercus to Snedden, 23.4.1914, AG 512 2/7.

78  Both mantles and boots were incorporated into the relevant warehouse departments for the purposes of net profit calculations.

## CHAPTER 13

1  *Cyclopedia*, p. 337; Report to Ordinary General Meeting, 9.2.1902, AG 512 8/6.

2  Ross to J.S. Ross, 20.9.1914, AG 512 4/14.

3  Report to Ordinary General Meeting, 7.9.1903, AG 512 8/6.

4  Hercus to Ross, 15.3.1907, AG 512 4/5.

5  Hercus to W. Strange & Co. 23.3.1903, AG 512 2/2; Ross to Boys, 25.11.1903, AG 512 4/5.

6  Report to Ordinary General Meeting, 12.9.1905, AG 512 8/6.

7  Ross to Glendining, 19.11.1904, AG 512 4/13.

8  Ross to George, 7.9.1903, AG 512 4/5; Report to Ordinary General Meeting, 7.9.1903, AG 512 8/6.

9  Ross to A. Hanna, 12.12.1902, AG 512 2/2.

10  Ross to Hanna, 29.1.1903, AG 512 2/2.

11  Ross to Hanna, 1.8.1903, AG 512 2/2.

12  Hercus to Hanna, 5.8.1903, AG 512 2/2.

13  Ross to George, 7.9.1903, AG 512 4/5.

14  Ross to Brown, 25.9.1903, AG 512 4/5.

15   Ross to Glendining, 19.4.1904, AG 512 4/13.
16   Ross to Glendining, 19.11.1904, AG 512 4/13.
17   Hercus to Ross, 3.9.1904, AG 512 2/3.
18   Hercus to Ross, 31.10.1904, AG 512 2/3.
19   Hercus to Snedden, 26.10.1904, AG 512 2/3.
20   Ross to Hercus, 9.12.1904, AG 512 4/13.
21   Ross to Jones, 30.12.1904, AG 512 4/13.
22   Hercus to Snedden, 7.5.1906, AG 512 2/4.
23   Hercus to Snedden, 10.12.1904, AG 512 2/3.
24   Hercus to Snedden, 19.9.1906, AG 512 2/4.
25   Ross to J.S. Ross, 18.6.1906, AG 512 4/5.
26   Ross to J.S. Ross, 19.3.1906, AG 512 4/5.
27   Report to Ordinary General Meeting, 17.9.1906, AG 512 8/6.
28   Ross to J. Currie, 17.10.1906, AG 512 4/5; T. Hodgson, *The Heart of Colonial Auckland* (Auckland, 1992), p. 35.
29   Ross to Hercus, 30.12.1904, AG 512 4/13.
30   Ross to J.S. Ross, 16.10.1906, Ross to J. Currie, architect, 17.10.1906, Ross to Ross & Glendining Ltd, Auckland, 28.8.1906, AG 512 4/6.
31   Hercus to J.S. Ross, 18.9.1906, AG 512 2/4.
32   Ross to (illegible), typed document, p. 478, AG 512 4/5.
33   Report to Ordinary General Meeting, 24.9.1907, AG 512 8/6.
34   Ross to J.S. Ross, 15.11.1907, AG 512 4/6.
35   Hercus to Snedden, 21.10.1907, AG 512 2/5.
36   Unpublished MS, p. 23, AG 512 15/8. Glendining had typed personal letters in the late 1880s but whether he continued thereafter is not known.
37   Half-yearly balances, AG 512 15/8, 15/9.
38   Assets and Financial Management Register, AG 512 15/14; Report to Ordinary General Meeting, 14.9.1910, AG 512 8/6.
39   Ross to J.S. Ross, 1.4.1907, AG 512 4/5.
40   Ross Private Account, Half-yearly balances, AG 512 15/7.
41   Hercus to Jones, 14.12.1907, AG 512 2/5.
42   Ross to J.S. Ross, 15.1.1908, AG 512 4/6.
43   Hercus to G. Eissenhardt, Greymouth, 8.2.1908; Hercus to P. Hayman, 21.2.1908, AG 512 2/6.
44   Hercus to Eissenhardt, 30.10.1908, AG 512 2/5.
45   Hercus to Jones, 14.12.1907, AG 512 2/5.
46   Ross to J.S. Ross, 18.2.1914, AG 512 4/14.
47   Ross & Glendining to W.R. Wilson, 2.3.1904, AG 512 2/5.
48   Half-yearly balances, AG 512 15/7–15/10.
49   Hercus to Brodie, 22.3.1907, AG 512 2/5.
50   Hercus to W. Greig & A. Blacklock, Wellington, 25.9.1908; Hercus to Snedden, 27.3.1909, AG 512 2/5.
51   Hercus to Ross, 20.1.1900, AG 512 2/1.
52   Ross to Hercus, 12.1.1901, AG 512 4/13; Hercus to Jones, 12.3.1901, 4.9.1901, AG 512 2/1.
53   Half-yearly balances, AG 512 15/8, 15/9.
54   Ross to J.S. Ross, 16.8.1911, 19.11.1911, 5.11.1913, 26.11.1913, 17.12.1913, AG 512 4/4.
55   Hercus to Jones, 8.4.1911, 7.10.1911, AG 512 2/6.
56   Hercus to Jones, 24.4.1906, AG 512 2/4.
57   Ross to Hercus, 15.4.1905, AG 512 4/13.
58   Ross to Glendining, 5.5.1905, AG 512 4/13.
59   Ross to J.S. Ross, 18.9.1907, AG 512 4/6.
60   Ross to J.S. Ross, 31.12.1907 AG 512 4/6.
61   Ross to J.S. Ross, 2.12.1905, AG 512 4/5.
62   Ross & Glendining Ltd to Commissioner of Taxes, 5.9.1910, AG 512 2/6.
63   Hercus to W. Greig & A. Blacklock, Wellington, 25.9.1908, AG 512 2/5.
64   Half-yearly balances, 1900–1914, AG

512 15/8–15/10; Hercus to Brodie, 14.3.1895, AG 512 2/3.

65   Hercus to Wilson, Napier, 15.9.1905, AG 512 2/4.

66   Hercus to Brodie, 8.3.1904, 29.9.1904, AG 512 2/5; 19.6.1906, AG 2/4; 22.3.1907, 23.9.1906, AG 512 2/5.

67   Hercus to Brodie, 15.9.1905, AG 512 2/4.

68   Hercus to Brodie, 11.11.1911; Hercus to Dunlop, 12.4.1912; AG 512 2/6; Ross to J.S. Ross, 7.12.1911, AG 512 4/4.

69   Ross to J.S. Ross, 19.6.1912, AG 512 4/14.

70   Ross to J.S. Ross, 11.8.1909, AG 512 4/6.

71   Hercus to Strain, 11.4.1896, AG 512 1/17.

72   Ross to Jones, 4.4.1901, AG 512 4/13.

73   Hercus to Strain, 22.7.1903, AG 512 2/2.

74   Hercus to Henderson, 7.11.1903, AG 512 2/3.

75   Hercus to Henderson, 18.11.1903; 3.11.1904, AG 512 2/3.

76   Hercus to Henderson, 29.9.1904, AG 512 2/3.

77   Hercus to Henderson, 10.3.1906, AG 512 2/4.

78   Hercus to Henderson, 18.9.1906, AG 512 2/4.

79   Ross to J.S. Ross, 1.9.1909, AG 512 4/6.

80   Ross to J.S. Ross, 8.9.1909, AG 512 4/6.

81   Ross to J.S. Ross, 22.9.1909, AG 512 4/6.

82   Ross to J.S. Ross, 20.9.1909, AG 512 4/6.

83   Ross to J.S. Ross, 15.12.1909, AG 512 4/6.

84   Hercus to Davidson, 7.10.1911, 17.11.1912, AG 512 2/6.

85   Hercus to Snedden, 27.3.1909, AG 512 2/5.

86   Ibid.

87   Hercus to Snedden, 27.9.1910, AG 512 2/6.

88   Hercus to Snedden, 27.9.1910 & 7.4.1911, AG 512 2/6.

89   Half-yearly balances, 15/8, 15/9, 15/10, AG 512.

CHAPTER 14

1   Hercus to Jones, 10.6.1902, AG 512 2/2.

2   Hercus to Boys, 23.6.1902, AG 512 2/2.

3   Hercus to Ross, 7.3.1905, AG 512 2/3.

4   Hercus to Boys, 11.3.1905, AG 512 2/3.

5   Ross to J.S. Ross, 11.6.1907, AG 512 4/5.

6   Ross to J.S. Ross, 24.4.1906, AG 512 4/5.

7   Ross to J.S. Ross, 19.3.1906, AG 512 4/5.

8   Ross to J.S. Ross, 11.6.1907, AG 512 4/5.

9   Ross to J.S. Ross, 15.1.1908, AG 512 4/6.

10   Ross to J.S. Ross, 12.2.1908, AG 512 4/6.

11   Ross to J.S. Ross, 15.4.1908, AG 512 4/6.

12   Ross to Ross & Glendining Ltd, London, 27.5.1908, loose leaf, AG 512 4/6.

13   Ross to J.S. Ross, 17.2.1909, AG 512 4/6.

14   Ross to J.S. Ross, 1.6.1910, AG 512 4/6.

15   Ross to Boys, 1.6.1910, AG 512 4/6.

16   Ross to J.S. Ross, 15.1.1911, 19.6.1912, AG 512 4/14.

17   Ross to J.S. Ross, 14.10.1910, AG 512 4/14.

18   Ross to J.S. Ross, 1.3.1911, AG 512 4/14.

19   The colony of New Zealand was formally proclaimed a Dominion on 26 September 1907.

20   Ross to J.S. Ross, 4.10.1910, AG 512 4/6.

21   Ross to J.S. Ross, 18.1.1912, AG 512 4/14.

22   Ross to J.S. Ross, 23.12.1911, AG 512 4/14.

23   Ross to J.S. Ross, 24.3.1909, AG 512 4/6; Ross to Boys, 5.6.1911, AG 512 4/14.

24   Ross to J.S. Ross, 16.8.1911, AG 512 4/14, Ross to Boys, 29.2.1912, AG 512 4/14.

25   Ross to Boys, 29.2.1912, 29.5.1912, AG 512 4/14.

26 Ross to J.S. Ross, 22.5.1912, AG 512
4/14.
27 Ross to McKenzie, 30.4.1913, AG 512
4/14.
28 Ross to J.S. Ross, 17.6.1914, AG 512
4/14.
29 Ross to J.S. Ross, 18.2.1914, AG 512
4/14.
30 Ross to J.S. Ross, 15.4.1914, AG 512
4/14.
31 Ross to J.S. Ross, 17.6.1914, AG 512
4/14.
32 Ross to J.S. Ross, 22.4.1914, AG 512
4/14

CHAPTER 15
1 Ross to J.S. Ross, 21.8.1914, AG 512
4/14.
2 Ross to J.S. Ross, 12.8.1914, AG 512
4/14.
3 Ross to J.S. Ross, 21.9.1914, AG 512
4/14.
4 Hercus to Jones, 6.10.1914, AG 512
2/7.
5 Hercus to Runciman, Napier,
9.10.1914, AG 512 2/7.
6 Hercus to Davidson, 5.10.1914, AG
512 2/7.
7 Ross to J.S. Ross, 15.9.1914, AG 512
4/14.
8 Ross to J.S. Ross, 18.11.1914, AG 512
4/14.
9 Ross to J.S. Ross, 7.12.1914, AG 512
4/14.
10 Ross to J.S. Ross, 19.2.1915, AG 512
4/14.
11 Ross to J.S. Ross, 14.5.1915, AG 512
4/14.
12 Ross to Thomson, 25.5.1915, AG 512
4/14.
13 Ross & Glendining Ltd to the
Honourable Arthur Meyer, 8.10.1915,
AG 512 2/7.
14 Hercus to Group Commander, Otago
Military District, 26.11.1915, AG 512
2/7.
15 Ross to J.S. Ross, 10.6.1915,
19.7.1915, AG 512 4/14.
16 Ross to Netting, 12.11.1915, AG 512
4/15.
17 Hercus to Evans, 24.2.1915, AG 512
2/7.
18 Ross to J.S. Ross, 10.6.1915, AG 512
4/14.

19 Ross to J.S. Ross, 7.12.1915, AG 512
4/15.
20 Ross to J.S. Ross, 19.7.1915, AG 512
4/15.
21 Ross to Netting, 13.11.1915, AG 512
4/15.
22 Ross to J.S. Ross, 7.12.1915, AG 512
4/15.
23 Ross to J.S. Ross, 10.6.1915,
20.8.1915, AG 512 4/15.
24 Ross to J.S. Ross, 9.11.1915, AG 512
4/15.
25 Hercus to R.C. Glendining,
4.12.1915, AG 512 2/7.
26 Hercus to Hill, 6.1.1916, AG 512 2/7.
27 Ross to J.S. Ross, 7.3.1916, AG 512
4/15.
28 Ross to J.S. Ross, 10.4.1916, AG 512
4/15.
29 Ross to J.S. Ross, 17.3.1916,
28.3.1916, 12.5.1916, AG 512 4/15.
30 Ross to J.S. Ross, 17.4.1917, AG 512
4/15.
31 Ross to J.S. Ross, 12.5.1916, AG 512
4/15.
32 Ross to J.S. Ross, 20.6.1916, AG 512
4/15.
33 Ross to J.S. Ross, 15.8.1916, AG 512
4/15.
34 Ross to J.S. Ross, 1.9.1916, AG 512,
4/15.
35 Ross to J.S. Ross, 16.4.1915, AG 512
4/14.
36 Ross to J.S. Ross, 12.5.1916, AG 512
4/15.
37 Ross to J.S. Ross, 1.9.1916, AG 512
4/15.
38 Ross to J.S. Ross, 24.10.1916, AG 512
4/15.
39 Ross to J.S. Ross, 24.11.1916, AG 512
4/15.
40 Hercus to Minister of Munitions,
7.11.1916, AG 512 2/7.
41 J.S. Ross to Ross, 25.7.1917, AG 512
4/7.
42 J.S. Ross to Ross, 25.2.1918, AG 512
4/7; Ross to J.S Ross, 10.6.1918, AG
512 4/15.
43 Ross to J.S. Ross, 22.12.1916, AG 512
4/15.
44 Ross to J.S. Ross, 18.1.1917, AG 512
4/15.
45 Ross to J.S. Ross, 13.3.1917, AG 512
4/7.

46  Ross to T.C. Ross, 26.3.1917, AG 512 4/7.
47  Ross to J.S. Ross, 1.11.1917, AG 512 4/15; J.S. Ross to Ross, 29.1.1918, AG 512 4/7.
48  J.S. Ross to P. Keith, Thurso, 23.11.1917, AG 512 4/7.
49  J.S. Ross to Ross, 1.1.1918, AG 512 4/7.
50  J.S. Ross to Ross, 7.5.1918, AG 512 4/8.
51  J.S. Ross to Ross, 26.8.1918, 4.9.1918, AG 512 4/8.
52  Ross to J.S. Ross, 21.11.1918, AG 512 4/15.
53  Ross to Netting, 30.10.1919, AG 512 4/15.
54  Ross to J.S. Ross, 13.8.1916, AG 512 4/15.
55  J.S. Ross to Ross, 1.12.1916, 15.12.1916, 12.1.1917, AG 512 4/7.
56  J.S. Ross to Ross, 27.3.1917, AG 512 4/7.
57  J.S. Ross to Ross, 27.2.1917; J.S. Ross to Jones, 13.3.1917, AG 512 4/7.
58  Ross & Glendining Ltd to New Zealand Government Offices, London, 24.1.1918, AG 512 4/7.
59  J.S. Ross to Ross, 27.3. 1917, 5.11.1917, AG 512 4/7.
60  J.S. Ross to Ross, 13.3.1917, AG 512 4/7.
61  Ross to J.S. Ross, 1.5.1917, AG 512 4/15.
62  J.S. Ross to T.C. Ross, 26.3.1917, AG 512 4/7.
63  J.S. Ross to Ross, 19.6.1917, AG 512 4/7.
64  J.S. Ross to Ross, 5.11.1917, AG 512 4/7.
65  Ross & Glendining Ltd, London to Head Office, 3.7.1917, AG 512 4/7.
66  Ross & Glendining Ltd, London, July 1917, AG 512 4/7.
67  J.S. Ross to Ross, 5.11.1917, AG 512 4/7.
68  J.S. Ross to Ross, 18.12.1917, AG 512 4/7.
69  J.S. Ross to Ross, 19.1.1918, J.S. Ross to Dr James Glendining, 6.2.1918, AG 512 4/7.
70  J.S. Ross to Ross, 25.7.1917, 20.11.1917; J.S. Ross to Fanny Ross, 24.11.1917; J.S. Ross to J. Glendining, 4.12.1917, AG 512 4/7.
71  Ross to J.S. Ross, 28.3.1916, AG 512 4/15.
72  Ross & Glendining Ltd, London, circular to branches, 17.6.1918, AG 512 4/8.
73  J.S. Ross to Jones, 30.7.1918, 4.9.1918, AG 512 4/8.
74  T.C. Ross to J.S. Ross, 18.3.1918, AG 512 4/16.
75  Ross to J.S. Ross, 16.5.1918, AG 512 4/15.
76  J.S. Ross to Ross, 28.3.1918, AG 512 4/8.
77  J.S. Ross to Ross & Glendining Ltd, Dunedin, 3.6.1918, AG 512 4/8.
78  J.S. Ross to Jones, 4.9.1918, AG 512 4/8.
79  Ross to J.S. Ross, 16.4.1918, AG 512 4/15.
80  Ross to J.S. Ross, 6.9.1918, AG 512 4/15.
81  Ross to J.S. Ross, 4.11.1918, AG 512 4/8.
82  Capital and Undivided Profit and Reserves, 1901–1925, AG 512 15/14.
83  Ross to J.S. Ross, 17.4.1917, 26.6.1917, AG 512 4/15; List of Depositors, Half-yearly balances, AG 512 15/10.
84  Ross to J.S. Ross, 30.8.1917, AG 512 4/15.
85  Ross to J.S. Ross, 11.1917, AG 512 4/15.
86  Ross to J.S. Ross, 26.9.1918, AG 512 4/15.
87  Ross to J.S. Ross, 12.9.1916, AG 512 4/15.
88  Ross to J.S. Ross, 12.12.1918, AG 512 4/15.

**CHAPTER 16**

1  Lloyd Prichard, *op. cit.*, p. 294; Tom Brooking, 'Economic Transformation', in G.W. Rice, ed., *The Oxford History of New Zealand*, second edition (Auckland 2000) p. 231.
2  Oxley & Greasley, (2000), *op. cit.*, Table 1A.
3  J.S. Ross to Ross, 21.11.1918, AG 512 4/8.
4  J.S. Ross to Ross, 19.11.1918, AG 512 4/8.

5   J.S. Ross to T. Lucas, 28.11.1918, AG 512 4/8.

6   Ross to J.S. Ross, 21.11.1918, AG 512 4/8.

7   Ross to J.S Ross, 12.12.1918, AG 512 4/8.

8   T.C. Ross to Netting, 17.1.1919, AG 512 4/6.

9   T.C. Ross to J.S. Ross, 17.1.1919, AG 512 4/6.

10  J.S. Ross to Ross, 21.1.1919, AG 512 4/8.

11  Ross to J.S. Ross, 14.12.1918, AG 512 4/15.

12  Ross & Glendining Ltd to all branches, 24.1.1919, AG 512 2/8.

13  J.S. Ross to Ross, 31.1.1919, AG 512 4/8.

14  Circular Letter to Ross & Glendining Ltd, Dunedin, 10.2.1919, AG 512 4/8.

15  T.C. Ross to J.S. Ross, 12.12.1918, 24.12.1918, AG 512 4/16.

16  J.S. Ross to Evans, 27.1.1919, J.S. Ross to T.C. Ross, 18.2.1919, AG 512 4/8.

17  Ross to J.S. Ross, 27.2.1919, AG 512 4/8.

18  Hercus to Netting, 31.1.1920, AG 512 4/10.

19  T.C. Ross to Netting, 27.10.1923, AG 512 4/16.

20  Ross to J.S. Ross, 26.8.1918, AG 512 4/10.

21  J.S. Ross to Ross, 3.1.1919; J.S Ross to Jones 3.1.1919, AG 512 4/8.

22  Ross to J.S. Ross, 3.1.1919, AG 512 4/15; T.C. Ross to J.S. Ross, 18.1.1919, 20.1.1919, AG 512 4/16.

23  J.S. Ross to James Evans, 16.7.1919, AG 512 4/11.

24  Ross to J.S. Ross, 2.8.1919, AG 512 4/15; J.S. Ross to T.C. Ross, 5.1.1920, AG 512 4/8.

25  Hercus circular, 19.8.1919, AG 512 2/8; T.C. Ross to J.S. Ross, 1.10.1919, AG 512 4/16.

26  T.C. Ross to J.S. Ross, 17.11.1919, AG 512 4/16.

27  Managers' Conference Resolutions, 14.11.1919, AG 512 8/1.

28  J.S. Ross to Ross, 18.2.1919, AG 512 4/9.

29  J.S. Ross to Snedden, 10.7.1919, AG 512 4/7; J.S. Ross to Ross, 22.12.1919, AG 512 4/8.

30  Ross to J.S. Ross, 1.10.1919, AG 512 4/15.

31  Ross to J.S. Ross, 31.10.1919, 17.11.1919, AG 512 4/15; Employees' Participating Bonus Scheme, AG 512 8/1.

32  Report and Balance Sheet, 10.10.1919, AG 512 8/6.

33  J.S. Ross to Ross, 6.2.1920, AG 512 4/8.

34  Ross to J.S. Ross, 26.9.1918, AG 512 4/15.

35  Ross to J.S. Ross, 16.10.1919, AG 512 4/15.

36  Ross to J.S. Ross, 6.12.1919, AG 512 4/15.

37  *Ibid.*

38  Hercus to Auckland Branch, 15.1.1920, AG 512 4/10.

39  Hercus to Auckland Branch, 18.2.1920, AG 512 4/10.

40  Half-yearly analysis of results, AG 512 15/12.

41  Hercus to Auckland Branch, 15.1.1920, AG 512 4/10.

42  Ross to Geo. Willis, Adelaide, 6.12.1919. AG 512 4/15; T.C. Ross to J.S. Ross, 22.1.1920, AG 512 4/6.

43  Hercus to H. Glendining, 9.2.1920, AG 512 2/8; T.C. Ross to J.S. Ross, 4.3.1920, AG 512 4/16.

44  Half-yearly analysis of results, AG 512 15/12.

45  T.C. Ross to Auckland Branch, 16.2.1920; AG 512 4/10; Ross & Glendining to Auckland branch, 27.4.1920, AG 512 2/8.

46  Ross & Glendining to Wellington Branch, 29.1.1920, AG 512 2/8; Notes for Annual Report 1920, AG 512 Box 8.

47  T.C. Ross to J.S. Ross, 27.7.1918, AG 512 4/16.

48  Ross to J.S. Ross, 11.5.1920, AG 512 4/15.

49  A.T. Inglis Minute Books, 6.6.1919, Hocken Library, Miss. MS 0711-00; Ross to McKenzie, London, 19.2.1920, AG 512 4/5; Ross & Glendining Ltd to J.J. Arthur, 9.6.1919, AG 512 2/8.

50 T.C. Ross to Robert Burns, Onehunga Woollen Mills, 28.4.1919, AG 512 4/16.

51 Ross to J.S. Ross, 16.10.1919, AG 512 4/15.

52 Ross & Glendining Ltd to Controller, Imperial Government Supplies, 19.11.1919; Ross to McKenzie, London, 19.2.1920, AG 512 2/8.

53 Ross to Netting, 5.9.1919, 6.12.1919, 31.1.1920, 24.6.1920, AG 512 4/15.

54 Ross to Netting, 7.5.1921, AG 512 4/15.

55 Ross to Netting, 31.3.1920, 12.8.1920, AG 512 4/15.

56 Ross to Netting, 24.6.1920, AG 512 4/15.

57 T.C. Ross to Netting, 12.10.1920, AG 512 4/16.

58 Hercus to Invercargill Branch, 10.9.1919, AG 512 2/8.

59 T.C. Ross to London Office, 17.6.1921, AG 512 4/8.

60 T.C. Ross to Netting, 27.1.1920, AG 512 4/16.

61 T.C. Ross to London Office, 12.9.1922, 28.11.122, AG 512 4/12.

62 T.C. Ross to London Office, 17.6.1921, AG 512 4/12; T.C. Ross to London Office, 22.9.1922; T.C. Ross to Dalgety & Co., Dunedin, 28.9.1922, AG 512 4/12.

63 J.S. Ross to Ross, 17.12.1919, AG 512 4/8.

64 J.S. Ross to Ross, 23.10.1919, AG 512 4/8.

65 J.S. Ross to T.C. Ross, 13.12.1919, AG 512 4/8.

66 T.C. Ross to Netting, 6.6.1919, AG 512 4/16.

67 T.C. Ross to J.S. Ross, 13.2.1920, AG 512 4/16.

68 Ross & Glendining Ltd to Department of Immigration, 17.5.1920, AG 512 2/8.

69 Ross & Glendining Ltd to London Office, 5.6.1920, AG 512 2/8.

70 Hercus to London Office, 16.4.1920, AG 512 2/8.

71 Hercus to London Office, 1.10.1919, AG 512 2/8; Ross to J.S. Ross, 19.1.1920, AG 512 4/15.

72 T.C. Ross to Trotter, Galashiels, 15.11.1921, AG 512 4/16.

73 Ross & Glendining Ltd to Kingston, Sydney, 12.1919; Ross & Glendining Ltd. to Lee, Sydney, 3.1.1920, AG 512 2/8.

74 T.C. Ross to London Office, 21.4.1922, AG 512 4/12.

75 Ross & Glendining Ltd to Bank of New South Wales, 22.12.1919, AG 512 4/9.

76 T.C. Ross to J.S. Ross 17.11.1919, AG 512 4/16.

77 Hercus to Netting, 26.4.1920, AG 512 4/6.

78 Return of soldier-employees, 31.3.1920, AG 512 4/10. Report and Balance Sheet, 12.10.1920, AG 512 8/6.

79 Hercus to Dunlop, 14.10.1920, AG 512 4/10.

80 Ross to Netting, 16.7.1920, 25.11.1920; Ross to C. James, 22.3.1921, AG 512 4/15.

81 Hercus to Bank of New South Wales, Dunedin, 5.10.1920, AG 512 4/10.

82 Hercus to Bank of New South Wales, 18.10.1920, AG 512 4/10.

83 Hercus to Registrar of Joint Stock Companies, Dunedin, 11.11.1920, AG 512 4/10.

84 T.C. Ross to Netting, 27.1.1921, AG 512 4/16.

85 Ross to Netting, 20.4.1921, AG 512 4/15; T.C. Ross to Netting, 3.5.1921, AG 512 4/16; J.S. Ross to Bank of New South Wales, 2.4.1921, AG 512 4/10.

86 Hercus to Bank of New South Wales, 11.3.1921, AG 512 4/10.

87 T.C. Ross to Netting, 3.5.1921, AG 512 4/16.

88 Ross to Snedden, 12.4.1922, AG 512 4/15.

89 T.C. Ross to J.S. Ross, 1.2.1920, 3.5.1921, 22.7.1922, AG 512 4/16; Share values and dividends, 1901–1925, AG 512 15/4. Half-yearly balances, AG 512 15/11.

90 Ross & Glendining Ltd to Chief Inspector, Bank of New South Wales, Wellington, 21.6.1922, AG 512 4/10.

91 T.C. Ross to Netting, 27.10.1923, 6.7.1924, AG 512 4/16.

92 Auckland Branch to Head Office, 3.9.1925, AG 512 6/1.

93  Directors' Meeting – Fair Minutes, 5.2.1924, AG 512 8/1.

94  *Ibid.*

95  Directors' Meeting – Fair Minutes, 29.7.1924, AG 512 8/1.

96  Head Office to Auckland Branch, 31.7.1924, AG 512 6/1.

97  Directors' Meeting – Fair Minutes, 8.11.1927, AG 512 8/1; T.C. Ross to Netting, 13.8.1927, 27.10.1927, 1.12.1928, AG 512 4/16.

98  Directors' Meeting – Fair Minutes, 12.8.1924, AG 512 8/1.

99  Head Office to Auckland Branch, 30.11.1926, AG 512 6/1.

100  Head Office to Samuel Vaile & Sons, 27.1.1925, AG 512 6/1.

101  Auckland Branch to Head Office 18.11.1926, AG 512 6/1; Directors' Meeting – Fair Minutes, 4.8.1931, AG 512 8/1.

102  T.C. Ross to London Office, 26.8.1922, AG 512 4/12.

103  Hercus to Ross, 15.12.1922, AG 512 4/10.

104  T.C. Ross to Netting, 1.5.1923, AG 512 4/16.

105  T.C. Ross to Trotter, 7.9.1923, AG 512 4/16.

106  Report by F.C.Gosling, 22.4.1924, AG 512, Box 11; Directors' Meeting, Fair Minutes, 25.9.1923–4.6.1924, AG 512 8/1.

107  Directors' Meeting, Fair Minutes, 1.7.1924–18.11.1924, AG 512 8/1.

108  T.C. Ross to London Office, 25.3.1925, AG 512 4/5; T.C. Ross to Netting, 28.3.1925, AG 512 4/16.

109  T.C. Ross to Netting, 3.7.1926, AG 512 4/16.

110  Ross to Netting, 30.9.1921, AG 512 4/15.

CHAPTER 17

1  Ross to J.S. Ross, 20.1.1906, AG 512 4/5.

2  Ross & Glendining Ltd, Summary of Capital and Shares 1925, DAAB Acc 95 236, National Archives, Dunedin.

3  Ross to J.S. Ross, 5.5.1909, 22.9.1909, AG 512 4/6; 7.12.1910, AG 512 4/14.

4  Ross to J.S. Ross, 5.4.1911, AG 512 4/14; 3.9.1915, AG 512 4/15.

5  Ross to J.S. Ross, 29.2.1911, AG 512 4/14.

6  Ross to J.S. Ross, 3.11.1909, AG 512 4/6.

7  Ross to J.S. Ross, 27.3.1912, AG 512 14/4.

8  J.S. Ross to Dr J. Glendining, 23.6.1917, AG 512 4/7.

9  Ross to J.S. Ross, 20.10.1909, 17.8.1910, AG 512 4/6.

10  Ross to J.S. Ross, 5.11.1913, AG 512 4/14.

11  Ross to J.S. Ross, 23.5.1916, AG 512 4/15.

12  Ross to J.S. Ross, 12.5.1909, AG 512 4/6.

13  Ross to T. Brown, 6.11.1906, AG 512 4/5.

14  Ross to J.S. Ross, 4.12.1907, 11.12.1907, AG 512 4/6.

15  Ross to J.S. Ross, 17.8.1910, AG 512 4/6.

16  Ross to J.S. Ross, 20.6.1911, AG 512 4/14.

17  Ross to J.S. Ross, 1.7.1913, AG 512 4/14.

18  Ross to J.S. Ross, 5.12.1917, AG 512 4/15.

19  Ross to J.S. Ross, 6.7.1917, 30.8.1917, AG 512 4/15.

20  Ross to J.S. Ross, 31.5.1911, AG 512 4/14.

21  Ross to J.S. Ross, 7.3.1916, AG 512 4/15.

22  Ross to J.S. Ross, 7.2.1916, 5.8.1916, 5.12.1916, AG 512 4/15.

23  Ross to J.S. Ross, 22.11.1917, 5.12.1917, AG 512 4/15.

24  Ross to Netting, 20.4.1921, AG 512 4/15.

25  Ross to D. George, 18.11.1904, AG 512 4/13.

26  Ross to J.S. Ross, 12.5.1906, AG 512 4/5.

27  Ross to T.C. Ross, 1.9.1906, AG 512 4/5.

28  Ross to J.S. Ross, 20.2.1907, 16.4.1907, AG 512 4/5.

29  J.S. Ross to T.C. Ross, 5.6.1917, AG 512 4/7.

30  Ross to George, 18.11.1904, AG 512 4/13.

31  Ross to W. Ross, 3.11.1906, AG 512 4/5.

32  Ross to J.S. Ross, 1.6.1910, AG 512 4/6.

33  Ross to J.S. Ross, 4.1.1911; Ross to Dr Fitzgerald, 4.6.1913, AG 512 4/14; Ross to J.S. Ross, 24.10.1917, AG 512 4/15.

34  T.C. Ross to J.S. Ross, 2.2.1918, AG 512 4/16.

35  T.C. Ross to Netting, 17.1.1919, AG 512 4/16.

36  J.S. Ross to Ross, 30.1.1917, AG 512 4/7.

37  Ross to J.S. Ross, 27.3.1917, AG 512 /15.

38  J.S. Ross to T.C. Ross, 20.4.1917, AG 512 4/7.

39  J.S. Ross to T.C. Ross, 5.6.1917, AG 512 4/7.

40  Ross to J.S. Ross, 6.7.1917, AG 512 4/15.

41  Ross to J.S. Ross, 30.8.1917, AG 512 4/15.

42  Ross to J.S. Ross, 27.12.1917, AG 512 4/15.

43  Ross to J.S. Ross, 26.9.1918, AG 12 4/15.

44  Ross to J.S. Ross, 10.10.1919, AG 512 4/15.

45  Obituary, *Otago Daily Times*, 25.6.1917.

46  K.C. McDonald, *op. cit.*, p. 242; Ross & Glendining Ltd to Drainage Engineer, 27.5.1904, AG 512 2/3.

47  Hercus to London Office, 14.8.1907, AG 512 3/1.

48  McDonald, *op. cit.*, p. 287.

49  Hercus to London Office, 18.9.1907, AG 512 3/1.

50  Ross to J.S. Ross, 21.7.1917, AG 512 4/15.

51  Ross to J.S. Ross, 1.7.1913, AG 512 4/14; W.P. Morrell, *The University of Otago: A Centennial History* (Dunedin, 1969), p. 124.

52  Alison Clarke, *A Living Tradition – A Centennial History of Knox College* (Dunedin, 2009).

53  Morrell, *op. cit.*, pp. 199–201.

54  Ross to J.S. Ross, 9.1.1909, 29.12.1909, AG 512 4/6.

55  Morrell, *op. cit.*, p. 201.

56  Obituary, *Otago Daily Times*, 6.1.1927, p. 9.

57  Ross to Rev. W. McBeath, 4.3.1901, AG 512 4/13.

58  Ross to William Black, Halkirk, 25.3.1908, AG 512 4/6.

59  Ross to Black, 4.11.1908, AG 512 4/6.

60  Ross to Black, 6.7.1907, AG 512 4/6.

61  Ross to niece, Ella, 7.12.1909, AG 512 4/6.

62  Ross to J.S. Ross, 1.6.1910, AG 512 /6.

63  Ross to J.S. Ross, 22.9.1909, AG 512 4/6.

64  Obituary, *Otago Daily Times*, 6.1.1927 p. 9.

65  Ross to J.S. Ross, 6.8.1913, AG 512 4/14.

66  Board Minutes, 24.2.1925, AG 512 8/1.

67  T.C. Ross, Letter Book, 5.11.1927, AG 512 4/16.

68  Board Minutes, 3.8.1922, 28.7.1925, AG 512 8/1, Obituary, *Otago Witness*, 17.8.1926, p. 28.

## CHAPTER 18

1  Lloyd Prichard, *op. cit.*, p. 314.

2  Directors' Meeting – Fair Minutes, 15.2.1927, 15.3.1927, AG 512 8/1.

3  T.C. Ross to J.S. Ross, 11.3.1927, AG 512 4/16.

4  T.C. Ross to Netting, 21.10.1927, AG 512 4/16.

5  National Industrial Conference, *AJHR* 1928, H35.

6  Estimated from Greasley & Oxley (2000), *op. cit.*, Table 1A.

7  W.B. Sutch, *The Quest for Security in New Zealand* (Wellington, 1966), pp. 129–39.

8  John Singleton, 'Auckland Business: The National and International Context' in Ian Hunter & Diana Morrow, eds, *City of Enterprise: Perspectives on Auckland Business History* (Auckland, 2006), pp. 16–18.

9  Directors' Meeting – Fair Minutes, 29.3.1926, 27.4.1926, AG 512 8/1.

10  Directors' Meeting – Fair Minutes, 8.2.1926, AG 512 8/1.

11  T.C. Ross to J.S. Ross, 11.3.1927, AG 512 4/6.

12  T.C. Ross to Netting, 21.10.1927, AG 512 4/6; Directors' Meeting – Fair Minutes, 8.11.1927, AG 512 8/1.

13  Directors' Meeting – Fair Minutes, 19.10.1926, AG 512 8/1.

14  Directors' Meeting – Fair Minutes, 1.2.1927, 21.6.1927, 31.1.1928, 22.5.1928, AG 512 8/1.

15  T.C. Ross to Netting, 21.10.1927, AG 512 4/16.
16  Director's Meeting – Fair Minutes, 8.11.1927, AG 512 8/1.
17  T.C. Ross to Netting, 22.3.1929, AG 512 4/16.
18  Head Office to L.C. Miller, Auckland Manager, 6.4.1927, AG 512 6/1.
19  Auckland Branch to Head Office, 23.8.1927, AG 512 6/1.
20  T.C. Ross to Netting, 9.2.1929, AG 512 4/16; Netting to J.S. Ross, 1.1.1929, 29.5.1931, AG 512 4/5.
21  Wanganui Branch to Head Office, 25.4.1928, AG 512 6/2.
22  Directors' Meeting – Fair Minutes, 22.5.1928, 19.6.1928, AG 512 8/1.
23  T.C. Ross to J.S. Ross, 28.3.1927, AG 512 4/16; Directors' Meeting – Fair Minutes, 2.8.1928, 11.9.1928, AG 512 8/1.
24  T.C. Ross to Trotter, 7.9.1923, AG 512 4/6.
25  T.C. Ross to A. Higginbottom, Wanganui, 16.10.1926, AG 512 4/16; Head Office to London Office, 6.12.1926, 12.8.1927, AG 512 4/12.
26  T.C. Ross to J.S. Ross, 28.3.1927, AG 512 4/16.
27  T.C. Ross to J.S. Ross, 22.4.1927, 3.6.1927, 16.6.1927, AG 512 4/16.
28  T.C. Ross to J.S. Ross, 23.5.1927, 3.6.1927, AG 512 4/16.
29  T.C. Ross to Netting, 5.12.1927, AG 512 4/16.
30  Head Office to London Office, 12.2.1927, 2.6.1927, AG 512 4/12.
31  T.C. Ross to London Office, 2.4.1928, AG 512 4/12.
32  T.C. Ross to Netting, 22.3.1929, 22.4.1929, AG 512 4/12.
33  T.C. Ross to J. Ewen, Auckland, 11.12.1922, AG 512 4/12.
34  T.C. Ross to London Office, 23.4.1928, AG 512 4/12.
35  T.C. Ross to London Office, 7.9.1928, 5.10.1928, AG 512 4/12.
36  T.C. Ross to Netting, 22.3.1929, 22.4.1929, AG 512 4/16.
37  T.C. Ross to Netting, 18.5.1929, AG 512 4/16.
38  Tony Simpson, *The Slump*, (Auckland, 1990), pp. 41–2.
39  Directors' Meeting – Fair Minutes, 18.12.1931, AG 512 8/1.
40  Half-yearly balances, 1928–1953, AG 512 15/13.
41  Directors' Meeting – Fair Minutes, 18.2.1932, 16.11.1932, 29.6.1933, AG 512 8/1.
42  W. Ashcroft to Head Office, 27.2.1931, AG 512 17/7.
43  L.C. Miller to Head Office, 12.2.1931, AG 512 17/7.
44  Ashcroft to Head Office, 27.2.1931, AG 512 17/7.
45  Wellington Branch to Napier 6.5.1931; Head Office to Wellington Branch, 29.5.1931, AG 512 17/4.
46  Annual Balance Sheet, 14.9.1934, AG 512 7/1.
47  R.S.Glendining to Head Office, 20.2.1931, AG 512 17/7.
48  R.S.Glendining to Head Office, 24.2.1931, 25.2.1931, 9.3.1931, AG 512 17/7.
49  Ashcroft to Head Office, 9.8.1931; Head Office to Ashcroft, 18.8.1931, AG 512 17/7.
50  Directors' Meeting – Fair Minutes, 12.5.1931, 6.9.1931, 6.4.1932, 1.6.1932, 24.6.1932, AG 512 8/1.
51  Netting to J.S Ross, 2.1.1931, 10.11.1931, 1.3.1932, AG 512 6/5.
52  T.C. Ross to Netting, 21.2.1931, AG 512 4/16.
53  T.C. Ross to London Office, 13.4.1931, AG 512 4/12.
54  Lloyd Prichard, *op. cit.*, pp. 383–4.
55  T.C. Ross to Netting, 2.3.1931, AG 512 4/16.
56  T.C. Ross to Netting, 13.6.1931, AG 512 4/16.
57  Lloyd Prichard, *op. cit.*, p. 382.
58  T.C. Ross to Netting, 27.11.1931, AG 512 4/16.
59  Macky, Logan Caldwell Ltd balance sheets, AG 512 Box 10; Directors' Meeting – Fair Minutes, 17.5.1933, AG 512 8/1.
60  T.C. Ross to Netting, 7.1.1933, AG 512 4/16; Directors' Meeting – Fair Minutes, 29.3.1933, AG 512 8/1.
61  T.C. Ross to Netting, 20.3.1932, AG 512 4/16; Submission to Tariff Commission, 1933, AG 512 19/3.
62  Directors' Meeting – Fair Minutes, 14.4.1931, AG 512 8/1; Half-yearly balances 1931–1934, AG 512 15/12.

63 T.C. Ross to Netting, 3.9.1932, AG 512 4/16.
64 Netting to J.S. Ross, 28.10.1933, 9.6.1923, AG 512 6/5; T.C. Ross to Netting, 22.1.1934, AG 512 4/16.
65 *NZOYB*, 1937, p. 659.
66 Lloyd Prichard, *op. cit.*, p. 385.
67 T.C. Ross to Netting, 7.1.1933, 17.2.1933, AG 512 4/16.
68 Submissions to Tariff Commission, 1934, AG 512 8/1.
69 Lloyd Prichard, *op. cit.*, p. 361.
70 Submissions to Tariff Commission, 1934, AG 512 19/3.
71 Directors' Meeting – Fair Minutes 4.5.1932, AG 512 8/1.
72 Annual Report, 5.9.1934, AG 512 7/1.
73 Directors' Meeting – Fair Minutes, 15.6.1933, AG 512 8/1; Factory Returns, 1922–1946, AG 512 19/9.
74 T.C. Ross to London Office, 17.2.1934, AG 512 4/12.
75 T.C. Ross to London Office, 17.8.1934, AG 512 4/12.
76 T.C. Ross to Netting, 15.9.1934, AG 512 4/16.
77 T.C. Ross to J. Ross, 13.10.1934, AG 512 4/16.
78 Directors' Meeting – Fair Minutes, 15.8.1932, 7.9.1932, AG 512 8/; Netting to J.S. Ross, 28.10.1932, AG 512 6/5.
79 Directors' Meeting – Fair Minutes, 4.5.1932, 24.6.1932, 30.11.1932, AG 512 8/1.
80 Directors' Meeting – Fair Minutes, 4.7.1934, AG 512 8/1.
81 *NZOYB*, 1937, pp. 646–7, 688.
82 Annual Report 5.9.1934, AG 512 8/8.
83 Annual Report 1937, AG 512 8/8.
84 General Plant Account, AG 512 15/18; Factory Returns, 1922–1946, AG 512 19/9.
85 T.C. Ross to J.S. Ross, 2.6.1937, AG 512 4/14.
86 T.C. Ross to J.S. Ross, 30.4.1937, AG 512 4/14.
87 Newspaper clipping, AG 512 Box 10.
88 Lloyd Prichard, *op. cit.*, p. 374.
89 Annual Report, 8.9.1938, AG 512 8/8.
90 *AJHR*, 1938, Vol. 1, B-16, p. 7; *AJHR*, 1940, Vol 1, B-16, p. 5.
91 Sutch, *op. cit.*, pp. 223–5.
92 Annual Report, 1.9.1939, AG 512 8/8.

**CHAPTER 19**

1 J.V.T Baker, *The New Zealand People at War, 1939–1945* (Wellington, 1945), pp. 31–9.
2 *NZOYB*, 1942, p. 182.
3 Baker, *op. cit.*, pp. 71, 97.
4 *NZOYB*, 1940, pp. 785–7.
5 *NZOYB*, 1943, p. 591.
6 National Archives of New Zealand, 26.8.1940, IC 57/43.
7 Roslyn Mills to Head Office, 15.8.1941, AG 512 Box 11; *AJHR*, 1940, H19, p. 9; Annual Report, 30.8.1940, 8/8.
8 Baker, *op. cit.*, p. 283.
9 Roslyn Mills to Head Office, 15.8.1941, AG 512, Box 11.
10 *New Zealand Draper and Allied Retailer*, 7.3.1943, p. 4.
11 *New Zealand Draper*, 7.6.1945, p. 6.
12 Annual Report, AG 512 8/8.
13 Flyer, 4.9.1939, AG 512 Box 8.
14 Half-yearly analysis, AG 512 15/13; Annual Report, 30.8.1940; Minutes, Ordinary General Meeting, 9.9.1941, AG 512 8/8.
15 Minutes, Ordinary General Meeting, 9.9.1941, AG 512 8/8.
16 Factory Returns, 1922–1946, AG 512 19/9.
17 Minutes, Ordinary General Meeting, 9.9.1941, AG 512 8/8; Operational Survey, May 1963, Appendix E, AG 512 19/1.
18 National Archives, IC 1, 57/43.
19 New Zealand Woollen Manufacturers Deputation to Prime Minister, 26.8.1940, National Archives, IC 1, 57/4/3.
20 Roslyn Mills to Head Office, 15.8.1941, AG 512, Box 11.
21 *Ibid.*
22 Minutes, Ordinary General Meeting, 9.9.1941, AG 512 8/8.
23 Baker, *op. cit.*, p. 81.
24 Bruce Woollen Mills to Factory Controller, 5.2.1942, National Archives, IC 1, 57/4/3.
25 *Ibid.*
26 *NZOYB*, 1942, p. 650.
27 Baker, *op. cit.*, pp. 99–102.
28 Ross & Glendining Ltd to Factory Controller, 5.11.1943, National Archives, IC 1, 57/4/3.

29   I am indebted to Dr Gael Ferguson for this information.

30   Memorandum, Controller of Textiles to Factory Controller, 28.10.1942, National Archives, IC 1, 57/4/3.

31   Ross & Glendining Ltd to Factory Controller, 5.11.1943, National Archives, IC 1, 57/4/3.

32   Ross & Glendining Ltd to Factory Controller, November 1943, National Archives, IC 1, 57/4/3.

33   Controller of Manpower to Factory Controller 10.1.1944, National Archives IC 1, 57/4/3.

34   Manpower Direction 1.1.1943 to 31.5.1945, National Archives, IC 1, 57/4/3.

35   Factory Returns, 1942–46, AG 512 19/9; Annual Report, 14.9.1944, AG 512 8/8.

36   New Zealand Draper, 7.3.1943, p. 5; 7.4.1944, p. 6.

37   New Zealand Draper, 7.3.1943, p. 3; 7.5.1943, pp. 2–4.

38   Head Office to London Office, 17.1.1941, AG 512 6/6; The March of Time: One Hundred Years with Ross & Glendining (Dunedin, 1967), p. 30.

39   Head Office to London Office, 2.4.1943, 14.7.1944, 4.2.1947, AG 512 6/6.

40   Head Office to London Office, 18.2.1941, AG 512 6/6.

41   Head Office to London Office, 25.2.1943, AG 512 6/6.

42   National Archives, IC 1, 9/13, pt. 7.

43   New Zealand Draper, 7.5.1943, p. 3.

44   New Zealand Draper, 7.4.1944, p. 7.

45   New Zealand Draper, 7.11.1944, p. 3.

46   National Archives, IC 1, 9 /13 pt. 7.

47   National Archives IC 1, 9/13 pt.7.

48   Mill and Factory Returns, AG 512 19/9.

49   John Singleton & Paul L. Robertson, Economic Relations Between Britain and Australasia, 1945–1970 (Basingstoke, 2002), pp. 76–7.

50   New Zealand Draper, 8.10.1945, pp. 11–12.

51   Ibid.

52   New Zealand Draper, 7.6.1945, p. 7.

53   Factory Controller to Minister of Supply, 13.7.1945, National Archives, IC 1, 9/13 pt. 7.

54   NZOYB, 1946, p. 603.

55   Annual Report, 12.9.1946, AG 512 8/8.

56   Pension Scheme, 14.5.1946, AG 512 Box 8; Annual Report, 12.9.1946; Minutes of Ordinary General Meeting, 15.9.1949, AG 512 8/8.

57   NZOYB, 1956, pp. 297, 319.

58   Board Report, May 1963, AG 512 19/1.

59   Ibid.

60   Ibid.

61   NZOYB, 1947–49, p. 701.

62   H.L. Bockett, Dept. of Labour & Employment to the Secretary, Department of Industries & Commerce, National Archives, IC 1, 9/13 pt. 7.

63   National Archives, IC 1, 9/13 pt. 7.

64   Roslyn: The Saga of a Woollen Mill (Whitcombe & Tombs Ltd, undated and unpaginated); Minutes of Ordinary General Meeting, 15.9.1949, AG 512 8/8.

65   Report on Annual Accounts, 1950, AG 512 8/8.

66   Minutes of Ordinary General Meeting, 15.9.1949, AG 512 8/8.

67   A.W. Jeavons to Dunedin Drainage Board, 1950, AG 512 Box 10.

68   City of Dunedin Council to Ross & Glendining Ltd, 17.8.1950, AG 512 Box 10.

69   Report on Annual Accounts 1950, 1952 & 1953, AG 512 8/8.

70   Annual Report 1949; Report on Annual Accounts, 1947 & 1949, AG 512 8/8.

71   National Archives, IC1 9/13 pt.1.

72   Unpublished MS, AG 512 Box 10.

73   I am grateful to Manuka Henare for this information.

74   Minutes of Ordinary General Meeting 1949; Report on Annual Accounts 1950, AG 512 8/8.

75   Annual Reports 1947, 1948, 1949; Reports on Annual Accounts 1947, 1949; Minutes of Ordinary General Meeting, 15.9.1949, AG 512 8/8.

76   Report on Annual Accounts 1949; Minutes of Ordinary General Meeting, AG 512 8/8.

77   Minutes of Ordinary General Meeting, AG 512 8/8.

78  *NZOYB*, 1956, p. 291.
79  *NZOYB*, 1956, pp. 490, 707.
80  S.R.H. Jones, 'Government Policy and Industry Structure in New Zealand', *Australian Economic History Review'*, Vol. 39, (November, 1999), pp. 203–4.
81  *NZOYB*, 1956, pp. 282, 695, 983.
82  R. Chapman, 'From Labour to National', in G.W. Rice, ed., *The Oxford History of New Zealand*, second edition (Auckland, 2000) pp. 373–5.
83  Reports on Annual Accounts, 1949, 1950, 1952; Annual Report 1951, AG 512 8/8.
84  Report on Annual Accounts, 1950; Annual Report 1952, AG 512 8/8.
85  Report on Annual Accounts 1952, AG 512 8/8.
86  *New Zealand Draper*, 22.4.1953, p. 18; *NZOYB*, 1956, pp. 836–7.
87  Report on Annual Accounts, 1953, AG 512 8/8.

**CHAPTER 20**
1  Annual Reports, 17.9.1953, 3.9,1954, AG 512 8/8.
2  Board Report, May 1963, p. 11, AG 512 19/1; E.O.Hunter, 'Productivity of Distribution', Background Paper 15, Industrial Development Conference, June 1960, pp. 1–2.
3  *Ibid.*
4  *New Zealand Draper*, 22.6.1953, p. 35; 22.11.1953, p. 2; Sir Jack Harris Bt, *Memoirs of a Century* (Wellington, 2007), p. 79.
5  Annual Report, 17.9.1953, AG 512 8/8.
6  Board Report, May 1963, pp. 4–5, AG 512 19/1.
7  *Ibid.*
8  *Ibid.*
9  Annual Report, 1952, AG 512 8/8.
10  Reports on Annual Accounts, 1952, 1953, 1954; Annual Report 1953, AG 512 8/8.
11  *Ibid.*
12  Board Report, May 1963, p. 3, AG 512 19/1.
13  Annual Report, 3.9.1954, AG 512 19/1.
14  Annual Report, 3.9.1954,; Annual General Meeting Proceedings, 8.8.1955, AG 512 8/8.
15  Board Report, May 1963, pp. 1–24, AG 512 19/1.
16  Report on Annual Accounts, 1955; Annual Report, 26.9.1955; Proceedings of Annual General Meeting, 1956, AG 512 8/8.
17  Proceedings of Annual General Meeting, Speech by J. Sutherland Ross, 8.10.1956, AG 512 8/8; *N.Z. Financial Times*, December 1957, p. 95.
18  Proceedings of Annual General Meeting, Speech by J. Sutherland Ross, 5.10.1955, AG 512 8/8.
19  *N.Z. Financial Times*, December 1957, p. 97; Proceedings of Annual General Meeting, 8.10.1956, AG 512 8/8.
20  Proceedings of Annual General Meeting, Speech by E.O.Hunter, 5.10.1955, AG 512 8/8.
21  Proceedings of Annual General Meeting, Speech by J. Sutherland Ross, 8.10.1956; Board Report, May 1963, p. 12, AG 512 19/1; *New Zealand Draper*, 22.5.1959.
22  Board Report, May 1963, pp. 3, 9, AG 512 19/1.
23  Sutch, *op. cit.*, p. 415; Malcolm McKinnon, *Treasury: The New Zealand Treasury 1840–2000* (Auckland, 2003), p. 218.
24  Proceedings of Annual General Meeting, 16.10.1957, AG 512 8/8.
25  Board Report, May 1963, p. 16, AG 512 19/1.
26  *New Zealand Draper*, 22.9.1956, pp. 16–17; 22.5.1957, p. 6; 22.7.1957, p. 29; 22.11.1961, p. 39.
27  Annual Report, 1955; Proceedings of Annual General Meeting, 16.10.1957, AG 512 8/8; Board Report, May 1963, AG 512 19/1.
28  Annual Report, 27.9.1957, AG 512 8/8.
29  Annual Report, 26.9.1958, AG 512 8/8.
30  Board Report, May 1963, p. 16, AG 512 19/1.
31  Board Report, May 1963, p. 10, AG 512 19/1.
32  Proceedings of Annual General Meeting 16.10.1957, AG 512 8/8.
33  Annual Report, 26.9.1960, AG 512 8/8.
34  Annual Report, 26.9.1958, AG 512 8/8; Board Report, May 1963, pp. 9–10, AG 512 19/1.

35 Annual Report, 27.9.1956, AG 512 8/8.

36 *Otago Daily Times,* 2.2.1959, p. 4.

37 McKinnon, *op cit.*, pp. 218–20.

38 Annual Report, 15.9.1959. Profits were apparently over-reported, the amended profit figure being reported in the text above. Board Report, May 1963, p. 8, AG 512 19/1.

39 Annual Report, 28.9.1961, AG 512 8/8; Board Report, May 1963, pp. 12–13, AG 512 19/1.

40 *New Zealand Draper,* 22.1.1960, p. 22.

41 Board Report, May 1963, p. 13, AG 512 19/1.

42 *Ibid*, pp. 13–14; Annual Report, 28.9.1961, AG 512 8/8.

43 *New Zealand Draper,* 22.2.1960, pp. 22–4, 36.

44 Board Report, May 1963, p. 17, AG 512 19/1.

45 *Ibid*, pp. 17–18.

46 *Ibid*, p. 18; *New Zealand Draper*, 22.8.1960, p. 26.

47 Board Report, May 1963, pp. 6, 7, AG 512 19/1.

48 Board Report, May 1963, pp. 20–22; Notes of Footwear Meeting held at Head Office, 14.8.1963, AG 512 19/1.

49 *Ibid*, pp. 21–3; Ewing, McDonald Pty to Ross & Glendining Ltd 24.5.1963, AG 512 15/17.

50 Board Report, May 1963, pp. 24–5, AG 512 19/1.

51 Letter from E.O. Hunter to shareholders, 8.8.1963, AG 512 8/8; Barr, Burgess, Stewart to Ross & Glendining Ltd, 2.7.1963, AG 512 9/1.

52 *Ibid.*

53 Chairman's Remarks, Proceedings of Annual General Meeting, 10.9.1963, AG 512 8/8.

54 *Ibid.*

55 *Ibid.*

56 Ross and Glendining Ltd Results, *Dominion,* 30.9.1963.

57 Proceedings of Annual General Meeting, 10.10.1963, AG 512 8/8.

58 *Ibid.*

59 *R & G Reporter,* November 1964, Vol. 1, No. 2, p. 3; December 1965, Vol. 2, No. 6, p. 3.

CHAPTER 21

1 *NZOYB,* 1965, pp. 737–8.

2 *Ibid,* 1967, 628–9.

3 *NZOYB,* 1965 p. 622.

4 Annual Report, 12.10.1962, AG 512 8/8.

5 National Archives, Industry and Commerce Files, IC 1, 9/12 pt. 1; *NZ Financial Times,* November 1957, p. 50.

6 Annual Report, 24.9.1964, AG 512 8/8.

7 Minutes, Directors' Meeting, 4.4.1966, AG 512 19/2.

8 *R & G Reporter,* Vol. 1, No. 2, November 1964, p. 3.

9 Annual Report, 24.9.1964, AG 512 8/8.

10 *R & G Reporter,* Vol. 2, No. 6, December 1965, p. 1.

11 *R & G Reporter,* Vol. 1, No. 1, September 1964, pp. 1, 7.

12 *Ibid,* p. 2; Annual Report, 24.9.1964, AG 512 8/8.

13 Report From Henderson Underwear Factory, 9.7.1963, AG 512 19/1

14 Annual Reports, 12.10.1964 & 12.10.1965, AG 512 8/8.

15 *R & G Reporter,* Vol. 1, No. 1, September 1964, p. 5.

16 *Ibid,* p. 6.

17 *Ibid,* p. 3.

18 Board Report, May 1963, pp. 23–5, AG 512 19/1; Annual Report, 24.9.1964, AG 51 8/8; *R & G Reporter*, Vol. 1, No. 2, November 1964, p. 3.

19 Annual Report, 29.9.1965, AG 512 8/8.

20 *R & G Reporter,* Vol. 2, No. 4, July 1965, p. 5.

21 *R & G Reporter,* Vol. 2, No. 6, December 1965, p. 1

22 *Ibid.*

23 *Ibid*; Annual Report, 29.9.1965, AG 512 8/8.

24 *R & G Reporter,* Vol. 2, No. 6, December 1965, p. 2.

25 *Ibid*, pp. 2–6; Vol. 3, No. 1, January 1966, p. 1; Vol. 3, No. 2, March 1966, p. 3.

26 Draft statement by Ross & Glendining Ltd as required by the Companies Amendment Act, 1963, 7.4.1966, AG 512 19/2.

27   Minutes of Special Meeting of Directors, 4.4.1966, AG 512 19/2.
28   Steve Jones, *op.cit.*, pp. 57–60.
29   *Unibox*, Vol. 1, No. 6, July 1966, p. 3.
30   Minutes of Special Meeting of Directors, 4.4.1966, AG 512 19/2.
31   *Ibid.*; Letter to Shareholders, 21.4.1966, AG 512 19/2.
32   C.R. Grey to D.I. Ross, 5.4.1966, AG 512 19/2.
33   'The brains behind the bid', newspaper cutting, 19.5.1966, AG 512 19/2.
34   C.R.Grey to D.I. Ross, 28.4.1966, AG 512 19/2.
35   D.I. Ross to C.R.Grey, 2.5.1966, AG 512 19/2.
36   'The brains behind the bid', newpaper cutting, 19.5.1966, AG 512 19/2; *Unibox*, Vol. 1, No. 6, July 1966, p. 1.
37   *Unibox*, Vol. 4, No. 6, July 1966, p. 1.
38   Circular to customers, 3.8.1966, AG 512 19/2.
39   UEB Annual Reports, 1967, p. 6; 1968, p. 8; 1969, p. 7; 1970, p. 7.
40   UEB Annual Report, 1968, p. 8.
41   Stewart, *op. cit.*, pp. 92–3, 97.
42   McLean, *Spinning Yarns*, pp. 159–60.
43   *Ibid*, 97–9, 118–19.
44   UEB, Annual Report 1976, pp. 5, 22.
45   McLean, *Spinning Yarns,* pp. 189–91.

### EPILOGUE

1   Geoffrey Jones, *Merchants to Multinationals* (Oxford University Press, 2002).
2   Michael King, *The Penguin History of New Zealand* (Auckland, 2003), p. 234.
3   For a useful corrective of this view, see J. McAloon, 'Long Slow Boom: Manufacturing in New Zealand, 1945–1970', *Australian Economic History Review,* Vol. 46, No. 1 (2006).
4   Board Report, May 1963, AG 512 19/1.
5   Harris, *Memoirs of a Century* (Wellington, 2003), pp. 78–85.

# GLOSSARY

*Terms used in woollen and worsted production*

**Backwashing** Scoured wool is immersed in a solution containing a small amount of oil, to make combing easier.

**Carbonising** Wool is soaked in chemicals, then baked and crushed in order to remove vegetable matter. Usually employed in the production of woollens rather than
worsteds.

**Carding engine** A machine containing a series of interacting rollers faced with wire bristles which remove vegetable matter and progressively tease out wool into a fine web. The web is then taken off the engine as a rope or sliver of wool.

**Combing** Aligns strands of long staple wool preparatory to spinning worsted yarns, taking out shorter strands and vegetable matter as it does so.

**Gill boxes** Help remove vegetable matter and straighten wool prior to combing.

**Heddle** Wires lifting alternate threads of warp on the loom so that the shuttle carrying the weft can pass between them, creating the weave.

**Hosiery frame** A machine that contains a number of needles, each with a hook and latch on it, the action of which produces a knitting motion.

**Jacquard loom** A hosiery frame fitted with apparatus to produce figured patterns.

**Mule spinning** A cross between the spinning jenny and Arkwright's water frame, the mule first draws out rovings and then a spindle twists the wool to produce yarn.

**Ring spinning** A more modern form of spinning, particularly well suited to lower-quality fibres. Unlike mule spinning, it is a continuous rather than two-stage process.

**Roving** A sliver or rope of wool drawn out and slightly twisted.

**Scouring** Occurring after a bale of wool has been opened, this process removes the natural grease, oil and dirt from the fleece. After washing with a scouring agent, the wool is dried and ready for processing. Dyeing might take place now or later.

**Shoddy** Inferior woollen yarn produced by mixing waste and rags with new wool.

**Shots-per-minute**  The number of times the shuttle passes from one side of the loom to the other.

**Shuttle**  Carries the weft from one side of the loom to the other, between threads of warp.

**Sliver**  Scoured wool which has been carded and drawn into a long rope. Worsted yarns are combed and twisted after an initial card and then spun.

**Spindle**  A tapered rod that spins yarn, the spun yarn being collected on a bobbin. Each mule consists of many spindles.

**Tape condenser**  Produces thin rovings of wool by dividing slivers and then rolling or condensing them ready for spinning. Imparts a slight twist.

**Warp**  Yarns which run the length of the loom and which tend to be stronger than the weft.

**Weft**  Yarns carried across the width of the loom by the shuttle.

**Winding**  Yarns are wound either in parallel onto a warp beam on the loom, which unwinds as weaving proceeds, or onto a bobbin that sits in the shuttle.

**Wool fineness**  Fineness depends on breed, health and nutrition. Nowadays measured in microns, fineness ranges from as low as 10 microns for Merino sheep to over 25 for poorer qualities.

**Woollen tops**  A sliver of long-stapled wool.

**Woollen yarn**  Usually made from shorter-staple wool, yarn relies on the natural matting of fibres rather than combing and close twisting to produce a continuous thread. Woollen cloth has a nap that is usually raised and cropped.

**Worsted yarn**  Yarn made from long-staple wool which has been combed to align fibres, then closely twisted. Used for high-quality cloths, knitting and embroidery.

# INDEX

*A number in **bold** indicates an illustration. A number followed by t indicates a table.*
*An en dash (–) between two numbers indicates continuous treatment of a topic, a tilde (~)*
*only that a topic is referred to on each page in the range.*